Fodor's

NEW YORK CITY

**FODOR'S
TRAVEL PUBLICATIONS**

NEW YORK • TORONTO
LONDON • SYDNEY • AUCKLAND

WWW.FODORS.COM

CONTENTS

114

69
216

CONTENTS | NEW YORK

3

UNDERSTANDING NEW YORK

Understanding New York is an introduction to the city, its geography, economy, history and its people. Living New York gets under the skin of New York today, while The Story of New York takes you through the city's past.

UNDERSTANDING NEW YORK

New York City is an international center for entertainment, fashion, creative arts and finance. It has great shopping, dynamic theater, superb concert halls and clubs, world-class museums, gorgeous parks and gardens, and sports events all year long. The variety and quality of restaurants is incomparable. As a world financial center, it soars and plummets with the fluctuations on Wall Street. New Yorkers move fast, talk fast and are passionate about politics and style. They come in all shapes, sizes, colors and ethnicities; the city's multiculturalism is part of its charm. Although known for being brusque, New Yorkers are often surprisingly warm. Sometimes infuriating, the city is never dull. And chances are, with its vibrant whirl of activity, it's nothing like home.

THE MANHATTAN LAYOUT

Manhattan is just one of five boroughs that comprise New York City. The others, sometimes known as the Outer Boroughs, are the Bronx, Brooklyn, Queens and Staten Island. Manhattan is the long, narrow island jutting southwest off the mainland and is the smallest borough at 13.5 miles (22km) long and 2.25 miles (3.5km) wide. On the east side of the island is the East River. On the west is the Hudson River. To the north is the Harlem River. Upper New York Bay—the city's fine harbor—is to the south.

In Manhattan, most streets are numbered and laid out in a grid. The exception to this is Lower Manhattan, south of 14th Street, which grew up before the grid system was established. On the grid, "avenues" run from north to south, and "streets" run east and west. Broadway cuts across town diagonally from northwest to southeast. First Avenue is on the eastern side of town, while Twelfth Avenue is on the western side. Fifth Avenue divides the city into the East Side and the West Side (except south of Washington Square, where Broadway becomes the east–west divide).

No matter where you are in Manhattan, if you are heading north you're going "uptown" and if you're heading south you're going "downtown." If you want to travel east or west, you want to go "crosstown."

CLIMATE

From January to March, New York can be very cold, with occasional blizzards, but cheaper air fares and hotel rooms can make it worth your while to visit then—and sometimes the weather can be temperate. The best times to visit are in late April and May, when temperatures are generally no lower than 61°F (16°C), and attractions are crowded only at peak times, and in September to early November, when temperatures range from 50°F (10°C) to 77°F (25°C). The city is hot and humid in July and August, with extremes of 95°F (35°C) or higher, but almost everything is air-conditioned.

STREET LIFE

Walking is the best way to fully appreciate the city, with its architectural splendors, intriguing sculptures, pretty fountains, beautiful parks and iconic landmarks. The street life is entertaining and colorful. Spanish, Chinese, Russian, Yiddish, Korean, Greek and English are just a few of the languages spoken by New Yorkers.

MANHATTAN'S NEIGHBORHOODS AT A GLANCE

LOWER MANHATTAN

Financial District The oldest part of the city and nexus of the securities industry anchored by the New York Stock Exchange and Wall Street.

TriBeCa Short for *Tri*angle *Be*low *Ca*nal, it is defined by Canal and Barclay streets and Broadway and the Hudson River. A mixed-use neighborhood of gritty warehouse lofts, loft-style restaurants and galleries.

Chinatown The area stretching over about 30 blocks, from Kenmare and Delancey streets to East Broadway and Worth Street, and from Broadway to Allen Street. Throngs of people shop for fish, meat, vegetables and herbal remedies or dine in the affordable restaurants.

Little Italy A section of Mulberry Street, with tourist-restaurants plus some genuine delis and pastry stores.

SoHo An ultra-expensive, chic shopping and gallery district, crowded with non-residents on weekends.

Lower East Side Bordered roughly by East Houston Street, Forsyth Street and the East River, this old immigrant quarter, once filled with crowded tenements, is now a nightlife hot spot with bars and nightclubs.

DOWNTOWN AND CHELSEA

Greenwich Village/West Village 14th Street to Houston Street and from the Hudson River to Bowery and Fourth Avenue. Boutiques line west Bleecker Street.

NoHo Between SoHo and Greenwich Village (from Houston to Eighth streets and Mercer to Bowery/Third Avenue), this youth-oriented neighborhood has plenty of fashionable shopping, bars and restaurants.

East Village Filled with restaurants, bars and a youth-oriented street scene.

Union Square/Flatiron District Hot neighborhood south of the Flatiron Building on 22nd Street and around Madison Square with bars, restaurants and clubs. From 14th to 23rd streets and Park Avenue to Sixth Avenue.

Chelsea Center of the gay community. Numerous warehouse/garage galleries along 24th Street, and a lively club and restaurant scene. Stretches from 14th to 30th streets and from Sixth Avenue to the Hudson River.

MIDTOWN

Hell's Kitchen The latest neighborhood undergoing gentrification (from Eighth Avenue to the Hudson River between 30th and 59th streets).

Midtown Commercial heart of the city between 34th and 59th streets on the West Side and from 40th to 59th streets on the East Side.

Times Square/Theater District The area around 42nd Street and Broadway is now occupied by major corporations and national chain stores, as well as new hotels, clubs and theaters.

CENTRAL PARK AND AROUND

Upper East Side From 59th to 96th streets and from Fifth Avenue to the East River. Madison Avenue is the ultra-chic shopping street.

East/Spanish Harlem From 96th to 142nd streets, and between Park Avenue and the East River. A mixed neighborhood of Italians, African-Americans and Hispanics.

Upper West Side Broadway cuts right through this section that extends from 59th to 125th streets between the Hudson River and Central Park West.

Harlem Stretching from 110th Street to the Harlem River and from Fifth to St. Nicholas avenues, Harlem is the city's most famous black community.

EXCURSIONS

The Bronx North of and linked to Manhattan by bridges and subway. Home of the New York Botanical Garden, the Bronx Zoo and Yankee Stadium.

Brooklyn Southeast of Manhattan and connected by bridges, a tunnel and subway, it is New York's most populous borough. Take in great views of Manhattan from Brooklyn Heights.

Queens A 20-minute subway trip east from Manhattan takes you to Queens, one of New York's fastest-growing and most ethnically diverse areas.

Staten Island The most southerly and least populous borough, with attractions such as Historic Richmond Town. Good views of Manhattan and the Statue of Liberty from the ferry.

LOWER MANHATTAN

Charging Bull sculpture at Bowling Green (▷ 91) by Arturo Di Modica (1989) reminds many stock-market traders who pass by daily that better times are ahead.

Century 21 (▷ 95) For seriously discounted designer wear and a crowd scene worthy of the annals of shopping.

Dean & DeLuca (▷ 95) Everything in this fancy food emporium is absolutely the best of its kind. A sensuous browsing and tasting experience.

The Immigrants (▷ 66) by Luis Sanguino (1973) is a heartrending sculpture in Battery Park evoking the hardships of early immigrants.

National September 11 Memorial (▷ 87) is a moving tribute to those who died in the terrorist attacks on the twin towers of the World Trade Center site.

Nobu (▷ 104) Nobu Matsuhisa's sushi is inspirational at this stylish restaurant.

Pravda (▷ 100) Sixty-five different vodkas, plus caviar and Russian snacks may tempt you to visit this trendsetter bar.

Soho Grand (▷ 105) First of the hip downtown hostelries where pets get the red-carpet welcome.

The Sphere (▷ 66) Fritz Koenig's 22-ton symbol of global peace, rescued from the plaza between the twin towers after 9/11, is now a memorial to the victims.

Staten Island Ferry (▷ 56) A free trip across the harbor giving fabulous views of the city. Just hop on.

Statue of Liberty (▷ 84–85) America's symbol of freedom is by Frédéric-Auguste Bartholdi (1885). Take the ferry to Liberty Island for a close-up look or to climb the 354 steps to the crown.

DOWNTOWN AND CHELSEA

Babbo (▷ 134) Mario Batali's flagship is the place to sample his lusty cuisine.

Flatiron Building (▷ 113) New York's first skyscraper got its nickname from its triangular shape.

Jeffrey (▷ 125) The shoe department at this expensive clothing store is stellar, and the best place to see high-designer selections in a single location.

Marcel (▷ 141) Chic on the cheap (by New York hotel standards) is the order of the day here.

Union Square (▷ 121) New York chefs buy produce from the green market, one of the best in the country.

MIDTOWN

42nd Street/Times Square (▷ 172–173 and 168–170) Architecture as performing art—the luminous facades of pulsating color are best at night.

B & H Photo (▷ 176) The professional place for cameras, video equipment and film, all at great prices.

Le Bernardin (▷ 187) Everything about this seafood specialist is perfect—the service, the flowers and the exquisitely refined, thoughtful cuisine.

Chrysler Building (▷ 148–149) An art deco masterpiece, this is a shrine to the Chrysler automobile.

DB Bistro Moderne (▷ 187) Eating at one of Daniel Boulud's restaurants is a must for every food-loving visitor. This is the most relaxed and joyous of them all.

Empire State Building (▷ 152–154) Take the elevator to the 86th Floor Observatory for stunning views

Above *Fine specimens at the American Museum of Natural History*
Opposite *The Chrysler Building—a city icon*

of Manhattan, the rivers and far into the distance, especially at night when the city is illuminated.

FAO Schwarz (▷ 177) The ultimate toy store, as seen in the film *Big* with Tom Hanks.

Flute (▷ 180) A luxury subterranean retreat serving 20 different champagnes by the glass, this bar is perfect for pre- or post-theater.

Four Seasons (▷ 188) Established in 1959, this modern restaurant is the darling of the city's movers and shakers. Christian Albin's cuisine is another bonus.

Four Seasons (▷ 191) A hotel legendary for its service and its immense bathtubs.

International Center of Photography (▷ 151) More than 60,000 photographs by top names are on display in this exhibition space.

King Cole Bar (▷ 181) Where the Bloody Mary was invented, Maxfield Parrish's mural adds vibrant color to this bar in the St. Regis Hotel.

Library (▷ 192) A boutique hotel and book-lovers' haunt notable for its minimalist design and good service.

Metro (▷ 192) One of the best value hotels in the city, Metro is art deco and stylish.

Museum of Modern Art (▷ 162–163) Now doubled in size after architect Yoshio Taniguchi's expansion, MoMA displays masterworks of sculpture and painting.

New York Public Library (▷ 159) Beaux Arts magnificence was funded by donations and bequests.

Le Parker Meridien (▷ 193) This very French uptown hotel with hip downtown style has a pool with a view and a rooftop jogging track.

P. J. Clarke's (▷ 183) A beloved New York saloon, this is home to a rakish crowd.

Prometheus (▷ 166) by Paul Manship (1934) is Rockefeller Center's famous gold-leaf and bronze statue overlooking the ice-skating rink.

Ritz-Carlton (▷ 243) The opulent Central Park star offers superb service, the latest techno amenities and the only La Prairie spa in the United States.

St. Regis (▷ 195) A gilded Beaux Arts beauty, this hotel is just off Fifth Avenue.

Rockefeller Center and Grand Central Terminal (▷ 164–167 and 156–157) These two architectural gems are worth a self-guided tour.

Salon De Ning (▷ 183) Who can resist a rooftop bar in Midtown?

Tiffany & Co. (▷ 178) Superb silver, crystal and other luxury gifts are the attraction at this famous American name, in the jewelry business since 1837.

Top of the Rock (▷ 167) affords views over Manhattan and Central Park from atop the G. E. Building.

Top of the Tower (▷ 184) A nostalgic 26th-floor piano-bar overlooking the East River.

CENTRAL PARK AND AROUND

Alice in Wonderland (▷ 213) by José de Creeft (1959) perches on a giant mushroom while the March Hare holds out a watch and the Mad Hatter looks on.

American Museum of Natural History (▷ 204–207) Not only for dinosaur fossils and moon rocks, this is also a stunning modern planetarium complex.

Barneys (▷ 230) For cutting-edge fashion. Don't miss the handbag department.

Bloomingdale's (▷ 230) This department store is so very New York.

Carlyle (▷ 242) This hotel is considered the city's most discreet retreat.

Central Park (▷ 208–213) New York's green lung is Frederick Law Olmsted's masterpiece of landscape architecture, housing the Metropolitan Museum of Art.

Frick Collection (▷ 215) A large collection of masterpieces by Rembrandt, Vermeer, El Greco and Goya is housed in Henry Clay Frick's splendid mansion.

Guggenheim Museum (▷ 216–217) Frank Lloyd Wright's only New York building is a whirling wonder both inside and out.

Jean-Georges (▷ 239) All of Jean-Georges Vongerichten's restaurants (Jo Jo, 66, Mercer Kitchen and Spice Market) showcase his brilliance, but this is his flagship.

MObar (▷ 243) This romantic hot spot is in the Mandarin Oriental Hotel.

Per Se (▷ 240) Thrilling cuisine by Thomas Keller, of French Laundry, Napa Valley fame, makes this the city's most coveted reservation.

Sherry-Lehmann (▷ 232) An education; the inventory of international wine selections is worth $10 million.

Trump International Hotel and Tower (▷ 243) Enjoy breathtaking views of Central Park from the stylish hotel.

TOP EXPERIENCES

Empire State Building (▷ 152–154) The Observation Deck offers a panoramic view of all Manhattan, which is very romantic at sunset.

A Broadway show Seeing one is a quintessential New York experience and various discount pricing schemes make it more affordable (▷ 170, Tips; ▷ 283).

Bronx Zoo (▷ 256–257) Always entertaining—the people are sometimes as interesting as the animals.

Waldorf-Astoria Hotel (▷ 195) A study in opulence. Ogle the amazing floral displays in the lobby.

A walk across Brooklyn Bridge (▷ 68–69) This landmark bridge offers a terrific view of the skyscrapers in Lower Manhattan and the East River.

Statue of Liberty and Ellis Island (▷ 84–85 and 72–74) Take the ferry ride to see Lady Liberty, and if you're feeling energetic climb the steps to the crown, and the Ellis Island memorial to 12 million immigrants.

Guggenheim Museum (▷ 216–217) Frank Lloyd Wright's spiral-shaped building showcases an exceptional collection of modern and contemporary art.

Central Park (▷ 208–213) Stroll along the paths and down the tree-lined Mall to Bethesda Fountain and the lake beyond to experience New York's quiet side.

Shopping along Fifth Avenue (▷ 155) Savor one of the world's finest shopping streets with visits to Saks Fifth Avenue, Tiffany & Co., FAO Schwarz and more.

Cathedral Church of St. John the Divine (▷ 227) The largest Gothic church in the world is vast, with chapels dedicated to national, ethnic and social groups.

Chinatown (▷ 70–71) Explore the largest, busiest and most colorful ethnic neighborhood and eat in a Chinese restaurant.

Times Square (▷ 168–170) New York's popular landmark offers flashy neon signs, animated advertisements and an exciting vibe that makes this bustling cultural scene memorable.

Yankee Stadium (▷ 258–259) **and Citi Field** These are the places to go for baseball when the New York Yankees or the New York Mets (▷ 267) are in town.

Frick Collection (▷ 215) The opulent home of steel magnate Henry Clay Frick is filled with fine Old Master paintings, French furniture and museum quality artworks that showcase the wealthy lifestyle of New York during the gilded age.

Metropolitan Museum of Art (▷ 209–211) Magnificent displays of fabulous art from cultures around the world feature an astonishing number of masterpieces. The daily Museum Highlights Tour provides an excellent introduction to the collection.

Below Walk or bicycle across the one-mile (1.6km) wooden, pedestrian walkway of Brooklyn Bridge to glimpse a spectacular view of the Manhattan skyline

LIVING NEW YORK

THE URBAN LANDSCAPE

Manhattan is only 13.5 miles (22km) long and 2.25 miles (3.5km) wide. Geologically it consists of bedrock made of gneiss, marble or mica schist. These two factors, plus population density, have played major roles in shaping the city's land- and streetscape, making it more vertical than most. Tall buildings line the streets, and people think nothing of riding elevators to their 50th-floor offices. Daily the population swells as commuters pour into Manhattan from the suburbs, creating a crowded environment that throbs with energy. Commuters access the city via ferry, tunnels and bridges, the most graceful of which are the Brooklyn (1883) and George Washington (1931) bridges. North of 14th Street the streets are laid out in a grid. There are few open spaces or green parks to provide relief—only one or two squares, such as Union, Washington and Madison, or small pockets of asphalt with benches, statues and fountains. Instead, there is one vast park, Central Park, which separates the Upper East Side and the Upper West Side and functions as the city's playground.

THE GRID AND THE WARREN

Most visitors to New York City quickly grasp the logic of the streetscape north of 14th Street. A series of broad north–south avenues is crossed by east–west streets, numbered logically. Below 14th Street things get more complicated. Here the narrow streets twist and turn, reminiscent of a medieval city, and have names rather than numbers. This came about because the city grew haphazardly and there were only a few long arteries connecting farms and villages. So in 1811 an orderly grid of 12 broad avenues and 155 streets was established, subdivided into lots measuring 25 by 100ft (7.5 by 30m). It was thought that traffic would be heaviest on the east–west routes, so more streets than avenues were planned. This pattern remains.

Clockwise from above From the top of the Empire State Building even other skyscrapers can look tiny; Central Park provides a haven for recreation and relaxation in the city; commuting on the subway is part of daily life in New York City

UNDERGROUND CITY

First-time visitors to Manhattan often notice the rooftop water towers, fire hydrants, potholes and, weirdest of all, steam-belching funnels. The last give an inkling of what lies below—a multilevel network of electric and telephone cables, plus steam, water, gas and sewage pipes, all laid above the subway. A large water tunnel under the subway supplies the city's drinking water. The subway alone has 660 miles (1,062km) of track and 490 stations. There's 100 million miles of telephone cable. City water comes from upstate New York reservoirs, and the 1,500 million gallons a day is delivered by more than 6,000 miles (9,654km) of tunnel and water mains. Installed before 1930 and made of cast iron, they can rupture, which causes chaos. When the piped gases build up, they cause manhole explosions. The steam-belching funnels help to relieve the pressure and stop the 60,000 manholes from erupting.

ROBERT MOSES— NEW YORK'S BARON HAUSSMANN

Robert Moses (1888–1981), who served on the Parks and Planning commissions, had a huge impact on the city's overall design, in a similar way to Baron Haussmann in Paris. Between 1924 and 1968, Moses transformed New York City, building 17 parkways, 14 expressways (including the Brooklyn–Queens Expressway), the FDR and Harlem River drives, the Robert F. Kennedy and Verrazano bridges, Lincoln Center and Stuyvesant Town. In the process he destroyed whole neighborhoods, tearing down slums and relocating residents in public housing in Harlem, the Lower East Side, the Bronx and Brooklyn. Not surprisingly, the citizens got angry. And when Moses moved to route cars through Washington Square and put parking lots in Central Park the citizens mobilized in an attempt to preserve the small scale of their neighborhoods. Still, Moses left a gigantic imprint on the city.

WAKING UP TO THE WATERFRONT

For years New York City's 580 miles (930km) of waterfront lay blighted, the site of rusting piers, crumbling warehouses and refuse-strewn lots. Now it's as if the city has woken up to its potential pleasures, as citizens go kayaking, fishing and sailing. A 28-mile (45km) bicycle path now encircles Manhattan, and the waterfront has been converted into a park with a promenade and gardens stretching from the Battery to 58th Street. It's hard to pinpoint when this regeneration began. In the 1980s, South Street Seaport with its retail outlets and museum, Battery Park City and Chelsea piers were important beginnings to the process, followed by Riverbank State Park (1993). The rest has followed, culminating in Stuyvesant Cove Park (2002) and Hudson River Park (2003).

URBAN GARDENS

New York City has one large park and only two major botanical gardens, so resident horticulturists create their own gardens in unlikely corners. If you look up at the residential buildings you might see green fronds peeking out from the roofline. Some of these roof gardens are luxurious indeed, planted with trees and flowers and decorated with urns and statues. In contrast are the hundreds of community gardens, usually created on vacant city-owned lots, which serve as neighborhood social centers. The impetus for such gardens can be traced to 1972 and a garden at Bowery and Houston tended by the Green Guerrillas. Mayor Giuliani sought to destroy such gardens and battled with neighborhood activists, but Mayor Michael Bloomberg has moved quickly to try to make peace.

New York City is a city of immigrants. Between 1892 and 1924, 12 million immigrants poured through Ellis Island, many heading to the Lower East Side. Today, the gateways are Kennedy and Newark airports, and the immigrants' destinations are often the ethnic mosaics of Brooklyn and Queens, where such high schools as New Town have students who speak 30 different languages, and where the Central Library caters to a population that speaks nearly 40 languages. The Dutch, of course, were the first immigrants. They were interested in talent and enterprise and opened the city to immigrants of all sorts—Huguenots, Jews, Germans, Africans (slave and free) and the English, Scottish, French and Irish. At the turn of the 20th century, large numbers of Jews, Italians and Russians arrived, and after 1965, people from the Caribbean, Central America and Asia. The percentage of foreign-born citizens has always fluctuated. At 36 percent, it is today at its highest. The lowest was in 1970 (18 percent). The total population of New York City is 8.4 million, of which 35 percent are white, 27 percent Hispanic, 25 percent black and 12 percent Asian.

INTERNATIONAL EXPRESS—THE NUMBER 7 TRAIN

While Staten Island is New York's fastest-growing borough, with a growth rate of nearly 11 percent (according to the Department of City Planning), Queens continues to be a key point of arrival for new immigrants—Indians, Colombians, Ecuadorians and Peruvians in Jackson Heights; Dominicans, Colombians and Mexicans in Corona; Chinese, Koreans and Vietnamese in Flushing. Queens is the city's new melting pot—the new gateway to America. A ride on the number 7 train will confirm this. The first few stations (40th to 61st streets and Queens Boulevard) are in Sunnyside and Woodside, where the most recent influx of Irish immigrants has settled. It then proceeds along Roosevelt Avenue, stopping in Jackson Heights (74th Street), Corona (111th Street) and, finally, Flushing.

Clockwise from above *New York's Chinatown, with its colorful street signs, is the largest in the United States, and has been home to immigrants from China, Taiwan, Korea and Vietnam for more than 150 years; immigrants from all over the world make a home in New York; the African Burial Ground at Broadway and Duane*

TRACING AFRICAN-AMERICAN HERITAGE

A scholar interested in researching black history in New York would begin at the Schomburg Center on 125th Street. Documents here chart the growth of the community from 14,000 in 1830 to more than 2 million today, along with the lives of such famous black New Yorkers as abolitionists Henry Highland Garnet and Alexander Crummell, and civil rights leaders Adam Clayton Powell and Malcolm X. A casual visitor might start at the African Burial Ground at Broadway and Duane. Here, from 1712 to 1794, 10,000–20,000 black people were buried as they were excluded from the Trinity Church graveyard. Few traces remain of Manhattan's 19th-century black communities, but much is found in Harlem: the church where Adam Clayton Powell, Sr. and Jr. preached, at 138th Street; the mosque associated with Malcolm X; and many Harlem Renaissance sites.

UNDERSTANDING YIDDISH

Every New Yorker knows what *chutzpah*, *mensch* and *kvetch* mean, and what the difference is between *shlep*, *shlemiel* and *schmozzle*. New York has the largest Jewish community outside Israel, but it's not its size so much as its spirit that counts. The greatest number of Jews came in the late 19th century, fleeing pogroms in Russia and Eastern Europe and settling on the Lower East Side. Their story is told in Irving Howe's history, *World of Our Fathers*. A tale of struggle rewarded by success and assimilation, it's a journey seen in the contrast between Woody Allen's Jewish outsider and Jerry Seinfeld's totally assimilated incidental Jew. Successful Jews moved from the Lower East Side and Brooklyn to the Upper West Side and to the suburbs. They became financiers, doctors, lawyers, stand-up comedians and schoolteachers, and passed along Yiddish.

HISPANICS—SECOND IN STRENGTH

The 1961 movie *West Side Story* depicted the struggle of Puerto Rican immigrants living in New York, the city's first Hispanic community. Today, joined by nationals from Cuba, Ecuador, Colombia, El Salvador, the Dominican Republic and Mexico, Hispanics are the city's largest minority, representing 27 percent of the population. The Hispanic influence can be seen everywhere, from media and music to politics and cuisine. Turn on the TV and you'll find Telemundo and Univision offering Spanish talk shows and steamy soap operas. Scan a newspaper stand and you will see the Hispanic publications *El Diario/La Prensa, Hoy, El Nacional* and *El Tiempo*. Baseball teams are peppered with Hispanic names; the Latino music craze continues, as more artists cross over in the footsteps of Ricky Martin; and chefs deliver the latest Spanish and Latino cuisine at such hot spots as Pipa and Casa Mono.

BOLLYWOOD ON THE HUDSON

Before 1965 only a few South Asian students lived in the city, but after 1965, the Indian, Pakistani, Bangladeshi, Sri Lankan and Nepalese presence increased noticeably. Gradually Asian cuisine and music registered on the consciousness of New Yorkers. Now fusion is occurring between Asian cultures and those of other national origin. Witness Panjaba MC and Jay-Z's hit *Beware of the Boys*, in which hip-hop meets British *bhangra*. In the 1970s more Asian professionals settled in Queens. Jackson Heights became the principal commercial center, with Sam and Raj's appliance store opening in 1976 on 74th Street. Here are stores selling saris, South Asian DVDs, music and cooking staples. There are also several Hindu temples. Furthermore, it's not uncommon to walk past venues like Madison Square Garden and see top Bollywood entertainers headlining their marquees.

There are so many great buildings in New York that it can be overwhelming. Many others have also been lost to redevelopment, and that too is overwhelming, but not surprising, given the city's commercial nature. Skyscrapers dominate the island of Manhattan, a building style made possible by the confluence of several factors — the geological bedrock, the availability of steel, and the techniques of engineering. City governments had always emphasized growth and innovation, which helped create such real-estate moguls as John Jacob Astor, William Zeckendorf, Harry Helmsley and Donald Trump. Zoning laws arrived only in 1916 and conservation came even later. Robert Moses razed whole neighborhoods, and between 1900 and 1965 many architectural gems were replaced with inferior substitutes. New Yorkers finally woke up in 1965, after Penn Station was demolished and replaced with the underground station there today. A Landmarks Preservation Commission was founded, but it still had to be reaffirmed by the Supreme Court in 1978 when the fabric of Grand Central Terminal was threatened with redevelopment.

BEYOND SIGNATURE SKYSCRAPERS

Yes, the Empire State and Chrysler buildings are two stunning skyscrapers, but they're not alone. The Bayard Condict Building (1898) on Bleecker Street is the only example of Louis Sullivan's work in the city. Later skyscrapers often incorporated elements from earlier eras, as did Daniel Burnham's Renaissance Revival Flatiron Building (1902). Raymond Hood's Radiator Building is a beauty — black brick and blue-green tiles with gold ornamentation. The Seagram Building on Park Avenue, by Mies van der Rohe and Philip Johnson, is a good example of 1950s' modernism. Architects are still building the skyscrapers of tomorrow — Daniel Libeskind's design was chosen for the new complex being built at the site of the former World Trade Center.

Clockwise from above *Grand Central Terminal is a magnificent public space and one of the city's finest landmarks; the Woolworth Building, designed by Cass Gilbert, has stunning interior decoration; tenements with their characteristic fire escapes in SoHo*

BROWNSTONES AND TENEMENTS

Besides skyscrapers there are plenty of other building types to appreciate. Brownstones — named after the sandstone from the banks of the Connecticut and Hackensack rivers — line the streets of Greenwich Village, Chelsea and other districts. Today they make elegant residences. In the mid-19th century, cast iron was used for the facades of factories, shops and warehouses, many in SoHo. They seem to be carved in stone, but are in fact some of the first pre-fabs ever made. The most spectacular examples are at Nos. 260–561 Broadway and Mercer Street in SoHo.

Humble tenements with fire escapes are also city trademarks. Built to house the 19th-century immigrants, they were narrow, cramped and insanitary, but cheap — $2–$3 per month. Examples still line the streets of the Lower East Side and East Village. Today the rent is 500 times more.

MEWS, AND OTHER NOOKS AND CRANNIES

Visitors soon discover Midtown's pocket parks and plazas, but if you wander farther you'll find more charming oddities. Pomander Walk (West 94th and 95th streets), for example, is 16 two-story Tudor-style cottages. Sniffen Court, 150–158 East 36th Street, is a beguiling collection of brick carriage houses now used as residences. The Village has several oddities. The enclaves of Patchin Place (1848), West 10th Street, and Milligan Place (1852), on Sixth Avenue between West 10th and 11th streets, were originally built to house Basque waiters, who worked at the Brevoort House on Fifth Avenue. Later residents were more famous — among them e. e. cummings. Along Bedford Street, between Morton and Commerce, stands the narrowest house in the city — it's only 9ft (3m) wide and was home to poet, playwright and feminist Edna St. Vincent Millay in 1924.

SCULPTORS AND PAINTERS HELP TO GILD THE LILY

Visitors often focus on the number and size of Manhattan skyscrapers, failing to notice the many embellishments created by famous and not so famous stonemasons, sculptors and painters. Daniel Chester French adorned the US Custom House with monumental portraits of Asia, America, Europe and Africa. Reginald Marsh painted the interiors, celebrating the maritime wealth of the city. The lower facades of the art deco Rockefeller Center are encrusted with sculptures and bas-reliefs. Lee Lawrie's *Wisdom* hovers above the entrance to the G. E. Building, while inside José Maria Sert's mural, *Man's Conquests*, covers the walls. Portraits of Mary Pickford and Ethel Barrymore by Alexander Stirling Calder grace the Miller Building at West 46th Street and Seventh Avenue. French artist Marc Chagall adorned the Metropolitan Opera House with two murals.

CASS GILBERT

Cass Gilbert stands out as the designer of some of the city's most beautiful and luxuriant buildings. Venture into the Woolworth Building (1910–1913) at 233 Broadway, for example. Frank W. Woolworth, who paid the $15.5 million price tag in cash, certainly got his money's worth. The exterior soars 792ft (241m) without a setback. The interior decoration is stunning. The vaulted lobby is swathed in veined marble, gold leaf and mosaic, and decorated with humorous sculptures, including one of Cass Gilbert himself holding the building and another of Woolworth counting his dimes. Gilbert's other great building is the Beaux Arts US Custom House (1907) at No. 1 Bowling Green, a suitably grand repository for the wealth of the early city. He also contributed the New York Life Insurance Building (1907) at 51 Madison Avenue, between 26th and 27th streets, and the postmodern curtain wall Federal Courthouse on Foley Square (1936).

Most New Yorkers are not born in the city. They come to it. They come for many reasons, most of which involve dreams of success and the money, power and fame that follow. So the city is full of competitive people trying to make it on stage, in music, in real estate, on Wall Street, Madison Avenue or in any other arena. Even though many citizens seem to be in a constant state of "success overdrive," there are other factors that affect the rhythms of city life. New York is not monolithic. It's a cluster of neighborhoods, each with a different ambience and energy. The West Village wakes up late and operates at a slow pace; the East Village wakes up very late and parties very late; Washington Heights is loud and moves to a Dominican rhythm; Beekman Place is always subdued. The city may stay open 24 hours, but each individual neighborhood plays its own rhythmic variation.

EXERCISE, EXERCISE!

Although a recent study reported that 35 percent of New Yorkers are overweight or obese, you would not know it from the frequent sightings of earnest New Yorkers pumping iron or running on treadmills. Most executives receive a standard gym membership as part of their remuneration package and many have personal trainers, who show them how to work the machines and set their fitness goals. Of course, the Old Guard have their clubs, where they go to swim, exercise or get a massage — the Knickerbocker, the Union, the Colony or the Harmonie are examples. After these come luxury gyms like the Sports Club/ L. A. Average New Yorkers are more likely to join Bally Fitness or Crunch and take aerobics classes. It's all part of the endless regimen of health and beauty.

Clockwise from above *Yellow cabs first hit the streets more than a hundred years ago, in 1907; skateboarding and bicycling are popular ways to keep fit in Central Park; Trinity Church is one of the numerous places of worship in the city*

YELLOW CABS—LOVE OR HATE?

The average New Yorker rides the bus or the subway, but many prefer to hail a cab, one of around 13,000 licensed to roam the city streets. You can't miss the yellow chariots. They have been in business since 1907. Early operators were so corrupt that in 1923 a Taxi and Limousine Commission began issuing licenses. LaGuardia sold the first medallion for $10 in 1937. Today they cost as much as $379,000. Every immigrant group has driven cabs—initially Jewish settlers, Italians and Irish and more recently people from Russia, Africa, Haiti and South Asia. They often receive only 24 hours of instruction. Some cabs perform some wild maneuvers to grab passengers. The bulletproof partitions separating passenger from driver were installed in 1967. Most recently, touch-screen GPS units and credit card machines have been the cause of strikes.

NEW YORK SOLUTIONS TO SINGLEDOM

There are 100 million "singles" in the United States. Several million of them live in New York and many are looking for the perfect mate, supporting a veritable marriage market industry. Even in the 1860s, matrimonial brokers' advertisements ran in the press. For example, John Johnson and Co. offered services to "ladies wishing agreeable and wealthy husbands," and to men desiring "beautiful, rich and accomplished wives." If you scan the ads in the local media, you'll find little has changed. Now, though, individuals advertise themselves, posting photographs in such publications as *New York Magazine,* revealing their most intimate data online at itsjustlunch.com, or signing up for TV shows such as *Perfect Partner* and *Boy Meets Boy.* There are singles groups of all kinds, from speed-dating specialists to one for tall people only.

CONVENIENCE GREASES THE DAILY WHEELS

To the average New Yorker, speed and convenience take precedence over everything else. Time is, after all, money. So meals on the run are habitual. Workers en route to their offices and exercisers sporting Adidas, stop for an Egg McMuffin at McDonald's or coffee and a danish at Starbucks. At lunch, New Yorkers "order in" a sandwich or salad and soft drink, instead of going out for a leisurely meal. Or if they have a corporate cafeteria they go there. Some of these are extraordinary, the most famous being the Philippe Starck version at Condé Nast. If workers do go out, it will often be to "brown bag it," taking a sandwich to a park.

At night, they may go home and order a take-out from one of the many neighborhood menus that they keep by their phone—Thai, Chinese, Mexican, Indian, Italian or Japanese.

WORSHIP AT YOUR CHOICE OF ALTAR

Many visitors are surprised to learn how religious New Yorkers are and how many people attend religious services. From the city's founding it has offered an array of religious options, when Anglicans, Presbyterians, Quakers, Anabaptists, Jews, Catholics and Lutherans co-existed. Today, Christians, Buddhists, Hindus, Sikhs, members of the Jewish community and Muslims all have a place to worship in the city. If you want to understand a culture, attend one of its religious services. In New York, head to Harlem and hear the enthusiastic gospel choirs raising the roofs of the Baptist churches, or go to West 113th Street to the Mosque of Islamic Brotherhood. Take the train to the Hindu temples or Sikh gurdwaras in Queens, or drop in to one of the Buddhist temples in Chinatown. Or visit St. John the Divine or St. Patrick's.

THE ARTS

New York City leads the nation in arts and entertainment innovation and provision. It's the world's center of contemporary art, and also has a phenomenal collection of performing arts companies in dance, music and theater. The city's cultural groups have also led the way in finding innovative fundraising solutions to finance their endeavors. For years, although they have received some funding from government, city cultural institutions and groups have developed their own funding resources—private donors, bequests, memberships, bookstores and other types of ancillary profit center. The arts scene is constantly evolving. There is an uptown mainstream scene and a downtown more experimental scene, and within each shifts are always occurring—SoHo galleries migrating to Chelsea, for example. Don't worry: Whatever excites you in the arts can be found in New York.

CULTURE AND MONEY
Wealthy dynasties have always served as patrons of the arts, and New York's are no different. Mayor Bloomberg donates a large part of his fortune to cultural institutions, as do many in the Social Register. Today, billions of dollars are likely to be dispensed each year by more than 500 city-based foundations. These cultural donors are copying earlier magnates whose names still resonate throughout the city—Astor, Carnegie, Morgan, Rockefeller, Vanderbilt and Whitney. John D. Rockefeller gave away $1.5 million annually and launched the Rockefeller Foundation in 1913 with $100 million. His son, John, Jr., founded Rockefeller University and donated the Cloisters, Fort Tryon Park and the site for the United Nations building. John Jacob Astor left $400,000 for a library, which Brooke Astor, the wife of John Jacob's great-great grandson, still supports.

Clockwise from above *The Lion Opera Ballet performing in New York; soundboard making at the Steinway factory; names up in lights—Broadway shows are advertised in Times Square*

NEW YORK, NEW YORK, IT'S A HELLUVA TOWN

The film industry may have moved from New York to Hollywood after World War I, but it is still a film town, thanks to the renovation of old studios and the encouragement of the Mayor's Office of Film. Filmmakers have long conducted a love affair with the city, sometimes using fake studio backdrops, as they did in *King Kong*, and other times filming the reality on location. The directors most associated with New York are Martin Scorsese, Paul Mazursky, Sidney Lumet, John Cassavetes, Spike Lee and Wes Anderson *(The Royal Tenenbaums)*. But the love affair goes back a long way to such films as *Miracle on 34th Street* (1947), *The Naked City* (1948) and *On the Waterfront* (1954).

If you are looking for an architectural tour of New York plus an insight into its collective unconscious, treat yourself to any Woody Allen film.

THEY STILL MAKE STEINWAYS IN NEW YORK

The name Steinway signifies the best pianos in the world, and it has done so since 1853, when Henry Steinweg started the company. The company was so successful that by 1873 the family was able to build a company town in Astoria, Queens, complete with factory, housing, a school and other amenities. At one time, the company made 6,000 grand pianos a year, but the industry collapsed in 1927 with the introduction of radio and the phonograph. The company survived, although the family sold it in 1972. Today it continues to operate with 450 workers, who handcraft about 3,000 grand pianos (and 600 uprights) a year, which cost from $25,000 to $147,000. Even though the year-long process is the same as it was in 1853, each one has a different musical personality, depending on the wood and other subjective factors.

CHELSEA—NEW CENTER OF CONTEMPORARY ART

Although the acclaimed Dia Center for the Arts has closed its Chelsea gallery and is looking for a new home, in the late 1980s and early 1990s it made Chelsea the new vortex for contemporary art, surpassing SoHo and 57th Street.

Since then, the area between 19th and 29th streets and 10th and 11th avenues has grown into a large gallery district with more than 200 spaces. All the former big names in SoHo and Uptown are now represented in the gallery district—Matthew Marks, Larry Gagosian, Mary Boone, Pace Wildenstein, Paula Cooper, Robert Miller, Barbara Gladstone, Holly Solomon and Sonnabend. Some galleries have vast hangar-like spaces, large enough to accommodate massive works produced by such artists as Richard Serra. In some cases entire buildings (529 West 20th Street and 526 West 26th Street, for example) now house multiple galleries.

THE CHALLENGE OF BROADWAY

Every year Broadway is reported to be teetering on the edge of economic disaster and is accused of abandoning serious theater for warmed-over revivals. It's tough to make money on Broadway. Back in 1866, *Black Crook,* a musical melodrama, ran for only 475 performances and took in $1.1 million, easily recouping the $24,000 investment. Today a musical costs on average $8 million to produce and stage, and the show has to run for at least 520 performances just to break even.

When producers have to rely on tourists to fill the seats, it gets really tough. Success then depends on low costs, good press, a Tony Award and lots of luck. Few shows meet the test. In fact, about 80 percent of Broadway shows fail to recoup their investments. So producers turn to locations off- and off-off Broadway, where costs are lower and they can afford to nurture new playwrights.

The New York Times

Summarizing New York City politics is difficult. It's a complex city divided into five boroughs—Manhattan, Brooklyn, the Bronx, Queens and Staten Island—populated by around 8 million people of different ethnic origins and religious beliefs, and with diverse socio-economic interests. As a consequence, city politics are often contentious, with ethnic rivalries playing a large part in the political process. The municipal employee unions—police, fire, teachers, sanitation and transit—also play a major role in city politics and can make the city a more, or less, pleasant place in which to live and work. As far as national politics goes, New York City is firmly Democratic, even though it has voted for three Republicans in the last four mayoral elections. Only Staten Island votes pretty solidly Republican. The print media cut across party lines. The *New York Times*, the *Daily News* and *Newsday* lean toward the liberal side while the *Wall Street Journal*, the fledgling *New York Sun* and Rupert Murdoch's *New York Post* take a more conservative tack.

WHO'S IN CHARGE?

It's hard for outsiders to determine who is in charge. Under the federal system, the responsibilities are divided among the federal, state and municipal governments. Although there have been many powerful mayors—LaGuardia, Koch, and Giuliani in particular—their power is limited by the state governor, the state assembly and senate, the borough presidents and the city council, to name the major challengers. In 2009, for example, even though Mayor Bloomberg presided over a city with 38 percent of the state's population, he was battling Governor Patterson over the allocation of federal stimulus funds for health care.

The city lives under a tough set of fiscal rules imposed by the state 30 years ago, with four agencies monitoring city finances. If the city fails to balance the budget or pay its debt, the state will assume financial control.

Clockwise from above The New York Times *is traditionally a liberal newspaper; Madison Avenue is the powerhouse of the US advertising industry; Mayor Michael Bloomberg's 2003 ban on smoking in all public places did not go down well with New Yorkers*

EDUCATION IS THE TOPIC OF THE DAY

From the 1960s to the early 1990s crime and race dominated the headlines, but under Mayor Giuliani crime dropped dramatically and although race continued to play a divisive role, it diminished as a headline issue. Today, education is such a compelling issue that among the wealthy even getting into the "right" nursery school matters. Although there are top-notch schools (Stuyvesant, Bronx Science), the public (state) school system has been in crisis. It educates 1.1 million students in nearly 1,700 schools. Bloomberg has staked his reputation on reforming it by streamlining the bureaucracy and imposing a standard curriculum and standardized tests. Teachers and students are held accountable for good grades.

THE SMOKING EDICT

Mayor Giuliani disciplined New Yorkers for such "bad behavior" as jaywalking, panhandling, staging scatological art shows, squeegeeing and sleeping on, or occupying, two seats on the subway. Initially, New Yorkers grumbled, but came to appreciate the improvement in the quality of life that followed.

When Mayor Bloomberg tried to implement similar policies, he ran into resistance, particularly when he banned smoking from all public spaces, including bars. Bar and nightclub owners, libertarians and dedicated smokers were irate. A few years on, everyone has calmed down. In fact smokers even admit to enjoying smoke-free interiors and the camaraderie of smoking outside with others. Business has not been adversely affected.

GOSSIP

Gossip has a high profile in New York City because power, money, sex and celebrity drive society and gossip helps keep score on who's in and who's out. Gossip may have begun with Mrs William Astor and her list of 400 fashionable society members and continued on the zebra-striped banquettes at El Morocco and at Walter Winchell's table at the Stork Club. Now it's not confined to the tabloid newspapers. They may not be called gossip columns, but that's what they are: the *New York Times* has "Boldface Names;" *New York Magazine* has "The Intelligencer;" The *New Yorker* calls it the "Talk of the Town" and *Town & Country* insists that it's "Parties." Tina Brown leavened *Vanity Fair* with it. Everyone has to read the *New York Post's* Liz Smith, Cindy Adams and Page Six. It's becoming even more center stage, as the *Star* moves into Manhattan and gossip drives the content of *Us Weekly* and *People*.

MADISON AVENUE

Madison Avenue may be the Golden Mile of designer retailing, but it is also synonymous with one of the largest and most important city industries. Well over $100 billion a year is spent on advertising, with several billion more going to focus groups alone. With consumer spending accounting for 60 percent of the national economy and 22,000 new packaged products being launched annually, advertising plays a huge marketing role.

New York City remains the advertising capital of the United States, because all the national TV networks and major publishing companies have their headquarters or offices here. Although the advertising companies are not necessarily on or near Madison Avenue anymore—Saatchi & Saatchi is at 375 Hudson in the West Village—they do need to be near media buyers and sellers, so that they can participate readily in the seasonal media buying frenzy.

In spite of their reputation as indoor-dwellers, vast numbers of New Yorkers have a passion for sunshine, fresh air and healthy outdoor activity. This trend has been growing in recent years, prompting the city to undertake one of its most ambitious projects to date. Although the New York Greenway is only partly completed (the whole project will take years), long stretches exist and are an urban oasis for outdoor lovers. Of course, the ultimate outdoor space in New York — the green heart of the city — is Central Park. On sunny days, New Yorkers flock to the park to stroll along the well-tended paths and enjoy the gardens, woodlands and open meadow-like spaces that offer an oasis away from the concrete canyons of Manhattan. The city has other popular parks too, including Riverside Park, Battery Park and the new elevated High Line park, which opened in 2009. New Yorkers are also rediscovering their love affair with the 500 miles (800km)-plus of scenic city waterfront. Water tours are springing up everywhere, as are boat rental and tour operations that offer a chance to paddle a canoe or kayak along the city's waterfront. And city dwellers have long known that a ferry ride to Staten Island offers a romantic way to see the city from the water.

CENTRAL PARK
The Queen of Parks, this remarkable 843 acre (340ha) green space has been the verdant center of the city since it was designed and created by then-farmer Frederick Law Olmsted and architect Calvert Vaux in 1851. Today it entertains young and old alike with 58 miles (95km) of trails and bicycle paths, several lakes, open plazas, restaurants and plenty of quiet green nooks for relaxation. Favorite things to do in the park include visiting the 5 acre (2ha) wildlife center (zoo), renting a rowboat at the Loeb Boat House, attending a performance of Shakespeare in the Park at the Delacorte Theater, or enjoying refreshments in the garden at Tavern on the Green. Kids will love Conservatory Water where the fanciful sculptures based on *Alice in Wonderland* and Hans Christian Andersen stories are a big hit.

Clockwise from above *The extensive waterfront offers many opportunities for walking; Conservatory Garden in Central Park is the city's oldest floral garden; the Liberty Island ferry affords tremendous views of the cityscape*

ROOFTOPS AND HIGH PLACES

One of the favored ways to get outdoors in New York is to enjoy dining or drinks in a rooftop garden. The quality of these is often expressed by the quality of the view and ambience of the gardens. The long-term champion on both counts may be the elegant Rooftop Restaurant which graces the fifth floor of the Museum of Modern Art and offers spectacular views of the Abby Aldrich Rockefeller Sculpture Garden and the city skyline. Another top contender is the über-chic 230 Fifth, which is the largest rooftop in the city. For a family-friendly venue, head to the Metropolitan Art Museum's Roof Garden Café.

ON THE WATER

One of the best ways to see the city is from the water, and there are many great options available for doing this. One of the best ways to enjoy and appreciate spectacular harbor views of the south end of the city and the Statue of Liberty is aboard the Staten Island Ferry. Best of all, it's free! Easily the most romantic of the many commercial harbor tours is the two-hour cruise aboard the beautiful sailing schooner *Pioneer*, which leaves from South Street Seaport. Do-it-yourselfers will also find numerous kayak rental operations that allow you to explore the city waterways under your own power, or join a guided tour to do the same.

SMALL PARKS AND GREENWAYS

Beyond Central Park, New York offers a wealth of other opportunities to enjoy the outdoors. The most impressive of these is also the newest. The New York Greenway will eventually be a dedicated pedestrian and bicycle route that will encircle the city and provide more than 350 miles (560km) of multi-modal cycling and jogging paths in Manhattan and the other four boroughs. Roughly half finished, many miles of the existing route follow the city's waterfront offering splendid views. The Greenway links several of the city's popular parks which are well worth exploring, including the beautiful and lush Riverside Park on the city's west side and the elegant Battery Park at Manhattan's southernmost tip.

FLORAL GARDENS

With the current passion for all things green, it's easier than ever to find flower-lined paths and fragrant green spaces within the city. One of the city's oldest and best-known gardens is the Conservatory Garden in Central Park which offers 6 acres (2.5ha) of floral abundance. New to the city is the open and airy British Memorial Garden in Lower Manhattan, which commemorates British lives lost on 9/11. If you want to retreat from the world, the best place to do it is in the medieval monastic walled gardens of The Cloisters, way up the island. Still, the best gardens lie just outside the confines of Manhattan. They include the phenomenal New York Botanical Gardens in the Bronx, as well as the lovely, themed Brooklyn Botanical Garden.

New York City has always been a money-making city. John Jacob Astor made his fortune in real estate, J. P. Morgan in banking, Cornelius Vanderbilt in transportation and John D. Rockefeller in oil. Today wealth is still made in finance, real estate and commodities, but the new money is more in technology and communications and less in manufacturing and trade. Manufacturing has moved south or to Mexico and Asia, while the once mighty port business has shifted to New Jersey. New York is still the financial capital of the United States and the center of banking and insurance. The securities industry is vital to the city's economy. When it is booming, the city flourishes and when it declines, the city does too. When the dot-com bubble burst in March 2000 and was followed a year and half later by the tragedy of 9/11, the city suffered and by fall 2002 the city had a projected deficit of $5 billion. Under Mayor Bloomberg the city staged a remarkable economic recovery. However, the city deficit increased again with the economic recession that began in 2008.

SEVENTH AVENUE HANGS ON

From the 1930s to the 1950s, the garment industry was the biggest in the city. Cutters, pattern-makers and sewing-machine operators and button- and zipper-makers jammed the blocks between 36th and 38th streets from Madison to Eighth Avenue. (Seventh Avenue is called Fashion Avenue between 23rd and 42nd streets.) Today the only evidences of the trade are the racks being pushed along the sidewalks and the "seconds" bins. Most manufacturing has gone to low-cost countries like China. What remains is on the Lower East Side, and in Chinatown and Queens, where Chinese, Thai and Dominicans staff sweatshops. The Garment Industry Development Corporation is working to reinvigorate the industry.

THE NYSE, AMEX AND NASDAQ—THE THREE PILLARS

The New York Stock Exchange (NYSE), whose 1,366 seats are for sale by auction, is the most prestigious of the three. The first seats sold in 1868 for $4,000; in 2005 a seat sold for $3.5 million. Only the most carefully scrutinized companies—about 2,800 of them—are listed on the NYSE, which has a global market capitalization of $26.4 trillion, with an average daily trading value of $83.6 billion. Those who could not afford to join the NYSE started the Amex. It was originally called the Curb Market because the brokers did their business at the curbside. It was acquired by NYSE Euronet (NYX) in 2008, and rebranded to NYSE Amex Equities in 2009.

In 1971 the National Association of Securities Dealers Automated Quotation (Nasdaq) was launched as the world's first electronic stock market. It lists 3,800 mostly high-growth companies.

Above *The Broad Street building has housed the New York Stock Exchange since 1903*

THE STORY OF NEW YORK

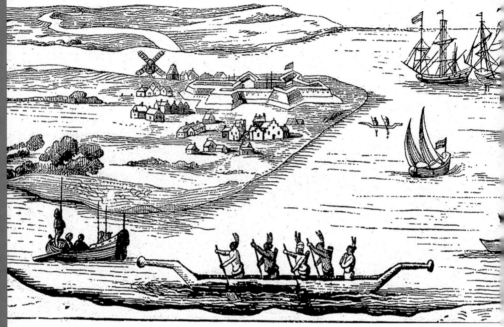

t' Fort nieuw Amsterdam op de Manhatans.

In the 16th century the area now known as Manhattan was a land of natural beauty, populated by wild animals and Native American tribes. Early explorers' engravings and vellum maps depict the hilly terrain and early settlements, including the Native American longhouses near Coney Island. In the early 16th century, Giovanni da Verrazano, a Florentine navigator and merchant working for the French, attempted to find the supposed Northwest Passage, a more direct route between Europe and Asia. Instead, he found himself sailing into the wonderful natural harbor that is now New York Harbor on April 17, 1524, and was greeted by the astonished native Algonquians. However, not much exploring went on until the arrival in 1609 of the English navigator Henry Hudson who reported to Europe on the quality of fur. The Dutch, recognizing the potential, went into business and brought traders to settle the area. One farm belonged to Jonas Bronck, whose name has stuck firmly to the area known today as the Bronx. In 1664 the English seized the territory and named it New York.

NATIVE AMERICANS

During the early colonial days, the Algonquians were often at war with each other and with the Iroquois. To protect themselves, the tribes lived in tight-knit groups under strong chiefs.

In the beginning, the Algonquians were a friendly people and showed the Dutch colonists where to hunt, farm and fish. The Native Americans enjoyed trading just as much as the Dutch, but then, as the colonists tried to take land away, fighting broke out. The Dutch attacked two encampments, killing 80 Native Americans, and started a very bloody war. Reports of this fighting got back to Holland, discouraging emigration to the New World.

Clockwise from above *Manhattan was named New Amsterdam after the Dutch took control; a view of Fort George and the early settlement of New York; Peter Stuyvesant's lack of a limb never held him back*

DUTCH COLONY

Peter Minuit bought Manhattan Island in 1626 for a cool $24 worth of kettles, axes and cloth. However, the Native Americans he paid did not share his concept of land ownership and did not understand the sale; furthermore, the transaction was made with the Canarsie tribe, who were merely passing by on that day. Dutch garrisons built a windmill, a fort, a barracks, a jail, a church, a tavern and a governor's house. There were about 120 houses by 1656, and about 300 four years later. Merchants and traders ran the municipal government and everyone was happy until the Dutch governor tried introducing measures to civilize the rowdy populace.

PETER STUYVESANT

The early colonists were a fairly lawless lot, and drunkenness and violence were common. Then, in 1647, the one-legged Peter Stuyvesant stepped in as governor. Under his strict control, law and order were established, along with a school, hospital, prison and post office. But Stuyvesant was not popular, and he eventually surrendered to English attackers, then returned to Holland in 1665 to defend himself against charges of misconduct. In 1667, he came back to his New York farm, the *bouwerij* that has given its name to New York's Bowery. Stuyvesant died in 1672 and was buried on his farm, now the site of St. Mark's Church-in-the-Bowery (▷ 120).

THE ENGLISH

In 1609 English navigator Henry Hudson first sailed up the river that now bears his name. He drew attention to the abundance of otter, beaver, mink and wildcat and on the possibilities of the fur trade. In 1664, with 8,000 unhappy Dutch colonists living on the island, now known as New Amsterdam, Colonel Richard Nicolls easily seized the territory from the Dutch on the orders of King Charles II of England. The king's brother, the Duke of York, took control and changed the colony's name to New York. The terms of the surrender were generous, and not a single Dutch resident took Nicolls up on his offer to repatriate them. Nicolls became governor and was both efficient and popular. In 1673, when a war between Holland and England broke out, New York returned to Dutch control, but it bounced back to the English in 1674 under the terms of the Treaty of Westminster.

FREEDOM OF THE PRESS

German immigrant John Peter Zenger became the editor of the *New York Weekly Journal* in 1733 and quickly grew unpopular with Governor William Cosby. His opposition to the governor's arbitrary acts gained support from lawyers, merchants and others of independent spirit. In 1734 he was arrested for seditious libel. His lawyer, Andrew Hamilton, refuted the libel charge on the basis that the offensive article was not actually false. The court disagreed, stating that whether or not the publication was true was irrelevant and that merely publishing such wicked words about the government was enough to convict.

However, Hamilton's eloquent appeal to the judge and jury resulted in Zenger's acquittal and a victory for freedom of the press. This set a precedent against judicial tyranny in libel suits and thus led eventually to the First Amendment to the Constitution.

THE·LIBRARY·OF·COLUMBIA·UNIVERSITY

King's College, now Columbia University (▷ 203), was established in 1754 by royal charter of King George II of Britain. As the American colonies grew more independently minded, students such as Alexander Hamilton emerged to become America's patriot leaders. In 1765 a Stamp Act passed by Parliament in London taxed marriage licenses, playing cards, newspapers and 40 other necessities of life, and infuriated the colonists. Leading opposition to the Stamp Act, New York sent a formal protest to the king; 28 delegates from nine colonies attended the Stamp Act Congress in New York. After protests that included suspension of all port activity for nearly two weeks, Parliament repealed the Act in March 1766. New York joined the fight against taxation that led to the American Revolution. Although New York did not see a great deal of action, it was Britain's military headquarters and was the only city occupied by the British throughout the conflict. When the war ended, many loyalists left America for the West Indies or Canada and the population dwindled to 12,000. But within six years of the British departure, New York had become America's most vibrant city.

BRITISH OCCUPATION

The city's Tories, who supported the British Crown, were jubilant when British troops entered New York in June 1776. Patriots surrounded the city, denying the British easy communications with other colonies. Under military occupation, the city suffered terrible fires and loss of life and property. A fire on September 21, 1776 destroyed a quarter of the city, including Trinity Church (▷ 79). On August 3, 1778, 100 houses burned. The guerrilla war between the two opposing sides involved cattle-rustling, abductions and deliberate burning of crops. American prisoners of war were either incarcerated in a crowded, appalling dungeon on Liberty Street or in ships anchored in the harbor. Almost 11,000 soldiers perished in the horrendous conditions.

Clockwise from above *The impressive entrance to the library of Columbia University; the inauguration of the first president, George Washington, on the balcony of Federal Hall*

THE TEA PARTY

The British Parliament approved the Tea Act in 1773, giving the British East India Company a monopoly on all the tea sold in the colonies. The angry Manhattan Sons of Liberty encouraged the public to repel the tea ships; New Yorkers boycotted all establishments offering East India tea.

On December 16, 1773, the Boston Tea Party, a protest in which a group of men masquerading as Mohawks dumped 342 cases of East India tea into Boston Harbor, further fueled radicalism in New York. Britain passed the Intolerable Acts which closed Boston's port, alarming New Yorkers. On April 22, 1774, New York had its own Tea Party and dumped 18 boxes of tea into the bay. This led to the establishment of the revolutionary government in New York State.

DEFEAT ON LONG ISLAND

After forcing the British General William Howe to evacuate Boston in March 1776, General George Washington arrived in Manhattan on April 13. Knowing that he would meet General Howe's army again, forts were built in Brooklyn Heights and Lower Manhattan. On July 2, Howe's force landed on Staten Island. On July 9, the Declaration of Independence was read to Washington's soldiers on Bowling Green. The delighted soldiers and civilians tore down the statue of King George III and melted it down to make bullets—42,088 of them. Meanwhile, Howe's army moved to the south of Brooklyn, where his 20,000 British regulars surprised Washington's 7,000 militiamen. The Battle of Long Island, a terrible defeat for Washington, left 2,000 Americans dead.

BENEDICT ARNOLD

In today's United States, the name Benedict Arnold is synonymous with traitor. After Arnold had fought for General Washington against the British at Lake Champlain and in Connecticut, he was placed in command of Philadelphia in 1778. But he became disillusioned with Congress after he was overlooked for promotion. He knew British General Clinton was bribing Americans to desert and he began a treasonable correspondence with Clinton. He was in the process of making plans to surrender West Point, the military academy then under his command, to the British when the plot was revealed. Arnold managed to escape and became a leader of British troops in New York. After the British surrendered, Arnold and his wife moved to England, where they were deeply unpopular.

FROM GENERAL TO PRESIDENT

On November 25, 1783, General Washington made his ceremonial entry into New York and gave a farewell address to his troops in front of Fraunces Tavern at 54 Pearl Street, then returned to his home at Mount Vernon in Virginia. On February 4, 1789, he was unanimously chosen as president of the new United States at a convention in Philadelphia.

On April 30, 1789, Washington took the oath of office on the balcony of L'Enfant's Federal Hall, on the site of today's Federal Hall National Monument (▷ 67). Thousands of supporters lined Murray's Wharf at the end of Wall Street as Washington arrived by ceremonial barge. The cheering crowds, waving their hats, then followed him on his route through the downtown streets of the city.

Savings Bank.   *Erie Canal.*   *Opera House.*

The first half of the 19th century brought New York conflict, epidemics and disaster, as well as an explosion of commerce and riches. During the War of 1812 between the United States and Britain, New York's port was blockaded. Ten years later, a yellow fever epidemic broke out in Front Street, and in 1832 a cholera epidemic killed 4,000. The Great Fire of 1835 gutted 700 buildings in a 17-block area below Wall Street; in 1845, another fire destroyed 300 buildings in Lower Manhattan. The achievement that brought growth, prosperity and international commerce to the city was the building of the Erie Canal in 1825, a project of Governor DeWitt Clinton. In following years, men went from rags to riches practically overnight. Cornelius Vanderbilt (1794–1877), an uneducated Staten Island farm boy, became one of the wealthiest men in America when he took control of much of the shipping business in the harbor and along the Hudson River to Albany. The swelling city needed news. William Cullen Bryant, whose name is now associated with Bryant Park, became editor of the *New York Evening Post* in 1829. In 1841 Horace Greeley became the founding editor of the *New York Tribune*, while other newspapers also flourished.

KNICKERBOCKER
The word "knickerbocker" was a literary invention of author Washington Irving (1783–1859) in his *Diedrich Knickerbocker's History of New York* (1809). A satire on pedantry, manners, politics and history told by an imaginary Dutch colonist, Knickerbocker, it won Irving much acclaim in the United States and Europe. New Yorkers of Dutch descent, and by extension the entire city, became known as Knickerbockers. The group of writers including Irving, novelist James Fenimore Cooper and poet William Cullen Bryant was known as the Knickerbocker Group. In 1946, the "New York Knickerbockers" pseudonym (shortened to New York Knicks) was adopted by the professional basketball team which plays its home games at Madison Square Gardens in Manhattan.

Clockwise from above *The Erie Canal gave the farmlands of the Midwest a route to the port of New York; engineer John Randel, Jr. devised the street grid system in 1811; John Jacob Astor bequeathed his library to the city*

ERIE CANAL

The Erie Canal, connecting the Hudson River and the Great Lakes, made New York the only eastern port with a waterway route to the farmlands of the Midwest, and instantly turned the city into America's thriving center of commerce. It was New York governor DeWitt Clinton who oversaw the $7-million project, which skeptics at the time called "Clinton's Folly."

The 10-day canal trip from New York to Buffalo meant that goods from around the world could be transported via New York to the interior of the New World. There was an explosion of new office space and warehouse development along the harbor, and New York began its career as a major world trading center.

ARTIST AND INVENTOR

By 1825, many of the most respected American painters were living in New York— that is, the ones who stayed in the country and did not go to Paris. A significant artist of the Romantic School and a successful portrait painter, Samuel F. B. Morse is best remembered as the inventor of the Morse Code.

He moved permanently to New York in 1824 and became a founder of the National Academy of Design in 1826. *The House of Representatives* (1822–23), one of Morse's most notable paintings, includes more than 80 portraits of politicians. By the early 1830s, he was more interested in electrical experiments than in painting, and in 1844 he tapped out in code the famous message, "What hath God wrought?"

JOHN JACOB ASTOR

By 1808, John Jacob Astor—who emigrated to America from Germany in 1783—had amassed a fortune in the fur trade and was the sole owner of the American Fur Company. When he grew fat and his health deteriorated, he sold the company and took up real estate. After he invested in farmland north of New York City, in what is now the heart of Manhattan, the city's rapid expansion turned his farmland into a goldmine. Astor House, the biggest hotel in the world at the time, stood on what is now City Hall Park (▷ 65) and was the first building to bear the family's name. The Astor Library, which he bequeathed to the city, is now part of the New York Public Library (▷ 159).

GRID SYSTEM

New York City's grid system of streets was devised in 1811, at a time when the population was increasing rapidly. In need of new streets for the undeveloped land north of Washington Square, city officials accepted the plans put forward by engineer and surveyor John Randel, Jr.

The commissioners dismissed the idea of ovals, circles or stars and opted for the economy of straight lines and right angles, while no street was to be less than 50 feet (15m) wide, and no main street less than 60 feet (18m) wide. The Commissioner's Plan called for 2,000 long, narrow blocks, disregarded the contours of the land, and provided for neither parks nor open spaces.

By 1875 more than a million people lived in New York. The poor, many of them recent immigrants, lived in tenements that bred hatred, violence and disease, especially tuberculosis. Jacob Riis published a book of photographs, *How the Other Half Lives* (1890), which called the public's attention to the atrocious living conditions. As a result, reformers like Theodore Roosevelt and Frances Perkins joined a crusade to rid the city of these inhumane dwellings. The enormous task of transportation in the growing city was a major problem. In 1858, about 35 million passengers used horse-drawn trams to move around. In the 1860s, trains were a welcome improvement. Washington Bridge, opened in 1889, made it easier to go from Manhattan to the Bronx. Commissioner George Waring reorganized the sanitation system and, in 1893, New York began chlorinating its drinking water. Progressive reformers brought education to immigrant children and they were offered free medical examinations in 1895.

ELIZABETH BLACKWELL

Elizabeth Blackwell came from Bristol, England, to New York in 1832 to train as a doctor. She applied to eight medical schools before being accepted at Geneva Medical School. Graduating in 1847, she was ostracized by the profession because she was a woman. With great determination, she opened a dispensary for the poor in the slums of the Lower East Side. In 1857 she founded the New York Infirmary for Indigent Women and Children (the New York Infirmary). In 1868, after creating a training school for nurses, she founded the Women's Medical College of the New York Infirmary. She died in 1910, in Hastings, England.

Clockwise from above *Abraham Lincoln proclaimed the emancipation of slaves in 1863; immigrants poured into the city in the second half of the 19th century; a cartoon satirizing William Marcy "Boss" Tweed (1823–78), the corrupt politician who defrauded New York City of $30 million*

SLAVERY

By the middle of the 18th century, New York had the highest concentration of slaves north of Virginia. They were sold at the slave market at the foot of Wall Street until slavery was abolished in New York State in 1827. But slavery was to continue, especially in the South, for another 38 years. New York provided a pivotal stage for its demise. On February 27, 1860, Abraham Lincoln arrived in New York City to give his celebrated antislavery address in the Great Hall of the Cooper Union Foundation Building on East Seventh Street, now a designated historic landmark. His eloquent defense of the Constitution and the call for the freedom of slaves helped him secure the Republican presidential nomination.

TAMMANY HALL

In 1850 William Marcy Tweed organized the formation of a volunteer fire department, a move which made him popular enough to get elected to city and state posts.

In the 1860s and 1870s, under Tweed's direction, corrupt politicians at the Democratic Party headquarters, Tammany Hall, ran the party by a combination of bribery, coercion and vote rigging.

Having swindled the city authorities at every opportunity, Tweed was finally caught after the Tweed Ring reneged on a deal with the sheriff, who went to the press with his story. *The New York Times* revealed the truth, and on November 19, 1873, Tweed was sentenced to 12 years in prison.

DRAFT RIOTS 1863

A dearth of volunteers for the Civil War led to conscription in 1862. In New York, as in other places, the draft met with great opposition and bounty hunters found substitutes for men who could pay. Others with $300 in their pocket could pay to be exempt.

The cost of living in New York had doubled and the mostly Irish dock workers had gone on strike for higher wages; they were furious when African-Americans were brought in to work. Under the circumstances the Irish workers could see no reason why they should be required to fight for black freedom and bitterly resented conscription. Four days of rioting in scorching heat ended on July 17, 1863, but not before 120 men had died, mostly African-Americans killed by Irish immigrant laborers.

JEWISH IMMIGRANTS

The first Jewish people, 27 of them, arrived in New York in 1633. The pogroms in Russia and Eastern Europe caused the great influx of Jewish immigrants at the turn of the 19th century. In 1892, around 81,000 Jewish people arrived at Ellis Island (▷ 72–74) and 258,000 more between 1905 and 1906. They crowded into the tenements on the Lower East Side (▷ 75), alongside the Irish, who had arrived in the country earlier and who resented the newcomers. Given that many of the city police officers of the day were Irish, it is hardly surprising that Mayor McClellan's police commissioner claimed that 50 percent of the city's crimes were committed by Jewish people. The outraged Jewish community then forced him to make a full public retraction.

By 1900 Greater New York had a population of 3.5 million and was the world's second-largest city after London. In Manhattan, 42,700 tenements housed the 1.5 million poor in dire conditions. By the 1920s a campaign to restrict immigration resulted in legislation that brought a decline in the number of newcomers from Poland, Russia and Italy. The great metropolis experienced terrible disasters and celebrated remarkable triumphs. In 1901, a heatwave killed nearly 100 New Yorkers in just 24 hours. The first skyscrapers went up, starting with the Flatiron Building in 1902, symbolizing the city's wealth and hopes for the future. Writer John J. Fitz Gerald first coined the city's nickname "Big Apple" in 1921. Meanwhile, Prohibition drove New Yorkers to illegal speakeasies. Many went uptown to Harlem for nights of pleasure. Then, on October 24, 1929, the New York stock market collapsed, bringing the Roaring Twenties to a sudden halt. The resulting Great Depression lasted a decade. After World War II the city experienced an economic boom and became a major political player when the United Nations headquarters was established in the city.

HARLEM

Jazz flourished in Harlem in the 1920s and 1930s as white New Yorkers discovered establishments such as the Cotton Club, famous for its "Colored Revues" and as the home of Duke Ellington, the Great Orchestrator of Jazz. Ellington's band, the Washingtonians, and his arrangements dominated big-band jazz for three decades. In 1932, he wrote a song whose title served as a slogan for the next 10 years: *It Don't Mean a Thing If It Ain't Got That Swing*. Cotton Club owner Owney Madden, a gangster and bootlegger, strictly enforced segregation. The Depression took the swing out of these Harlem nightspots, and the Cotton Club moved downtown to West 48th Street, eventually closing in 1940.

Clockwise from above *New Yorkers got their kicks on Coney Island's Boardwalk, thanks to the subway; since 1904 the subway system has been an important factor in New Yorkers' daily life; Edwardian New York is apparent in the 20-floor Flatiron Building*

TRIANGLE SHIRTWAIST FIRE

Sweatshops in the Lower East Side at the beginning of the 20th century employed immigrant families in dreadful conditions on very low pay. Wages were increased after a series of strikes, but the tragedy of the Triangle Shirtwaist Fire in 1911 was to bring improvements in factory safety standards.

The factory, on the top three floors of a 10-story building at the corner of Washington Place and Greene Street, employed 600 workers, mainly young women. They were ready to go home when the fire broke out. Many doors to the fire escapes were locked, as was common during working hours, and 146 workers perished, some leaping to their deaths. Public outrage brought new legislation for safety in the workplace.

TIN PAN ALLEY

By 1900 New York was the place to be for the young, ambitious songwriter. Theaters were flourishing and music publishers needed as many songs as they could get their hands on. Hundreds of composers and small publishing firms crowded into the abandoned brownstones on 28th Street, between Fifth Avenue and Broadway, and the area became known as Tin Pan Alley because of the cacophony coming from the open windows. Two of the great songwriters of this era were George and Ira Gershwin, sons of Russian immigrants. At 15 years old, George was the youngest song demonstrator. The brothers' many hits included the classics *I Got Rhythm*, *Embraceable You* and *Somebody Loves Me*. George died of a brain tumor in 1937 at the age of 38.

THE SUBWAY

The elevated railways, financed by Jay Gould, Russell Sage and J. P. Morgan in the 1860s, improved public transportation, but were already inadequate by 1900. It was time to go underground. The Interborough Rapid Transit Company was born. The first line, 22 miles (35km) long, opened in 1904, carrying 600,000 passengers each day. It was a huge success and the profits enabled the city to expand the system. In 1921, New York and New Jersey joined forces to create the Port of New York Authority to develop and operate transportation. Delightful Coney Island, with its family entertainment, vaudeville and exhibitions, became accessible to everyone, thanks to New York's subways, which now total 660 miles (1,062km) in length, across 22 lines.

ORGANIZED CRIME

Just before Mayor William O'Dwyer, first elected as New York's mayor in 1946, began a re-election campaign, the *Brooklyn Eagle* published some extremely damning news about the mayor's connection to organized crime in the city. The newspaper charged that police officers and judges were being paid off in return for protection for 4,000 bookies. The mayor fled to Florida "for health reasons." In the hope of avoiding prosecution, more than 110 police officers resigned.

In August 1950, the mayor also resigned. Subpoenaed and left with little alternative, O'Dwyer had to admit he knew all about the corruption and that he too had associations with mobsters. Yet for a lack of hard evidence of willful wrongdoing, he went unpunished.

The years between 1950 and 2000 swung back and forth between economic booms (1950s, 1980s, 1990s) and financial crisis (1970s), and Wall Street struggled and soared with the times. New York's Abstract Expressionist painters inspired the art world in the late 1940s and 1950s; the Pop Artists shocked and thrilled the public from the late 1950s to the 1970s. Music and theater got a massive boost when the Lincoln Center was built in the 1960s. The number of Asian and Hispanic immigrants swelled, with Hispanics eventually overtaking the African-American population as the city's largest minority group. In 1989 the city elected its first black mayor, David Dinkins, who beat Rudolph Giuliani. Crime soared in the 1970s and 1980s, and vandals defaced landmarks and public buildings with graffiti. After Rudolph Giuliani was elected mayor in 1994, the number of recorded crimes dropped from 430,460 per year in 1993 to 161,956 in 2001, and the city had bright hopes for the future.

GREENWICH VILLAGE

By the 1950s, New York was America's cultural marketplace and Greenwich Village, with its cheap rents and bohemian flair, attracted America's finest artists and writers. Cedar Street Tavern at 24 University Place was the favorite Village hang-out for Abstract Expressionist painters Jackson Pollock, Willem de Kooning and Franz Kline. Regulars at the San Remo bar on the corner of Bleecker and MacDougal streets included writers James Agee, James Baldwin, Allen Ginsberg, Jack Kerouac and William Burroughs. It was here that the word "Beatnik" entered the language. Writers Dylan Thomas and Norman Mailer preferred the White Horse at Hudson and West 11th Street. Mailer's disregard for the Beats produced the Hip Generation.

Clockwise from above *The Lincoln Center was part of a 12-block urban renewal project in the 1960s, replacing tenement buildings in the Upper West Side; Woody Allen; Astronaut John Glenn was greeted with a tickertape parade*

WOODY ALLEN

Allan Konigsberg changed his name when he started out as a comedian in Greenwich Village comedy clubs. He went on to make about a movie a year after 1965, most of them about New Yorkers. In 1977 for *Annie Hall* the brainy, scrawny actor and director won Oscars for Best Director and Best Screenplay.

He sometimes shows up on Monday night at the Café Carlyle (35 East 76th Street at Madison Avenue) to play clarinet with the resident jazz band.

His 1992 affair with and later marriage to the adopted daughter of his then partner, fellow actor Mia Farrow, shook his fans and seriously damaged his subsequent career.

ED KOCH

The Big Apple was in such dire financial straits in the 1970s that it seemed only a miracle could prevent a collapse. In October 1975, for instance, the city was only 53 minutes from defaulting on its almost $477 million debt. After the Federal government proved unwilling to extend a hand, money from teacher pension funds inched the city back from the brink of disaster. When Ed Koch ran for mayor, he vowed to restore prosperity. He kept his promise after winning the 1977 election, and was re-elected by a landslide victory in 1981. His tax cuts, along with changes to investment banking, restored corporate America's confidence in New York.

SWEET SUCCESS

In 1962, astronaut John Glenn, the first American to orbit the earth, arrived in New York and jubilant throngs lined Broadway for a tickertape parade, an honor bestowed only on visiting heads of state, generals, victorious baseball teams, athletes and great politicians. New Yorkers flung 3,474 tons of tickertape, more than anyone had ever seen before, from the windows of office buildings and skyscrapers along the route.

In 1969 the New York Mets rose from ninth place in the National League, defeating the Baltimore Orioles in the World Series and ending up with their first victory pennant. But they received only a tickertape flurry compared to the blizzard that welcomed John Glenn.

ANDY WARHOL

Pop Art changed the art scene when Andy Warhol opened his Factory in 1963. His Coca-Cola bottle, Campbell's Soup cans and multicolor silk-screen images of icons Marilyn Monroe, Elvis Presley and Jackie Kennedy were as astonishing at the time as the openly gay lifestyle he confidently espoused in an era when "homophobic" wasn't even a word. As a movie director he filmed *Kiss* and *Blow Job* in friends' apartments on the Lower East Side and in Greenwich Village. He lived as a recluse for the last 13 years of his life at 57 East 66th Street and died in 1987 rather bizarrely after routine gallbladder surgery.

New York City's financial situation was not rosy at the start of the millennium. Mayor Rudolph Giuliani had cut taxes by $3 billion, and the city was heavily in debt. Then came the terrorist attack on September 11, 2001, that killed nearly 3,000 people, destroyed millions of square feet of office space and closed the Stock Exchange for four days. Mayor Giuliani's courage and compassion was admired by all. For plain-speaking Michael Bloomberg, elected in 2002, Giuliani was a hard act to follow. The billionaire businessman won re-election in 2005, and again in 2009. Bloomberg turned the $6 billion deficit into a $3 billion surplus. In 2011, the National September 11 Memorial, built on the site of the former World Trade Center twin towers, opened to the public on the 10th anniversary of the tragedy.

Above *Nightlife thrives in a city made safer and healthier by the reforms of its 21st-century mayors*

CRIME

In 2003, New York happily boasted that it was America's safest large city, and given its history of disturbing crime statistics, this is good news. New York was ranked 160th in total crime among 205 American cities. The 15-year trend of crime reduction, with homicides at a 40-year low, is continuing. It was the controversial, aggressive policing during the Giuliani years that helped to cut crime by 62 percent. The mayor beefed up the police force with 4,000 new officers and sent them out to tackle jaywalking, sleeping on subways, defacing property, and other petty crime and quality of life issues. Mayor Bloomberg has continued to fight crime.

SOCIAL REFORMS

Bloomberg's trendsetting social reforms have gained followers in municipalities across the United States and Europe. The smoking ban was extended in 2003 to include all commercial establishments and, in 2011, to parks and beaches as well. In 2008, New York became the first city in the US to ban trans-fat in all restaurants. Bloomberg made education reform a top priority, and achieved an 18 percent increase in the high school graduation rate.

In 2007 he announced an aggressive program to improve the environment by reducing pollution and traffic congestion. Hybrid taxicabs will be one of the early changes, along with planting 1 million trees.

ON THE MOVE

On the Move gives you detailed advice and information about the various options for traveling to New York before explaining the best ways to get around the city once you are there. Handy tips help you with everything from buying tickets to renting a car.

ON THE MOVE NEW YORK

ARRIVING

ARRIVING BY AIR

You can fly direct to New York from most major European, American and other cities around the world. International carriers fly into John F. Kennedy International Airport, 15 miles (24km) from Manhattan, on Jamaica Bay, and Newark Liberty International Airport, 16 miles (26km) west of town. LaGuardia Airport handles mainly domestic flights and is 8 miles (13km) from Manhattan in Queens.

Above *The city has three major airports*

TRANSPORTATION FROM MAJOR AIRPORTS

	JOHN F. KENNEDY INTERNATIONAL AIRPORT (JFK)	LAGUARDIA AIRPORT (LGA)
Distance from Manhattan:	15 miles (24km).	8 miles (13km).
Journey time to Manhattan:	Taxi 45–60 minutes, subway 60–100 minutes.	Taxi 20–35 minutes, bus 40–50 minutes.
Ground transportation information:	Baggage claim level of all terminals.	Baggage claim level of all terminals.
Transport	**Shuttle/subway** » The subway costs $2.25 but you will need to buy a MetroCard (▷ 45). **AirTrain** » Buy your ticket ($5 each way) at the station, or from a vending machine in the airport. » The AirTrain connects to the LIRR at Jamaica station, subways at Howard Beach/JFK Airport station and Sutphin Boulevard-Archer Avenue/Jamaica station, and local bus lines.	**Bus** » Follow the "Ground Transportation" signs out of the terminal. You will see the M60 bus stop sign at the curb. » The fare is $2.25, but you save on the transfer if you use a MetroCard (▷ 45). » Take the M60 to 106th Street at Broadway. » Get off at Lexington Avenue to catch the 4, 5 and 6 subway trains; at Malcolm X Boulevard for the 2 and 3 trains; at St. Nicholas Avenue for the A, B, C and D trains; at 116th Street-Columbia University for the 1 train. » The bus runs daily 24 hours, at least every 30 minutes and more frequently during the day. » For current information, visit www.mta.info/nyct/service/airport.htm.

John F. Kennedy International Airport (JFK)

JFK has nine passenger terminals. Terminal 7 handles all British Airways flights, jetBlue uses Terminal 5, and Delta Terminals 2, 3 and 4. There are information desks, restaurants and concession stands in all terminals. An AirTrain links the airport and the New York subway, local bus lines and the Long Island Railroad (LIRR).

LaGuardia Airport (LGA)

Most domestic flights go through LaGuardia Airport, with United Airlines and Continental Airlines operating the lion's share. For assistance, look for the Customer Service Agents in their red jackets or go to the information desk between concourse C and D on the departure level. There are restaurants in the USAir and Delta terminals, which are accessible via a free shuttle service.

Newark Liberty International Airport (EWR)

Major carriers that fly into this airport include Virgin Atlantic, British Airways, Lufthansa and Continental Airlines. All passenger terminals— A, B and C—have restaurants on the concourse level, and the information desk is in Terminal B, lower level. The AirTrain system links the airport with the NJ Transit, Amtrak and the LIRR, and is quick and cheap.

LEAVING THE AIRPORT

After collecting your bags and going through Customs, you can get into the city in several ways (▷ below).

TAXIS

Taxi stands are outside all the terminals. Dispatchers work peak hours at JFK and LaGuardia, and 24 hours a day at Newark (▷ 53).

Tip your drivers 15 to 20 percent.
» At JFK, you are charged a flat rate of $45, plus round-trip tolls and tip.
» At LaGuardia, you pay by the meter ($24–$30), plus tolls and tip.
» At Newark, dispatchers ask you where you are going. Give an address and you will be quoted the fare ($50–$75, plus tolls, tip and a $5 surcharge).

TIP

» Avoid airport hustlers offering taxi services. City cabs and car services are a better option from outside terminals in designated areas.

NEWARK LIBERTY INTERNATIONAL AIRPORT (EWR)

16 miles (26km).

Taxi 50–60 minutes, AirTrain 30 minutes.

On the baggage claim level.

AirTrain

» This modern speedy monorail/rail link operated by NJ Transit and Amtrak is comfortable, fast and easy, provided you do not have a lot of baggage.

» Follow signs to the AirTrain from any Newark arrivals terminal.

» Buy your ticket at the station (NJ Transit trains $12.50/children under 5 free) or from a vending machine in the airport or at the train station.

» The AirTrain takes you to Penn Station at Eighth Avenue and 31st Street in Manhattan.

» Do not get off at Newark's Penn Station if you want to go to Manhattan—stay on board until the next stop to reach New York's Penn Station. From there, you can easily catch a cab, the subway or a bus to your hotel.

» NJ Transit trains run two to three times an hour during peak travel times, once an hour off-peak.

» It is easy to make connections to destinations beyond Manhattan from the Newark International Airport Station. For details, phone NJ Transit 973/275-5555 or visit www.njtransit.com, or phone Amtrak 800/ USA-RAIL or visit www.amtrak.com.

ADDITIONAL INFORMATION

Telephone contact

The Air-Ride number, 800/247-7433, describing transportation to and from all three airports, is answered by an operator Monday to Friday between 8am and 6pm; at all other times you get recorded information.

NYC and Co.

810 Seventh Avenue, New York, NY 10019
212/484-1222
www.nycgo.com

Contact NYC and Co. to order the *Official Visitor Guide* listing hotels, restaurants, theaters, attractions and events. The visitor's kit also includes a map, brochures, a newsletter and information on services.

PRIVATE TRANSPORTATION FROM MAJOR AIRPORTS
New York Airport Service Express Bus
www.nyairportservice.com

Follow the "Ground Transportation" signs to the pick-up point outside the terminal.

☎ 718/560-3915

From JFK
This service runs between 6.05am and 11pm, and travel time is 45 to 65 minutes, longer during rush hour. The trip to the Port Authority Bus Terminal, at 42nd Street and Eighth Avenue, costs $15 ($27 round trip). The journey to Grand Central Terminal at Vanderbilt Avenue and 42nd Street or to Bryant Park costs $15 ($27 round trip), or $27 round trip to hotels between 31st and 60th streets. The service to New York's Penn Station costs $15 ($27 round trip).

From LaGuardia
This service runs between 7.30am and 11pm, and travel time is 30 to 45 minutes, longer during rush hour. The journey costs $12 ($21 for a round trip) to Port Authority Bus Terminal at 42nd Street and Eighth Avenue or Grand Central Terminal at Vanderbilt Avenue and 42nd Street or Bryant Park, and $21 for a round trip to hotels between 31st and 60th streets. From Grand Central there are onward connections from the 30-minute journeys to Penn Station (also $21 for a round trip from LaGuardia).

Right *A local bus on Madison Avenue*

SuperShuttle
www.supershuttle.com

Go to the Ground Transportation desk and dial SuperShuttle on the courtesy phone in the baggage claim area of JFK, LaGuardia or Newark airports. Vans run 24 hours a day, throughout all five boroughs of New York City. Reservations are not required. The fares range from $20 to $30.

☎ 800/258-3826 or 212/ 315-3006

Coach USA
www.coachusa.com

Operating only out of Newark Airport, Coach USA takes passengers to Grand Central Terminal, at Vanderbilt Avenue and 42nd Street; to the Port Authority Bus Terminal, at Eighth Avenue and 42nd Street; and to Fifth Avenue—Bryant Park on 42nd Street, opposite the New York Public Library. The bus leaves every 15 minutes to Midtown (every 30 minutes 11.15pm–6.45am) and costs $15 ($25 round trip); children under 12 ride free.

☎ 877/8-NEWARK (639275)

SECURITY AT CUSTOMS
Since 9/11, security has been stepped up at airports, tunnels, bridges and train stations. To facilitate departure, do cooperate. Do not carry sharp items on your person or in your carry-on bags.

Empty your pockets into the tray provided before walking through the security detection scanner. Be prepared to open your bags to be hand searched or remove your shoes for inspection, or to allow a security officer to scan your body with a hand-held scanner.

ARRIVING BY ROAD
Driving into Manhattan is not for the faint-hearted and once you've got into the city, you then have the problem of finding somewhere to park. Always expect lengthy delays on the bridges and tunnels that cross to the island of Manhattan, especially on the bridges that cross the East River (repairs are ongoing). It is best to avoid the morning, lunchtime and evening rush-hour traffic if you can.

ARRIVING BY RAIL
Most commuter trains operating from Connecticut and the suburbs north of the city serve Grand Central Terminal (on 42nd Street at Park Avenue, ▷ 156–157).

Amtrak's long-distance trains from across the United States pull into Penn Station at 31st Street and Seventh Avenue.

For journeys to and from Long Island and New Jersey, the Long Island Railroad and New Jersey Transit are the trains to catch, also operating out of Penn Station.

The best way to see Manhattan is on foot. Streets in most Manhattan neighborhoods are safe both by day and after dark. However, walking takes time, and if you want to visit several museums or neighborhoods, or if the weather is bad, the subways are a better option. They are easy to use, inexpensive, and relatively clean and safe. Buses are more pleasant than subways because you get a chance to see street life as you travel, although you need to pay with correct change, and during rush hour traffic slows your progress—sometimes it's faster to walk.

OPTIONS

If you will be in New York for seven days or more, buy a MetroCard to save money on transit fares. You swipe the card at the subway turnstile or as you get on the bus, and you do not have to worry about having the correct change. Taxis are the quickest way for many to travel but the most expensive. When you take a cab, don't forget to tip the driver 15 percent or more.

Driving your own car in New York is not usually the best option for getting around. Besides the traffic, you will need to park on the street, and garages are expensive. If you do arrive in New York by car, the best course is to leave your car in a garage until you are ready to leave town (head for the eastern or western fringes of Manhattan if saving money matters more to you than convenience).

WALKING IN NEW YORK

» Always use crosswalks; jaywalking is against the law.
» Stay to the right as you would when driving.
» When the light changes and you are about to cross, check the intersection to make sure that no drivers or bicyclists have decided to make a dash through the light. This is not uncommon.

METROCARD

What is it?
A magnetically encoded card that debits the fare when you swipe it through the turnstile in the subway or the fare box on a bus.

What about transfers?
When you use a MetroCard for a trip, transfers between subways and buses within a two-hour period are free.

Where can I buy one?
From staffed subway booths (cash only), special vending machines in most subway stations (cash, credit cards, debit cards), drugstores like Rite Aid, Hudson News at Penn Station and Grand Central Terminal, or at the Times Square Visitor Center at 1560 Broadway between 46th and 47th streets (cash, credit cards, debit cards). Many hotels sell them, too.

What's the cost?
Pay-Per-Ride MetroCard: choose how many rides to buy when you purchase the card. Cards can be swiped four times in succession, so are good for up to four people traveling together. Just swipe, walk through, and hand the card to the person behind you, who swipes, walks through, and hands it to the person behind. You can refill these cards—that is, put more rides on them—in the vending machines located in most subway stations. Just put the card in, indicate how much money you want to spend, and insert your credit card or cash.

Unlimited Ride MetroCard: $29 buys a 7-Day Card, $104 buys a 30-Day Card. These can't be used by more than one person—an 18-minute interval must elapse between successful card swipes at the same station. These cards go into effect the first time you use them, not the day you buy them.

Can I get a discount?
Seniors and visitors with disabilities can get reductions, but you must fill out an application for a Reduced-Fare MetroCard or an AutoGate Reduced-Fare MetroCard (to enable wheelchair users or visitors with disabilities who are accompanied by a service animal to access the subway via the AutoGate). You can download it online, or phone 718/330-1234 for more information.

How do you use a MetroCard?
When you swipe your card, the turnstile indicator shows how much money is left on the card. If you swipe the card too fast or too slowly, the indicator asks you to swipe it again. If this happens, swipe it again. Do not go to a different turnstile, as you may end up paying twice.

Where can I get more information?
Phone 718/330-1234, from Monday through Friday between 6am and 10pm or visit www.mta.nyc.ny.us/metrocard

The Metropolitan Transit Authority (MTA) runs the subway system. It runs 24 hours a day, seven days a week. Rush hour is roughly between 7.30 and 9.30am and again from 4.30 to 6.30pm Monday through Friday except holidays. The subway is quick, inexpensive, efficient, generally safe, and fairly easy to figure out.

TIP

» New Yorkers refer to subway lines as trains. "Take the A train" means "Take subway line A."

Fares are $2.25 ($1.10 for seniors and people with disabilities); children under 44 inches (1.12m) ride free. The best way to pay is by MetroCard (▷ 45). A single-ride ticket purchased from a vending machine is $2.50.

Passengers should give their seats to the elderly and infirm, move to the center of the train so as not to block the doors, and walk not run.

SUBWAY HELP

» Station clerks are very helpful, and many subway stations are manned.

» For help in English, call 718/330-1234, 24 hours a day.
» For help in other languages, call 718/330-4847, between 7am and 7pm.

FINDING A SUBWAY

» In the station look for the signs with colored circles showing the subway line letter (A, B, C, etc.) or

UNDERSTANDING THE SUBWAY MAP

MTA maps are free and easy to understand. You can get them in any subway station, at information centers and in hotel lobbies.

The map (▷ 47) shows each line as a different color, but it is the number or letter that you need to know. No one refers to trains by color.

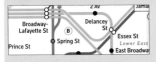

Solid black circles on the colored lines indicate stops for local trains, which make more stops than express trains.

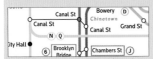

Black and white lines connecting white and black circles indicate free subway transfers.

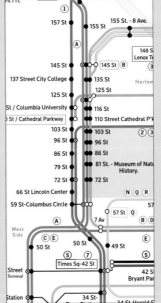

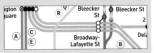

White circles on the colored lines indicate express train stops. Express trains skip about three stops for every one they make.

Below the name of every stop, the letters or numbers of the lines that stop there are indicated. Boldface type, for example **B**, indicates that the line offers a full-time service. Lightface type, for example B, indicates a part-time service. At 72nd Street, you see B, **C**, indicating part-time service on line B and full-time on C.

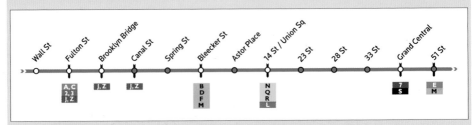

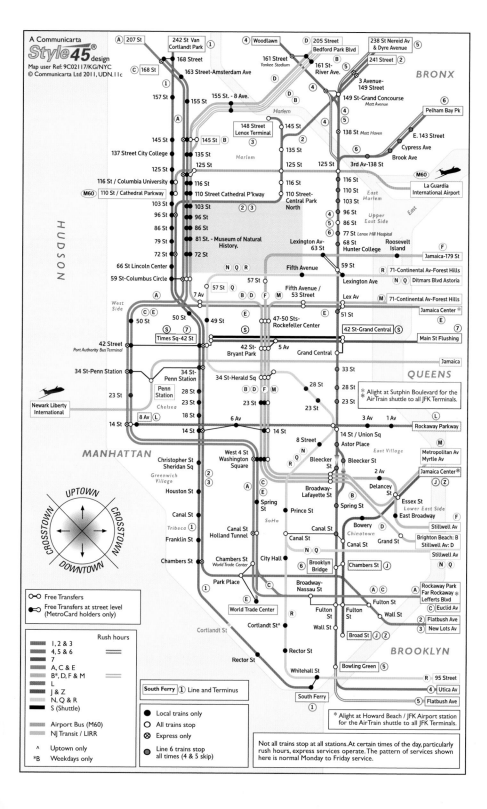

the subway line numbers of the trains that stop there.

» If you need help finding a subway station, ask a police officer or step into a hotel lobby, museum or store to ask. Most people working in such places are used to helping tourists but even regular New Yorkers on the street do so quite happily.

TIP
» The Lower East Side and the East Village are not well served by subways. If you are traveling to or from these areas at night, it is best to take a taxi.

FINDING THE RIGHT SUBWAY LINE
» After you have paid and walked through the turnstile, look for the colored circles. Find the line you want, and follow the signs. Above the platform edge, signs indicate the trains that stop there, their destinations and hours of operation. Changes to the line's service are usually posted, but signs are not very large, so you need to look carefully.

» Uptown or downtown? If you want to go north of where you are, no matter where in the city you happen to be, you want an uptown train. If you want to go south of where you are, you want a downtown train. Some stations are Uptown Only or Downtown Only— clearly marked at street level. If you find the color circle with the number or letter you want and know that you want to go north, for example, do not go into a subway entrance marked Downtown Only—any train you catch there will take you in the opposite direction. Trains headed in the right direction are nearby—the entrance is usually across the street.

» On the front and side of every train, the route number or letter is displayed. Make sure you look for this before getting on the train to be sure it is the one you want.

» If you really want to be sure, stand in the middle of the platform, halfway between the two ends of the train, and when the train

HOW TO USE THE SUBWAY

» Although the New York subway once had a bad reputation for safety, trains are now safer and cleaner. However, pickpockets and beggars are perennial, so keep a close eye on your bags. Keep your money well hidden and do not wear expensive jewelry or even jewelry that looks expensive.

» Do not wait for trains near the edge of the platform; stand back a bit.

» If there are few people on the platform or if you are alone, stand under the yellow sign "During Off Hours Trains

Stop Here." When the train stops, the conductor sticks his or her head out the window from a middle car, which is where he or she rides, and you should, as well.

» Let passengers get off first before getting on.

» Stay out of empty cars.

» After 11pm or midnight, take a taxi until you know your way around in the subway.

» If you find yourself on an express train speeding past your destination, get off at the next stop and either take the same line back to where you got on or ask the station clerk for directions. Be prepared to pay an extra fare to re-enter the platform; at some stations, you may need to exit the station, cross the street, and re-enter the station on the other side to catch the train that's going in the right direction for you.

rolls into the station, look for the conductor leaning out of a window in the center car—he or she can tell you where the train is headed.

KNOWING WHEN TO GET OFF
» Conductors make announcements before each stop. On new trains, these are recorded.
» Every subway car has a map posted on the wall by a door, so you can make sure you are traveling in the right direction and can see how many stops you need to go.
» Look for signs on the station walls as you pull into the station.

LEAVING THE SUBWAY
After you get off the train, go upstairs (usually a stairway, but sometimes an escalator). You have to go through the turnstiles to exit the station, but you do not need to use your MetroCard again. Make sure you choose the right exit for your destination.

DISRUPTIONS
» Subway lines are occasionally closed or re-routed for maintenance or construction work. Weekly service advisories for all lines are posted on the MTA website and alternative route directions are given (http://travel.mtanyct.info/serviceadvisory/).
» Weekend service is sometimes altered on some lines to allow for maintenance. Announcements are posted in the affected stations.

IN CASE OF EMERGENCY
» Look for a police officer. Transit Bureau Police patrol the subways.
» Find a phone and call 911 (free).
» Go to the station clerk booth.
» On the subway train, make your way to the middle of the train to find the conductor or to the front of the first car to find the operator.

TRAVELERS WITH DISABILITIES
Not all subways are wheelchair accessible. You can find information on the 30 or more stations that are by visiting http://mta.info/accessibility/.

Above *An elevated section of the subway*
Left *Using a ticket machine at Times Square subway station*
Opposite *A line 6 train arrives at Grand Central subway station*

TRAINS MOST USEFUL FOR VISITORS	
4, 5 and 6	The trains run up and down the east side of Manhattan, to the Bronx and to Brooklyn.
1, 2, 3, A, B, C, D, E and F	The trains run up and down the west side of Manhattan, to the Bronx and to Brooklyn.
N, R and Q	The trains run from Brooklyn and Queens in and out of Manhattan.
S	The train runs between Times Square and Grand Central Terminal, operating as a shuttle.
L	The train runs across 14th Street to Brooklyn.

BUSES

The Metropolitan Transit Authority (MTA) runs the city's buses, and fares are the same as for subways (▷ 46–49). You can use your MetroCard (▷ 45) or exact change to pay for your ride. Bus drivers do not give change, so travel with plenty of quarters if you do not buy the more practical and economical MetroCard. Buses are slower than subways. Buses run 24 hours a day on most routes but less often at night, and on weekends. Drivers are helpful, so if you need advice, don't be afraid to ask.

FINDING A BUS

» Go to a designated bus stop, recognized by the yellow-painted curb and blue-and-white sign.
» Look at the posted Guide-A-Ride boxes, showing the route map and service schedule.
» Most major avenues have their own bus routes, running north or south.
» Stops for crosstown buses, running east and west, are strategically located on major streets across Manhattan.

GETTING ON AND OFF

Board buses at the front. Swipe your MetroCard or pay in exact change. Leave seats in front for the elderly, the infirm and adults with small children. You will notice a tape strip above and beside the windows. To indicate to the driver where you wish to get off, push on this about one block before your stop. Front doors open automatically; to exit by the back, wait for the green light above the doors. Press the yellow tape on the doors to open them.

WHICH BUS TO TAKE

The routes given below are the ones most used by visitors for the main attractions. If you need further guidance, see the Bus Route Chart (▷ 52), or pick up an MTA bus map from any visitor center (▷ 282), subway station or hotel lobby.

North–South buses
» **M1, M2, M3** and **M4** basically run north up Madison and south down Fifth. These buses take you to the museums along Fifth Avenue,

ADDRESS LOCATOR

To locate the cross street of an address on an avenue:

» Drop the last digit of the street number.
» Divide by 2.
» Add or subtract the number given below.
» The answer is approximately the nearest number cross street (for example 54th Street).

Avenues		
A, B, C, D, First, Second add 3		
Third, Eighth	add 10	
Fourth	add 8	
Sixth	subtract 12	
Seventh	add 12	
Ninth	add 13	
Tenth	add 14	
Amsterdam	add 60	
Broadway	(23rd to	
	192nd St)	subtract 30
Fifth	up to 200	add 13
	up to 400	add 16
	up to 600	add 18
	up to 775	add 20
	up to 1286	drop last digit
		and subtract 18
	up to 1500	add 45
	above 2000	add 24
Central Park West		divide by 10
		and add 60
Columbus		add 60
Lexington		add 22
Madison		add 26
Park		add 35

also called Museum Mile; M4 travels as far north as The Cloisters in Fort Tryon Park (▷ 260–261).

» **M5** runs from Central Park South down Fifth Avenue past Rockefeller Center, the New York Public Library and the Empire State Building, then east on Eighth Avenue and south on Broadway through Greenwich Village, SoHo and the Financial District to South Ferry. It returns up Sixth Avenue, passing near Times Square and rejoining Broadway at Central Park South before continuing north along Riverside Drive to Washington Heights.

» **M7** runs from 14th Street and West 146th Street/Malcolm X Boulevard, up Sixth Avenue, over Broadway, up Amsterdam Avenue, and across 116th Street, then up Malcolm X Boulevard to 146th Street. On the return, it travels south on Columbus, Seventh Avenue and Broadway back to Union Square.

» **M9** runs from Union Square to Battery Park along Manhattan's Lower East Side.

» **M10** runs from West 31st Street/ Seventh Avenue (Penn Station) to West 159th Street/Frederick Douglass Boulevard. It travels up Central Park West, via the American Museum of Natural History.

» **M11** runs along the west side of Manhattan, north on Tenth Avenue/ Amsterdam Avenue into Harlem.

» **M15** runs from South Ferry, north along the East Side to Second Avenue/East 126th Street.

» **M60** runs from West 106th Street/ Broadway to LaGuardia Airport.

» **M100** runs from West 220th Street/Broadway to East 127th Street/Second Avenue.

Crosstown buses

» **M8** runs from Avenue D to West Street through the East Village and Greenwich Village.

» **M14A** and **M14D** run from the Chelsea Piers to Lower East Side.

» **M21** circles through West Village on West Houston, Washington and Spring streets, then up Sixth Avenue and east on Houston to the northern edge of SoHo and the Lower East Side to the East River, before circling back to Houston via FDR Drive, Lewis and Columbia streets.

» **M34** runs from Jacob Javits Convention Center at 11th Avenue/ West 34th Street to the Ferry Terminal at East 34th Street.

» **M42** runs along 42nd Street from Circle Line Pier to the United Nations Headquarters.

» **M72** runs from the Upper West Side to the Upper East Side from West 68th Street/Freedom Place to East 72nd Street/York Avenue.

» **M79** runs from West 79th Street/ Riverside Drive to East 79th Street/ East End Avenue.

SAFETY

Buses are safe throughout the day and evening, but after 10pm it is best to take a taxi. If a beggar asks you for money, just shake your head and don't converse.

TRAVELERS WITH DISABILITIES

Buses are equipped with wheelchair lifts, and drivers can make the buses "kneel" by lowering the front step.

Left *A typical bus stop*
Opposite *New York City Port Authority Bus Terminal*

MAIN TOURIST BUS ROUTES

Certain bus routes link key attractions. All routes shown are circular (north to south section of M15 shown only). Start and end stops are given as well as stops near to main attractions.

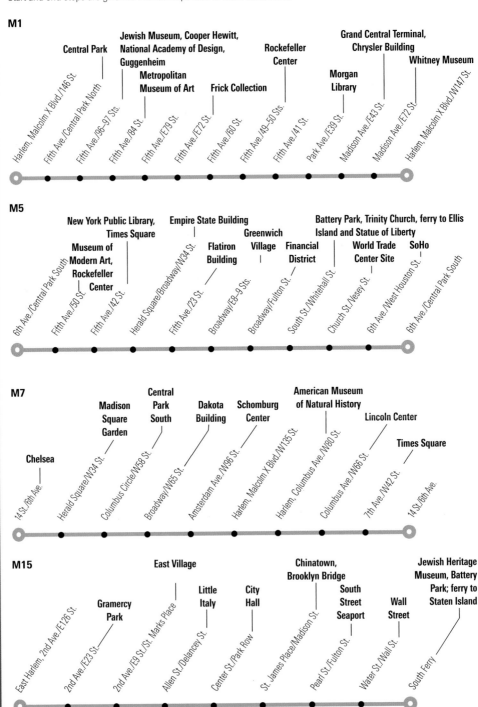

M1

Central Park

Jewish Museum, Cooper Hewitt, National Academy of Design, Guggenheim

Metropolitan Museum of Art

Frick Collection

Rockefeller Center

Morgan Library

Grand Central Terminal, Chrysler Building

Whitney Museum

Harlem, Malcolm X Blvd./146 St.
Fifth Ave./Central Park North
Fifth Ave./96–97 Sts.
Fifth Ave./84 St.
Fifth Ave./E79 St.
Fifth Ave./E72 St.
Fifth Ave./60 St.
Fifth Ave./49–50 Sts.
Fifth Ave./41 St.
Park Ave./E39 St.
Madison Ave./E43 St.
Madison Ave./E72 St.
Harlem, Malcolm X Blvd./W147 St.

M5

New York Public Library, Times Square

Museum of Modern Art, Rockefeller Center

Empire State Building

Flatiron Building

Greenwich Village

Financial District

Battery Park, Trinity Church, ferry to Ellis Island and Statue of Liberty

World Trade Center Site

SoHo

6th Ave./Central Park South
Fifth Ave./50 St.
Fifth Ave./42 St.
Herald Square/Broadway/W34 St.
Fifth Ave./23 St.
Broadway/E8–9 Sts.
Broadway/Fulton St.
South St./Whitehall St.
Church St./Vesey St.
6th Ave./West Houston St.
6th Ave./Central Park South

M7

Chelsea

Madison Square Garden

Central Park South

Dakota Building

Schomburg Center

American Museum of Natural History

Lincoln Center

Times Square

14 St./6th Ave.
Herald Square/W34 St.
Columbus Circle/W58 St.
Broadway/W65 St.
Amsterdam Ave./W96 St.
Harlem, Malcolm X Blvd./W135 St.
Harlem, Columbus Ave./W80 St.
Columbus Ave./W66 St.
7th Ave./W42 St.
14 St./6th Ave.

M15

Gramercy Park

East Village

Little Italy

City Hall

Chinatown, Brooklyn Bridge

South Street Seaport

Wall Street

Jewish Heritage Museum, Battery Park; ferry to Staten Island

East Harlem, 2nd Ave./E126 St.
2nd Ave./E23 St.
2nd Ave./E9 St./St. Marks Place
Allen St./Delancey St.
Center St./Park Row
St. James Place/Madison St.
Pearl St./Fulton St.
Water St./Wall St.
South Ferry

TAXIS AND CAR SERVICES

New York's official taxicabs are licensed by the Taxi and Limousine Commission (TLC). They are easily recognizable; they are always yellow, always display the rates on the door, and always have a light on the roof and a flat bronze medallion on the hood. Do not get into any other taxi; only yellow cabs with the distinctive markings are legally licensed. Car services operated by private companies are available at an hourly rate and must be arranged in advance; they are not allowed to pick up passengers who hail them. Limousines are also available to rent.

HOW TO GET A TAXI

You can hail a taxi on any street by holding out your arm at the curb. When the light on the roof is turned on, the taxi is available, unless the "Off Duty" lights are also turned on. Usually you don't have to wait long before getting one, but it sometimes takes a while—after the theater, in the theater district and just about anywhere with the approach of rush hour time (4pm). Try to hail a taxi in the direction you would like to travel, which saves travel time and money. The best way to direct the driver is by giving the cross street and the avenue—for example, 42nd Street and Fifth Avenue. As you near your destination, you can let the driver know the exact address. Many taxi drivers do not have a great command of the English language, so speak clearly and not too quickly when giving addresses.

HOW MUCH IS THE FARE?

» As soon as you get into the cab, the meter is turned on; this flag-drop fare is $2.50.

» After that, it's 40 cents per one-fifth mile (0.3km) or 40 cents per minute in stopped or slow traffic.
» Tolls at tunnels and bridges cost extra. The driver may ask you for the toll money as you approach or may pay it himself then charge you at the end of the journey. Tolls range from $8 to $16. For more information on toll charges, visit www.panynj.gov
» Between 8pm and 6am, you pay a night surcharge of 50 cents; during weekday peak hours from 4 to 8pm the surcharge is $1.
» Tip your driver between 15 percent and 20 percent on the fare excluding tolls.
» Note down the taxi driver's four-digit medallion identity number, which is posted on the divider behind the driver's head and ask for a receipt. These will be useful if you accidentally leave one of your possessions in the taxi or if you want to make a complaint.
» There is no extra charge per passenger, but taxis cannot take more than four people. There is also no extra charge for luggage.

KNOW YOUR RIGHTS

Drivers are required by law to:
» Be polite;
» Take passengers anywhere in the five boroughs, to Westchester and Nassau counties, and to Newark Airport;
» Provide air conditioning;
» Turn off the radio if asked;
» Refrain from smoking while a passenger is in the taxi.

For full information on the Taxi Rider's Bill of Rights, call the 24-hour Consumer Hotline 311 or visit www.nyc.gov/taxi or http://www.nyc.gov/html/tlc/html/passenger/taxicab_rights.shtml.

TRAVELERS WITH DISABILITIES

Taxis are required to carry passengers with folding wheelchairs, as well as those with guide dogs and therapy dogs.

CAR SERVICES

Most car services have a two-hour minimum rental period and rates start at $42 per hour. Try Allstate Car and Limousine Service (tel 212/333-3333), Carmel (tel 212/666-6666) or Dial 7 (tel 212/777-7777). The Yellow Pages has a complete listing. Alternatively, you can contract with a car service, through a concierge. It might be possible to agree a pre-set rate for a specific trip.

TIP

» Fasten your seatbelt. All taxis are required by law to provide them and passengers in the front seat are required to wear them.

Left *A distinctive yellow New York taxi*

DRIVING

Driving in New York City is not for everyone. Garage parking runs to $40 a day or more, and finding on-street parking is nearly impossible; restrictions are designed to discourage drivers from using their cars. Plus tow trucks are out in force, and to get your car back if it's towed, you have to pay a hefty fine — in cash, often in a neighborhood you would rather not visit. Traffic is taxing during rush hours, between 7.30 and 9.30am and again from 4.30 to 6.30pm. Generally, drivers are aggressive, unpredictable, or both.

DRIVING CUSTOMS AND LAWS

» Most streets in New York are one-way. Newcomers from Britain and Australia need to remember to drive on the right.

» No right turn is permitted on red lights in New York City.

» Drivers must wear seatbelts. By law, front-seat passengers and children aged 4 to 10 in the back seat must also wear them. Children under 4 ride in child safety-seats.

» Passing (overtaking) is permitted on the inside and outside lanes of Interstate Highways.

PARKING

» Check street parking signs carefully. For street cleaning, parking is prohibited on alternate sides of the street on different days.

» For on-street parking you may need to feed the parking meter with change, sometimes on an hourly basis. In Midtown, look for Mini Meters, kiosks that dispense timed parking chits to leave locked inside your car, visible to parking inspectors.

» Do not park within 15ft (4.6m) of a fire hydrant.

» Never leave anything inside a parked vehicle, not even in the trunk (boot). Even an empty shopping bag can provoke a thief's curiosity — and lead to a broken window or locks.

» Parking garages are easy to find but cost in the range of $15 for the first hour to $40 a day, with special rates if you arrive before 10 or 11am. Midtown is the priciest area; to save money, park closer to the rivers.

CAR RENTALS

Car rental companies are at all three major airports and at various

---

ROAD SIGNS

Regulatory information appears on signs with a white background.

Warning information appears on signs with a yellow background.

Give way to other traffic

Intersection lane control

Left reverse turn ahead

Sharp curve to the right

Intersection within curve

Y intersection ahead

T intersection ahead

Give way to other traffic ahead

High occupancy vehicle lane ahead

Divided highway

Divided highway ahead

Stop ahead

Advisory speed on deceleration lane for exit

locations around the city. Prices vary, but as a rule, a one-day weekday rental costs between $75 and $100, weekly rates run between $210 and $300, and weekend rates run around $65 for one day to $175 for two days. If you require a specific type of car then make sure the rental company is aware of your needs: generally you will be reserving the rental rate and not an actual car model when you make your booking. When working out costs, remember to consider the 13.63 percent tax in addition to the quoted price and remember that rates are calculated using the 24-hour clock. Most rental companies will offer various insurance packages which may include Collision Damage Waiver (CDW), Loss Damage Waiver (LDW), Physical Damage Waiver (PDW) or Additional Liability Insurance (ALI) in their cover. Another charge to look out for is the "dropping off" charge levied when you want to leave the car in a different place to where you collected it. This charge can be quite high if you journey interstate. Most car rental companies have a stock of childrens' car safety seats; request these when you make your booking.

CAR RENTAL COMPANIES		
NAME	TELEPHONE	WEBSITE
Alamo	877/222-9075	www.alamo.com
Avis	800/331-1212	www.avis.com
Budget	800/527-0700	www.budget.com
Dollar	800/800-3665	www.dollar.com
Hertz	800/654-3131	www.hertz.com
National	877/222-9058	www.nationalcar.com

TIPS

To rent a car you must:
» Be 25 years old to rent a car from most companies (and be aware that some companies may have an upper age limit, too);
» Have a valid driver's license bearing your photo;
» Produce a major credit card and, if you're not an American citizen, your passport;
» Have your own insurance or purchase maximum insurance from the rental company;
» Make sure you fill up with a full tank of fuel when you return the car or the company will fill it up and add the cost to your bill.

Above *A traffic police officer*
Left *Exits from expressways and major streets are clearly signed*

SPEED LIMITS	
Major streets	30mph (48kph)
Residential areas	25mph (40kph)
Major expressways (in New York City)	50mph (80kph)
Highways in rural areas out of town	55mph (88kph)

ALTERNATIVES

Depending on where you want to go, your trip around the city can be an exciting and unmissable travel experience in itself.

FERRIES

Ferries offer a comfortable ride with spectacular views. The free Staten Island Ferry has been running since 1905; it gives you a great view of the Statue of Liberty and New York Harbor. Boats depart from Whitehall Terminal 1 (Whitehall Street, tel 718/727-2508, www.nyc.gov) and operate from Staten Island to Manhattan round the clock, except on holidays, roughly every 30 minutes during the day and hourly at night. Vehicles are not allowed on the ferry at the present time. The trip, 5.2 miles (8.4km), takes 25 minutes. Listed below are only some of the ferry commuter services available. For sightseeing cruises, ▷ 270.

NY Waterway (tel 800/53-FERRY, www.nywaterway.com) operates commuter ferries from New Jersey to points in Manhattan and from Manhattan to Yankee Stadium and Citi Field using several piers: Midtown at West 39th Street, Pier 11 at Wall Street, and the World Financial Center. Ferries run between 6am and 9.30pm, depending on location. Harbor sightseeing cruises are available.

New York Water Taxi (tel 212/742-1969, www.nywatertaxi.com) runs a shuttle between several piers around Manhattan, including Chelsea Piers on West 26th Street and at Pier 45 at Christopher Street.

Circle Line operates sightseeing cruises (▷ 270).

NYC Department of Transportation (tel 311) can give you information on all New York City ferries.

PEDICABS

On weekends and evenings in Greenwich Village, SoHo, Times Square, Midtown and the East Village, consider a pedicab for a unique view of town. Some drivers are licensed NYC tour guides. Most fares from Manhattan Rickshaw (tel 212/604-4729, www.manhattanrickshaw.com) are from $15–$30 and upwards, depending on the distance. Consult a driver or contact the company by telephone. Pedicabs can be hailed in the street; there are no stands.

CARRIAGES

A good old-fashioned carriage ride around Central Park can be an idyllic experience. Carriages stand at Fifth Avenue and Central Park South. Most charge $40 for 20 minutes. For specific information call Central Park Carriages (547 West 37th Street, tel 212/736-0680, www.centralparkcarriages.com).

Below *New York Water Taxi operates a shuttle service between piers*

If you want to sample life away from the metropolis for a day then head out to the boroughs. If you have more time, travel north into the beautiful Hudson Valley, with its pretty towns and historical buildings, or go south to Philadelphia or Washington, D.C. Trains and buses serve all major routes out of town if you decide not to take to the road yourself.

BY RAIL

New York has two train stations: Grand Central Terminal on the east side and Pennsylvania Station on the west.

» Local Metro-North commuter trains run in and out of Grand Central Terminal to the New York and Connecticut suburbs. Information: 212/532-4900 or 800/METRO-INFO; www.mta.info/mnr.

» Long Island Railroad (LIRR) runs commuter trains to and from Long Island. Information: 718/217-5477; www.mta.info.

» PATH connects Manhattan to New Jersey. Information: 201/216-6000 or 800/234-7284; www.panynj.gov/path.

» Amtrak's high-speed Acela trains serve Penn Station as well as Boston, Philadelphia and Washington, D.C. Amtrak also operates a daily service to cities throughout the US. Information: 800/872-7245 or 212/630-6400; www.amtrak.com.

BY ROAD

Long-distance and commuter buses, as well as airport buses, operate from the Port Authority Bus Terminal (625 Eighth Avenue, tel 212/564-8484), which is New York's main bus station.

Greyhound® buses (tel 800/231-2222; www.greyhound.com) travel to cities and towns across the United States.

Bolt Bus (www.boltbus.com) and Megabus (www.megabus.com) run between New York City and Boston, Washington, D.C. and Philadelphia. Both these companies provide free Wi-Fi on board. The buses are a good alternative to Greyhound, as fares are often cheaper. They leave from around Penn Station.

Below *Passengers waiting for their train at Grand Central Terminal*

BUS VERSUS TRAIN

All prices are based on pre-booked one-way tickets. To ensure availability, bookings should be made at least 24 hours in advance. Some train journeys involve transfers; contact Amtrak for information.

ALBANY–HUDSON RIVER VALLEY
Train 2 hours 30 min. $39
Bus 2 hours 49 min. $20

HARTFORD
Train 2 hours 45 min. $37
Bus 2 hours 20 min. $15

BOSTON
Train Acela Express 3 hours 30 min. $115
Bus 4 hours 20 min. $39

PHILADELPHIA
Train 1 hour 30 min. $49
Bus 2 hours. $20

WASHINGTON, D.C.
Train 3 hours 15 min. $78
Bus 4 hours 20 min. $35

CHICAGO
Train 19 hours, reservations only. $186
Bus 17 hours 15 min, reservations only. $154

ATLANTA
Train 18 hours, reservations only. $256
Bus 18–22 hours. $130

Thanks to the Americans with Disabilities Act, New York City is a fairly accessible place for wheelchair users. Most streets are level with curbs, cut at corners. Buses have lifts for wheelchairs, and taxis are required to pick up those with folding wheelchairs or guide dogs.

GETTING AROUND

All three airports serving New York are wheelchair accessible and have restrooms for travelers with disabilities as well as TDD telephones in all terminals.

Most subway stations provide elevators and ramps, and there are tactile and audio features on ticket vending machines. If you use a wheelchair, alert the station clerk, who will collect your fare and buzz you through the entry gate near the turnstile; customers can enter the subway with a special AutoGate MetroCard (▷ 45).

The MTA buses have wheelchair lifts at the rear of most vehicles, operated by the bus driver. Once on board, the driver makes sure that the wheelchair is secure. The buses are also fitted with a device that lowers the front of the vehicle so that people with impaired mobility are able to board and alight safely.

The car rental companies Avis and Hertz have some hand-operated cars for rent (▷ 55). There are car rental desks at each airport.

Many theaters offer discounts to people with disabilities, and most cultural events are sign-language interpreted. Museums are accessible, but some old buildings have not yet been converted.

USEFUL CONTACTS

If you have accessibility concerns and require information on visiting sights, contact individual venues or any of the following.

Mayor's Office for People with Disabilities (tel 212/788-2830; www.nyc.gov/mopd) will send the free, large-type book *Access New York* to people who phone. It provides a guide to accessing city services, also available online, as is *Exercise Your Ability*, a guide to sports and recreation for people with disabilities, published by the New York City Sports Commission.

Metropolitan Transit Authority (tel 718/393-4999, TTY 711; 877/337-2017 for Access-a-Ride) provides information on New York's public transportation system.

Gray Line Air Shuttle (tel 212/445-0848; www.grayline.com) provides transportation between the three major airports and area hotels with 24-hour notice.

Theater Development Fund (TDF; tel 212/912-9770; www.tdf.org) has accessibility programs to aid theatergoers with disabilities, from special seating to open captioning and sign-language performances.

Society for Accessible Travel and Hospitality (SATH; tel 212/447-7284; www.sath.org) gives information on travel worldwide.

Big Apple Greeter (tel 212/669-8159, 212/669-8159, TDD 212/669-8273; www.bigapplegreeter.org) provides free tours of New York's neighborhoods with native New Yorkers. If you wish, you may ask for a volunteer guide with a disability. Reserve tours at least six weeks in advance.

Scoot Around (tel 888/441-7575; www.scootaround.com) provides wheelchairs and scooters for rental.

Hospital Audiences (tel 212/575-7676; www.hospitalaudiences.org) arranges seats at theaters, concert halls and other venues.

Hands On Sign Interpreted Performances (tel 212/740-3087; www.handson.org) can tell you where you will find sign language interpreters at exhibitions, performances and film screenings.

AT&T Relay Operator (tel voice 1-800/682-8706, TTY 1-800/682-8786; http://relayservices.att.com/). Operators act as interpreter between a TTY user and a voice telephone user. The operator reads the TTY user's typed message back to the other party.

REGIONS

This chapter is divided into four regions of New York (▷ 7). Region names are for the purposes of this book only and places of interest are listed alphabetically in each region.

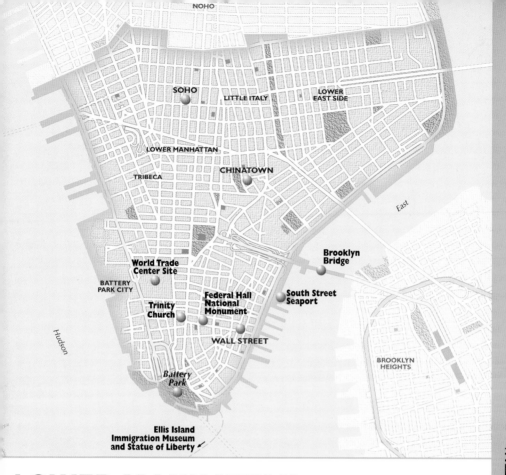

LOWER MANHATTAN

If there is one city that represents America's raucous, can-do, anything-is-possible spirit, it is New York. Lower Manhattan was the first area of today's city to be settled, by the Dutch in 1625, and the area known as South Street Seaport thrived in the 17th century by providing dockage for large commercial ships. By the early 1670s the British were firmly in control of the city which they named New York.

Twelve million immigrants arrived at Ellis Island between 1892 and 1954, and today the Ellis Island Immigration Museum tells the powerful story of America's immigrants through photos, exhibits and oral histories. Nearby, the Statue of Liberty provided the first glimpse of America for immigrants and visitors alike, representing freedom, liberty and hope. There are cruises that take visitors to both Ellis Island and the Statue of Liberty, or there is the free Staten Island Ferry that provides views of the Statue of Liberty, New York Harbor and the Manhattan skyline.

The financial district is best known for Wall Street and the New York Stock Exchange, the world's largest securities trader (which is no longer open to the public). Wall Street is surprisingly narrow, for it was originally an 18th-century lane, and is lined with tall neoclassical buildings. Nearby, the towers of the new World Trade Center are being built, slowly rising above the National September 11 Memorial and Museum.

Lower Manhattan grew as successive waves of immigrants arrived at Ellis Island and settled in New York, forming the now historic neighborhoods. Chinatown is home to many of New York's most recent Asian immigrants, and offers visitors fabulous ethnic restaurants and shopping, as well as colorful, bustling streets and sidewalks lined with merchants selling all manner of goods to throngs of pedestrians. The SoHo neighborhood was once the center of 19th-century industry, and the cast-iron buildings of that era now house trendy loft apartments, shops and popular nightspots. TriBeCa is known for art galleries and boutique shops, while the Lower East Side is in transition with the traditional Jewish neighborhood gradually being modernized by wealthy, hip newcomers.

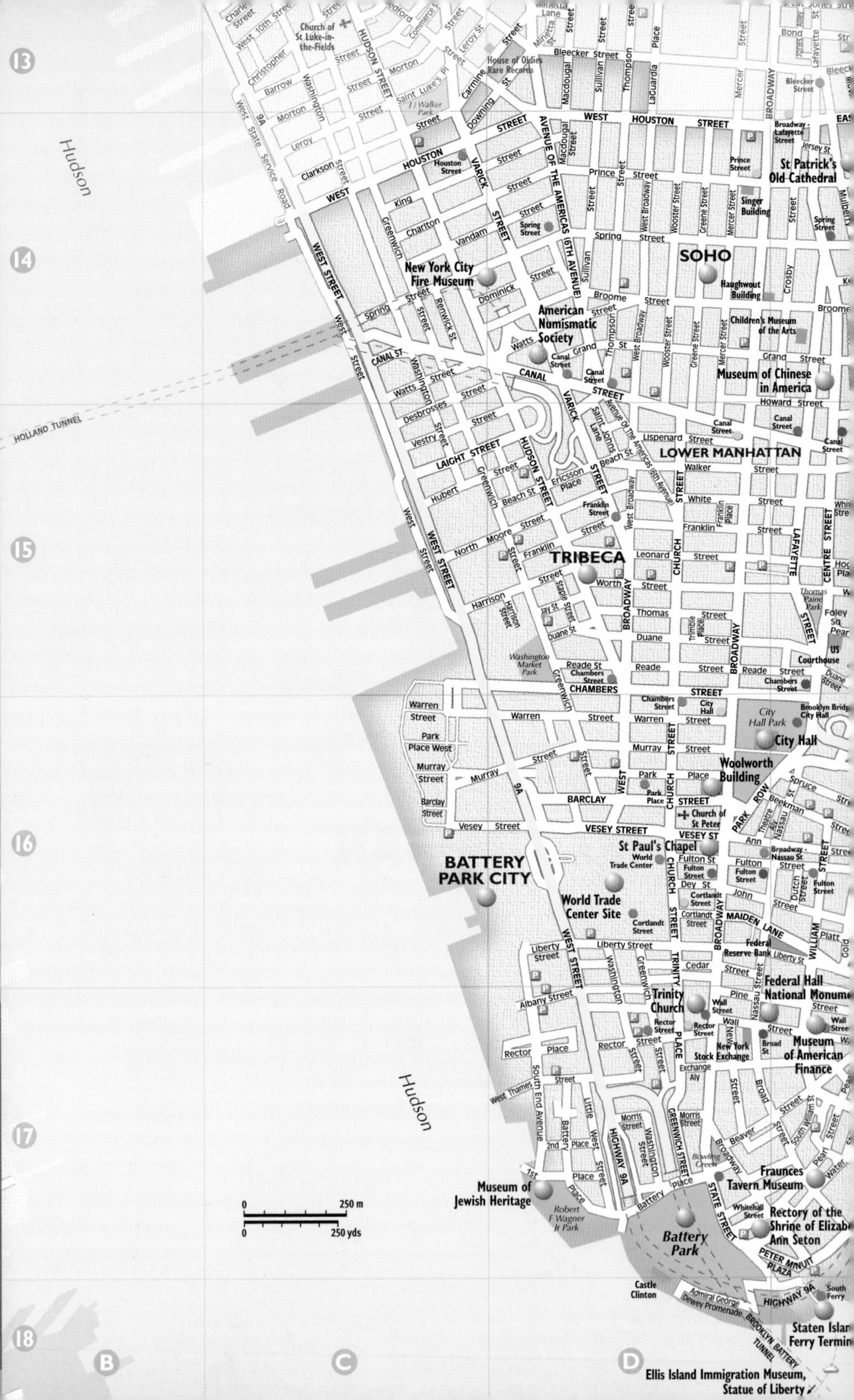

13

14

15

16

17

18

B C D

Hudson

Hudson

HOLLAND TUNNEL

Church of St Luke-in-the-Fields

House of Oldies Rare Records

St Patrick's Old Cathedral

Broadway-Lafayette Street

Prince Street

Singer Building

Spring Street

SOHO

Raughwout Building

New York City Fire Museum

American Numismatic Society

Children's Museum of the Arts

Museum of Chinese in America

Canal Street

LOWER MANHATTAN

TRIBECA

Thomas Paine Park

Foley Sq

US Courthouse

Washington Market Park

Reade St Chambers Street

CHAMBERS

City Hall Park

Brooklyn Bridge City Hall

City Hall

Woolworth Building

Church of St Peter

St Paul's Chapel

World Trade Center

Broadway-Nassau Street

BATTERY PARK CITY

World Trade Center Site

Federal Reserve Bank

MAIDEN LANE

Trinity Church

Federal Hall National Monument

New York Stock Exchange

Museum of American Finance

Museum of Jewish Heritage

Robert F Wagner Jr Park

Fraunces Tavern Museum

Rectory of the Shrine of Elizabeth Ann Seton

Battery Park

Castle Clinton

Admiral George Dewey Promenade

HIGHWAY 9A

BROOKLYN BATTERY TUNNEL

PETER MINUIT PLAZA

Staten Island Ferry Terminal

Ellis Island Immigration Museum, Statue of Liberty

0   250 m
0   250 yds

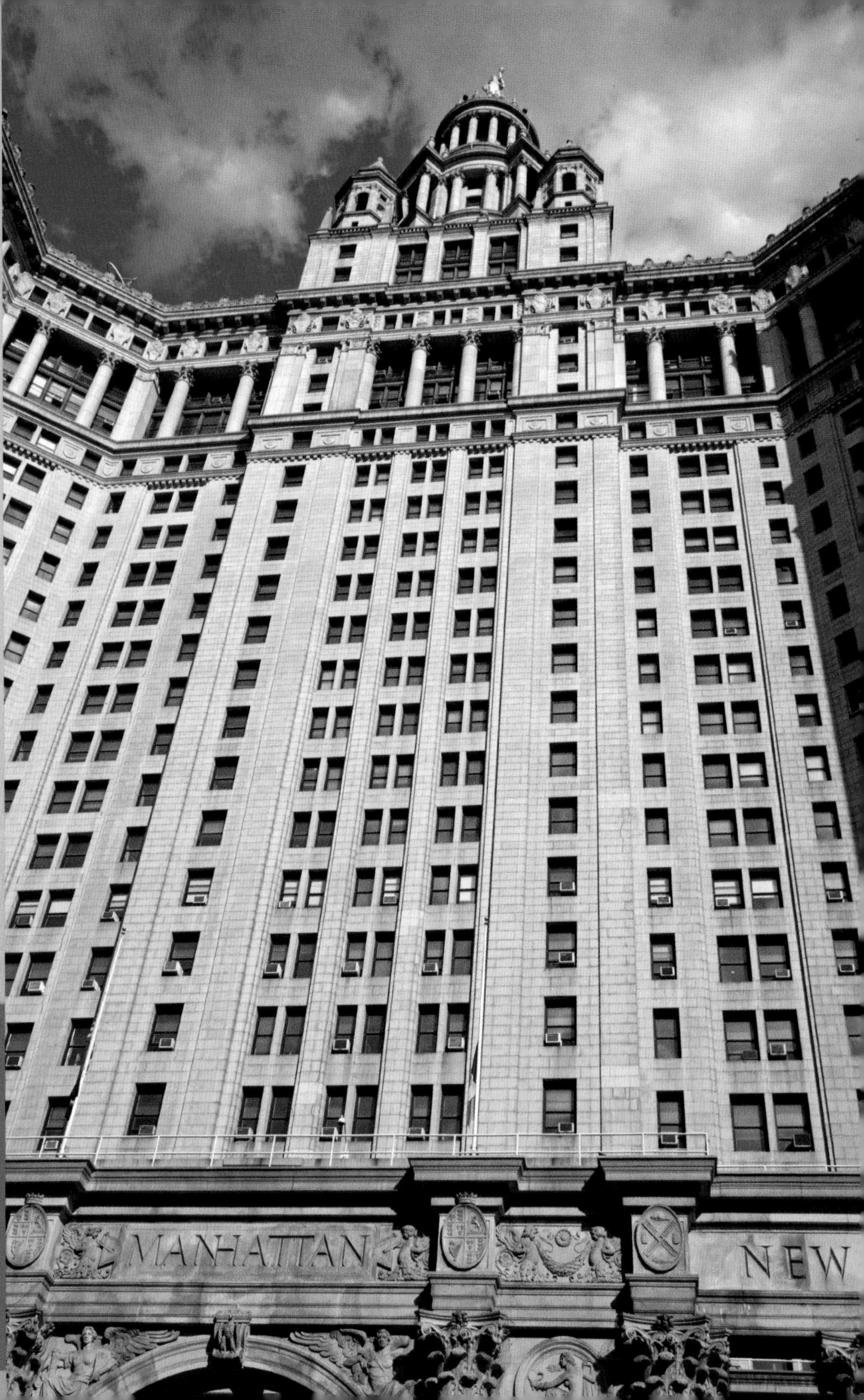
MANHATTAN
NEW

AMERICAN NUMISMATIC SOCIETY AT THE FEDERAL RESERVE BANK OF NEW YORK

www.numismatics.org

This society has a huge collection of coins, estimated at around 800,000 items, as well as maps and photographs. The society's library, educational and research facilities are open to the public. Exhibitions documenting the heritage of US coins and medals and the history of money are held nearby at The Federal Reserve Bank of New York, 44 Maiden Lane.

➕ 62 D14 ✉ 75 Varick Street, 11th Floor, 10013 ☎ 212/571-4470 🕐 Mon–Fri 9.30–4.30 🎟 Free 🚇 1, A, C, E 🚌 M1, M5, M20

BATTERY PARK

▷ 66.

BATTERY PARK CITY

www.batteryparkcity.org

From Pier A to Chambers Street, the $4-billion Battery Park City was created in the 1970s. It's a great place for a stroll along the waterfront, or for watching the boats on the Hudson River. Cesar Pelli's World Financial Center (1987) sits amid residential towers, plazas and parks. The Gardens of Remembrance were planted here two months after 9/11.

➕ 62 C16 ✉ Southwest tip of Manhattan 🚇 1, 2, 3, N, R 🚌 M1, M5, M9, M15, M20

BROOKLYN BRIDGE

▷ 68–69.

CHINATOWN

▷ 70–71.

CITY HALL AND CIVIC CENTER

www.nyc.gov

Built between 1802 and 1812 in the Federal style with French influence, City Hall is one of New York's most elegant buildings. It is where the City Council meets and the mayor has his office. Tours are available on weekdays (free), by reservation only. The surrounding Civic Center area includes City Hall Park and Foley Square, several city, state

and federal government offices and police headquarters, including the New York State Supreme Court, the US Courthouse and the New York City Criminal Courts Building.

➕ 62 D16 ✉ Broadway and Chambers Street, 10007 ☎ 311 or 212/639-9675 🚇 2, 3, 4, 6, N, R 🚌 M1, M5, M15 ✈ Tours by appointment ☎ 212/788-2656

ELLIS ISLAND IMMIGRATION MUSEUM

▷ 72–74.

FEDERAL HALL NATIONAL MONUMENT

▷ 67.

FRAUNCES TAVERN MUSEUM

www.frauncestavernmuseum.org

The 18th-century Queen's Head Tavern on this site, run by Samuel Fraunces, was visited in 1783 by George Washington. In the Long Room, now reproduced in the style of a dining room of the period, he met with fellow officers and gave his famous farewell address at the end of the American Revolution. The current structure is a 1907 reconstruction sponsored by the Sons of the Revolution and now, together with adjacent 19th-century buildings, contains a museum of early American history and culture. Children can dress up in costume and try writing with quills. Separate from the museum is a restaurant serving all-American dishes.

➕ 62 E17 ✉ 54 Pearl Street, 10004 ☎ 212/425-1778; restaurant 212/968-1776 🕐 Mon–Sat 12–5 (also Sun Memorial Day–Labor Day) 🎟 Adult $17, child (6–18) $4 🚇 4, 5 🚌 M5, M15 🍴 🏛

Opposite *Elegant City Hall* **Below** *Fraunces Tavern contains a museum of American history*

INFORMATION

www.thebattery.org

✚ 62 D17 ✉ Southwest tip of Manhattan on the Hudson River ⓢ 1, 4, 5, N, R 🚌 M5, M15, M20

TIP

» If you enter the park from Bowling Green subway station, you will pass the damaged 22-ton bronze *Sphere*, which once stood between the twin towers of the World Trade Center. The sculpture was recovered and placed temporarily in the park as a memorial to the victims of the 9/11 attack.

Above *Spectacular views take in New York Bay to the south and the Financial District skyscrapers rising to the north*

BATTERY PARK

These 21 acres (8.5ha), at the southern tip of Manhattan, are the site of Castle Clinton, a national monument, where you can buy tickets for the ferries to Liberty Island (▷ 84–85) and Ellis Island (▷ 72–74). The park's meandering paths are scattered with large, poignant memorials to more than 200 years of war dead. With its terrific view of the harbor, it is a pleasant place to get away from the busy, skyscraper-packed Financial District. Once a rocky ledge, Battery Park was created with landfill to protect the island from British attack in 1811, and it was named for the cannons that stood here.

CASTLE CLINTON

Castle Clinton was built between 1807 and 1809 for defense. In 1823 the US government ceded it to the city, and it became a center for theatrical and musical entertainment, hosting such events as the triumphal 1850 appearance of the Swedish soprano Jenny Lind. From 1855 to 1890 almost 8 million immigrants passed through Castle Clinton, when it was the immigration processing center, recalled by the statue in front of the castle, *The Immigrants* by Luis Sanguino. In 1892 immigration processing moved to Ellis Island. From 1896 to 1911, Castle Clinton was home to New York's first aquarium, now at Coney Island. Dioramas in the small museum depict Castle Clinton's history.

THE HARBOR

At the south end of Battery Park is the terminal for the Staten Island Ferry. From here, looking out across the city's harbor, you have a magnificent view of the Statue of Liberty, Ellis Island, Governors Island, and the Verrazano Narrows Bridge with the Atlantic Ocean beyond. Just past Slip 6 is a sculpture by Marisol, the *American Merchant Mariners' Memorial*, dedicated to all merchant mariners who have served the United States since the Revolutionary War. Throughout the park vendors sell everything from T-shirts to ice cream.

FEDERAL HALL NATIONAL MONUMENT

As you approach the Federal Hall National Monument there's no escaping the massive bronze John Quincy Adams Ward statue of George Washington on the front steps. This Doric-columned, Greek Revival building resembles a simplified Parthenon, and looks a bit out of place among Wall Street's massive structures. Inside, the rotunda has 16 marble Corinthian columns, a domed ceiling and ornate bronze railings. One exhibit explores the Constitution; another showcases the Bible used to administer the oath to Washington.

A HISTORIC SITE

New York's first City Hall was built on this site in 1699 and petty offenders were flogged in front of the building. In 1789 it was reconstructed by Pierre L'Enfant, who later designed Washington, D.C., and the First Continental Congress met here to draft the Bill of Rights, guaranteeing the rights to freedom of worship, speech, press, assembly, keeping and bearing arms, trial by jury, and the right against unreasonable searches and seizures. April 30, 1789, the day Washington took the oath of office, was an occasion for massive celebrations. The building remained the nation's first capitol until 1790, when the "famed deal" between Thomas Jefferson and Alexander Hamilton moved the seat of government along the Potomac River.

Many other important historic events took place on this site. Newspaper publisher John Peter Zenger was imprisoned here for seditious libel in 1734; a brilliant defense by lawyer Andrew Hamilton secured him victory in court and was an important step towards freedom of the press (▷ 29). In 1765, the Stamp Act Congress assembled here to protest taxation without representation. In 1787, after the colonies won their independence, the First Continental Congress met here to establish procedures for the creation of new states. The state, war and treasury departments were established here, as was the Supreme Court. Customs stayed for 20 years before moving to Wall Street. The building became a National Historic Site on May 26, 1939, and a National Memorial to George Washington on August 11, 1955.

INFORMATION

www.nps.gov/feha

✚ 62 D17 ✉ 26 Wall Street, 10005
☎ 212/825-6990 🕐 Mon–Fri 9–5
♿ Free 🚇 4, 5 🚌 M9, M15 🎫 Free guided tours at 10, 11, 1, 2 and 3

Above *On the site of the nation's first capitol, the first president of the newly created United States, George Washington, took the oath of office*

INFORMATION

✚ 63 F16 ✉ From southern Manhattan over the East River to Brooklyn ✋ Free
🚇 2, 3, 4, 5, 6, N, R 🚌 M9, M15, M22, M103

Above *The bridge has been described as the crowning glory of an age memorable for great industrial achievements*

INTRODUCTION

This remarkable feat of 19th-century engineering, designed by John Roebling and built between 1867 and 1883, was the world's first steel suspension bridge. It spans a mile (1.6km) across the East River, roughly between Cadman Plaza in Brooklyn and Park Row in Manhattan.

The construction of the bridge cost several lives, including that of the chief engineer. While doing the final survey for the bridge, John Roebling suffered a severe injury to his foot. He survived the amputation of his toes, but died on July 22, 1869, of the resulting tetanus infection. His son, Washington Roebling, an engineer with the Union Army during the Civil War, took over as chief engineer. Working underwater on the caissons one day in 1872, Washington surfaced too quickly and was partially paralyzed by the resulting attack of the bends, also known as decompression sickness. He carried on, directing construction from his window in Brooklyn Heights with the aid of a telescope, while his wife Emily marched back and forth delivering his instructions to workers. Of the 600 laborers who worked on this project, 20 lost their lives in construction accidents.

When the bridge opened in May 1883, the public marveled at the Gothic-inspired span with its stone pylons and web of steel cables. Roebling's understanding of aerodynamic stability was very advanced for the time and he was the first to introduce radiating stays extending from the tops of the towers to the lower end of the suspender cables. It is estimated that 150,000 people walked across Brooklyn Bridge on opening day—but not Roebling, who refused to come after a bitter dispute with the company that financed the project. Disaster struck days later. A woman stumbled and fell while walking across. As people tried to see what was happening, there was much pushing and shoving. It was Memorial Day, a national holiday commemorating American servicemen killed in action, so there were great crowds on the bridge. A rumor started that the bridge was about to collapse, and everyone panicked and rushed toward land. Twelve people were trampled to death in the stampede and many were injured. On a cheerier note, in 1884 the great circus entertainer P. T. Barnum led 21 elephants across the bridge, which bore the weight without incident.

WHAT TO SEE

THE BRIDGE TODAY

As you walk along the wooden pedestrian walkway, you will come to a viewing spot where a bronze plaque gives information about the Roeblings. Take a look at the map etched in metal alloy, so that you know which skyscrapers are which among the towers looming ahead.

American poet Walt Whitman described the bridge and the views as the best medicine his soul had ever experienced. He might balk at the number of skyscrapers, and probably at the number of bicycle-riders, roller skaters and joggers racing across it today, but they have their own lane so pedestrians can stroll at their own pace and in safety.

The twin Gothic arches tower 277ft (84m) above the East River. The bridge was repainted in 1973, in its original beige and light brown. The walkway was reconstructed in 1983. In recent years the bridge has again been painted and the approaches strengthened at a cost of $500 million.

TIP

» Walk across the bridge at dusk on a summer evening as the sun slowly sets behind Liberty Island and the city lights begin to twinkle.

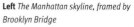

Left *The Manhattan skyline, framed by Brooklyn Bridge*
Below *The pedestrian walkway is a mile (1.6km) long*

REGIONS LOWER MANHATTAN • SIGHTS

INFORMATION

www.explorechinatown.com

✚ 63 E15 ✉ Between Little Italy and the Lower East Side, bounded by Canal and Worth streets between Broadway and Bowery 🚇 J, M, N, Q, R, Z, 6 🚌 M22, M103 🍴 Hundreds of restaurants 🍵 Ten Ren Tea Time, 79 Mott Street 10013 ☎ 212/732-7178 🛈 Kiosk at Canal Street and Baxter Street 🕐 Daily 10–6 🛍 Dozens of souvenir shops; a few concentrate in the mini-mall at 15 Elizabeth Street

INTRODUCTION

Chinatown, northeast of City Hall and below Canal Street, has been home to generations of immigrants from China, Hong Kong, Taiwan, Korea, Vietnam and other Asian countries for more than 150 years. Now covering 3 square miles (8sq km), it has all but crowded out its neighbors, Little Italy and the Lower East Side. For cheap restaurants, bargain clothing, souvenirs, and exotic herbs and spices, no other Manhattan neighborhood compares.

The district occupied by today's densely populated Chinatown was dominated by the hog and cattle industry in the 17th and early 18th centuries; many streets were named for prominent local butchers (including Joshua Pell and John Mott). During the 1800s, the area was populated by Irish and German immigrants; some of New York's dirtiest and most crowded tenements were around the intersection of today's Mosco, Worth and Baxter streets, then known as the Five Points—the setting for Martin Scorsese's 2002 movie *Gangs of New York*. Chinese immigrants arrived in the late 1870s.

WHAT TO SEE

MUSEUM OF CHINESE IN AMERICA

The popular Museum of Chinese in America (▷ 76) has large, modern exhibition galleries set around a central courtyard. Exhibits are captivating, drawing visitors into the experience of Chinese culture as well as displaying ancient artifacts. History and culture are not only preserved, but the new *Archeology of Change* exhibit captures the changing landscape of Chinatown through five landmarks.

SHOPPING

Chinatown's most popular streets for shoppers are Canal Street and Mott Street. The variety of shops ranges from chic boutiques to ancient antiques, souvenirs and food markets. Look for exotic Chinese vegetables, herbs, spices, ducks' feet and neat rows of fish on shaved ice. The ornate storefront

Above *Signs are in Cantonese and English along Chinatown's busy shopping streets*

at 32 Mott Street dates to 1891, the oldest storefront in Chinatown; the store is now home to Good Fortune Gifts (tel 212/791-9989) offering feng shui products, snuff bottles and teapots.

EASTERN STATES BUDDHIST TEMPLE
Visit this small temple, a place of prayer, compassion and community, to admire the statues of Buddha and three altars adorned with flowers and fruit frequented by local Buddhists who light incense and pray. The temple is known for its collection of 100 golden Buddhas.
✉ 64 Mott Street ☎ 212/966-6229

COLUMBUS PARK
From 8am to 9pm residents of Chinatown gather in Columbus Park (67 Mulberry Street, near Bayard Street, tel 212/408-0100). T'ai chi practice begins early in the morning, and by early afternoon the park is filled with neighbors playing mah-jong, Chinese chess, betting on dominoes, sitting in the shade socializing, or playing basketball. Fortune-tellers will read palms, and artists offer their paintings for sale.

MORE TO SEE
CONFUCIUS SQUARE
The statue of Confucius, located in Confucius Square on Bowery Street, was sculpted by Liu Shih and has been a Chinatown landmark since 1976. The great teacher is dressed in a long toga and stands atop a pedestal of green marble inscribed with his teachings.

CHINATOWN ICE CREAM FACTORY
For 30 years this family business, one of Chinatown's oldest, has created and served homemade American-style ice cream with a delicious Chinese twist to visitors from all over the world. The Asian flavors are excellent, with options like green tea, almond cookie, ginger and Zen butter.

KIM LAU CHINESE MEMORIAL ARCH
Located in Chatham Square, also known as Kimlau Square, at Bowery and East Broadway, this arch commemorates the Chinese-Americans who died in World War II. A statue of imperial commissioner Lieutenant B. R. Kim Lau, who fought against the opium smuggling that led to the Opium Wars, stands facing the arch.

TIPS

» Go to Chinatown to enjoy the colorful, crowded, noisy and exotic atmosphere, which is very different to the rest of Manhattan.

» Eat at a Chinese restaurant, where entrées are usually served family style. Choose a restaurant where lots of Chinese are eating for the probability of good food, and then be adventurous when you order. But you may want to skip dessert and head over to the ice cream shop at the Chinatown Ice Cream Factory.

Below *Columbus Park is a popular meeting place for Chinatown's residents*

INFORMATION

www.nps.gov/ellis
www.ellisisland.org

✚ Off map 62 E18 ✉ Ellis Island, New York 10004 ☎ Information 212/363-3200, ferry 877/523-9849; audiotours, café and gift shop 212/344-0996 ⏰ Daily 9.30–5, last outbound ferry departs 3.30. Extended hours in summer ✋ Museum free, including film. Ferry ticket: adult $13, child (4–12) $5. Audiotours $8 🎫 Buy tickets in Castle Clinton, Battery Park. Ferry runs approximately every 30 min daily 9–3.30, depending on season 🚇 1, 4, 5 🚌 M5, M15, M20 ⚑ Park rangers periodically conduct tours; check schedules on arrival 🍴 Ellis Island Café serves burgers, pizza, sandwiches, soft drinks and beer and wine. Outdoor seating 🏛

Above *The museum building seen from the water*

INTRODUCTION

Ellis Island is a deeply moving memorial to the 12 million immigrants who arrived from distant lands between 1892 and 1954. Permanent exhibits include passports, clothing, baggage and family heirlooms donated by immigrants and their families. Dutch settlers named this 3-acre (1.2ha) island Oyster Island because of the abundance of oyster beds in the area. In the 1760s, after the execution of pirates on the island, it was known as Gibbet Island. It then came under the ownership of Samuel Ellis, and when the city of New York bought it after his death in 1807, it was renamed again. Expanded by landfill to 272 acres (110ha), it became home to Fort Gibson and housed munitions. The original wooden fort burned down in 1897.

IMMIGRATION

From 1892 Ellis Island replaced Castle Clinton as the inspection center for newly landed immigrants. The architectural firm Boring & Tilton designed its current Beaux Arts buildings. Until 1924, while the island was active, 70 percent of the immigrants to the US passed through the receiving facility; it served as a hospital, detention facility and transportation station. First- and second-class passengers were processed on board ship in more comfortable quarters, but steerage passengers were herded onto the island. Because it was assumed that these huddled masses came from countries with substandard hygiene, no one was allowed to sleep on a bed provided by Uncle Sam without first having a bath. Public Health Service doctors examined every person and if they detected signs of heart problems, mental problems or moral degradation, they would return the individual to their homeland. Eyes were examined for signs of trachoma, a highly contagious eye disease that led to blindness and even death; doctors, who came to be called "buttonhook men," used their fingers or a button-hook to turn eyelids inside out in search of redness caused by inflammation. Via translators, immigrants had to answer questions about their finances, their intended residence, and any waiting relatives. They had to prove they were strong, intelligent and able to find work. Fearful, many immigrants gave contradictory answers and corrupt immigration officers took advantage of many by accepting bribes when they gave a "wrong" answer. Inspectors questioned 400 to 500 individuals each day, spending only a few minutes with each.

The bureaucracy was daunting, and Ellis Island became known as the Island of Tears, although most new arrivals received the landing card that allowed them to enter the US. Despite this, immigrants were often overcharged for their first train tickets in their new homeland so that many began their new lives in the poverty and squalor of New York City tenements.

AFTER WORLD WAR I
During World War I, the island came under US Army control and was used as a hospital. In 1924, after changes in legislation, prospective immigrants were checked in US consulates abroad and Ellis Island became a deportation center for illegal aliens. A new immigration building, a ferry house and a recreation building were added between 1934 and 1936 under the Public Works Administration. During World War II, the US Army used the island to detain enemy aliens. Between 1945 and 1954, the buildings were abandoned and deteriorated. In 1952, despite a proposal to convert the main building into a museum, it remained unused and was closed in 1954. In 1965, President Lyndon Baines Johnson designated the island part of the Statue of Liberty National Monument. In the 1980s, architects Beyer Blinder Belle led a massive restoration project. The museum opened in 1990.

GETTING THERE
To reach Ellis Island, buy a ferry ticket at Castle Clinton in Battery Park (▷ 66). Boarding is on a first-come, first-served basis, so in spring and summer, catch the ferry early to avoid long lines. From Battery Park, take the Statue Cruises-Statue of Liberty ferry; en route you can stop at Liberty Island (▷ 84–85). Upon arrival at Ellis Island, walk under the glass-and-metal canopy from the ferry slip to the museum, an ornate Beaux Arts building with fanciful copper-domed turrets. The magnificent arched portals must have been both imposing and intimidating to the arriving immigrants. There are three floors with permanent and changing exhibits about the immigration process, the living conditions of the detainees, memorabilia and displays on the building itself and its restoration. Upon entering, collect your free ticket for the 30-minute film *Island of Hope, Island of Tears*. The audiotour is also well worth getting.

WHAT TO SEE
FIRST FLOOR
The Peopling of America **Exhibit,** in the old railroad ticket office, provides information on the history of immigration to the US from as early as the 17th century. Trace migration patterns on the 6ft (180cm) globe.
The American Family Immigration History Center helps anyone to research their ancestors using high-tech facilities. Visit the website at www.ellisisland.org.

SECOND FLOOR
The Registry Room is reached by climbing the stairs to the Great Hall, as every immigrant did, with doctors scrutinizing their walk for physical impairment. The voices of thousands of people speaking in many different languages filled this hall as inspectors and their interpreters questioned each adult and asked any child who looked old enough to give his or her name. The inspectors asked each immigrant up to 29 questions he or she had already answered on the ship's manifest. If the immigrants' answers did not match their previous answers, they were detained and questioned further. It was a harrowing experience for people who had traveled far, leaving family and possessions behind and enduring a long and difficult journey across the Atlantic. The railings that were here to keep the immigrants in orderly lines were removed in 1911 and replaced with benches. Today visitors pay tribute to the immigrants in this quiet space.

TIPS
» Allow at least three hours; the museum alone usually takes two to three hours. Add extra time to visit the gift shop if you are interested in immigration or genealogy.
» Stop by the Information Booth to check the times of the daily free tours given by park rangers.

REGIONS LOWER MANHATTAN • SIGHTS

IN THE GROUNDS

The American Immigrant Wall of Honor displays the names of more than 700,000 immigrants whose descendants made donations to the Ellis Island Restoration Project. It serves as a memorial to all those who passed through here as they fled persecution and disease, poverty and hopelessness.

MUSEUM GUIDE
KEY TO MAIN ROOMS

THIRD FLOOR

17: *Restoring a Landmark:* photographs of the restoration
16: *Silent Voices:* large photographs of the abandoned building before restoration
15: *Treasures from Home:* immigrants' memorabilia
14: *Ellis Island Chronicles:* detailed models depicting the island's history 1897–1940
13: Dormitory Room: early 20th-century furnished room showing cramped conditions
12: Changing exhibits

SECOND FLOOR

11: *Peak Immigration Years:* photographs, memorabilia and recorded commentaries on immigration 1880–1924
10: Theater 2: shows *Island of Hope, Island of Tears* film, where immigrants tell their stories
9: Registry Room: the now empty great hall where immigrants were processed
8: *Through America's Gate:* 14 rooms with exhibits on the inspection process and the "Stairs of Separation"

FIRST FLOOR

7: Shop
6: Ellis Island Café
5: Theater 1: shows *Island of Hope, Island of Tears* film, where immigrants tell their stories
4: *The Peopling of America:* immigration patterns from 17th century to the present, and a Word Tree explaining the origins of words
3: Baggage Room: immigrants' suitcases and bags
2: Learning Center
1: American Family Immigration History Center

In 1916 the spectacular arched ceiling with Guastavino tiles and the red Ludowici tiled floor were added. During the 1980s' restoration, only 17 of the 28,000 tiles needed replacing.

In the West Wing is an exhibit re-creating the step-by-step immigration process. In the East Wing, photographs and memorabilia explore the immigrants' hopes and expectations, fears and hardships. You can also listen to first-hand accounts of the process.

THIRD FLOOR

Treasures from Home displays more than 1,000 objects, including clothing, jewelry, family heirlooms and photographs donated by immigrants and their descendants. There are touching reminders of the life each person left behind and of the bright future they were hoping to find. A wedding dress, a grandmother's bracelet, a child's teddy bear—all testify to the heartbreaking sacrifices made by people desperate to find freedom and prosperity.

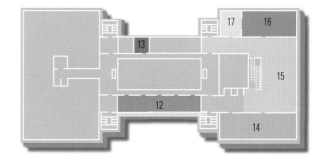

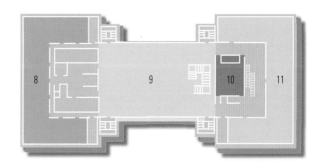

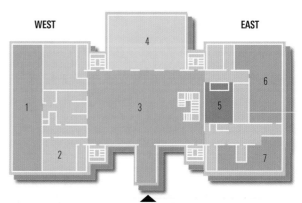

WEST   EAST

MAIN ENTRANCE

LITTLE ITALY

Once the overcrowded destination of Italian immigrants, Little Italy is shrinking under pressure from New York's burgeoning Chinatown (▷ 70–71). A few blocks along Mulberry Street are chock-a-block with Italian restaurants and grocery stores with displays of cheese, olives and salami. Exhibits in the Italian American Museum (155 Mulberry Street/ Grand Street, tel 212/965-9000; www.italianamericanmuseum. org; Wed–Thu, Sat–Sun 11–6, Fri 11–8; donation) display the rich heritage they brought to New York. Descendants of the initial immigrants still gather for family occasions. In mid-September the Feast of San Gennaro, patron saint of Naples, fills Mulberry Street, the main artery, from Canal Street to Spring Street with gaudy lights and carnival booths.

🕇 63 E14 ✉ Between Canal, Lafayette, and Houston streets and the Bowery 🚇 6 🚌 M21, M103

LOWER EAST SIDE

A slum tenement here was the next stop for most 19th-century immigrants after the ordeal of Ellis Island. The squalor, stench and disease in these overcrowded apartments during the area's heyday—from the mid-19th century until the 1920s—can barely be imagined today. Few of the original town houses survived the frenzied 19th-century building of tenement blocks, but most of those that did also survived later rebuilding.

Today, although there is little to admire in the architecture, the area is thick with history. It is also one of New York shoppers' best bargain-hunting destinations, particularly on Sundays. Almost every day except Saturday (when stores are closed), the discount garment stores in the streets off Delancey and Orchard streets are crowded. Ethnic food shops in the area are wonderful; Essex Street Market (Mon–Sat) is a great place to appreciate the ethnic mix of residents.

🕇 63 F14 ✉ East of the Bowery, south of East Houston to the East River 🚇 F, J, M, Z 🚌 M9, M14A, M21

LOWER EAST SIDE TENEMENT MUSEUM

www.tenement.org

Four re-created apartments in a typical, five-story tenement dating from 1863 give a disturbing insight into how the other half lived, or at least managed to exist, in the overcrowded, insanitary conditions common on the Lower East Side between the 1870s and 1920s.

Some 10,000 seekers of the American Dream and refugees from violent pogroms passed through this building over 70 years, as you learn on a guided tour. Fewer people go on each of these—never more than 15—than lived in a typical apartment. None of this is really for kids. For them, take in the interactive living history program, where they can try on period clothes and talk to "Victoria Confino," a Jewish teenager who lived here in 1916.

🕇 63 F14 ✉ 108 Orchard Street, between Broome and Delancey streets ☎ 212/982-8420 🕐 Guided tours only; available from the Visitor Center. Times vary but normally every 30 or 40 min daily 10–5 🖐 Adult $20, under 5 free. Advance tickets (advisable) ☎ 866/606-7232 🚇 F, J, M, Z 🚌 M9, M14A, M15 🈂 🎫 Guided tours

MUSEUM OF AMERICAN FINANCE

www.moaf.org

On the site of Alexander Hamilton's law office, once the headquarters of multimillionaire John D. Rockefeller's Standard Oil Company, this four-room, Smithsonian Museum affiliate celebrates America's spirit of entrepreneurship with exhibits of coins, tickertape from the Wall Street Crash of 1929, curiously interesting photographs and murals of Wall Street and other documents and artifacts. Interactive financial news terminals help children understand the stock market. Special exhibitions have included informative displays about banknote engraving and counterfeiting.

🕇 62 E17 ✉ 48 Wall Street, 10005 ☎ 212/908-4110 🕐 Tue–Sat 10–4 🖐 Adult $8, child 6 and under free 🚇 2, 3, 4, 5, J, Z 🚌 M5, M15 🈂

Left Go to Little Italy to experience the flavors and colors of the Mediterranean

MUSEUM OF CHINESE IN AMERICA

www.mocanyc.org

MoCA's 14,000 square-foot (1,300sq m) space in a former machine shop was designed by architect Maya Lin. The walls of the building's central skylit courtyard have been left untouched to reveal the original brick; the courtyard opens into the exhibition galleries and the auditorium. The galleries present the stories and artifacts of Chinese immigrants spanning a 200-year period. The artifacts, photographs, historical documents, musical instruments and clothing reflect the hardships, triumphs and daily life of the immigrants. Videos and photographs are projected onto screens accompanied by narrated oral histories which present the real-life stories of Chinese immigrants.

Changing exhibits of modern Chinese artists are featured in one of the main exhibition galleries. 62 E14 ⊠ 211–215 Center Street, 10013 ☎ 212/619-4785 ⚫ Mon and Fri 11–5, Thu 11–9, Sat–Sun 10–5 💷 Adult $7, under 12 free 🚇 N, Q, R, Z 🚌 M103

MUSEUM OF JEWISH HERITAGE

www.mjhnyc.org

This museum, opened in 1996 and designed by Kevin Roche and John Dinkeloo in a hexagonal shape to represent the Star of David, houses an exhibition of 20th-century Jewish history and culture. Presenting the story of Jewish suffering, survival and renewal, the museum has three main sections: Jewish Life a Century Ago, The War Against the Jews, and Jewish Renewal.

Displays take you back to the now-vanished worlds of a century ago, through the horror of industrialized mass murder, to the resurgence of hope in a world not yet free of hatred and intolerance. Film clips, interspersed with displays of physical objects, include testimonies from Steven Spielberg's *Survivors of the Shoah* project and also footage from the museum's own archives.

Above *Architects from Tokyo designed the building for the New Museum of Contemporary Art, opened in 2007*

62 D17 ⊠ 36 Battery Place, 10280 ☎ 646/437-4202 ⚫ Sun–Tue, Thu 10–5.45, Wed 10–8, Fri 10–5, eve of Jewish holidays 10–3; closed Jewish holidays and Thanksgiving 💷 Adult $12, under 12 free 🚇 4, 5 🚌 M5, M20 💳 🖥 🖼

NEW MUSEUM OF CONTEMPORARY ART

www.newmuseum.org

The museum has been inviting international contemporary artists to mount shows of experimental work since 1977. It presents several major exhibitions each year as well as shows in a space dedicated to digital art, experimental video and sound works.

In late 2007 the museum moved into its current home in this stunning building designed by Tokyo-based architects SANAA. In addition to several purpose-built galleries it contains a theater, a floor for educational facilities, café, shop and a top-floor events space with roof terraces. 63 E14 ⊠ 235 Bowery at Prince Street ☎ 212/219-1222 ⚫ Wed–Sun 11–6 (Thu to 9pm) 💷 Adult $12, free Thu evenings, under 18 free 🚇 6, N, R 🚌 M103 🖥 🖼

NEW YORK CITY FIRE MUSEUM

www.nycfiremuseum.org

A former firehouse of Rescue Company No.1, built in 1904, this museum packs three floors with firefighting paraphernalia, the most comprehensive collection in the United States.

Equipment from the 1700s to the present includes buckets, pumps, horse-drawn fire engines, a fire hydrant and more equipment, and there's an exhibit on fire safety. Firefighters are usually around to share stories.

This is one of the best places in the city to pay tribute to the 343 firefighters who lost their lives on September 11, 2001. You can also see exhibits relating to the disaster.
✚ 62 D14 ✉ 278 Spring Street at Hudson/Varick, 10013 ☎ 212/691-1303 🕐 Tue–Sat 10–5, Sun 10–4 ✋ Adult $8, child (under 12) $5 🚇 C, E 🚌 M15, M21 ☛ Tours by appointment 🎫

NEW YORK CITY POLICE MUSEUM

www.nycpolicemuseum.org

This museum exhibits a collection of uniforms, ceremonial batons, New York Police Department (NYPD) shields, handguns, and even the machine gun used by Al Capone's gang to assassinate Frankie Yale, the first homicide in New York by such a weapon. Visit a prison cell and see the display on vintage weapons and notorious criminals, which includes arrest records. Learn about fingerprinting and forensics, then view the NYPD Hall of Heroes, which now has a memorial to the 23 police officers who died in the attack on the World Trade Center. "Policing a Changed City" covers the way New York has become one of the world's safest cities.
✚ 63 E17 ✉ 100 Old Slip, 10005 ☎ 212/480-3100 🕐 Mon–Sat 10–5, Sun 12–5 ✋ Adult $8, child (3–18) $5 🚇 2, 3, N, Q 🚌 M15 🎫

RECTORY OF THE SHRINE OF ELIZABETH ANN SETON

www.setonshrine.com

From 1801 to 1803, this red-brick town house was the home of the New York socialite and mother of five, Elizabeth Ann Seton, the first American-born woman to be canonized by the Roman Catholic Church. Born in 1774, she converted to Catholicism as an adult and became a spiritual leader and educator. She founded the first order of nuns in the US, the Sisters of Charity. Her legacy includes six religious communities with more than 5,000 members, schools, and social service centers and hospitals across the world. Pope Paul VI declared her a saint in 1975.
✚ 62 D17 ✉ 7 State Street, 10004 ☎ 212/ 269-6865 🕐 Mon–Fri, ring bell for admission 🚇 1, 4, 5 🚌 M5, M15, M20

ST. PATRICK'S OLD CATHEDRAL

www.oldcathedral.org

French architect Joseph François Mangin had been busy with the building of City Hall until 1809, when he began work on this Gothic structure, the first Roman Catholic cathedral of New York. At 120ft long (36m) and 80ft (24m) wide, it opened in 1815, when the area was populated by Irish immigrants. The work of enlarging the cathedral was under way in 1866, when a fire destroyed it. Restored by 1868, the cathedral remained the seat of the archdiocese until the dedication of the new St. Patrick's in 1879, when the old cathedral was demoted to parish church. Now restored, the interior is grand and gloomy, the timber roof is supported on iron columns and there is a good organ.
✚ 62 E14 ✉ 260–264 Mulberry Street, 10013 ☎ 212/226-8075 🕐 Daily 8–5 but hours may vary 🚇 N, Q, R 🚌 M5, M21, M103

Below *Displays in the New York City Fire Museum*

ST. PAUL'S CHAPEL
www.saintpaulschapel.org

Modeled on London's St. Martin-in-the-Fields, this church was built of local stone between 1764 and 1768, with the spire added in 1796. In 1789 the inaugural prayer service for George Washington, the first president, was held here. Pierre L'Enfant, the soldier-architect who designed the Federal Hall, is credited with the altar. After his inauguration, Washington worshiped here regularly and his pew, together with Governor Clinton's, is preserved. St. Paul's escaped damage from the attack on the nearby World Trade Center on 9/11, and became a refuge for rescue workers during the aftermath. Moving tributes to those who lost their lives fill the aisles.

✚ 62 D16 ✉ 209 Broadway, between Fulton and Vesey streets, 10007 ☎ 212/233-4164 🕐 Mon–Fri 10–6, Sat 10–4, Sun 7–3 🚇 4, 5 🚌 M5, M22 ✋

SOHO
▷ 80–81.

SOUTH STREET SEAPORT
▷ 82–83.

STATEN ISLAND FERRY
www.nyc.gov/dot

These commuter craft are—for tourists—a free, hour-long, round trip in the harbor: past the Statue of Liberty (▷ 84–85), Ellis Island (▷ 72–74) and Governors Island, with the Verrazano Narrows Bridge in the distance. In good weather, try for one of the old orange and green boats—the white boats have no outside deck. To get the best view, sit on the right side. Avoid rush hours, and disembark at Staten Island. On your right as you get off, look for the boat-loading sign, which directs you to the next loading dock.

✚ 62 E18 ✉ Whitehall Terminal, 1 Whitehall Street, 10004 ☎ Dial 311 for ferry information 🕐 Daily 24 hours, every 15 min during rush hour, every 30 or 60 min nights and weekends ✋ Free 🚇 1, 4, 5, R 🚌 M5, M15, M20

Above *Cass Gilbert's neo-Gothic Woolworth Building was the tallest in the world in 1913*

STATUE OF LIBERTY
▷ 84–85.

TRIBECA
TriBeCa (pronounced *try-beck-a*), the *Tri*angle *Be*low *Ca*nal Street, is where artists went in the late 1970s after SoHo (▷ 80–81) became unaffordable to all but the very rich. They converted cast-iron warehouses into loft apartments, and now a wealthy group has moved in along with antiques and design shops and fine restaurants. Notable buildings include 2 White Street, dating from 1809; the Fleming Smith warehouse at 451 Washington Street, home of long-established Capsouto Frères bistro; and the Corinthian-columned, cast-iron 47 Worth Street.

✚ 62 D15 ✉ Between Hudson River and Broadway, Chambers and Canal streets 🚇 1, 2, 3, A, C, E 🚌 M20

TRINITY CHURCH
▷ 79.

WALL STREET
▷ 86.

WOOLWORTH BUILDING
F. W. Woolworth, the department store mogul, hired fashionable architect Cass Gilbert to build the tallest building in the world in 1913. At 792ft (241m), this terracotta-faced, neo-Gothic masterpiece held the record until the Chrysler Building was completed in 1929 (▷ 148–149). Inside, the lobby is a marvel of Skyros marble, with murals of *Labor and Commerce* and plaster depictions of some of the builders, including Gilbert with a model of the building and Woolworth counting his cash.

✚ 62 D16 ✉ 233 Broadway, 10007 🚇 2, 3, 4, 5, 6, N, R 🚌 M5, M22

TRINITY CHURCH

As you walk up Broadway, north of Bowling Green, you come to Trinity Church. Now dwarfed by the surrounding skyscrapers, Richard Upjohn's 1846 rose-pink sandstone masterpiece, with beautiful stained-glass windows and an eight-sided, 280ft (85m) spire, was once the tallest building in New York. The church bell was presented to the church in 1704 by the Bishop of London.

As you enter, notice the biblical scenes on the bronze doors, designed by Richard Morris Hunt and donated in memory of John Jacob Astor III. Look for the white marble altar, the wooden vault and the screen of the Chapel of All Saints. To the left, at the back of the church, is a small museum (Mon–Fri 9–5, Sat 9–3, Sun 1–3.45) selling postcards, pamphlets outlining the church's history, books and videos, and gifts. The 30-minute guided tours of the church start from this museum. Check the website for details of classical music concerts and other events which take place regularly. Men must remove their hats as a sign of respect, even in the dead of winter, or they will be reminded to do so by one of the church wardens.

THE FIRST CHURCH

In 1697, by royal charter, the Anglican parish of Trinity became one of the largest landholders in Manhattan; the first church was put up the next year, only to burn in the great fire of 1776, when the British army occupied New York. You will find the royal charter for the church on display in the museum. During the struggle for independence, Trinity Church was a Loyalist bastion, but when the revolution ended, so did the Loyalists' hold on the city. A second building on the same spot was structurally flawed and was torn down in 1839. British architect Richard Upjohn, together with James Renwick, Jr., were commissioned to build the third Trinity Church. In the process, Upjohn made his reputation and went on to design many more churches.

Before you leave the church, stroll around the small churchyard, a green oasis that is now estimated to be worth several million dollars for its prime location. Here are the graves of steamboat inventor Robert Fulton, statesman Alexander Hamilton, killed in a duel with Aaron Burr, and Francis Lewis, a signatory to the Declaration of Independence. The large cross in the churchyard is dedicated to Caroline Webster Schermerhorn Astor, the queen of high society in the 1800s.

INFORMATION

www.trinitywallstreet.org
✚ 62 D17 ✉ Broadway at Wall Street, 10006 ☎ 212/602-0800 🚇 Mon–Fri 7–6, Sat 8–4, Sun 7–4 🚇 4, 5, 2, 3 🚌 M5 🎧 Free guided tours daily 2pm

REGIONS LOWER MANHATTAN • SIGHTS

Above *A historic church tucked away among Lower Manhattan's skyscrapers, Trinity Church is the final resting place of a handful of great Americans*

79

INFORMATION

✚ 62 D14 ✉ Canal Street to Houston
Street, between Sixth Avenue and
Lafayette Street Ⓢ C, E, N, R, 6 🚌 M5,
M21 🍽 Rocky's, 45 Spring Street
☎ 212/ 274-9756 ◻ Le Pain Quotidien,
100 Grand Street ☎ 212/625-9009 🏛

INTRODUCTION

This area *South* of *Ho*uston (pronounced *how-stun*)—which actually extends as far south as Canal Street, and runs from Sixth Avenue on the west to Lafayette Street on the east—started out in the 19th century as an industrial zone. Architects kept catalogs of cast-iron window frames, balustrades and columns, then pieced together what they liked; an Italian Renaissance motif was very popular. Fashion moved uptown in the early 20th century, taking industry and business out of the area. Development stalled; nothing went up—but nothing came down, either. Rents plummeted, opening up opportunities for artists and sculptors in need of cheap accommodations and studio space. Preservationists caught wind of the phenomenon and soon all New York was singing the praises of SoHo.

Today, there are 50 cast-iron structures on Greene Street alone. The most admired include the Haughwout Building at the corner of Broome Street and Broadway, the Little Singer Building at 561 Broadway, and the St. Nicholas Hotel, where Mark Twain met his future wife, at 521–523 Broadway. Across the street at 504 Broadway, Harry Houdini worked as a tie-cutter before his career as an escape artist took off. It was in the Haughwout Building that Elisha Graves Otis installed his first passenger elevator; unfortunately it is no longer in the building. (▷ 88–89 for a walk around this neighborhood.)

WHAT TO SEE

GALLERIES

By the 1970s, SoHo was one of the most desirable addresses in town; rents shot up and struggling artists left. But many dealers and galleries thrived, like the Leo Castelli Gallery, which exhibited Andy Warhol, Frank Stella and Roy Lichtenstein in the 1960s, at 420 Broadway.

By the end of the 20th century there were about 200 other art galleries, as well as more photography galleries than anywhere else in New York. Today many of the galleries have moved to Chelsea (▷ 113) and, to a lesser extent, to TriBeCa (▷ 78), but some remain. The Peter Blum Gallery at 99 Wooster Street (tel 212/343-0441) exhibits artists working in a variety of media, including photographs, drawings, sculpture and cartoons. Nearby, at 461 Broome Street, the Animazing Gallery (tel 212/226-7374) specializes in original animation, illustration and distinctive fine art.

Above *Stylish boutiques and stores, fashionable restaurants, fascinating architecture and plenty of art galleries make up the SoHo scene*

Two tiny art museums offer very different and unique works of art for anyone looking for an original SoHo experience. The innovative New York Earth Room (tel 212/989-5566; Wed–Sun 12–6) at 141 Wooster Street, displays 14 tons of soil in a second-floor apartment in a residential building. The innovative earth sculpture was created by Walter De Maria in 1977. Expect an unusual, earthy, peaceful and sensory encounter with urban nature. The Museum of Comic and Cartoon Art (tel 212/254-3511; www.moccany.org; Tue–Sun 12–5; adult $6) at 594 Broadway, Suite 401 (between Houston and Prince) displays every genre of this art form. Special exhibits feature works by some of the world's finest illustrators, focusing on the craft with respect to historical time and place. Displays can include animation, comic books, caricature, graphic novels and computer-generated art.

SHOPPING

Stores followed the galleries, pushing out both galleries and artists. But in the interim, many well-to-do New Yorkers moved into the loft spaces on the buildings' upper floors, attracting still other high-end retailers to SoHo, along with chic cafés and lots of bars and music venues. Rents for apartments here can rise to $15,000 per month.

No matter what the season, SoHo's streets offer the ultimate New York retail experience.

Left *A SoHo designer boutique*
Below *SoHo loft spaces are sought-after apartments*

INFORMATION

www.southstreetseaport.com
www.southstreetseaportmuseum.org

🕂 63 E16 ✉ South of Brooklyn Bridge at Fulton Street ☎ Museum: 212/748-8786 🅸 Most shops Mon–Sat 10–9, Sun 11–8. Museum: Apr–Dec Tue–Sun 10–6; Jan–Mar Thu–Sun 10–5 (ships open 12–4), shops 12–5, Mon 10–5 Schermerhorn Row galleries only 🖐 Museum: adult $15, child (5–12) $12 🅸 12 Fulton Street ☎ 212/732-7678 or 212/748-8600 🅸 Apr–Oct daily 10–6; rest of year daily 10–5 🚇 2, 3, 4, 5 🚌 M15 🚶 Guided walking tours: ask at the ticket booth across from Pier 17 🍴 30 restaurants and food outlets ☕ Seaport Café on Pier 17 ☎ 212/964-1120; Nestlé Toll House Café ☎ 212/374-6300

Above *Historic ships are berthed between piers 15 and 17*

INTRODUCTION

The South Street Seaport Museum, at 207 Front Street, opened in 1967 and was the original draw to this then-neglected area, leading to a complete restoration project. Schermerhorn Row is the most significant historical landmark in the South Street Seaport complex. Nos. 191 and 193 Front Street were built in the 1790s by Peter Schermerhorn, a leading merchant from a prominent New York family. He built further groups of four-story Georgian and Federal-style warehouses and counting houses on Fulton Street in 1812. The stone warehouse at 167–171 John Street was built in 1849 for A. A. Low & Brothers. By the 1860s, the South Street area was no longer the hub of commercial port activity and only the Fulton Fish Market remained. In the 1980s the Rouse Company moved in to start restoring.

This "museum without walls" is a 12-square-block landmark district at the eastern edge of downtown Manhattan on the East River. Buildings include the Pier 17 Pavilion, the South Street Seaport Museum and retail outlets on the surrounding blocks. Begin your visit at Pier 17, where the eateries and shops are concentrated. Pick up a visitors' leaflet from one of the many display racks at the entrance to the pier. The clear, well-labeled map and listing of the stores and restaurants will enable you to decide the route that appeals to you most.

Plans are underway for a historic renovation coupled with a pedestrian friendly expansion of the Seaport in the coming years. The historic Tin Building will be restored, the shopping mall will be reconfigured, neighborhood markets and shops added, and additional space for year-round events.

WHAT TO SEE

PIER 17
From this impressive three-story glass-and-steel pier, transformed into a shopping center with dozens of restaurants and eateries, you can enjoy the magnificent views of the East River from the outdoor terrace.

SOUTH STREET SEAPORT MUSEUM
Historic Ships
Berthed between piers 15 and 17, the collection of ships includes the 1911 *Peking*, a four-masted cargo vessel built by Blohm and Voss in Hamburg, Germany, which made several trips around Cape Horn. After numerous voyages between Europe and South America, then serving as a stationary school ship for the British, it came to New York in 1975. The *Pioneer*, a schooner built in 1885, takes visitors on a 2.5-hour harbor cruise, including close-up views of the Statue of Liberty and Governors Island (call for hours and reservations, tel 212/748-8786).

World Port New York
The museum's core exhibition, with 24 galleries on the upper floors of the renovated Schermerhorn Row and the A. A. Low Building, explores the history of the port from colonial times to the present.

THE TITANIC MEMORIAL LIGHTHOUSE
At the Water Street entrance to the seaport, this monument to the victims of the *Titanic*, which sank on April 15, 1912, on its maiden voyage from Southampton, England, to New York, was put up in 1913 overlooking the East River. It was moved to its present site in 1968. John Jacob Astor, owner of the Astoria Hotel, which stood on the site of the Empire State Building, was one of the 1,513 people who died.

TIP
» If you plan to take a harbor cruise, reserve in advance to avoid disappointment.

Below *A landmark district of historic buildings, a maritime museum, and more than 100 shops, cafés and restaurants occupies the waterfront*

REGIONS • LOWER MANHATTAN • SIGHTS

INFORMATION

www.nps.gov/stli
www.statuecruises.com

✚ Off map 62 D18 ✉ Liberty Island in New York Harbor ☎ General information 212/363-3200, ferry tickets 877/523-9849 🕐 Daily 9.30–5, extended hours in peak season 🖐 Ferry tickets (good for a round trip that includes a stop at Ellis Island) adult $13, child (4–12) $5. Free admission to Liberty Island and the Statue of Liberty. Crown tickets are $3, sold with ferry tickets — advance reservations required 🚇 1, 4, 5 🚌 M5, M15, M20 🍴 Refreshments on ferries; café on Liberty Island ♿ On ferries

Above *The Statue of Liberty is the city's most important landmark*

INTRODUCTION

A symbol of freedom and democracy, the Statue of Liberty was the first sight for millions of immigrants as they approached their new homeland. As you sail toward her today, it's easy to imagine how they felt.

When the Statue of Liberty was unveiled on October 28, 1886, thousands of spectators were filled with awe. Nearly three times the height of the Colossus of Rhodes, one of the Seven Wonders of the World, this gift from the people of France was in recognition of the friendship established between the two countries during the American Revolution. The French statesman Edouard de Laboulay proposed that the statue be made in France, but that the pedestal be made by the Americans. Alexandre-Gustave Eiffel, who designed the Eiffel Tower in Paris, came up with the concept of a revolutionary support system of interlocking angle irons for the enormous statue, which was designed by Frédéric-Auguste Bartholdi.

Paying for the project was a problem for both nations and great effort was put into fundraising events, such as theatrical performances, art exhibitions, auctions and prize-fights. The public showed little interest until Joseph Pulitzer, who established the Pulitzer Prize, criticized the rich in his newspaper *The World* for failing to help finance the pedestal construction and reprimanded the middle classes for expecting the rich to provide all the money. Donations then poured in and the pedestal was completed in 1886. The French shipped the statue in June 1885; it took four months to assemble.

WHAT TO SEE
VITAL STATISTICS
Lady Liberty, as she is often affectionately called, was installed on Bedloe's Island, renamed Liberty Island in 1956. By presidential proclamation the Statue of Liberty became a National Monument in 1924; the United Nations designated her a World Heritage Site in 1984. After almost 100 years, the statue needed some attention; an $87-million restoration project ended with fireworks to celebrate the statue's centennial, coinciding with Independence Day, on July 4, 1986. Her measurements are impressive. She weighs 225 tons and measures 151ft 1in (46.05m) from the top of the base to the torch. Her hands measure a whopping 16ft 5in (5m) and even her nose is 4ft 6in (1.37m). Richard Morris Hunt's magnificent pedestal measures 154ft (46.9m).

VISITING LADY LIBERTY
She can be fully appreciated only up close, and many consider the strenuous climb up 354 narrow steps into the statue's crown for views of the harbor to be the high point of a visit. Access to the crown is limited to just 10 visitors per hour, only 240 each day, and advance tickets are mandatory. Early morning is the best time for the climb as the staircase is cramped and hot in the summer with no air conditioning.

It is still worth taking the trip across the harbor to peer up at this impressive monument to liberty and freedom, even if crown tickets are not available. For a panoramic view of the harbor, you can climb to an observation deck on the 16th floor at the top of the pedestal.

The museum displays the original Statue of Liberty Torch, numerous models of the statue including a full size replica of the Lady's face, and a collection of historic posters and postcards.

To visit Liberty Island, take the Statue of Liberty & Ellis Island Ferry from Battery Park. In advance, buy tickets online, by telephone or at the ticket office. In person, use the CityPass (▷ 274) or get your ticket from Castle Clinton ticket office (▷ 66). Lines are long during peak season so, as there are no reservations, arrive early. Everyone must clear security, including x-ray inspection of baggage and metal detectors, before boarding the ferry and again before entering the statue. There is a Time Pass system (free) for visiting the museum and pedestal observation deck. During peak periods it's best to order tickets in advance and request a time pass from the ferry company (tel 1-877/523-9849, www.statuecruises.com).

Above *Ferries ply the water between Battery Park and Liberty Island, giving their passengers a close-up view of the famous statue*

INFORMATION

www.downtownny.com

✠ 63 E17 ✉ Financial District 🚇 2, 3, 4, 5 🚌 M5, M15, M22 🚇 A number of insider tours are offered by the Wall Street Experience (www.thewallstreetexperience.com; tel 212/608-0130) 🍴 The Bailey Pub & Brasserie, 52 William Street ☎ 212/859-2200 🕐 Daily 11am–1am 🍴 Mangia, 40 Wall Street ☎ 212/425-4040 🕐 Mon–Fri 7am–4pm

TIP

» As the Financial District is deserted on weekends, visit on a weekday when this little street becomes a superhighway for stockbrokers in dark suits.

WALL STREET

The heart of New York's financial center and the historic site of George Washington's inauguration, this symbol of wealth is in fact a narrow 18th-century lane running from Broadway to South Street. The New York Stock Exchange (closed to the public since 9/11) stands on the corner of Broad Street and Wall Street. At the west end of the street on Broadway, framed between towering office buildings, is the Gothic Revival Trinity Church (▷ 79)—an impressive sight, and a great photo opportunity, with the many US flags waving from their perches on the buildings along the street. Stop in front of Federal Hall National Monument (▷ 67); a statue of George Washington marks the spot where the first president took the oath of office. The two skyscrapers at Nos. 40 and 55 Wall Street rise up 930ft (283m) and 951ft (290m) respectively. This is an area steeped in history, evidenced by the many plaques, cornerstones, markers and notices. Take a look at the J. P. Morgan Bank headquarters at No. 60. Its bold arcade vies for attention as one of the tallest skyscrapers in the Financial District. Visit the white marble lobby.

Wall Street was named for the northern wall erected in 1653 to defend New Amsterdam from Native Americans. North of this wall were the *bouwerijs* (farms). After the English defeated the Dutch, and New Amsterdam was renamed New York, the wall started to crumble and in 1699 it was torn down. The bastion stones from the Dutch wall were carted off and used in the foundation of City Hall (▷ 65).

THE FIRST TRANSACTION

In 1792, 22 brokers and merchants stood in front of a buttonwood tree on Wall Street and made their first trading agreement. They were actively trading government securities, seeking to establish fixed commissions on transactions and favoring brokers who were signatories. This "Buttonwood Agreement," as it was called, eventually gave birth to the New York Stock Exchange. Their open-air trading activities moved indoors, probably to taverns, until premises on William Street were acquired in the 1860s.

The telegraphic ticker, new in 1867, has been replaced by today's latest market information display technology. The adrenaline rushes as hundreds of brokers on the trading floor, the size of a football field, trade billions of shares in about 3,000 companies. Sadly, this frenetic trading cannot be viewed live, because the Stock Exchange is closed indefinitely to visitors. Call 212/656-3000 for further information.

Below *This world-famous financial district has been trading since 1792*

WORLD TRADE CENTER SITE (GROUND ZERO)

Ground Zero looks like nothing so much as a construction site, but seeing this corner of Lower Manhattan brings home vividly the horrors of 9/11. The World Trade Center once filled seven buildings on the 16 acres (6.5ha) bordered by Church Street, Liberty Street, Park Place and West Street. The center's twin towers became the tallest buildings in the world in 1973, and for the next 28 years more than a million people visited every year, thrilling to the views from the open-air rooftop observation level. Then, on the morning of September 11, 2001, New Yorkers and the rest of the world watched with horror on their televisions as two hijacked commercial jets slammed into the towers. A total of 2,752 people were killed, 343 of them firefighters. When the towers collapsed, six buildings were destroyed and about 100,000 jobs were lost. Streets like Church and Vesey were completely enshrouded in thick white dust, people were in shock, and emergency crews and firefighters rushed to the scene, hoping to find survivors, but there were very few. When the fires were eventually extinguished, Ground Zero was all that was left.

LOOKING TO THE FUTURE

Within a year, clean-up crews had completed their gruesome task and workers had started rebuilding subway stations. The Lower Manhattan Development Corporation (LMDC) staged a design competition, inviting top architects to create plans for the site. Six were unveiled in July 2002; all were rejected. Calling for more plans, the LMDC got responses from 406 teams of architects, and in March 2003 the governor and the mayor announced the winner: Daniel Libeskind, a Polish immigrant who arrived in the US in 1960, at the age of 13.

The National September 11 Memorial, built on the site of the twin towers, opened in 2011, on the 10th anniversary of the tragedy. Consisting of two waterfalls plunging 30ft (9m) into reflecting pools that disappear into a center void, it is surrounded by a memorial park. The underground museum, which opens in 2012, will have interactive exhibits and provide contemplative areas.

Formerly known as the Freedom Tower, the One World Trade Center building is under construction, and will be a symbolic 1,776ft (541m) high, representing the year that the Declaration of Independence was signed. Completion of the office tower, observation deck and restaurant is scheduled for 2013. Three additional high-rise office towers are planned for the site, and two of the three are currently under construction.

INFORMATION

www.national911memorial.org
www.tributewtc.org
www.projectrebirth.org
✚ 62 D16 ✉ Church to West streets, Liberty to Vesey streets 🚇 1, E, N, R
🚌 M5, M20

TIP

» The National September 11 Memorial and Museum and the Downtown Alliance have an information kiosk open seven days a week. The kiosk is located on Vesey Street across from the entrance to the World Trade Center PATH station.
» You can take a walking tour of the World Trade Center Site with a guide who has personal experience of the 9/11 tragedy. Go to the Tribute WTC Visitor Center, 120 Liberty Street.

Above *The two pools of the National September 11 Memorial occupy the exact footprint of the Twin Towers; each pool is surrounded with metal ledges in which the names of the victims of have been incised*

SOHO'S PUCK BUILDING TO THE SOHO GRAND HOTEL

If you enjoy gallery-hopping or architecture, put this walk at the top of your list. SoHo, *South of Houston* (pronounced *how-stun*), a landmark district famous for the prefabricated cast-iron facades of its buildings, is full of galleries showing some of the city's most interesting contemporary artists.

THE WALK

Distance: 2 miles (3.2km)
Time: 1.5 to 2 hours
Start at: Broadway/Lafayette subway station
End at: Canal Street subway station

HOW TO GET THERE

Subway F and downtown 6;
bus M5.

★ Leave the Broadway/Lafayette Street subway and turn right (south) on Lafayette.

❶ The restored Puck Building is at 295 Lafayette Street. Don't miss the statue of Puck, decorated with gold leaf, above the door. Here the satirical magazine *Puck* was published, in German (1876–96) and in English (1877–1918). A plaque on the Houston Street side of the building relates its history. With its complex brickwork, the building was instantly revered as a prime example of classic New York commercial design.

Continue south along Lafayette, and turn right on Prince Street, then left on Broadway.

❷ The Little Singer Building at 561 Broadway was designed by Ernest Flagg. It was very avant-garde in 1904 with its curled steel, recessed glass and textured terracotta. It suggested the next great architectural step: replacing cast-iron floor supports with steel—the basis of the modern skyscraper.

Walk two blocks south to the corner of Broadway and Broome. Look across Broadway to the northeast corner of Broome and Broadway.

❸ The 1857 Haughwout Building is SoHo's oldest cast-iron beauty. Cast-iron facades were stylish, cheap, easy to assemble and recyclable. The Haughwout Building architect based the facade on a window arch from a Venice library, repeating it 92 times. The first Otis elevator was installed here, giving rise to ever-higher buildings.

Turn right onto Broome Street and right again onto Mercer Street. Go north on Mercer.

❹ Stop for drinks at Bar 89, two doors down—and make sure you check out the now-you-see-through-them-now-you-don't doors on the toilet facilities on the mezzanine.

Continue to Prince Street and turn left (west), then go left again onto

Opposite *The Little Singer Building was a forerunner of modern skyscrapers*

Greene Street, where there are more cast-iron buildings.

5 Many of these structures started out as warehouses. By 1962, a lot of them had been abandoned, and there were plans to raze the neighborhood and build a new highway, but the area was saved when residents protested. Rents were low here at the time so many artists, attracted to the huge, light-filled spaces, set up their homes and studios here; by the 1970s, artists had almost completely taken over the neighborhood. Landmark designation for the neighborhood came in 1973. As you walk south on Greene Street, watch for Nos. 72–76, known as the King of Greene Street, with cast-iron Corinthian columns, and Nos. 28–30, the Queen of Greene Street, with a Second Empire roof.

On the opposite side of Greene Street, at No. 65, the William Bennett Gallery displays original works and rare prints by Picasso, Dalí, Warhol, Miró and other artists. Return along Greene to Grand Street and turn right. Walk one block west to Wooster Street and turn right.

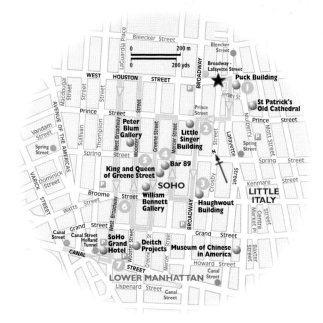

6 On Wooster Street, the Peter Blum Gallery at No. 99 is worth a visit. Artists exhibit paintings, drawings, sculptures, photographs and cartoons. Nearby at No. 18 is the fashionable Deitch Projects in a huge loft. At No. 141, the innovative New York Earth Room exhibits great mounds of earth.

When you reach West Houston Street, turn left and walk one block west to West Broadway, where you turn left again and walk south all the way down to Canal Street.

7 Just north of Canal Street is the SoHo Grand Hotel. Have a look at the postmodern industrial interiors, then join the hip crowds at the bar.

Continue south on West Broadway, and turn right at Canal Street. You'll see the Canal Street station for A, C and E subway lines two blocks down the street and, two blocks beyond that, the 1 and 2 subway stations.

WHEN TO GO
To make the most of this walk, go when the art galleries are open, generally Tuesday to Sunday from 10 to 6.

WHERE TO EAT
BAR 89
✉ 89 Mercer Street ☎ 212/274-0989

PLACE TO VISIT
NEW YORK EARTH ROOM
✉ 141 Wooster Street ☎ 212/989-5566
🕐 Wed–Sun 12–3, 3.30–6 ✋ Free

Left *The gold Puck statue outside the building of the same name*

BOWLING GREEN TO SCHERMERHORN ROW

New York City began as a settlement here in the 17th century, so if you are interested in the city's history, this is the walk for you. From Bowling Green to South Street Seaport, this area encompasses some of the city's greatest treasures.

THE WALK

Distance: 2.5 miles (4km)
Time: 2 to 2.5 hours
Start at: Bowling Green subway station
End at: Fulton Street subway station (A, 2, 3)

HOW TO GET THERE

Subway 4, 5; bus M5.

★ Leave Bowling Green station, and you'll see Battery Park ahead of you. Taking the path to the right, walk toward Castle Clinton.

❶ Castle Clinton (tel 212/ 344-7220; Mon–Sun 8.30–5) was the immigrant clearing center before Ellis Island. You'll pass a temporary memorial to the victims of the World Trade Center, *The Sphere*, a sculpture which once stood between the towers as a symbol of world peace and is now a

symbol of hope. In 1850, P. T. Barnum brought Europe's greatest soprano, Jenny Lind, to Castle Clinton, securing international stardom for both "the Swedish nightingale" and for himself as her promoter. Inside the gate to your right, a small museum has dioramas depicting the castle's various uses from fort and entertainment center to ticket office for boat trips to Liberty Island and the Statue of Liberty (▷ 84–85) and Ellis Island Immigration Museum (▷ 72–74).

Leave through the gate straight ahead and walk to your right, keeping to the path as it veers left past Slip 6.

❷ In the water, just beyond Slip 6, is the site of the *American Merchant Mariners' Memorial,* a sculpture of

a sinking ship by Marisol, dedicated to all merchant mariners who have served the United States from the Revolutionary War to the present.

Turn back and walk east past the ferries to Slip 3. Walk up the steps to your left.

❸ Albino Manca's sculpture of a bronze eagle with a funeral wreath, the *East Coast Memorial*, honors the memory of all the people who died in American waters during World War II.

Take the path west back toward Castle Clinton and turn right at the east gate. Walk past the Hope Garden to the point where Battery Place, Broadway and State Street meet. This small park is Bowling Green, where a statue of King

Opposite Two of the historic ships in South Street Seaport

George III was torn down by fervent nationalists in 1776.

4 The imposing neoclassical US Custom House on the right of the park houses the National Museum of the American Indian. Inside the Great Hall, the impressive rotunda is well worth viewing.

Pass Bowling Green and walk north on Broadway, passing Arturo Di Modica's bronze *Charging Bull* on your right. Continue past this symbol of stockmarket prosperity to Trinity Church, on your left.

5 Trinity Church is historic (▷ 79). Many famous people are buried in the churchyard, including statesman Alexander Hamilton, steamboat inventor Robert Fulton and Captain James Lawrence, whose last words ("Don't give up the ship") are now legendary.

As you leave the churchyard, cross to the east side of Broadway and continue east on famous Wall Street, straight ahead.

6 Wall Street (▷ 86) is where you will find the New York Stock Exchange, now closed to the public, halfway down the street on your right. No. 40 is the Trump Building. The Museum of American Finance is at No. 48.

Walk east on Wall Street to William Street and go left, then left again onto Pine Street.

7 On Pine Street, steps lead up to the Chase Manhattan Plaza, where sculptor Jean Dubuffet's *Group of Trees* takes center stage. Below the plaza is Isamu Noguchi's *Sunken Garden* sculpture.

Return to William Street by descending the steps, right of the *Group of Trees*. Turn left to view the four abstract metal sculptures in

Louise Nevelson Plaza. Across the street from the largest sculpture is the Federal Reserve Bank, designed to look like a Florentine palazzo. Just past the bank is Maiden Lane. Here turn left onto Maiden Lane, then right onto Nassau Street, and then right again onto John Street. At No. 44 is the United Methodist Church, with a fine Palladian front window. Continue east on John Street for five blocks, then left onto Water Street.

8 South Street Seaport Historic District (▷ 82–83) is more shopping mall than historic, but the atmosphere is festive and you have fine views of the East River, Brooklyn Bridge and the river craft. At the northern end of Water Street is Manhattan's oldest saloon, the Bridge Café, dating from 1847, where you can have a drink and a meal.

Turn right (east) onto Dover Street, then right again onto Front Street. When you get to Beekman Street, turn left to the city's former fish market, Fulton Street Market. Go across South Street and walk to the end of Pier 17, and go up the steps for a spectacular view of Brooklyn

Bridge (▷ 68–69). Then head toward South Street, cross over and continue straight ahead along Fulton Street.

9 Schermerhorn Row, the Federal-style buildings along this street, were built as warehouses or counting houses in the early 1800s and named for the developer.

Continue west on Fulton Street to William Street and the subway station.

WHEN TO GO
To fully appreciate the bustle of Wall Street it is best to do this walk on weekdays.

WHERE TO EAT
Any of the eateries at South Street Seaport.

BRIDGE CAFÉ
✉ 279 Water Street ☎ 212/227-3344

PLACE TO VISIT
NATIONAL MUSEUM OF THE AMERICAN INDIAN
www.nmai.si.edu
✉ 1 Bowling Green ☎ 212/514-3700
🕐 Mon–Wed, Fri–Sun 10–5, Thu 10–8
✋ Free

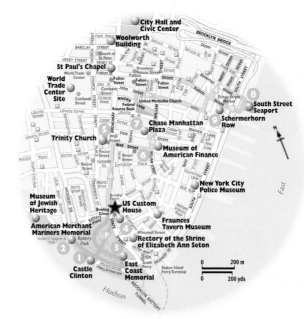

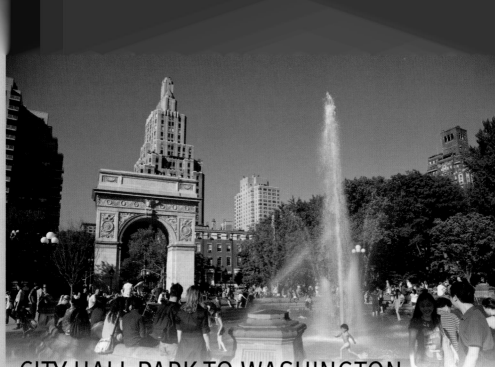

CITY HALL PARK TO WASHINGTON SQUARE PARK

Starting out from City Hall Park, you'll walk past the famous Woolworth Building, the world's tallest building until 1930 when the Chrysler Building spired even higher. Beyond lies Ground Zero, the site of the World Trade Center. You'll continue to SoHo and what remains of once-bustling Little Italy.

THE WALK
Distance: 3 miles (4.8km)
Time: 2 to 2.5 hours
Start at: Park Place subway station
End at: West 4th Street/Washington Square

HOW TO GET THERE
Subway 2, 3; bus M5.

★ When you leave Park Place subway station, City Hall and its park are on your left at the northern end of City Hall Park.

❶ The principal designer of City Hall (▷ 65) was Joseph François Mangin, who also worked on the place de la Concorde in Paris. This mini-palace is where the mayor and city council have their offices. A wrought-iron fence keeps the rest of us out. In the park in front of City Hall is a statue of Nathan Hale, a spy for Washington's army, hanged by the English in 1776. Just before his execution he uttered his famous last words of regret that he had "but one life to lose for my country." The same area was the site of the 1863 Draft Riots (▷ 35). Behind City Hall facing Chambers Street is the old Tweed Courthouse, now the Department of Education. In 1872, when Boss Tweed (▷ 35) ran the city and milked taxpayers of millions of dollars, the estimated cost of constructing the courthouse was $250,000. By the time Tweed paid off friends and lined his own pockets to the tune of some $10 million, the tab was $14 million. Tweed died penniless in jail in 1878.

Across Broadway is Cass Gilbert's Woolworth Building (▷ 78), between Park Place and Barclay Street, a skyscraper with lavish Gothic ornamentation.

Continue south down Broadway.

❷ St. Paul's Chapel (▷ 78), on Broadway between Fulton and Vesey streets, is Manhattan's only remaining pre-Revolution building. George Washington worshiped here when New York was the nation's capital; his pew is inside.

Turn right on Fulton Street and continue west.

❸ Along the fence protecting the site of the World Trade Center (also

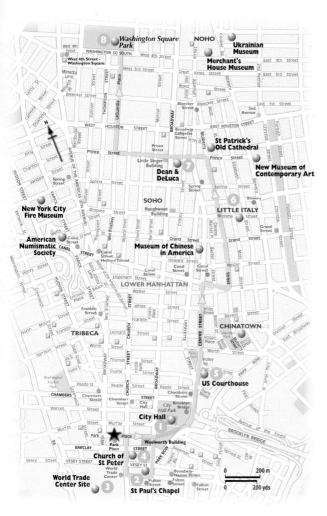

Opposite *Washington Memorial Arch in Washington Square Park*

known as Ground Zero, ▷ 87) at the end of Fulton Street, on Church Street, photos, flags, candles, flowers, teddy bears and other poignant memorials to the victims of the 9/11 tragedy can still be seen. Reconstruction on this site is well underway. The National September 11 Memorial (▷ 87) opened here on that date in 2011, on the 10th anniversary of the terrorist attacks, and a memorial museum is due to open in 2012. The surrounding park is filled with 300 oak trees.

Turn right on Church Street.

❹ At the corner of Church and Barclay streets is the Church of St. Peter, New York's oldest Catholic parish church,which dates to 1785.

Turn right on Park Place and you'll see City Hall Park ahead. Walk east through the park to get a good view of Brooklyn Bridge. Take Park Row to Centre Street and walk north to the US Courthouse.

❺ The US Courthouse, designed by architect Cass Gilbert, stands on the corner of Centre Street and Foley Square.

A little farther north are the criminal courts. As you approach Canal Street, the proximity to Chinatown becomes obvious: open-fronted shops sell everything from Chinese lanterns to refrigerator magnets and made-in-China trinkets. When you reach the corner of Centre Street and Canal Street, turn right. Walk two blocks east, then turn left on Mulberry Street and walk north.

❻ You are now in the heart of Little Italy (▷ 75), with a handful of Italian restaurants and cafés. Two blocks north, at 195 Grand Street, is Ferrara Café, founded in 1892, with strong coffee and sweet pastries.

Continue north on Mulberry Street to Prince Street, and turn left.

❼ On the southeast corner of Prince Street and Broadway is Dean & DeLuca, a temple to food and cuisine offering beautiful displays of the finest pastries, meats, fish and produce, plus good coffee at the front counter. Cross Broadway and continue along Prince Street and turn right on West Broadway toward Houston Street.

As you cross Houston Street, West Broadway becomes LaGuardia Place.

❽ Three blocks north is Washington Square Park. Once a hanging ground and a burial site for more than 10,000 unidentified paupers, this space became a public park in 1828.

After a rest in the park, you can catch a downtown train from West 4th Street/Washington Square back to Chambers Street near City Hall.

WHEN TO GO
The area around City Hall Park is at its liveliest on weekdays.

WHERE TO EAT
FERRARA CAFÉ
✉ 195 Grand Street, between Mulberry and Mott streets ☎ 212/226-6150

SHOPPING

37=1

www.jeanyu.com

Jean Yu makes dresses, lingerie and separates of rich silks. The garter belts are to die for. Prices are high.
✚ 106 E14 ✉ 37 Crosby Street, between Grand and Broome streets ☎ 212/226-0067 🕐 Tue–Fri 1–6 (appointment only) 🚇 Canal Street (N, R) 🚌 M5

ALIFE RIVINGTON CLUB (SHOES)

The unmarked steel door opens onto a space paneled in cherry wood, where sneakers are treated as high fashion, and you can find limited-edition lines in bright colors.
✚ 107 F14 ✉ 158 Rivington Street, between Clinton and Suffolk streets ☎ 212/375-8128 🕐 Mon–Sat 11–7, Sun 12–6 🚇 Delancey Street/Essex Street (F, J, Z) 🚌 M9

APC

Atelier Production and Creation doesn't immediately suggest what you'll find here—good-looking and well-constructed Parisian-style basics. You can buy entire outfits, including cotton T-shirts, turtlenecks, sweatshirts, dress shirts, leather jackets and some extremely stylish jeans.
✚ 106 D14 ✉ 131 Mercer Street, between Prince and Spring streets ☎ 212/966-9685 🕐 Mon–Sat 11–7, Sun 12–6 🚇 Prince Street (N, R) 🚌 M5

BCBG BY MAX AZRIA

www.bcbg.com

Bon Chic, Bon Genre brings you great style and fine quality from designer Max Azria. The women's fashions are stylish and sexy, suitable for daytime or night-time wear. Eye-catching accessories too, all at fair prices. Also at 770 Madison Avenue.
✚ 106 D14 ✉ #1B, 120 Wooster Street, between Prince and Spring streets ☎ 212/625-2723 🕐 Mon–Sat 11–7, Sun 12–6 🚇 Prince Street (N, R) 🚌 M5, M21

BROOKS BROTHERS

www.brooksbrothers.com

Brooks Brothers has been dressing New Yorkers in classic style for nearly 200 years. Those who love its signature preppy look can find well-cut basics from underwear to white shirts, as well as made-to-measure suits and dress shirts. It sells a range of women's separates as well as menswear, and the service is generally excellent.

Above *SoHo has some of the hippest stores in the city*

94

✚ 106 D16 ✉ 1 Liberty Plaza at Broadway ☎ 212/267-2400 🕐 Mon–Fri 9–8, Sat 10.30–7, Sun 12–6 🚇 Fulton Street (4, 5, J, Z) 🚌 M5, M22

CENTURY 21

www.c21stores.com
Customers do their trying on in the aisles at this resource for discounted designer fashions. Look for Prada, Armani and Jil Sander among other designers at 40 to 75 percent off or more.
✚ 106 D16 ✉ 22 Cortlandt Street, between Broadway and Church Street ☎ 212/227-9092 🕐 Mon–Wed 7.45am–9pm, Thu–Fri 7.45am–9.30pm, Sat 10–9, Sun 11–8 🚇 Fulton Street (4, 5) 🚌 M5

DEAN & DELUCA

www.deandeluca.com
A wonderful place to browse. Absolutely everything here is top quality—pastries, cheeses, meats, fishes, chocolates and packaged products, plus the baskets of hand-picked fruits and vegetables. There's also a coffee bar. There is another branch at 1150 Madison Avenue.
✚ 106 E14 ✉ 560 Broadway at Prince Street ☎ 212/226-6800 🕐 Mon–Fri 7.30am–8pm, Sat–Sun 8–8 🚇 Prince Street (N, R) 🚌 M5

DOLCE VITA

http://shopdolcevita.com
High prices needn't freeze you out of designer footwear. This acclaimed brand has all the coolest styles in boots, flats, heels, pumps, platforms and wedges at good prices.
✚ 107 F14 ✉ 159 Ludlow Street at Stanton Street ☎ 212/529-2111 🕐 Mon–Sat 12–8, Sun 12–7 🚇 Delancey Street/Essex Street (F, J, M, Z) 🚌 M9, M14a, M15

DOYLE AND DOYLE

www.doyledoyle.com
Doyle and Doyle offers some very alluring, historic estate jewelry in prime condition.
✚ 107 F13 ✉ 189 Orchard Street, between Houston and Stanton streets ☎ 212/677-9991 🕐 Tue–Fri 1–7 (Thu until 8), Sat–Sun 12–7 🚇 Lower East Side/Second Avenue (F) 🚌 M9, M15

EDITH MACHINIST

Everything from boots to ballet shoes, military-style jackets to furs, evening wear and jewelry comes through this Lower East Side shop, including designer names minus the high prices.
✚ 107 F14 ✉ 104 Rivington Street, between Ludlow and Essex streets ☎ 212/979-9992 🕐 Mon–Fri 1–8, Sat 12–8, Sun 12–7 🚇 Delancey Street/Essex Street (F, J, M, Z) 🚌 M9, M14a

EILEEN FISHER

www.eileenfisher.com
New Yorkers love these easy-to-wear clothes—they are versatile enough to take a woman right through the day with minimal changes. This is the flagship store featuring Eileen Fisher's entire line, all made of natural fabrics. March and August sales are a big draw. Other stores are on Madison Avenue (at 53rd and 79th Streets) and Fifth Avenue (at 22nd).
✚ 106 D14 ✉ 395 West Broadway, between Spring and Broome streets ☎ 212/431-4567 🕐 Mon–Thu 11–7, Fri–Sat 11–8, Sun 12–6 🚇 Spring Street (C, E) 🚌 M5

EMPORIO ARMANI

www.emporioarmani.com
At this flagship of Giorgio Armani's less expensive line, you get the same great design at a fraction of the price.
✚ 106 D14 ✉ 410 West Broadway at Spring Street ☎ 646/613-8099 🕐 Mon–

Sat 11–7, Sun 12–6 🚇 Spring Street (C, E), Prince Street (N, R) 🚌 M5

FOLEY & CORINNA

www.foleyandcorinna.com
Fashionistas and celebrities flock here to see the famous silk and vintage lace butterfly blouses, mohair and cashmere knit coats and other romantic hippie-chic fashions created by Dana Foley, who began her career at a city flea market. Partner Anna Corinna selects the vintage clothing and accessories.
✚ 107 E13 ✉ 114 Stanton Street, between Ludlow and Essex streets ☎ 212/529-2338 🕐 Sun–Mon 12–7, Tue–Sat 12–8 🚇 Delancey Street/Essex Street (F, J, M, Z) 🚌 M15, M21

GAS BIJOUX

www.gasbijoux.com
This outpost of the St. Tropez and Paris jeweler has lovely inspirational handmade jewelry featuring semi-precious stones. There are two more branches on Bleecker Street and Columbus Avenue.
✚ 107 E14 ✉ 238 Mott Street, between Prince and Spring streets ☎ 212/334-7290 🕐 Mon–Sat 11–7, Sun 12–6 🚇 Broadway-Lafayette (F, S) 🚌 M1, M103

INA

www.inanyc.com
The designer resale stock, discounted by 30 to 50 percent,

Below *Dean & DeLuca is a magnet for New York's gourmets*

changes daily, as models turn in their cast-offs. Look for Diane Von Furstenberg and Anna Sui. There's usually a fantastic array of Manolos, Pradas and Sigerson Morrisons, too. ✚ 106 D14 ✉ 101 Thompson Street, between Spring and Prince streets ☎ 212/941-4757 ◷ Sun 12–7, Mon–Sat 12–8 Ⓜ Spring Street (C, E), Prince Street (N, R) 🚌 M5, M21

ISSEY MIYAKE
www.isseymiyake.com
This TriBeCa store, designed by Frank Gehry and his protégé Gordon Kipping, stocks all of Miyake's lines including the A-POC ("a piece of cloth"), each item created from a seamless cloth.
✚ 106 D15 ✉ 119 Hudson Street at North Moore Street ☎ 212/226-0100 ◷ Mon–Sat 11–7, Sun 12–6 Ⓜ Franklin Street (1, 9) 🚌 M20

J & R MUSIC AND COMPUTER WORLD
www.jr.com
This store stocks every conceivable brand of audio, video, computer, camera and cell phone, plus software and household appliances. Prices are excellent, and the staff are knowledgeable and helpful. The Music Store has separate stores for jazz, classical and pop.
✚ 106 D16 ✉ 23 Park Row (across from City Hall Park) ☎ 212/238-9000 ◷ Mon–Wed 10–7, Thu–Fri 10–7.30, Sat–Sun 11–7 Ⓜ Park Place (2, 3), City Hall (N, R), Brooklyn Bridge/City Hall (4, 5, 6) 🚌 M9, M22

KAM MAN FOODS
The Chinese food hall overflows with exotic products, from live fish and edible birds' nests to ginseng priced at hundreds of dollars. It also sells inexpensive Asian cookware.
✚ 107 E15 ✉ 200 Canal Street at Mott Street ☎ 212/571-0330 ◷ Daily 8.30am–8.45pm Ⓜ Canal Street (J, M, Z) 🚌 M103

KATE SPADE
www.katespade.com
The former *Mademoiselle* accessories editor, Kate started

out in 1993, making handbags that emphasized utility, color and fabric. She opened her first store in 1996, and now sells a full line of exquisite nylon, leather and fabric bags, plus luggage, stationery, eyeglasses, fragrance and beauty products.
✚ 106 D14 ✉ 454 Broome Street at Mercer Street ☎ 212/274-1991 ◷ Mon–Sat 11–7, Sun 12–6 Ⓜ Prince Street (N, R) 🚌 M5

KATE'S PAPERIE
www.katespaperie.com
Expensive but beautiful gifts can be found at this elegant store. Gorgeous stationery, handsome journals and date books, photo frames, alluring and exquisite wrapping papers and ribbons, a variety of writing tools, and all kinds of ingenious paper items are attractively displayed.
✚ 106 E14 ✉ 435 Broome Street between Broadway and Crosby Street ☎ 212/941-9816 ◷ Mon–Sat 10–8, Sun 11–7 Ⓜ Spring Street (6) 🚌 M5

KELLY CHRISTY
www.kellychristyhats.net
Kelly Christy makes eye-catching hats for men and women in all kinds of fabrics and in every conceivable style, from fedora to beret. Every hat is named to reflect a mood or character—recent examples are "Miss Marple" and "Let's skate." Prices vary according to complexity and exclusivity of style and fabric, and start at about $200.
✚ 106 D14 ✉ 453 Broome Street at Mercer Street ☎ 212/965-0686 ◷ By appointment Ⓜ Spring Street (6, A, C, E), Prince Street (N, R) 🚌 M21, M103

KENNETH COLE
www.kennethcole.com
Good, clean styling and quality for the money have made Kenneth Cole a major fashion player. He started with urban shoes, but has expanded to include such fashionable footwear as satin pumps with ankle straps, plus sportswear, handbags, fragrance and other accessories.
✚ 106 D14 ✉ 595 Broadway between Houston and Prince streets ☎ 212/965-

0283 ◷ Mon–Sat 10–8, Sun 11–7 Ⓜ Broadway-Lafayette (B, D, F, M), Prince Street (N, R) 🚌 M5, M21

KIRNA ZABETE
www.kirnazabete.com
Beth Buccini and Sarah Easley assemble their choice of the avant-garde designers at this pretty store. You might find knitwear by Giambattista Valli, sunglasses and bags by Balenciaga, T-shirts by Alexander Wang, leather jackets by Rick Owens, plus exciting ranges by other renowned designers such as Stella McCartney, Azzedine Alaïa, Balmain and Proenza Schouler.
✚ 106 D14 ✉ 96 Greene Street, between Prince and Spring streets ☎ 212/941-9656 ◷ Mon–Sat 11–7, Sun 12–6 Ⓜ Prince Street (N, R) 🚌 M5

MARC JACOBS
www.marcjacobs.com
Marc Jacobs is one of the hottest designers, turning out luxurious, updated vintage designs in soft, feminine colors. He also has two stores on Bleecker Street, one selling accessories, the other his less expensive Marc by Marc Jacobs line, which includes his must-have cargo pants.
✚ 106 D14 ✉ 163 Mercer Street, between Houston and Prince streets ☎ 212/343-1490 ◷ Mon–Sat 11–7, Sun 12–6 Ⓜ Prince Street (N, R) 🚌 M5

ME & RO
www.meandrojewelry.com
The collection of Michelle Quan and Robin Renzi uses precious and semi-precious stones in stackable rings, bangles, necklaces and other pieces with a lotus petal motif or Sanskrit and Tibetan calligraphy.
✚ 107 E14 ✉ 241 Elizabeth Street, between Houston and Prince streets ☎ 917/237-9215 ◷ Mon–Sat 11–7, Sun 12–6 Ⓜ Broadway-Lafayette (F, S) 🚌 M21, M103

MODELL'S
www.modells.com
Savvy New Yorkers come here to get the best deal on their running and athletic shoes (Adidas, New

Balance, Reebok). The chain also stocks sports attire and equipment, from treadmills and trampolines to baseball and yoga gear. Sports fans appreciate the reasonable prices on NFL, NBA and MLB team souvenirs and memorabilia.

106 D15 ✉ 55 Chambers Street ☎ 212/732-8484 🕐 Mon–Fri 8.30–8, Sat 10–7, Sun 11–6 🚇 Chambers Street (E), City Hall (R), Park Place (1, 2, 3) 🚌 M5, M22

THE MYSTERIOUS BOOKSHOP

www.mysteriousbookshop.com

An essential stop for every compulsive mystery reader, this bookshop caters as well to the collectors of first editions and rare volumes. Sherlock Holmes, Raymond Chandler, P. D. James and Patricia Highsmith can all be found here. Recommendations from owner Otto Penzler are reliable, sure-fire winners.

106 D16 ✉ 58 Warren Street at Church Street, TriBeCa ☎ 212/587-1011 🕐 Mon–Sun 11–7 🚇 Chambers Street (1, 2, 3, A, C, E) 🚌 M20, M22

PATRICIA FIELD

www.patriciafield.com

Patricia Field's latest and largest shop sells camp fashions made of rubber, PVC, leather, spandex, plastic and feathers. Styles range from bustiers and garter belts to micro minis. Not for the faint of heart, accessories, wigs and cosmetics are equally outrageous.

107 E13 ✉ 302 Bowery, between Bleecker and Houston streets ☎ 212/966-4066 🕐 Mon–Thu 11–8, Fri–Sat 11–9, Sun 11–7 🚇 2nd Avenue (F), Bleecker Street (4, 5, 6) 🚌 M21, M103

PEARL PAINT

www.pearlpaint.com

You won't find a better place for fine arts supplies at discounted prices than this multilevel store. The choice of oils, acrylics and other mediums, brushes, easels, markers, pens, pastels, sketchbooks, photo frames and sculpting tools is superb.

106 D15 ✉ 308 Canal Street, between Mercer Street and Broadway ☎ 212/431-7932 🕐 Mon–Fri 9–7, Sat 10–7, Sun 10–6 🚇 Canal Street (N, R) 🚌 M5

PEARL RIVER

www.pearlriver.com

New Yorkers who have moved out of town often return to this store to browse the enticing bargains— Asian-style robes, embroidered silk slippers, good-looking ceramics, Asian cuisine ingredients, paper lanterns, and many other attractive and appealing objects.

106 D14 ✉ 477 Broadway, between Broome and Grand streets ☎ 212/431-4770 🕐 Daily 10–7 🚇 Canal Street (N, R) 🚌 M5

THE PUMA STORE

www.puma.com

Puma has made a dramatic return to the fashion scene in recent seasons, with shoes in shades of olive and beige, as well as hot, vibrant colors like canary yellow and lime green.

106 D14 ✉ 521 Broadway, between Spring and Broome streets ☎ 212/334-7861 🕐 Mon–Thu 10–8, Fri–Sat 10–9, Sun 11–7 🚇 Prince Street (N, R) 🚌 M5

Above *Kirna Zabete stocks designer ranges*

RESURRECTION VINTAGE

www.resurrectionvintage.com

This store has vintage designer clothes—Pucci slips, pieces by Miyake and Vivienne Westwood, and 80s-style skateboard clothes from Alva, Thrasher and others. The owners sell their own lines.

➕ 107 E14 ✉ 217 Mott Street, between Spring and Prince streets ☎ 212/625-1374 🕔 Mon–Sat 11–7, Sun 12–7 🚇 Broadway-Lafayette (B, D, F, M) or Spring Street (6) 🚌 M21, M103

SIGERSON MORRISON

www.sigersonmorrison.com

The shoes from this exciting designer are not as pricey as Manolos but are stunning nonetheless. Colors range across the spectrum from red to lavender, and materials include pony skin, suede, satin and metallic leather. Styles range from slingback stilettos to flats and boots.

➕ 107 E14 ✉ 28 Prince Street, between Mott and Elizabeth streets ☎ 212/219-3893 🕔 Mon–Sat 11–7, Sun 12–6 🚇 Broadway-Lafayette (F, S), Prince Street (N, R) 🚌 M21, M103

SPACE.NK

www.spacenk.com

SoHo is the perfect location for the Stateside opening of British founder Nicky Kinnaird's must-have brand of beauty products. This spacious boutique is a temple of temptation, stocked with her lines in skin care and hair products, carefully sourced from specialists around the world. You'll find all the top names and latest innovations in moisturizers, masks, make-up, fragrances, bath products and much more on the well-stocked shelves. You can also book facials and other treatments.

➕ 106 D14 ✉ 99 Greene Street, between Spring and Prince streets ☎ 212/941-4200 🕔 Mon–Sat 11–7, Sun 12–7 🚇 Spring Street (6), Broadway-Lafayette (B, D, F) 🚌 M5, M21

STEVEN ALAN

www.stevenalan.com

Radical fashions for daring fashionistas. The store stocks the

Above Designer clothes from yesteryear can be found at Resurrection Vintage

very latest international designers such as Vanessa Bruno, Alice Roi and Kateyone Adeli.

➕ 106 D15 ✉ 103 Franklin Street, between West Broadway and Church Street ☎ 212/343-0692 🕔 Mon–Sat 11.30–7 (Thu until 8), Sun 12–6 🚇 Franklin Street (1) 🚌 M5, M20

ENTERTAINMENT AND NIGHTLIFE

ARLENE'S GROCERY

www.arlenesgrocery.net

This former bodega is one of the best rock clubs in the city. The bar is pleasant, and the back room casually comfortable. It's the place to hear up-and-comers.

➕ 107 F14 ✉ 95 Stanton Street, between Ludlow and Orchard streets ☎ 212/995-1652 🕔 Daily 6pm–4am ✋ Varies 🚇 Lower East Side/Second Avenue (F) 🚌 M15, M21

BARRAMUNDI

www.barramundiny.com

Manhattanites enjoy the woodsy Adirondack accents at this funky bar. The martinis and caipirihnas taste fine, and the crowd is friendly.

➕ 107 F14 ✉ 67 Clinton Street, between Rivington and Stanton streets ☎ 212/529-

6900 🕔 Daily 6pm–4am 🚇 Delancey Street/Essex Street (F, J, M, Z) 🚌 M9, M14a, M21

BOWERY BALLROOM

www.boweryballroom.com

When Patti Smith came out of retirement, it was to this rollicking tri-level venue in a 1929 Beaux Arts building that she returned. The club has comfortable lounges, good sound systems, a large stage and excellent sight lines. Beth Orton, Soul Asylum, David Byrne and Counting Crows have played here.

➕ 107 E14 ✉ 6 Delancey Street, between Bowery and Chrystie streets ☎ 212/533-2111 🎟 $13–$35 🚇 Delancey Street/Essex Street (F, J, M, Z) 🚌 M103

THE BUBBLE LOUNGE

www.bubblelounge.com

This 1930s-style lounge celebrates champagne by serving more than 24 types by the glass and 350 by the bottle, amid luxurious red sofas, marble tables and light orbs.

➕ 106 D15 ✉ 228 West Broadway, between Franklin and White streets ☎ 212/431-3433 🕔 Mon–Wed 5pm–1am, Thu 5pm–2am, Fri–Sat 5pm–4am 🚇 Franklin Street (1) 🚌 M20

EAR INN

http://earinn.com

This 1817 bar near the Hudson River used to cater to sailors and stevedores and now attracts writers and artists.

✚ 106 C14 ✉ 326 Spring Street, between Greenwich and Washington streets ☎ 212/431-9750 🕐 Daily noon–4am 🚇 Spring Street (C, E), Canal Street (1) 🚌 M20

ELEMENT

www.elementny.com

Opened in 2006 in a former bank building (which was once the studio of artist Jasper Johns), Element was quickly acclaimed as one of the city's best dance clubs in an online poll. Attractions include a powerful sound system and a huge hardwood dance floor.

✚ 107 F13 ✉ 225 East Houston Street at Essex ☎ 212/254-2200 🕐 Thu–Sun 10pm–4am 🚇 Lower East Side/Second Avenue (F) 🚌 M9, M14a, M21

FANELLI CAFE

Open the etched-glass doors and step through, and you could be in London. A few artists still gather here, and you can get pub food in the back room.

✚ 106 D14 ✉ 94 Prince Street at Mercer Street ☎ 212/226-9412 🕐 Mon–Thu 10am–1am, Fri–Sat 10am–2am, Sun 11.30am–1am 🚇 Prince Street (N, R) 🚌 M5, M21

FILM FORUM

www.filmforum.com

The leading cinema for independent films, Film Forum also shows domestic and foreign documentaries, as well as revivals of classics.

✚ 106 D14 ✉ 209 West Houston Street, between Sixth Avenue and Varick Street (Seventh Avenue) ☎ 212/727-8110 or 212/727-8112 💵 $12.50 🚇 Houston Street (1) 🚌 M5, M20, M21

FLEA THEATER

www.theflea.org

Interestingly named, Flea Theater is home to the Bat Theater Company, which presents works by playwrights who are breaking boundaries—society's or their own.

✚ 106 D15 ✉ 41 White Street, between Broadway and Church Street ☎ 212/226-2407 🚇 Canal Street (A, C, E) 🚌 M5

HAPPY ENDING

www.happyendinglounge.com

This duplex lounge reveals traces of its former life as a massage parlor, from the showerheads to the tiled sauna alcoves and the circular booths (which used to be tubs). Innovative drinks are served.

✚ 107 E14 ✉ 302 Broome Street, between Eldridge and Forsythe streets ☎ 212/334-9676 🕐 Tue 10pm–4am, Wed–Sat 7pm–4am 🚇 Delancey Street/Essex Street (F, J, M, Z)

HOUSING WORKS USED BOOK CAFÉ

www.housingworks.org

This bookstore with a gallery has become a major literary hub for readings, parties and events. Every third Friday of the month, there's an acoustic music concert. All monies go to support homeless people.

✚ 106 E14 ✉ 126 Crosby Street at Jersey Street ☎ 212/334-3324 🕐 Mon–Fri 10–9, Sat–Sun 12–7 (readings/events vary) 💵 Free–$20 🚇 Prince Street (N, R), Broadway-Lafayette (B, D, F, M), Bleecker Street (6) 🚌 M5, M21

JAZZ GALLERY

www.jazzgallery.org

The Jazz Gallery opened in 1995. This exhibition and performance space is used for jazz-oriented and jazz-influenced art, literature, drama and music.

✚ 106 C14 ✉ 290 Hudson Street, between Dominick and Spring streets ☎ 212/242-1063 🕐 Times vary, check program 💵 $10–$25 🚇 Spring Street (C, E), Houston Street (1) 🚌 M20, M21

JOYCE SOHO

www.joyce.org

This theater offers cutting-edge dance, often with an alternative perspective. Rehearsals are open to the public.

✚ 106 D14 ✉ 155 Mercer Street, between Houston and Prince streets

☎ 212/431-9233 or 212/334-7479 💵 $19–$40 🚇 Prince Street (N, R) 🚌 M5, M21

KUSH

www.thekushnyc.com

Exotic Moroccan-inspired décor sets the stage for the hip crowd at this seductive lounge, with its private alcoves and sunken hookah lounge. Global music spins on the turntable most nights.

✚ 107 E14 ✉ 191 Chrystie Street, between Stanton and Rivington streets ☎ 212/677-7328 🕐 Tue–Sun times vary 🚇 Lower East Side/Second Avenue (F), Bowery (J, M, Z) 🚌 M21, M103

LANDMARK SUNSHINE CINEMA

www.landmarktheatres.com

This five-screener offers a medley of movies, from challenging documentaries such as *Bowling for Columbine*, foreign films and oldies, to first-run movies. Seating is raked and more comfortable than at other similar movie houses.

✚ 107 E13 ✉ 143 East Houston Street, between First and Second avenues ☎ 212/260-7829 💵 $12.50 🚇 Second Avenue (F) 🚌 M15, M21

MANHATTAN ENSEMBLE THEATER

www.met.com

Home to the Manhattan Ensemble, which was founded by David Fishelson, this theater presents new plays that may well be by well-known playwrights.

✚ 106 D14 ✉ 55 Mercer Street, between Broome and Grand streets ☎ 212/925-1900 🚇 Canal Street (J, M, N, Q), Spring Street (C, E) 🚌 M5

MERC BAR

www.mercbar.com

The ultra-hip have moved on, but this bar has comfortable seating, seductive lighting and groovy music. The front banquettes are great places for people-watching in the summer months.

✚ 106 D14 ✉ 151 Mercer Street, between Houston and Prince streets ☎ 212/966-2727 🕐 Sun–Thu 5pm–1am,

Fri–Sat 5pm–3.30am 🚇 Broadway-Lafayette (F, S), Bleecker Street (6) 🚌 M5, M21

MERCURY LOUNGE
www.mercuryloungenyc.com
This is a regular stop for sampling the downtown music scene. Bands—both local and international—perform back to back in one amazing, raucous room. You might find Holly Go Lightly, who sang with punk Brit Billy Childish, doing garage rock, for example. The adjacent lounge is more serene.
➕ 107 F13 ✉ 217 East Houston Street, between First Avenue and Avenue A ☎ 212/260-4700 🕐 Daily 8pm–3am ✋ $8–$20 🚇 Lower East Side/Second Avenue (F, V) 🚌 M14, M21

Ñ
A tiny narrow bar, Ñ serves sangria with tasty tapas. There is a good selection of sherry and excellent Spanish wines.

Below *Cocktail bars and lounges abound in Lower Manhattan*

➕ 106 E14 ✉ 33 Crosby Street, between Broome and Grand streets ☎ 212/219-8856 🕐 Sun–Thu 5pm–2am, Fri–Sat 5pm–4am 🚇 Spring Street (6) 🚌 M5

PERFORMING GARAGE
www.thewoostergroup.org
Home to the Wooster Group, an Obie-winning troupe founded in 1975 by Jim Clayburgh, Willem Dafoe, Spalding Gray and others. The group produces and develops experimental entertainment and theater.
➕ 106 D14 ✉ 33 Wooster Street at Grand Street ☎ 212/966-9796 🚇 Canal Street (A, C, E) 🚌 M5

PIANOS
www.pianosnyc.com
Don't expect piano entertainment at this bi-level bar—the name is a relic of a previous occupant. Go for the alternative music on Friday, Sunday and Monday.
➕ 107 F14 ✉ 158 Ludlow Street, between Stanton and Rivington streets ☎ 212/505-3733 🕐 Daily 3pm–4am ✋ $8–$10 🚇 DeLancey Street/Essex Street (F, J, M, Z) 🚌 M9, M14a, M15

POETS HOUSE
www.poetshouse.org
Poets House is a 45,000-volume poetry library and meeting place with panoramic views of the Hudson River and Statue of Liberty. It has regular readings and lectures, and offers poetry workshops run by established poets.
➕ 106 C16 ✉ 10 River Terrace at Battery Park City ☎ 212/431-7920 ✋ Free–$7 🚇 Chambers Street (1, 2, 3, L, A, C) 🚌 M20, M22

PRAVDA
www.pravdany.com
Caviar and other Russian snacks accompany the vodka at this classy lounge. An amazing 65 different vodkas are available, many infused with a variety of exotic ingredients like ginger, mango or horseradish.
➕ 106 E14 ✉ 281 Lafayette Street, between Houston and Prince streets ☎ 212/226-4944 🕐 Mon–Thu 5pm–1am,

Fri–Sat 5pm–3am, Sun 6pm–1am (closed Sun, Jul–Aug) 🚇 Broadway-Lafayette (F, S), Bleecker Street (6) 🚌 M5, M21

SLIPPER ROOM
www.slipperroom.com
The name Slipper Room captures the mood of this lounge, which claims to be "New York's True Home of Burlesque." Shows feature aspiring cabaret artists, stand-up comedy and live music. Try the cocktails while being entertained.
➕ 107 F14 ✉ 167 Orchard Street at Stanton Street ☎ 212/253-7246 🕐 Daily 8pm–4am 🚇 Lower East Side/Second Avenue (F) 🚌 M15, M21

SOB'S
www.sobs.com
Since 1982 this club (Sounds of Brazil) has been at the forefront of Afro-Latino music. The featured band might play hip-hop and rap or driving Latin salsa with Haitian, reggae and Bhangra music, too.
➕ 106 C14 ✉ 204 Varick Street at Houston Street ☎ 212/243-4940 🕐 Show times and opening hours vary; call for details ✋ $20 minimum 🚇 Houston Street (1) 🚌 M20, M21

WILLIAM BENNETT GALLERY
www.williambennettgallery.com
This renowned veteran in the heart of the SoHo arts district exhibits original works and rare prints by Dalí, Picasso, Miró and Warhol among its offerings of contemporary art. Artworks are also on display in the basement, and you are welcome to drop in whether you're a collector looking to buy or if you're just browsing.
➕ 106 D14 ✉ 65 Greene Street between Spring and Broome streets ☎ 212/965-8707 🕐 Daily 11–7 🚇 Prince Street (N, R), Spring Street (C, E, 6) 🚌 M5, M21

SPORTS AND ACTIVITIES
NEW YORK KAYAK COMPANY
www.nykayak.com
This company offers classes and guided tours by kayak. The tours last two or three hours.

106 C14 ✉ Pier 40 at Houston Street, ☎ 212/924-1327 ⏱ Tours early May to mid-Oct ✋ Classes: $50 per hr; tours: $100–$150 🚇 Houston Street (1) 🚌 M21

PATRIOT TOURS
▷ 270.

HEALTH AND BEAUTY
SOHO SANCTUARY
www.sohosanctuary.com
This spa and yoga studio achieved a well-deserved reputation when actor Julia Roberts made frequent visits. It offers a full range of facials, therapeutic body wraps and massage.
106 D14 ✉ 119 Mercer Street near Prince Street ☎ 212/334-5550 ⏱ Tue–Fri 10–8, Sat 10–7, Sun 12–6, Mon 3–8 ✋ Facial $125–$250, massage $75–$210 🚇 Prince Street (N, R) 🚌 M5

FOR CHILDREN
CHILDREN'S MUSEUM OF THE ARTS
www.cmany.org
Children aged from 1 to 11 are welcome at this playground-cum-museum, which offers all kinds of hands-on art projects.
106 E14 ✉ 182 Lafayette Street, between Broome and Grand streets ☎ 212/274-0986 ⏱ Wed, Fri–Sun 12–5, Thu 12–6 ✋ $10, child (under 1) free 🚇 Spring Street (6), Prince Street (N, R) 🚌 M5

ELLIS ISLAND
▷ 72–74.

MUSEUM OF COMIC AND CARTOON ART
www.moccany.org
Adults seeking to relive their childhoods and older kids who love their super heroes enjoy coming here. The museum aims to promote the art of telling stories through pictures. Exhibits are dedicated to the works of such seminal figures as Harvey Kurtzman, founder of *MAD* magazine, or are theme-oriented like the recent Infinite Canvas exhibit, which explored the world of web-based comics.
106 D14 ✉ 594 Broadway (4th floor), between Houston and Prince ☎ 212/254-3511 ⏱ Tue–Sun 12–5 ✋ $6, under 12

free 🚇 Broadway-Lafayette (B, D, F, 6), Prince Street (N, R) 🚌 M5

SOUTH STREET SEAPORT MUSEUM AND MARKETPLACE
▷ 82–83.

STATEN ISLAND FERRY
www.siferry.com
The view from the decks of the harbor, the Statue of Liberty and the Lower Manhattan skyline is stunning—and free.
106 E18 ✉ Whitehall Terminal, 1 Whitehall Street ☎ 311 ⏱ Daily 24 hours ✋ Free 🚇 South Ferry (1), Whitehall Street (N, R) 🚌 M5, M15

STATUE OF LIBERTY
▷ 84–85.

Below *Ride the Staten Island Ferry for great free views of the harbor*

PRICES AND SYMBOLS

The prices given are the average for a two-course lunch (L) and a three-course dinner (D) for one person, without drinks. The wine price is for the least expensive bottle.

For a key to the symbols, ▷ 2.

AQUAGRILL

www.aquagrill.com

The day's fresh selection of seafood—cod, halibut, grouper, monkfish, tuna—can be prepared to your specifications, roasted, poached or grilled, or served in such dishes as sea bass with smoked pepper and crispy bacon in thyme vinaigrette. The oyster bar offers about 24 varieties.

✚ 106 D14 ✉ 210 Spring Street at Sixth Avenue ☎ 212/274-0505 ◷ Mon–Thu 12–3, 6–10.45, Fri 12–3, 6–11.45, Sat 12–3.45, 6–11.45, Sun 12–3.45, 6–10.30 🍴 L $30, D $50, Wine $31 🚇 Spring Street (C, E) 🚌 M5

THE BAILEY

www.thebaileynyc.com

Located just off Wall Street, the Bailey pub and brasserie is a favorite with both Financial District workers and residents. The bar area is especially lively at lunch and the end of the day, and serves a simple pub-style menu. Sink into comfortable red banquettes in the adjoining brasserie, which offers excellent yet surprisingly inexpensive meals, from salads and sandwiches to succulent steaks and a daily plat du jour.

✚ 106 E17 ✉ 52 William Street at Pine Street ☎ 212/859-2200 ◷ Daily 7am–1am 🍴 L $25, D $30, Wine $32 🚇 Broadway/Nassau Street (A, C); Wall Street (2, 3, 4, 5) 🚌 M5, M15

BALTHAZAR

www.balthazarny.com

Keith McNally has cloned a classic Paris brasserie. Bistro fare includes the seafood platter piled high with oysters, clams, shrimp and scallops; chicken paprika; and skate in brown butter. The place is crowded and vibrant and loaded with celebrity cachet. Bread and pastries come from the adjacent bakery. The wine list features a selection of totally French varieties.

✚ 106 E14 ✉ 80 Spring Street, between Broadway and Lafayette Street ☎ 212/965-1414 ◷ Mon–Thu 7.30–11.30, 12–5, 6–12, Fri 7.30–11.30, 12–5, 6–1, Sat 8–4, 6–1, Sun 8–4, 5.30–12 🍴 L $40, D $50, Wine $33 🚇 Prince Street (N, R), Spring Street (6) 🚌 M5

BAR PITTI

Actors, writers, fashion designers and Village residents gather at this European-style *boîte*. In summer, the sidewalk dining affords the chance to observe the comings and goings at hot spot Da Silvano. Your best bet is to select one of the reliable meat, fish or pasta chalkboard specials. Otherwise, choose one of the typical pastas, perhaps spaghetti with clam sauce. Credit cards are not accepted.

✚ 106 D13 ✉ 268 Sixth Avenue, between Bleecker and Houston streets ☎ 212/982-3300 ◷ Daily 12–12 🍴 L $25, D $38, Wine $30 🚇 West 4th (A, C, F), Houston Street (1) 🚌 M5

BIG WONG KING

At this Manhattan restaurant you're guaranteed a cheap, tasty meal. Don't expect tablecloths or efficient service. You're here for noodles (with duck, chicken, shrimp), congee and other standard Cantonese dishes. Credit cards are not accepted.

✚ 107 E15 ✉ 67 Mott Street, between Bayard and Canal streets ☎ 212/964-0540 ◷ Daily 8.30am–9pm 🍴 L $15, D $20 🚇 Canal Street (J, M, N, Q, R, Z, 6) 🚌 M103

BLUE RIBBON BAKERY

www.blueribbonrestaurants.com

Sandwiches made with house-baked breads and tasty small plates—mushroom ravioli, sweet *sopressata,* smoked red trout—draw crowds at lunch, while such dinner entrées as New Orleans barbecue shrimp and filet mignon with tomato, onion and watercress salad and potato cake draw night-time customers. There is a wide choice of cheese and an extensive wine list. The restaurant's hundred-year-old brick oven produces the tantalizing fresh-baked lunch sandwich and dinner breads. The dessert menu features crème brûlée, bread puddings and sundaes.

Opposite *Fresh flavors on a plate*

✚ 106 C13 ✉ 34 Downing Street at Bedford Street ☎ 212/691-0404 🕐 Daily 4pm–2am 🍴 L $25, D $50, Wine $28 🚇 Houston Street (1) 🚌 M5, M20, M21

BOULEY

www.davidbouley.com

The new Bouley is down the street from the old restaurant. David Bouley has created a romantic candle-lit atmosphere, with vaulted ceiling, fireplace and Impressionist paintings. Entrées include chicken with black truffle and fresh almond purée, or cod with black onion crust. The desserts are the real show here: try the caramelized Anjou pear with biscuit, chocolate and a scoop of vanilla-flavored ice cream, or the complex chocolate frivolous with multiple components and textures.

✚ 106 D15 ✉ 163 Duane Street at Hudson ☎ 212/964-2525 🕐 Daily 11.30–3, 5–11 🍴 L $55, D $75, Wine $45 🚇 Chambers Street (A, C, E, 1, 2, 3) 🚌 M5, M20

BREAD

This small casual café makes delicious paninis, soups, salads and daily plates. Try the gazpacho in summer and the prosciutto di Parma with truffle oil, bruschetta, spicy shrimp salad, and delicious bread and tomato soup in winter. There is a choice of wines with 12 wines sold by the glass.

✚ 107 E14 ✉ 20 Spring Street, between Elizabeth and Mott streets ☎ 212/334-1015 🕐 Sun–Thu 10.30–midnight, Fri–Sat 10.30–1am 🍴 L $15, D $25 🚇 Spring Street (6), Bowery (J, M, Z), Grand Street (S) 🚌 M103

BRIDGE CAFÉ

www.bridgecafenyc.com

In New York they don't come much older than the Bridge Café, a tavern that was first opened in 1794 and still has the feel of the 18th century. The bright red wood-framed building stands in the shadow of Brooklyn Bridge. With a colorful history as a brothel and a speakeasy, today the tavern has a fine bar menu and is terrific for a Sunday brunch.

✚ 107 E16 ✉ 279 Water Street, between Dover Street and Peck Slip ☎ 212/227-3344 🕐 Tue–Thu 11.45am–11pm, Fri 11.45am–midnight, Sat 5pm–midnight, Sun–Mon 11.45–4 🚇 Fulton Street/Broadway/Nassau Street (2, 3, J, Z) 🚌 M15

DIM SUM GO GO

At this small, modernist restaurant you can find the latest in Chinese cuisine: dim sum, presented in bamboo steamers or on pupu platters. Expect jicama and lotus root dumplings, crabmeat stuffed in green spinach dough, wood mushrooms and carrot dumplings.

✚ 107 E15 ✉ 5 East Broadway, between Catherine and Oliver streets ☎ 212/732-0797 🕐 Daily 10am–11pm 🍴 L $23, D $32 🚇 East Broadway (F), Canal Street (J, M, N, R, Q, Z, 6) 🚌 M9, M15, M22

HAMPTON CHUTNEY

www.hamptonchutney.com

South Indian dosas and uttapas are the specialties of this counter-style eatery. The classic dosa is filled with spiced potato here, but many Western-inspired variations are offered, from avocado, tomato, arugula and jack cheese, to tuna with cilantro-chutney dressing. Good sandwiches on black, sourdough and other breads, too. Chai and lassi are the choice drinks.

✚ 106 E14 ✉ 68 Prince Street, between Crosby and Lafayette streets ☎ 212/226-9996 🕐 Daily 11–9 🍴 $15 🚇 Prince Street (N, R), Broadway-Lafayette (F), Spring Street (6) 🚌 M5

THE HARRISON

www.theharrison.com

With its tufted leather banquettes and weathered wood paneling, this friendly, inviting restaurant is the kind of neighborhood spot where people drop in regularly. The food is brimming with flavor; the skillet calves' liver comes with bacon, onion and potato strudel in a rich sherry sauce, while sautéed skate is redolent of treviso, pancetta and preserved lemon.

✚ 106 D15 ✉ 355 Greenwich Street at Harrison Street ☎ 212/274-9310 🕐 Mon–Thu 12–2.30, 5.30–10.30, Fri 12–2.30, 5.30–11, Sat 5.30–11, Sun 5–10 🍴 L $30, D $55, Wine $36 🚇 Franklin Street (1) 🚌 M20

KATZ'S DELI

www.katzdeli.com

The site of the climactic scene in *When Harry Met Sally* is the last remaining deli in what was once a thriving Jewish neighborhood. Opened in 1888, it upholds deli traditions: nondescript surroundings and immense knishes and pastrami sandwiches. They make their own salami, the corned beef takes 30 days to cure, and the sandwiches, platters and meats are served in large portions. Bustling Katz's serves presidents, movie stars and hungry visitors from around the world as well as locals. Credit cards are accepted only on bills of $20 and more.

✚ 107 F13 ✉ 205 East Houston Street, between Ludlow and Orchard streets ☎ 212/254-2246 🕐 Sun, Wed–Thu 8am–10.45pm, Mon–Tue 8am–9.45pm, Fri–Sat 8am–2.45am 🍴 L $20, D $30 🚇 Lower East Side/Second Avenue (F) 🚌 M9, M14a, M21

LUPA

www.luparestaurant.com

Lupa, the moderately priced restaurant owned by beloved Food Channel host Mario Batali and two partners, has the feel of a casual Roman trattoria. The cuisine starts with ultra-fresh staples, many of which are made on the premises, notably the pasta, sausages and cheeses featured as appetizers. The simple, intense main dishes range from a classic saltimbocca to *bucatini all'amatriciana,* made with bacon, onions and cilantro. Side dishes such as braised escarole and cauliflower with capers are worthy additions to the menu.

✚ 106 D13 ✉ 170 Thompson Street, between Bleecker and Houston streets ☎ 212/982-5089 🕐 Daily 12–12 🍴 L $32, D $45, Wine $27 🚇 West 4th Street (A, C, E, F) 🚌 M5, M21

MARK JOSEPH STEAKHOUSE

www.markjosephsteakhouse.com

Those who have had enough of Peter Luger's sawdust-on-the-floor style claim that this sleek and more modern meat specialist is the city's best steakhouse. The porterhouse is the choice cut. Finish with the apple galette or a slice of pecan pie.

107 E16 ✉ 261 Water Street at Peck Slip ☎ 212/277-0020 ◷ Mon–Thu 11.30–9.45, Fri 11.30–10.45, Sat 5–10.45 ✋ L $40, D $65, Wine $40 ⊡ Broadway/ Nassau Street (A, C), Fulton Street (J, M, Z, 2, 3, 4, 5) ⊟ M15

NAM

www.namnyc.com

Nam stands out for its style and its authentic and unique dishes. Particularly alluring are appetizers. *Banh xeo,* for example, is a crêpe filled with mushrooms, bean sprouts, coconut-flavored rice, shrimp and chicken; *ca tim nuong* consists of grilled Asian eggplant (aubergine) with ginger, lime, garlic and a little chili. Among the many main dishes, crisp red snapper and chicken with chili lemongrass sauce make good dinner choices.

106 D15 ✉ 110 Reade Street at West Broadway ☎ 212/267-1777 ◷ Mon–Fri 12–2pm, Sun–Thu 5.30–10, Fri–Sat 5.30–11 ✋ L $25, D $39, Wine $28 ⊡ Chambers Street (1) ⊟ M20

NOBU

www.noburestaurants.com

Celebrities flock to Drew Nieporent's TriBeCa hot spot for the artistic sushi and sashimi fashioned by chef Nobu Matsuhisa. The *omakase* menu will deliver the chef's inspirations for the day. Or choose from baby abalone, live scallop or sashimi drizzled with garlic and ginger-flavored olive oil. Masu sake is served in small cedar cups with salted rims; finish with green tea crème caramel. Reservations are hard to come by; the next best thing is to drop in to Next Door Nobu.

106 D15 ✉ 105 Hudson Street, between Franklin and North Moore streets ☎ 212/219-0500 ◷ Mon–Fri 11.45–2.15, 5.45–10.15, Sat–Sun 5.45–10.15 ✋ L $40,

D $60, *omakase* $100, $120 or $150, Wine $35 ⊡ Franklin Street (1) ⊟ M20

NYONYA

You can sample some of Malaysia's appealing, sometimes spicy dishes at this plain favorite. You have a wide choice of rice, noodle, casserole and other dishes; start with a roti (Indian pancake) or the satays, and follow with a fiery sambal or a curry made with lemongrass, chili and coconut milk. Credit cards are not accepted.

107 E14 ✉ 194 Grand Street, between Mott and Mulberry streets ☎ 212/334-3669 ◷ Sun–Thu 11am–11.30pm, Fri–Sat 11am–midnight ✋ L $20, D $25 ⊡ Grand Street (B, D) ⊟ M103

ODEON

www.theodeonrestaurant.com

In the early 1980s this cafeteria-turned-hip-bistro was the incubator of the downtown scene. Odeon still has Venetian blinds on the windows and chrome stools at the bar, but nowadays it caters to neighborhood residents as well as downtown celebrities, with a typical bistro menu of onion soup gratinée, moules and steak frites. This is a great late-night stop.

106 D15 ✉ 145 West Broadway, between Thomas and Duane streets ☎ 212/233-0507 ◷ Mon–Tue 11.30am–midnight, Wed 11.30am–1am, Thu–Fri 11.30am–2am, Sat 10am–2am, Sun 10am–midnight ✋ L $32, D $45, Wine $38 ⊡ Chambers Street (A, C, E), Chambers Street (1, 2, 3) ⊟ M5, M20

PEASANT

www.peasantnyc.com

This cozy storefront has become a popular chef's hang-out. As the name suggests, it produces bold rustic Italian cuisine from its wood-fired ovens. Wood-roasted sardines, roasted clams and really fine pizzas are carefully prepared. The grilled fishes are flavored with the best olive oil, lemon and herbs.

107 E14 ✉ 194 Elizabeth Street, between Prince and Spring streets ☎ 212/965-9511 ◷ Tue–Thu 6–11, Fri–Sat 6–11.30, Sun 6–10.30 ✋ D $45,

Wine $20 ⊡ Bowery (J, M, Z), Spring Street (6) ⊟ M5

TOMOE SUSHI

http://tomoesushi.com

This plain sushi parlor does a brisk trade among students and other sushi aficionados, drawn by its reasonable prices. About 30 different sushi choices and 30 varieties of *maki* rolls are available, along with hot dishes and noodles.

106 D13 ✉ 172 Thompson Street, between Bleecker and Houston streets ☎ 212/777-9346 ◷ Mon 5–11, Tue–Sat 1–3, 5–11, Sun 5–10 ✋ L $28, D $44 ⊡ West 4th Street (A, C, E, F) ⊟ M5, M21

TRAVERTINE

www.travertinenyc.com

One of the hottest restaurants on the trendy NoLita dining scene, Travertine attracts celebrities. Chef Danae Cappelletto blends a range of culinary influences in her Italian Mediterranean cuisine, with dishes such as garganelli with shitake mushrooms, baby brussels sprouts and brown butter, or her delicious spice-rubbed braised pork belly. The pasta is homemade daily. Behind the understated facade is an elegant yet casual space. Desserts include self-saucing chocolate pudding.

107 E14 ✉ 19 Kenmare Street, between Elizabeth Street and the Bowery ☎ 212/966-1810 ◷ Tue–Sun 6pm–1 or 2am ✋ D $50, Wine $35 ⊡ Spring Street (6), Bowery (J, Z) ⊟ M5, M21, M103

WD-50

www.wd-50.com

Wylie Dufresne made the Lower East Side a dining destination when he cooked at 71 Clinton Street. His own place is a postmodern dining room where he mixes exciting flavor combinations—octopus with celery pesto, pineapple and almonds, striped bass with passion fruit. Desserts are also creative.

107 F14 ✉ 50 Clinton Street, between Stanton and Rivington streets (east side of the street) ☎ 212/477-2900 ◷ Wed–Sat 6–11, Sun 6–10 ✋ D $60, Wine $56 ⊡ Delancey Street/Essex Street (F, J, M, Z) ⊟ M9, M21

PRICES AND SYMBOLS

Prices are the lowest and highest for a double room for one night. Breakfast is included unless noted otherwise. All the hotels listed accept credit cards unless otherwise stated. Note that rates vary widely throughout the year.

For a key to the symbols, ▷ 2.

COSMOPOLITAN HOTEL– TRIBECA

www.cosmohotel.com

This hotel has a great downtown location and attractive rooms. They are all furnished with Scandinavian-style pieces, and they have private bath, TV and telephone.
➕ 106 D15 ✉ 95 West Broadway at Chambers Street, 10007 ☎ 212/566-1900 ✋ $99–$279 🛈 125 🚇 Chambers Street (1, 2, 3), Chambers Street (A, C) 🚌 M20

HOTEL AZURE

www.hotelazure.com

The Azure is a compact boutique hotel in SoHo, which is smoke-free. Room rates include a newspaper and bottled water. Rooms are simple but bright and modern, with lots of blue and white, and all have free high-speed Internet, direct-dial phones with voice mail and 32-inch flat-screen TVs with cable.
➕ 106 E15 ✉ 120 Lafayette Street at Canal Street, 10013 ☎ 212/925-4378 ✋ $269–$400 🛈 28 🚇 Canal Street (6) 🚌 M5

MERCER

www.mercerhotel.com

The Hollywood crowd loves this East Coast version of Andre Balaz's Château Marmont. The SoHo location is ultra-hip, but the place is discreet, comfortable and tranquil. The loft-style rooms are spacious and minimalist. Christian Liaigre used neutral colors, glass, fabrics like linen, and rich woods from Africa. Spacious bathrooms are standard, and most offer marble tubs for two. If that's not enough,

Above *Lower Manhattan has some lovely boutique hotels*

then the Mercer Kitchen under star chef Jean Georges Vongerichten is the clincher. Access to a nearby fitness center is provided.
➕ 106 D14 ✉ 147 Mercer Street, between Prince and Spring streets, 10012 ☎ 212/966-6060 ✋ $425–$820, suite from $1,500 🛈 75 rooms and suites 🚇 Prince St (N, R) 🚌 M5, M21

OFF-SOHO SUITES

www.offsoho.com

These suites, with bedroom and living/dining areas, are on the Lower East Side, the last of Manhattan's gentrified neighborhoods. Savvy travelers will appreciate the low prices. Ideal for two couples traveling together, as each suite shares a kitchen and bath, they are equipped with cable TV, telephone, modular jack and minibar.
➕ 107 E14 ✉ 11 Rivington Street, between Chrystie and Bowery streets, 10002 ☎ 212/979-9815 ✋ $179–$459, quads $299–$379 🛈 38 suites 🚇 Bowery (J, Z) 🚌 M103

SOHO GRAND

www.sohogrand.com

Since the CEO of Hartz pet food owns this stylish downtown hotel, it puts out a welcome mat for animals. It was a pioneer, too, when it opened in art-oriented SoHo. A cast-iron staircase studded with coke-bottle glass leads up to the vibrant lobby. Cool tones create the ambience in the rooms, but there are plenty of guest comforts— bathrobes, Frette linens, velvet drapes, plus DVD, WiFi, restaurant and two bars.
➕ 106 D14 ✉ 310 West Broadway, between Canal and Grand streets, 10013 ☎ 212/965-3000 ✋ From $229, suite $3,500 🛈 363 rooms and suites 🚇 Canal Street (A, C, E) 🚌 M5

TRIBECA GRAND

www.tribecagrand.com

With its luxurious 98-seat private screening room, this hotel, close to SoHo and the Village, caters to the independent film crowd. The lobby opens to a dramatic atrium lounge/ restaurant. The rooms are modern and come with such gadgets as wireless keyboards, a bathroom TV with waterproof remote, Bose radio and fax/printer. Bliss and Kiehl products in the bathroom and the Dean & DeLuca snacks are alluring extras. The business center is well equipped, and the workstations have flat-panel screens. Hartz owns the place, so pets are welcome.
➕ 106 D15 ✉ 2 Avenue of the Americas at White Street, 10013 ☎ 212/519-6600 ✋ Doubles from $279, suite from $799 🛈 203 rooms 🚇 Franklin Street (1) 🚌 M20

Charles Street
West 10th Street
Christopher
Bedford Street
Commerce Street
Barrow
Morton
Washington
Morton Street
Leroy
Clarkson Street
King
Charlton
Vandam
Spring Street

13
14
15
16
17
18

Hudson

Church of St. Luke-in-the-Fields
House of Oldies Rare Records
Saint Luke's Pl.
J J Walker Park

Minetta Lane
Minetta Street
Thompson St
LaGuardia Place
Great Jones Street
Bond Street
Lafayette
Bleecker Street

Bar Pitti
Blue Ribbon Bakery
Lupa
Tomoe Sushi

Bleecker Street
Bleecker St

HOUSTON Street
Houston Street
WEST HOUSTON STREET

Prince Street
West Broadway
Wooster Street
Greene Street
Mercer Street

Mercer
Singer Building
St Patrick's Old Cathedral
Jersey St
Prince Street
Hampton
Chutne

Aquagrill
Balthazar
Spring Street
Spring Street

New York City Fire Museum
Broome
Dominick
Watts

SOHO
Haughwout Building
Crosby
Broome
Grand
Children's Museum of the Arts
Grand
Museum of Chinese in America
Howard Street

American Numismatic Society
Canal Grand
Canal Street
SoHo Grand
Hotel Azure

CANAL ST
Desbrosses
Vestry
Laight Street
Hubert
Beach St
Greenwich
Hudson Street
Ericsson Place
VARICK

Lispenard
Walker
White
Franklin
Leonard
Worth
Thomas
Duane
Reade St
Chambers

LOWER MANHATTAN
CENTRE STREET
LAFAYETTE STREET

Tribeca Grand
TRIBECA
Nobu
The Harrison
Odeon
Bouley
Nam

CHURCH
BROADWAY

North Moore
Franklin Street
Harrison
Jay St
Staple St
Duane
Thomas Paine Park
Foley
Pear
US Courthouse

Washington Market Park
Reade St
Chambers Street
Cosmopolitan Hotel-Tribeca
City Hall

Warren Street
Park Place West
Murray Street
Barclay Street

Greenwich
Park Place
Murray
Warren
City Hall Park
Brooklyn Bridge City Hall
City Hall

Woolworth Building
Church of St Peter
Spruce Street
Beekman
PARK ROW
Ann

9A
Vesey Street
VESEY STREET
VESEY ST

BATTERY PARK CITY

St Paul's Chapel
World Trade Center
World Trade Center Site
Fulton St
Dey St
John
Cortlandt Street
Liberty

Broadway-Nassau St Street
Fulton
Dutch Street
Nassau Street
William Street
MAIDEN LANE
Platt
Gold
Maiden

Federal Reserve Bank
Cedar
Pine
Wall Street
Liberty St

Albany Street
Rector Street
Rector Place
Trinity Church
Wall Street
The Bailey
Museum of American Finance

New York Stock Exchange
Exchange Aly
Broad St
Beaver

West Thames Street
South End Avenue
Morris Street
Battery Place
Washington Street
GREENWICH STREET
Bridge St

Hudson

Museum of Jewish Heritage
Robert F Wagner Jr Park
Bowling Green
Battery Place

Fraunces Tavern Museum
STATE STREET
Whitehall Street
Rector of the Shrine of Elizabeth Ann Seton
PETER MINUIT PLAZA

Battery Park

Castle Clinton
Admiral George Dewey Promenade
HIGHWAY 9A
BROOKLYN BATTERY TUNNEL

Staten Island Ferry Termi

HOLLAND TUNNEL

0 ___ 250 m
0 ___ 250 yds

Ellis Island Immigration Museum, Statue of Liberty

B **C** **D**

East
River
Park

East 3rd Street

East Houston Street

Katz's Deli

WD-50

New Museum of Contemporary Art

Off-SoHo Suites

Peasant

LOWER EAST SIDE

Bread

Travertine

LITTLE ITALY

Lower East Side Tenement Museum

Nyonya

CHINATOWN

Big Wong King

Dim Sum Go Go

Seward Park

Corlears Hook Park

Williamsburg Bridge Approach

Hamilton Fish Park

Baruch Place

East Broadway

Rutgers Park

Manhattan Bridge

Franklin Delano Roosevelt Drive (FDR)

Avenue of the Finest

East
River

BROOKLYN BRIDGE

Bridge Café

Mark Joseph Steakhouse

Fulton Street Market

South Street Seaport

WALL STREET

New York City Police Museum

Empire-Fulton Ferry State Park

New Dock Street

BROOKLYN-QUEENS EXPRESSWAY

Plymouth Church of the Pilgrims

High Street Brooklyn Bridge

Cadman Plaza Park

BROOKLYN HEIGHTS

Federal Building

US Post Office & Courthouse

Supreme Court of New York

Brooklyn Historical Society

Cathedral of Our Lady of Lebanon

Grace Court Aly

Grace Church

Brooklyn Borough Hall

Borough Hall

E   F   G   H

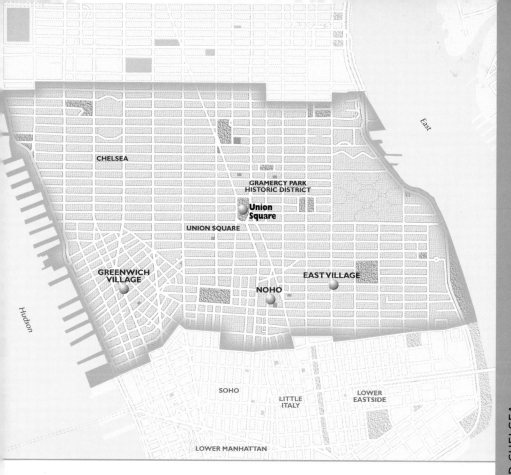

CHELSEA

GRAMERCY PARK
HISTORIC DISTRICT

Union Square

UNION SQUARE

GREENWICH
VILLAGE

EAST VILLAGE

NOHO

SOHO

LITTLE
ITALY

LOWER
EASTSIDE

LOWER MANHATTAN

Hudson

East

DOWNTOWN AND CHELSEA

Don't let the Downtown moniker fool you, for this section of Manhattan is all about unique neighborhoods brimming with one-of-a-kind coffeeshops, cafés, bars and boutiques. The museums here are smaller, the buildings only mid-rise, and young, hip professionals and students mingle with the established residents.

The East Village was settled in the 1800s, first by the Irish, then Germans followed by the Ukrainians whose influence has been the most lasting. The Ukrainian Museum commemorates the Ukrainian history of the neighborhood through folk art, crafts, costumes and artworks. Musicians and artists took up residence in the 1950s and 1960s, and the area reached its artistic heyday in the 1980s. New York University has expanded into this neighborhood of brownstones and historic residences.

Now a chic neighborhood with a large population of celebrities, Greenwich Village was the bohemian district of New York from the late 1800s through the mid-1900s when it attracted colorful, artistic personalities and alternative lifestyles. Cherry Lane Theatre, the oldest continuously running off-Broadway theater, opened here in 1924. The performing arts scene is still vibrant, with many off-Broadway and off-off-Broadway theaters. Washington Square is the heart of the neighborhood, where street musicians, students and chess players gather in warm weather. The Washington Memorial Arch was built in 1889, and many artists have painted it over the years. Nearby, Washington Mews is a pretty cobblestone street lined with the former stables and servants' quarters for the town houses along the north side of the park, known as The Row.

Union Square is a popular, centrally located gathering place in Manhattan. Numerous subway lines intersect in the bustling 14th Street/Union Square station, and many expensive restaurants and bars surround the square. New York's premier green market is held here four days a week, drawing crowds who come to shop for fresh produce.

West 36th Street
West 35th Street
West 34th Street
34th Street Penn Station
West 33rd Street
West 31st Street
West 30th Street
West 29th Street
West 28th Street
Chelsea Park
West 27th Street
West 26th Street
West 25th Street
West 24th Street
Chelsea Waterside Park
West 23rd Street
West 22nd Street
Chelsea Art Museum
West 21st Street
West 20th Street
West 19th Street
West 18th Street
West 17th Street
West 16th Street
West 15th Street
WEST 14TH STREET
West 13th Street
Little West 12th Street
Bloomfield Street
Gansevoort Street
Horatio Street
Jane Street
West 12th Street
Bethune Street
Bank Street
West 11th Street
Perry Street
Charles Lane
Charles Street

GREENWICH VILLAGE

Christopher Street
Sheridan Square
McNulty's Rare Teas and Choice Coffee Shop
Church of St Luke-in-the-Fields

Hudson

West 10th
Christopher
Barrow
Morton
Leroy
Clarkson Street

Macy's
34th Street Herald Square
Empire State Building
Madison Square Garden
Pennsylvania Station
28th Street
23rd Street
18th Street
Rubin Museum of Art
8th Avenue
14th Street
6th Avenue
Washington
Greenwich
Waverly
Bank Street
Perry Street
Charles Street
Jefferson Market Library
Christopher Park
Washington
Grove Street
Bedford
Commerce St
Leroy St
House of Oldies Rare Records
J J Walker Park
Saint Luke's Pl
Carmine Street
Downing

Little Church Around the Corner
West 29th Street
28th Street
West 28th St
West 27th Street
West 26th Street
West 25th Street
Madison Square Park
West 24th Street
23rd Street
Flatiron Building
West 22nd Street
West 21st Street
West 20th Street
West 19th Street
West 18th Street
West 17th Street
West 16th Street
14th Street
UNION SQUARE
WEST 14TH STREET   EAST 14
West 13th Street
Forbes Magazine Galleries
West 12th Street
West 11th Street
West 10th Street
West 9th Street
West 8th Street
Mac Dougal Alley
Washington Mews
WASHINGTON SQUARE NORTH
Washington Square Park
WASHINGTON SQUARE SOUTH
West 4th Street Washington Square
Minetta Lane
Bleecker Street
Macdougal Street
Sullivan Street
Thompson Street
LaGuardia Place

WEST HOUSTON
Houston Street
Prince Street
Spring Street
King
Charlton
Vandam
New York City Fire Museum
Spring
Dominick
American Numismatic Society
CANAL

West 36th Street   East 36
West 35th Street   East 35
WEST 34TH STREET   EAST 34
West 33rd Street   East 33
West 32nd Street   East 32
West 31st Street   East 31
West 30th Street   East 30

Hudson

10

11

12

13

14

10TH AVENUE
11TH AVENUE
12TH AVENUE
9TH AVENUE
8TH AVENUE
7TH AVENUE
FASHION AVENUE
Avenue of the Americas (6th Avenue)
5th Avenue
Broadway
WEST STREET
9A

A   B   C   D

250 m
250 yds

Morgan Library

33rd Street

East 36th Street

East 35th Street

East 34th Street

EAST 34TH STREET

East 33rd Street

Lexington Avenue
3rd Avenue
2nd Avenue
1st Avenue
FDR DRIVE SERVICE ROAD

East 30th Street

East 29th Street

28th Street

East 28th Street

Mt. Carmel Place

East 27th Street

East 26th Street

East 25th Street

Metropolitan Life Insurance Tower

25th St

East 24th St

East 24th Street

East 23rd Street

East Levy Place

Waterside Plaza

23rd Street

East 22nd Street

Peter Cooper Road

GRAMERCY PARK HISTORIC DISTRICT

Gramercy Park North
Gramercy Park
Gramercy Park South

East 21st Street

East 20th Street Service Drive

East 20th Street

Theodore Roosevelt Birthplace

Block Beautiful

East 19th Street

East 18th Street

20th Street Loop

East 17th Street

1st Avenue Loop

Stuyvesant Walk

Avenue C Loop

Rutherford Place

Stuyvesant Square

Perlman Place

Nathan D. Perlman Place

Stuyvesant Oval

East 16th Street

East 16th Street

3rd Avenue

Irving Place

East 15th Street

1st Avenue

14th Street Loop

Union Square

SQUARE EAST

ET 14th Street Union Square

EAST 14TH STREET SERVICE DRIVE

EAST 14TH STREET

East 13th Street

East 13th Street

East 12th Street

East 12th Street

4th Avenue

East 11th Street

East 11th Place

Grace Church

St Mark's Church-in-the-Bowery

East 10th Street

East 10th Street

BROADWAY

Stuyvesant Street

East 9th Street

East 9th Street

Wanamaker Place

Astor Place

Saint Marks Place

East 8th Street

8th Street NYU

Astor Place

Cooper Sq.

EAST VILLAGE

East 7th Street

Tompkins Square Park

NOHO

Ukrainian Museum

East 6th Street

East 5th Street

East 5th Walk

Washington Place

East 5th Street

4th Street

Merchant's House Museum

East 4th Street

East 4th Walk

Great Jones Street

Bond Street

Bleecker Street

East 3rd Street

East 3rd Street

Louis Street

Mangin Street

Bowery

Mercer

LaFayette Street

Bleecker Street

Mott Street

East 2nd Street

East 1st Street

2nd Avenue

EAST HOUSTON STREET

Hamilton Fish Park

Attorney Avenue

Columbia

Baruch Place

Broadway - Lafayette Street

Prince Street

St Patrick's Old Cathedral

Prince Street

Stanton Street

Attorney Street

Stanton Street

Rivington St

HO

Jersey Street

Singer Building

New Museum of Contemporary Art

Mulberry Street
Elizabeth Street
Bowery
Chrystie Street
Forsyth Street
Eldridge Street
Allen Street
Orchard Street
Ludlow Street
Essex Street
Norfolk Street
Suffolk Street
Clinton Street
Attorney Street
Ridge Street
Pitt Street
Willett Street
Sheriff Street
Columbia Street
Lewis Street

Spring Street

Rivington Street

Delancey Street

WILLIAMSBURG BRIDGE APPROACH

Spring Street

DELANCEY STREET

Roosevelt Drive

HO
Haughwout Building

Kenmare Street

Bowery

Essex Street

LOWER EAST SIDE

Broome Street

Lower East Side Tenement Museum

Children's Museum of the Arts

LITTLE ITALY

Broome Street

Grand Street

Seward Park

Henry Street

Madison Street

Jackson Street

Corlears Hook Park

Museum of Chinese in America

Grand Street

Centre Market Pl

Mott Street

Chrystie Street

Forsyth Street

BOWERY

Eldridge Street

Allen Street

Orchard Street

Ludlow Street

Essex Street

Norfolk Street

Suffolk Street

Clinton Street

Ridge Street

Pitt Street

Cherry Street

East River Park

FRANKLIN DELANO ROOSEVELT DRIVE (FDR)

East River

E   F   G

111

CHELSEA

Galleries, studios and dance and media centers add the artsy edge to this now-stylish district. Before World War I the US movie industry developed in disused warehouses and theaters here before moving to California. The Kitchen, at 512 West 19th Street, has film, music and dance. Between 19th and 29th streets, and Tenth and Eleventh avenues, the Chelsea Art District is packed with galleries. The Chelsea Art Museum (556 West 22nd Street, tel 212/255-0719) holds contemporary exhibitions. The Rubin Museum of Art (150 West 17th Street at Seventh Avenue, tel 212/620-5000) has Tibetan and Himalayan art.

West of the West Side Highway, a series of piers on the Hudson, known as Chelsea Piers, forms a sports and entertainment complex with ice skating, roller skating, swimming and restaurants.

🕂 110 C11 ✉ Seventh to Eleventh avenues, between 14th and 28th streets 🚇 C, E 🚌 M20 🍴 🖥 📷

EAST VILLAGE AND NOHO
▷ 114–115.

FLATIRON BUILDING AND DISTRICT

Squeezed into the angle where Broadway crosses Fifth Avenue, the Flatiron Building, at 285ft (87m), was originally known as the Fuller Building, built to designs by Daniel Burnham in 1902. The proportions have attracted photographers ever since. Below 23rd Street, Fifth and Sixth avenues and Broadway were once the swankiest shopping district of New York, and this stretch of Sixth Avenue was called Ladies' Mile. Department stores brought commercialism and a new style of architecture to the area. Just northeast of the Flatiron Building is Madison Square Park.

Above *Publishing magnate Malcolm Forbes' collections are on display here*
Opposite *Chelsea is a chic, artsy district in a former warehousing area*

🕂 110 D11 ✉ 175 Fifth Avenue at Broadway, 10017 🚇 N, R 🚌 M2, M3, M5, M6

FORBES MAGAZINE GALLERIES

www.forbesgalleries.com
Publishing magnate and adventurer Malcolm Forbes (1919–90) had a passion for collecting, and the former home of the Macmillan publishing house, now the offices of *Forbes* magazine, has a gallery that displays the result: old Monopoly games, model boats, battlefields with model soldiers, about 3,000 historical documents (including Abraham Lincoln's *Emancipation Proclamation)* and, among a display of objets d'art, a dozen of the fabled, bejeweled Easter eggs crafted for Russian czars by the house of Fabergé. Children enjoy the antique toy collection, the model boats and other watercraft.

🕂 110 D12 ✉ 60–62 Fifth Avenue at 12th Street, 10011 ☎ 212/206-5548 🕐 Tue–Wed, Fri–Sat 10–4; call to confirm hours on day of visit 🎫 Free 🚇 1, 4, 5, 6, N, R, A, C, E, B, D 🚌 M1, M2, M3, M5

GRACE CHURCH

www.gracechurchnyc.org
By the time James Renwick, Jr. began building churches, the Gothic Revival was in full swing. Renwick, like Richard Upjohn, who designed Trinity Church (▷ 79) on Lower Broadway—once the tallest building in New York City—took up the style with enthusiasm. Grace Church, completed in 1846, was one result; another was the massive, Gothic Revival St. Patrick's Cathedral (▷ 160), on Fifth Avenue at 50th Street.

Grace Church's original wood steeple was replaced by marble in 1888. It stands on the first bend of Broadway, so that it anchors the view along Broadway from downtown. The complex that surrounds the church includes Renwick's Grace House (1881) and the Rectory, and, on Fourth Avenue South, Renwick's fine Grace Memorial House.

🕂 111 E12 ✉ 800 Broadway at 10th Street, 10004 ☎ 212/254-2000 🕐 Mon–Fri 10–4, Sun for services only 🚇 N, R, 6 🚌 M1, M7

INFORMATION

✚ 111 E13 ✉ South of 14th Street, east of Bowery 🚇 4, 5, 6 🚌 M8, M15

INTRODUCTION

This is a funky area of vintage-clothing shops, ethnic diners, innovative restaurants and trendy clubs, with historic sites. The East Village and NoHo (*North of Ho*uston) extend between 14th Street and Houston Street, between Broadway and Avenue B. Once farmland owned by Dutch governor Peter Stuyvesant, this area was home to Irish, German, Jewish, Ukrainian and Italian immigrants in the 1800s and 1900s. Today you can visit the Ukrainian Museum (▷ 120) to appreciate the culture of immigrants from the Ukraine.

New York's second-oldest church, St. Mark's Church-in-the-Bowery (▷ 120), on Second Avenue at 10th Street, is on land that was once part of the Stuyvesant farm; the old governor is buried in the churchyard. Poet W. H. Auden, who lived at 77 St. Marks Place from 1953 to 1972, was a parishioner.

In the 1830s the richest of the rich lived at 428–434 Lafayette Street, south of Astor Place, known as Colonnade Row. Among them were John Jacob Astor, some of the Vanderbilts, and the Delano family. Today only four of the original nine houses remain. Cooper Union, at 51 Astor Place, was founded by one of America's great engineering geniuses, Peter Cooper. Now a designated New York landmark, the building was completed in 1859 and was where Abraham Lincoln made the antislavery speech that helped earn him the Republican Party's presidential nomination. In the 1870s, wealthy New York women attended services at Grace Church (▷ 113), designed by architect James Renwick, Jr., one of the finest examples of Gothic Revival architecture in the United States.

WHAT TO SEE

JEWISH, RUSSIAN AND TURKISH HERITAGE

At the beginning of the 20th century, Second Avenue between Houston Street and 14th Street became a center of Yiddish culture and came to be known as the Jewish Rialto. Edward G. Robinson and Walter Matthau got their start in the Yiddish theater here. Although the much-loved Second Avenue Deli has been driven out by rent rises, plaques in the sidewalk outside its old location

Above *Alternative culture thrives in the East Village*

at No. 156 honor Yiddish theater stars. The Christadora House, on the corner of 9th Street and Avenue B, was where George Gershwin gave his first public recital. On 10th Street, between First Avenue and Avenue A, the Russian and Turkish Baths (tel 212/674-9250) opened in 1892; unlike many similar establishments, it has survived to become a New York institution. Inside, the baths are not glamorous but poignantly evoke 19th-century New York.

A BOHEMIAN DISTRICT

In the 1960s and 1970s, the East Village was a focal point of the American hippie culture. Anarchist Abbie Hoffman lived on St. Marks Place and Allen Ginsberg, Timothy Leary, Andy Warhol and a motley collection of Hell's Angels, Hare Krishnas and political rebels frequented the area, often meeting for protest rallies and rock concerts in Tompkins Square Park. For years, until a 1990s restoration, the area attracted the homeless and drug-users. Today it is lovely by day, but still best avoided after dark.

The Joseph Papp Public Theater on Lafayette Street is one of the city's most famous off-Broadway theaters. Impresario Joseph Papp rescued the old Astor Library from demolition, and his theater opened in 1967 with the original production of the musical *Hair*.

The mix of ethnic restaurants in the East Village gives visitors a choice of great food at budget prices. For more stylish dining at higher prices, head for NoHo, the area around Lafayette Street and Broadway between Bleecker and Fourth streets.

The farthest area east, known unofficially as Alphabet City because the streets are designated by letters not numbers, is less accessible by subway, so it's best to arrive and leave by taxi. The area has some chic shops and fashionable bistros.

TIPS

» Skip the area east of Avenue B— it's not really worth visiting and can be intimidating.

» Check local listings to find out what's on at theaters.

» Visit in late afternoon or early evening for a stroll and an inexpensive dinner.

Left and below *There is a wealth of places to eat in the East Village, from ethnic restaurants to stylish bistros*

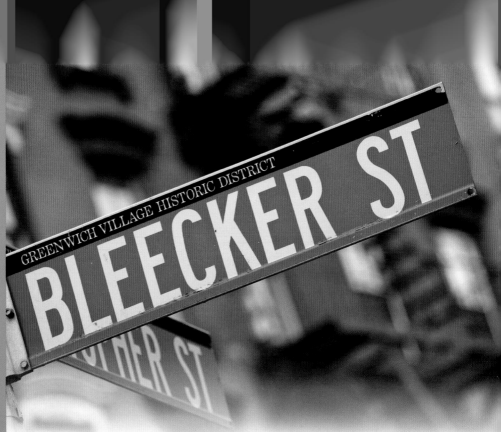

INFORMATION

➕ 110 C13 ✉ From Broadway west to the Hudson River, between Houston Street to the south and 14th Street to the north 🚇 A, B, C, D, E, F, M, N, R, 1, 2, 3 🚌 M1, M2, M3, M5, M8, M20 🍴 A huge number of restaurants on Bleecker Street, Greenwich Avenue and streets in between provide a choice of international cuisines 🍕 John's Pizzeria (▷ 136–137) 🛍 Shops on Bleecker Street and Greenwich Avenue and many others ℹ️ Information centers at Sixth Avenue and Christopher Street and at Astor Place Triangle, both Jul 1–Labor Day daily 12–6

Above *Lively Bleecker Street has great shops and cafés*

INTRODUCTION

In this fascinating, once bohemian, now celebrity-studded area, bursting with funky shops, unique bookstores, sidewalk cafés and cool clubs, famous artists, writers and radical thinkers lived and hung out.

Broadway divides Greenwich Village into the East Village (▷ 114–115) and the West Village. Bleecker Street is the main thoroughfare of the West Village and is full of cafés, restaurants and shops. Coffeehouses, music and poetry still thrive, and this is definitely a lively place for a late night out, whether you take in the bars and clubs, or just go for a stroll.

By 1700 Greenwich Village, named after Greenwich in London, England, had become a small village of wood-framed houses and tree-lined, mud streets north of the city. A single grand estate, Richmond Hill, built by a British paymaster-general at what is today the intersection of Varick and Charleston streets, was George Washington's headquarters during the attempt to defend New York in 1776 and was later home to vice-presidents John Adams (1767–1848) and Aaron Burr (1756–1836). Burr sold much of the land to John Jacob Astor, who divided it up into 456 lots, which he leased for a tidy little profit.

The streets grew up, sometimes along former cowpaths, before the grid street plan was introduced in 1811. When yellow fever struck in the 1820s, half the population fled the city, and prominent families looking for fresh air settled in Greenwich Village, tearing down most of the original frame houses and rebuilding in brick. The Village was a fashionable residential area by July 4, 1826, when Washington Military Parade Ground (Washington Square) was officially opened to celebrate the 50th anniversary of the signing of the Declaration of Independence. African-Americans moved in after the Draft Riots in 1863 and soon Italian immigrants from Little Italy were spilling over into the neighborhood. Tenements and factories were built, and wealthy New Yorkers moved to northern districts.

In the early 1900s, social changes and new zoning laws created cheap housing, attracting artists looking for studio space and low rents. Intellectuals, writers and rebels took up residence, creating a bohemian enclave. Social critics, including suffragists, anarchists and Communist sympathizers, turned the Village into a hotbed of disaffection. Writers such as Henry James, O. Henry, Mark Twain, Edgar Allen Poe and Stephen Crane all lived here. The Village's artist-residents, including Edward Hopper, Jackson Pollock, Franz Kline and Willem de Kooning, created a new American style. Today, the Village is one of the liveliest parts of the city, and maintains its artsy overtones, despite being an expensive place to live, popular with wealthy professionals.

WHAT TO SEE

CHRISTOPHER PARK
Bordered by Christopher Street, West Fourth Street and Seventh Avenue, Christopher Park is home to George Segal's life-size sculpture *Gay Liberation*, which depicts a gay couple standing in front of a bench where two lesbians sit. Behind them is the Stonewall Bar & Grill, where riots in 1969 sparked the nation's Gay Liberation movement. Christopher Street is a focal point of gay life in New York City.

CHUMLEY'S
At 86 Bedford Street, near Grove Street, this former speakeasy is not easy to find—it has no sign outside and the number does not appear on the front of the building. Over time many New York writers, including John Steinbeck (1902–68), have found solace in a drop or two here. Photos of famous patrons decorate the interior walls. The bar has appeared in movies, including Woody Allen's *Sweet and Lowdown*. Chumley's is currently closed for renovation.

JEFFERSON MARKET LIBRARY
In 1885, a survey of architects found this Gothic building (originally the Jefferson Market Courthouse) at 425 Sixth Avenue, designed by Calvert Vaux and Frederick Clarke Withers between 1874 and 1877, to be the fifth most beautiful building in the United States. The richly ornamented facades include a pediment depicting the trial scene from Shakespeare's *The Merchant of*

TIPS
» Enjoy the outrageous costumes and partying up and down Sixth Avenue at the Village Halloween Parade.

» Stop at the Village Chess Shop at 230 Thompson Street, between Bleecker and West 3rd streets, for a friendly game of chess (www.chess-shop.com).

» Chumley's has been closed since a chimney collapsed in 2007. Repairs are underway, and it is due to reopen in 2012.

Below *George Segal's sculpture* Gay Liberation *was installed in Christopher Park in 1992*

ADDRESS GUIDE

ARTISTS

24 University Place: The site of the Cedar Street Tavern, where Jackson Pollock, Franz Kline and Willem de Kooning shared ideas, along with Beat writers Allen Ginsberg and Jack Kerouac.

8 West 8th Street: The first address of the Whitney Museum of American Art (▷ 222–225).

Garrick Theater, Bleecker Street: Crowds flocked here for seven months to see Andy Warhol's movie *Flesh*, which premiered in October 1968.

WRITERS

145 Bleecker Street: Home to James Fenimore Cooper, author of *The Last of the Mohicans*, in 1833.

172 Bleecker Street: Where James Agee wrote the screenplay for *The African Queen*.

130–132 MacDougal Street: Louisa May Alcott stayed in this house and, it is believed, wrote *Little Women* here.

137 MacDougal Street: Home to the Liberal Club. Writers such as Upton Sinclair, Jack London, Theodore Dreiser and Sinclair Lewis regularly met in the house that once stood here.

85 West 3rd Street: Edgar Allen Poe lived on the third floor in 1845 (his was the last window on the right).

11 Commerce Street: Washington Irving wrote *The Legend of Sleepy Hollow* while living here.

14 West 10th Street: Home of Mark Twain when he moved to New York at the age of 65.

RADICALS

12 Charles Street: Home of suffragette Crystal Eastman and a suffragist gathering place.

91 Greenwich Avenue: Where *The Masses* was published. This left-wing publication backed the Communist Party and was a precursor to the counter-culture of the 1960s.

147 West 4th Street: John Reed rented a room in this house while he wrote *Ten Days That Shook the World*.

Venice. The building's tower was originally used by firewatchers, who had an uninterrupted view of the village from the balcony. The original bell used to summon volunteer firefighters still hangs in the tower. After years of neglect, the building was about to be demolished when local activists saved it and it became a branch of the New York Public Library in 1967, housing a special collection of books on New York and Greenwich Village history. The Adult Reading Room was once a civil court, the Children's Room was originally a police court, and the brick-arched basement that was once a holding area for prisoners is now the Reference Room.

SHERIDAN SQUARE

Sheridan Square is at the point where Seventh Avenue, West Fourth Street and Barrow Street intersect. Named for the Civil War general Philip Henry Sheridan, it is the site of the first protests that culminated in the Draft Riots of 1863 when 120 were killed, mostly African-Americans, by Irish immigrants (▷ 35). You can see the statue of General Sheridan in Christopher Park.

WASHINGTON MEMORIAL ARCH IN WASHINGTON SQUARE

Built in 1889 as the entrance to the park at the base of Fifth Avenue, the original triumphal arch commemorated the centenary of George Washington's inauguration. Architect Stanford White designed the first arch, which was made of wood, plaster and papier mâché. It was so successful that a fund to erect a permanent stone arch of the same design soon raised $134,000. The arch you see today, 30ft (9m) across and 77ft (23m) high, became the gateway to fashionable Fifth Avenue in the 1950s, when cars passed directly underneath it and the avenue cut through the park; it is a treasured city icon.

Many artists have painted or drawn the arch, including Childe Hassam in his 1894 *Washington Arch, Spring*. Many New Yorkers feel that New York University's 12-story Helen and Martin Kimmel Center on Fifth Avenue at Washington Square North detracts from the magnificence of the arch.

WASHINGTON MEWS

As you approach Memorial Arch from Fifth Avenue, on your left is a little cobblestone street called Washington Mews. Originally the houses here were the stables and servants' quarters for the elite town houses on Washington Square North, known as "The Row," a street lined with fashionable homes built in 1833 by John Jacob Astor and Cornelius Vanderbilt.

The delightful old houses lining Washington Mews have long been sought as residences by artists and painters, including Gertrude Vanderbilt Whitney, founder of the Whitney Museum of American Art (▷ 222–225). Members of the faculty of New York University have more recently taken up residence.

WASHINGTON SQUARE PARK

Washington Square is the heart of Greenwich Village. In warm weather the park is alive with street musicians, students, skateboarders, inline skaters, the occasional film crew and chess players (bring your own set), so this lively little park is great for people-watching.

Originally the site was marshland and a hunting ground; until the 1820s, criminals were hanged from the large elm in the northwest corner, and from 1797 until 1926 it was a potters' field, where paupers were buried. The remains of about 10,000 people rest here in peace, if not quiet. Washington Square was eventually acquired by the city, cleared, and laid out as a military parade ground. The Common Council then purchased more land, and the 9 acres (3.5ha) became the city's largest park in the 1840s. In 1963 the city closed the park to traffic, making it even more attractive to the students in the area. By the 1970s, alcohol and drug abusers had taken over. A clean-up over the past decade has left it the mellow, genial place you see today.

GRAMERCY PARK HISTORIC DISTRICT

Copied from historic London squares by the developer Samuel Ruggles in 1831, Gramercy Park is the only private park in New York City and is still surrounded by the original high iron railings. The elegant area, full of attractive buildings, has long been favored by well-to-do citizens. At No. 16 Gramercy Park South the actor Edwin Booth, brother of Lincoln's assassin, lived in a brownstone. Booth's statue is inside the park. At No. 15, Samuel Tilden, Governor of New York from 1875 to 1877, installed steel doors and a tunnel to 19th Street in fear of the mob.

➕ 111 E11 ✉ Between Park Avenue South and Third Avenue from 18th to 21st streets 🚇 N, Q, R, 6 🚌 M1, M2, M3, M23, M101, M102, M103

GREENWICH VILLAGE

▷ 116–118.

LITTLE CHURCH AROUND THE CORNER

www.littlechurch.org

The Episcopal Church of the Transfiguration is affectionately called the Little Church Around the Corner. Nothing could better demonstrate changed attitudes to all things theatrical than the way in which this charming little church acquired its nickname. In 1870, a nearby church declined to conduct funeral rites for actors, and directed one such request to "the little church around the corner." It's been favored by theater folk ever since.

An English-style lychgate leads to the church, set back from the street in a quiet garden. The interior maintains the intimate, modest atmosphere with carved wooden pillars and beams.

➕ 110 D10 ✉ East 29th Street, between Fifth and Madison avenues ☎ 212/ 684-6770 🕐 Daily 9–5 🚇 1, 6, N, R 🚌 M2, M3, M5

MERCHANT'S HOUSE MUSEUM

www.merchantshouse.com

This museum is an 1832 time capsule, one of six Federal-style row houses with a gracious Greek Revival doorway. Bought by wealthy merchant Thomas Tredwell in 1835, the house was lived in by his daughter for 93 years. Renovated after her death in 1933, it was opened to the public as a museum in 1936 with the original furnishings and personal family possessions. It is the only 19th-century house in Manhattan to be so well preserved. Seven rooms on three floors and a secret garden are on view. Miss Tredwell is thought to have been the model for a character in Henry James' *Washington Square*.

➕ 111 E13 ✉ 29 East 4th Street, between Lafayette Street and the Bowery, 10003 ☎ 212/777-1089 🕐 Thu–Mon 12–5 💵 Adult $10, under 12 free 🚇 6, N, R 🚌 M5, M103 ☛ Tours Fri 2pm 🏛

METROPOLITAN LIFE INSURANCE TOWER

Met Life's 1893 main building on 23rd Street stands on the site of the Madison Square Presbyterian Church, whose minister savagely attacked the corrupt politicians who ran the city in 1892. This 54-story tower, built in 1909, was their revenge. Planned as the tallest building in the world and a proud symbol of Met Life's prominence, it was soon overtaken by the Woolworth Building (▷ 78). The Met's campanile was 700ft (213m); in 1913, the Woolworth surpassed it by 92ft (28m). In 1962, the tower was stripped of its original ornamentation, leaving the gold dome and the huge clock faces.

➕ 111 D11 ✉ 1 Madison Avenue 🚇 N, R, 6 🚌 M1, M3

Above *An avenue in Gramercy Park*

Left *St. Mark's Church-in-the-Bowery*

ST. MARK'S CHURCH-IN-THE-BOWERY

http://stmarksbowery.org

Peter Stuyvesant, New Amsterdam's last Dutch governor, had a *bouwerij* (farm) in the quiet countryside north of the bustling settlement. As the city expanded and land values soared, Stuyvesant's grandson sold off plots for development. In 1779, a year after the Stuyvesant mansion was destroyed by fire, his great-grandson sold the site of Stuyvesant's private chapel to the Episcopal Church for a nominal dollar. And so it was that St. Mark's Church-in-the-Bowery was built and named. The original church was Federal-style; in keeping with the area's increasing affluence it later acquired a cast-iron portico. Stuyvesant and six generations of his descendants are buried in the graveyard.

✚ 111 E12 ✉ East 10th Street, at Second Avenue, 10004 ☎ 212/674-6377 🎫 Events only 🚇 6, N, R 🚌 M8, M15

THEODORE ROOSEVELT BIRTHPLACE

www.nps.gov/thrb

Theodore (Teddy) Roosevelt, the great outdoorsman and 26th president of the United States, was born in New York in 1858 and spent his first 14 years in a fashionable brownstone just off Broadway. The house was demolished just before his death in 1919, but the lot where the house stood was acquired in 1923 by the Women's Roosevelt Memorial Association, which commissioned a female architect to reconstruct it as it had been in Roosevelt's youth.

Rooms are furnished with objects preserved from the original house. The "lion's room" is filled with hunting and outdoor memorabilia. Roosevelt was sickly as a child, and a small gym that was intended to build up his health adjoins the nursery. There is also an exhibition about his eventful life.

✚ 111 D11 ✉ 28 East 20th Street, between Park Avenue South and Broadway, 10003 ☎ 212/260-1616 🎫 Guided tour only (30 min) Tue–Sat at 10, 11, 1, 2, 3, 4 ✋ Free 🚇 6, N, R 🚌 M1, M2, M23

UKRAINIAN MUSEUM

www.ukrainianmuseum.org

Ukrainian immigrants came to America in the 19th century and many stayed in New York, living in tenements on the Lower East Side. Committed to preserving the cultural heritage of Ukrainians, this museum displays folk art items, including traditional costumes, decorative brass and silver jewelry, decorated Easter eggs, ceramics and woven and embroidered ritual cloths used as talismans at important events. It also curates shows of works by important Ukrainian artists.

✚ 111 E13 ✉ 222 East Sixth Street, between Second and Third Avenues, 10003 ☎ 212/228-0110 🎫 Wed–Sun 11.30–5 ✋ Adult $8, under 12 free 🚇 6 🚌 M101, M102, M103 ☕ 🏛

Below *Theodore Roosevelt Birthplace is a replica of the original house*

UNION SQUARE

On a sunny day, the park is a pleasant place to people-watch and relax. There are also sculptures of Washington (1856) and Lincoln (1866), both by Henry Kirke Brown, and Lafayette by Statue of Liberty sculptor Frédéric-Auguste Bartholdi. Nearby are the Center for Jewish History at 15 West 16th Street; the eclectic Forbes Magazine Galleries at 62 Fifth Avenue at 12th Street (▷ 113); and Theodore Roosevelt's reconstructed birthplace at 28 East 20th Street.

At last count there were some 100 restaurants in the Union Square area, including some of the city's top tables. In September, at a fundraiser called Harvest in the Square, you can sample signature dishes of top neighborhood chefs. Also in September, the free outdoor Manhattan Short Film Festival screens 14 of the world's best short films and gives new film-makers a chance to compete for prizes.

A VARIED HISTORY

Run down and with a threatening atmosphere in the 1970s, Union Square is thriving and proud today. Every Monday, Wednesday, Friday and Saturday, a green market—one of the best farmers' markets in the United States—draws New Yorkers from all over the city and inspires local chefs. The bright idea of Barry Benepe (director of the green market)—who saw it as a way to simultaneously help Hudson Valley farmers and improve the neighborhood—it encouraged other communities to set up similar markets.

Union Square went residential in the 1840s, and America's greatest concentration of theaters, nightclubs, restaurants, hotels and luxury shopping followed. Union Square Park was laid out for the wealthy residents. In the 1800s, Ladies' Mile—Broadway and Sixth Avenue between 15th and 24th streets—was the height of fashionable shopping, until the turn of the 20th century when wealth moved uptown and the area deteriorated. In the late 1800s, Union Square was the center for demonstrations and political protests. In the early 1930s the editorial offices of *The New Masses* and the offices of the Communist Party's Yiddish-language paper moved here. A renovation of the square in 1936 discouraged further demonstrations.

INFORMATION

www.unionsquarenyc.org

✚ 111 D12 ✉ From East 12th Street to East 20th Street, between Third and Fifth avenues Ⓜ 4, 5, 6, L, N, Q, R 🚌 M1, M2, M3 🚶 Free walking tour Sat 2pm, meet at the Lincoln statue near the Pavilion Building in Union Square Park 🍴 Old Town Bar & Restaurant, 45 East 18th Street between Broadway and Park Avenue ☎ 212/529-6732

Below *Relax in the shade of the trees in Union Square's gardens*

GREENWICH VILLAGE: IFC CENTER TO WASHINGTON SQUARE

Some of the country's finest literature and most radical ideas have developed in the area covered by this stroll. From the revolutionary Thomas Paine, who decried taxation without representation in colonial times, to the Stonewall rioters, whose protests sparked the gay liberation movement beginning in 1969, Village people have long been at the forefront of liberalism in America.

THE WALK

Distance: 1.9 miles (3km)
Time: 2 hours
Start/End at: West 4th Street/Washington Square subway station

HOW TO GET THERE

Subway A, B, C, D, E, F, M; bus M5.

★ Leave the subway on Avenue of the Americas (Sixth Avenue), cross the avenue at West Fourth Street and position yourself in front of the IFC Center. Turn to your left (as you face the theater) and head along the avenue to Carmine Street. Turn right.

❶ Along Carmine Street you pass first the Unoppressive, Non-Imperialist Bargain Books store on the left and then the House of Oldies Rare Records (on the right), both worth a browse.

Continue to Seventh Avenue South, cross it, and turn right. At St. Luke's Place (also called Leroy Street), go left. On your left you will pass J. J. Walker Park, once a graveyard, which locals claim is the resting place of the lost son of Louis XVI and Marie Antoinette. The brick and brownstone houses along this street date from the 1850s. Theodore Dreiser wrote *An American Tragedy* while he was living at No. 16. At Hudson Street, turn right, and walk two blocks to Barrow Street where you turn left.

❷ On Barrow Street, take a look at the pretty garden behind the Church of St. Luke-in-the-Fields, built in 1822. The gate is on your right just before you reach Greenwich Street. Backtrack along Barrow Street to Hudson Street, and stop for a snack or light lunch at the popular

Belgian café, Petite Abeille. Go across Hudson Street to 81 Barrow Street, where a plaque gives some architectural history of the area. Continue heading east on Barrow, then turn right onto Commerce Street. To the right at the bend in Commerce Street is the Cherry Lane Theatre.

❸ Cherry Lane Theatre, an off-Broadway venue, was founded in 1924 by the Pulitzer Prize-winning poet Edna St. Vincent Millay. Samuel Beckett's *Waiting for Godot* and *Endgame* both premiered here, as have plays by Edward Albee, David Mamet and many other distinguished writers.

Continue east on Commerce Street for one block and then turn right on Bedford Street. Notice the first two houses on your right.

Opposite *Christopher Park is the site of George Segal's* Gay Liberation *sculpture*

❹ The Isaacs-Hendricks House, 77 Bedford Street, is the oldest in the West Village. The narrowest house in the city is at No. 75, which was home to Edna St. Vincent Millay in 1923–24. The actor Cary Grant also lived here when he was young.

Return along Bedford Street, past Chumley's, a famous speakeasy, which put in an appearance in Warren Beatty's *Reds* and Woody Allen's *Sweet and Lowdown*. John Steinbeck, Eugene O'Neill, e. e. cummings and F. Scott Fitzgerald are among past patrons. The building is currently closed for renovation. When you reach Grove Street, turn left.

❺ The pretty, leafy Grove Court, 10–12 Grove Street, was once dubbed "Ale Alley" because of the original Irish tenants' fondness for a brew.

Return to the corner of Grove and Bedford streets. The oldest wooden house in the Village stands at 17 Grove Street. Continue one block roughly north on Bedford Street to Christopher Street, and turn right.

❻ The long-established McNulty's Rare Teas and Choice Coffee Shop is at 109 Christopher Street, and from its looks it hasn't changed much since it opened in 1895. Go in and enjoy the aroma.

Continue east on Christopher Street and cross Seventh Avenue South.

❼ Tiny Christopher Park, which was part of a tobacco farm from 1633 to 1638, is to your right. Stop for a rest on the bench next to George Segal's sculpture *Gay Liberation*, then look behind you at the Stonewall Bar and Club, where gay resistance to police arrests provoked the Stonewall Riot in 1969, the start of the gay rights movement. There's a modest plaque on the building. Christopher Street

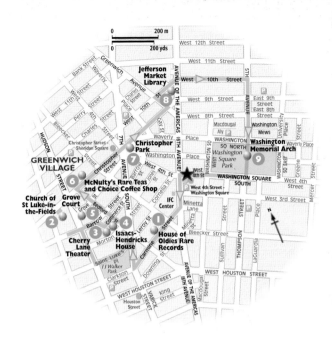

is also called Stonewall Place from the park up to Greenwich Avenue.

Walk along the Stonewall side of Christopher Street to Greenwich Avenue, and turn left. Go north one block, turn right onto West 10th Street and you'll come to Patchin Place; No. 4 was famously the home of e. e. cummings. Continue on West 10th Street one block east.

❽ The ornate landmark Jefferson Market Library, at 425 Sixth Avenue, is a former courthouse built in 1877. The tower originally served as a fire-watching lookout.

Continue on West 10th Street, crossing Avenue of the Americas, until you come to Fifth Avenue. Turn right and walk four blocks south on Fifth Avenue, through Washington Memorial Arch.

❾ The original wooden arch was erected in 1889, in honor of George Washington 100 years after his inauguration. The marble Stanford White arch you see now was erected in 1895. The residential

Washington Mews, on the east side of Fifth Avenue just north of the arch, were built as carriage houses for the wealthy residents of the fine town houses on Washington Square Park south of the arch. In the mews, John Dos Passos lived at No. 14A and Sherwood Anderson at No. 54. Washington Square Park, the focus of Greenwich Village, was once a potter's field and was the site of public executions until the early 19th century.

Walk straight through the park to Washington Square South and turn right. This becomes West Fourth Street, and ahead are the entrances to the subway on Avenue of the Americas.

WHEN TO GO
If you want to visit shops along the way, it is best to do this walk between 10 and 5 Monday to Saturday.

WHERE TO EAT
PETITE ABEILLE
✉ 466 Hudson Street ☎ 212/741-6479
🕐 24 hours

SHOPPING

ABC CARPET AND HOME

www.abchome.com

Fabrics, furnishings and artifacts from around the world are artfully displayed on 10 floors. Provencal armoires, Venetian chandeliers and Kashmiri silks keep company with rugs from India, Nepal and China.

✚ 142 D11 ✉ 888 Broadway, between 19th and 20th streets ☎ 212/473-3000 ⏰ Mon–Sat 10–7 (Thu until 8), Sun 12–6 🚇 23rd Street (N, R) 🚌 M1, M2, M3, M5

ALEXANDER MCQUEEN

www.alexandermcqueen.com

The late British fashion designer, who died in 2010, made his name at Givenchy and went on to design at Gucci. He began his career on Savile Row and at theatrical costumer Angels and Bermans.

✚ 142 B12 ✉ 417 West 14th Street, between Ninth Avenue and Washington Street ☎ 212/645-1797 ⏰ Mon–Sat 11–7, Sun 12.30–6 🚇 14th Street (A, C, E), Eighth Avenue (L) 🚌 M11, M14

ANNA

www.annanyc.com

Designer Kathy Kemp named her label after her grandmother, who taught her how to sew. Everyone from punk rock babes to uptown trendies makes a beeline for her East Village boutique to check out her latest offbeat designs.

✚ 143 F13 ✉ 150 East 3rd Street at Avenue A ☎ 212/358-0195 ⏰ Mon–Sat 1–8, Sun 1–7 🚇 Second Avenue (F), Essex Street (J, M, Z) 🚌 M1, M14a, M21

AN REN

A small, colorful boutique featuring coats, jackets and tops finely crafted from top-of-the-line fabrics, An Ren sells modern styles with carefully detailed craftsmanship. Many pieces skilfully combine several fabrics and textures. Look for interesting designs, varied colorways and details such as large buttons and contrasting stitching.

✚ 143 E13 ✉ 315 East Ninth Street, between First and Second avenues ☎ 212/388-9486 ⏰ Mon–Fri 1–8, Sat 12–8, Sun 12–7 🚇 Astor Place (6) 🚌 M8, M15, M103

BARNES & NOBLE

www.barnesandnoble.com

Although not the original of this megachain, this is the flagship store. Like most of the other branches, this store has a café and comfortable chairs for reading, and sells music, software and magazines as well as books. The main college bookstore is at Fifth Avenue and 18th Street.

✚ 143 D12 ✉ Union Square North at 33 East 17th Street, between Broadway and Park Avenue South ☎ 212/253-0810 ⏰ Daily 10–10 🚇 14th Street/Union Square (4, 5, 6, L, N, Q, R) 🚌 M1, M2, M3, M5

BROADWAY PANHANDLER

www.broadwaypanhandler.com

Originally selling to professional kitchens, Broadway Panhandler now offers the very best cookware, tools, appliances and gadgets to domestic cooks at decent prices. There are hundreds of different types of pots, pans and skillets—about 10,000 items in all. Special weekend demonstrations bring in the likes of Jean-Georges Vongerichten, Eric Ripert and Jacques Pépin.

✚ 143 D13 ✉ 65 East 8th Street, between Broadway and University ☎ 212/966-3434 ⏰ Mon–Sat 11–7 (Thu until 8), Sun 11–6 🚇 8th Street (N, R) 🚌 M1, M8

CASWELL MASSEY

www.caswell-massey.com

This apothecary, founded in 1752, provided perfume to George

Washington and Dolly Madison and continues to produce a range of delicious floral scents such as freesia, lilac, rose, geranium and lily of the valley. You can find rosewater and glycerine soap, sandalwood massage oil and appealing gift sets.
✛ 142 D11 ✉ Space 59, Limelight Marketplace, 47 West 20th Street at 6th Avenue ☎ 212/359-5559 🕔 Mon–Sat 10–9, Sun 11–8 🚇 23rd Street (F, M) 🚌 M5, M7, M23

CHELSEA MARKET
www.chelseamarket.com
On the first floor of this building, you can put together an entire meal, including table decorations. You'll find bakers, fishmongers, florists, wine merchants and Buon Italia, which sells cheeses, sausages, oils, sauces and other Italian products.
✛ 142 C12 ✉ 75 Ninth Avenue, between 15th and 16th streets ☎ 212/243-6005 🕔 Mon–Sat 7am–9pm, Sun 8–7 🚇 14th Street (A, C, E) 🚌 M11, M14

DARLING
www.darlingnyc.com
Former Broadway costume designer Ann French Emonts offers traffic-stopping sexy silk dresses, formal gowns and business dresses.
✛ 142 C12 ✉ 1 Horatio Street ☎ 212/367-3750 🕔 Mon–Sat 12–7, Sun 12–6 🚇 Eighth Avenue/14th Street (A, C, E, L) 🚌 M20

DIANE VON FURSTENBERG
www.dvf.com
Famous for her signature wrap dresses, Diane von Furstenberg encouraged women to "feel like a woman, wear a dress." Her DVF label includes sports and swimwear, accessories and cosmetics.
✛ 142 B12 ✉ 874 Washington Street at 14th Street ☎ 646/486-4800 🕔 Mon–Sat 11–7 (Thu until 8), Sun 12–6 🚇 14th Street (A, C, E) 🚌 M11, M14A, M14D, M20

DIESEL
www.diesel.com
This Italian clothes house always keeps one step ahead of the latest trends. Diesel jeans are de rigueur and so, too, are the shoes and bags. Also at 770 Lexington Avenue.
✛ 143 D12 ✉ 1 Union Square West at University Place ☎ 646/336-8552 🕔 Mon–Sat 11–9, Sun 11–8 🚇 14th Street/Union Square (L, N, Q, R, 4, 5, 6) 🚌 M2, M3, M5, M14

DISC-O-RAMA
http://discorama.com
From vinyl LPs to the latest CD by top pop artists, you'll find it here at a saving. Rock, pop, R&B, hip-hop, country, jazz, classical, reggae and more, as well as DVDs, books and used CDs and records.
✛ 142 D13 ✉ 44 West 8th Street ☎ 212/206-8417 🕔 Mon–Thu 10am–11pm, Fri–Sat 10–midnight, Sun 12–8 🚇 West Fourth Street/Washington Square (A, B, C, D, E) 🚌 M1, M5, M8

JAZZ RECORD CENTER
www.jazzrecordcenter.com
This store stocks all the great jazz names and labels, plus books, videos and ephemera. It specializes in rare and out-of-print recordings.
✛ 142 C11 ✉ 236 West 26th Street, between Seventh and Eighth avenues (8th floor, room 804) ☎ 212/675-4480 🕔 Mon–Sat 10–6 🚇 28th Street (1) 🚌 M7, M20

JEFFREY
www.jeffreynewyork.com
It took courage for former Barneys shoe buyer Jeffrey Kalinsky to open this giant boutique in the blighted Meatpacking District before it became hip. Naturally, the shoe department is stellar, chock full of Manolos and other designer names. You will also find fashions by such leaders as Fendi, Jil Sander, Celine, Prada, Gucci and Dolce & Gabbana.
✛ 142 B12 ✉ 449 West 14th Street, between Ninth and Tenth avenues ☎ 212/206-1272 🕔 Mon–Fri 10–8 (Thu until 9), Sat 10–7, Sun 12.30–6 🚇 14th Street (A, C, E), Eighth Avenue (L) 🚌 M11, M14

JUSSARA LEE
www.jussaralee.com
This Korean-Brazilian designer's clothes have an edge but are eminently wearable. Coats, dresses, tops, pants, skirts and bathing suits are elegantly displayed here.
✛ 142 B12 ✉ 11 Little West 12th Street, between Washington Street and Ninth Avenue ☎ 212/242-4128 🕔 Mon–Sat 11–7, Sun 12–7 🚇 14th Street (A, C, E) 🚌 M11, M14

KIEHL'S
www.kiehls.com
Kiehl's is now owned by cosmetics giant L'Oréal. It has been selling homeopathic remedies and natural cosmetics and treatment products since its inception in 1851.
✛ 143 E12 ✉ 109 Third Avenue, between East 13th and 14th streets ☎ 212/677-3171 🕔 Mon–Sat 10–8, Sun 11–6 🚇 14th Street/Union Square (L, N, Q, R, 4, 5, 6), Third Avenue (L) 🚌 M101, M102, M103

LOEHMANN'S
www.loehmanns.com
This place has been a name on the discount shopping scene ever since Frieda Mueller Loehmann began selling well-priced skirts and blouses out of her Brooklyn home in 1920. This flagship store has five floors.
✛ 142 C12 ✉ 101 Seventh Avenue at 16th Street ☎ 212/352-0856 🕔 Mon–Sat 9–9, Sun 11–7 🚇 14th Street (1, 2, 3) 🚌 M7, M14, M20

OLD NAVY
www.oldnavy.com
This huge store features affordable basics for men, women, boys, girls and infants, as well as a complete line of accessories. There is even clothing for pets.
✛ 142 D12 ✉ 610 Sixth Avenue at 18th Street ☎ 212/645-0663 🕔 Mon–Sat 9am–9.30pm, Sun 10–8 🚇 Sixth Avenue/14th Street (F, L, M) 🚌 M5, M7

PARAGON SPORTING GOODS
www.paragonsports.com
New Yorkers come here to buy clothes and equipment for every conceivable sport or pastime. It stocks camping and hiking gear, binoculars, golfing gear, skis, surfboards and tennis racquets.
✛ 142 D12 ✉ 867 Broadway at 18th Street ☎ 212/255-8889 🕔 Mon–Sat 10–8,

Sun 11–7 🚇 14th Street/Union Square (L, N, Q, R, 4, 5, 6) 🚌 M7

LA PETITE COQUETTE
www.thelittleflirt.com
This may well be the best lingerie store in the city. In a boudoir setting, it sells swimwear and sexy top-of-the-line, multi-hued lingerie.
✚ 142 D13 ✉ 51 University Place, between 9th and 10th streets ☎ 888/473-5799 🕐 Mon–Sat 11–7 (Thu until 8), Sun 12–6 🚇 8th Street (N, R) 🚌 M5, M8

ST. MARKS BOOKSHOP
www.stmarksbookshop.com
This counterculture bookstore offers political and alternative titles plus general books.
✚ 143 E13 ✉ 31 Third Avenue, between St. Marks Place and Ninth Street on east side ☎ 212/260-7853 🕐 Mon–Sat 10am–midnight, Sun 11am–midnight 🚇 Astor Place (4, 5, 6) 🚌 M8, M103

SCREAMING MIMI'S
www.screamingmimis.com
The stock at this old-timer ranges from 1940s to 1980s. It's well displayed and in good condition. Cool and hip still, even though *Sex and the City* made it famous.
✚ 143 E13 ✉ 382 Lafayette Street, between Great Jones and West 4th streets ☎ 212/677-6464 🕐 Mon–Sat 12–8, Sun 1–7 🚇 Broadway-Lafayette (B, D, F, M) 🚌 M21, M103

SHAKESPEARE & CO
www.shakeandco.com
One of the city's few surviving small independent book chains. As the name suggests, it leans toward literary and small press titles.
✚ 143 D13 ✉ 716 Broadway, between West 4th Street and Washington Place ☎ 212/529-1330 🕐 Mon–Sat 10–9.30, Sun 11–8 🚇 Astor Place (4, 5, 6), 8th Street (N, R), West 4th Street (A, C, E, F) 🚌 M1, M5, M8

SHELLY STEFFEE
www.shellysteffee.com
The sign outside reads "Design Studio" and the clothes are displayed, in a museum-like fashion. The designs are sexy and fun.

✚ 142 C12 ✉ 34 Gansevoort Street between Hudson Street and Ninth Avenue ☎ 917/408-0408 🕐 Sun–Tue 11.30–7, Wed–Sat 11.30–9 🚇 14th Street (A, C, E) 🚌 M11, M14A

STELLA MCCARTNEY
www.stellamccartney.com
Stella McCartney began her rise to stardom at Chloe and continues in partnership with Gucci. In this store, fitting rooms are lined with marquetry or hand-printed fabric. Her full line of well-tailored but nicely draped fashions is for sale.
✚ 142 B12 ✉ 429 West 14th Street, between Ninth and Tenth avenues ☎ 212/255-1556 🕐 Mon–Sat 11–7, Sun 12.30–6 🚇 14th Street (A, C, E), Eighth Avenue (L) 🚌 M11, M14

STRAND BOOKSTORE
www.strandbooks.com
Here you can pore over stacks of publishers' review copies, sold at half price. The management claims to shelve 18 miles (29km) of books.
✚ 143 E12 ✉ 828 Broadway at 12th Street ☎ 212/473-1452 🕐 Mon–Sat 9.30am–10.30pm, Sun 11–10.30 🚇 14th Street/Union Square (L, N, Q, R, 4, 5, 6) 🚌 M1, M5

THREE LIVES
www.threelives.com
The proprietor of this store stocks an amazing variety of titles given the size of the place. A real neighborhood store, and one of the last personal bookstores in the city.
✚ 142 C13 ✉ 154 West 10th Street at Waverly Place (southwest corner) ☎ 212/741-2069 🕐 Wed–Sat 11–8.30, Sun 12–7, Mon–Tue 12–8 🚇 Christopher Street (1), West 4th Street (A, B, C, D, E, F) 🚌 M5, M8, M20

UNION SQUARE GREEN MARKET
Drop by this busy market to get a sense of the agricultural scene outside the city and to participate in a city happening.
✚ 143 D12 ✉ Union Square 🕐 Mon, Wed, Fri, Sat from 8am 🚇 14th Street/Union Square (L, N, Q, R, 4, 5, 6) 🚌 M1, M2, M3, M5

VILLAGE CHESS SHOP
www.chess-shop.com
From beautifully carved chess sets in fine woods, stones and metals, to artworks, this shop has all your chess needs. You can even drop in for a game.
✚ 142 D13 ✉ 230 Thompson Street between West 3rd and Bleecker streets ☎ 212/475-9580 🕐 Daily 24 hours 🚇 West 4th Street-Washington Square (A, B, C, D, E, F, M) 🚌 M5, M21

ZERO
http://zeromariacornejo.com
In this store you'll see avant-garde capes, jackets and coats, which Maria Cornejo sews in the back.
✚ 143 E13 ✉ 33 Bleecker Street, between Lafayette and Bowery streets ☎ 212/925-3849 🕐 Mon–Sat 11–7, Sun 12.30–6.30 🚇 Prince Street (N, R) 🚌 M5, M21

ENTERTAINMENT AND NIGHTLIFE
49 GROVE
www.49grovenyc.com
In the deep-purple lounge you'll find comfortable couches to sink right into, while bottles or cocktails are brought to your table as the city's fashion crowd mingle. The music is hip-hop, house, funk, and garage and the prices are seriously high, even by New York club standards.
✚ 142 C13 ✉ 49 Grove Street at Bleecker Street ☎ 212/727-1100 🕐 Thu–Sat 10pm–4am 🚇 Christopher Street/Sheridan Square (1), Fourth Street/Washington Square (A, B, C, D, E, F) 🚌 M5

ACTOR'S PLAYHOUSE
www.nyactorsplayhouse.com
This small downstairs venue, which has been around for 40 years, presents musical revues, often with a gay theme.
✚ 142 C13 ✉ 100 Seventh Avenue South, between Bleecker and West Fourth streets ☎ 212/255-6452 🚇 Christopher Street/Sheridan Square (1) 🚌 M20

ANGELIKA FILM CENTER
www.angelikafilmcenter.com
This multiplex principally shows foreign films with English subtitles,

plus films by such artists as Atom Egoyan and other independent moviemakers.

➕ 143 D13 ✉ Mercer and Houston streets ☎ 212/995-2570 💲 $13 🚇 Broadway-Lafayette (B, D, F), Bleecker Street (6) 🚌 M5, M21

ANGEL'S SHARE

Tucked away upstairs in a Japanese restaurant, this tiny bar is named for the alcohol that evaporates while whiskey is aging. The lychee daiquiri is delicious.

➕ 143 E12 ✉ 8 Stuyvesant Street (2nd floor), between Ninth Street and Third Avenue ☎ 212/777-5415 🕐 Mon–Thu 6pm–1.30am, Fri–Sat 6pm–2.30am 🚇 Astor Place (6) 🚌 103

ANTHOLOGY FILM ARCHIVES

www.anthologyfilmarchives.org
Shows new film-makers along with old and rare vintage pieces and occasional tributes to directors.

➕ 143 E13 ✉ 32 Second Avenue at East Second Street ☎ 212/505-5181 💲 $9 🚇 Astor Place (6), Lower East Side/Second Avenue (F) 🚌 M15, M21

ARTHUR'S TAVERN

www.arthurstavernnyc.com
This funky down-home bar has jazz, Dixieland or blues most nights.

➕ 142 C13 ✉ 57 Grove Street between Seventh Avenue South and Bleecker Street ☎ 212/675-6879 🕐 Tue–Sat 6.30pm–4am, Sun–Mon 8pm–4am 💲 Free 🚇 Christopher Street/Sheridan Square (1) 🚌 M8, M20

AUTOMATIC SLIM'S

An outpost of the original Automatic Slim's in Memphis, the kid brother in the Meatpacking District brings a soulful Southern feel, with a fun atmosphere and good music.

➕ 142 C13 ✉ 733 Washington Street at Bank Street ☎ 212/645-8660 🕐 Tue–Wed 5.30pm–2am, Thu–Sat 5.30pm–4am 🚇 Christopher Street/Sheridan Square (1), 14th Street (A, C, E) 🚌 M20

B BAR

www.bbarandgrill.com
B Bar has cooled as a hot spot, but its Tuesday night extravaganza,

Beige, still draws gay society and other beauties. Large outdoor summer patio.

➕ 143 E13 ✉ 40 East Fourth Street at Bowery ☎ 212/475-2220 🕐 Mon 11am–2am, Tue, Thu–Fri 11am–4am, Wed 11.30am–3am, Sat 10am–4am, Sun 10am–2am 🚇 Broadway-Lafayette (B, D, F, M), Bleecker Street (6) 🚌 M103

BITTER END

www.bitterend.com
The cradle of the antiwar folk music scene in the 1960s, the Bitter End is much more rock-oriented today. Performances every night.

➕ 142 D13 ✉ 147 Bleecker Street at Thompson Street ☎ 212/673-7030 🕐 Mon–Thu, Sun 7pm–2am, Fri–Sat 7.30pm–4am 💲 $7–$15 🚇 West Fourth Street (A, B, C, D, E, F) 🚌 M5, M21

BLIND TIGER ALE HOUSE

www.blindtigeralehouse.com
Grab a window seat and you can watch the Bleecker Street scene while sipping a boutique ale or one of around 30 uncommon American brews on tap. Knowledgeable bartenders will help you choose one to your liking. It also serves some of the best bar food in the city.

➕ 142 C13 ✉ 281 Bleecker Street at Jones Street ☎ 212/462-4682 🕐 Daily 11.30am–4am 💲 Free 🚇 West 4th Street/Washington Square (A, B, C, D, E, F, M), Christopher Street (1) 🚌 M5, M8, M20

BLUE NOTE

www.bluenotejazz.com
Tiny and ultra-expensive, the Blue Note is jammed with fans grooving to the sounds of contemporary leaders in jazz, blues, Latin and R&B. Monday night showcases up-and-coming local musicians.

➕ 142 D13 ✉ 131 West 3rd Street at Sixth Avenue ☎ 212/475-8592 🕐 Daily at 8pm and 10.30pm (and 12.30am weekends) 💲 $20–$65 at tables, $10–45 at bar, plus $5 minimum 🚇 West Fourth Street (A, B, C, D, E, F) 🚌 M5, M8

BOWERY POETRY CLUB

www.bowerypoetry.com
All kinds of poets and performance artists play here. There are shows

almost every night, and weekend lunchtime performances, too.

➕ 143 E13 ✉ 308 Bowery, between Bleecker and Houston streets ☎ 212/614-0505 💲 $5–$15 🚇 Bleecker Street (6), Broadway-Lafayette (B, D, F, M) 🚌 M21, M103

CAFÉ WHA?

www.cafewha.com
This legendary Village club helped launch the careers of Bob Dylan, Jimi Hendrix and Bruce Springsteen. It's still a popular hangout, with a house band and guest artists every night, and encompassing a range of musical styles from modern rock and R&B to jazz, funk and soul. There are two shows nightly at 9.30 and 11.45.

➕ 142 D13 ✉ 115 MacDougal Street between Bleecker and West 3rd streets ☎ 212/254-3706 🕐 Nightly 8.30pm–3am 💲 $5–$15; free Wed and most Sun 🚇 West 4th Street/Washington Square (A, B, C, D, E, F, M) 🚌 M5, M8, M21

CHERRY LANE

www.cherrylanetheatre.org
In 1924 Edna St. Vincent Millay and others turned a warehouse into a theater. Today the Cherry Lane Alternative continues the theater's tradition of producing emerging playwrights.

➕ 142 C13 ✉ 38 Commerce Street, between Hudson and Bedford streets ☎ 212/989-2020 🚇 Christopher Street/Sheridan Square (1) 🚌 M20, M21

CIELO

www.cieloclub.com
Great DJs and a fantastic sound system have made this one of the best clubs not only in the Meatpacking District but in all of New York. The hottest electronic dance music moves the crowds on the sunken dance floor. Top international DJs are often featured.

➕ 142 B12 ✉ 18 Little West 12th Street between Ninth Avenue and Washington Street ☎ 212/645-5700 🕐 Mon, Wed–Sat 10pm–4am; Sun, Tue for special events 💲 $12–$25; free before 11 or midnight 🚇 14th Street (A, C, E), Eighth Avenue (L) 🚌 M11, M14, M20

CINEMA VILLAGE
www.cinemavillage.com
Renovated in 2000, this independent cinema, housed in a former fire station, now has three screens. Documentaries and old movies are the staples.
✚ 142 D12 ✉ 22 East 12th Street, between University Place and Fifth Avenue ☎ 212/924-3363 🖐 $11 🚇 14th Street/Union Square (L, N, Q, R, 4, 5, 6) 🚌 M1, M2, M3, M5, M14

COMEDY CELLAR
www.comedycellar.com
A cave-like venue that features nationally known comedians—Seinfeld, Stewart, Williams et al. Full dinner and drinks menu in the club, and also upstairs in the Olive Tree Café and Bar.
✚ 142 D13 ✉ 117 MacDougal Street, between West 3rd and Bleecker streets ☎ 212/254-3480 🕐 Sun–Thu shows at 9 and 11pm; Fri shows at 8, 9.45, 11.30pm; Sat shows at 7.30, 9.15, 11pm and 12.45am 🖐 $10–$18, plus 2-drink minimum 🚇 West 4th Street (A, B, C, D, E, F, M) 🚌 M5

COMMON GROUND
www.commongroundnyc.com
A few blocks north of Tompkins Square Park is this bar that looks like a bar should, with shelves filled with books, and even chandeliers giving it a hint of Victorian London. Nothing Victorian about the patrons, though, a mix of office workers and locals, enjoying either the bar snacks or the extremely tasty main plates on offer. Wednesday is trivia night, and there's an open-mic night on Sunday.
✚ 143 F12 ✉ 206 Avenue A, between 12th and 13th streets ☎ 212/228-6231 🕐 Mon–Wed 4pm–2am, Thu–Fri 4–4, Sat noon–4am, Sun noon–2am (kitchen closes midnight) 🚇 First Avenue (L) 🚌 M14A

COOPER UNION GREAT HALL
www.cooper.edu/ce
Everything from fado (Portuguese folk music) and contemporary classical music to Afro-Brazilian drum groups and samba bands can be heard at a private tuition-free

college for the Advancement of Science and Art. Abraham Lincoln spoke here in 1860.
✚ 143 E13 ✉ Seventh Street at Third Avenue ☎ 212/353-4195 🖐 Free–$25 🚇 Astor Place (6), 8th Street (N, R) 🚌 M8, M101, M102, M103

CORNELIA STREET CAFÉ
www.corneliastreetcafe.com
This subterranean space hosts everything from structured free jazz and cabaret to poetry and performance art.
✚ 142 C13 ✉ 29 Cornelia Street, between Bleecker and West 3rd streets ☎ 212/989-9319 🕐 Daily 10am–10.45pm (late shows Fri–Sat) 🖐 $10–$15, plus $7–$10 drinks minimum 🚇 West 4th Street (A, B, C, D, E, F) 🚌 M5, M20

DANCE THEATER WORKSHOP
www.dancetheaterworkshop.org
In 1965 Jeff Duncan, Art Bauman and Jack Moore founded this choreographers' collective. It still promises innovative performances here and at other city venues. Many famous dancers have begun careers here—Bill T. Jones, Mark Morris, Ann Carlson, Eiko and Koma—plus such theatrical talents as Bill Irwin, Whoopi Goldberg and Paul Zaloom.
✚ 142 C11 ✉ 219 West 19th Street at Seventh Avenue ☎ 212/691-6500 🚇 18th Street (1) 🚌 M14, M20

DARYL ROTH THEATER
www.darylroththeater.com
Theater producer Daryl Roth, who has produced five Pulitzer Prize-winning plays, owns this theater in an old bank building. The space is dramatic.
✚ 143 D12 ✉ 101 East 15th Street at Union Square ☎ 212/375-1110 🚇 14th Street/Union Square (L, N, Q, R, 4, 5, 6) 🚌 M1, M2, M3, M14

D.B.A.
Serious drinkers appreciate the massive selection of single malts (90) and beers (16 on tap and 260 in bottles) at this friendly bar. The backyard garden is great in summer.
✚ 143 E13 ✉ 41 First Avenue, between East 2nd and 3rd streets ☎ 212/475-5097

🕐 Daily 1pm–4am 🚇 Lower East Side/Second Avenue (F) 🚌 M15

DECIBEL
www.sakebardecibel.com
Subterranean, funky and cramped, this Japanese bar has a huge selection of sake.
✚ 143 E13 ✉ 240 East 9th Street, between Second and Third avenues ☎ 212/979-2733 🕐 Mon–Sat 6pm–2.50am, Sun 6pm–12.50am 🚇 Astor Place (6) 🚌 M8, M103

THE DUPLEX
www.theduplex.com
A launching pad for Woody Allen, Joan Rivers and Rodney Dangerfield, the tradition continues in the upstairs cabaret room. There is a piano bar downstairs.
✚ 142 C13 ✉ 61 Christopher Street at Seventh Avenue South ☎ 212/255-5438 🕐 Nightly, check program 🖐 Cover varies, plus 2-drink minimum 🚇 Christopher Street/Sheridan Square (1) 🚌 M8, M20

ENOTECA I TRULLI
www.itrulli.com/
This light and airy wine bar offers some 50 wines by the glass at the marble bar. Accompany them with first-class cured meats, cheeses and olives from I Trulli next door.
✚ 143 E11 ✉ 122 East 27th Street between Park Avenue South and Lexington Avenue ☎ 212/481-7372 🕐 Mon–Sat 5–12, Sun 5–10 🚇 28th Street (6) 🚌 M101, M102, M103

FAT CAT BILLIARDS
http://fatcatmusic.org/
For a New York experience it's hard to beat going into a basement bar and playing pool. The Fat Cat has 10 tables, along with 10 ping-pong tables, 10 shuffleboard tables and three *foosball* (table football) machines. A good range of beers too, from around the world, and live music including jazz and salsa every night of the week.
✚ 142 C13 ✉ 75 Christopher Street at Seventh Avenue ☎ 212/675-6056 🕐 Mon–Thu 2pm–5am, Fri–Sun noon–5am 🖐 Pool $5–$7 per hour, $3 cover on music nights 🚇 Christopher Street/Sheridan

Square (1), Fourth Street/Washington Square (A, B, C, D, E, F) 🚌 M8, M20

FLANNERY'S BAR

www.flannerysny.com

Flannery's has been one of New York's best Irish bars for more than 20 years. There are DJs twice a week, darts tournaments Wednesday and Saturday, and a rock and blues jam with the house band on Sundays.

✚ 142 C12 ✉ 205 West 14th Street at Seventh Avenue ☎ 212/229-2122 🕐 Mon–Sat 8pm–4am, Sun noon–4am 🍸 $5 cover on darts nights 🚇 14th Street (1, 2, 3, A, C, E), Eighth Avenue (L) 🚌 M14A, M14D

GLASS BAR

www.indigochelsea.com

You might think you're on cloud nine after a couple of drinks at this fantastic rooftop bar in Chelsea's Hotel Indigo. The glass walls after which it's named give you bird's eye views from the 23rd floor, while you relax in comfy chaise lounges, sipping cocktails or wine.

✚ 142 C11 ✉ 127 West 28th Street between Sixth and Seventh avenues ☎ 212/973-9000 🕐 Daily 11am–2am 🍸 Free 🚇 28th Street (1) 🚌 M5, M7, M20

GOTHAM COMEDY CLUB

www.gothamcomedyclub.com

Old and new hands on the comedy scene play this elegant club in the Flatiron District.

✚ 142 C11 ✉ 208 West 23rd Street, between Seventh and Eighth avenues ☎ 212/367-9000 🕐 Two to three shows nightly, times vary 🍸 $12–$30 🚇 23rd Street (1) 🚌 M7, M20, M23

HOME

www.homeguesthouse.com

Long banquettes run the length of some of the walls of this Chelsea nightclub, which oozes style and atmosphere with its low lights, red wood floors, candles and couches. If rock and pop music is too staid, try Guest House down the street.

✚ 142 B11 ✉ 532 West 27th Street, between Tenth and Eleventh avenues

☎ 212/273-3700 🕐 Daily 10pm–4am 🚇 28th Street (1), 23rd Street (C, E) 🚌 M23

INCUBATOR ARTS PROJECT

www.incubatorarts.org

An offshoot of writer-director Richard Foreman's Ontological-Hysteric Theater, the Incubator continues in the vanguard of cutting-edge arts by providing a home for independent theater artists to premiere their original works, as well as programs for experimental performing artists. There is also a concert series.

✚ 143 E12 ✉ St. Mark's Church, 131 East 10th Street, between Second and Third avenues ☎ 212/420-1916 🚇 Astor Place (6), Eighth Street (N, R) 🚌 M8, M15

JAZZ STANDARD

www.jazzstandard.com

The Union Square Café's Danny Myers established this popular downstairs venue with food from his ground-floor restaurant Blue Smoke. It's a sleek, comfortable place for music and a meal. There are two sets nightly, with an additional late show on weekends.

✚ 143 E11 ✉ 116 East 27th Street between Park Avenue South and Lexington Avenue ☎ 212/576-2232 🕐 Daily 6.30pm–3am (shows at 7.30, 9.30, 11.30 Fri–Sat) 🍸 $20–$30 🚇 28th Street (6) 🚌 M1, M2, M3, M101, M102, M103

JOE'S PUB

www.joespub.com

A favorite cabaret club of many New Yorkers, named after Public Theater founder Joe Papp. It's comfortable the way a club should be, with couches and tables. DJs spin during Late Night at Joe's.

✚ 143 E13 ✉ Public Theater, 425 Lafayette Street, between Astor Place and East 4th Street ☎ 212/967-7555 or 212/539-8778 🕐 Daily 6pm–4am (show times vary) 🍸 From $10, plus 2-drink minimum 🚇 Astor Place (6) 🚌 M1, M8

THE JOYCE THEATER

www.joyce.org

The city's premier dance venue hosts top international and domestic

dance companies and showcases such important dance series as Altogether Different. Expect to see the Eliot Feld Ballet, Pilobolus Dance Theater and many others.

✚ 142 C12 ✉ 175 Eighth Avenue, southwest corner of 19th Street ☎ 212/691-9740 or 212/242-0800 🚇 23rd Street (C, E) 🚌 M20, M23

THE JUDSON MEMORIAL CHURCH

www.judson.org

For many decades this Baptist Church has nurtured avant-garde artists. It's most famous for hosting the late Judson Poets Theater, but the Memorial Church still hosts a number of avante-garde arts programs and performances, including theater, music and experimental dance.

✚ 142 D13 ✉ 55 Washington Square South ☎ 212/477-0351 🚇 West Fourth Street (A, B, C, D, E, F) 🚌 M5, M8

THE KITCHEN

www.thekitchen.org

At this fixture of the downtown scene established in 1971, the careers of such artists as Philip Glass, Laurie Anderson, Eric Bogosian, Robert Mapplethorpe and Cindy Sherman were nurtured. It's still going strong.

✚ 142 B12 ✉ 512 West 19th Street, between Tenth and Eleventh avenues ☎ 212/255-5793 🍸 $10–$20 🚇 23rd Street (C, E) 🚌 M11, M23

LABYRINTH THEATER COMPANY

www.labtheater.org

Thirteen actors founded the LAByrinth Repertory Company in 1992 to enable members to write, direct and act. It has 60 international members, who produce plays at Bank Street Theater.

✚ 142 B13 ✉ 155 Bank Street, between Bethune and West 11th streets ☎ 212/513-1080 🚇 Christopher Street (1) 🚌 M20

LITTLE TOWN NYC

www.littletownnyc.com

Sip cocktails and fine wines at this fine old neighborhood bar. The exposed brick and simple wood furniture give it a rustic feel. The pinot noir flavoured wine cellar sorbet is an unusual treat.

➕ 143 E12 ✉ 118 East 15th Street at Irving Place ☎ 212/677-6300 🕐 Daily 11am–1am 🖐 Free 🚇 14th Street/Union Square (4, 5, 6) 🚌 M1, M2, M3, M14

LOUNGE

http://crimescenebar.com

If you like a bar with character then Lounge fits the bill with a hip atmosphere and a gritty party buzz. This trendy lounge attracts an up-and-coming clientele. Weeknights offer DJs; weekends are party nights.

➕ 143 E13 ✉ 310 Bowery at Bleecker Street ☎ 212/477-1166 🕐 Mon–Fri 3pm–4am, Sat 3pm–5am 🚇 Bleecker Street (6), Lower East Side/Second Avenue (F) 🚌 M103

MCSORLEY'S OLD ALE HOUSE

www.mcsorleysnewyork.com/

McSorley's, established in 1854, refused to admit women until 1970. The walls are plastered with old newspaper clippings. Students are the principal patrons today.

➕ 143 E13 ✉ 15 East Seventh Street, between Second and Third avenues ☎ 212/473-9148 🕐 Mon–Sat 11am–1am, Sun 1–1 🚇 Astor Place (6), Eighth Street (N, R) 🚌 M8, M15, M101, M102, M103

LA MAMA EXPERIMENTAL THEATRE CLUB

www.lamama.org

One of the most famous off-off-Broadway theaters was founded in 1961 by Ellen Stewart to nurture new playwrights. It has three theaters: the Annex, the First Floor and the Club, a cabaret space.

➕ 143 E13 ✉ 74A East Fourth Street, between Second Avenue and Bowery ☎ 212/475-7710 🚇 Astor Place (6) 🚌 M8, M15

MARIE'S CRISIS

A mixed crowd of gays and straights gather around the upright piano and sing along to Broadway show tunes at this popular downstairs bar.

➕ 142 C13 ✉ 59 Grove Street ☎ 212/243-9323 🕐 Daily 4–4 🚇 Christopher Street/Sheridan Square (1) 🚌 M20

MARQUEE

www.marqueeny.com

This club has a lot of buzz and attracts a celebrity crowd who appreciate its plush comforts, French elegance and cabaret room. Baby Tuesday caters to the fashion industry. The crowd is mainly straight, but there's a smattering of fashion-conscious gays, too. Hiphop, house, funk and soul are the main musical themes.

➕ 142 B11 ✉ 289 Tenth Avenue, between 26th and 27th streets ☎ 646/473-0202 🕐 Tue–Sat 10pm–4am 🖐 Cover $20 🚇 23rd Street (C, E) 🚌 M11

MERCE CUNNINGHAM STUDIO

www.merce.org

The Studio Performance Series for Emerging Choreographers uses this large studio space from September to July. It seats 99. Cunningham, now in his 90s, still teaches here.

➕ 142 C13 ✉ 55 Bethune Street at Washington Street (11th floor) ☎ 212/255-8240 🖐 $15 🚇 14th Street (A, C, E), 14th Street (1, 2, 3) 🚌 M11, M14A, M20

MINETTA LANE

This Greenwich Village theater is a major off-Broadway player.

➕ 142 D13 ✉ 18 Minetta Lane ☎ 212/420-8000 🚇 West Fourth Street (A, B, C, D, E, F, M) 🚌 M5, M8

NEW SCHOOL

www.nsu.newschool.edu

The prestigious university stages concerts, lectures and readings by writers such as Edmund White, poetry, film shows and discussions.

➕ 142 D12 ✉ Tishman Hall, 66 West 12th Street, between Fifth and Sixth avenues ☎ 212/229-5488 🚇 14th Street (F, M) 🚌 M5, M7, M14

NEW YORK THEATRE WORKSHOP

www.nytw.org

A main player on the Manhattan theater scene. *Rent* began life here,

and the workshop has staged Caryl Churchill and Athol Fugard.

➕ 143 E13 ✉ 79 East Fourth Street, between Second Avenue and Bowery ☎ 212/780-9037 or 212/460-5475 🚇 Broadway-Lafayette (B, D, F, M), Bleecker Street (6) 🚌 M5, M21

NUYORICAN POETS CAFÉ

www.nuyorican.org

Originally a platform for Puerto Rican poets and artists, the café is still famous for its Wednesday and Friday night poetry slams. Expect to see theater, screenplay readings and even Latin jazz. Take a cab.

➕ 143 F13 ✉ 236 East Third Street, between Avenues B and C ☎ 212/780-9386 🕐 Tue–Sat 7–12, Sun 4–12 🚇 Lower East Side/Second Avenue (F) 🚌 M9, M21

OLD TOWN BAR

www.oldtownbar.com

At this authentic hang-out, dating from 1892, look for the private booths. Tiled floors, a long mirrored bar, pressed-tin ceiling and original gas lamps complete the look. No jukebox, conversation reigns.

➕ 143 D12 ✉ 45 East 18th Street, between Broadway and Park Avenue ☎ 212/529-6732 🕐 Mon–Fri 11.30am–1am, Sat–Sun noon–1am 🚇 14th Street/Union Square (L, N, Q, R, 4, 5, 6) 🚌 M1, M2, M3, M5, M14

THE PARK

www.theparknyc.com

This gargantuan complex features a glass-enclosed atrium with a fireplace. The main dining room has windows onto the outdoor garden dining area. The Penthouse and the Red Room are open late on Fridays and Saturdays.

➕ 142 B12 ✉ 118 Tenth Avenue between West 17th and 18th streets ☎ 212/352-3313 🕐 Mon–Wed 11.30am–midnight, Thu 11.30am–2am, Fri 11.30am–4am, Sat 10am–4am, Sun 10am–midnight 🚇 14th Street (A, C, E), Eighth Avenue (L) 🚌 M11, M14D

PEOPLE'S IMPROV THEATER

www.thepit-nyc.com

Improvisation at this theater comes with the addition of caustic social commentary. Audience participation is encouraged.

⊞ 142 D10 ⊠ 123 East 24th Street, between Park and Lexington avenues ☎ 212/563-7488 🕐 Several shows daily, times vary 🖐 Free–$15 🚇 22nd Street (6) 🚌 M23, M101, M102, M103

PETE'S TAVERN

www.petestavern.com

The writer O. Henry supposedly wrote *The Gift of the Magi* in a beer-stained booth here. In summer, snag a sidewalk table if you can, for some great people-watching.

⊞ 143 E12 ⊠ 129 East 18th Street at Irving Place ☎ 212/473-7676 🕐 Daily 11am–2.30am 🚇 14th Street/Union Square (L, N, Q, R, 4, 5, 6) 🚌 M1, M2, M3

THE POETRY PROJECT

www.poetryproject.org

This legendary outpost in the East Village, which hosted W. H. Auden, Allen Ginsberg and many others, has poetry readings, workshops and other events. See the website for a current schedule.

⊞ 143 E12 ⊠ St. Mark's Church-in-the-Bowery, 131 East 10th Street at Second Avenue ☎ 212/674-0910 🖐 $8 most events 🚇 Astor Place (6), First Avenue (L) 🚌 M8, M15

IL POSTO ACCANTO

www.ilpostoaccanto.com/

This is a friendly and welcoming wine bar. Order appetizers to go with one of 30 Italian wines sold by the glass.

⊞ 143 F13 ⊠ 190 East 2nd Street, between Avenues A and B ☎ 212/228-3562 🕐 Mon, Sat–Sun 5.30pm–3am, Tue–Fri noon–3am 🚇 Lower East Side/Second Avenue (F) 🚌 M14A, M21

QUAD CINEMA

www.quadcinema.com

This four-screen art house shows foreign and independent films and works by new directors.

⊞ 142 D12 ⊠ 34 West 13th Street, between Fifth and Sixth avenues ☎ 212/255-8800 or 212/255-2243 🖐 $11 🕐 14th Street (F), 14th Street/Union Square (L, N, Q, R, 4, 5, 6) 🚌 M2, M3, M5, M14

RF LOUNGE

http://rflounge.com/

Couches and antique chairs are clustered around the fireplace in the upstairs bar, which attracts an over-35 crowd. There is a convivial restaurant downstairs.

⊞ 142 C13 ⊠ 531 Hudson Street, between Charles and West 10th streets ☎ 917/262-0836 🖐 $5 before 11pm, $10 after 🕐 Daily 3pm–4am 🚇 Christopher Street (1) 🚌 M8, M20

RODEO BAR

www.rodeobar.com

This Southern-style roadhouse serves Tex-Mex food and margaritas, along with nightly live bluegrass, country, rockabilly or alt-country.

⊞ 143 E11 ⊠ 375 Third Avenue at East 27th Street ☎ 212/683-6500 🕐 Daily 11.30am–2am (music Sun–Wed 8.30–11pm, Thu 9.30pm–midnight, Fri–Sat 11pm–2am) 🖐 Free 🚇 28th Street (6) 🚌 M101, M102, M103

SING SING KARAOKE

www.karaokesingsing.com

Take to the stage at one of the oldest and best karaoke bars in New York City. The song list numbers more than 20,000 songs and is updated regularly so you can always try your hand at the latest hits. There is a second location at 81 Avenue A.

⊞ 143 E13 ⊠ 9 St. Marks Place between Second and Third avenues ☎ 212/387-7800 🕐 Daily 1pm–4am 🖐 Free 🚇 Astor Place (6) 🚌 M8, M15, M101, M102, M103

STAR LOUNGE

www.starloungechelsea.com

In the basement of the Hotel Chelsea, the Star Lounge is a fashionable late-night spot with three rooms: Room 100 is an exclusive VIP lounge, Room 200 a nightclub with regular DJ sessions, and Room 300 a retro-style gentlemen's bar.

⊞ 142 C11 ⊠ Hotel Chelsea, 222 West 23rd Street, between Seventh and Eighth avenues ☎ 212/255-4646 🕐 Tue–Sat 6pm–4am 🚇 23rd Street (1) 🚌 M7, M20, M23

STONEWALL INN

www.stonewall-place.com

It's nondescript, but this place has acquired near-mythic status for the gay movement. Here in 1969 some transvestites, using their stilettos, took a stand against the police.

⊞ 142 C13 ⊠ 53 Christopher Street between Seventh Avenue South and Waverly Place ☎ 212/488-2705 🕐 Mon–Sat 3pm–4am, Sun noon–4am 🚇 Christopher Street/Sheridan Square (1) 🚌 M8, M20

SUGARCANE

www.sushisamba.com

The DJ spins Brazilian-Caribbean sounds at this atmospheric bar. The sultry lounge of the partner SushiSamba restaurant next door kicks off with Samba Hour drinks and shared plate special (Sun–Thu 4–7) and continues through late-night cocktails.

⊞ 143 D11 ⊠ 245 Park Avenue South, between 19th and 20th streets ☎ 212 475-9377 🕐 Mon–Wed 5.45–1, Thu–Sat 5.45–2, Sun 5.45–midnight 🚇 23rd Street (6), 23rd Street (N, R) 🚌 M1, M2, M3

SULLIVAN HALL

www.sullivanhallnyc.com

An eclectic variety of music styles is performed here, but don't expect to hear hard core or heavy metal.

⊞ 142 D13 ⊠ 214 Sullivan Street, between Bleecker and West Third streets ☎ 212/477-2782 🕐 Nightly 🖐 $10–$20 🚇 West Fourth Street (A, B, C, D, E, F, M), Bleecker Street (6) 🚌 M5, M21

SWIFT HIBERNIAN LOUNGE

www.swiftnycbar.com

Numerous brews are on tap at this slice of Dublin named for satirist Jonathan Swift. There's Irish music on Tuesdays at 9.30pm, and DJs Thursdays, Fridays and Saturdays.

⊞ 143 E13 ⊠ 34 East Fourth Street, between Bowery and Lafayette Street ☎ 212/260-3600 🕐 Daily noon–4am 🚇 Broadway-Lafayette (B, D, F, M), Bleecker Street (6) 🚌 M21, M103

TEMPLE BAR

www.templebarnyc.com

This ultra-expensive bar attracts models and their coterie.

✚ 143 E13 ✉ 332 Lafayette Street, between Houston and Bleecker streets ☎ 212/925-4242 🕐 Mon–Thu 5–1, Fri–Sat 5–2 🚇 Broadway-Lafayette (B, D, F, M), Bleecker Street (6) 🚌 M5, M21

TERRA BLUES
www.terrablues.com
At this second-floor club, acoustic acts warm up the crowd for the nightly blues show.
✚ 142 D13 ✉ 149 Bleecker Street between LaGuardia Place and Thompson Street ☎ 212/777-7776 🕐 Nightly at 7pm, blues show 10pm ✋ From $5, plus 2-drink minimum 🚇 West Fourth Street (A, B, C, D, E, F) 🚌 M5, M21

THEATER FOR THE NEW CITY
www.theaterforthenewcity.net
Thought-provoking, often politically inspired dramas are the repertory of this community-oriented company, founded in 1970.
✚ 143 E13 ✉ 155 First Avenue, between Ninth and Tenth streets ☎ 212/254-1109 🚇 Astor Place (6) 🚌 M8, M15

VILLAGE UNDERGROUND
www.thevillageunderground.com
A subterranean club with a good line-up of artists ranging from salsa bands to blues artists.
✚ 142 D13 ✉ 130 West Third Street, between Sixth Avenue and MacDougal Street ☎ 212/777-7745 🚇 West Fourth Street (A, B, C, D, E, F, M) 🚌 M5

VILLAGE VANGUARD
www.villagevanguard.com
Founded by Max Gordon in 1935, it's still the premier jazz club in the city, presided over by Lorraine Gordon since her husband died in 1989. The Vanguard is intimate, has terrific acoustics and features top-flight artists—Lester Young, Thelonious Monk, John Coltrane, Keith Jarrett and Miles Davis have played here. Now evenings often morph into a vibrant jam session.
✚ 142 C12 ✉ 178 Seventh Avenue at West 11th Street ☎ 212/255-4037 🕐 Daily from 8pm (sets Sun–Fri 9 and 11, Sat 9, 11 and sometimes 12.30) ✋ Cover $25 per set plus 1-drink minimum 🚇 14th Street (1, 2, 3) 🚌 M14, M20

VINEYARD THEATRE
www.vineyardtheatre.org
Located in a residential tower, this off-Broadway theater has staged Pulitzer Prize-winning plays before they went to Broadway. The auditorium seats 120.
✚ 143 E12 ✉ 108 East 15th Street, between Union Square and Irving Place ☎ 212/353-3366, 212/353-0303 🚇 14th Street/Union Square (L, N, Q, R, 4, 5, 6) 🚌 M14, M101, M102, M103

WHITE HORSE TAVERN
Dylan Thomas, Brendan Behan and Jack Kerouac all slaked their thirst here. In summer, the benches and picnic tables make perfect perches for Village people-watching.
✚ 142 C13 ✉ 567 Hudson Street at 11th Street ☎ 212/989-3956 🕐 Sun–Thu 11am–1.30am, Fri–Sat 11am–3.30am 🚇 Christopher Street/Sheridan Square (1), 14th Street (A, C, E) 🚌 M20

ZINC BAR
www.zincbar.com
Music-lovers and musicians alike come to this casual, tiny bar to hear both talented newcomers and established names such as George Benson and Max Roach. There's usually Brazilian music on Saturdays and Sundays.
✚ 142 D13 ✉ 82 West Third Street near Thompson Street ☎ 212/477-9462 🕐 Sun–Thu 6pm–2.30am, Fri–Sat 6pm–3am (show times vary) ✋ Cover $10–$20 🚇 West Fourth Street (A, B, C, D, E, F, M), Houston Street (1), Bleecker Street (6) 🚌 M5, M21

SPORTS AND ACTIVITIES
BOWLMOR LANES
www.bowlmor.com
This funky bowling alley has 42 lanes with automatic scoring. At Monday's Night Strike (10pm–2am), DJs spin music as you bowl.
✚ 143 D12 ✉ 110 University Place, between 12th and 13th streets ☎ 212/255-8188 🕐 Sun–Tue 11am–1am, Wed–Thu 11am–2am, Fri–Sat 11am–3am ✋ $8.45–$9.95 per game (shoe rental $5.50). Night Strike $24 🚇 14th Street/Union Square (L, N, Q, R, 4, 5, 6) 🚌 M1, M2, M3, M5, M14

CHELSEA PIERS
www.chelseapiers.com
The city's ultimate sports complex is built on four Hudson River piers. In summer, the beach, sundecks, large pool and kayaking layout are inviting. There's a climbing wall as well as 200-meter and quarter-mile tracks, an ice rink, and rows of cardiovascular, circuit and strength-training equipment. There are courts for basketball, indoor sand volleyball and touch football, plus a boxing ring, golf driving range and batting cages. Some 125 classes a week offer everything from aerobics to yoga. Other facilities include a sports medicine clinic, café and spa.
✚ 142 A11 ✉ Piers 59–62 at 23rd Street and the Hudson River ☎ 212/336-6666 🕐 Daily 6am–midnight ✋ Day passes available 🚇 23rd Street (C, E) 🚌 M23

MANHATTAN KAYAK COMPANY
www.manhattankayak.com
This company offers instruction and more than 30 local tours for all abilities. Longer tours go to the Verrazano Bridge and farther.
✚ 142 A11 ✉ Pier 66, 26th Street and 12th Avenue ☎ 212/924-1788 🕐 Mid-Apr to Oct ✋ Tours $35–$250 🚇 Eighth Avenue (C, E) then M23 bus 🚌 M23

NEW YORK GALLERY TOURS
▷ 270.

SLATE
www.slate-ny.com
This is one of the city's best billiard-pool halls, with 31 tables.
✚ 142 D11 ✉ 54 West 21st Street, between Fifth and Sixth avenues ☎ 212/989-0096 🕐 Mon–Sat noon–4am, Sun 12–12 ✋ $15–$17 per hour 🚇 23rd Street (F, M, N, R) 🚌 M2, M3, M5, M7, M23

HEALTH AND BEAUTY
ACQUA BEAUTY BAR
www.acquabeautybar.com
Treatments include an Indonesian "ritual of beauty," an Adlay (Asian wheat) body scrub and an indulgent Garden of Eastern Delights, combining a mist facial with a shiatsu massage. You can still get

a reviving Swedish massage and expert French manicure or pedicure. ✚ 142 D12 ✉ 7 East 14th Street near Fifth Avenue ☎ 212/620-4329 🕐 Mon–Fri 10–9, Sat 10–8, Sun 10–7 ✋ Facial $135–$250, manicure $12–$22, massage $100–$110 🚇 Union Square/14th Street (L, N, Q, R) 🚌 M1, M2, M3, M5, M14

BALLY TOTAL FITNESS
www.ballyfitness.com
This national chain has several facilities in Manhattan. The Sixth Avenue club has more than 70 pieces of cardiovascular equipment, 73 pieces of resistance-training equipment, personal trainers and classes in yoga and Pilates. ✚ 142 D12 ✉ 641 Avenue of the Americas at 19th Street ☎ 212/645-4565 🕐 Mon–Fri 5–10, Sat 9–6, Sun 9–5 🚇 Day pass $15 🚇 18th Street (1) 🚌 M5, M7

CLAY
www.insideclay.com
Sleek, serene and minimal, Clay combines bodywork therapies with exercise (weights, cardio-boxing, yoga). The fireside lounge and rooftop deck are bonuses. ✚ 142 D12 ✉ 25 West 14th Street, between Fifth and Sixth avenues ☎ 212/206-9200 🕐 Mon–Thu 5.30am–11pm, Fri 5.30am–10pm, Sat–Sun 8–9 ✋ Massage $110–$145 🚇 14th Street/ Union Square (L, N, Q, R, 4, 5, 6) 🚌 M2, M3, M5, M14

CRUNCH FITNESS
www.crunch.com
Crunch, which has 12 locations in the city, is the premier brand of Bally Fitness. The instructors are first rate, and the studio is known for its innovative classes, from street stomp to cycle karaoke. ✚ 143 E12 ✉ 113 Fourth Avenue at 12th Street ☎ 212/533-0001 🕐 Mon–Thu 5am–11pm, Fri 5am–10pm, Sat 7am–9pm, Sun 8am–9pm ✋ Day pass $16 🚇 14th Street/Union Square (L, N, Q, R, 4, 5, 6) 🚌 M1, M2, M3, M5, M14

GREAT JONES SPA
www.greatjonesspa.com
The Great Jones Spa blends organic principles (a raw food café) with unashamed indulgence. They provide a kind of feng shui for the body, and the facilities are as impressive as the ambience is relaxing. There are water cures, acupuncture, detoxifying and spa treatments. ✚ 143 E13 ✉ 29 Great Jones Street at Lafayette ☎ 212/505-3185 🕐 Mon 4–10pm, Tue–Sun 9am–10pm ✋ Manicure $25–$40, facial $130–$250, massage $140–$230 🚇 Bleecker Street (6) 🚌 M5

JENIETTE
www.jeniette.com
Since 1979 this East Village salon has been providing good manicures, pedicures, facials and massage at much lower prices than uptown. Jeniette uses Dinur products. ✚ 143 D12 ✉ 58 East 13th Street, between University Place and Broadway ☎ 212/529-1616 🕐 Mon, Wed, Sat 10–7, Tue, Thu, Fri 10–8, Sun 11–6 ✋ Manicure $11–$20, facial from $65, massage $75–$170 🚇 14th Street/Union Square (L, N, Q, R, 4, 5, 6) 🚌 M1, M5, M14

NEW YORK HEALTH AND RACQUET CLUB
www.nyhrc.com
The 10 Manhattan branches of this chain offer sports and classes from t'ai chi to aqua-cise. Each branch has a pool. Members have access to a beach and tennis club in New Rochelle, and a yacht docked at 23rd Street. ✚ 142 D12 ✉ 24 East 13th Street, between Fifth Avenue and University Place ☎ 212/924-4600 🕐 Mon–Fri 6am–11pm, Sat–Sun 8am–9pm ✋ Day pass $20 🚇 14th Street/Union Square (L, N, Q, R, 4, 5, 6) 🚌 M1, M2, M3, M5, M14

NEW YORK SPORT CLUBS
www.mysportsclubs.com
This chain has close to 100 locations around town, consisting mostly of aerobic studios with cardio-fitness machines and free weights, plus a full program of exercise classes— cardio-kickboxing, step, abs, Pilates and yoga. Massage treatments are available. ✚ 142 C12 ✉ 128 Eighth Avenue at 16th Street ☎ 212/627-0065 🕐 Mon–Thu 6am–11pm, Fri 6am–10pm, Sat–Sun 8am–9pm ✋ Day pass $25 🚇 18th Street (1) 🚌 M20

OASIS DAY SPA
www.nydayspa.com
Candlelight and soft music enhance this popular spa, which offers 15 massage treatments. There is also a hair and nail salon. ✚ 143 D10 ✉ 1 Park Avenue, between 32nd and 33rd streets ☎ 212/254-7722 🕐 Mon–Fri 10–10, Sat–Sun 9–9 ✋ Facial $70–$155, massage $65–$185 🚇 33rd Street (6) 🚌 M1, M2, M3

RESCUE BEAUTY LOUNGE
www.rescuebeauty.com
Rescue takes a medical approach to pampering, maintaining hospital standards of cleanliness. This is the place to get the ultimate manicure. ✚ 142 C12 ✉ 34 Gansevoort Street, between Hudson and Greenwich streets, second floor ☎ 212/206-6409 🕐 Tue–Fri 11–8, Sat–Sun 10–6 ✋ Manicure $30–$70, pedicure $50–$125, facial $85–$225 🚇 14th Street (A, C, E), Eighth Avenue (L) 🚌 M11, M20

FOR CHILDREN
FORBES MAGAZINE GALLERIES
▷ 113.

TADA THEATER AND DANCE ALLIANCE
www.tadatheater.com
Young professionals aged 8 to 17 put on shows and revues at this theater company-and-school. ✚ 142 D11 ✉ 15 West 28th Street at Sixth Avenue ☎ 212/252-1619 ✋ Adult $25, child $8 🚇 23rd Street (F, M) 🚌 M5, M7, M23

THEATREWORKS USA
www.theatreworksusa.org
Plays and musicals for children are specialties here. Performers deliver favorites such as *The Lion, the Witch and the Wardrobe*. ✚ 142 C13 ✉ Lucille Lortel Theatre, 121 Christopher Street, between Hudson and Bleecker ☎ 212/647-1100 or 800/497-5007 🕐 Call for details ✋ $25 🚇 Christopher Street/Sheridan Square (1) 🚌 M8, M20

PRICES AND SYMBOLS

The prices given are the average for a two-course lunch (L) and a three-course dinner (D) for one person, without drinks. The wine price is for the least expensive bottle.

For a key to the symbols, ▷ 2.

ALMOND

www.almondnyc.com

The freshest farm-to-table fare is served from the kitchens at this popular American bistro, set in the elegant Gramercy Park Historic District. The atmosphere is warm and relaxing, with hardwood floors, golden walls, antique mirrors and soft candlelight. The menu ranges from bistro favorites like steak frites to house-smoked trout and goat cheese ravioli, with such plats du jour as risotto or rack of lamb. The weekend brunch menu is full of treats like almond hash made with duck confit, and a wonderful classic eggs Benedict.

✚ 143 D11 ✉ 12 East 22nd Street between Broadway and Park Avenue South ☎ 212/228-7557 🕐 Mon–Thu 12–2.45, 6–11, Fri 12–2.45, 6–12, Sat 11–3, 6–12, Sun 11–4, 6–10 ✋ L $27, D $45, Wine $28 🚇 23rd Street (N, R, 6) 🚌 M1, M2, M3, M5, M23

ANGELICA KITCHEN

www.angelicakitchen.com

This ecological restaurant proves that vegetarian cuisine does not have to be bland. Go for the hearty soups, chili or tasty noodle dishes and sandwiches. There is no alcohol, and credit cards are not accepted.

✚ 143 E12 ✉ 300 East 12th Street, between First and Second avenues ☎ 212/228-2909 🕐 Daily 11.30–10.30 ✋ L $18, D $26 🚇 14th Street/Union Square (4, 5, 6, L, N, Q, R) 🚌 M14, M15

ANNISA

www.annisarestaurant.com

At this minimalist restaurant chef Anita Lo cooks fusion cuisine. For appetizers, oysters might arrive with three root vegetables, while roasted *kabocha* squash and *maiiake* mushrooms could be combined with bitter chocolate. Smoked lamb hominy is enriched with chili and lime. Credit cards are not accepted.

✚ 142 C13 ✉ 13 Barrow Street, between Bleecker and West Fourth streets ☎ 212/741-6699 🕐 Mon–Sat 5.30–10.30, Sun 5.30–9.30 ✋ D $65, 5-course tasting $78, 9 courses $98, Wine $40 🚇 West 4th Street (A, C, E, F), Christopher Street/Sheridan Square (1) 🚌 M20, M21

BABBO

www.babbonyc.com

Mario Batali has a lust for life that's infectious and an originality that is breathtaking. He has authored numerous cookery books and has a prime-time PBS series. At Babbo, his flagship restaurant, the welcome is warm and the food some of the freshest and lustiest anywhere. Try the handmade beef cheek ravioli or the prosciutto with spicy fig jam. The all-Italian wine list is a revelation.

✚ 142 D13 ✉ 110 Waverly Place, between MacDougal Street and Sixth Avenue ☎ 212/777-0303 🕐 Mon–Sat 5.30–11.15, Sun 5–10.45 ✋ D $70, Wine $30 🚇 West Fourth Street (A, B, C, D, E, F, M) 🚌 M5

BANJARA

www.banjaranyc.com

Sixth Street is lined with Indian restaurants, but Banjara is the best of the lot. Northern Indian cuisine is the specialty. The tandoori dishes are particularly good with their fine smoky flavor. Also appealing are the pasanda lamb, cooked in a yogurt-based curry sauce, and the *palak ghost*—lamb in a purée of spinach, tomatoes, ginger and cumin seeds.

Opposite *The vegetarian Angelica Kitchen*

✚ 143 E13 ✉ 97 First Avenue at Sixth Street ☎ 212/477-5956 🕐 Daily 12–12 ✋ L $20, D $30, Wine $19 🚇 Astor Place (6) 🚌 M8, M15

BLUE HILL
www.bluehillnyc.com
Candlelight and bouquets set the inviting tone of this below-ground dining room. It's named for a farm in Massachusetts where the chef finds his seasonal, locally grown ingredients. Expect corn shoots in June, squash and apples in fall. The menu offers such dishes as fall mushrooms braised and steamed with fingerling potato tart, followed by roasted trout with a pistou of vegetables with puréed basil, or poached duck with a stew of organic carrots with toasted spices. Desserts are enticing.
✚ 142 D13 ✉ 75 Washington Place, between MacDougal and Sixth Avenue ☎ 212/539-1776 🕐 Mon–Sat 5.30–11, Sun 5.30–10 ✋ D $65, Wine $35 🚇 West Fourth Street (A, B, C, D, E, F, M) 🚌 M5

BLUE SMOKE
www.bluesmoke.com
The secret of barbecue is slow cooking and well-blended spices. Danny Meyer studied it for three years and traveled 62,000 miles before opening this rustic red-hot restaurant. Barbecue addicts drool over the rib sampler. Eight beers are on tap, while the bourbon whiskey and wine list pairs well with the food. A good jazz room downstairs shares the upstairs menu.
✚ 143 E11 ✉ 116 East 27th Street, between Park Avenue South and Lexington Avenue ☎ 212/447-7733 🕐 Sun–Mon 11.30–10, Tue–Thu 11.30–11, Fri–Sat 11.30am–1am ✋ L $35, D $54, Wine $32 🚇 23rd Street (6) 🚌 M1, M101, M102, M103

BOND ST
www.bondstrestaurant.com
The buzz has lessened at this sleek Japanese spot in a SoHo brownstone, but the glistening sushi and sashimi are as beautiful as ever. Among the appetizers, expect seared duck with shitake and truffle glaze, or monkfish filet with spicy-and-sour salsa. Desserts are innovative Japanese. Traditional tatami rooms are upstairs; downstairs there's a fashionable lounge serving exotic *saketinis*.
✚ 143 E13 ✉ 6 Bond Street, between Broadway and Lafayette Street ☎ 212/777-2500 🕐 Sun–Tue 6–10.30, Wed–Thu 6–11, Fri–Sat 6–11.30 ✋ D $55, *omakase* $80–$120, Wine $44 🚇 Broadway-Lafayette (B, D, F, M) 🚌 M5, M21

CASA MONO
www.casamononyc.com
Mario Batali has turned to Spain for inspiration at this small tapas bar reminiscent of those found in Barcelona and Madrid. It's crowded and noisy and the dishes invite experimentation. There might be bacalao croquettes with orange flavored aioli, cockles with scrambled eggs and Serrano ham, or oxtails with *piquillo* peppers along with more substantial dishes and great artisanal cheeses. Affordable wine and sherry selection.
✚ 143 E12 ✉ 52 Irving Place at 17th Street ☎ 212/253-2773 🕐 Daily 12–12 ✋ L $25, D $42, Wine $30 🚇 14th Street/Union Square (L, N, Q, R) 🚌 M1, M2, M3, M101, M102, M103

I COPPI
www.icoppinyc.com
This restaurant is like a piece of Tuscany in Manhattan. Wood tables and rush-seated chairs create a rustic charm accompanied by music from the opera. Tuna carpaccio is paper-thin and spiked with green peppercorn sauce; sliced pears with Gorgonzola and stracchino cheese make for a perfect salad. Among the *secondi,* there might be grilled wild boar, or wild striped bass with capers and black olives.
✚ 143 F13 ✉ 432 East 9th Street, between First Avenue and Avenue A ☎ 212/254-2263 🕐 Mon–Tue 5.30–10, Wed–Thu, Sun 5.30–10.30, Fri–Sat 5.30–11. Also brunch Sat–Sun 11.30–3 ✋ Brunch $15, D $50, Wine $30 🚇 Astor Place (6) 🚌 M8, M14, M15

CORNER BISTRO
www.cornerbistrony.com
The graffiti-covered tables and booths at this plain West Village bar remain the best place in town to grab burgers. Made with 8oz (225g) ground chuck, they come plain or topped with bacon or blue cheese. Other sandwiches and chili are also available. The jukebox has great sounds and the beer is good. Credit cards are not accepted.
✚ 142 C12 ✉ 331 West Fourth Street, between Jane Street and Eighth Avenue ☎ 212/242-9502 🕐 Mon–Sat 11.30am–4am, Sun noon–4am ✋ L $10, D $16 🚇 14th Street (A, C, E) 🚌 M14, M20

CRAFT AND CRAFTBAR
www.craftrestaurant.com
When Tom Colicchio conceived Craft he wanted diners to create their own dishes from a menu that was just a list of ingredients. This is still the focus, but the chef now supplies more direction. Most dishes are roasted (striped bass, quail) or braised (red snapper, short ribs). Desserts can be fresh fruits, intense sorbets or decadent confections like the toffee steamed pudding. The cheeses are stunning. The leather, copper and steel, and plain wood furnishings and fittings recall the Arts and Crafts movement. Craftbar serves sandwiches and oysters.
✚ 143 D11 ✉ 43 East 19th Street, between Broadway and Park Avenue South ☎ 212/780-0880 🕐 Sun–Thu 5.30–10, Fri–Sat 5.30–11 ✋ D $75, Wine $40 🚇 23rd Street (N, R), 23rd Street (6) 🚌 M1, M2, M3, M23

CREMA RESTAURANTE
www.cremarestaurante.com
Julieta Ballasteros has consistently been voted among the top two Mexican chefs in New York, by Zagat. Her Chelsea restaurant combines the zingy flavors of Mexico with the subtlety of fine French cuisine, with dishes such as a casserole of cheese and Mexican chorizo served with corn tortillas. Leave room for unusual desserts like the pumpkin cheesecake.

✚ 142 D12 ✉ 111 West 17th Street, between Sixth and Seventh avenues ☎ 212/ 691-4477 🕐 Tue–Wed, Sun 12–11, Thu–Sat 12–12 🖐 L $25, D $50, Wine $22 🚇 18th Street (1), 14th Street (F, M) 🚌 M5, M7, M20

DEVI

www.devinyc.com

The décor and food will transport you to India in a minute. Dishes draw inspiration from street food and regional cuisine. Goan shrimp are cooked with *balchao*, a vinegar based sauce; fishes are baked in banana leaf; Manchurian cauliflower is a mixture of tomato sauce with scallions and chilies. All are redolent with cilantro (coriander), mint, tamarind and coconut.

✚ 142 D12 ✉ 8 East 18th Street, between Fifth Avenue and Broadway ☎ 212/691-1300 🕐 Mon–Fri 12–2.30, 5.30–11, Sat 5.30–11, Sun 5–10 🖐 L $40, D $50, chef's tasting menu $85, Wine $36 🚇 14th Street/Union Square (L, N, Q, R, 4, 5, 6) 🚌 M1, M2, M3, M5

DOS CAMINOS

www.doscaminos.com

The space is celebratory, the bar stocks 150 tequilas, and the fare covers all Mexican bases— guacamole made tableside; shrimp, scallop and tuna ceviche; chicken mole; and pan-roasted snapper with pineapple-passion fruit sauce. Desserts are ice creams and sorbets such as guava-mango sorbet.

✚ 143 E11 ✉ 373 Park Avenue South, between 26th and 27th streets ☎ 212/294-1000 🕐 Daily 11.30–4, Sun–Mon 5–10, Tue–Thu 5–11, Fri–Sat 5–midnight 🖐 L $30, D $50, Wine $35 🚇 28th Street (6) 🚌 M1, M2, M3, M23

ELEVEN MADISON PARK

www.elevenmadisonpark.com

This dramatic dining space, once the brokers' hall of the Metropolitan Life insurance company, is worthy of the cuisine. The dishes on the menu are listed only according to the main ingredients available, and diners can state their likes and dislikes and let the team of chefs prepare their dishes individually.

It's somewhere between a formal menu and a tasting menu, so if you want lobster with lemon and coconut, that's what you can have. The international wine list leans to the French.

✚ 143 D11 ✉ 11 Madison Avenue at 24th Street ☎ 212/889-0905 🕐 Mon–Fri 12–2, 5.30–10, Sat 5.30–10 🖐 L $56, D $125, Wine $40 🚇 23rd Street (6) 🚌 M1, M2, M3

GNOCCO

www.gnocco.com

No prizes for guessing the house specialty here—delicious home-made gnocco which are fried and served with either a sauce or a cold meat plate and not to be confused with gnocchi. Either way these, and the other fresh pasta dishes, are Italian cooking at its best. The intimate dining room conceals a lovely garden dining area out back, and the service is relaxed and amiable Italian-style.

✚ 143 F12 ✉ 337 East 10th Street, between A and B avenues ☎ 212/677-1913 🕐 Mon–Fri 5–12, Sat–Sun 12–4, 5–12 🖐 L $20, D $50, Wine $31 🚇 Astor Place (6), First Avenue (L) 🚌 M8, M9, M14a

GOTHAM BAR & GRILL

www.gothambarandgrill.com

Unique among Manhattan celebrity chefs, Alfred Portale has not yet created his own mini-chain. This may be why his fresh-tasting, dramatically presented contemporary cuisine continues to excite even after more than 20 years. Rack of lamb is Portale's signature dish, but you can't go wrong with the truffle-crusted halibut with verjus sauce or the Snake River Farms pork with caramelized *cipollini* onions. The warm apple and mango tartes Tatin and the warm Gotham chocolate cake are sublime.

✚ 142 D12 ✉ 12 East 12th Street, between Fifth Avenue and University Place ☎ 212/620-4020 🕐 Mon–Fri noon–2.15, Mon–Thu 5.30–10, Fri 5.30–11, Sat 5–11, Sun 5–10 🖐 L $40, D $80, Wine $45 🚇 14th Street/Union Square (L, N, Q, R, 4, 5, 6) 🚌 M2, M3, M5

GRAMERCY TAVERN

www.gramercytavern.com

Danny Meyer's stellar restaurant, under Executive Chef Michael Anthony, still shines. Both the main dining room (made up from a warren of several cozy rooms) and the more casual tavern in the front of the building are both striking and comfortable. The truly warm hospitality and the seamless service make this one of the city's top tables. You can't go wrong on this menu, which offers a seared foie gras paired with a rhubarb tart, arugula (rocket) and sherry vinegar, and a roasted monkfish wrapped with pancetta. Twenty-five wines from the superb list are available by the glass. Desserts are just as delightful as the main dishes.

✚ 142 D11 ✉ 42 East 20th Street, between Broadway and Park Avenue South ☎ 212/477-0777 🕐 Dining room: Mon–Fri noon–2, Sun–Thu 5.30–10, Fri–Sat 5.30–11; Tavern: Sun–Thu noon–11, Fri–Sat 12–12 🖐 L $45, tasting menu $58, D 3-course prix fixe $88, tasting menu $116; Tavern L $30, D $40, Wine $32 🚇 23rd Street (N, R) 🚌 M1, M2, M3, M5

HOLY BASIL

www.holybasilrestaurant.com

This is one of the city's best Thai restaurants. Here, the kitchen balances the flavors of sweet and salt associated with the cuisine. The stars are the fish dishes, such as the whole crisp fish, which you can order in red chili sauce or a delicious tamarind sauce. Wine selections pair well with the food.

✚ 143 E13 ✉ 149 Second Avenue, between East Ninth and Tenth streets ☎ 212/460-5557 🕐 Mon–Thu 5–11.30, Fri 5–midnight, Sat 4–midnight, Sun 4–11 🖐 D $32, Wine $23 🚇 Astor Place (6) 🚌 M8, M15

JOHN'S PIZZERIA

www.johnspizzerianyc.com

The pizza served at this John's Pizzeria is frequently touted as the best in the city, and it is extraordinarily good indeed. Note that this is not a pizza parlor; slices are not available. Instead, take a booth and order a whole pie loaded with toppings—more than 50 are available. Credit cards are not accepted here.

✚ 142 C13 ✉ 278 Bleecker Street, between Sixth and Seventh avenues ☎ 212/243-1680 🕐 Daily 11.30–11.30 ✋ L $25, D $35, Wine $19 🚇 West 4th Street (A, B, C, D, E, F, M), Christopher Street/Sheridan Square (1) 🚌 M5, M20

KESTÉ PIZZERIA
www.kestepizzeria.com
You might think the last thing New York needs is another pizza parlor, but Kesté opened to great acclaim and diners are flocking to this cozy Village hot spot. It's worth paying a little bit more for these authentic Neapolitan pizzas, crafted by chef Roberto Caporuscio who was raised on a dairy farm outside Naples. Even the simple Regina Margharita is memorable, made with the freshest, sweetest tomatoes, while the long list of pies features ingredients from truffle spread to imported olives, cured meats and smoked mozzarella.

✚ 142 C13 ✉ 271 Bleecker Street, between Jones and Cornelia streets ☎ 212/243-1500 🕐 Mon–Sat 12–3.30, 5–11, Sun 12–3.30, 5–10 ✋ L $20 D $25, Wine $20 🚇 West 4th Street/ Washington Square (A, B, C, D, E, F, M), Christopher Street (1) 🚌 M5, M8, M20

MANATUS
www.manatusnyc.com
Manatus is the kind of old-fashioned diner-style restaurant that is increasingly hard to find in New York. It's nothing fancy, but it's comfortable, spacious, inexpensive and best of all, open 24 hours. The food is good too, with classic Greek and Italian dishes on the menu alongside fresh seafood, roasts and chicken sauté dishes, and an array of sandwiches, burgers, wraps, salads and breakfast dishes. There is a full bar, and outdoor patio.

✚ 142 C13 ✉ 340 Bleecker Street between West 10th and Christopher streets ☎ 212/989-7042 🕐 Daily 24 hours ✋ L $15, D $25, Wine $15 🚇 Christopher Street (1) 🚌 M8, M20

MERMAID INN
www.themermaidnyc.com
This is the closest that Manhattan can come to a seafood shack, complete with ocean paraphernalia and navigational charts. The menu opens with a small selection of raw shellfish and follows with everything from chowder and spaghetti *fra diavolo* to *zaruela* brimming with lobster tail, cod and squid. No desserts are available, except whatever the house provides as complimentary.

✚ 143 E13 ✉ 96 Second Avenue, between Fifth and Sixth streets ☎ 212/674-5870 🕐 Mon 5.30–10, Tue–Thu 5.30–11, Fri–Sat 5–11.30, Sun 5–10 ✋ D $42, Wine $30 🚇 Astor Place (6), Eighth Street (N, R) 🚌 M15, M103

MESA GRILL
www.mesagrill.com
When Bobby Flay opened this restaurant in 1991, he introduced New Yorkers to the spices of the Southwest, and the place continues to excite. The red walls recall Sedona rock, the shrimp and fresh corn with black pepper tamale is hot off the grill, and the cactus pear margaritas cool the heat. Follow the cornmeal-crusted oysters and mango *habanero* sauce with 16-spice chicken in cilantro (coriander)-pumpkin seed sauce. Brunches are distinctive as well—it's not everywhere you'll find tequila-smoked-salmon quesadilla.

✚ 142 D12 ✉ 102 Fifth Avenue, between 15th and 16th streets ☎ 212/807-7400 🕐 Mon–Thu 12–2.30, 5.30–10.30, Fri 12–2.30, 5.30–11, Sat 11.30–2.30, 5–11, Sun 11.30–3, 5.30–10.30 ✋ L $30, D $57, Wine $28 🚇 14th Street/Union Square (L, N, Q, R, 4, 5, 6) 🚌 M2, M3, M5, M14

NEGRIL VILLAGE
www.negrilvillage.com
The neo-Caribbean dishes sit wonderfully on the tongue at this sultry restaurant. It's hard to choose between the succulent curried goat, and such specialties as the ackee and the saltfish. Tropical desserts include key lime cheesecake with mango coulis. The downstairs

rum lounge pours an amazing 50 different rums.

✚ 142 D13 ✉ 70 West Third Street, between La Guardia Place and Thompson Street ☎ 212/477-2804 🕐 Mon–Thu 12–12, Fri–Sat noon–3am, Sun 11.30am–midnight ✋ L $22, D $40, Wine $20 🚇 West 4th Street (A, B, C, D, E, F, M) 🚌 M5, M21

NORTH SQUARE
www.northsquareny.com
On the north side of Washington Square Park, this relaxed, bistro-style restaurant features the inventive cooking of chef Yoel Cruz. His Mediterranean-influenced dishes include lobster risotto to start, followed by herb-crusted yellowfin tuna, seared sea scallops or filet mignon au poivre, topped off by butterscotch banana bread pudding or other sublime desserts. The Sunday Jazz Brunch is a treat. The restaurant is in the Washington Square Hotel, a favorite of musicians playing in the Village clubs. Norah Jones worked here as a waitress before her rise to fame.

✚ 142 D13 ✉ 103 Waverly Place at MacDougal Street ☎ 212/254-1200 🕐 Mon–Sat 7.30–11, 12–3.30, 5.30–10.30, Sun 7.30–11, 12–4, 5.30–10 ✋ L $25, D $40, Wine $24 🚇 West 4th Street/ Washington Square (A, B, C, D, E, F, M) 🚌 M1, M2, M3, M5, M8

OTTO ENOTECA PIZZERIA
www.ottopizzeria.com
Mario Batali continues to apply his genius to educating the average American palate to real Italian cuisine and wine. Here, the arena is pizza, which you can have with marinara, or—a better idea—in one of the combinations dreamed up by Mario, such as topped with porcini and taleggio or with tomato, fennel, bottarga (silver mullet roe), pecorino and mozzarella. The wine card is extraordinary, and the gelati are the best in the city, period.

✚ 142 D13 ✉ 1 Fifth Avenue at Eighth Street ☎ 212/995-9559 🕐 Daily 11.30am–midnight ✋ L $24, D $39, Wine $32 🚇 West 4th Street (A, B, C, D, E, F, M) 🚌 M2, M3, M5, M8

LA PALAPA

www.lapalapa.com

At this dark and sultry Mexican, the cooking reveals the complex flavors of *epazote,* cactus pads, avocado leaves and chilies. The balance is always right, whether in the shrimp with red mole sauce, or the baked cod with *guajillo,* garlic and achiote barbecue sauce. Meat dishes are also well spiced. Then there are the extras — pinto beans with smoked bacon and chayotes in spicy cream.

✚ 143 E13 ✉ 77 St. Marks Place, between First and Second avenues ☎ 212/777-2537 🕔 Mon–Fri 12–12, Sat–Sun 11am–midnight ✋ L $25, D $40, Wine $28 🚇 Astor Place (6) 🚌 M8, M15

PARADOU

www.paradounyc.com

A taste of Provence in the Meatpacking District, Paradou is popular with lovers of good hearty French cooking. The garden gives a country feel, and with dishes such as cassoulet, duck *magret* and venison pot-au-feu on the menu, you could almost be in Provence.

✚ 142 B12 ✉ 8 Little West 12th Street, between Ninth Avenue and Washington Street ☎ 212/463-8345 🕔 Mon–Thu 6–11, Fri–Sat 11am–midnight, Sun 11–7 ✋ D $45, Wine $36 🚇 14th Street (A, C, E), Eighth Avenue (L) 🚌 M11, M14A

PASTIS

www.pastisny.com

At Pastis, you could just as easily be in Paris. Every detail rings true: the zinc bar, the smoky mirrors, the tiles and the French ads. Then there are the *plats* (dishes) — onion soup gratinée, croque-monsieur, skate *au beurre noir,* steak and moules frites, and, at breakfast, brioche and egg dishes. Anglophiles can order fish and chips and beans on toast. Wine is served in tumblers. Expect to have to wait for a table.

✚ 142 C12 ✉ 9 Ninth Avenue at Little 12th Street ☎ 212/929-4844 🕔 Mon–Wed 8–11.30, noon–1am, Thu 8–11.30, noon–2am, Fri 8–11.30, noon–3am, Sat 9–4.30, 6–3, Sun 9–4.30, 6–1 ✋ L $35, D $48, Wine $24 🚇 14th Street (A, C, E) 🚌 M11, M14

PEARL OYSTER BAR

www.pearloysterbar.com

The fiercely loyal patrons of this spot with a marble bar don't mind lining up for New England favorites such as oysters, creamy chowder and the fried oyster sandwiches doused in rémoulade sauce. The pièce de résistance is the delicious lobster roll encased in a toasted bun.

✚ 142 D13 ✉ 18 Cornelia Street ☎ 212/691-8211 🕔 Mon–Fri noon–2.30, Mon–Sat 6–11 ✋ L $32, D $44, Wine $28 🚇 West 4th Street (A, B, C, D, E, F, M) 🚌 M5, M20

PERIYALI

www.periyali.com

This was the first authentic Greek restaurant to open in Manhattan, and it has remained a premier Greek destination. The ambience is warm and appealing (white plaster, dark wood beams and attractive displays of appetizers). Everything is carefully prepared, from the fragrant *avgolemono* soup to the grilled lamb chops with fresh rosemary.

✚ 142 D11 ✉ 35 West 20th Street, between Fifth and Sixth avenues ☎ 212/463-7890 🕔 Mon–Fri noon–3, Mon–Thu 5–11, Fri–Sat 5.30–11.30, Sun 5–10 ✋ L $35, D $50, Wine $40 🚇 23rd Street (N, R) 🚌 M2, M3, M5, M7, M23

PIPA

www.pipa-nyc.com

Douglas Rodriguez does Spanish at this lively restaurant, whose name means "great time." You can make a meal of the tapas — succulent fried oysters with banana-and-lentil salad, horseradish aioli and crispy bacon; shrimp with garlic oil and chilies; or sautéed chorizo. Follow up with a rice, meat or fish dish, or perhaps a paella. The white or red sangria are perfect accompaniments, or go for one of the rum drinks.

✚ 143 D12 ✉ ABC Carpet and Home, 38 East 19th Street, between Broadway and Park Avenue South ☎ 212/677-2233 🕔 Mon–Wed 12–5, 5.30–11, Thu–Fri 12–5, 5.30–12, Sat 11–5, 5.30–12, Sun 11–5, 5.30–10.30 ✋ L $24, D $44, Wine $32 🚇 Fourth Street/Union Square (L, N, Q, R, 4, 5, 6) 🚌 M1, M2, M3, M5

PRUNE

www.prunerestaurant.com

Everything is meticulously prepared and beautifully presented at this small, idiosyncratic restaurant. Dinner entrées might include roast duck with green olives, or whole grilled fish with fennel oil and salt. Vegetable accompaniments include roast beets and bitter greens salad with oil and lemon juice.

✚ 143 E13 ✉ 54 East First Street, between First and Second avenues ☎ 212/677-6221 🕔 Mon–Fri 11.30–3.30, 5.30–11, Sat–Sun 10–3.30, 5.30–11 ✋ L $24, D $55, Wine $32 🚇 Lower East Side/Second Avenue (F) 🚌 M15, M21

THE RED CAT

www.theredcat.com

A downtown art crowd packs this vivacious bistro in a narrow crimson room illuminated by large Moroccan lanterns. The contemporary kitchen puts plenty of flavor into its creations — take, for example, the crisp skate wing in caper brown butter, or the calves' liver au poivre. Tasty Parmesan fries spiked with mustard aioli are one of the most popular side orders. Desserts are eclectic but equally delicious. The wine list is carefully chosen.

✚ 142 B11 ✉ 227 Tenth Avenue, between West 23rd and 24th streets ☎ 212/242-1122 🕔 Tue–Sat 12–2.30, Mon–Thu 5–11, Fri–Sat 5–12, Sun 5–10 ✋ L $30, D $55, Wine $28 🚇 23rd Street (C, E) 🚌 M11, M23

SPICE MARKET

www.jean-georges.com

Beguiling and theatrical are the only words to describe this Southeast Asian space swathed in teak, lit by silk lanterns and dotted with palm trees. It's Jean-Georges Vongerichten's stage for exciting spicy street food. Roll the spring rolls in lettuce with fresh mint and cilantro (coriander) and dip them in sweet lime and rice vinegar broth, sample the fiery pork vindaloo or the black pepper shrimp with pineapple.

✚ 142 C12 ✉ 403 West 13th Street at Ninth Avenue ☎ 212/675-2322

🕐 Sun–Wed 12–12, Thu–Sat noon–1am
✋ L $30, D $45, Wine $35 🚇 14th Street
(A, C, E, L) 🚌 M11

THE SPOTTED PIG

www.thespottedpig.com

Chef April Bloomfeld draws crowds
at this small "gastro pub." She
comes most recently from London's
River Café and delivers some gutsy
cuisine—veal kidneys, lamb with
salsa verde, roast cod with parsley
sauce and her beloved *gnudi*
(gnocchi with sheep's milk ricotta
and brown butter and sage).

➕ 142 C13 ✉ 314 West 11th Street
at Greenwich Street ☎ 212/620-0393
🕐 Mon–Fri noon–2am, Sat–Sun
11am–2am ✋ L $25, D $50, Wine $32
🚇 Christopher Street (1), 14th Street (A, C,
E, L) 🚌 M11, M20

STRIP HOUSE

www.striphouse.com

Recalling a 19th-century bordello
with its tufted leather banquettes
and swathe of velvet, this place
serves up juicy succulent beef,
notably the New York strip. Other
cuts are available along with a
couple of fish dishes, wild striped
bass with artichokes, pancetta and
basil sauce, for example.

➕ 142 D12 ✉ 13 East 12th Street,
between Fifth Avenue and University Place
☎ 212/328-0000 🕐 Mon–Sat 5–11.15,
Sun 5–10 ✋ D $65, Wine $35 🚇 14th
Street/Union Square (L, N, Q, R, 4, 5, 6)
🚌 M2, M3, M5

SUEÑOS

www.suenosnyc.com

The Mexican cooking with a
contemporary twist is hailed by
the *New York Times* as the most
exciting Mexican food in the city.
The menu features familiar dishes,
tortillas, quesadillas and guacamole,
but re-invented. Entrées include
tamarind-glazed steak.

➕ 142 C12 ✉ 311 West 17th Street,
between Eighth and Ninth avenues
☎ 212/243-1333 🕐 Tue–Thu 5–11,
Fri–Sat 5–midnight, Sun 5–10 ✋ D $40,
3-course prix fixe $30, Wine $26 🚇 14th
Street (A, C, E), Eighth Avenue (L) 🚌 M11,
M14D, M20

TAMARIND

www.tamarinde22.com

The dining room of this Indian
restaurant is sleek and comfortable
(although noisy), and the wine list
expansive. The flavor of tamarind
infuses many dishes, such as
shrimp cooked in coconut sauce
flavored with curry leaves and
smoked tamarind, but there are
other flavors as well—the she-crab
soup with sweet spices, ginger and
saffron is another winner. The lamb
vindaloo is authentically spiced, as
are many of the vegetarian dishes.
Some are refreshingly new—*bhindi
do piazza*, which is okra-flavored
with brown onions and dried
mango, for example. Even the
desserts shine.

➕ 143 D11 ✉ 41–43 East 22nd Street,
between Broadway and Park Avenue South
☎ 212/674-7400 🕐 Daily 11.30–3, Sun–
Thu 5.30–11.30, Fri–Sat 11.30–midnight
✋ L $24, D $40, Wine $30 🚇 23rd Street
(N, R), 23rd Street (6) 🚌 M1, M2, M3,
M5, M23

UNION SQUARE CAFÉ

www.unionsquarecafe.com

Led by chefs Michael Romano
and Carmen Quagliata, the menu
features a fusion of American and
Italian cuisine. The compositions
include spaghettini with flaked
halibut in a garlic, chili and wine

Below *A burger bar in Downtown*

sauce, or pan-roasted chicken
with asparagus bread pudding and
mushrooms. Weekly classics may
include filet mignon of tuna or pan-
roasted quail. For dessert there is
warm rustic apple crostata with sour
cream ice cream, or the signature
warm banana tart with vanilla ice
cream and macadamia brittle.

➕ 142 D12 ✉ 21 East 16th Street,
between Fifth Avenue and Union Square
West ☎ 212/243-4020 🕐 Daily noon–2,
Mon–Thu 5.30–10, Fri–Sun 5.30–11
✋ L $42, D $62, Wine $34 🚇 14th Street/
Union Square (L, N, Q, R, 4, 5, 6)
🚌 M2, M3, M5, M14

VERITAS

www.veritas-nyc.com

With 3,200 selections, Veritas has
the most comprehensive wine list
in the city. And the kitchen offers
some gutsy cuisine to go with
the wines. Expect pepper-crusted
venison with Armagnac or juniper,
or braised veal in Barolo reduction.
Even a dish like red snapper brings
a surprise—here it arrives in Thai
red curry *nage*. Hot chocolate
and doughnuts is the magnificent
signature dessert.

➕ 143 D11 ✉ 43 East 20th Street,
between Broadway and Park Avenue South
☎ 212/353-3700 🕐 Daily 5–12 ✋ D $65,
Wine $39 🚇 23rd Street (N, R, 6) 🚌 M1,
M2, M3, M5, M23

PRICES AND SYMBOLS

Prices are the lowest and highest for a double room for one night. Breakfast is included unless noted otherwise. All the hotels listed accept credit cards unless otherwise stated. Note that rates vary widely throughout the year.

For a key to the symbols, ▷ 2.

ABINGDON GUEST HOUSE

www.abingdonguesthouse.com
Located in two historic three-story red-brick town houses above a coffee shop in Greenwich Village, the guest house is unmarked. The nine rooms are individually decorated and well furnished with antiques. Amenities include private bath (with hairdryer), cable TV and free WiFi Internet access. The patio garden is a bonus.

✚ 142 C12 ✉ 21 Eighth Avenue at West 12th Street, 10014 ☎ 212/243-5384 🖐 $209–$279 (minimum stay 2 nights weekdays, 3 nights weekends) ❶ 9 🚇 14th Street (A, C, E), Christopher Street/Sheridan Square (1) 🚌 M20, M14

CHELSEA

www.hotelchelsea.com
Many renowned artists and bohemians have stayed or lived here since the Chelsea opened in 1884, including Mark Twain and Dylan Thomas. The rooms vary in size and décor. Serena's, the bar opened by Serena Bass, attracts a Brit-pack crowd.

✚ 142 C11 ✉ 222 West 23rd Street, between Seventh and Eighth avenues, 10011 ☎ 212/243-3700 🖐 From $139, suites from $269 ❶ 375 rooms 🚇 23rd Street (C, E, 1) 🚌 M20, M23

CHELSEA LODGE

www.chelsealodge.com
In very fashionable Chelsea, this small hotel occupies a handsome red-brick town house, which has been lovingly restored by the owners. The rooms are decorated in plain American country style with patterned wallpaper and eclectic furnishings. Most have hardwood floors and small TVs, plus sink and shower. The toilet is in the hall.

✚ 142 C11 ✉ 318 West 20th Street, between Eighth and Ninth avenues, 10001 ☎ 212/243-4499 🖐 $134 ❶ 22 🚇 23rd Street (C, E) 🚌 M11, M20

GERSHWIN

www.gershwinhotel.com
The Gershwin attracts young budget travelers, who stay in plain doubles, though more comfortable

conventional rooms and suites are also available. Rooms have cable TV and phone. On weekends, live bands play in the Gallery Lounge.
🚊 142 D11 ✉ 7 East 27th Street, between Fifth and Madison avenues, 10016 ☎ 212/545-8000 ✋ $119, suite from $249, dorm for two $53, women only dorm $43, coed dorm $39 🚹 130 rooms, 6 suites 🚇 28th Street (N, R) 🚌 M2, M3

GIRAFFE
www.hotelgiraffe.com
A small boutique hotel in the Flatiron neighborhood evokes the 1920s and 1930s. Each floor has only seven rooms, decorated in glamorous colors and materials. Many have balconies. There is an on-premises restaurant, plus access to a nearby health club.
🚊 143 E11 ✉ 365 Park Avenue South, between 26th and 27th streets, 10016 ☎ 212/685-7700 ✋ $219–$559, suite from $389, including wine and cheese (weekday evenings) 🚹 51 rooms, 21 suites 🚇 23rd Street (6) 🚌 M1

HOTEL GANSEVOORT
www.hotelgansevoort.com
This Meatpacking District hotel adopts South Beach style with such dramatic features as heated rooftop pool, kaleidoscopic illuminated glass columns that change color and mood, and a Japanese restaurant with a fetching outdoor courtyard bar-dining area. Rooms are decorated in minimalist style and hues, and feature the latest amenities—plasma TVs and complimentary WiFi. A spa and fitness center occupy a lower level.
🚊 142 C12 ✉ 18 Ninth Avenue at 13th Street, 10014 ☎ 212/206-6700 ✋ Doubles from $395, suite from $675 🚹 167 rooms, 20 suites 🏊 🍽 🚇 14th Street (A, C, E) 🚌 M11

INN AT IRVING PLACE
www.innatirving.com
These two 1834 town houses have plenty of ersatz atmosphere. Rooms have fireplaces and four-poster beds

dressed with Frette linens, plus antique reproductions. Amenities include two-line telephones with data port, VCRs and CD players. Guests sit on tufted chairs around the fireplaces in Lady Mendl's at afternoon tea. There is a lounge.
🚊 142 E12 ✉ 56 Irving Place, between East 17th and 18th streets, 10003 ☎ 212/533-4600 ✋ $445–$645 🚹 12 rooms and suites 🚇 14th Street/Union Square (L, N, Q, R, 4, 5, 6) 🚌 M1, M2, M3, M14

THE INN ON 23RD
www.innon23rd.com
If you prefer a bed-and-breakfast, then this inn in a 19th-century town house (with an elevator) has much to offer. The Fisherman family has furnished it with heirlooms and eclectic pieces. The rooms have such modern amenities as dual-line phone (local calls are free). Bathrooms are small. Guest amenities include a second-floor library and an honor bar with liquor, wine and beer, plus a microwave.
🚊 142 C11 ✉ 131 West 23rd Street, between Sixth and Seventh avenues, 10011 ☎ 212/463-0330 ✋ $219–$269, suite from $329 🚹 14 🚇 23rd Street (F, M, 1) 🚌 M5, M7, M20, M23

LARCHMONT
www.larchmonthotel.com
This is a great place on an extra-quiet side street in Greenwich Village. It has plenty of character and appeals to travelers who don't mind shared bathrooms (bathrobe and slippers provided). The rooms are attractive, ultra clean and well equipped with air conditioning, cable TV and telephone.
🚊 142 D12 ✉ 27 West 11th Street, between Fifth and Sixth avenues, 10011 ☎ 212/989-9333 ✋ $90–$249 🚹 58 🚇 14th Street (F, M), Sixth Avenue (L) 🚌 M2, M3, M5, M8

MARCEL
www.hotelmarcelnewyork.com
Modern and chic, the recent transformation of the Marcel presents a sophisticated, hip style throughout. Graphic prints

and animal patterns set off the comfortable, ultramodern guest rooms that feature custom designed beds with down comforters and Frette linens, marble bathrooms, LCD flat-screen TVs and iPod docking stations. Restaurant Inoteca features Northern Italian cuisine and a European-style breakfast buffet is available daily.
🚊 143 E11 ✉ 201 East 24th Street, between Second and Third avenues, 10011 ☎ 212/696-3800 ✋ $249–$650 🚹 135 rooms and suites 🚇 23rd Street (6) 🚌 M15, M23, M101, M102, M103

MARITIME HOTEL
www.themaritimehotel.com
In Chelsea and close to nightlife central, the Meatpacking District, this hotel was formerly the headquarters of the Maritime Union. The rooms are small and cabin-like with teak paneling and porthole windows. Furnishings are modern and the rooms feature the latest technology—flat-panel TVs and high-speed internet access. It has two attention-grabbing restaurants. Matsura is a dramatic basement supper-club style Japanese restaurant; there's also a Mediterranean café with a large outdoor terrace garden landscaped with magnolia trees and lily pond.
🚊 142 C12 ✉ 363 West 16th Street at Ninth Avenue, 10011 ☎ 212/242-4300 ✋ $265–$400 🚹 121 rooms, 5 suites 🚇 14th Street (A, C, E) 🚌 M11

WASHINGTON SQUARE
www.washingtonsquarehotel.com
On the northwest corner of Washington Square Park, this small hotel has a casual bohemian air. The rooms are stylishly chic, decorated with old photos of movie stars, and the hotel has had many illustrious guests including Bob Dylan, Joan Baez and Bill Cosby. Facilities include an attractive restaurant-lounge (with occasional jazz).
🚊 142 D13 ✉ 103 Waverly Place, between Fifth and Sixth avenues, 10011 ☎ 212/777-9515 ✋ $249–$400 🚹 150 🍽 🚇 West 4th Street (A, B, C, D, E, F, M) 🚌 M5, M8

West 36th Street
West 35th Street
West 34th Street
West 33rd Street
West 31st Street
West 30th Street
West 29th Street
West 28th Street
West 27th Street
West 26th Street
West 25th Street
West 24th Street
West 23rd Street
West 22nd Street
West 21st Street
West 20th Street
West 19th Street
West 18th Street
West 17th Street
West 16th Street
West 15th Street

West 36th Street
West 35th Street
WEST 34th STREET
West 33rd Street
West 32nd Street
West 31st Street
West 30th Street
West 29th Street
West 28th Street
West 27th Street
West 26th Street
West 25th Street
West 24th Street
West 23rd Street
West 22nd Street
West 21st Street
West 20th Street
West 19th Street
West 18th Street
West 17th Street
West 16th Street

East 36th Street
East 35th Street
EAST 34th STREET

Macy's
34th Street Penn Station
34th Street Penn Station
34th Street Herald Square
Empire State Building
Madison Square Garden
Pennsylvania Station

12TH AVENUE
11th AVENUE
10TH AVENUE
9TH AVENUE
8TH AVENUE
7TH AVENUE
Avenue of the Americas (6th Avenue)
5th

Chelsea Park
Chelsea Waterside Park
Chelsea Art Museum

Little Church Around the Corn
Gershwin
Inn on 23rd Street
Metropolitan Insurance Tow
Flatiron Building
Madison Square Park

Red Cat
Chelsea
Chelsea

CHELSEA

Periyali
Gramercy Tavern
Devi
Union Square Café
Mesa Grill

Chelsea Lodge
Sueños
Maritime Hotel

Crema Restaurante
Rubin Museum of Art

UNION SQUA
WEST 14TH STREET

9A

Spice Market
Hotel Gansevoort
Paradou
Pastis
Corner Bistro
Abingdon Guest House
Spotted Pig

GREENWICH VILLAGE

Strip House
Forbes Magazine Galleries
Larchmont
Gotham Bar & Grill

Jefferson Market Library

Washington Square North
Otto Enoteca Pizzeria
Babbo
Blue Hill
Manatus
Tangerine
Annisa
Kesté Pizzeria
John's Pizzeria
Pearl Oyster Bar
Negri Villa

Church of St Luke-in-the-Fields
House of Oldies Rare Records

Washington Square Park

Hudson

New York City Fire Museum

American Numismatic Society

0   250 m
0   250 yds

East 36th Street
East 35th Street
East 34th Street
East 33rd Street
East 30th Street
East 29th Street
East 28th Street

Blue
Smoke

Giraffe Dos Caminos

East 27th Street
East 26th Street
East 25th Street

Marcel

East 24th Street

Eleven
Madison Park

East 23rd Street

Tamarind

**GRAMERCY PARK
HISTORIC DISTRICT**

Gramercy Park North

East 22nd Street

ritas

Gramercy Park South

East 21st Street
East 20th Street

Craft and
Craftbar

Block Beautiful

East 19th Street
East 18th Street

Pipa

Casa Mono

Inn at
Irving Place

East 17th Street
East 16th Street
East 15th Street

Union
Square

Stuyvesant
Square

Stuyvesant
Oval

Stuyvesant
Walk

East 16th
Street

East 15th Street

EAST 14TH STREET   **EAST 14TH STREET SERVICE DRIVE**   **EAST 14TH STREET**

East 13th Street

Grace
Church

Angelica Kitchen

St Mark's Church
-in-the-Bowery

East 12th Street
East 11th Street

Gnocco

East 10th Street

Holy Basil

East 9th Street

I Coppi

La
Palapa

Saint Marks Place

EAST VILLAGE

Tompkins
Square Park

East 8th Street
East 7th Street

NOHO

Ukrainian
Museum

Mermaid
Inn

Banjara

East 6th Street
East 5th Street

East 5th Walk

Merchant's
House Museum

East 4th Street

East 4th Walk

Bond St

East 3rd Street
East 2nd Street

Prune

East 1st Street

EAST HOUSTON STREET

Hamilton
Fish Park

East Houston Street

**Broadway –
Lafayette
Street**

St Patrick's
Old Cathedral

New Museum of
Contemporary Art

LITTLE ITALY

Children's Museum
of the Arts

Museum of Chinese
in America

**LOWER
EAST SIDE**

Lower East Side
Tenement Museum

Seward
Park

Corlears
Hook
Park

143

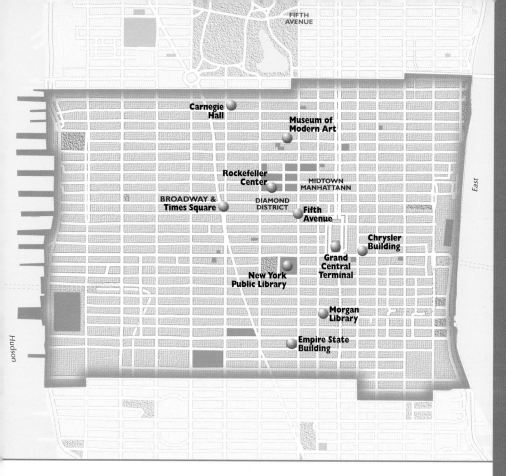

Map labels:
- FIFTH AVENUE
- Carnegie Hall
- Museum of Modern Art
- Rockefeller Center
- MIDTOWN MANHATTANN
- BROADWAY & Times Square
- DIAMOND DISTRICT
- Fifth Avenue
- Chrysler Building
- Grand Central Terminal
- New York Public Library
- Morgan Library
- Empire State Building
- East
- Hudson

MIDTOWN

The Midtown skyline boasts many of New York City's finest towers and spires. Spectacular modern skyscrapers, ranging from the Citigroup Center wedge to the tall Trump Tower and the gleaming United Nations Building, are accompanied by the art deco spires of the Empire State Building and the Chrysler Building.

New York's famous entertainment intersection, Times Square, is well known for the crystal ball that drops at midnight every New Year's Eve. And for the nightly drama as throngs of theatergoers and visitors move beneath the blazing neon billboards and electronic advertisements.

The Empire State Building is New York's most famous skyscraper, and a visit to the 86th Floor Observatory presents amazing views of Manhattan. At night the tower is bathed in light, and on some nights colored lights denote special dates, including red for Valentine's Day and green for St. Patrick's Day.

Fifth Avenue from the Empire State Building north is a paradise for shoppers of luxury merchandise. Tiffany & Co. and Cartier for jewelry, department stores Saks Fifth Avenue and Bergdorf Goodman, and the wonderful FAO Schwarz toy store are just a few examples of the many big name offerings.

Lovers of art and architecture have many choices in Midtown, beginning with Grand Central Terminal, the city's magnificent Beaux Arts train station. Here high-arched windows flood the main concourse with natural light and, overhead, the vaulted ceiling is decorated with a mural of constellations. Another Beaux Arts building, the marble New York Library, has a vast, richly paneled cathedral-like reading room that is almost two blocks long. For modern art from the late 19th century to the present, the Museum of Modern Art displays famous paintings by noted artists, including Van Gogh, Cézanne and Picasso, and sculpture in the Abby Aldrich Rockefeller Sculpture Garden.

West 63rd Street
HIGHWAY 9A
West End Avenue
West 62nd Street
Amsterdam Avenue
Lincoln Center
West 65th Street
Central Park West
BROADWAY

West 61st Street
West 62nd Street
West Drive

West 61st Street
Columbus Avenue
Museum of Biblical Art

⑦

West 60th Street

West 59th Street
59th Street Columbus Circle
COLUMBUS CIRCLE
Central

12th Av
West 58th Street
57th Street

WEST 57TH STREET

12th Avenue
11th Avenue
West 56th Street
10th Avenue
West 55th Street
9th Avenue
West 54th Street
8th Avenue
BROADWAY
7th Avenue
Carnegie Hall

⑧
De Witt Clinton Park
West 53rd Street
West 54th Street
7th Avenue

12th Avenue
West 52nd Street

West 51st Street

West 50th Street

12th
West 49th Street
50th Street
50th Street
49th Street

West 48th Street

West 47th Street

West 46th Street
BROADWAY

Hudson
West 46th Street
Intrepid Sea, Air and Space Museum
West 45th Street
10th AVENUE
9th Avenue

⑨
9A
West 44th Street
8th Avenue
Times Square

11th Avenue
West 43rd Street

WEST 42ND STREET
Holy Cross Church
Reuters Building
Times Square 42nd Street

West 41st Street
42nd Street Port Authority Bus Terminal
New Amsterdam Theater

West 40th Street

HIGHWAY 495
West 39th Street
DYER AVENUE
8TH AVENUE
FASHION

West 38th Street

Jacob K Javits Convention Center
West 37th Street

West 36th Street
AVENUE

West 35th Street
Macy

West 34th Street
34th Street Penn Station
34th Street Penn Station

⑩
West 33rd Street
Madison Square Garden
Pennsylvania Station

0   250 m
0   250 yds
West 31st Street

11th Avenue
West 30th Street

West 29th Street
10th AVENUE
9TH AVENUE
8TH AVENUE
7TH AVENUE
28th Street

West 28th Street

12th AVENUE
West 27th Street
Chelsea Park

⑪

A   West 26th Street   B   C

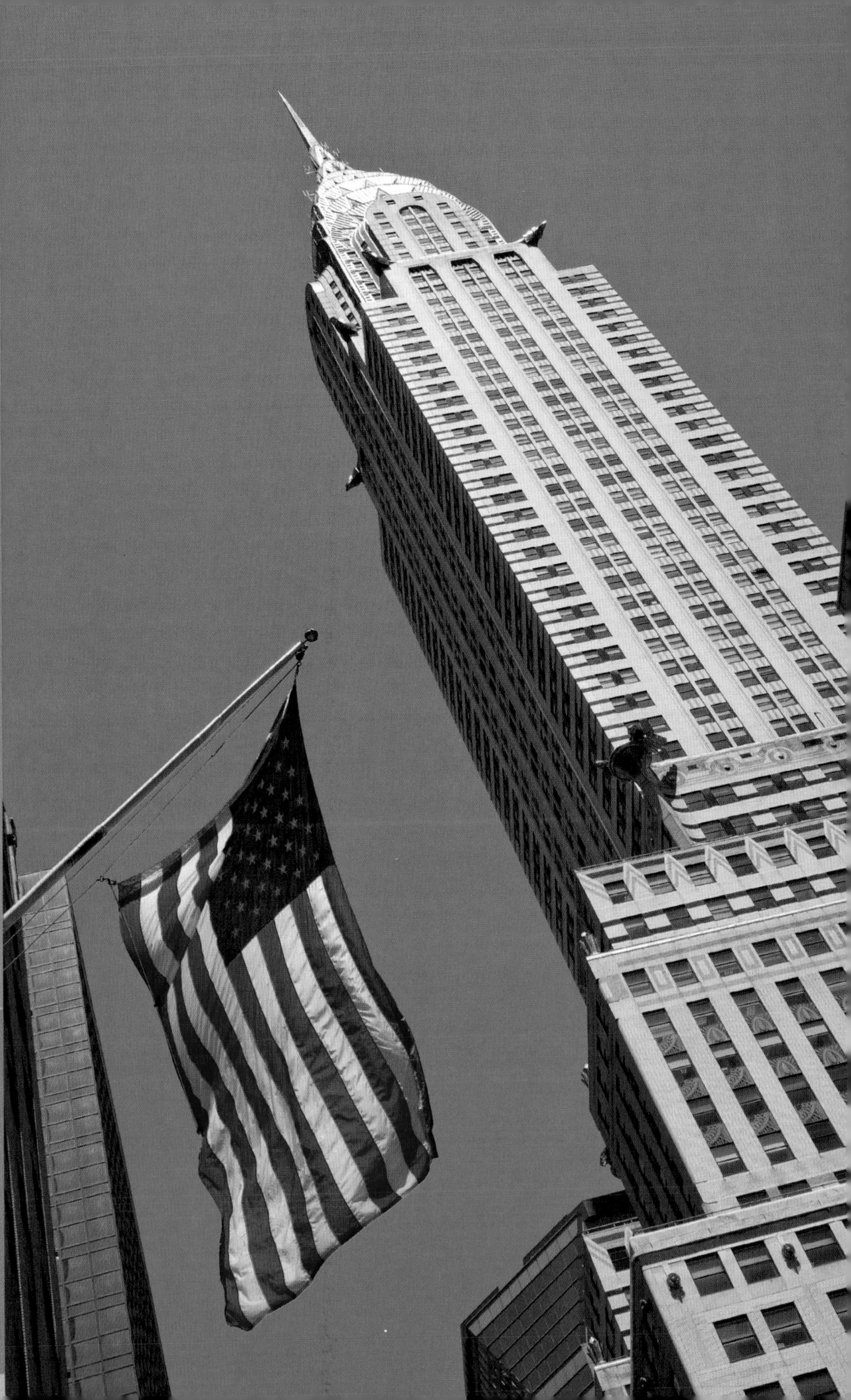

CHRYSLER BUILDING

The Chrysler Building's diamond-honed Enduro KA-2 steel is as incandescent today as it was in 1929. From the street, look up at the spire with its pattern of 30 radiating triangular windows. Note the 9ft (3m) pineapples on the spire and the mighty, gargoyle-like eagle heads at the corners of the building. Around the 30th floor, a brick frieze depicts hubcaps. Go inside to view the lobby's sumptuous walls of African marble and steel and the Parisian-style elevators. The elaborate ceiling was painted by Edward Trumbull.

Walter Chrysler, the third-biggest automobile manufacturer in America, spent $2 million of his own money to buy the skyscraper's site. Chrysler had been an automobile mechanic for most of his life and had very little formal education, but when it came to machines he was a genius. After saving General Motors a fortune with his new techniques, he moved to New York from Chicago at the age of 45. Already earning a million dollars a year, he produced his first line of Chryslers in January 1924. They appealed to the rich and were a symbol of wealth and luxury—they were the right product for the booming 1920s. For Chrysler, building a skyscraper more fantastic than anything anyone had ever seen was a challenge he could not resist.

THE TALLEST BUILDING IN THE WORLD

In late 1929, architect William Van Alen watched anxiously as the spire was raised above the 77-story structure to make it, at 1,048ft (320m), the world's tallest building, beating the Bank of the Manhattan Company Building at 40 Wall Street. It held the title for only a short time. Opened on May 1, 1931, the 1,250ft (381m) Empire State Building surpassed it. Securing an object at such a height had never been done before, and the job had been kept so secret that no reporters were around when it actually happened—probably on October 24, 1929, the day before the Wall Street Crash. The spire was as daring as it was ingenious and took the city by surprise. Many thought the building a crass piece of architectural advertising; today it is a symbol of an age when anything was possible.

In 1978, the Chrysler Building was designated a New York City Landmark. In 1997, Tishman Speyer Properties took it over and restored the art deco lobby. The lancet crown was first switched on in 1981.

INFORMATION

147 E9 405 Lexington Avenue at 42nd Street Mon–Fri 8–6 4, 5, 6, 7, S M42, M101, M102, M103

Above *New York's most stunning art deco skyscraper has a magnificent lobby with walls of African marble and steel*
Opposite *With its shining stainless-steel spire, the Chrysler Building is an icon*

REGIONS MIDTOWN • SIGHTS

www.carnegiehall.org

146 C8 ✉ 154 West 57th Street at Seventh Avenue, 10019 ☎ 212/247-7800 ③ For performance schedule, check website or phone 212/903-9765 ✋ Check website or phone 212/247-7800 ☞ One-hour tours Oct–Jun Mon–Fri 11.30am, 2pm, 3pm, Sat 11.30, 12.30, Sun 12.30 when concert schedule permits; adult $10, child (under 12) $4 N, Q, R M5, M7, M10, M20, M57 🍴 ⌨

CARNEGIE HALL

This superb Italian-Renaissance-inspired concert hall took seven years to build, opening in 1891. With 2,804 seats and excellent acoustics, it remains one of New York's most highly prized music centers. The Rose Museum on the second floor (mid-Sep to end Jun daily 11–4.30 and available to concert patrons in the evenings; free) has archival treasures relating to the history of the building and famous figures who have performed here.

EARLY HISTORY

Late 19th-century New York was an important place but it did not have a concert hall. When the steel magnate Andrew Carnegie heard this, he put up the $2 million needed to construct the building, on the condition that the city provide the land on which to build it: at that time New York was a stretch of vacant lots, coal yards and row houses. Chief architect William B. Tuthill was a gifted amateur cellist, and was determined to get the acoustics right. Tchaikovsky opened the hall, making his American conducting debut in 1891. In the years since, the world's greatest musicians, including Rachmaninov, Horowitz, Stravinsky, Ravel and George Gershwin, have all performed here. The New York Philharmonic orchestra made this its home until moving to the Lincoln Center (▷ 218–219) on the Upper West Side in 1962.

The second building, added in 1894, housed famous musicians, architects, dancing classes and agencies. In 1894 the green mansard roof of the main building was removed to build the studio floor. There is a small recital hall within the original building and an elegant auditorium, which was a movie theater until 1997.

THE HALL TODAY

In the 1960s, Carnegie Hall was saved from demolition largely by violinist Isaac Stern. So it is for good reason that the main auditorium is named after him. The Weill Recital Hall features singers and chamber groups; Zankel Hall offers contemporary innovative programming. Between 1981 and 1990, Carnegie Hall underwent a $50-million renovation. The modern 60-story office tower next door, sensitively designed by César Pelli, was built in 1990.

Below *The outstanding acoustics of this famous concert hall attract the world's most gifted musicians*

INTREPID SEA, AIR & SPACE MUSEUM

www.intrepidmuseum.org

The veteran aircraft carrier *Intrepid*, built in 1943, makes a fascinating museum. It is 898ft (274m) long, weighs 42,000 tons, and had a crew of 3,500. On the Flight Deck you can inspect aircraft, including a Lockheed A-12 Blackbird, a Russian MIG and a Cobra helicopter. You can tour the destroyer *Edson* and the submarine *Growler*; take a seven-minute SR-2 flight simulator ride; and rent a two-hour audiotour. The museum reopened in 2008 following restoration and painting of *Intrepid,* refurbishment of the 16 aircraft onboard, rebuilding of Pier 86 and completion of the Intrepid Sea, Air & Space Museum. The Hangar Deck exhibits have been redesigned and new exhibits have been added, including an interactive wind tunnel.

✛ 146 A9 ✉ Hudson River Pier 86, west end of 46th Street, 10036 ☎ 212/245-0072 🕐 Apr–Oct Mon–Fri 10–5, Sat–Sun 10–6; Nov–Mar Tue–Sun 10–5 🖐 Adult $24, child (7–17) $19, child (3–6) $12, under 2/those on active duty with ID free 🚈 A, C, E 🚌 M34, M42, M50 👆 Free tours

Above *Exterior of the Daily News Building*
Below *Intrepid Sea, Air & Space Museum*

CHRYSLER BUILDING
▷ 148–149.

DAILY NEWS BUILDING

Founder of the *Daily News*, James Patterson, commissioned this modernist steel-and-concrete song of praise to journalism in 1925. It was one of the first skyscrapers in New York not built in Gothic style. On the first floor, outside and in, abstract art deco ornamentation contrasts with the modernist strips on the upper facade. Inside, the lobby is still mostly original. Note the revolving globe, 12ft (3.5m) in diameter; the frieze representing the early days of the paper; and the clock that gives the time in 17 time zones. The floor is laid out like a giant compass. In 1995, the *Daily News* moved out and the building was renamed the News Building.

✛ 147 E9 ✉ 220 East 42nd Street, between Second and Third avenues, 10036 🕐 Daily 9–5, lobby only 🚈 4, 5, 6, 7 🚌 M42, M103

EMPIRE STATE BUILDING
▷ 152–154.

GRAND CENTRAL TERMINAL
▷ 156–157.

INTERNATIONAL CENTER OF PHOTOGRAPHY

www.icp.org

In the heart of Midtown Manhattan, the ICP is both a school and a museum. The permanent collection has 60,000 photographs ranging from old daguerreotypes to iris prints, mainly from American and European reportage and documentation from the 1930s to the present. There are photographs by Henri Cartier-Bresson, Elliott Erwitt and Harold Edgerton, along with 13,000 original prints by Weegee, who photographed crime scenes and New York nightlife in the 1930s and 1940s.

✛ 147 D9 ✉ 1133 Avenue of the Americas at 43rd Street, 10036 ☎ 212/857-0000 🕐 Tue–Wed 10–6, Thu–Fri 10–8,

INTRODUCTION

In 1827, William B. Astor bought the farm where the Empire State Building now stands for $20,500, and in 1897 the first Waldorf-Astoria hotel was constructed. In 1928 the hotel was sold for $20 million and demolished to make way for the present structure. Excavation began in 1930. The developer was General Motors' vice-president, John Jacob Raskob, who wanted to create the world's tallest structure as quickly as possible. As a result, designs decorating the limestone facade and the chromium-steel windows were machine-stamped. Completed in 1931, and $5 million under budget, the Empire State Building replaced the Chrysler Building as the world's tallest building and held this title until surpassed by the World Trade Center in 1971. Since 9/11 it has again become the tallest building in New York City, although the new One World Trade Center building (▷ 87), currently under construction, will be taller.

The Depression and then World War II put an end to the city's prosperity and much of its office space stood vacant. The Empire State Building was dubbed the Empty State Building. However, the Observatory was so popular that the income from admission charges paid the taxes on the building. In 1933 the thriller *King Kong* was released and the Empire State Building became a movie star. Concerns about the stability of the building were put to rest on July 28, 1945, when a US Army B-25 bomber crashed into the 78th and 79th floors, killing 13 people and causing extensive damage.

The main entrance is on Fifth Avenue, then you pass through a security checkpoint. There is no coat check (cloakroom). If you have not purchased a ticket in advance, take the escalator or elevator to the Concourse level and the Observatory ticket office. Signs indicate the waiting time and visibility. After buying your tickets, go back up the escalator to the main floor and follow the signs to the Observatory elevators on the second floor. Elevators let you out on the 80th floor, where staff direct you to the Tower elevator to the 86th floor. Viewing areas are indoors and outdoors.

INFORMATION

www.esbnyc.com

⊞ 147 D10 ✉ 350 Fifth Avenue, at East 34th Street, 10118 ☎ 212/736-3100 🕔 Daily 8am–2am, last elevator ascends at 1.15am 💰 Adult $20, child (12–17) $18, child (6–11) $15, under 5s free, military in uniform free. 102nd Floor Observatory $17 extra 🚇 6 to 33rd Street or B, D, F, M, N, Q, R, to 34th Street/ Herald Square 🚌 M1, M2, M3, M4, M16, M34 🎧 Observatory audiotour $8, corresponds to signs on the observation deck so you know exactly what buildings you are seeing 🍴 🏛

Above *Millions of visitors a year go up to the 86th Floor Observatory for spectacular panoramas of the great metropolis*
Opposite *This New York City icon is the most famous skyscraper in the world*

TIPS

» To avoid waiting in line for tickets, buy them online, or in advance at the NYC & Company Visitor Center (tel 212/484-1222) at 810 Seventh Avenue between 52nd and 53rd streets.

» Come on a clear day and bring some quarters for the binoculars outside.

» The elevators carry only 16 people at a time, so be patient.

» Dusk is a popular time, so buy a ticket in advance if you can. Starry nights are magical and you can stay until closing time. There is no time limit on your visit.

» The Express Pass ($45) puts you first in each of the lines for security, tickets and elevators.

STATISTICS

» The Empire State Building weighs 365,000 tons; took 7 million man-hours to build; and is made up of 60,000 tons of steel, 2.5 million feet (760,000m) of electrical wire, 10 million bricks, 62 miles (100km) of water pipes, 6,500 windows, 72 elevators, 7 miles (11km) of elevator shafts, 1,860 steps, and a foundation that extends 55ft (17m) below street level.

» The purchase price for the land, the site of the old Waldorf-Astoria Hotel, was $15 million; construction costs were $25 million. Construction time was an amazing 14 months. The building opened on May 1, 1931.

» With 102 stories, the Empire State Building stands 1,454ft (449m) tall, including the pinnacle. Eighty-six stories are usable office space. The Observation Tower is 16 stories.

» The TV antenna, installed in 1985, is 22 stories high.

» More than 3.8 million visitors ascend annually. The stupendous 360-degree view extends for around 80 miles (130km) on a clear day.

» The Fleet Empire State Building Run-Up Race, a New York Road Runners Club event, was first run in 1978 and is now held annually in February. Competitors run up 1,567 steps. The current record is 9 minutes 33 seconds.

WHAT TO SEE

FIFTH AVENUE LOBBY

Interesting exhibits show off memorabilia from New York's museums, galleries and artists. The art deco lobby is exceptional, with floor-to-ceiling marble walls obtained from quarries in France, Germany, Italy and Belgium, and a dazzling metal relief sculpture of the building.

34TH-STREET LOBBY

Eight huge color panels by artists Roy Sparkia and Renee Nemerov depict the Seven Wonders of the Ancient World and the eighth wonder from the modern world. The tallest Wonder of the Ancient World is the 600ft (183m) Lighthouse of Pharos.

CONCOURSE LEVEL

In addition to the Observatory ticket office, there is a collection of photographs of famous people who have visited the Empire State Building, including Queen Elizabeth II and Fidel Castro.

SECOND FLOOR

Special exhibits about New York City and its museums, cultural institutions and tourist attractions are on this floor. NY SKYRIDE (tel 212/279-9777; www. skyride.com; daily 8am–10pm; adult $29, child (6–12) $19, under 6s free) gives a thrilling simulated tour of the city via the same simulator hardware that is used to train 747 commercial pilots.

86TH FLOOR OBSERVATORY

The most popular observation deck, the 86th floor has an outdoor deck without glass walls. Here the wind blows and the view on a clear day encompasses an 80-mile (130km) sweep with a magnificent panoramic view of the city. On the outside deck you can get close-up views of the surrounding buildings and area using the high-powered binoculars. There is also an indoor, enclosed deck, which is useful if it's raining.

102ND FLOOR OBSERVATORY

The highest observation deck on the 102nd floor reopened in November 2005. Separate admission tickets must be bought at the Observatory ticket office on the second floor, at an additional cost. The view is much the same as from the 86th-floor deck, and although this deck is smaller the vantage point is much higher and the glass windows offer shelter from the wind.

FLOODLIGHTS

Powerful floodlights illuminate the upper 30 floors between 9pm and midnight every night. Significant colors are used for special occasions—red, white and blue for Independence Day (July 4); green on St. Patrick's Day (Mar 17); red, black and green on Martin Luther King Day (third Mon in Jan); yellow and white for Easter; lavender and white on Gay Pride Day (Jun); red and green for Christmas. The stainless-steel window frames glimmer by day and night. In spring and fall during the bird migration season, the lights are turned off on foggy nights because the light shining through the fog confuses them.

THE TOWER

Broadcast cameras and microwave antennae on the east and west sides of the building monitor city traffic conditions for major TV and radio stations. The National Broadcasting Company (NBC) sent out the United States' first experimental transmission from the TV station here on December 22, 1931. Since 1965, FM radio has been transmitting from the tower, as has the New York Telephone Company.

FIFTH AVENUE

The Empire State Building was completed in 1931, on Fifth Avenue at 34th Street. From its 86th Floor Observatory all of Fifth Avenue stretches out below you. The avenue begins downtown in Washington Square Park. Nearby, at No. 47, the Salmagundi Club, in an elegant Italianate brownstone, is America's oldest club for artists, founded in 1871. At No. 62 are the Forbes Magazine Galleries (▷ 113). At 23rd Street is Manhattan's first skyscraper, the triangular Flatiron Building (▷ 113).

St. Patrick's Cathedral (▷ 160) is between 50th and 51st streets. At No. 645 is the Olympic Tower, the headquarters of the late Aristotle Onassis's empire, with shops, offices, apartments and a restaurant. These two landmarks are at the heart of a section of luxury shopping, between 49th and 59th streets. Tiffany & Co., founded in 1837, is now at 57th Street. Along with Saks Fifth Avenue, between 50th and 51st, and Bergdorf Goodman, also at 57th Street, are many other high-end retailers. Beyond the Trump Tower (▷ 171), Central Park (▷ 208–213) spreads out on the west side.

MANSIONS AND MUSEUMS

In the 19th century, Fifth Avenue was the fashionable address for the very wealthy, such as coke-and-steel tycoon Henry Clay Frick, tobacco magnate James Duke and railroad baron Jay Gould, who built increasingly large mansions. Some of them were demolished in the 1920s to make way for luxury apartments, but many remain. The first one, at No. 998, built in 1912, was such a success that it became the model that hundreds copied in form and detail. The starched doormen are an indication of the wealth of the residents, who enjoy spectacular views of Central Park. Henry Clay Frick's mansion at 70th Street is now open to the public, displaying the outstanding Frick Collection (▷ 215) of European art in a residential setting. Andrew Carnegie's 64-room home at 91st Street is now the Cooper-Hewitt National Design Museum (▷ 203). The Jewish Museum, at 92nd Street, occupies another fine old home. The stretch between 79th and 104th streets is also punctuated by museums and has become known as Museum Mile, with the Metropolitan Museum of Art, the Guggenheim Museum (▷ 216–217) and the Museum of the City of New York (▷ 220).

INFORMATION

✛ 147 D9 ✉ From Washington Square north to the Harlem River 🚇 4, 5, 6 🚌 M1, M2, M3, M4, M5

TIP

» Be sure to catch a parade on Fifth. The St. Patrick's Day Parade on March 17 is the biggest, but there are others. Check the NYC & Company events calendar for details. Crowds are so thick on the sidewalks during parades that you will not be able to shop or sightsee.

Above *Fifth Avenue is one of New York's most fashionable streets, with luxury shopping, excellent museums and a few landmark skyscrapers*

INFORMATION

www.grandcentralterminal.com
⊞ 147 D9 ✉ East 42nd Street at Park
Avenue, 10017 ☎ 212/532-4900; for
travel information 718/330-1234, or tours
212/935-3960 ⏰ Daily 5.30am–2am
✋ Free 🚇 4, 5, 6, 7, S 🚌 M1, M2,
M3, M4, M42, M101, M102 🎧 Excellent
free tour by the Municipal Arts Society
on Wed at 12.30. Meet at the information
desk, under the clock, in the main
concourse 🍴 Grand Central Oyster Bar
& Restaurant on the lower level; Mon–Sat
☎ 212/490-6650, www.oysterbarny.com.
Michael Jordan's The Steak House N.Y.C.
serves just that ☎ 212/328-0000, www.
theglaziergroup.com. ☎ 212/687-4600,
www.charliepalmer.com/properties/
metrazur 🏪 68 specialist shops on the
mezzanine and lower levels

INTRODUCTION

New York's most magnificent public space and one of the city's finest
landmarks, Grand Central is full of sophisticated shops and interesting places
for a quick bite. Every day, trains running on 48 pairs of railroad tracks bring
in half a million commuters from the northern suburbs. New York Central
Railroad magnate Cornelius Vanderbilt ordered the construction of Grand
Central Terminal. Built between 1903 and 1913, it replaced the 42nd Street
Terminal, an iron and glass train shed dating from 1871. At the turn of the
20th century, this area was the northern edge of the city, but as the new
station flourished, stores, hotels, restaurants and offices grew up around it. By
the 1920s it had become a boulevard graced with luxury apartment buildings.

Grand Central is an outstanding example of Beaux Arts design, with
triumphal arches filled with glass and steel, a grand waiting room, sumptuous
concourse, superb vaulted ceiling and imposing sculptures of Roman deities.
The innovative design, by engineer William Wilgus and architects Reed &
Stem, included extensive tunnels, a ramp system instead of stairs to keep
people moving, and upper and lower level concourses. Architect Whitney
Warren, a Vanderbilt cousin, was responsible for the outstanding facades
and interior. The public was delighted with this marvel, but by the 1970s, the
station had acquired layers of grime and was not a place to linger. The steel
was rusty, the asbestos was falling out and the stairways stank: it had become
a symbol of urban decay.

In 1978, a New York City developer proposed building a 55-story office
tower on top of the station, obliterating the facade. After a series of legal

challenges, a US Supreme Court decision sided with the New York City Landmarks law and saved it from this fate. Jacqueline Kennedy Onassis was a prime force in the battle against the tower. Restoration was completed in 1998 under architects Beyer Blinder Belle, who examined 4,500 of Warren's original drawings and blueprints. Over a period of four years, 80-year-old wiring and plumbing were replaced, air conditioning was installed and new entrances were built. All of this was done while the station continued to operate, and not a single train was late or delayed owing to construction.

Enter Grand Central on 42nd Street at Park Avenue in order to experience the full impact and grandeur of the main concourse. As you enter, the feeling of space, sophistication and city bustle creates an awesome introduction to Manhattan. The careful $200-million renovation project that has restored its grandeur fills even cynical New Yorkers with civic pride. Notice the 75ft (23m) windows, the Tennessee marble floor, the brass clock over the central kiosk, and the gold-and-nickel chandeliers. Stroll around the arcades leading to Lexington Avenue and the lower level where you'll find restaurants and shops, including Banana Republic, L'Occitane, Papyrus, M.A.C. Cosmetics, Grande Harvest Wines and Li-Lac Chocolates. Off the main concourse is the Grand Central Market, packed with fresh produce. The New York Transit Museum Annex & Store is worth visiting if you've got time. A maze of underground walkways links the terminal to surrounding streets; you can stay underground as far north as 48th and Park streets.

WHAT TO SEE

THE MAIN CONCOURSE CEILING

With 59 electric stars replicating the zodiac constellations, in reverse, the design is based on an illustration from a medieval manuscript. It is not known whether the ceiling's French creator, Paul Helleu, was aware that depicting the heavens in reverse, or from God's point of view, was a common practice of medieval illustrators. The main concourse itself is 375ft long (114m) and 120ft wide (36m).

JULES ALEXIS COUTAN'S SCULPTURE

Mercury, the Roman god of travel and commerce, is the central figure of this 1935 sculpture over the south entrance. He is supported by Minerva and Hercules, representing mental and physical strength.

GRAND CENTRAL OYSTER BAR AND RESTAURANT

This restaurant, with its low-vaulted ceiling, is worth seeing. The tiles are by Guastavino. Order a bowl of clam chowder—either Manhattan (tomato-based) or New England (cream-based) style (▷ 188).

THE CAMPBELL APARTMENT

This elegant (if pricey) cocktail bar was built by John Campbell as an office and pied-à-terre in the 1920s in the style of a 13th-century Florentine palazzo, with its stained-glass windows by Louis Comfort Tiffany and elegant dark paneling. Follow signs to the small staircase across from Michael Jordan's The Steak House off the west balcony.

NEW YORK TRANSIT MUSEUM GALLERY & STORE

This gallery annex has changing exhibits on the history, impact and future of public transportation (tel 212/878-0106, http://mta.info/mta/museum).

SPECIAL EVENTS

Exhibitions, food tastings, treasure hunts and concerts take place regularly. The Christmas Market in Vanderbilt Hall showcases the work of dozens of innovative regional craftspeople and retailers.

TIPS

» Take one of the free area tours sponsored by Grand Central Partnership (GCP), one of the largest business improvement districts, every Friday at 12.30, rain or shine. Meet in the sculpture court at 120 Park Avenue, on the southwest corner with 42nd Street.

» For lunch in New York, the food concourse on the lower level is fun, with its many interesting options from Cajun pizza to Vietnamese sandwiches. But go early—after 12.30 it's next to impossible to find a seat.

» Don't rush, take your time to enjoy the shopping, restaurants and most of all the architecture. This is not just a train station, it's a New York experience.

» When you leave the building, walk a couple of blocks south to 40th Street, then turn around and look back at Coutan's neoclassical sculpture over the south entrance.

Opposite *The main concourse is a fine example of Beaux Arts style*
Below *The brass four-faced clock tells the time from all angles*

MTA METRO-NORTH
TRAIN INFORMATION

www.themorgan.org
✚ 147 D10 ✉ 225 Madison Avenue
at 36th Street, 10016 ☎ 212/685-0008
🕓 Tue–Thu 10.30–5, Fri 10.30–9, Sat
10–6, Sun 11–6 ✋ Adult $15, under 12
with adult free; free Fri evening 7–9, with
live music 🚇 4, 5, 6, 7 🚌 M2, M3, M4
🍽 Morgan Court Café serves lunch and
afternoon tea 📚 Bookshop closes
15 min before galleries

MORGAN LIBRARY

By the end of the 19th century, John Pierpont Morgan was one of New York's wealthiest financiers. To fulfill his desire to match Europe's greatest libraries, he began his opulent private library of European cultural treasures: illuminated and literary manuscripts, paintings, prints and furniture. His travels abroad resulted in this priceless collection of nearly 10,000 drawings and prints, including some by Leonardo da Vinci and Albrecht Dürer. In 1902, he commissioned Charles McKim to design the magnificent Renaissance-style building. Later additions include those by Benjamin Morris in 1928, the annex, which was Morgan's private residence, at 231 Madison Avenue, and the garden courtyard in the 1990s.

The complex underwent more renovations between 2003 and 2006, which gave it twice the gallery space, an enlarged auditorium, a café, more shop and storage space, and a better-equipped Reading Room. Musical performances, lectures, readings and other public programs are offered throughout the year.

MORGAN'S STUDY

The West Room of the library remains as Morgan left it when he died in 1913. He used it as a study and his huge wooden desk is still here, along with the Italian Renaissance paintings lining the walls. From the study you pass green-veined marble columns as you proceed toward the rotunda and the East Room. The beautiful three-tiered, walnut and bronze bookcases are almost as amazing as the ceiling covered with frescoes and the signs of the zodiac. Notice the 16th-century Flemish tapestry above the fireplace. But it is the collection of letters and manuscripts that most intrigues.

Morgan acquired nearly 600 medieval and Renaissance manuscripts, including the 9th-century Lindau Gospels, a rare vellum copy of the Gutenberg Bible, and the medieval Dutch masterpiece *The Hours of Catherine of Cleves*. He also purchased handwritten scores by such composers as Beethoven, Mozart and Puccini, which are protected under glass. The collection also includes manuscripts by high-calibre authors such as Jane Austen, Charles Dickens, Henry David Thoreau and Mark Twain.

Below The Adoration of the Magi, *from a choirbook executed in around 1540*

NEW YORK PUBLIC LIBRARY

Some things in New York are surprises, and this amazing research library is one of them. The massive white marble building, one of the first major commissions of the firm Carrère & Hastings in 1911, is absolutely gorgeous. Half of its $9-million cost was donated by steel magnate and philanthropist Andrew Carnegie (1835–1919). The two lions at the foot of the staircase fronting the museum are New York icons affectionately named Patience and Fortitude by New York's 1930s' mayor, Fiorello LaGuardia; in the gift shop they adorn tote bags, spoons, charm bracelets, bookends, paperweights and more.

Up the imposing staircase and through the triple-arched portico is beautiful Astor Hall, named after John Jacob Astor (1763–1848), whose private library, along with that of James Lenox, was the foundation of this great collection. (Former New York governor Samuel J. Tilden bequeathed the $2.4 million to combine the libraries and erect the building.) Wall Street financier Stephen A. Schwarzman donated $100 million toward its renovation, and in 2011 the building was discreetly renamed for him.

WHAT TO SEE, AND WHERE

Upon entering, pick up a floor plan at the information desk and ask about free tours around the library. Gottesman Hall, straight ahead, displays temporary exhibits. The DeWitt Wallace Periodical Room, to the left, is embellished with Richard Haas murals of New York magazine and newspaper offices. At the top of the marble stairs is the McGraw Rotunda. The stupendous Main Reading Room is to your right. Across the hall is the Edna Barnes Salomon Room, now a designated computer room.

This is not a lending library (though there are more than 80 libraries in Manhattan and the outer boroughs). Occasionally, you can see important items here from the vast collection, which includes a Gutenberg Bible, a 1493 folio edition of a letter written by Christopher Columbus describing his discoveries in the New World, a first folio edition of Shakespeare's works from 1623, and an early draft of Thomas Jefferson's Declaration of Independence.

INFORMATION

www.nypl.org

✚ 147 D9 ✉ Fifth Avenue and 42nd Street, 10018 ☎ 212/930-0800 🕐 Mon, Thu–Sat 10–6, Tue–Wed 10–8, Sun 1–5 🖐 Free 🚇 B, D, F, M 🚌 M1, M2, M3, M4, M42 📷 Free tours Mon–Sat 11 and 2, Sun 2 from Astor Hall 🗓

Above *The Main Reading Room in the grand and beautifully restored Beaux Arts New York Public Library*

MUNICIPAL ART SOCIETY

www.mas.org

Founded in 1893, MAS is a non-profit, private, membership society aiming to promote a "more livable city." It advocates excellence in architecture, design and planning, public art and the preservation of historic buildings, and believes sensible development is critical to the city's economic health and social well-being. The MAS also organizes exhibitions and walking tours. The guides on these informative tours are highly qualified and give insights into the history and significance of the urban scene. Exhibitions are held at the headquarters on the 16th floor of the Steinway Building, and are open to the public free of charge.

✚ 147 D8 ✉ 111 West 57th Street, 16th floor, 10022 ☎ 212/935-3960 information; 212/935-2075 for tours and meeting places ⏲ Mon–Sat 10–6 (Wed to 8), Sun 11–5 ✋ Guided walking tours $15; some walking and bus tours are more expensive

MUSEUM OF MODERN ART
▷ 162–163.

NEW YORK PUBLIC LIBRARY
▷ 159.

PALEY CENTER FOR MEDIA

www.paleycenter.org

Formerly called the Museum of Television and Radio, the new name reflects the growing range of media in modern times. William S. Paley (1901–90), former chairman of CBS, donated the land for this 17-story building, erected in 1989, to a design by architects Philip Johnson and John Burgee. Theaters, screening rooms, three public galleries and individual viewing and listening consoles are your access to the museum's collection of tapes of 100,000 programs and commercials celebrating nearly 100 years. Thousands of new programs are added every year. When you arrive, make a reservation to use the computer catalog on the fourth floor to locate what interests you, then reserve it and watch it in one of the museum's consoles. Or take in a show or two at one of the theaters.

✚ 147 D8 ✉ 25 West 52nd Street, between Fifth and Sixth avenues, 10019 ☎ 212/621-6800 ⏲ Wed–Sun noon–6, Thu until 8, Fri theater programs until 9 ✋ Adult $10, under 14 $5 🚇 E 🚌 M1, M2, M3, M4 🛍 🍴 📷

ROCKEFELLER CENTER
▷ 164–167.

ST. PATRICK'S CATHEDRAL

www.saintpatrickscathedral.org

Each year the largest Roman Catholic cathedral in the United States, seating about 2,200, welcomes more than 3 million visitors. Designed by James Renwick, Jr., this Gothic Revival cathedral was inspired by European originals, most notably Cologne Cathedral in Germany. The spires are 330ft (100m) above street level. The pietà inside is three times the size of the one in St. Peter's in Rome. Tiffany & Co. designed the beautiful St. Michael and St. Louis altar. Work began on the church in 1853 and it was consecrated in 1879. The cathedral's arrival encouraged the rich and powerful to move north and contributed to the development of Fifth Avenue's many sumptuous mansions.

✚ 147 D8 ✉ Fifth Avenue, between 50th and 51st streets, 10022 ☎ 212/753-2261 ⏲ Daily 6.30am–8.45pm 🚇 6, B, D, E, F 🚌 M1, M2, M3, M4, M5

Opposite *A neoclassical entrance for the 1989 17-story building designed to house the Paley Center for Media*
Below *The striking Gothic Revival interior of St. Patrick's Cathedral*

THE PALEY CENTER FOR MEDIA

INFORMATION

www.moma.org
✚ 147 D8 ✉ 11 West 53rd Street,
10019 ☎ 212/708-9400 ◷ Sat–Mon
10.30–5.30, Wed–Thu 10.30–5.30, Fri
10.30–8; closed Tue ✋ Adult $20, under
16 with adult free, free Fri 4–8 ⊕ Fifth
Avenue/53rd Street (E), 47th–50th streets/
Rockefeller Center (B, D, F) 🚌 M1,
M2, M3, M4, M5 ✈ Audio programs
free; gallery talks daily at 11.30am and
1pm (free) 🖥 1 restaurant, 2 cafés
📖 MoMA Design and Book Store at
museum ☎ 212/708-9700; MoMA
Design Store, 44 West 53rd Street
☎ 212/767-1050

INTRODUCTION

When MoMA opened in 1929 it occupied six rooms on 57th Street. Today, after a dramatic $425 million renovation by architect Yoshio Taniguchi, it offers an unparalleled collection of modern and contemporary art. The new MoMA opened in November 2004 to much acclaim. Taniguchi's redesign doubled the institution's space, allowing it to display much more of its superb collection. Visitors can now enter from 53rd or 54th streets to view the galleries, which are clustered around a 110ft tall (34m) atrium, which diffuses light throughout the building and gives great views of the sculpture garden, which features Aristide Maillol's *The River*, Henry Moore's *Family Group* and other works in an inviting outdoor setting.

WHAT TO SEE

FOURTH AND FIFTH FLOORS

The permanent collection, spanning art from the late 19th century to the late 1960s, is displayed on the fourth and fifth floors. The works are presented in chronological sequence to create a comprehensive history of modern art. The 12 galleries on the fifth floor cover Postimpressionism, Cubism, Italian Futurism, Austrian and German Expressionism, Social Realism and Surrealism. Each boasts a string of masterpieces; Vincent Van Gogh's *The Starry Night* and Salvador Dalí's *The Persistence of Memory* are just two of the most celebrated examples. One gallery is devoted entirely to Matisse. Fourth-floor galleries present works from the late 1940s to the late 1960s and include works by such major artists as Willem de Kooning, Jasper Johns, Francis Bacon and Andy Warhol, as well as some splendid examples of Jackson Pollock's work.

SECOND AND THIRD FLOORS

Contemporary works created since 1970 are shown in the second-floor galleries, which also include a dedicated media gallery. The collections of drawings, photography, architecture and design are found on the third floor. The drawing collection contains 7,000 works from 1880 onward and the photography collection 25,000 works, which document the development of photography from the 1840s. The photograph collection ranges from Henri Cartier-Bresson to Diane Arbus, highlighted by William Fox Talbot's *Lace* and

Above *Among the many fine works in the Museum of Modern Art is Van Gogh's* The Starry Night *(1889)*

Paul Strand's *Fifth Avenue, New York*. With 19,000 films and 4 million film stills, the Film and Media Department is also impressive. The sixth floor is reserved for special exhibits.

MARC CHAGALL, OIL ON CANVAS: *I AND THE VILLAGE*
Painted in 1911, a year after Chagall (1887–1985) arrived in Paris, *I and the Village* portrays his memories of his native community outside Vitebsk. Here Chagall's personalized version of Cubism used a disjunctive geometric structure to evoke the rural and magical. Objects jumble together, representing the peasants and animals living side by side with a mutual dependence. The peasant's flowering sprig symbolizes the tree of life, the reward of a harmonious relationship between man and animal.

PAUL GAUGUIN, OIL ON BURLAP: *THE SEED OF THE AREOI*
In this 1892 portrait of a Polynesian goddess sitting on a blue-and-white cloth, Gauguin (1848–1903) combines elements from multiple cultures to portray the island in sharp contrast to the European world. The pose derives from ancient Egypt, with Javanese style used for the arm position based on a relief from the Temple of Borobudur. The eclectic use of color is pure Gauguin, and not reflective of the island's visual reality.

AUGUSTE RODIN, BRONZE: *MONUMENT TO BALZAC*
This 1898 cast Bronze by Rodin (1840–1917) was commissioned in honor of France's great novelist, Honoré de Balzac (1799–1850). Rodin strived to capture the spirit of the man rather than his physical appearance, although he clothed him in a robe similar to the one he often wore while writing.

Left *The world's greatest collection of painting and sculpture from the late 19th century to the present is on display in this modern space*

Sex joints drove out reputable business, and by the 1970s the district was crawling with hookers, pimps and other dubious characters.

During the 1990s, an aggressive clean-up operation—which included legislation against noise, gambling and prostitution, as well as new zoning laws—transformed the area. There's no question that the current state of the square and surrounding area has been an amazing show of effective planning, and a great triumph for the city.

Begin your visit at the Times Square Information Center, originally the attractive landmark Embassy Theater and now dominated by a branch of McDonald's. Even if you don't need information, take a look at the grand foyer. Over time, many of the old theaters have been renovated and now have landmark status. A special security force patrols the streets, and the area is as safe as any crowded urban neighborhood can be. If your visit to New York happens to coincide with New Year's Eve and you don't mind dense crowds, join the throngs in Times Square to see the glass ball drop at midnight to ring in the New Year. It's a great New York tradition.

WHAT TO SEE

ED SULLIVAN THEATER
Built by Arthur Hammerstein as a memorial to his father, Oscar Hammerstein I, this theater was formerly called the Hammerstein Theater. The neo-Gothic vestibules, lobbies and auditorium are unique on Broadway. Used as a dance hall for many years, it made history when it became a television studio. *The Ed Sullivan Show*, the longest-running TV show in history, was broadcast from here during the 1950s and 1960s. Today it is perhaps even more famous as the home of the *Late Show with David Letterman*.

✉ 1697–1699 Broadway, between West 53rd and West 54th streets

Opposite and below *Times Square is New York at its flashiest: neon signs, huge billboards, live TV broadcasts, stores and family-friendly theme restaurants, not to mention theaters*

REGIONS MIDTOWN • SIGHTS

169

TIPS

» Broadway extends from Lower Manhattan to beyond Manhattan's northern tip, but Broadway as most visitors understand it refers to the area north–south between West 53rd and West 40th streets and east–west from Sixth to Eighth avenues. Most theaters are not on Broadway but on side streets.

» The TKTS booth is located at Times Square "under the Red Steps" in Father Duffy Square on Broadway and 47th Street (www.tdf.org; open Mon, Wed–Sat 3–8, Tue 2–8, Sun 3–half an hour before curtain time, 10–2 for Wed and Sat matinées, 11–3 for Sun matinees; only cash or traveler's checks). It sells day-of-show tickets for on and off-Broadway performances at 20–50 percent off face value. By 6pm the line is short.

» Times Square Information Center has a Metropolitan Transit Authority desk for transit maps and MetroCards; a Broadway Ticket Center selling full-price tickets; an HSBC Bank Center with ATMs and currency-exchange machines; computers with free internet access; free brochures and leaflets — some with discount.

LYCEUM THEATRE

The oldest New York theater, saved from demolition in 1939, it is Broadway's most imposing structure with its magnificent Beaux Arts facade and powerful neo-Baroque columns. Inside are marble walls with murals by James Wall Finn. Many of Broadway's highly acclaimed comedies and dramas have been performed here, as well as classics by the National Actors Theatre. Such famous names as Ethel Barrymore, Bette Davis, Joseph Cotton, Melvyn Douglas, Alan Bates and Lauren Bacall have all performed at the Lyceum. ✉ 149 West 45th Street ☎ 212/239-6200

NEW VICTORY THEATER

www.newvictory.org
Built by Oscar Hammerstein I in 1899 and once known as Minsky's, the New Victory was restored and remodeled in 1995 and is the city's first full-time family-oriented performing arts center. ✉ 209 West 42nd Street

PARAMOUNT THEATRE BUILDING

The tallest building in Times Square when it was completed in 1927, the Paramount is crowned by a four-faced clock with a glass globe, a focal point of the area that is visible for miles when it's illuminated. The World Wrestling Entertainment's 2,000-seat theme restaurant, WWE New York, whose sign boasts the latest in fiber-optic technology, is in the old theater space; a 30ft (9m) video screen and 110 monitors ensure that every diner can watch live broadcasts of shows like *Raw* and *Smackdown!*, and appearances by WWE stars. Other entertainments vary from concerts to magic shows. ✉ 1501 Broadway

TV SHOW TICKETS GUIDE

Tickets for live tapings of TV shows are free but usually hard to obtain because of the high demand, especially the immensely popular *Late Show with David Letterman*. If you are seriously addicted to a show and you know six months in advance that you'll be in New York, you can always register your preferred dates online.

Many studios hand out stand-by tickets on the day of taping, but you have to get up early and stand in line. In the dead of winter, you stand a better chance, as snow and cold winds put some people off. For more information call NYC & Company on 212/484-1222. You can also phone or check show websites for information on ticket availability, waiting lists and stand-by tickets. When you attend a show, take photo ID, as it may be required.

Late Show with David Letterman

Register at www.cbs.com/latenight/lateshow or telephone 212/ 247-6497 for stand-by tickets on the day of taping at 11am sharp. You must be 18 or over to attend. You can request two tickets (maximum) in advance by filling out the request form online, or in person at the theater. Tapings are held at the Ed Sullivan Theater (▷ 169).

Good Morning, America

Visit www.abcnews.go.com/GMA and you may be lucky and get to join Robin Roberts and George Stephanopoulos in their street-facing studio on Broadway at 44th Street. The show runs Monday to Friday from 7am to 9am. Tickets can only be reserved online for individuals.

Left *Broadway is by far New York's longest street*

SEAGRAM BUILDING

Erected in 1958 with interiors by Philip Johnson, this is New York City's only Mies van der Rohe building. The decision to set it toward the back of the granite-paved plaza was daring at the time, especially given real-estate values, but it ignited a taste for pedestrian plazas that lingers in Manhattan to this day.

The building is also notable as the site of the esteemed Four Seasons restaurant, famed venue for power lunches, and of the bustling Brasserie restaurant.

✚ 147 E8 ✉ 375 Park Avenue, 10022 ☎ 212/572-7000 🕐 Mon–Fri 9–5

TIMES SQUARE AND BROADWAY

▷ 168–170.

TRUMP TOWER

Not to be confused with the older Trump Building, originally the Manhattan Company Building, or with other Trump structures about town, this one rose in the 1980s as a glass monument to affluent lifestyles. Upper floors contain 263 plush apartments. (Trump himself was one of the first to move in.) Below them, the interior is a six-story atrium with escalators, waterfalls and glittering boutiques surrounded by pink marble, mirrors and shrubbery. It's ridiculously ostentatious but still quite a sight.

✚ 147 D8 ✉ 725 Fifth Avenue, 10022 ☎ 212/832-2000 🕐 8am–10pm 🚇 E, M, N, R 🚌 M1, M2, M3, M4 🏛

UNITED NATIONS HEADQUARTERS

www.un.org

At the end of World War II John D. Rockefeller, Jr. donated $8.5 million to purchase this site for the United Nations complex. The 544ft (166m) Secretariat building that dominates the site opened in 1950. Alongside are the General Assembly building, the Conference building (fronting the river) and the Dag Hammarskjöld Library. Fittingly, architects from many countries contributed to the designs. A 45-minute guided tour covers the General Assembly Hall and Security Council Chamber. You can see donated exhibits such as stained glass by Marc Chagall, a replica sputnik and, in the park, sculptures by Barbara Hepworth and Henry Moore. Visit the landscaped grounds, with beautiful views. Arrive early at peak times.

✚ 147 F9 ✉ United Nations Plaza, 10017 ☎ 212/963-8687 🕐 Daily 9–4.45; closed Sat, Sun in Jan and Feb 🖐 Adult $16, child (5–12) $9, under 5 not admitted 🚇 4, 5, 6, 7 🚌 M15, M42 🔲 Tours every half-hour Mon–Fri 9.45–4.45 🍴 🏛

Below *The United Nations headquarters (foreground) is a symbol of peace and unity*

42nd STREET TO THE UN HEADQUARTERS

This walk along 42nd Street is architecturally fascinating, taking you past some of the finest buildings in the city, including nine designated landmarks. It's a great stroll for families. Times Square is exciting and surprising, with its flashing billboards, electronic news and stock tickers, theater marquees and posters. The walk ends at the United Nations complex in a quiet, peaceful spot alongside the East River.

THE WALK

Distance: 1.5 miles (2.4km)
Time: 2 hours
Start at: 42nd Street/Port Authority subway
End at: United Nations Building, 46th Street and First Avenue

HOW TO GET THERE

Subway A; bus M20, M42, M50, M104.

★ Leave the 42nd Street/Port Authority subway station and turn right, then proceed to the intersection of West 42nd Street and Eighth Avenue.

❶ Times Square and 42nd Street are famous today for their theaters, giant neon advertisements and megastores. Look back toward Ninth Avenue and you will catch a glimpse of an older side of the area: Holy Cross Church, one of its oldest buildings, dates from 1887.

Face east toward Seventh Avenue and you'll see the gleaming spire of the Chrysler Building in the distance. Walk east toward it, passing the AMC 25-screen multiplex, formerly the Empire Theater, on your right. Next door is Madame Tussauds and next to that the Candler Building.

❷ The Candler Building was named for a salesman for the Coca-Cola Company, which built this white terracotta tower in 1914. Two doors farther east is the New Amsterdam Theater, lavishly restored by the Walt Disney Company with an outstanding art nouveau lobby.

To see the building directly opposite, the New Victory Theater, you will need to cross this very busy street, so continue east to the traffic lights and use the crosswalk. The New Victory Theater, once known

as Minsky's, was built in 1899 by Oscar Hammerstein I. Restoration in 1995 has retained the beautiful old-fashioned interior. Continue east along West 42nd Street on this side of the street. Two doors east of the New Victory is the Reuters Building, and just east of that, Times Square (▷ 168–170), the triangle created by 42nd Street, Seventh Avenue and Broadway.

❸ The 25-story tower at No. 1 Times Square became the home of the *New York Times* on December 31, 1904; the inaugural fireworks display was almost outshone by the illuminated globe lowered from the roof to herald the New Year. Almost 100 years later, the globe is still lowered every New Year's Eve, and for many New Yorkers and visitors Times Square is still the place to celebrate the holiday. The tower now functions as an office block.

On the southeast corner of West 42nd Street and Broadway, on the right, is the former Knickerbocker Hotel, commissioned by Colonel John Jacob Astor. The songwriter George M. Cohan lived here for a time. The building now houses studios and showrooms.

Continue east along 42nd Street, crossing Broadway and Sixth Avenue (now officially known as Avenue of the Americas).

4 The flashy glass building leaning away from traffic on the north side of 42nd Street, 41 West 42nd Street, is the W. R. Grace Building, built in 1974 by architects Skidmore, Owings and Merrill.

Cross to the south side of the street and Bryant Park. Bryant Park sits on top of the subterranean stacks of the New York Public Library. During the World's Fair of 1853, the first to be held on United States soil, the park was the site of the Crystal Palace. To reach the library, continue east along 42nd Street to Fifth Avenue. The library rises ahead of you on the southwest corner of 42nd Street and Fifth Avenue.

5 The majestic Beaux Arts New York Public Library (▷ 159) is guarded by two stone lions, Patience and Fortitude, who sit at the base of an imposing front

stairway. Inside the building, the marble entrance area on the first floor and the usually packed second-floor Main Reading Room are well worth a look.

Return to 42nd Street and continue along east, crossing Madison Avenue. On your left at Park Avenue is Grand Central Terminal. Cross the street and plunge in.

6 Inside Grand Central Terminal (▷ 156–157), look at the ceiling in the main concourse, decorated with the constellations of the zodiac, and glimpse the dining concourse downstairs.

Back on 42nd Street, continue east to Lexington Avenue and the Chanin Building (on the southwest corner). Named for the brothers who developed the Times Square Theater District, the building features an art deco bas-relief, the work of Edward Trumbull. Continue to the northwest corner for the Chrysler Building.

7 The Chrysler Building (▷ 148–149) is one of the world's great 20th-century buildings—completed in 1929. Around the 30th floor a brick frieze depicts hubcaps, and there are also 9ft (3m)-high pineapples and giant stainless-steel radiator caps. The art deco foyer is made of African marble and steel.

Continue to 220 East 42nd Street and you'll come to the Daily News Building.

8 The Daily News Building (▷ 151) was until 1995 the home of America's first tabloid newspaper.

Cross Second Avenue and continue on 42nd Street until you come to an area with steps on both sides of the street. These lead to the charming Tudor City apartments. From the top of the steps there is a splendid view of the United Nations Building, the East River and, beyond it, the borough of Queens. Turn left onto Tudor City Place, then right onto 43rd Street. Here, steps lead down to Ralph Bunche Park. Cross United Nations Plaza (as First Avenue is called here) and turn left.

9 At the United Nations Headquarters (▷ 171), view the General Assembly lobby (foyer) and stroll through the gardens. The entrance to the complex is on 46th Street. John D. Rockefeller, Jr. donated the $8.5 million for the site.

WHEN TO GO
Crowds will not be out in full force if you begin your walk on a weekday morning before 10. If you wish to visit the United Nations Building at the end of the walk, arrive early— the last tour begins at 4.45pm.

WHERE TO EAT
The dining concourse at Grand Central Terminal, 42nd Street at Park Avenue, is just the place to refuel; for variety at affordable prices, it can't be beaten. The Oyster Bar & Restaurant (tel 212/490-6650), on the same level, offers excellent seafood, but at higher prices.

PLACE TO VISIT
MADAME TUSSAUDS WAX MUSEUM
✉ 234 West 42nd Street ☎ 212/512-9600 or 866/841-3505 🕐 Daily 10–10 💵 Adult $36, child (4–12) $29

Opposite *The Paramount Building in Times Square*

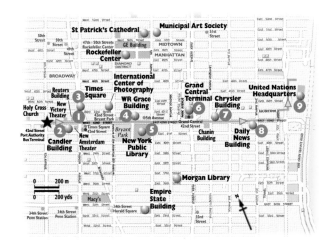

MACY'S TO ROCKEFELLER CENTER

Some of New York's most striking sights are along this route—the Empire State Building, the Diamond District and Rockefeller Plaza, where you may be tempted to stop in at the NBC Experience Store to pick up a *Will & Grace*, *Friends* or *Law & Order* T-shirt.

THE WALK
Distance: 3 miles (4.8km)
Time: 2.5 hours
Start at: 34th Street/Penn Station subway station
End at: 34th Street/Herald Square

HOW TO GET THERE
Subway 1, 2, 3; bus M34.

★ Leave the 34th Street/Penn Station subway so you come out onto West 34th Street at Seventh Avenue (also known as Fashion Avenue).

❶ You are standing in front of Macy's, arguably New York's most famous department store. Encompassing two entire city blocks, this store is so big you could spend days here.

Head east on West 34th Street. Continue to Broadway, cross it and turn left onto Sixth Avenue (Avenue of the Americas), keeping to the right as you go through the

intersection. Six blocks north on Sixth, past lots of shops and banks, is Bryant Park on your right, where you can rest or get a coffee in the park. Continue north past the park. At the corner of 43rd Street is the International Center of Photography (▷ 151).

❷ The Diamond District is concentrated on 47th Street between Fifth and Sixth avenues. Notice the diamond-motif street lights illuminating the corners. Millions of dollars-worth of gems are traded daily in businesses here.

Continue north on Sixth Avenue.

❸ At 49th Street you'll see the 70-story G.E. Building tower to the right at 30 Rockefeller Plaza. This building is the headquarters of General Electric and NBC (National Broadcasting Corporation) and is part of the Rockefeller Center (▷ 164–167), a city landmark. The first floor of the building is

worth visiting; note José Maria Sert's sepia murals depicting the progress of man. From Top of the Rock observation decks, on floors 67–70 of the G.E. Building, there are spectacular views.

Continue on Avenue of the Americas (Sixth Avenue) to 50th Street.

❹ Stop to admire the landmark art deco Radio City Music Hall (▷ 167), another city landmark and important element of the Rockefeller Center. Most famous for its Rockettes Christmas spectacular, it also hosts other music shows throughout the year. This was the world's largest indoor theater when it opened in 1932. Hour-long guided tours are worth the time and the money. The block-long entry, with its 24-carat-gold ceiling and two-ton glass chandeliers, is spectacular. Just past Radio City, at 1290 Avenue of the Americas, is the AXA Financial Center. Stop in to view

Opposite *Entrance to Macy's department store, decorated for Christmas*
Below *Rockefeller Center*

the lobby's multi-panel murals by Thomas Hart Benton depicting the nation's economic and social life on the eve of the Depression.

Back on Avenue of the Americas, go north a block to 52nd Street and turn right. The CBS Building, constructed in a dark granite in 1965, is on the corner of Avenue of the Americas and 52nd Street, a part of which is also known as Swing Street because of the many jazz clubs that flourished along here after the repeal of Prohibition.

5 At 25 West 52nd Street is the Paley Center for Media (▷ 160). Next door at No. 21 is the 21 Club, a still-fashionable hang-out, now a fine restaurant. Note the jockeys above the door.

At the corner of 52nd Street and Fifth Avenue, turn right and walk south a block.

6 At St. Patrick's Cathedral (▷ 160), the largest Catholic cathedral in America, the flying buttresses and 330ft (100m) twin spires vie for your attention.

Turn left on 51st Street, and walk east past the cathedral to Madison Avenue. Cross Madison Avenue.

7 On the southeast corner of 51st and Madison is the New York Palace Hotel, which rises out of the Villard Houses, twin brownstone mansions built in 1884 by the Bavarian-born journalist, financier and railroad tycoon Henry Villard.

Continue walking east on 51st as far as Park Avenue. Turn left and walk one block north.

8 The bronze-glass tower at 375 Park Avenue is the Seagram Building (▷ 171), a lively place in summer and a delight at Christmas

with a tree and lights. Diagonally across the avenue is Lever House, built in 1952 with an avant-garde metal- and glass-curtain wall that reflects everything around.

Go left on East 53rd Street, walk west to Sixth Avenue and turn left again. Walk four blocks south.

9 The Rockefeller Center is a great place to shop, stop for a snack or just wander around.

From here you can take the subway to Herald Square.

WHEN TO GO
Avoid this walk on Sunday if you want to shop and visit St. Patrick's Cathedral. Monday to Saturday from 10 to 6 is best.

WHERE TO EAT
The Sea Grill at Rockefeller Center (212/332-7610) or Rock Center Café, 20 West 50th Street (212/332-7620).

PLACES TO VISIT
PALEY CENTER FOR MEDIA
✉ 25 West 52nd Street ☎ 212/621-6800
🕐 Wed–Sun 12–6, Thu until 8

RADIO CITY MUSIC HALL
✉ 1260 Sixth Avenue ☎ 212/247-4777
🕐 Daily 11–3 🎧 Hour-long behind-the-scenes tours every 30 min

SHOPPING

APPLE STORE

www.apple.com

The transparent glass cube that marks the entrance to Apple's flagship New York store has become a Fifth Avenue landmark. From iPads to MacBooks, all of Apple's latest gadgets are on show, along with slick accessories. There's also a schedule of workshops and events to please everyone.

➕ 197 D7 ✉ 676 Fifth Avenue at 59th Street ☎ 212/336-1440 🕐 Daily, 24 hours 🚇 Fifth Avenue/59th Street (N, Q, R) 🚌 M1, M2, M3, M4, M5, M31, M57

B & H PHOTO

www.bhphotovideo.com

Even if you're not in the market for a new camera, you might want to make a detour to this vast store to pick up inexpensive supplies. You'll find every conceivable brand and type of camera, plus darkroom equipment and other accessories. Don't expect service—come knowing what you want to buy.

➕ 196 C10 ✉ 420 Ninth Avenue, between West 33rd and 34th streets ☎ 212/444-5000 🕐 Mon–Thu 9–7, Fri 9–2, Sun 10–6. Closed Sat 🚇 34th Street/ Penn Station (A, C, E) 🚌 M11, M34

BERGDORF GOODMAN

www.bergdorfgoodman.com

Some shoppers actually dress up to visit this luxurious store, which showcases classics and new talent. The store is beautifully laid out, the shoe department marvelous and the designer boutiques extraordinary. The men's store is just across the street.

➕ 197 D7 ✉ 754 Fifth Avenue, between 57th and 58th streets ☎ 212/753-7300 🕐 Mon–Fri 10–8, Sat 10–7, Sun 12–6 🚇 Fifth Avenue/59th Street (N, Q, R) 🚌 M3, M5, M57

CARTIER

www.cartier.com

Cartier opened in Paris in 1847 and has been famous for beautiful design ever since, creating such signature pieces as the three-band ring and the Portico Mystery Clock. Richard Burton went to Cartier for the diamond he gave to Elizabeth Taylor. Today, Cartier sells jewelry and watches, leather goods and other luxuries.

➕ 197 D8 ✉ 653 Fifth Avenue, between 51st and 52nd streets ☎ 212/753-0111 🕐 Mon–Fri 10–6, Sat 10–5.30, Sun 12–5 🚇 Fifth Avenue/53rd Street (E, M) 🚌 M1, M2, M3, M4, M50

CHANEL

www.chanel.com

Coco Chanel created the little black dress and slacks for women. Now Karl Lagerfeld designs the styles and the accessories, shoes and scents to go with them. Two stores on Madison Avenue sell accessories and jewelry only.

➕ 197 D7 ✉ 15 East 57th Street, between Madison and Fifth avenues ☎ 212/355-5050 🕐 Mon–Fri 10–6.30 (Thu until 7), Sat 10–6, Sun 12–5 🚇 Lexington Avenue/59th Street (N, Q, R, 4, 5, 6) 🚌 M1, M2, M3, M4, M57

COACH

www.coach.com

This successful leather purveyor has a line of classics as well as seasonal collections. There are nine other branches in the city.

➕ 197 D7 ✉ 595 Madison Avenue, between East 57th and 58th streets ☎ 212/754-0041 🕐 Mon–Sat 10–8, Sun 11–6 🚇 Fifth Avenue/59th Street (N, Q, R), 59th Street (4, 5, 6) 🚌 M1, M2, M3, M4, M57

COLE HAAN

www.colehaan.com

Nike now owns this maker of traditional, good-quality shoes and is jazzing it up with new ideas, colors and styles.

✚ 197 D8 ✉ 620 Fifth Avenue at 50th Street ☎ 212/765-9747 🕐 Mon–Fri 10–8, Sat 10–7, Sun 12–6 🚇 47th–50th streets/ Rockefeller Center (B, D, F, M) 🚌 M1, M2, M3, M4

EUGENIA KIM
www.eugeniakim.com

Former *Allure* editor Kim fell into her career when she fashioned a hand-feathered cloche for herself, went shopping, and attracted attention from shop owners. Her hats are dashing, flamboyant, beautifully crafted, and expensive, made of straw and cotton, and trimmed with feathers, leather and ribbons.

✚ 196 C10 ✉ 347 West 36th Street, between Eighth and Ninth avenues ☎ 212/674-1345 🕐 Mon–Fri by appointment only 🚇 34th Street-Penn Station (1, 2, 3, A, C, E) 🚌 M11, M16, M20

FAO SCHWARZ
www.fao.com

This famous store has been in Manhattan since 1876. It stocks action figures, stuffed toys, books, games, dolls, educational toys, electronics, furniture and fashions.

✚ 197 D7 ✉ 767 Fifth Avenue, between 58th and 59th streets ☎ 212/644-9400 🕐 Mon–Thu 9.30–7, Fri–Sat 9.30–8, Sun 10–7 🚇 59th Street/Fifth Avenue (N, Q, R) 🚌 M1, M2, M3, M4

FENDI
www.fendi.com

The Fendi label conveys money and glitz. This flagship store sells the full line: handbags, shoes, accessories and furs.

✚ 197 D8 ✉ 677 Fifth Avenue, between 53rd and 54th streets ☎ 212/759-4646 🕐 Mon–Sat 10–7, Sun 12–6 🚇 Fifth Avenue/53rd Street (E, M) 🚌 M1, M2, M3, M4, M57

GUCCI
www.gucci.com

Gucci and Fifth Avenue were made for each other, both being combinations of the chic and the commercial. Gucci is the biggest-selling Italian brand in the world, and this is its flagship store.

✚ 197 D8 ✉ 725 Fifth Avenue at East 54th Street ☎ 212/826-2600. Also at 840 Madison Avenue, between 69th and 70th streets ☎ 212/717-2619 🕐 Mon–Sat 10–7, Sun 12–6; Madison Avenue: Mon–Sat 10–6 (Thu until 7), Sun 12–5 🚇 Fifth Avenue/53rd Street (E, M), 68th Street (6) 🚌 M1, M2, M3, M4

HAMMACHER SCHLEMMER
www.hammacher.com

Ingenuity meets the future. At this longtime innovator, which started as a hardware store on the Bowery in 1848, you will find such items as the upside-down tomato garden and the Roomba, a robotic cleaning device that navigates whole rooms effortlessly removing dust from carpets and floors.

✚ 197 E7 ✉ 147 East 57th Street, between Lexington and Third avenues ☎ 212/421-9000 🕐 Mon–Sat 10–6 🚇 59th Street (4, 5, 6) 🚌 M31, M57, M101, M102, M103

HENRI BENDEL
www.henribendel.com

Henri Bendel is synonymous with sophistication and elegance. The inventory of goods is similar to Bergdorf's, but the displays reveal the store's élan. If you want to see works by the hottest new designers, check out the New Creators boutique, which features such names as Michael Soheil, Peter Som, Alice Roi, Zac Posen and Behnaz Sarafpour.

✚ 197 D8 ✉ 712 Fifth Avenue at 56th Street ☎ 212/247-1100 🕐 Mon–Sat 10–8, Sun 12–7 🚇 Fifth Avenue/59th Street (N, Q, R), Fifth Avenue/53rd Street (E, M) 🚌 M3, M5, M57

LACOSTE
www.lacoste.com

The alligator has been around since French tennis champion René Lacoste, nicknamed "alligator," sold his first polo shirt in 1933. Today, Christophe Lemaire is re-energizing the company, adding fragrance, home fabrics, eyewear, underwear and footwear to the selection of golf, tennis and yachting sportswear.

✚ 197 D8 ✉ 575 Madison Avenue, between East 54th and 55th streets ☎ 212/750-8115 🕐 Mon–Sat 10–7 (Thu until 8), Sun 12–5 🚇 Fifth Avenue/53rd Street (E, M), 51st Street/Lexington (6) 🚌 M1, M2, M3, M4

LORD & TAYLOR
www.lordandtaylor.com

This classic, established in 1826, targets traditional shoppers, from Greenwich matrons to young working women. The Christmas windows are a must-see.

✚ 197 D9 ✉ 424 Fifth Avenue, between 38th and 39th streets ☎ 212/391-3344 🕐 Mon–Sat 10–9, Sun 11–7 🚇 42nd Street (B, D, F, M) 🚌 M2, M3, M5

MACY'S
www.macys.com

Macy's calls itself the "world's largest department store." The Cellar stocks housewares and culinary delights, and clothing, generally mainstream, comes from a range of well-known names. The store has excellent seasonal sales, and currently sponsors the Thanksgiving Day parade and the July 4th fireworks.

✚ 197 D10 ✉ Herald Square at 34th Street and Broadway ☎ 212/695-4400 🕐 Mon–Sat 10–9.30, Sun 11–8.30 🚇 34th Street/Herald Square (B, D, F, M, N, Q, R) 🚌 M5, M7, M34

MANOLO BLAHNIK
www.manoloblahnik.com

The sexy, strappy sandals, plain stiletto pumps, slingbacks and mules are beloved of the fashion and celebrity crowd, who willlingly pay $450 and up for these most glamorous accessories. They're fashioned from pony skin and other elegant materials in a brilliant palette.

✚ 197 D8 ✉ 31 West 54th Street, between Fifth and Sixth avenues ☎ 212/582-3007 🕐 Mon–Fri 10.30–6, Sat 10.30–5.30, closed Sun 🚇 Fifth Avenue/53rd Street (E, M) 🚌 M5, M7

MICHAEL C. FINA

www.michaelcfina.com

This family-owned business, which specializes in engagement and wedding rings, also sells beautiful jewelry, tablewear, stylish home décor, designer bath accessories and a range of gift items from art glass to figurines to collectibles.

➕ 197 D9 ✉ 545 Fifth Avenue at 45th Street ☎ 800/289-3462 🕐 Mon–Fri 11–7 (Wed until 8), Sat–Sun 11–6 🚇 Fifth Avenue (7), 42nd Street (B, D, F, M) 🚌 M1, M2, M3, M4, M5, M42

MORRELL & COMPANY

www.morrellwine.com

Morrell, in business since 1947, is the other great wine shop in Manhattan after Sherry-Lehmann (▷ 232). It has its own wine bar and café next door.

➕ 197 D8 ✉ 1 Rockefeller Plaza ☎ 212/688-9370 🕐 Mon–Sat 10–7 🚇 47th–50th streets/Rockefeller Center (B, D, F, M) 🚌 M1, M2, M3, M4, M50

PAUL STUART

www.paulstuart.com

This pricey haberdashery opened in 1938. It sells fine-quality suits, Italian dress shirts, Irish argyles and other good-looking traditional fashions for men. Women will find silk cashmere turtlenecks, pinstripe pantsuits and leather jackets.

➕ 197 D9 ✉ Madison Avenue at East 45th Street ☎ 212/682-0320 🕐 Mon–Wed, Fri 8–6.30, Thu 8–7, Sat 9–6 🚇 42nd Street (B, D, F, M), 42nd Street/Grand Central (4, 5, 6, 7, S) 🚌 M1, M2, M3, M4, M5

POSMAN BOOKSELLERS

www.posmanbooks.com

A general bookstore which offers a good selection of journals and sharp insightful staff recommendations.

➕ 197 D9 ✉ 9 Grand Central Terminal (Vanderbilt Avenue and 42nd Street) ☎ 212/983-1111 🕐 Mon–Fri 8am–9pm, Sat 10–7, Sun 10–6 🚇 42nd Street (4, 5, 6) 🚌 M1, M2, M3, M4, M42

RIZZOLI

www.rizzoliusa.com

This store has an excellent stock of art, design, and fashion books.

➕ 197 D7 ✉ 31 West 57th Street, between Fifth and Sixth avenues (north side) ☎ 212/759-2424 🕐 Mon–Fri 10–7.30, Sat 10.30–7, Sun 11–7 🚇 Fifth Avenue/59th Street (N, Q, R), 57th Street (F) 🚌 M1, M2, M3, M4, M5, M7, M57

SAKS FIFTH AVENUE

www.saksfifthavenue.com

Saks offers a very fine selection of clothing by an excellent range of established and up-and-coming designers for men and women.

➕ 197 D8 ✉ 611 Fifth Avenue, between 49th and 50th streets ☎ 212/753-4000 🕐 Mon–Sat 10–8, Sun 12–7 🚇 Fifth Avenue/53rd Street (E), 47th–50th streets/Rockefeller Center (B, D, F, M) 🚌 M1, M2, M3, M4, M50

SEPHORA

www.sephora.com

This popular European chain has an efficient self-service orientation and sells more than 200 brands of beauty products, from Adrienne Vittadini to Philosophy. There's a scent-testing bar, and treatments by skin type.

➕ 196 C9 ✉ 1500 Broadway, between 43rd and 44th streets ☎ 212/944-6789 🕐 Daily 10am–midnight 🚇 Times Square (N, Q, R, 1, 2, 3) 🚌 M7, M20, M42

SHANGHAI TANG

www.shanghaitang.com

Asian styling informs fashions at this store. Chinese frog closures detail women's jackets and blouses fashioned from pagoda prints. Kung fu and Fuji jackets with mandarin collars are favorites for men.

➕ 197 D7 ✉ 600 Madison Avenue, between East 57th and 58th streets ☎ 212/888-0111 🕐 Mon–Sat 10.30–7 (Thu until 8), Sun 12–6 🚇 59th Street (4, 5, 6), Lexington Avenue/53rd Street (F) 🚌 M1, M2, M3, M4

SUAREZ HANDBAGS

www.suarezny.com

Here are copies of designer handbags for a fraction of the price.

➕ 197 D8 ✉ 450 Park Avenue at East 56th Street ☎ 212/753-3758 🕐 Mon–Sat 10–6 🚇 59th Street (4, 5, 6) 🚌 M1, M2, M3, M4

THOMAS PINK

www.thomaspink.com

This British store sells formal, business and casual shirts for men and women in strikingly beautiful colors and patterns.

➕ 197 D8 ✉ 520 Madison Avenue, between East 53rd and 54th streets ☎ 212/838-1928 🕐 Mon–Fri 10–7 (Thu until 8), Sat 10–6, Sun 12–6 🚇 Fifth Avenue/53rd Street (E, M), 51st Street (6) 🚌 M1, M2, M3, M4

TIFFANY & CO.

www.tiffany.com

Tiffany is famous for its silver and crystal. Some items are amazingly expensive, but it also displays more moderately priced luxury gifts—embossed note cards and singular silver pieces. All are packaged in the signature duck-egg blue box tied with red or white ribbon, introduced when the store opened in 1837.

➕ 197 D8 ✉ Fifth Avenue at 57th Street ☎ 212/755-8000 🕐 Mon–Sat 10–7, Sun 12–5 🚇 Fifth Avenue/59th Street (N, Q, R), 57th Street (F) 🚌 M1, M2, M3, M4

ENTERTAINMENT AND NIGHTLIFE

ALVIN AILEY AMERICAN DANCE THEATER

www.alvinailey.org

This black modern dance company has its permanent home in this 285-seat theater and 12 studios. Even if you don't go to a performance, see them working out in the studios.

➕ 196 C8 ✉ 405 West 55th Street at Ninth Avenue ☎ 212/405-9000 ✋ $25–$110 🚇 Columbus Circle (1, A, B, C, D), 57th Street/Seventh Avenue (N, R, Q) 🚌 M11

AMBASSADOR THEATRE

www.ambassadortheater.com

Opened in 1921, this 1,088-seat auditorium is wider than it is deep, so viewing is good but with a mezzanine overhang.

➕ 196 C8 ✉ 219 West 49th Street, between Broadway and Eighth Avenue ☎ 212/239-6200 🕐 Sat–Sun 2.30, Mon–Tue and Thu–Sat 8, Sun 7 🚇 50th Street/Seventh Avenue (1), 49th Street (N, R) 🚌 M7, M20, M50, M104

AMERICAN AIRLINES THEATRE

www.roundabouttheatre.org

This restored 1918 theater is now the home of the Roundabout Theatre Company, founded in 1965 to perform the classics and new plays at affordable prices.

✚ 196 C9 ✉ 227 West 42nd Street, between Seventh and Eighth avenues ☎ 212/719-1300 ⏰ Tue–Sat 7.30, matinees Wed, Sat–Sun 2 🚇 42nd Street/Times Square (N, Q, R, S, 1, 2, 3, 7) 🚌 M7, M20, M42, M104

AUGUST WILSON THEATRE

The Theater Guild commissioned this striking theater with its Tuscan-style facade. The theater opened in 1925.

✚ 196 C8 ✉ 245 West 52nd Street, between Broadway and Eighth Avenue ☎ 212/239-6200 ⏰ Tue 7, Wed–Sat 8, matinees Wed, Sat 2, Sun 3 🚇 50th Street (1), 50th Street (C, E) 🚌 M7, M20, M50, M104

B. B. KING BLUES CLUB AND GRILL

www.bbkingblues.com

Little Richard and Roberta Flack, among others, have entertained at this large bi-level club. On Sunday a gospel choir shakes up the Sunday brunch from 12.30 to 2.30, and Saturday brunch features the music of The Beatles from 11 to 2.

✚ 196 C9 ✉ 237 West 42nd Street ☎ 212/997-4144 ⏰ Daily 11am–1am; shows at 8pm and 10.30pm 🚇 42nd Street/Times Square (N, Q, R, S, 1, 2, 3, 7) 🚌 M20, M42, M104

BELASCO

www.shubertorganization.com

Named for David Belasco, the bishop of Broadway, this gem of a theater with 1,016 seats has some gorgeous Tiffany lamps and murals by Everett Shinn. Avoid the side orchestra seats.

✚ 197 D9 ✉ 111 West 44th Street, between Broadway and Sixth Avenue ☎ 212/239-6200 ⏰ Tue–Sat 8, matinees Wed, Sat 2, Sun 3 🚇 42nd Street/Times Square (N, R, S, 1, 2, 3, 7), 42nd Street/Sixth Avenue (B, D, F, M) 🚌 M5, M7, M20, M42, M104

BERNARD B. JACOBS THEATRE

www.shubertorganization.com

Laurence Olivier starred in *The Entertainer* on this stage, which opened in 1927.

✚ 196 C9 ✉ 242 West 45th Street, between Broadway and Eighth Avenue ☎ 212/239-6200 ⏰ Tue–Sat 8, matinees Wed 2, Sun 3 🚇 42nd Street/Times Square (N, Q, R, S, 1, 2, 3, 7), 42nd Street/Eighth Avenue (A, C, E) 🚌 M7, M20, M42, M104

BIRDLAND

www.birdlandjazz.com

Charlie Parker inspired the original Birdland, which opened in 1949, and he was its first headliner. This is perhaps the most elegant jazz club in town. Expect to hear everyone from Kurt Elling to Diana Krall.

✚ 196 C9 ✉ 315 West 44th Street, between Eighth and Ninth avenues ☎ 212/581-3080 ⏰ Shows daily, times vary ✋ $20–$50 plus $10 minimum 🚇 42nd Street (A, C, E) 🚌 M11, M20, M42

BOOTH THEATRE

www.shubertorganization.com

Numerous hits have played at this Italianate theater dating to 1913 and named after actor Edwin Booth.

✚ 196 C9 ✉ 222 West 45th Street, between Broadway and Eighth Avenue ☎ 212/239-6200 ⏰ Mon, Wed, Fri–Sat 8, Tue 7, matinees Wed and Sat 2, Sun 3 🚇 42nd Street/Times Square (N, Q, R, S, 1, 2, 3, 7) 🚌 M7, M20, M42, M104

BROADHURST THEATRE

www.shubertorganization.com

Named after Anglo-American playwright George Broadhurst, this theater was built by the Shuberts and has welcomed star-studded casts since opening in 1918.

✚ 196 C9 ✉ 235 West 44th Street, between Broadway and Eighth Avenue ☎ 212/639-6200 ⏰ Tue–Sat 8, matinees Wed, Sat 2, Sun 3 🚇 42nd Street/Times Square (N, Q, R, S, 1, 2, 3, 7) 🚌 M7, M20, M42, M104

BROADWAY THEATRE

www.shubertorganization.com

This 1,761-seat theater was built as a movie house in 1924. Avoid the back of the house if you can.

✚ 196 C8 ✉ 1681 Broadway, between 52nd and 53rd streets ☎ 212/239-6200 ⏰ Tue–Sat 8, matinees Wed, Sat 2, Sun 3 🚇 50th Street/Eighth Avenue (C, E), 50th Street/Seventh Avenue (1) 🚌 M7, M20, M50, M104

BROOKS ATKINSON THEATRE

www.brooksatkinsontheater.com

Built in 1926, this ornate theater is named for longtime *New York Times* theater critic Brooks Atkinson. With 1,069 seats, you may feel you're too far from the stage if you sit in the rear mezzanine.

✚ 196 C9 ✉ 256 West 47th Street, between Broadway and Eighth Avenue ☎ 212/307-4100 ⏰ Tue–Sat 8, matinees Wed, Sat 2, Sun 3 🚇 50th Street/Eighth Avenue (C, E), 50th Street/Seventh Avenue (1) 🚌 M20, M50, M104

CAMPBELL APARTMENT

It's worth seeking out this quintessential New York bar. Originally designed as an office for wealthy businessman John W. Campbell, it's dark and richly decorated in a Renaissance style. Today it caters to suburbanites en route to their homes in Connecticut and Westchester County.

✚ 197 D9 ✉ 15 Vanderbilt Avenue in Grand Central Terminal (southwest corner) ☎ 212/953-0409 ⏰ Mon–Thu noon–1am, Fri noon–2am, Sat 3pm–2am, Sun 3pm–11pm 🚇 42nd Street/Grand Central (4, 5, 6, S) 🚌 M42

CARNEGIE HALL

www.carnegiehall.org

"Practice, practice, practice" is the answer to the old chestnut of a question, "How do you get to Carnegie Hall?" Many well-practiced international conductors and artists have played in this famous hall, which was built with Carnegie money in 1891, from Tchaikovsky and Mahler to the Beatles and the Rolling Stones. Programming includes the great orchestras of the world, top-class instrumentalists, the New York Pops under Skitch Henderson, and performers of jazz, folk, pop and comedy. A small free museum on the second floor (tel

212/903-9629) displays associated memorabilia.
✚ 196 C8 ✉ Seventh Avenue at West 57th Street ☎ 212/247-7800 🕐 Museum: daily 11–4.30; tours (tel 212/903-9765) Mon–Fri 11.30, 2 and 3, Sat 11.30, 12.30, Sun 12.30 ✋ $10–$102 🚇 57th Street (N, Q, R) 🚌 M7, M57

CAROLINES ON BROADWAY
www.carolines.com
First opened by Caroline Hirsch as a cabaret in Chelsea in 1981, the club gained a name throughout the 1980s and 1990s for comedy. Now in its glitzy Times Square venue, it presents live entertainment 365 nights a year.
✚ 196 C8 ✉ 1626 Broadway, between 49th and 50th streets ☎ 212/757-4100 🕐 Nightly, check program ✋ $20–$50, plus 2-drink minimum 🚇 50th Street (1) 🚌 M20, M50

CENTRAL SYNAGOGUE
www.centralsynagogue.org
Concerts at the synagogue often feature well-known or overlooked Jewish composers.
✚ 197 E8 ✉ 123 East 55th Street at Lexington Avenue ☎ 212/415-5500 or 212/838-5122 🚇 51st Street (6) 🚌 M57, M101, M102, M103

CHICAGO CITY LIMITS
www.chicagocitylimits.com
This comedy revue company relocated from Chicago in 1979. The resident troupe puts on improv shows. Don't sit in the front row if you're worried about being heckled.
✚ 196 C8 ✉ 318 West 53rd Street at Eighth Avenue ☎ 212/888-5233 🕐 Sun–Thu 9, Fri 8, Sat 8 and 10 ✋ $15 plus 2-drink minimum 🚇 50th Street (C, E) 🚌 M11

CIRCLE IN THE SQUARE (UPTOWN)
Opened in 1972, this theater is in the same building as the Gershwin theater. All 681 seats have good sight lines.
✚ 196 C8 ✉ 1633 Broadway at 50th Street ☎ 212/239-6200 🕐 Tue 7, Wed–Sat 8, matinees Wed 2, Sat 11.30, 3.30 🚇 50th Street/Eighth Avenue (C, E),

50th Street/Seventh Avenue (1) 🚌 M7, M20, M50, M104

CORT THEATRE
www.shubertorganization.com
Named for producer John Cort, this 1,082-seat space was built in 1912, to model the Petit Trianon, Versailles. All seats have good views.
✚ 196 C8 ✉ 138 West 48th Street, between Sixth and Seventh avenues ☎ 212/239-6200 🕐 Tue–Sat 8, matinees Wed, Sat 2, Sun 3 🚇 47th–50th streets/Rockefeller Center (B, D, F, M) 🚌 M7, M20, M50, M104

DON'T TELL MAMA
www.donttellmamanyc.com
Diverse singers and cabaret artists perform here nightly.
✚ 196 C9 ✉ 343 West 46th Street between Eighth and Ninth avenues ☎ 212/757-0788 ✋ Cover, drink minimum 🚇 42nd Street (A, C, E) 🚌 M11, M20

ETHEL BARRYMORE THEATRE
www.shubertorganization.com
Ethel Barrymore starred in The Kingdom of God to open this theater in 1928. Fred Astaire gave his last stage performance here in The Gay Divorcée in the 1930s.
✚ 196 C9 ✉ 243 West 47th Street, between Seventh and Eighth avenues ☎ 212/239-6200 🕐 Tue–Sat 8, matinees Wed, Sat–Sun 2 🚇 50th Street (C, E), 50th Street (1), 49th Street (N, Q, R) 🚌 M7, M20, M104

EUGENE O'NEILL
Opened in 1926, this theater was named for the great playwright in 1959.
✚ 196 C8 ✉ 230 West 49th Street, between Broadway and Eighth Avenue ☎ 212/239-6200 🕐 Tue–Thu 7, Fri 8, Sat 2 and 8, Sun 2 and 7 🚇 50th Street/Eighth Avenue (C, E), 50th Street/Seventh Avenue (1) 🚌 M7, M20, M50, M104

FLUTE
www.flutebar.com
Perfect, if pricey, for an after-theater celebration, this gilt-and-mirror subterranean bar serves 20 champagnes by the glass. Snag one of the private curtained alcoves.

✚ 196 C8 ✉ 205 West 54th Street, between Seventh Avenue and Broadway ☎ 212/265-5169 🕐 Sun–Wed 4–2, Thu 4–3, Fri–Sat 4–4 🚇 Seventh Avenue (B, D, E) 🚌 M7, M20, M104

FOXWOODS THEATRE
www.foxwoodstheatre.com
The Lyric (1903) and the Apollo (1920) were combined to create this 1,839-seat house ideal for spectacular musicals. Most seats have good sight lines.
✚ 196 C9 ✉ 213 West 42nd Street, between Seventh and Eighth avenues ☎ 212/556-4750 or 212/307-4100 🕐 Wed 1.30 and 7.30, Tue and Thu 7.30, Fri 8, Sat 2 and 8, Sun 3 🚇 42nd Street/Times Square (N, Q, R, S, 1, 2, 3, 7), 42nd Street/Eighth Avenue (A, C, E) 🚌 M7, M20, M42, M104

GERALD SCHOENFELD THEATRE
www.shubertorganization.com
Drama and comedy from Noël Coward's Present Laughter to the Royal Shakespeare Company's Nicholas Nickleby have played at this 1918 theater.
✚ 196 C9 ✉ 236 West 45th Street, between Broadway and Eighth Avenue ☎ 212/239-6200 🕐 Wed–Sat 8, Mon 8, Tue 7, matinees Wed, Sat 2, Sun 3 🚇 42nd Street/Times Square (N, Q, R, S, 1, 2, 3, 7), 42nd Street/Eighth Avenue (A, C, E) 🚌 M7, M20, M42, M104

GERSHWIN
www.gershwin-theater.com
Owned by the Broadway producers the Nederlanders, the Gershwin opened in 1972. The auditorium is on the second floor. It was renamed in 1983 after George and Ira.
✚ 196 C8 ✉ 222 West 51st Street, between Broadway and Eighth Avenue ☎ 212/307-4100 🕐 Tue 7, Wed–Sat 8, matinees Wed, Sat 2, Sun 3 🚇 50th Street/Eighth Avenue (C, E), 50th Street/Seventh Avenue (1) 🚌 M7, M20, M50, M104

HELEN HAYES THEATRE
This small Colonial Revival-style theater was built in 1912 to house new and experimental productions.
✚ 196 C9 ✉ 240 West 44th Street, between Seventh and Eighth avenues

☎ 212/944-9450 or 212/239-6200 🕓 Mon and Thu–Sat 8, Tue 7, Sun 2 and 7 🚇 42nd Street/Times Square (N, Q, R, S, 1, 2, 3, 7), 42nd Street/Eighth Avenue (A, C, E) 🚌 M7, M20, M42, M104

HUDSON TERRACE
www.hudsonterracenyc.com
With fine views over the Hudson river, this elegant rooftop bar at the western edge of Midtown is a perfect place for watching sunsets. The décor features heirloom woods, handcrafted tiles, banquette seating and floor-to-ceiling windows, with a retractable roof for fine weather. Dress code is business-casual. Events range from DJ nights to the popular Beer Garden.
➕ 196 B9 ✉ 621 West 46th Street between Eleventh and Twelfth avenues ☎ 212/315-9400 🕓 Tue–Wed 5pm–1am, Thu–Fri 5pm–4am, Sat 10pm–4am 🍸 Varies with events 🚇 42nd Street (A, C, E) 🚌 M42, M50

IMPERIAL THEATRE
www.shubertorganization.com
Gypsy, Fiddler on the Roof and *Les Misérables* played here.
➕ 196 C9 ✉ 249 West 45th Street, between Broadway and Eighth Avenue ☎ 212/239-6200 🕓 Mon–Sat 8, matinees Wed, Sat 2 🚇 42nd Street/Times Square (N, Q, R, S, 1, 2, 3, 7), 42nd Street/Eighth Avenue (A, C, E) 🚌 M7, M20, M42, M104

IRIDIUM
www.iridiumjazzclub.com
At this chic club, top R&B and jazz names appear.
➕ 196 C8 ✉ 1650 Broadway at 51st Street ☎ 212/582-2121 🕓 Mon–Thu 5–midnight (sets at 8 and 10), Wed–Sun 7pm–2am (sets at 8, 10 and 11.30) 🍸 $25–$95 ($5 minimum at bar, $10 at table) 🚇 49th Street (N, R), 50th Street (1) 🚌 M7, M50

IRISH ARTS CENTER
www.irishartscenter.org
Comedy, theater, film and music with a Celtic-Gaelic flavor are performed here all week.
➕ 196 B8 ✉ 553 West 51st Street, between Tenth and Eleventh avenues ☎ 212/757-3318 🚇 50th Street (C, E) 🚌 M11, M50

JAPAN SOCIETY
www.japansociety.org
Japanese music concerts, dance, theater and cultural events are held in the Lila Acheson Wallace Auditorium.
➕ 197 E9 ✉ 333 East 47th Street, between First and Second avenues ☎ 212/832-1155 🚇 51st Street (6) 🚌 M15, M50

JOE ALLEN
www.joeallenrestaurant.com
It's really a restaurant, but the bar is ideal for a pre- or post-theater drink.
➕ 196 C9 ✉ 326 West 46th Street, between Eighth and Ninth avenues ☎ 212/581-6464 🕓 Mon–Tue, Thu 12–11.45, Wed, Sun 11.30am–11.45pm, Fri 12–12, Sat 11.30am–midnight 🚇 42nd Street (A, C, E) 🚌 M42

JULIA MILES THEATER
www.womensproject.org
Founded in 1978 by Julia Miles, the Women's Project Theatre is the nation's pre-eminent women's theater company.
➕ 196 B8 ✉ 424 West 55th Street ☎ 212/765-1706, tickets 212/757-3900 🚇 59th Street (A, B, C, D, 1) 🚌 M11, M57

KING COLE BAR
http://kingcolebar.com
Named for the 1906 Maxfield Parrish mural *Old King Cole*, this bar claims to have invented the Bloody Mary. It serves excellent cognacs, grappas and single malts.
➕ 197 D8 ✉ St. Regis Hotel, 2 East 55th Street, between Fifth and Madison avenues ☎ 212/753-4500 🕓 Mon–Thu, Sun 4pm–12.30am, Fri–Sat 4pm–1am 🚇 Fifth Avenue/53rd Street (E, M) 🚌 M1

LANDMARK TAVERN
www.thelandmarktavern.org
The Landmark Tavern is worthy of its name, since it opened in 1868. The mahogany bar, antique mirrors and tile floor provide a historic patina. The pub fare is good.
➕ 196 B9 ✉ 626 Eleventh Avenue at the southeast corner of 46th Street ☎ 212/247-2562 🕓 Daily 11.30am–3am (kitchen closes at 11pm) 🚇 42nd Street (A, C, E), 50th Street (C, E) 🚌 M50

THE LAURIE BEECHMAN THEATRE
www.beechmantheatre.com
Located in the West Bank Café, this 100-seat cabaret venue stages performances by some impressive Broadway and cabaret artists, from Barbra Streisand to comedian Joan Rivers, who does regular shows here.
➕ 196 C9 ✉ 407 West 42nd Street, between 9th and 10th avenues ☎ 212/695-6909 🕓 Daily from 7pm 🍸 $15–$20 🚇 42nd Street (A, C, E) 🚌 M11, M16, M42

LONGACRE THEATRE
www.shubertorganization.com
Named for Longacre Square, today's Times Square, this 1,091-seat theater opened in 1913. Orchestra seats have the best sight lines.
➕ 196 C8 ✉ 220 West 48th Street, between Broadway and Eighth Avenue ☎ 212/239-6200 🕓 Tue–Fri 8, Sat 5 and 9, Sun 3 and 7 🚇 50th Street/Seventh Avenue (1), 49th Street (N, R), 47th–50th streets/ Rockefeller Center (B, D, F, M) 🚌 M20, M42, M50, M104

LUNT-FONTANNE THEATRE
http://luntfontannetheatre.com
Designed by Carrère and Hastings in 1910, the theater was gutted in 1958. It was the New York home of *The Sound of Music*.
➕ 196 C9 ✉ 205 West 46th Street, between Broadway and Eighth Avenue ☎ 212/575-9200 or 212/307-4747 🕓 Mon–Sat 8, matinees Wed, Sat 2 🚇 42nd Street/Times Square (N, Q, R, S, W, 1, 2, 3, 7), 50th Street/Seventh Avenue (1, 9), 50th Street/Eighth Avenue (C, E) 🚌 M20, M42, M50, M104

LYCEUM THEATRE
www.shubertorganization.com
Built in 1903 in Beaux Arts style, this is the oldest theater still in use on Broadway.
➕ 196 C9 ✉ 149 West 45th Street, between Broadway and Sixth Avenue ☎ 212/239-6200 🕓 Tue–Sat 8, matinees Wed, Sat 2, Sun 3 🚇 49th Street (N, R), 47th–50th streets/Rockefeller Center (B, D, F) 🚌 M5, M7, M20, M42, M104

MADISON SQUARE GARDEN

www.thegarden.com

Located on top of Penn Station, this arena hosts sports events, concerts and other entertainment. Bob Dylan, Madonna, the Rolling Stones, Elton John and other star tours stop here. ✚ 196 C10 ✉ 4 Penn Plaza ☎ 212/465-6741 🚇 34th Street/Penn Station (A, C, E, 1, 2, 3) 🚌 M10, M16, M20, M34

MAJESTIC THEATRE

www.shubertorganization.com

This theater opened in 1927 and has hosted hits from *Carousel* to *Phantom of the Opera*, currently the longest-running show on Broadway. ✚ 196 C9 ✉ 245 West 44th Street, between Broadway and Eighth Avenue ☎ 212/239-6200 🕐 Mon–Sat 8, matinees Wed, Sat 2 🚇 42nd Street/Times Square (N, Q, R, S, 1, 2, 3, 7), 42nd Street/Eighth Avenue (A, C, E) 🚌 M7, M20, M42, M104

MINSKOFF THEATRE

www.minskofftheatre.com

This Nederlander theater, built in 1973, is rather impersonal. An escalator takes you to the fourth-floor orchestra. ✚ 196 C9 ✉ 200 West 45th Street, between Seventh and Eighth avenues ☎ 212/307-4100 🕐 Tue 7, Wed–Sat 8, matinees Wed, Sat 2, Sun 3 🚇 42nd Street/ Times Square (N, Q, R, S, 1, 2, 3, 7) 🚌 M7, M20, M42, M104

THE MINT SPACE

www.minttheater.org

Home of the Mint Theater, one of the most recognized companies off-off-Broadway, it performs plays often drawn from foreign traditions. ✚ 196 C9 ✉ 311 West 43rd Street, between Eighth and Ninth avenues ☎ 212/315-9434 or 212/315-0231 🚇 42nd Street (A, C, E) 🚌 M11, M20, M42

MOMA FILM

www.moma.org

MoMA offers an ambitious film program of documentaries, historic retrospectives and director tributes. ✚ 197 D8 ✉ 11 West 53rd Street ☎ 212/708-9480 ✋ $20 🚇 Rockefeller Center (B, D, F, M), 53rd Street/Fifth Avenue (E) 🚌 M1, M2, M3, M4, M5, M7

MUSIC BOX THEATRE

www.shubertorganization.com

Note the plaque, just inside the lobby, commemorating Irving Berlin, who built this theater in 1921 with producer Sam Harris to house his Music Box Revues. ✚ 196 C9 ✉ 239 West 45th Street, between Broadway and Eighth Avenue ☎ 212/239-6200 🕐 Tue–Sat 8, matinees Sat 2, Sun 3 🚇 42nd Street/Times Square (N, Q, R, S, 1, 2, 3, 7), 42nd Street/Eighth Avenue (A, C, E) 🚌 M7, M20, M42, M104

NEDERLANDER THEATRE

www.nederlandertheatre.org

When *Rent* moved from the East Village, it came to this theatre, and *Who's Afraid of Virginia Woolf?* opened here. Avoid the side seats. ✚ 196 C9 ✉ 208 West 41st Street, between Seventh and Eighth avenues ☎ 212/921-8000 or 212/307-4100 🕐 Mon–Tue, Thu–Sat 8, matinees Sat, Sun 2 🚇 42nd Street/Times Square (N, Q, R, S, 1, 2, 3, 7) 🚌 M7, M20, M42, M50, M104

THE NEGRO ENSEMBLE COMPANY

www.necinc.org

Founded in 1967, this group holds workshops for playwrights and actors; it also mounts productions. ✚ 196 C9 ✉ 303 West 42nd Street at Eighth Avenue ☎ 212/582-5860 🚇 42nd Street (A, C, E) 🚌 M16, M20, M42

NEIL SIMON THEATRE

www.neilsimontheatre.com

This ornate theater, opened in 1927, has been home to many musicals, including *Porgy and Bess, Funny Face* and *Hairspray*. It seats 1,334. ✚ 196 C8 ✉ 250 West 52nd Street, between Broadway and Eighth Avenue ☎ 212/757-8646 or 212/307-4100 🕐 Tue 7, Wed–Sat 8, matinees Wed, Sat 2, Sun 3 🚇 50th Street/Eighth Avenue (C, E), 50th Street/Seventh Avenue (1) 🚌 M7, M20, M50, M104

NEW AMSTERDAM THEATRE

http://disney.go.com

Florence Ziegfeld commissioned this art nouveau beauty in 1903. In 1997 the Walt Disney Company restored it with its murals, stucco, tiles and woodwork, and installed *The Lion King* for a run. Avoid the side seats. ✚ 196 C9 ✉ 214 West 42nd Street, between Seventh and Eighth avenues ☎ 212/282-2900 or 212/307-4747 or 212/282-2907 for tours 🕐 Wed–Sat 8, Sun 6.30, Wed and Sat 2, Sun 1 🚇 42nd Street/ Times Square (N, Q, R, S, 1, 2, 3, 7), 42nd Street/Eighth Avenue (A, C, E) 🚌 M7, M20, M42, M104

NEW YORK CITY CENTER

www.nycitycenter.org

The exotic Moorish-style building dating to 1922–24 hosts dance. The Dance Theater of Harlem, Alvin Ailey American Dance Theater, Paul Taylor Dance Company, American Ballet Theatre and the San Francisco Ballet have performed here. The Gilbert and Sullivan Players are residents. Originally a Shriner's temple, it became a "people's theater" in 1943. ✚ 196 C8 ✉ 131 West 55th Street, between Sixth and Seventh avenues ☎ 212/247-0430 or 212/581-1212 ✋ $25–$130 🚇 57th Street (N, Q, R) 🚌 M5, M7, M57

OAK ROOM

www.algonquinhotel.com

By nurturing such artists as Steve Ross, Michael Feinstein, Harry Connick, Jr. and Diana Krall, this room led a revival of cabaret. Dinner is available before the first show. ✚ 197 D9 ✉ Algonquin Hotel, 59 West 44th Street, between Fifth and Sixth avenues ☎ 212/419-9331 🕐 Tue–Thu 8.30, Fri–Sat 8.30 and 11, Sun 1 ✋ Music charge $50–$60, minimum brunch/dinner charge $30 🚇 42nd Street (B, D, F, M) 🚌 M1, M2, M3, M4, M5, M7

PADDY REILLY'S MUSIC BAR

http://paddyreillysmusicbar.us

The Celtic house band plays excellent Irish music on a small stage in this friendly bar with Guinness on tap. Wednesday and Saturday nights are open mic. ✚ 197 E10 ✉ 519 Second Avenue at 29th Street ☎ 212/686-1210 🕐 Daily 11am–4am ✋ $5–$15 🚇 28th Street (6) 🚌 M15

PALACE THEATRE

www.palacetheatreonbroadway.com

The Palace opened as a vaudeville house in 1913, and such legends as Bob Hope, Sophie Tucker, Jimmy Durante and the Marx Brothers all entertained here. The Nederlanders restored it in 1965.

✚ 196 C9 ⊠ 1564 Broadway, between 46th and 47th streets ☎ 212/730-8200 or 212/307-4747 ⏰ Tue 7, Mon and Wed–Sat 8, Sun 7.30, Wed and Sat–Sun 2 🚇 50th Street (1), 49th Street (N, Q, R) 🚌 M7, M20, M50, M104

PARIS THEATRE

www.theparistheatre.com

The films that play here are mostly foreign.

✚ 197 D7 ⊠ 4 West 58th Street, between Fifth and Sixth avenues ☎ 212/688-3800 ✋ $13 🚇 Fifth Avenue/59th Street (N, Q, R) 🚌 M1, M2, M3, M4, M57

P. J. CLARKE'S 1884

www.pjclarkes.com

The tiny building which houses P. J. Clarke's is overshadowed by skyscrapers. The bar played a major role in Billy Wilder's 1945 film *The Lost Weekend*.

✚ 197 E8 ⊠ 915 Third Avenue at 55th Street ☎ 212/317-1616 ⏰ Daily 11.30am–4am 🚇 59th Street (4, 5, 6)

PLAYWRIGHTS HORIZONS THEATER

www.playwrightshorizons.org

This company is dedicated to the production of new American plays and musicals. In its 37 years it has produced the work of more than 350 writers. The main stage seats 198 and the studio 96.

✚ 196 B9 ⊠ 416 West 42nd Street between Ninth and Tenth avenues ☎ 212/564-1235 🚇 42nd Street (A, C, E) 🚌 M11, M42

RADIO CITY MUSIC HALL

www.radiocity.com

This theater with plenty of art deco paraphernalia hosts stars like Barry Manilow and, of course, the Rockettes.

✚ 197 D8 ⊠ 1260 Sixth Avenue at 50th Street ☎ 212/247-4777 ⏰ 1-hour tours

daily 11–3 ✋ Tours: adult $22.50, child (under 12) $15.75 🚇 47th–50th streets/ Rockefeller Center (B, D, F, M) 🚌 M5, M7, M50

ROSELAND BALLROOM

www.roselandballroom.com

The original Roseland opened at 51st Street in 1919, but moved here in 1956. Once a legendary ballroom featuring the bands of Fletcher Henderson and Tommy Dorsey, today it hosts rock concerts and occasional sporting events.

✚ 196 C8 ⊠ 239 West 52nd Street, between Broadway and Eighth Avenue ☎ 212/247-0200 ✋ $25–$60 🚇 50th Street (1), 50th Street (C, E) 🚌 M7, M20, M50, M104

RUSSIAN VODKA ROOM

http://russianvodkaroom.com

A huge selection of flavored vodkas, apple-cinnamon and horseradish, for example, are poured into martinis or drunk straight, the preference of the Russians who gather at this old-style basement bar. The menu is inexpensive.

✚ 196 C8 ⊠ 265 West 52nd Street, between Broadway and Sixth Avenue ☎ 212/307-5835 ⏰ Mon–Thu 4–2, Fri–Sun 4–4 🚇 50th Street (C, E) 🚌 M7, M20, M104

ST. ANDREW'S

www.standrewsnyc.com

Scotch-lovers crowd the bar at this traditional pub-style restaurant. Here they select their favorites from about 175 or so single malts. Go early or late to avoid the crush.

✚ 196 C9 ⊠ 140 West 46th Street, between Broadway and Seventh Avenue ☎ 212/840-8413 ⏰ Daily 11.30am–4am 🚇 42nd Street (B, D, F, M) 🚌 M5, M7

ST. JAMES THEATRE

www.jujamcyn.com

Oklahoma!, The King and I, Hello Dolly and *The Producers* have all played in this Beaux Arts theater. Its mezzanine hangs over the orchestra.

✚ 196 C9 ⊠ 246 West 44th Street, between Seventh and Eighth avenues ☎ 212/239-5800 ⏰ Tue 7, Wed–Sat 8,

matinees Wed, Sat 2, Sun 3 🚇 42nd Street/ Times Square (N, Q, R, S, 1, 2, 3, 7), 42nd Street/Eighth Avenue (A, C, E) 🚌 M7, M20, M42, M104

SAKAGURA

www.sakagura.com

In the basement of a high-rise building, this bar seems lifted from Japan. Shelves are lined with more than 200 different types of sake, and you can order flights of four selections.

✚ 197 E9 ⊠ 211 East 43rd Street, between Second and Third avenues ☎ 212/953-7253 ⏰ Mon–Thu 11.30–2.20, 6–11.45, Fri 11.30–2.20, 6–12.45, Sat 6–12.45, Sun 6–10.45 🚇 42nd Street/Grand Central (4, 5, 6)

SALON DE NING

www.salondening.com

Who can resist an invitation to a well-dressed outdoor rooftop bar in the heart of Manhattan? You'll pay for the privilege, but that's what makes memories.

✚ 197 D8 ⊠ Peninsula Hotel, 700 Fifth Avenue at 55th Street ☎ 212/903-3097 ⏰ Mon–Sat 4–1, Sun 11.30–2.30, 4–1 🚇 59th Street/Fifth Avenue (E, M) 🚌 M1, M2, M3, M4, M5

SAMUEL J. FRIEDMAN THEATRE

www.mtc-nyc.org

This landmark theater opened in 1925 and hosted such winners as *Hair* and Neil Simon's *Barefoot in the Park*. It is the Broadway home of the Manhattan Theatre Club.

✚ 196 C9 ⊠ 261 West 47th Street, between Broadway and Eighth Avenue ☎ 212/239-6200 ⏰ Tue–Sat 8, Sun 7, Sat, Sun 2 🚇 50th Street (C, E), 50th Street (1) 🚌 M7, M20

SCANDINAVIA HOUSE

www.scandinaviahouse.org

Scandinavia House shows films by directors and actors from Denmark, Finland, Iceland, Norway and Sweden.

✚ 197 D10 ⊠ Victor Borge Hall, 58 Park Avenue, between East 37th and 38th streets ☎ 212/879-9779 ✋ $10 🚇 42nd Street/ Grand Central (4, 5, 6) 🚌 M1

SECOND STAGE THEATER

www.2st.com

Dutch architect Rem Koolhaas helped revamp the old bank building that is home to this company, which stages modern American plays.

✚ 196 C9 ✉ 305 West 43rd Street, between Eighth and Ninth avenues ☎ 212/246-4422 🚇 79th Street (1) 🚌 M79, M104

SHUBERT THEATRE

www.shubertorganization.com

This theater, opened in 1913, is the cornerstone of the Shubert empire.

✚ 196 C9 ✉ 225 West 44th Street, between Seventh and Eighth avenues ☎ 212/239-6200 🕐 Mon–Tue, Thu–Sat 8, Sun 7, matinees Sat, Sun 2 🚇 42nd Street/ Times Square (N, Q, R, S, 1, 2, 3, 7), 42nd Street/Eighth Avenue (A, C, E) 🚌 M7, M20, M42, M104

STUDIO 54

www.roundabouttheatre.org

This former discotheque is now a theater. The musical *Cabaret* has played here.

✚ 196 C8 ✉ 254 West 54th Street, between Broadway and Eighth Avenue ☎ 212/239-6200 🕐 Tue–Sat 8, matinees Sat, Sun, Wed 2 🚇 Seventh Avenue (B, D, E), 57th Street (N, R, Q) 🚌 M7, M27, M50, M57

SWING 46

www.swing46.com

At this 1940s-style jazz club, you can lindy and jitterbug to top-notch live bands. Friday and Saturday is always swing. The management provides lessons to neophytes.

✚ 196 C9 ✉ 349 West 46th Street, between Eighth and Ninth avenues ☎ 212/262-9554 🕐 Sun–Thu 5–12, Fri–Sat 9–1 ✋ $12–$15 🚇 42nd Street (A, C, E)

TAO

www.taorestaurant.com

A large golden Buddha presides over this loft space, so crowded with singles after work that it was featured in an episode of *Sex and the City*.

✚ 197 D7 ✉ 42 East 58th Street, between Madison and Park avenues ☎ 212/888-

2288 🕐 Tue–Fri 11.30am–1am, Sat 5–1, Sun 5–12, Mon–Wed 11.30am–midnight, 🚇 Fifth Avenue/59th Street (N, R), 59th Street (4, 5, 6)

THEATRE AT ST. CLEMENTS

www.stclementsnyc.org

Playwrights such as David Mamet and Terrence McNally have premiered works here. The plays often focus on contemporary issues.

✚ 196 B9 ✉ 423 West 46th Street, between Ninth and Tenth avenues ☎ 212/246-7277 or 212/279-4200 🕐 Varies 🚇 42nd Street (A, C, E) 🚌 M11, M42

TOP OF THE TOWER

www.thetopofthetower.com

This 26th-floor cocktail lounge is neither overhyped nor overpriced—a miracle for such a romantic place with bewitching views.

✚ 197 E8 ✉ Beekman Tower, 3 Mitchell Place on First Avenue at 49th Street ☎ 212/980-4796 🕐 Sun–Thu 5–1, Fri–Sat 5–2 🚇 51st Street (6), 53rd Street/ Lexington (E)

THE TOWN HALL

www.the-townhall-nyc.org

Founded in 1921 by the suffragist League for Political Education, this theater offers eclectic programming with Broadway songs, cabaret, opera, pop and world music as well as lectures and readings.

✚ 196 C9 ✉ 123 West 43rd Street, between Sixth Avenue and Broadway ☎ 212/840-2824 (recording) and 212/997-6661 (Mon–Sat 12–6) ✋ Free–$75 🚇 42nd Street/Times Square (N, Q, R, S, 1, 2, 3, 7), 42nd Street (B, D, F) 🚌 M5, M7, M42

THE TOWNHOUSE

www.townhouseny.com

Upscale gay professionals gather around the piano here.

✚ 197 E7 ✉ 236 East 58th Street at Second Avenue ☎ 212/754-4649 🕐 Sun–Wed 4–3, Thu–Sat 4–4 🚇 59th Street (4, 5, 6)

WALTER KERR

Named after the famous *New York Times* critic, this is an ideal house

for serious drama and classic comedy. Seats 947.

✚ 196 C8 ✉ 219 West 48th Street, between Broadway and Eighth Avenue ☎ 212/239-6200 🕐 Tue 7, Wed–Sat 8, matinees Wed, Sat 2, Sun 3 🚇 50th Street/ Eighth Avenue (C, E), 50th Street/Seventh Avenue (1) 🚌 M7, M10, M27, M50, M104

YORK THEATRE

www.yorktheatre.org

The material presented at the modern space in St. Peter's church at Citicorp Center is often experimental and challenging.

✚ 197 E8 ✉ 619 Lexington Avenue at 54th Street ☎ 212/935-5824 🚇 51st Street (6), Fifth Avenue/53rd Street (E) 🚌 M98, M101, M102, M103

SPORTS AND ACTIVITIES
DOWNTOWN BOATHOUSE

www.downtownboathouse.org

The Downtown Boathouse organization offers free kayaking trips and instruction on the Hudson River. It operates from several locations.

✚ 196 A8 ✉ Pier 96, Clinton Cove Park at 56th Street 🕐 Mid-May to mid-Oct ✋ Free 🚇 Columbus Circle (1) 🚌 M20

GRAND CENTRAL PARTNERSHIP TOURS

▷ 270.

NEW YORK KNICKS

www.nba.com/knicks

The Knicks are the city's hottest ticket. This team and the Boston Celtics are the only remaining charter members of the NBA. Walt Frazier, Bill Bradley and Willis Reed made them golden in the 1970s, and Patrick Ewing helped them to the play-offs in 1994 and 1999.

✚ 196 C10 ✉ Madison Square Garden, 2 Pennsylvania Plaza, Seventh Avenue, between West 31st and 33rd streets ☎ 212/465-5867 or 212/465-6741 (Madison Square Garden), 212/307-7171 for tickets, 212/465-5802 for tours ✋ $15–$3,000 🚇 34th Street/Penn Station (A, C, E, 1, 2, 3) 🚌 M20, M34

NEW YORK LIBERTY

www.wnba.com/liberty

The team has become a star in the Women's National Basketball Association (WNBA) and has played in WNBA finals.

✚ 196 C10 ✉ Madison Square Garden, 2 Pennsylvania Plaza, Seventh Avenue, between West 31st and 33rd streets ☎ 212/564-9622 💲 $10–$250 🚇 34th Street/Penn Station (A, C, E, 1, 2, 3) 🚌 M20, M34

ROCKEFELLER CENTER ICE RINK

www.therinkatrockcenter.com

It's dreamlike to glide on this legendary rink under the golden statue of Prometheus. There is a live DJ on Thursday from 7pm till 11pm.

✚ 197 D8 ✉ 1 Rockefeller Center Plaza, Fifth Avenue, between 49th and 50th streets ☎ 212/332-7654 🕐 Oct–late Apr several sessions daily, phone or visit website for timings 💲 Mon–Thu $5 lunch, $10 otherwise Fri–Sun and holidays $19; under 11 and seniors Mon–Thu $7.50, Fri–Sun and holidays $8.50, skate rental $7 🚇 47th–50th streets/Rockefeller Center (B, D, F) 🚌 M1, M2, M3, M4, M50

HEALTH AND BEAUTY

EQUINOX FITNESS CLUB

www.equinoxfitness.com

All 19 Equinox clubs in Manhattan are sleek and sophisticated and almost invariably offer spinning, Pilates, yoga, cardio-boxing and cardio machines.

✚ 197 D10 ✉ 1 Park Avenue at East 33rd Street ☎ 212/779-1727 🕐 Mon–Thu 5.30am–11pm, Fri 5.30am–10pm, Sat–Sun 8am–9pm 💲 $148 monthly membership, or $178 for all Equinox clubs 🚇 33rd Street (6) 🚌 M1, M2, M3, M4, M16, M34

MARIO BADESCU

www.mariobadescu.com

You might expect Mario Badescu, whose clients include Sharon Stone, Kate Moss and P. Diddy, to charge an arm and a leg to treat your hands and your feet, but his prices are very reasonable and if you want one spa session in New York, book it here.

✚ 197 E8 ✉ 320 East 52nd Street, between First and Second avenues

☎ 212/758-1065 🕐 Mon–Tue, Fri 8.30–6, Wed–Thu 8.30–8.30, Fri 8.30–6, Sat 9–5, Sun 10–6 💲 Facial $65, manicure $15, pedicure $25, massage $70 🚇 51st Street (6), Lexington Avenue-53rd Street (E, M) 🚌 M101, M102, M103

PIERRE MICHEL

www.pierremichelbeauty.com

The Cornelia range of beauty products is exclusively available in New York at this salon just off Park Avenue, where haircuts, facials, waxing, manicures and other indulgences are available.

✚ 197 E8 ✉ 135 East 57th Street (3rd Floor) between Park and Lexington avenues ☎ 212/755-9500 💲 Facial from $95, manicures $35 🚇 59th Street (4, 5, 6) 🚌 M31, M57, M101, M102, M103

FOR CHILDREN

CIRCLE LINE CRUISES

www.circleline42.com

Circling around Manhattan in a boat is the best way to grasp the contours of the island and the extraordinary city piled high upon it. Depending on the attention span of your kids, you can opt for the two-hour afternoon trip or the three-hour version. The narration can be great or mediocre, but the fresh air, the passing craft and the sights make it fun. The same company also runs day-long tours up the Hudson River.

✚ 196 A9 ✉ Pier 83, West 42nd Street and Hudson River ☎ 212/563-3200 🕐 Call for departure times and schedules 💲 $24–$36 🚇 42nd Street (A, C, E) then M42 🚌 M42, M50

FAO SCHWARZ

▷ 177.

LIBERTY HELICOPTERS

www.libertyhelicopters.com

Helicopters take off from the heliport on tours from 2 to 17 minutes hovering above the city and the Hudson River. If you can afford it, why not?

✚ 196 A10 ✉ West 30th Street and Twelfth Avenue ☎ 212/967-6464 💲 $150–$215 🚇 34th Street (A, C, E) 🚌 M11, M34

MADAME TUSSAUDS

www.madametussauds.com

The New York version of this world-famous London waxworks museum opened in 2000. It contains the usual collection of lifelike historical, political and cultural figures—here, geared to a New York audience. You'll probably see realistic replicas of such luminaries as comedian Joan Rivers, actor and director Woody Allen and basketball star Michael Jordan.

✚ 196 C9 ✉ 234 West 42nd Street, between Eighth and Seventh avenues ☎ 800/246-8872 🕐 Daily 10–10 💲 Adult $36, child (4–12) $29, under 4 free 🚇 42nd Street (A, C, E), 42nd Street/Times Square (N, Q, R, S, 1, 2, 3, 7) 🚌 M7, M16, M20, M42

NBC STUDIO TOUR

www.nbcstudiotour.com

Take one of the 70-minute tours of the NBC (National Broadcasting Company) network's studios where *The Today Show* and *Saturday Night Live* are produced. Visitors peek into studios and also see how shows are made.

✚ 197 D8 ✉ 30 Rockefeller Plaza, 49th Street, between Fifth and Sixth avenues ☎ 212/664-7174 🕐 Mon–Thu 8.30–5.30, Fri–Sat 8.30–6.30, Sun 9.15–4.30. Reservations recommended 💲 Adult $20, child (6–12) $17 (under 6 not admitted) 🚇 47th–50th streets/Rockefeller Center (B, D, F, M) 🚌 M1, M2, M3, M4, M5, M7, M50

SONY WONDER TECHNOLOGY LAB

www.sonywondertechlab.com

Interactive exhibits fill four floors here, demonstrating the latest developments in communications, robotics, medical technology and entertainment. It is not as much of a hard sell as you might expect. Reservations are needed and can be made one week to three months in advance.

✚ 197 D8 ✉ Sony Plaza, 550 Madison Avenue at East 56th Street ☎ 212/833-8100 🕐 Tue–Sat 9.30–5.30 💲 Free 🚇 Fifth Avenue/53rd Street (E), Fifth Avenue/59th Street (N, Q, R) 🚌 M1, M2, M3, M4

PRICES AND SYMBOLS

The prices given are the average for a two-course lunch (L) and a three-course dinner (D) for one person, without drinks. The wine price is for the least expensive bottle.

For a key to the symbols, ▷ 2.

'21' CLUB

www.21club.com

The hamburger makes headlines for its price ($32 and climbing), but this storied locale is about so much more than the sandwich. Two college students opened it as a speakeasy in Greenwich Village in 1920; it was frequented by Humphrey Bogart, F. Scott Fitzgerald and Joe Di Maggio after relocating to this town house in 1929. Old-fashioned and masculine, it purveys fist-size medallions of beef flambéed with cognac and Dijon, chicken hash and Dover sole, along with newer, lighter dishes like black sea bass in champagne sauce. The daily special ice creams, gussied up or plain, are the choice desserts, and the wine cellar is renowned. Jacket and tie required.

✚ 197 D8 ✉ 21 West 52nd Street, between Fifth and Sixth avenues
☎ 212/582-7200 🕐 Mon 5.30–10, Tue

12–2.30, 5–10, Wed–Thu 12–2.30, 5.30–10, Fri 12–2.30, 5.30–11, Sat 5–11 ✋ L $60, D $80, Wine $30 🚇 47th–50th streets (B, D, F, M) 🚌 M1, M2, M3, M4, M5, M7, M50

AQUAVIT

www.aquavit.org

In a sleek modern space, Chef Marcus Jemmark creates contemporary interpretations of Swedish–Scandinavian cuisine: oysters come with a mango-curry sorbet; mushroom broth is poured over delicately smoked arctic char. There's a wide selection of aquavits, plus 250 wines (15 by the glass). Jackets are required in the dining room, but the front café is more casual and offers more traditional Scandinavian fare.

✚ 197 D8 ✉ 65 East 55th Street, between Madison and Park avenues ☎ 212/307-7311 🕐 Mon–Fri 12–2.30, 5.30–10.30, Sat 5.30–10.30 ✋ L $42, D $84, tasting menu $110, Wine $38 🚇 Fifth Avenue (E, M) 🚌 M1, M2, M3, M4, M5, M7, M57

ARTISANAL

www.artisanalbistro.com

This gem is all about cheese, and the quality of the 250 varieties in the walk-in cheese vault is astonishing, ranging from *cabecou de*

Rocamadour to *callu de cabreddu*. Savor them straight or in a fondue. Not to worry if you don't eat cheese: escargots, moules and main dishes such as crisp skate wing with blood orange *Grenobloise* and steak frites complete the menu.

✚ 197 D10 ✉ 2 Park Avenue at 32nd Street ☎ 212/725-8585 🕐 Mon–Wed 11.45–4.30, 5–10, Thu–Fri 11.45–4.30, 5–11, Sat 10.30–4.30, 5–11, Sun 10.30–4.30, 5–9 ✋ L $40, D $54, Wine $35 🚇 33rd Street (6) 🚌 M1

BANN

www.bannnewyork.com

Innovative dishes featuring stylized versions of Korean cuisine are the focus of this restaurant. You can see the dishes being prepared in the open kitchen, where the flaming woks and exotic aromas provide an exciting and sensory dining experience. Start with marinated steak tartare over Asian pear, or seasoned crab and leek in spinach crêpes. Then move on to the authentic Korean barbecue featuring a variety of meats and seafood which are cooked tableside at smokeless grills. There are also a range of traditional entrées from tofu to black cod to beef short ribs, as well as rice and noodle dishes. Don't forget the kimchi—pickle dishes that are always on the Korean table.

✚ 196 C8 ✉ 350 West 50th Street, between Eighth and Ninth avenues ☎ 212/582-4446 🕐 Sun–Thu 12–10.30, Fri–Sat 12–11 ✋ L $15, D $45, Wine $34 🚇 50th Street (C, E, 1) 🚌 M11, M20, M50, M104

LE BERNARDIN
www.le-bernardin.com

Le Bernardin is the best seafood restaurant in the city. The teak-paneled room is spacious and comfortable, the service discreet and precise, and the food exquisite. Chef Eric Ripert's dishes are designed to show off the flavor and texture of the specific type of fish. Cod is served in a sage and garlic broth, halibut poached in lemongrass and coconut, and monkfish oven roasted and served with lemon-paprika sauce. Signature appetizers—tuna carpaccio; a scallop wrapped in a cabbage leaf with foie gras and truffles and steamed; and black bass ceviche topped with coriander, mint, jalapeños and tomatoes—are all gems. Desserts are inspirational.

✚ 196 C8 ✉ 155 West 51st Street, between Sixth and Seventh avenues ☎ 212/489-1515 🕐 Mon–Fri 12–2.30, Mon–Thu 5.30–10.30, Fri–Sat 5.30–11 ✋ L prix fixe $70, D 3-course prix fixe $115, Wine $50 🚇 47th–50th streets/Rockefeller Center (B, D, F, M), 49th Street (N, Q, R) 🚌 M5, M7, M50

BLUE FIN
www.bluefinnyc.com

The vast, theatrical Blue Fin offers the freshest fish, prepared simply in such dishes as salmon in a warm bacon sherry vinaigrette, or poached halibut in ancho-chili-and-vegetable broth. Sushi is available on the first floor of the two-story space, which has a floating staircase that looks out over a school of black fish suspended from

the ceiling against an undulating wall. There are 600 wines on the list, 30 by the glass.

✚ 196 C9 ✉ W Hotel, Times Square, 1567 Broadway at 47th Street ☎ 212/918-1400 🕐 Daily 7–11.30, 11.30–4, Sun–Mon 5–11, Tue–Thu 5–11.30, Fri–Sat 5–12 ✋ L $40, D $60, Wine $45 🚇 49th Street (N, Q, R), 50th Street (1) 🚌 M7, M20, M50, M104

BRASSERIE
www.patinagroup.com

From its theatrical entrance ramp to its buzzing bar, Brasserie is one very cool room and so very New York. The French-Mediterranean menu is satisfying, ranging as it does from salad Niçoise and burgers (with oyster mushrooms, bacon and roasted onions) to duck cassoulet and rice-crusted black sea bass in lemongrass and lime broth. Great sushi and a raw bar, too.

✚ 197 E8 ✉ 100 East 53rd Street, between Park and Lexington avenues ☎ 212/751-4840 🕐 Mon–Thu 7am–11pm, Fri 7am–midnight, Sat 11am–midnight, Sun 11–10 ✋ L $40, D $60, Wine $35 🚇 53rd Street/Lexington Avenue (E, M), 51st Street (6) 🚌 M1, M2, M3, M4, M50, M101, M102, M103

CHO DANG GOL
www.chodanggolny.com

This popular Korean place makes its own tofu daily, but it's not a vegetarian restaurant. The tasty tofu can be mixed with pork, squid and octopus, among other things, with a casserole being the house specialty. Korean wine is served, but most people opt for sake. Sweet-lovers should note there are no desserts.

✚ 197 D10 ✉ 55 West 35th Street, between Fifth and Sixth avenues ☎ 212/695-8222 🕐 Daily 11.30–10.30 ✋ L $30, D $30, Wine $14 🚇 34th St. Herald Square (B, D, F, N, Q, R, M), 34th St. Penn Station (1, 2, 3) 🚌 M5, M7, M16, M34

LE COLONIAL
www.lecolonialnyc.com

The French colonial ambience is a perfect backdrop for the Vietnamese cuisine at this striking spot. Start with *chao tom* (grilled shrimp wrapped around sugarcane with

angel-hair noodles, lettuce, mint and peanut dipping sauce) or the steamed ravioli with chicken and mushrooms. The steamed sea bass dishes are outstanding.

✚ 197 E7 ✉ 149 East 57th Street, between Lexington and Third avenues ☎ 212/752-0808 🕐 Mon 12–2.30, 5.30–11, Tue–Thu 12–2.30, 5.30–11.30, Fri 12–2.30, 5.30–12, Sat 5.30–12, Sun 5.30–11 ✋ L $35, D $50, Wine $38 🚇 59th Street (4, 5, 6), 59th Street/Lexington Avenue (N, Q, R) 🚌 M31, M57, M101, M102, M103

DAWAT
http://dawatrestaurant.com

Cookbook author Madhur Jaffrey consults at this comfortable Indian. The spices are skillfully blended to subtle effect in such dishes as shrimp in coconut sauce flavored with curry leaves and smoked tamarind; chicken tikka; and baby goat in cardamom sauce. There are rice and vegetarian specialties.

✚ 197 E7 ✉ 210 East 58th Street, between Second and Third avenues ☎ 212/355-7555 🕐 Mon–Sat 11.30–3, 5.30–11, Sun 5.30–11 ✋ L $60, D $65, tasting menus $50–$80, Wine $19 🚇 59th Street/Lexington Avenue (4, 5, 6) 🚌 M31, M32, M57, M101, M102, M103

DB BISTRO MODERNE
www.danielnyc.com

This most casual and contemporary of Daniel Boulud's restaurants is a great Theater District choice. It's famous for its $32 sirloin burger—a fistful of ground sirloin wrapped around red wine-braised short ribs with truffle and foie gras, served with tomato confit and fresh horseradish. Other delights include roast salmon with honeyed eggplant (aubergine) and stuffed zucchini (courgette) flowers, and Muscovy duck breast with blood orange jus.

✚ 197 D9 ✉ 55 West 44th Street, between Fifth and Sixth avenues ☎ 212/391-2400 🕐 Mon–Fri 7–10, 12–2.30, Mon 5–10, Tue 5–11, Wed–Thu 5–11, Fri 5–11.30, Sat 8–2.30, 5–11.30, Sun 8–2.30, 5–10 ✋ L $45, D $65, Wine $35 🚇 42nd Street/Grand Central (S, 4, 5, 6, 7), 42nd Street (B, D, F, M) 🚌 M1, M2, M3, M4, M42

ESCA

www.esca-nyc.com

Esca, another star in Mario Batali's firmament, prepares fish southern Italian style. The menu changes daily, but you might find Mediterranean sea bass in sea salt or Amalfi-style fritto misto, with crispy scrod, skate, calamari, steamers, oysters and shrimp. Appetizers run to crispy Neapolitan-style eel and juicy morsels from a serious raw bar.

✚ 196 C9 ✉ 402 West 43rd Street at Ninth Avenue ☎ 212/564-7272 ⏰ Mon–Sat 12–2.30, Mon 5–10.30, Tue–Sat 5–11.30, Sun 4.30–10.30 ✋ L $40, D $70, Wine $32 Ⓜ 42nd Street (A, C, E) 🚌 M11

FELIDIA

www.felidia-nyc.com

Felidia is a top Italian restaurant. The Istrian wedding pillows, stuffed with rum, raisins and three cheeses, are a signature dish, but chef Fortunato Nicotra has added regional dishes, such as roasted goose ravioli.

✚ 197 E7 ✉ 243 East 58th Street between Second and Third avenues ☎ 212/758-1479 ⏰ Mon–Thu 12–2.30, 5–11, Fri 12–2, 5–11.30, Sat 5–11.30 ✋ L $50, 3-course prix fixe $29.50, D $75, Wine $44 Ⓜ 59th Street (4, 5, 6) 🚌 M15, M31, M57, M101, M102, M103

FOUR SEASONS

www.fourseasonsrestaurant.com

This modernist power restaurant was designed by Philip Johnson and Mies van der Rohe. When it opened in 1959, it helped launch the city's food revolution. The square bar at the center of the Grill Room is a great cocktail spot. The pièce de résistance is the Pool Room, with a large fountain as centerpiece. Chef Christian Albin's signature dish is roast duck, which is carved tableside. The soufflés are famous.

✚ 197 E8 ✉ 99 East 52nd Street, between Park and Lexington avenues ☎ 212/754-9494 ⏰ Mon–Fri 12–2.30, 5–9.30, Sat 5–9.30 ✋ L $70, D $100, Wine $65 Ⓜ 51st Street (6), Fifth Avenue/53rd Street (E, M) 🚌 M1, M50, M101, M102, M103

GORDON RAMSAY AT THE LONDON

www.gordonramsay.com

In 2007 Ramsay won two Michelin stars. You'll need to book two months ahead—exactly two months ahead, as tables go as soon as they're available, with diners longing to experience Ramsay's ability to combine flavors and let every single one shine through in dishes like his baked fluke with almond bread, celery hearts, Concord grapes and champagne velouté.

✚ 196 C8 ✉ The London NYC Hotel, 151 West 54th Street between Sixth and Seventh avenues ☎ 212/468-8888 ⏰ Tue–Sat 5.30–10 ✋ D $135, 7-course menu prestige $185, Wine $40 Ⓜ Seventh Avenue (B, D, E), 57th Street (N, Q, R) 🚌 M5, M7

GRAND CENTRAL OYSTER BAR

www.oysterbarny.com

You don't have to love oysters to love this legendary room in the lower level of Grand Central. Since it opened in 1913 it has starred in many a movie. Today, it's jammed at lunch and busy in the early evening with people sampling the fresh fish choices, or slurping down oysters, all flown in daily from around the world. Choose from some 30 varieties of fresh oysters: East Coast, West Coast, Kumamoto, Wellfleet and many more. Or try the steamed mussels, lobsters, broiled scallops, grouper, sole, trout, bass or even fish and chips. You might like the renowned chowder-like panroasts. The wine list includes more than 50 varieties by the glass, and there is also a large beer list.

✚ 197 D9 ✉ Grand Central Terminal, 42nd Street and Park Avenue ☎ 212/490-6650 ⏰ Mon–Fri 11.30–9.30, Sat 12–9.30 ✋ L $35, D $45, Wine $30 Ⓜ 42nd Street/Grand Central (4, 5, 6) 🚌 M1, M2, M3

HELL'S KITCHEN

www.hellskitchen-nyc.com

Here, a contemporary interpretation of Mexican cuisine uses prime American ingredients. Start with calamari in smoked chipotle broth, or chayote and portobello mushroom roll with chipotle pepper sauce. The strong exotic drinks from the bar match the robust flavors.

✚ 196 C9 ✉ 679 Ninth Avenue, between West 46th and 47th streets ☎ 212/977-1588 ⏰ Sun–Wed 5–11, Thu–Sat 5–12 ✋ D $50, Wine $25 Ⓜ 42nd Street (A, C, E) 🚌 M11

MOLYVOS

www.molyvos.com

This large space with a café, a bar and two dining rooms, brings Greece to Manhattan. The dips and spreads are irresistible, including the garlicky roasted eggplant (aubergine) purée and the tzatziki, a blend of yogurt, cucumber, garlic, mint, dill and lemon. Outstanding are the cold meze such as grilled baby octopus with olives, fennel, lemon and oregano, and fava beans mashed with olive oil. Marinated lamb shanks, whole grilled fish and rabbit stew are main courses.

✚ 196 C8 ✉ 871 Seventh Avenue, between West 55th and 56th streets ☎ 212/582-7500 ⏰ Mon–Fri 12–3, 5.30–11, Sat 12–3, 5–11, Sun 12–11 ✋ L $38, D $60, Wine $38 Ⓜ Seventh Avenue (B, D, E), 57th Street (N, Q, R) 🚌 M7, M20

NAPLES 45

www.patinagroup.com

Authentic Neapolitan pizzas emerge piping hot from the wood-fired ovens, as do the fish of the day. The menu showcases southern Italian cooking with a good range of fish, chicken and steak dishes—and vegetarians won't leave unsatisfied, either. The *piccoli piatti,* or small plates, are popular appetizers, especially the steamed mussels and veal meatballs.

✚ 197 D9 ✉ Met Life Building, 200 Park Avenue at East 45th Street (entrance on 45th) ☎ 212/972-7000 ⏰ Mon–Fri 7.30am–10pm ✋ L $30, D $50, Wine $29 Ⓜ Grand Central/42nd Street (4, 5, 6, 7, S) 🚌 M1, M2, M3, M4, M50, M101, M102, M103

PAMPANO

www.modernmexican.com

Placido Domingo helped open this restaurant where chef Richard

Sandoval, who hails from Mexico City, via California, produces great contemporary Mexican using such ingredients as *huitlacoche, epazote,* pomegranate, *queso blanco* and every conceivable kind of pepper. The *chile rellenos* are roasted not fried and stuffed with seafood and tart manchego. Start with any one of the ceviches and continue with a seafood dish. Meat lovers are out of luck although the lamb in adobo orange sauce is tasty. The outdoor terrace is as close to the beach as you can get in midtown Manhattan.
➕ 197 E8 ✉ 209 East 49th Street, between Second and Third avenues ☎ 212/751-4545 🕐 Mon–Fri 11.30–2.30, Mon–Wed 5–10, Thu–Sat 5–10.30, Sun 5–9.30 ✋ L $35, D $60, Wine $32 🚇 51st Street (6) 🚌 M15, M50, M101, M102, M103

PAM REAL THAI

At this authentic Thai, the traditional favorites are all available: superb hot and milder curries, fiery salads made with green papaya, ground pork with lime dressing, noodle dishes and, best of all, duck with chili sauce and lime leaves. Bring your own bottle. Credit cards are not accepted.
➕ 196 B8 ✉ 404 West 49th Street, between Ninth and Tenth avenues ☎ 212/333-7500 🕐 Sun–Thu 11.30–11, Fri–Sat 11.30–11.30 ✋ L $16, D $24 🚇 50th Street (C, E, 1, 9) 🚌 M11, M50

SHUN LEE PALACE

www.shunleepalace.com
It's still the best Chinese restaurant in the city, even though it's been around since 1972. It may be expensive, but the dining rooms are comfortable and elegant and the Shanghai, Szechuan and Cantonese cuisine is beautifully presented. Besides such traditional dishes as crispy sea bass Hunan style and lobster in black bean sauce, you will find such extraordinary specialties as Grand Marnier prawns and red cooked short ribs Hang Chow style. There's a branch near the Lincoln Center at 43 West 65th Street between Central Park West and Columbus Avenue (tel 212/595-

8895)—a good bet for a leisurely meal or a pre-concert snack.
➕ 197 E8 ✉ 155 East 55th Street, between Lexington and Third avenues ☎ 212/371-8844 🕐 Mon–Sat noon–11.30, Sun noon–11 ✋ L $40, D $56, Wine $40 🚇 Lexington Avenue/53rd Street (E, M), 51st Street (6) 🚌 M31, M57, M101, M102, M103

SUGIYAMA

www.sugiyama-nyc.com
Here, the seasons inform chef Nao Sugiyama's Kaiseki cuisine. You have a choice of various 5-, 6- or 8-course dinners and post- or pre-theater. Each includes an appetizer, sashimi, soup, a sizzling dish on hot stone and dessert. The sashimi is exceptionally fresh, featuring uni (sea urchin), octopus, tuna, red snapper and more. The excellently prepared dishes are attractively presented, and offer a variety of flavors and textures, with soup, appetizers, vegetable creations and main dishes of seafood or meat. There is a wide selection of sake, available by the glass and bottle.
➕ 196 C8 ✉ 251 West 55th Street, between Broadway and Eighth Avenue ☎ 212/956-0670 🕐 Tue–Sat 5.30–11.45 ✋ D $58–$198, $32 pre-theater, Wine $28 🚇 59th Street/Columbus Circle (A, B, C, D, 1) 🚌 M7, M20, M104

SUSHI YASUDA

www.sushiyasuda.com
Here owner Naomichi Yasuda displays his artistry, selecting the best fish, evaluating its texture, masterfully cutting it to release the best flavor, and cooking and seasoning the rice to perfection. Then he crafts a meal for the individuals who sit down at his sushi bar, according to their tastes and experience, and to the size of their mouths. It's custom-made perfection, but naturally it comes at a high price. For a delightful meal request one of his eight tuna specialties or one of the eel pieces for which he is renowned.
➕ 197 E9 ✉ 204 East 43rd Street, between Second and Third avenues ☎ 212/972-1001 🕐 Mon–Fri 12–2.15,

6–10.15, Sat 6–10.15, closed Sun ✋ L $80, D $100, Wine $18 (sake) 🚇 42nd Street/Grand Central (S, 4, 5, 6, 7) 🚌 M15, M42, M101, M102, M103

UNCLE NICK'S

www.unclenicksgreekrestaurant.com
At this authentic Greek restaurant, there's always a fun, festive atmosphere. Start with a selection of hot and cold appetizers, followed by home-cooked traditional dishes such as moussaka, pastitsio and stuffed vine leaves. There are excellent grilled meats, chicken and quail, and seasonal seafood dishes that come straight off the boat.
➕ 196 C8 ✉ 747 Ninth Avenue between 50th and 51st streets ☎ 212/245-7992 🕐 Daily 11.30–11 ✋ L $18, D $30, Wine $18 🚇 50th Street (C, E), 49th Street (N, R) 🚌 M11, M50

UNCLE VANYA CAFÉ

Russian home cooking starts at this plain storefront restaurant: hearty borscht, beef dumplings with sour cream, stuffed cabbage rolls and beef Stroganoff with kasha. It's filling and inexpensive. Try one of the Georgian wines, if you dare.
➕ 196 C8 ✉ 315 West 54th Street, between Eighth and Ninth avenues ☎ 212/262-0542 🕐 Mon–Thu 12–11, Fri–Sat 12–12, Sun 2–10 ✋ L $20, D $25, Wine $25 🚇 50th Street (C, E) 🚌 M11, M20, M104

VIRGIL'S REAL BARBECUE

www.virgilsbbq.com
The aroma of hickory wood smoke alone is enough to draw you into Virgil's vast barbecue emporium. Here, the huge platters of Memphis-style barbecue or fried chicken arrive with grits or mashed potatoes and biscuits and gravy. Po'boys, also known as hero sandwiches, round out the Southern-style menu.
➕ 196 C9 ✉ 152 West 44th Street between Sixth Avenue and Broadway ☎ 212/921-9494 🕐 Mon 11–11, Tue–Fri 11.30am–midnight, Sat 9am–midnight, Sun 9am–11pm ✋ L $35, D $45 🚇 42nd Street/Times Square (N, Q, R, S, 1, 2, 3, 7), 42nd Street (B, D, F, M) 🚌 M5, M7, M42, M104

PRICES AND SYMBOLS

Prices are the lowest and highest for a double room for one night. Breakfast is included unless noted otherwise. All the hotels listed accept credit cards unless otherwise stated. Note that rates vary widely throughout the year.

For a key to the symbols, ▷ 2.

70 PARK AVENUE

www.70parkave.com

In quiet Murray Hill, Kimpton's first property in New York City has been designed in contemporary style, but with comfort in mind, even though the rooms are on the small side. Guest rooms are decorated in a gracious style, with at-home comfort. Deep soaking tubs invite tranquil repose in the well-appointed bathrooms. Yoga mats and a 24-hour yoga channel are also available. Technical equipment includes 42-inch flat-panel TVs, DVD/CD players, and wireless and wired high-speed Internet access. Pets are welcome. The Silverleaf Tavern offers contemporary American fare.

✚ 197 D10 ✉ 70 Park Avenue at 38th Street, 10016 ☎ 212/973-2400 💶 Doubles from $389, suites from $589 🛈 205 rooms and suites 🚇 Grand Central/42nd Street (4, 5, 6, 7) 🚌 M1, M2, M3, M4, M42

ALGONQUIN

www.algonquinhotel.com

It's famous for being the place where in the 1920s Robert Benchley, Dorothy Parker and the rest of the *Vanity Fair/New Yorker* crowd gathered regularly for lunch at the Round Table. The rooms are moderate in size and furnished with reproductions of American antiques. The wood-paneled Oak Room (▷ 182) is the city's best cabaret.

✚ 196 C9 ✉ 59 West 44th Street, between Fifth and Sixth avenues, 10036 ☎ 212/840-6800 💶 $300–$499, suite from $349 🛈 150 rooms, 24 suites 🖥 🚇 42nd Street (B, D, F, M) 🚌 M5, M7, M42

AMERICANA INN

www.theamericanainn.com

Rooms here are bright, modern and comfortable, if plainly decorated. They are equipped with cable TV and telephone. All rooms share a bath, and each floor has a kitchenette.

✚ 197 D9 ✉ 69 West 38th Street, between Fifth and Sixth avenues, 10018 ☎ 212/840-6700 💶 $110–$150 🛈 54 🚇 42nd Street (B, D, F, M) 🚌 M5, M7

AVALON

www.theavalonny.com

This small hotel is near the Empire State Building and has traditionally furnished rooms. Executive suites have fax, Bose radio and cordless phone. Complimentary breakfast and morning newspaper are set out in the mahogany-paneled library off the lobby.

✚ 197 D10 ✉ 16 East 32nd Street at Madison Avenue, 10016 ☎ 212/299-7000 💶 Double from $329, suite from $369 🛈 70 rooms, 30 suites 🚇 33rd Street (6) 🚌 M1, M2, M3, M4, M34

BEEKMAN TOWER

www.thebeekmanhotel.com

This all-suite hotel, in a 1928 art deco building near the UN, has accommodations that include bedroom, sitting room and fully equipped kitchen. The deluxe suites have such extras as VCRs and two-line phones. The bar/restaurant on the top floor is one of the most romantic aeries in the city. There is a fitness center on-premises.

✚ 197 E8 ✉ 3 Mitchell Place (East 49th Street and First Avenue), 10017 ☎ 212/355-7300 💶 From $220, 2-bedroom suite from $500 🛈 174 suites 🖥 🚇 51st Street (6) 🚌 M15

BELVEDERE

www.belvederehotelnyc.com

The most expensive hotel in the Empire Hotel group, the Belvedere has handsome sizable rooms with kitchenettes fitted with microwave, refrigerator and coffeemaker. Executive rooms and suites are also available. On the premises is the Churrascaria Plataforma, a Brazilian steakhouse.

╋ 196 C8 ✉ 319 West 48th Street, between Eighth and Ninth avenues, 10036 ☎ 212/245-7000 ✋ $194–$540 ⓘ 334 rooms and suites ⓠ 50th Street (C, E) 🚌 M11, M20, M50

BENJAMIN

www.thebenjamin.com

Conveniently situated in Midtown, this Manhattan Suites hotel offers good-looking rooms and excellent facilities in a handsome 1927 building. The rooms are furnished with mahogany pieces. Guests can select from a 10-type pillow menu. The Wellness Spa is a bonus. There is a restaurant and bar.

╋ 197 E8 ✉ 125 East 50th Street at Lexington Avenue, 10022 ☎ 212/715-2500 ✋ Doubles from $399, suites from $499 ⓘ 209 ⓠ 51st Street (6) 🚌 M50, M101, M102, M103

BLAKELY

www.blakelyny.com

The rooms are handsome with a traditional English flavor conveyed in foxhunt prints and cherry furnishings. Amenities include full kitchenettes with microwave and mini-fridge plus the latest in tech—flat-screen TVs, DVD/CD players, cordless phones and complimentary WiFi. Comforts run to Frette bathrobes and Penhaligon toiletries. There is a restaurant-bar and fitness center.

╋ 196 C8 ✉ 136 West 55th Street, between Sixth and Seventh avenues, 10019 ☎ 212/245-1800 ✋ $330–$435, suite from $585 ⓘ 58 rooms, 55 suites 🛇 ⓠ 57th Street (F, N, Q, R) 🚌 M5, M7, M57, M104

CASABLANCA

www.casablancahotel.com

Close to the Theater District, the boutique-style Casablanca is small and personal and offers stylish, modern, well-equipped guest rooms. The public areas have a distinctly Moroccan feel complete with tiles and rattan chairs.

╋ 196 C9 ✉ 147 West 43rd Street, between Sixth and Seventh avenues, 10036 ☎ 212/869-1212 ✋ Doubles from $279, suites from £369 ⓘ 40 rooms, 8 suites ⓠ 42nd Street/Times Square (N, Q, R, S, 1, 2, 3, 7, 9), 42nd Street (B, D, F, M) 🚌 M5, M7, M20, M42

DREAM HOTEL

www.dreamny.com

From the minute you enter the stylish lobby you know that this hotel is all about design. Sculptures, dramatic lighting and modern styling dominate the lobby. The rooms are dramatically furnished with blue satin headboards and lit blue, too. Bathrooms are minimalist. The rooms have the latest tech amenities—plasma TV, iPod with Bose speakers. Lounges are found in the lobby, on the rooftop and underground. Plus, Deepak Chopra has an Ayurvedic center here.

╋ 196 C8 ✉ 210 West 55th Street, between Broadway and Seventh Avenue, 10019 ☎ 212/247-2000 ✋ Doubles from $219, suite from $359 ⓘ 204 rooms and 16 suites ⓠ Seventh Avenue (B, D, E), 57th Street/Seventh Avenue (N, Q, R) 🚌 M7, M20

EDISON

www.edisonhotelnyc.com

Theater patrons appreciate this art deco 1931 hotel in the center of the Theater District. The entrance lobby is somewhat bland, but it is functional. The rooms are moderately priced and have cable TV and telephone. There is a restaurant and bar, too.

╋ 196 C9 ✉ 228 West 47th Street, between Broadway and Eighth Avenue, 10036 ☎ 212/840-5000. ✋ Doubles from $145, suites from $299 ⓘ 900 rooms and suites ⓠ 50th Street (C, E), 50th Street (1) 🚌 M7, M20, M50, M104

ELYSÉE

www.elyseehotel.com

This little gem of a hotel, built in 1926, has comfortable rooms decorated with fine French antique reproductions and luxurious fabrics. Bathrooms are marble and brass. The Monkey Bar, named for its murals, was once home to such regulars as actress Tallulah Bankhead. Guests have use of a nearby sports club.

╋ 197 D8 ✉ 60 East 54th Street, 10022 ☎ 212/753-1066 ✋ Doubles from $320, suites from $450, including Continental breakfast and wine and cheese (weekday evenings) ⓘ 87 rooms, 13 suites ⓠ 53rd Street/Fifth Avenue (E, M), 51st Street (6) 🚌 M1, M2, M3, M4, M50

FOUR SEASONS

www.fourseasons.com

The service at this hotel is legendary; staff are trained to cater to a guest's every whim. I. M. Pei designed the 53-story building, which opened in 1993. The rooms, averaging 600sq feet (55sq m), are the largest in the city and include a dressing area. The suites have walk-in closets and balconies with grand city views. The large fitness center contains a full spa, and the restaurant and bar are top range.

╋ 197 D7 ✉ 57 East 57th Street, between Madison and Park avenues, 10022 ☎ 212/758-5700 ✋ From $595, suite from $1,550 ⓘ 305 rooms, 63 suites 🛇 ⓠ 59th Street (4, 5, 6) 🚌 M1, M2, M3, M4

GRAND UNION

www.hotelgrandunion.com

This old-fashioned hotel in the trendsetting Flatiron neighborhood has clean basic rooms that are equipped with small refrigerators and phones with data ports.

╋ 197 D10 ✉ 34 East 32nd Street, between Madison and Park avenues, 10016 ☎ 212/683-5890 ✋ $175–$300 ⓘ 95 ⓠ 33rd Street (6) 🚌 M1, M2, M3, M34

HOTEL CHANDLER

www.hotelchandler.com

This 14-floor boutique hotel in the Murray Hill neighborhood occupies a 1903 Beaux Arts building, which has been carefully renovated and decorated in retro style. Rooms are small but chic, with CD and DVD, free high-speed internet, personal phone number and flat-screen TV. The 12:31 bar attracts a hip crowd. There is a fitness room with sauna.

✚ 197 D10 ✉ 12 East 31st Street, between Fifth and Madison avenues, 10016 ☎ 212/889-6363 💵 $209–$289, suite from $359 🛏 112 rooms, 9 suites 🍴 🚇 33rd Street (6) 🚌 M2, M3, M5

HOTEL ROGER WILLIAMS

www.therogernewyork.com

In 1997 Unique Hotels Group renovated this fine old hotel (1928). The good-sized rooms have been decorated in bright, bold colors. Stylish and spacious with modern furnishings, the rooms are stimulating and relaxing. Amenities include flat-screen plasma TV, ergonomic desk chair and high-speed internet. Bathrooms have hairdryers, Frette robes and Aveda toiletries. Cappuccino and espresso are available 24 hours. There's also a fitness studio.

✚ 197 D10 ✉ 131 Madison Avenue at 31st Street, 10016 ☎ 212/448-7000 💵 $445–$615, suite from $500 🛏 193 rooms, 1 suite 🍴 🚇 33rd Street (6) 🚌 M1, M2, M3

HUDSON

www.hudsonhotel.com

The Hudson is Ian Schrager's and Philippe Starck's latest "hotel as ongoing party." Guests arrive in the ivy-draped lobby via escalators encased in a chartreuse-green tube. Starck trademarks include oversized chairs and other objects like the 500-gallon (1,890-litre) watering can in the garden courtyard. The rooms are small and furnished with minimalist stainless-steel pieces, plus the latest technical amenities. The Library lounge has plenty of leather, a hearth and a dramatically lit antique billiard table. A long gilded table serves as a bar in the lounge, which converts into a dance club at night. The landscaped roof terrace is a bonus.

✚ 196 C7 ✉ 356 West 58th Street, between Eighth and Ninth avenues, 10019 ☎ 212/554-6000 💵 Doubles from $309, suites from $689 🛏 1,000 rooms, 11 suites 🚇 59th Street/Columbus Circle (A, B, C, D, 1) 🚌 M10, M20, M57

KIMBERLY

www.kimberlyhotel.com

This small personal hotel in Midtown has a European flavor. Originally built in 1985 as an apartment house, it has large rooms with fully equipped kitchens. Some rooms have balconies; they all have three dual-line phones and high-speed internet access. Guests also have membership at the New York Health and Racquet Clubs.

✚ 197 E8 ✉ 145 East 50th Street, between Third and Lexington avenues, 10022 ☎ 212/702-1600 💵 Doubles from $249, suites from $329 🛏 26 rooms, 158 suites 🚇 51st Street (6) 🚌 M50, M101, M102, M103

LIBRARY

www.libraryhotel.com

It's not just the design concept that book lovers appreciate at this boutique property, it's also the service. Each floor of the hotel is dedicated to a subject category from the Dewey Decimal system and each room has a collection of art and books related to a sub-category. The décor is modern and minimalist. Amenities include multi-line phones and free WiFi. Refreshments are served in the second-floor, book-lined Reading Room. There's also an American Bistro and Wine Bar and complimentary passes to a nearby fitness center.

✚ 197 D9 ✉ 299 Madison Avenue at 41st Street, 10017 ☎ 212/983-4500 💵 $345–$435, suite from $599, including breakfast and afternoon wine and cheese 🛏 52 rooms, 8 suites 🚇 Grand Central/42nd Street (S, 4, 5, 6, 7) 🚌 M1, M2, M3, M4, M42

MANSFIELD

www.mansfieldhotel.com

Occupying a 1904 Beaux Arts building with many original features,

this hotel is convenient for the theater and Midtown shopping. The elegantly furnished rooms have sleigh beds with steel mesh headboards, metal and fabric armoires, plus free WiFi. There is a nearby health club.

✚ 197 D9 ✉ 12 West 44th Street, between Fifth and Sixth avenues, 10036 ☎ 212/277-8700 💵 Doubles from $319, suites from $419 🛏 100 rooms, 24 suites 🚇 42nd Street (B, D, F, M) 🚌 M1, M2, M3, M4, M5, M42

METRO

www.hotelmetronyc.com

This has to be one of the best-value hotels in the city. It has a good Midtown location and plenty of art deco style. The rooms are classic, with earth-toned décor, nightstands and chairs, and are equipped with cable TV, and phone with data port. The marble bathrooms have hairdryers. Guests can relax in the library, which actually has books, or on the rooftop garden terrace. The Metro Grill provides room service.

✚ 197 D10 ✉ 45 West 35th Street, between Fifth and Sixth avenues, 10001 ☎ 212/947-2500 💵 $255–$410, suite from $375 🛏 181 rooms and suites 🚇 34th Street (B, D, F, M, N, Q, R) 🚌 M2, M3, M5, M7, M34

THE MICHELANGELO

www.michelangelohotel.com

The boutique Michelangelo hotel is in Midtown Manhattan, a block west of Radio City Music Hall and convenient for Broadway's theater district. It's the only US property of an Italian hotel chain, and the Italian influences are everywhere: the friendliness of the staff, the Italian marble in the reception and in guest bathrooms, and in the Limoncello restaurant. All the rooms are very spacious by New York standards and feature high-speed internet, CD players, voice mail and large whirlpool bathtubs.

✚ 196 C8 ✉ 152 West 51st Street, between Sixth and Seventh avenues, 10019 ☎ 212/765-0505 💵 From $320, suites from $489 🛏 179 rooms and suites 🚇 49th Street (N, R) 🚌 M1, M2

MODERNE

www.modernehotelnyc.com

This small retro-style hotel in a fine location near Carnegie Hall is reliable. The rooms are sleekly decorated (padded high-back bed, built-in nightstands, op art) and equipped with the latest gadgetry—VCR, CD player and telephone with data port—plus hairdryer and an extra phone in the bathroom.

➕ 196 C8 ✉ 243 West 55th Street, between Broadway and Eighth Avenue, 10019 ☎ 212/397-6767 ✋ Doubles from $289 ⓘ 34 Ⓢ Seventh Avenue (B, D, E), 59th Street/Columbus Circle (A, B, C, D, 1) 🚌 M10, M20, M104

MORGANS

www.morganshotel.com

In 1984 Ian Schrager opened this hotel, his first in New York City. The 2008 renovation created a smart, chic boutique hotel with an emphasis on clean lines and décor in white, gray and black tones. Lighting elements add an artistic flair throughout. Sophisticated and understated, the guest rooms are elegant, modern and comfortable. Crafted furnishings include stylish lighting, inlaid Corian table and wood-upholstered chair with fine linen bedding and down comforter. Bathrooms have whirlpool tubs and stainless-steel fixtures, striking granite floors and eye-catching black and white tiles. The rooms also have the latest amenities. The dramatic cellar bar and the restaurant Asia de Cuba attract a fashion-conscious crowd. Residents have complimentary access to a nearby fitness club.

➕ 197 D10 ✉ 237 Madison Avenue, between East 37th and 38th streets, 10016 ☎ 212/686-0300 ✋ Doubles from $329, suites from $489 ⓘ 113 rooms and suites Ⓢ 33rd Street (6), 42nd Street/Grand Central (S, 4, 5, 6, 7) 🚌 M1, M2, M3, M4, M42, M34

THE MUSE

www.themusehotel.com

Close to the Broadway theater district, the Muse pays homage to New York's performing arts with specially commissioned artworks in rooms and public areas. It's close by Rockefeller Center, too. The rooms and bathrooms are spacious and smartly decorated in contemporary style, with such amenities as in-room spa treatments, on-demand movies and high-speed Internet. Some rooms have balconies with city views. The Muse has a complimentary 24-hour fitness center, daily paper delivery and evening wine receptions.

➕ 196 C9 ✉ 130 West 46th Street, between Sixth and Seventh avenues, 10036 ☎ 212/485-2400 ✋ $439, suites from $559 ⓘ 181 rooms, 19 suites Ⓢ 42nd Street (B, D, F, M) 🚌 M7, M20, M50, M104

NEW YORK PALACE

www.newyorkpalace.com

Six landmark brownstones, designed by McKim, Mead and White make up the core of this luxury hotel. Owner Sultan of Brunei has spent lavishly on the décor of the public areas and the guest rooms. Several gorgeous Louis Comfort Tiffany windows and alabaster sculptures by Saint-Gaudens grace the interiors. The accommodations are located in a 55-story tower. Business travelers appreciate the executive amenities: fax, three phones and spacious desk. The restaurant Istana serves elegant, innovative takes on American classics for breakfast, lunch and dinner. A fitness center is available.

➕ 197 D8 ✉ 455 Madison Avenue, between 50th and 51st streets, 10022 ☎ 212/888-7000 ✋ $379–$680, suite from $829 ⓘ 813 rooms, 86 suites Ⓢ 51st Street (6) 🚌 M1, M2, M3, M4, M50

LE PARKER MERIDIEN

www.parkermeridien.com

The rooms in this French hotel are furnished with sleek modernist pieces and contain the latest amenities—32-inch TV, ergonomic chairs, fax, DVD, CD player and free high-speed internet access. There are several places to eat. Hip bistro-style Seppi's serves Mediterranean fare, while Norma's luxury all-day breakfast is famous. Burger Joint serves one of the best burgers in town. There is an excellent 42nd-floor fitness center with a rooftop jogging track.

➕ 197 D8 ✉ 119 West 56th Street, between Sixth and Seventh avenues, 10019 ☎ 212/245-5000 ✋ $269–$909, suite from $909 ⓘ 727 rooms and suites Ⓢ 57th Street (N, Q, R) 🚌 M5, M7, M57

Left *The New York Palace hotel*

REGIONS **MIDTOWN • STAYING**

PENINSULA

www.peninsula.com

This small hotel in a beautiful 23-story 1902 Beaux Arts building has a premier Fifth Avenue location. To complement the address, there are luxurious interiors and superb service. The rooms contain the latest amenities: fax, hands-free telephone, TV in the bathroom, free WiFi, free "Water Bar," and bedside electronic control of all the electrical systems. The furnishings are sumptuous and made even more so by the mood lighting. The Salon De Ning bar and terrace (▷ 183) is ideal for summertime trysts and Fives is an inviting bar/restaurant overlooking Fifth Avenue. A large, outstanding fitness center is also available for guests; there is an indoor pool, sundeck and spa.

➕ 197 D8 ✉ 700 Fifth Avenue at 55th Street, 10019 ☎ 212/956-2888 💷 $695–$895, suites from $1,095 ❶ 185 rooms, 54 suites 🏊 Indoor 🚇 59th Street/Fifth Avenue (E, M) 🚌 M1, M2, M3, M4, M5

THE POD HOTEL

www.thepodhotel.com

If space is not a factor, then the new Pod Hotel is New York's version of the increasing world trend for providing simple but small rooms for travelers on a budget or in a hurry. Designed like ships' cabins to maximize storage space, they still manage to provide bathrooms, safes, TVs, free WiFi and iPod docking stations. Some single rooms have shared bathrooms.

➕ 197 E8 ✉ 230 East 51st Street, between Second and Third avenues, 10022 ☎ 212/355-0300 💷 $169 twin bunk room, double from $189 ❶ 348 🚇 51st Street (6) 🚌 M15, M50, M101, M102, M103

RENAISSANCE NEW YORK HOTEL 57

www.hotel57.com

There is little wonder that travelers love this place. It has a great location, and the contemporary rooms are clean, comfortable and attractively decorated after a complete makeover. All guest rooms have cable TV and telephone with data port.

➕ 197 E8 ✉ 130 East 57th Street at Lexington, 10022 ☎ 212/753-8841 💷 From $239, suites from $368 ❶ 202 rooms and suites 🚇 59th Street (4, 5, 6) 🚌 M31, M57, M101, M102, M103

ROYALTON

www.royaltonhotel.com

The first hotel conceived by Ian Schrager, the late Steve Rubell and Philippe Starck became an instant magnet for the city's movers and shakers. The Royalton has a sexy, modern, sophisticated look. The lobby is decorated in wood, metal and glass, softened by suede-covered furnishings. Guest rooms are designed for comfort with luxurious bedding and either soaking tubs or slate and glass showers. Rooms have workspaces and flat-screen HD TVs. Bar Forty Four is a pleasant place for a drink. The fitness center is open 24 hours.

Above *The 1904 luxury St. Regis*

✚ 197 D9 ✉ 44 West 44th Street, between Fifth and Sixth avenues, 10036 ☎ 212/869-4400 ✋ Doubles from $399, suites from $699 ⓘ 165 rooms, 3 suites 📺 🍽 42nd Street (B, D, F, M) 🚌 M1, M2, M3, M4

ST. REGIS

www.stregis.com

Colonel John Jacob Astor IV conceived this beautiful 1904 Beaux Arts-style hotel. The hallmarks of luxury, marble, gold leaf, tapestries and Louis XVI furniture, are joined by the latest in technical wizardry. The service—each floor has 24-hour butler service—is also extraordinary. Suites have CD player/stereo, flat-screen TV, MP3 player, and high-speed internet. The King Cole Bar is famous for the 1932 murals painted by Maxfield Parrish and for the creation of the first Bloody Mary in 1934 (originally called the "Red Snapper"). Tea in the Astor Court is one of the city's best. There is a spa. ✚ 197 D8 ✉ 2 East 55th Street at Fifth Avenue, 10022 ☎ 212/753-4500 ✋ $755–$895, suites from $1,100 ⓘ 164 rooms, 65 suites 📺 🍽 Fifth Avenue/53rd Street (E, M) 🚌 M1, M2, M3, M4

SHOREHAM

www.shorehamhotel.com

This mid-size Midtown hotel, right behind the Museum of Modern Art, has been imaginatively updated and now boasts the latest looks and the most up-to-date technology and amenities in the rooms. Mesh headboards shimmer above the beds. The décor includes plenty of aluminum, plus plasma TVs and DVDs. Choice rooms are in the back. A restaurant and bar is available. ✚ 197 D8 ✉ 33 West 55th Street, between Fifth and Sixth avenues, 10019 ☎ 212/247-6700 ✋ Doubles from $359, suites from $419 ⓘ 143 rooms, 31 suites 🍽 53rd Street/Fifth Avenue (E, M) 🚌 M1, M2, M3, M4, M5, M7, M57

THIRTY THIRTY

www.thirtythirty-nyc.com

On the edge of the burgeoning Flatiron District in a refurbished 1902 building, this hotel is decent value. The rooms sport the latest minimal look, but they are small with European-style solutions—TVs suspended on walls and limited furnishings. They do have telephone with data port and hairdryer. Superior rooms have 27-inch TVs. ✚ 197 D10 ✉ 30 East 30th Street, between Madison and Park avenues, 10016 ☎ 212/689-1900 ✋ $219–$319 ⓘ 253 rooms and suites 🍽 33rd Street (6) 🚌 M1, M101, M103

TRAVEL INN

www.thetravelinnhotel.com

The benefits of this Manhattan hotel are the outdoor pool and the free parking. The rooms are simple but comfortable, with data port. ✚ 196 B9 ✉ 515 West 42nd Street, between Tenth and Eleventh avenues, 10036 ☎ 212/695-7171 ✋ $160–$400 ⓘ 160 🍽 Outdoor 🚇 42nd Street (A, C, E) 🚌 M42, M11

W NEW YORK – TIMES SQUARE

www.whotels.com

W is the hip Starwood Hotels chain. Here, as elsewhere in the group, the lobby is a living room space, where you can relax on ottomans or play board games. Natural elements are always evident, too: pots of grass, waterfalls, polished chunks of tree trunk as coffee tables and bouquets of grasses and seedpods, for example. Rooms are modern and equipped with Web TV, two-line phones, VCRs and CD players. Good food and beverage outlets polish the image—The Blue Fin Restaurant and the Living Room Bar. The spa and fitness center is a standout. ✚ 197 E8 ✉ 541 Lexington Avenue, between East 49th and 50th streets, 10022 ☎ 212/755-1200 ✋ $399–$469, suites from $649 ⓘ 509 rooms, 43 suites 📺 🍽 51st Street (6) 🚌 M50, M101, M102, M103

WALDORF-ASTORIA HOTEL AND TOWERS

www.waldorfastoria.com

The Waldorf opened in 1931 to rave reviews. The largest hotel in the world at the time, it remains monumental—some would say overwhelming. The Towers, which occupy the 28th to 42nd floors, have a separate entrance and the most luxurious rooms. The clubby Bull and Bear is popular for steaks, while Peacock Alley is famous for its afternoon tea. Oscar's is a very chic coffeeshop. Large fitness center; excellent business center. ✚ 197 D8 ✉ 301 Park Avenue, between 49th and 50th streets, 10022 ☎ 212/355-3000 ✋ Waldorf rooms from $319, suites from $489; Waldorf Towers rooms from $599, suites from $679 ⓘ 1,049 rooms, 197 suites (Waldorf), 58 rooms, 123 suites (Towers) 📺 🍽 51st Street (6) 🚌 M1, M2, M3, M4, M50

WARWICK

www.warwickhotelny.com

William Randolph Hearst built this hotel in 1927 as his East Coast hideaway. Many a movie celebrity settled into residence here, including Cary Grant. The large rooms have such rare amenities as walk-in closets and extra-large marble bathrooms, plus modern ones such as high-speed internet and two dual-line phones. Facilities include a restaurant, bar and fitness center. ✚ 197 D8 ✉ 65 West 54th Street at Sixth Avenue, 10019 ☎ 212/247-2700 ✋ $220–$500, suites from $485 ⓘ 359 rooms, 67 suites 📺 🍽 57th Street (F) 🚌 M5, M7, M57

WOLCOTT

www.wolcott.com

Close to the Empire State Building, this hotel has comfortable rooms decorated in an old-fashioned style (candy-stripe wallpaper, wing chair). The room amenities include cable TV, telephone with data port, hairdryer and air conditioning. There is a fitness room. ✚ 197 D10 ✉ 4 West 31st Street, between Fifth Avenue and Broadway, 10001 ☎ 212/268-2900 ✋ Doubles from $260, suites add $10 ⓘ 137 rooms, 63 suites 📺 🍽 28th Street (N, R), 34th Street/Herald Square (B, D, F, M, N, Q, R) 🚌 M2, M3, M4, M5, M7, M32

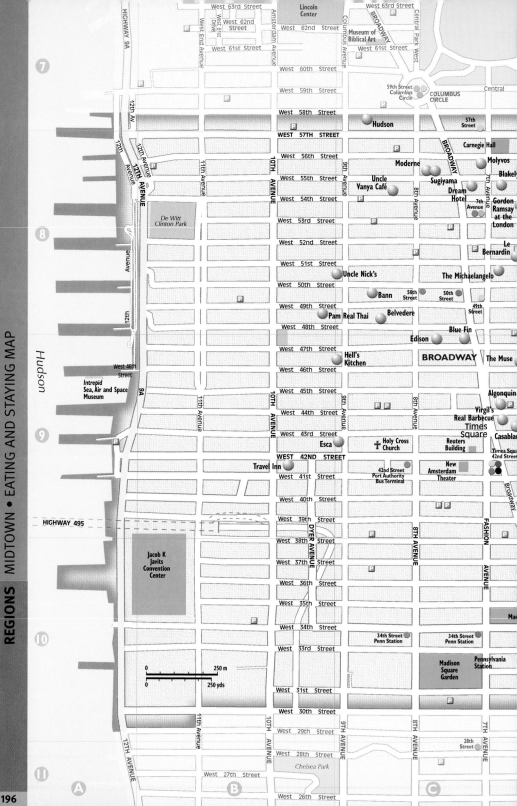

West 63rd Street
Lincoln Center
West 63rd Street
West 62nd Street
West 62nd Street
Museum of Biblical Art
West 61st Street
West 61st Street
Central Park West
BROADWAY

West 60th Street

HIGHWAY 9A
West End Avenue
Amsterdam Avenue
Columbus Avenue

West 59th Street

59th Street Columbus Circle
COLUMBUS CIRCLE
Central

West 58th Street

12th AV
12th Avenue
11th Avenue
10th AVENUE
9th Avenue
8th Avenue
7th Avenue

Hudson
57th Street

WEST 57TH STREET
Carnegie Hall

West 56th Street
BROADWAY

West 55th Street
Moderne
Molyvos
Blakel

Uncle Vanya Café
Sugiyama
Dream Hotel
Gordon Ramsay at the London

De Witt Clinton Park
West 54th Street
7th Avenue

West 53rd Street

West 52nd Street
Le Bernardin

West 51st Street
Uncle Nick's
The Michaelangelo

West 50th Street
Bann
50th Street
50th Street

West 49th Street
Pam Real Thai
Belvedere
49th Street

12th
West 48th Street
Blue Fin

West 47th Street
Edison

Hell's Kitchen
BROADWAY
The Muse

West 46th Street

West 46th Street
Intrepid Sea, Air and Space Museum

9A

West 45th Street
Algonquin

11th Avenue
10th AVENUE
9th Avenue
8th Avenue

West 44th Street
Virgil's Real Barbecue
Times Square

West 43rd Street
Holy Cross Church
Reuters Building
Casabla

Esca
Times Squ 42nd Street

WEST 42ND STREET

Travel Inn
West 41st Street
42nd Street Port Authority Bus Terminal
New Amsterdam Theater

West 40th Street
BROADWAY

HIGHWAY 495
West 39th Street

DYER AVENUE
West 38th Street
FASHION AVENUE

Jacob K Javits Convention Center
West 37th Street
8th AVENUE

West 36th Street

West 35th Street

West 34th Street
34th Street Penn Station
34th Street Penn Station
Mae

West 33rd Street

Madison Square Garden
Pennsylvania Station

0   250 m
0   250 yds
West 31st Street

11th Avenue
West 30th Street

10th AVENUE
West 29th Street

9th AVENUE
8th AVENUE
7th AVENUE

West 28th Street
28th Street

12th AVENUE
West 27th Street
Chelsea Park

A
West 26th Street
B
C

⑦ ⑧ ⑨ ⑩ ⑪

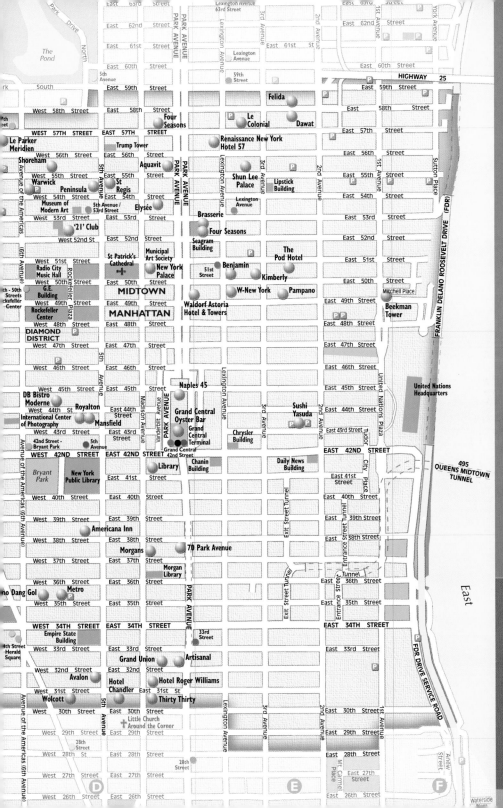

The Pond

Park Drive North

Park Drive

Lexington Avenue 63rd Street

East 63rd Street

East 62nd Street

East 61st Street

East 60th Street

3rd Avenue

2nd Avenue

York Avenue

East 59th Street

South

5th Avenue

Lexington Avenue

59th Street

HIGHWAY 25

East 59th Street

Felida

West 58th Street

East 58th Street

Street

East 58th Street

Street

Four Seasons

Le Colonial

Dawat

WEST 57TH STREET

EAST 57TH STREET

East 57th Street

Le Parker Meridien

Trump Tower

West 56th Street

East 56th Street

Renaissance New York Hotel 57

East 56th Street

Street

Shoreham

Aquavit

5th Avenue

West 55th Street

St Regis

Street

PARK AVENUE

Lexington Avenue

3rd Avenue

Shun Lee Palace

Lipstick Building

1st Avenue

East 55th Street

2nd Avenue

East 55th Street

Street

Warwick

Peninsula

West 54th Street

East 54th Street

East 54th Street

Museum of Modern Art

5th Avenue / 53rd Street

Elysée

Lexington Avenue

'21' Club

East 53rd Street

Brasserie

Four Seasons

East 53rd Street

Street

West 52nd St

East 52nd Street

Seagram Building

East 52nd Street

Street

Avenue of the Americas (6th Avenue)

St Patrick's Cathedral

Municipal Art Society

New York Palace

51st Street

Benjamin

The Pod Hotel

East 51st Street

West 51st Street

Radio City Music Hall

Rockefeller Plaza

West 50th Street

Kimberly

East 50th Street

G.E. Building

5th – 50th Streets Rockefeller Center

MIDTOWN

East 50th Street

W-New York

Pampano

East 50th Street

West 49th Street

East 49th Street

Street

Rockefeller Center

MANHATTAN

Waldorf Astoria Hotel & Towers

East 49th Street

Mitchell Place

Beekman Tower

West 48th Street

East 48th Street

Street

East 48th Street

DIAMOND DISTRICT

West 47th Street

East 47th Street

Street

East 47th Street

5th Avenue

West 46th Street

East 46th Street

Street

East 46th Street

DB Bistro Moderne

West 45th St

Naples 45

East 45th Street

Street

East 45th Street

Royalton

East 44th Street

Grand Central Oyster Bar

Sushi Yasuda

United Nations Headquarters

International Center of Photography

Mansfield

Madison Avenue

Vanderbilt Avenue

PARK AVENUE

Grand Central Terminal

3rd Avenue

2nd Avenue

East 43rd Street

West 43rd Street

5th Avenue

East 43rd Street

Chrysler Building

United Nations Plaza

42nd Street - Bryant Park

Grand Central 42nd Street

495 QUEENS MIDTOWN TUNNEL

WEST 42ND STREET

EAST 42ND STREET

EAST 42ND STREET

Avenue of the Americas (6th Avenue)

Bryant Park

New York Public Library

Library

Chanin Building

Daily News Building

East 41st Street

City Place

West 40th Street

East 40th Street

Street

East 40th Street

Exit Street Tunnel

Entrance Street Tunnel

East 39th Street

West 39th Street

East 39th Street

Street

Americana Inn

West 38th Street

East 38th Street

Street

70 Park Avenue

East 38th Street

Morgans

East 37th Street

Street

West 37th Street

Morgan Library

East 36th Street

West 36th Street

Metro

PARK AVENUE

Entrance Street Tunnel

East 36th Street

no Dang Gol

West 35th Street

Exit Street Tunnel

East 35th Street

East 35th Street

WEST 34TH STREET

EAST 34TH STREET

East 34th Street

EAST 34TH STREET

Empire State Building

West 33rd Street

33rd Street

East 33rd Street

FDR DRIVE SERVICE ROAD

4th Street Herald Square

Grand Union

Artisanal

East 33rd Street

West 32nd Street

East 32nd Street

Street

Avalon

Hotel Chandler

Hotel Roger Williams

East 31st Street

Wolcott

West 31st Street

5th Avenue

Thirty Thirty

West 30th Street

East 30th Street

Street

East 30th Street

Little Church Around the Corner

East 29th Street

East 29th Street

Anew Street

West 29th Street

28th Street

28th Street

East 28th Street

East 28th Street

Mt Carmel Place

West 28th St

East

West 27th Street

East 27th Street

28th Street

East 27th Street

East

West 26th Street

D

E

F

East 26th Street

Waterside

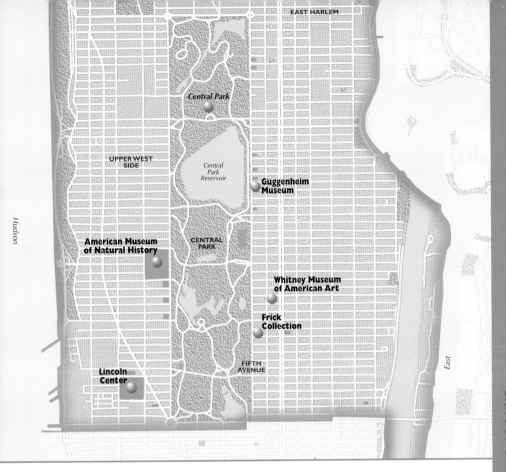

Central Park

EAST HARLEM

UPPER WEST
SIDE

Central
Park
Reservoir

Guggenheim
Museum

Hudson

American Museum
of Natural History

CENTRAL
PARK

Whitney Museum
of American Art

Frick
Collection

FIFTH
AVENUE

East

Lincoln
Center

CENTRAL PARK AND AROUND

New York's Central Park, a magnificent 843-acre (341ha) oasis of green, was designed by Frederick Law Olmsted and Calvert Vaux in 1858. Wealthy New Yorkers soon moved north and settled along the east and west sides of Central Park. Today Central Park East is best known for Museum Mile, where many fabulous museums are located along Fifth Avenue, while Central Park West is home to the Lincoln Center, trendy clubs and restaurants.

A daytime stroll through Central Park is the perfect way to see the highlights, and to escape the noise, congestion and frantic pace characteristic of Manhattan. The park offers vast expanses of grass, lakes and ponds, paths through the wooded Ramble as well as Belvedere Castle, Bethesda Fountain and the Victorian Gothic Dairy Building which houses the visitor center.

Of the many museums along Central Park East, the Guggenheim Museum displays an exceptional collection of modern and contemporary art in Frank Lloyd Wright's stunning spiral-ramped building. The Whitney Museum of American Art presents the entire range of American modern and contemporary art, while the Frick Collection showcases the wealthy lifestyle and mansion of steel magnate Henry Clay Frick, as well as his opulent furnishings and fine art collection.

The Lincoln Center performing arts complex houses the Metropolitan Opera, New York Philharmonic and the Juilliard School of Music, and provides more than a dozen venues for a broad variety of theater, music and children's performances. Nearby, the American Museum of Natural History is one of the largest in the world, with more than 30 million artifacts and specimens. The Rose Center for Earth and Space with its planetarium, the Hall of the Universe and Big Bang Theater is one of the highlights here, closely followed by the dinosaur exhibits in the five-story Theodore Roosevelt Rotunda.

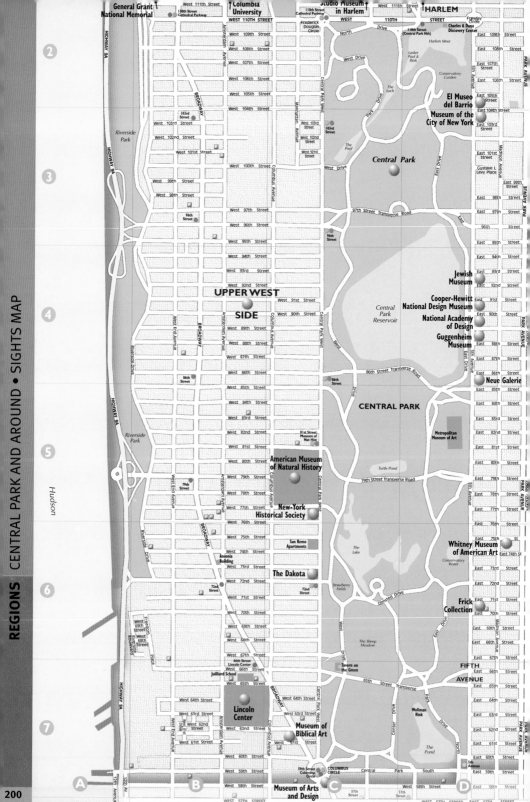

General Grant
National Memorial

Columbia
University

Studio Museum
in Harlem

HARLEM

West 111th Street

WEST 110TH STREET

110th Street
Cathedral Parkway

Frederick
Douglass
Circle

110th Street
Cathedral Parkway

West 111th Street

WEST
110TH
STREET

Charles A Dana
Discovery Center

110th Street
(Central Park Nth)

Harlem Meer

WEST 109th Street

West 109th Street

East 109th
Street

② WEST 108th Street

West 108th Street

East 108th
Street

West 107th Street

West Drive

Lasker
Pool &
Rink

East 107th
Street

WEST 106th Street

Conservatory
Garden

East 106th
Street

West 105th Street

El Museo
del Barrio

East 105th
Street

West 104th Street

The Loch

Museum of
the City of
New York

East 104th Street

West 103rd Street

103rd Street

West 103rd
Street

103rd
Street

West 102nd Street

West 102nd
Street

West 101st Street

The Pool

East 101st
Street

Gustave L
Levy Place

③ West 100th Street

West Drive

East 98th
Street

West 99th Street

West 98th Street

East 97th
Street

97th Street Transverse Road

97th
Street

West 97th Street

East 96th
Street

West 96th Street

96th
Street

West 95th Street

East 95th
Street

West 94th Street

East 94th
Street

West 93rd Street

Jewish
Museum

East 93rd
Street

West 92nd Street

Cooper-Hewitt
National Design Museum

East 92nd
Street

UPPER WEST
SIDE

West 91st Street

Central
Park
Reservoir

National Academy
of Design

East 91st
Street

④ West 90th Street

Guggenheim
Museum

East 90th
Street

West 89th Street

East 89th
Street

West 88th Street

East 88th
Street

West 87th Street

East 87th
Street

West 86th Street

86th Street Transverse Road

86th
Street

Neue Galerie

East 86th
Street

West 85th Street

West
Drive

East 85th
Street

West 84th Street

CENTRAL PARK

East 84th
Street

West 83rd Street

East 83rd
Street

81st Street
Museum of
Nat Hist

Metropolitan
Museum of Art

East 82nd
Street

West 82nd Street

⑤ West 81st Street

East 81st
Street

West 80th Street

American Museum
of Natural History

Turtle Pond

East 80th
Street

West 79th Street

79th Street Transverse Road

79th
Street

East 79th
Street

West 78th Street

East 78th
Street

New-York
Historical Society

West 77th Street

East 77th
Street

West 76th Street

East 76th
Street

West 75th Street

The Lake

East 75th St

West 74th Street

San Remo
Apartments

Whitney Museum
of American Art

East 74th St

Ansonia
Building

West 73rd Street

73rd
Street

Conservatory
Water

East 73rd
Street

The Dakota

⑥ West 72nd Street

72nd
Street

East 72nd
Street

West 71st Street

Frick
Collection

East 71st
Street

West 70th Street

The Sheep
Meadow

Strawberry
Fields

East 70th
Street

West 69th Street

Olmsted Drive

East 69th
Street

West 68th Street

East 68th
Street

West 67th Street

East 67th
Street

66th Street
Lincoln Center

Tavern on
the Green

FIFTH
AVENUE

West 66th Street

East 66th
Street

West 65th Street

65th Street Transverse

East 65th
Street

West 64th Street

Lincoln
Center

East 64th
Street

⑦ West 63rd Street

Wollman
Rink

East 63rd
Street

West 62nd Street

East 62nd
Street

West 61st Street

Museum of
Biblical Art

East 61st
Street

West 60th Street

The Pond

East 60th
Street

West 59th Street

Museum of Arts
and Design

59th Street
Columbus Circle

COLUMBUS
CIRCLE

Central Park South

East 59th
Street

WEST 57TH STREET

West 57th
Street

West 58th Street

WEST 57TH STREET

EAST 57TH STREET

Carnegie Hall

A   B   C   D

Highway 9A

Riverside Park

Amsterdam Avenue

Broadway

Columbus Avenue

Central Park West

Manhattan Avenue

West End Avenue

Riverside Drive

Hudson

Park Avenue

Madison Avenue

5th Avenue

Central Park

EAST HARLEM

East 111th Street
East 110th Street
East 109th Street
East 108th Street
East 107th Street
East 106th Street
East 105th Street
East 104th Street
East 103rd Street
East 102nd Street
East 101st Street
East 100th Street
East 99th Street
East 98th Street
East 97th Street
East 96th STREET
East 95th Street
East 94th Street
East 93rd Street
East 92nd Street
East 91st Street
East 90th Street
East 89th Street
East 88th Street
East 87th Street
East 86th Street
East 84th Street
East 83rd Street
East 82nd Street
East 81st Street
East 80th Street
East 79th Street
East 78th Street
East 77th Street
East 76th Street
East 75th Street
East 74th Street
East 73rd Street
East 72nd Street
East 71st Street
East 70th Street
East 69th Street
East 68th Street
East 67th Street
East 66th Street
East 65th Street
East 64th Street
East 63rd Street
East 62nd Street
East 61st St
East 60th Street
East 59th Street
East 58th Street
East 57th Street

103rd Street
103rd Street
101st Street
100th Street
98th Street

Lexington Avenue
3rd Avenue
2nd Avenue
1st Avenue
York Avenue

FRANKLIN DELANO ROOSEVELT DRIVE (FDR)

Gracie Mansion

Carl Schurz Park

John Jay Park

Asia Society and Museum

68th Street Hunter College

Lexington Avenue 63rd Street

Lexington Avenue

59th Street

Mount Vernon Hotel Museum and Garden

East HIGHWAY 25

Mill Rock Park

Wards Island Park

Ralph Demarco Park

23rd Road
23rd Drive
23rd Terrace

Astoria Park

Astoria Park South
25th Road
25th Road

26th Avenue
26th Avenue
27th Avenue
27th Road

Astoria Blvd
Newtown

30th Avenue

Astoria Boulevard

Welling Court
Hallets Cove Playground

30th Avenue

Vernon Boulevard

31st Avenue

31st Road

Socrates Sculpture Park

Broadway

33rd Avenue
33rd Road
33rd Avenue
33rd Road

Rainey Park

34th Avenue

35th Avenue

Ravenswood Playground

River Road

Roosevelt Island Bridge

East

QUEENS

Roosevelt Island

36th Avenue

21st STREET

57th Avenue

38th Avenue

39th Avenue

Roosevelt Island Main Street

40th Avenue

Queensbridge Park

11th Street Queensbridge

41st Road

QUEENSBORO BRIDGE

Main Street

HIGHWAY 25

Queens Plaza South

West Road

43rd

Main Street

0 — 250 m
0 — 250 yds

E   F   G   H

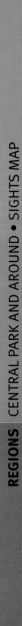

REGIONS CENTRAL PARK AND AROUND • SIGHTS MAP

201

AMERICAN MUSEUM OF NATURAL HISTORY
▷ 204–207.

ASIA SOCIETY AND MUSEUM
www.asiasociety.org
Founded by John D. Rockefeller III in 1956 to promote relations between America and Asian countries, the society mounts exhibitions, lectures, concerts and workshops. In 2001, a $30-million renovation of the 1981 building doubled the exhibition space. The collection is based on Rockefeller's donation of acquisitions from all over Asia, and ranges from 11th-century BC Chinese ceramics to Japanese prints and Cambodian sculptures to 19th-century objects.
✚ 201 E6 ✉ 725 Park Avenue at 70th Street, 10021 ☎ 212/288-6400 ⏰ Tue–Sun 11–6, Fri 11–9 (except July 4–Labor Day) 💰 Adult $10, under 16s and members free, Fri 6pm–9pm free for all (except July 1–Labor Day) Ⓢ 6 🚌 M1, M2, M3, M4, M66, M72, M103 🔲 🏛

CENTRAL PARK
▷ 208–213.

COLUMBIA UNIVERSITY
www.columbia.edu
Founded as King's College in 1754 as a rival to the by then well-established Harvard and Yale, this was New York's first college and the fifth-oldest in the nation, and is among the Ivy League's wealthiest universities. Originally located in the schoolhouse of Trinity Church (▷ 79), the college has occupied several Manhattan locations. It moved to the current 36-acre (15ha) campus, originally the site of Bloomingdale's Insane Asylum, in 1897. The heart of the campus is the magnificent Low Library, inspired by the Pantheon in Rome; academic buildings are arranged around it. In 1934 Low became the administrative center.
✚ Off map 200 B2 ✉ West 114th to 120th streets, 10027 ☎ 212/854-4900 ⏰ Low Library Visitor Center Mon–Fri 9–5 🚌 M4, M5, M11, M60, M104 🍴 🔲 🏛 🛈 Free guided tours weekdays 1pm

COOPER-HEWITT NATIONAL DESIGN MUSEUM
www.si.edu/ndm
This elegant, 64-room, wood-paneled Georgian mansion, built from 1899 to 1902, was the home of the industrialist and philanthropist Andrew Carnegie. It was the first private residence in New York to have an Otis elevator.

Today it houses one of the largest design collections in the world, with more than 250,000 items. The collection, originally from the Cooper Union School for the Advancement of Science, was donated in 1967 to the Smithsonian, which moved it here. It includes a drawing by Michelangelo, furniture designs by Frank Lloyd Wright and industrial design drawings by Donald Deskey and Henry Dreyfuss.
✚ 200 D4 ✉ 2 East 91st Street, 10128 ☎ 212/849-8400 ⏰ Closed for renovation until late 2013 Ⓢ 4, 5, 6 🚌 M1, M2, M3, M4 🍴 🏛

THE DAKOTA
A vaguely Germanic Upper West Side landmark, this marble-floored, mahogany-paneled structure was the first luxury apartment block on Central Park. Far beyond the city's bright lights, or even the power supply, it seemed as distant from the city as the Dakotas when it opened; the name was a joke on its remoteness. It wasn't long before the city moved uptown, however. Prices soared, and the rich and famous moved in—among them musician Leonard Bernstein and actress Lauren Bacall. John Lennon was tragically shot dead on the sidewalk outside the door, and his widow, Yoko Ono, still lives here.
✚ 200 C6 ✉ 1 West 72nd Street, 10023 Ⓢ B, C 🚌 M7, M10, M11

Opposite Alma Mater *statue outside the Low Library at Columbia University*
Below *The Asia Society was founded by John D. Rockefeller in 1956*

INFORMATION

www.amnh.org

✚ 200 C5 ✉ Central Park West at 79th Street, 10024-5912 ☎ 212/769-5100 🕐 Daily 10–5.45. Space shows Mon, Tue, Thu, Fri 10.30–4.30, Wed 11–4.30, Sat–Sun 10.30–5 every half hour (tickets can sell out, so buy in advance online or phone 212/769-5200) 👆 Museum and Rose Center suggested donation: adult $16, child (2–12) $9. Admission and Space Show suggested donation: adult $24, child (2–12) $14. Additional charge for IMAX and some special exhibitions 🚇 B, C 🚌 M7, M10, M11 🎧 Rose Center audiotours at desk near the Planetarium shop on the lower level, free. Hour-long guided Highlights Tour hourly 10.15–3.15, free. Free thematic Spotlight Tours change each month 🍴 Museum Food Court on the lower level (daily 11–4.45); Café on 4 on the fourth floor (Sat–Sun 11–4.45); Café on One on the first floor (daily 11–4.45); Starlight Café (Sat–Sun 11–4.45) 🎁

Above *The Rose Center glass cube is made up of 736 panes of glass*

INTRODUCTION

Increasing interest in natural history and the discovery of fossils, particularly of dinosaurs, across the United States provided the inspiration for this great museum, founded in 1869 by Albert S. Bickmore. Originally the museum was in the Arsenal building in Central Park. Construction on this site began in 1874, to plans conceived by Calvert Vaux and J. Wrey Mould. President Ulysses S. Grant laid the cornerstone, and President Rutherford B. Hayes formally opened the museum in 1877. Additions in many architectural styles have expanded the museum since. The Theodore Roosevelt Memorial Hall, finished in 1936, was designed by John Russell Pope. Roosevelt, a keen hunter and collector, donated specimens from his many expeditions, including a bat and the skull of a red squirrel. The museum also includes a research center with numerous laboratories, teaching and other facilities, and a library that has the largest collection of natural history books in the Western hemisphere. The collection of dinosaurs and other fossils is the largest in the world, and many of those on view are real, not cast reproductions.

There are three entrances to the museum: the main entrance on Central Park West, where you will see the impressive bronze statue of President Theodore Roosevelt on horseback; the Columbus Avenue entrance onto West 77th Street; and an entrance on West 81st Street into the Rose Center for Earth and Space, a planetarium with a narrated history of the universe. The museum has grown over the years and now has 40 grand exhibition halls, so you will have to decide what interests you most and save the rest for other visits. A good way to start a visit is to join one of the free Highlights Tours; you will hear about some of the museum's prized treasures and get orientation on the layout of the exhibits. Ask at the information desk inside the main entrance, where the tour begins. The tour guides are friendly, well informed, usually very entertaining and easy to spot: they hold up a yellow flag as they proceed through the museum. You can join in along the way.

WHAT TO SEE

ROTUNDA

Inside the main entrance is the Rotunda, a city landmark, where colorful murals depict great accomplishments of Theodore Roosevelt, the first New Yorker to become president of the United States. The *Barosaurus* in the middle of the Rotunda is the tallest mounted dinosaur in the world at 50ft (15m). The real bones are stored elsewhere; the ones you see here are casts.

ROSE CENTER FOR EARTH AND SPACE

Hayden Sphere

Part of the four-story, $210-million Rose Center for Earth and Space, which occupies a glass cube designed by James Polshek, the great Sphere contains the planetarium (access from first floor only). Take a 30-minute virtual ride through the Milky Way and find out about distant planets and superclusters through the fascinating commentary and stellar special effects. The spiral Cosmic Pathway winds down around the course of the Sphere.

FIRST FLOOR

Dzanga-Sangha Rainforest (Hall of Biodiversity)

The full-size rainforest diorama, 90ft (27m) long, 26ft (8m) wide and 18ft (5.5m) high, re-creates a forest from the Central African Republic. Visitors can go behind the glass into a world where high-resolution imagery, video, sound and smell take you into a rainforest experience. On the forest floor, insects, reptiles and small mammals scuttle through the saplings, shrubs, herbs, ferns and leaf litter; a stream runs past, and in the distance you may catch glimpses of elephants moving about, while birds and primates hang around in the tangle of overhead vines, branches and trunks.

Below *The dinosaur and fossil collection is the largest of its kind in the world*

TIPS

» Go on a free Highlights Tour.

» Purchase a CityPass (▷ 274), good for nine days, to save money and avoid standing in line for tickets.

» The gift shop has a wide range of jewelry, pottery, metalwork and glasswork from all over the world.

Blue Whale (Hall of Ocean Life)

One of the museum's favorite exhibits, the 94ft (29m) model of a blue whale dominates the state-of-the-art Hall of Ocean Life. Video projection screens and interactive computer stations help you to understand marine environments.

Discovery Room

Designed to interest children between the ages of 5 and 12, the Discovery Room has puzzles, games, scientific challenges and investigations to explore.

SECOND FLOOR

Elephant Diorama (Akeley Hall of African Mammals)

This venerable diorama, constructed in the 1930s, set the standard for natural history museum displays. The group of elephants is set amid vegetation typical of their natural habitat. Other dioramas in the hall show more of Africa's stunning wildlife.

THIRD FLOOR

Passenger pigeon (Hall of New York City Birds)

Two centuries ago, the passenger pigeon was one of the most abundant birds in North America. Now extinct, the bird's life is traced through vivid displays.

FOURTH FLOOR

Stegosaurus **and** ***Triceratops*** (Hall of Ornithischian Dinosaurs)

These two huge dinosaurs were vegetarians, protected from rapacious attacks by massive bony jaw plates. Begin with a visit to the Wallach Orientation Center for an overview of the six fossil halls. Did you know that the word dinosaur means "terrible lizard"?

Tyrannosaurus **and** ***Apatosaurus*** (Hall of Saurischian Dinosaurs)

You may feel very small when you enter the Hall of Saurischian Dinosaurs and meet the giants displayed here. *Tyrannosaurus rex* is an awesome sight, with the horrendous teeth of a meat-eater.

Above *A huge model blue whale hangs above the Hall of Ocean Life*

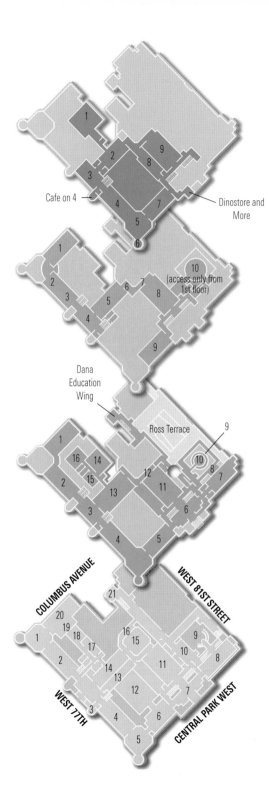

GALLERY GUIDE
KEY TO MAIN ROOMS

FOURTH FLOOR
1: Research library
2: Vertebrate origins
4: Advanced mammals
5: Primitive mammals
7: Ornithischian dinosaurs (*Stegosaurus* and *Triceratops*)
9: Saurischian dinosaurs (*Tyrannosaurus* and *Apatosaurus*)

THIRD FLOOR
1: Pacific peoples
2, 3: Plains and Woodlands Indians
4: Primates
5: North American birds
6: New York State mammals
7: New York City birds
8: African mammals
9: Reptiles and amphibians (including the world's largest lizard, the 10ft/3m Komodo dragon)
10: Hayden Planetarium Space Theater

SECOND FLOOR
1: South American peoples
2: Mexico and Central America
3: Birds of the world
4: Asian peoples
5: Asian mammals
6: Main entrance and Rotunda
7: Oceanic birds
8: Scales of the universe
9: Cosmic pathway
10: Big Bang
11: African mammals
13: African peoples

FIRST FLOOR
1: Ross Hall of Meteorites
2: Spitzer Hall of Human Origins
3: Discovery Room
4: New York state environment
5: North American forests
6: Hall of Biodiversity
7: Theodore Roosevelt Memorial Hall
8: Hall of Planet Earth
9: Cosmic pathway
10: Rose Gallery (space show boarding)
11: North American mammals
12: Hall of Ocean Life
14: Northwest Coast Indians
15: IMAX theater
19, 20: Gems and minerals (Star of India sapphire)

INFORMATION

www.centralparknyc.org

✚ 200 C3 ✉ Central Manhattan from 59th to 110th streets, between Fifth and Eighth avenues ☎ 212/310-6600 🕐 6am–1am 🚇 A, B, C, D, 1 to Columbus Circle (southwest corner) 🚌 M1, M2, M3, M4 to Fifth Avenue (East Side) and M10 (West Side) ℹ Look for park lamp posts to find out where you are in relation to city streets. The first two digits on the lamp post are those of the nearest street. There are direct-line emergency phones throughout the park and a 24-hour park police line (☎ 212/570-4820) you can call from mobile phones 🍴 Loeb Boathouse (▷ 239–240) 🍽 Bar and Grill at the Boathouse serves light meals and drinks from early spring to late October. Other cafés and food stalls throughout the park 🚶 Guided Central Park Conservancy Walking Tours (☎ 212/360-2726) and Central Park Bicycle Tours (☎ 212/541-8759); horse-drawn hansom cabs (☎ 212/736-0680)

INTRODUCTION

New York's "great green lung" was designed by Frederick Law Olmsted and Calvert Vaux in 1858—843 acres (341ha) of green space with woods, gardens, playing fields and a zoo. It's a great place for birdwatching, cycling, rowing, ice skating, inline skating, strolling or jogging along 58 miles (93km) of paths.

In the 1850s, many New Yorkers felt that their growing city needed a park. A large central site was chosen, and a competition in 1858 attracted 33 entries. A farmer, Frederick Law Olmsted, and an architect, Calvert Vaux, won the $2,000 commission. Olmsted was appointed superintendent of Central Park. Jacob Wrey Mould took on the ornamental side and designed the bridges, the Belvedere and the terrace. Construction took 16 years and cost more than $14 million. Three thousand workers, mostly unemployed Irish immigrants, and 400 horses moved stone and earth and planted 500,000 trees, shrubs and vines. The park got its own police force to discourage lawlessness. In 1925, the first of 19 playgrounds, the Heckscher Playground at 61st Street and Seventh Avenue, was constructed.

Between 1913 and 1919, decay took its toll on some of the fine designs. By 1934 Vaux's Marble Bridge was beyond repair and had to be demolished. In 1934, when parks commissioner Robert Moses moved the sheep from Sheep Meadow to Brooklyn's Prospect Park, the sheepfold, designed by Mould, was turned into a restaurant, the former Tavern on the Green. The addition of the Wollman Skating Rink came in 1951 and the Delacorte Theater in 1963. Many statues were added along the way. The 1970s brought another period of neglect and lawlessness and the park was for a while not a safe place to visit. But that changed after the Central Park Conservancy, headed by Elizabeth Barlow Rogers, took the initiative in the 1970s and 1980s to clean up the park and raise funds to establish a safer and cleaner space. The Sheep

Meadow, the first area to be restored by the conservancy, was reopened in 1981 and remains one of the safest, most pleasant areas of the park.

Several entrances lead into Central Park from Central Park South (59th Street) at the southern edge and 110th Street at the northern edge. The most popular entrance is at Grand Army Plaza, at 59th Street and Fifth Avenue. From Fifth Avenue on the east side, you can enter at 66th, 72nd, 79th, 85th, 97th and 102nd streets. On the west side, from Central Park West, you can enter at 66th, 72nd, 81st, 86th, 96th and 100th streets. North of 96th Street, the park is more rugged and less suitable for visitors with disabilities. Because there are so many different access points, study the map before entering, read about the highlights, then decide on a route through the park. Many roads that cut through the park are closed to vehicular traffic on weekends in summer, which makes it perfect for joggers, bikers, inline skaters and baby-strollers. There are bronze statues throughout the park, including monuments to Beethoven, Christopher Columbus, William Shakespeare and Mother Goose in the south end. At the entrance to the Delacorte Theater are lovely statues of Romeo and Juliet, and from Shakespeare's *The Tempest*, Prospero with his daughter, Miranda. Bring binoculars, especially in the Ramble or on the lake.

WHAT TO SEE
SOUTH QUADRANT
The Pond is a lovely first impression of Central Park for visitors who come in at Grand Army Plaza. The gilded bronze statue of Civil War Union General William Tecumseh Sherman by sculptor Augustus Saint-Gaudens is one of the most distinguished equestrian groupings in Western art. Along Central Park South, drivers of horse-drawn carriages wait for passengers. Nearby, the wooded Hallett Nature Sanctuary juts into the Pond, which has an island inhabited by turtles and birds and a lovely waterfall.

The Metropolitan Museum of Art (1000 Fifth Avenue at East 82nd Street, tel 212/535-7710; www.metmuseum.org; Tue–Thu, Sun 9.30–5.15, Fri–Sat 9.30–8; suggested donation adult $25, under 12 with adult free) was founded in 1870. The first donation was a Roman sarcophagus, but when multimillionaire J. P. Morgan was elected president of the Board of Trustees, world masterpieces became the main acquisitions. Significant donations of works by Old Masters, Louis Comfort Tiffany and Henri Matisse have been added to the museum's collection over the years. The grand main entrance has an impressive neoclassical facade. As you enter the Great Hall, pick up a museum plan at the information desk, and ask about the day's activities. Allow plenty of time—there is much to see. The collections number more than 2 million items, with around 100,000 on display at any given time, and it can be confusing if you simply wander around. If you wish to rent an audioguide or join a free guided tour, sign up at an information desk in the Great Hall.

With more than 35,000 works ranging from the Neolithic period to AD312, the Greek and Roman Art collection is one of the most comprehensive in North America. In the center of the Steinhardt Gallery is the marble statue of a *kouros* (youth), one of the earliest of such statues of boys to survive complete. Carved in Naxian marble in Attica, it is believed to have marked the grave of a young Athenian aristocrat. In the Belfer Court is a collection of terracotta pots, gemstones, figures and sculptures from the Neolithic period to the fifth century BC. There are interesting pieces from the Minoan Palace of Knossos in Crete and Roman copies of Hellenistic sculptures from classical Greece. Upstairs are bronze mirrors from the sixth century BC, painted amphoras from the fifth century BC, Corinthian and Hellenistic pottery, and bronze reliefs from the Etrusco-Roman period.

European Sculpture and Decorative Arts is one of the largest departments in the museum. In the Northern Renaissance and Florence galleries is

Above *There is plenty to see and do in Central Park*

Opposite *The Sherman Monument (1903) at Grand Army Plaza*

Above *The entrance to the Metropolitan Museum of Art is imposing from any angle*
Below *Diana by Augustus Saint-Gaudens in the Metropolitan Museum of Art's American Wing*

Bacchanal: A Faun Teased by Children, a sculpture by Rome's Gian Lorenzo Bernini (1598–1680), which he created when he was only 18. In the Louis XIV Gallery, the little oak, pine and walnut veneered desk, engraved with tortoiseshell, brass, ebony and rosewood, is one of a pair made in France for Louis XIV's small study in the Palace of Versailles by cabinetmaker Alexandre-Jean Oppenordt (1639–1715). In the English galleries are a rococo-style dining room from Kirtlington Park, Oxfordshire, and a lavish dining room from Lansdowne House, London. The French galleries include a Paris shopfront from 1775, a daybed made for Marie Antoinette in the boudoir of the Hôtel de Crillon, and in the Louis XVI Gallery, the king's desk from his study at Versailles. Not to be missed is the beautiful Petrie European Sculpture Court. Fountains and greenery and a splendid view of Central Park and Cleopatra's Needle provide a peaceful setting for fine Italian and French sculptures. Cleopatra's Needle was a gift from the Pasha of Egypt.

One of the Met's most popular areas, the American Wing has three floors and centers on the splendid Charles Englehard Court. Focusing on the development of art and design in America, the collection fills 25 rooms with period furniture and furnishings, more than 1,000 paintings by American artists, 600 sculptures, 2,500 drawings and numerous examples of the decorative arts. The Louis Comfort Tiffany vase, one of the first pieces of American glass in the collection, is a beautiful example of his Favrile glass peacock vases—the fan shaped like a peacock's outspread plumage, the eyes of sliced glass millefiori canes, and the graceful lines depicting each individual feather. *Washington Crossing the Delaware,* painted in 1851 by the German-born painter Emmanuel Gottlieb Leutze (1816–68), is an American icon depicting General George Washington's surprise attack on the Hessians at Trenton, New Jersey, on Christmas night 1776. The earliest interior in the American Wing, the Hart Room is from the home of Thomas Hart of Ipswich, Massachusetts. Built sometime between 1639 and 1674, this is a typical example of homes of the early New England settlers. In the airy Charles Englehard Court, linger to study Tiffany's *Garden Landscape and Fountain* and the beautiful stained-glass *Autumn Landscape*. The former was inspired by the Byzantine churches Tiffany saw while traveling in Europe. Turn to the right to see Tiffany's extravagant loggia from Laurelton Hall. The sculptures in this glass-enclosed garden are by American artists Augustus Saint-Gaudens, Frederick MacMonnies and Daniel Chester French. In Gallery 127 is the work of architect Frank Lloyd Wright. *Living Room from the Little House,* a very modern design in 1912, was designed for Francis Little. Paintings and sculptures by American artists on this floor include John Singleton Copely's *Midshipman August Brine, The Falls of Niagara* by S. F. B. Morse, James McNeill Whistler's *Arrangement in Flesh, Color and Black,* John Singer Sargent's *Madame X* (1884), Mary Cassatt's *Lady at the Tea Table* (1885), and from the Hudson River School Frederic Church's *Heart of the Andes*.

Highlights of the European paintings collection include *Virgin and Child with St. Anne* by Albrecht Dürer (1471–1528), *Cypresses* painted in 1889 by Vincent Van Gogh (1853–90), and *Terrace at Sainte-Adresse* (1867) by Claude Monet (1840–1926). Among the many Italian masters' works are Raphael's *Madonna Enthroned with Child and Saints* (1505), Titian's *Venus and the Lute Player* (c. 1560), Tintoretto's *Finding of Moses* (c. 1550), Botticelli's *Last Communion of St. Jerome* (c. 1450) and Caravaggio's *Musicians* (1504). Early Dutch painters include a Rembrandt *Self-Portrait* (1660), Vermeer's *Woman with a Water Jug* (1664) and works by de Hooch, van Goyen and others. French paintings include Poussin's *Rape of the Sabine Women* (c. 1635) and Jean Clouet's *Guillaume Budé*. Spanish works include El Greco's *View of Toledo* and *Grand Inquisitor Cardinal Don Fernando Niño de Guevara*. The English collection is represented by William Hogarth, Joshua Reynolds and Thomas Gainsborough. European paintings of the 19th century include

TIPS

» Don't stroll alone in deserted areas, and stay out of the park at night unless you are going to a play or concert. The park is now generally safe by day and after dark when there are crowds on hand. Police and park rangers patrol in vehicles, on skates and on horseback.

» Count on spending a half day or more here, depending on what you want to see.

» On the roads, watch out for bicycle traffic, and always look carefully when crossing.

» The park has 21 children's playgrounds. Many are state of the art and no two are alike.

Millet's *Autumn Landscape with a Flock of Turkeys* (1872–73) and many Impressionist and Postimpressionist paintings. Besides 100 works by Degas, there are paintings by Manet, Renoir, Seurat, Toulouse-Lautrec, Cézanne and Gauguin. One of Cézanne's best still lifes, *Still Life with Apples and a Pot of Primroses* (1895), is also worth seeing.

The Wildlife Center fills 5.5 acres (2ha) just north of Grand Army Plaza. This state-of-the-art zoo (tel 212/439-6500; Apr–Oct daily 10–5.30; rest of year 10–4.30; adult $12, child (3–12) $7) is home to more than 130 species from three climate zones: monkeys, crocodiles and snakes in the Rain Forest, Asian and North American animals in the Temperate Territory, and polar bears, penguins and polar foxes in the Polar Circle. The sea lion pool in the central courtyard is very popular, especially at feeding times (daily 11.30, 2 and 4). Young children can feed goats, sheep and a cow in the Children's Zoo. There are also daily animal shows in the Acorn Theater. North of the zoo, the George Delacorte Clock plays a nursery rhyme every hour on the hour as miniature animals glide around playing musical instruments. There is a café.

Wollman Memorial Rink (tel 212/439-6900, www.wollmanskatingrink.com; Mon–Tue 10–2.30, Wed–Thu 10–10, Fri–Sat 10am–11pm, Sun 10–9; Mon–Thu adult $10.50, child (under 12) $5.50, Fri–Sun $15, $5.75, respectively, skate rental $6.25) is filled with ice skaters in winter. With its classic New York views of the Midtown skyline and its terrace overlooking the rink, this is one of the park's gems. Lessons are available and there's a snack shop.

The Dairy (tel 212/794-6564; daily 10–5 year-round), a 19th-century building overlooking the Wollman Rink, has an exhibit about the history and design of the park. There's a 12ft (3.6m) model of the park.

Friedsam Memorial Carousel (tel 212/439-6900; Apr–Oct Mon–Fri 10–6, Sat–Sun 10–7; Jan–Mar Sat–Sun 10–dusk; Nov–Dec daily 10–dusk), in the middle of the park at 64th Street, is one of the largest carousels in the US, with 58 hand-carved, painted horses.

Above *The park's famous pond, Conservatory Water, is popular with model boat enthusiasts*

PARK GUIDE
SOUTH QUADRANT

The Arsenal (Mon–Fri 9–5), originally the New York State National Guard's munitions supply depot, was built between 1847 and 1851. Now a New York City Landmark, the Arsenal houses Olmsted and Vaux's original blueprint for Central Park, called the Greensward Plan. You can see it in a glass case on the third floor.

The Dairy, a Gothic Revival cottage, was once a place where children could go for a glass of fresh milk. It now houses a visitor center (tel 212/794-6564; daily 10–5) with video information terminals and a permanent exhibit on the history of the park.

To the west of the Dairy is the octagonal Chess and Checkers (draughts) House, where you can test your skills at one of the 24 chess tables.

RESERVOIR QUADRANT

As you walk, or run, around the reservoir, note the three pedestrian wrought-iron bridges, called 24, 27 and 28. New Yorkers call Bridge 28 the Gothic Arch because of its lace-like quality.

NORTH QUADRANT

The Charles A. Dana Discovery Center, opened in 1993 on the northern shore of the Harlem Meer, is a visitor and community center with free educational exhibits relating to Central Park (tel 212/860-1370; Apr–Oct Tue–Sun 10–5; Nov–Mar Wed–Sun 10–5).

Above *Conservatory Garden is a formal garden with a rustic atmosphere*

The Sheep Meadow is 15 acres (6ha) of grass where you can have a picnic, fly kites and sunbathe. Some 300 sprinkler heads keep the grass green and lush throughout the year. A flock of sheep grazed here until 1934; their sheepfold is now a visitor center, the former Tavern on the Green. On the east side of the meadow is a patch of pavement where you can watch talented roller skaters practice their moves.

Bethesda Terrace, in Olmsted and Vaux's original design, was "the heart of the park." By the 1980s it had fallen into disrepair and was rebuilt. Stand on the Upper Terrace for a splendid view of the lake and the wooded area known as the Ramble. The fountain, *Angel of the Waters* (1870), was the work of sculptor Emma Stebbins.

Strawberry Fields was created in 1981 with funds provided by Yoko Ono, widow of musician John Lennon, after his murder in 1980 outside The Dakota (▷ 203), and named after his song *Strawberry Fields Forever*. Italian craftsmen made the black-and-white mosaic embedded in the path near the entrance at West 72nd Street, directly across the street from The Dakota apartment building where he was killed. It is centered around the word "Imagine," recalling another of Lennon's most popular songs. Yoko Ono provides $1 million annually to the Central Park Conservancy for the upkeep of these 2.5 acres (1ha). Fans often stop to pay their respects and leave flowers or candles, and a huge crowd gathers every year on the singer's birthday (October 9) to sing, pray and celebrate his life and work.

Loeb Boathouse rents out rowboats and bicycles (mid-Apr to end Oct daily 10–5.30). Rowboats cost $12 for the first hour, $5 for each extra half hour; each boat takes up to four people. A $20 cash deposit is required. Renting a bicycle costs between $9 and $20 per hour, and you must leave a credit card, driver's license or a passport as a deposit. In June and August (weather permitting) another option is a gondola ride—not cheap at $30 per half hour, but memorable. A fast-food restaurant in the Boathouse offers cold drinks and snacks. The Boathouse Restaurant is a lovely spot, serving brunch and lunch year round, and dinner from April to November (reservations are a must, tel 212/517-2233). Birdwatchers record their observations in the Bird Register, inside the Boathouse, and other visitors' sightings also make for some interesting reading.

Conservatory Water is the park's famous pond. On Saturdays at 10am from spring through fall, the Model Yacht Club races its radio-powered craft. You can rent miniature boats. North of the pond is the delightful *Alice in Wonderland* sculpture, designed by José de Creeft in 1959, and to the west is the Hans Christian Andersen sculpture; children climb up on it to sit on his lap, and there are story hours on summer Saturdays at 11am.

Belvedere Castle (tel 212/772-0210; Apr–Oct Tue–Sun 10–5; Nov–Mar Wed–Sun 10–5) was Olmsted and Vaux's folly, an open-air flight of fancy that served as an elaborate scenic lookout across the lake. But during an extensive restoration in the early 1980s windows and doors were put in and it is now the Henry Luce Nature Observatory. Here you will find interesting displays—telescopes, microscopes, skeletons, feathers—intended to help children understand how naturalists observe the world. The US Weather Bureau has been operating from here since 1919, and you can get up-to-the-minute weather reports on the second floor. Also on this floor is a tree loft with a collection of papier-mâché models of bird species found in the park.

The Delacorte Theater, built in 1962, is where Shakespeare in the Park performances (▷ 235) delight large audiences in summer. Waiting in line for a free ticket (from 10am) is part of the experience—New Yorkers bring picnic baskets and books. The box office begins distributing tickets at 1pm. Tickets are also handed out at the Public Theater at 425 Lafayette Street on the day of the performance from 1 to 3pm.

RESERVOIR QUADRANT

The Jacqueline Kennedy Onassis Reservoir, named for the widow of President John F. Kennedy because of her fondness for the place and her contributions to the city, is noted for the 1.58-mile (2.54km) track around it. Joggers and walkers come here by the thousands every day. This 106-acre (43ha) body of water no longer supplies Manhattanites with fresh water, but it still feeds the other ponds in the park. In spring glorious ornamental cherry trees blossom on the slopes.

NORTH QUADRANT

The Conservatory Garden is 6 acres (2.5ha) of formal gardens with lovely fountains in an area that has been landscaped in a more rustic, naturalistic style than the southern part of the park. If you enter from Fifth Avenue at East 104th Street, you will pass through giant Parisian wrought-iron gates from the mansion of Cornelius Vanderbilt II.

Harlem Meer, Dutch for "little sea," is a pretty pond, well stocked with about 50,000 fish. Catch-and-release fishing (mid-Apr to mid-Oct Tue–Sat 10–3, Sun 10–1) is great entertainment for kids, big and small. Fishing rods can be rented at the Charles A. Dana Discovery Center.

Lasker Memorial Rink and Pool (skating: tel 917/492-3856; pool: 212/534-7639; Jul–Labor Day daily 11–3, 4–7; free), built in the 1960s, is an ice-skating rink from November through March and a roller-skating rink for the rest of the year. Skate rental is available. Very popular in summer, the swimming pool opens on July 1 and closes after Labor Day.

Above *The memorial to John Lennon in Strawberry Fields*
Below *Belvedere Castle is a lakeside folly in the South Quadrant*

EAST HARLEM

Above the Upper East Side is East Harlem, once known as Spanish Harlem and now as El Barrio (the neighborhood). Unlike Central Harlem, this area developed in the 1870s and 1880s. Its poor-quality working-class dwellings were home to immigrants—first the Irish and then, from the 1890s, Italians. As the Puerto Ricans moved on up the social and employment ladder, they made the area their own.

The city's Puerto Rican population numbered 45,000 by the 1930s and 600,000 by the 1960s; today more than a million Puerto Ricans live in New York, and Spanish is a second language. El Barrio has a vibrant Hispanic flavor, with family-owned businesses.

✚ 201 E2 ✉ Fifth to First avenues, East 97th to East 125th streets 🚇 4, 5, 6 🚌 M15, M101, M102, M103

EL MUSEO DEL BARRIO

www.elmuseo.org

Opened in 1969, this is one of the few museums in the United States dedicated to Puerto Rican, Latin American and Caribbean culture and art. There is a permanent display of hand-carved religious statuettes known as *santos de palo*, and another of artifacts from Caribbean cultures that welcomed Christopher Columbus to the New World in the 15th century. The glass facade and new galleries were added in 2009.

✚ 200 D2 ✉ 1230 Fifth Avenue, between 104th and 105th streets, 10029 ☎ 212/831-7272 🕐 Tue–Sat 11–6 (Wed until 9), Sun 1–5 💰 Suggested donation: adult $9 (senior free on Wed), under 12 free. Special exhibition rates apply; free Wed 6–9 and third Sat of month 🚇 6 🚌 M1, M2, M3, M4 🏛

FRICK COLLECTION

▷ 215.

GENERAL GRANT NATIONAL MEMORIAL

www.nps.gov/gegr

Known as Grant's Tomb, this may be the nation's largest and most impressive sepulcher. Rising dramatically 150ft (46m) next to the Hudson River, the squat, dome-topped granite building fronted by six Doric columns proclaims the wildly popular Civil War general, and later president, Ulysses S. Grant (1822–85).

The design, chosen after a competition, was copied from the fourth-century BC tomb of Mausolus at Halicarnassus. Work began soon after Grant's death, with contributions from more than 90,000 people, many of them African-Americans, for whom Grant's achievements at the head of the Union army outweighed his less successful efforts as president.

Inside the massive bronze doors, below the domed rotunda and set off by the gleaming white marble, two 9-ton polished black sarcophagi hold the remains of Grant and his wife, Julia.

✚ Off map 200 B2 ✉ Riverside Drive at West 122nd Street, 10027 ☎ 212/666-1640 🕐 Daily 9–5 🚇 A, 1 🚌 M4, M5, M104

Above *Ulysses S. Grant's tomb was completed in 1897*

GUGGENHEIM MUSEUM

▷ 216–217.

HARLEM

Harlem is forever linked with the speakeasies and jazz of the Prohibition era. The area declined in the middle of the last century into the bleak landscape that saw the departure of middle-class families in the 1960s. Today this has given way to housing renovation and a growing, upbeat population. There is much of architectural interest, and nightlife, jazz clubs and cultural attractions, including Manhattan's oldest residence, the Morris-Jumel Mansion Museum (65 Jumel Terrace, tel 212/923-8008, Wed–Sun 10–4, adult $5). After his second term as president, Bill Clinton opened an office in Harlem.

✚ Off map 200 D2 ✉ Fifth Avenue to Morningside Avenue, north of 110th Street 🚇 2, 3, A, B, C, D 🚌 M2, M3, M7, M10, M102 🏛 Harlem Tourist Center and Gift Shop, 2224 Frederick Douglass Boulevard

FRICK COLLECTION

Henry Clay Frick (1849–1919) has gone down in history as a ruthless businessman, staunchly anti-union, obsessed with acquiring wealth—in other words, a master entrepreneur. Frick had his own successful business, the Frick Coke Company in Pittsburgh, when Andrew Carnegie made him his partner in the Carnegie Steel Company. Together they made the Carnegie steel empire one of the most important businesses in the country, and both men became multimillionaires. Frick's sole interest outside the world of steel and coke was art. He collected works painted by many of the world's masters dating from the 14th to the 19th centuries. At the age of 64 he had a palatial residence on Fifth Avenue built as his private home and gallery, to plans drawn up by Carrère & Hastings. Frick and his wife lived in the home until their deaths—his in 1919, hers in 1931. Frick, in a generous move, bequeathed the house and paintings to the public.

After Frick's wife's death, the house was enlarged and became a museum in 1935. There is a reference library, the Frick Art Reference Library, next door on East 71st Street, designed by John Russell Pope, the architect of the National Gallery in Washington, D.C. The house is set back from Fifth Avenue behind an elevated garden designed by Russell Page. As part of multimillion dollar improvements, the stone wall surrounding the site was replaced in 2002 and the wrought-iron fence was restored.

ARTISTIC HIGHLIGHTS

Through the 16 galleries, the paintings are not arranged by period or national origin, but in the way Frick would have had them displayed in his home. The Fragonard Room shows the large Fragonard paintings depicting *The Progress of Love* and contains 18th-century French furniture and porcelain. In the Living Room are paintings by Holbein, El Greco, Titian and Bellini. Through the Library, past Italian bronzes and Chinese vases, is the West Gallery, where there are landscapes by John Constable and portraits by Rembrandt and Velázquez. Especially delightful is the East Gallery, with works by David, El Greco, Goya, Hogarth and Manet. After your visit, pause in the peaceful Garden Court (the enclosed Palm Court is the perfect oasis on a cold New York day), which occasionally hosts special exhibitions.

INFORMATION

www.frick.org

✚ 200 D6 ✉ 1 East 70th Street at Fifth Avenue, 10021 ☎ 212/288-0700

🕐 Tue–Sat 10–6, Sun 11–5; closed Mon; limited hours, 1–6, on Presidents' Day, Election Day and Veterans' Day

💲 Adult $18, no children under 10. Sun pay what you wish 11–1; ArtPhone audioguide free 🚇 6 🚌 M1, M2, M3, M4 🎁 Books, cards, CDs, videos and museum-inspired gifts

TIP

» Try to come for a chamber music concert (year round on occasional Sundays at 5pm). Check website for details.

Below The Purification of the Temple *(c.1600), an oil on canvas by El Greco (1541–1614) from the collection*

INFORMATION

www.guggenheim.org

✚ 200 D4 ✉ 1071 Fifth Avenue at 89th Street, 10028 ☎ 212/423-3500
🕐 Sun–Wed, Fri 10–5.45, Sat 10–7.45
💲 Adult $18, under 12 free, Sat 5.45–7.45 pay-as-you-wish 🚇 4, 5, 6 🚌 M1, M2, M3, M4 📖 Free Guggenheim Guide containing listing of exhibits and programs, available at admission desk
🛍 Fri–Wed 10.30–5.15, Thu 9.30–3, Fri 9.30–8 🍴 Sun–Wed, Fri 9.30–6.15, Thu 11–6, Sat 9.30–8.30 🎧 Free tours daily. Ask at the information desk. Audiotours free

Above *A masterpiece of modern architecture designed by Frank Lloyd Wright, the Guggenheim exhibits one of the world's finest collections of modern and contemporary art*

INTRODUCTION

The Solomon R. Guggenheim Museum, designed by Frank Lloyd Wright, opened in 1959. The inverted-ziggurat design, with its ramp encircling the walls, is as surprising today as it was when it was created. Solomon R. Guggenheim, a wealthy New Yorker whose father was a prominent 19th-century mining and smelting capitalist, used some of his wealth to buy works of art. He was content with Old Masters until 1927, when at the age of 66 he met baroness Hilla Rebay von Ehrenwiesen. The baroness favored European abstract art and introduced Guggenheim to such artists as Wassily Kandinsky, Fernand Léger and Robert Delaunay. It was she who suggested that Wright design a museum to house the great collection Guggenheim was amassing. Guggenheim died in 1949 and never saw the wondrous building, but Wright took on the job with enthusiasm and later pronounced it his "Pantheon."

As you enter, to your right is the admission desk, where you can pick up a free exhibitions program with a floor plan. As you look up at the five levels above the low white walls bordering the ramp you will see a tall, empty atrium-like space so dramatic that it is easy to forget that you came here primarily to see the modern art. Frank Lloyd Wright designed this building with the belief that the eye should not be confronted with angles and sudden changes of form when viewing works of art. From a logistical point of view, the best way to view the works hung here is to take the elevator up to the skylit top of the building and meander down the spiral ramp. However, the exhibits are often hung with the opposite path in mind.

WHAT TO SEE

PAUL CÉZANNE, *STILL LIFE: FLASK, GLASS AND JUG*
In this 1877 still life, Cézanne (1839–1906) perceived objects in space as being interrelated. He created an illusion of objects resting and flowing simultaneously, calling attention to the two-dimensional canvas. This painting, and others, made Cézanne the foremost precursor of Cubism.

PABLO PICASSO, *WOMAN IRONING*
Painted in 1904 at the end of his Blue Period, *Woman Ironing* is Picasso's (1881–1973) quintessential work of labor and fatigue, reminiscent of the years he spent among the Paris working class. His expressionist style, with angular contours and attenuated proportions, expresses the woman's movement poetically, making her the metaphor for the pathos of the working poor.

MAX ERNST, *ATTIREMENT OF THE BRIDE*
This 1940s' Surrealist painting by Max Ernst (1891–1976) evokes late 19th-century Symbolist painting, while the sleek, round-bellied figures recall motifs of 16th-century German art. The background architecture indicates the strong influence of the Italian painter Giorgio De Chirico. Ernst's invented alter-ego, the bird-man on the left, depicts the artist with a symbolic phallic spear. The picture-within-a-picture shows the same bride walking amid overgrown Classical ruins, indicating the role of the bride throughout history. Garish colors and beastly figures suggest something violent is about to happen.

Below *Under the rotunda, the ramp spirals downward*

Above *The Metropolitan Opera House and Lincoln Center Plaza*

INFORMATION

www.lincolncenter.org

✚ 200 B7 ✉ 70 Lincoln Center Plaza, 10023-6583 ☎ 212/875-5000 for main Lincoln Center 🚇 1 🚌 M5, M7, M10, M11, M66, M104 🎫 Guided tours of the Lincoln Center start from the tour desk in the David Rubenstein Atrium, daily 10–4, adult $15 (reservations ☎ 212/875-5350); Metropolitan Opera House backstage tours weekdays at 3.30 Oct–May only, Sun 10.30, adult $15 (reservations ☎ 212/865-5350) 🍽 Avery Fisher Hall: Arpeggio Food and Wine ☎ 212/874-7000 🕐 Tue–Sat for dinner, lunch on matinee days ☕ Avery Fisher Hall: Espresso Bar, 5pm–intermission nightly, opens at noon for matinees 📖 Metropolitan Opera Shop ☎ 212/580-4090; Other gift shops open for performances at various venues

INTRODUCTION

The Lincoln Center is the Upper West Side's performing arts center for the best in opera, classical music, chamber music, jazz, ballet and theater. With 14 venues offering everything from classical music to performances for children, the Lincoln Center is New York's premier center for performing arts. In the 1960s, a block of old tenements on the Upper West Side, where some of *West Side Story* was filmed, was demolished in a 12-block urban renewal project, and the Lincoln Center for the Performing Arts was built on the site. The initial investment for the Lincoln Center was more than $165 million. The state contributed the site and the remainder of the money came from private contributions and donations.

In 1962 the New York Philharmonic moved here from Carnegie Hall (▷ 150), which was threatened with demolition, but the acoustics were never good, so in 1973 Avery Fisher donated $10 million to improve them. The hall closed for a time to undergo this work, but musicians and music-lovers were still not satisfied, so in 1992 the hall underwent further renovation.

WHAT TO SEE

OPERA, BALLET, THEATER, JAZZ

The David H. Koch Theater is home to the New York City Opera and the New York City Ballet. The theater seats 2,700.

The Metropolitan Opera House, affectionately known as the Met, is home to both the opera company and the American Ballet Theater and seats 3,800. General manager Joe Volpe started as an apprentice carpenter and has worked his way up; he knows what attracts crowds and what doesn't.

The Guggenheim Bandshell in Damrosch Park, on 62nd Street near Amsterdam Avenue, hosts open-air concerts in summer.

The Lincoln Center Theater consists of the Vivian Beaumont Theater, with seating for 1,140, and the Mitzi E. Newhouse Theater, an off-Broadway venue.

Jazz, led by trumpeter and composer Wynton Marsalis, has moved to the massive new Time Warner headquarters at nearby Columbus Circle, after receiving a $10-million gift from the Coca-Cola Company. The $128-million jazz venue is the focal point of the building, with three main performance spaces (tel 212/258-9800).

THE JUILLIARD SCHOOL OF MUSIC

The Juilliard School of Music is the top music school in the United States. The campus includes the Alice Tully Hall, a wonderful venue for chamber music and solo recitals, and the Walter Reade Film Theater, where the New York Film Festival sends up sparks every fall.

RECENT RENOVATIONS

West 65th Street has been turned into a broad boulevard. This is a major portion of the $150-million redesign of the public areas and the center's buildings and grounds. The avant-garde design team of Diller and Scofidio, who are described as "artist architects," and specialize in experimental installations, were selected for the project. Changes include technologically sophisticated signs with information about events, a sweeping staircase into the Josie Roberson Plaza, and a renovation of its distinctive patterned paving, along with new lighting and water displays for the Revson Fountain at the plaza's heart. The opening of the David Rubenstein Atrium provides a centralized box office, information desk and gathering point for tours. The Elinor Bunin Munroe Film Center, opened in 2011, is the Lincoln Center's newest addition. The Claire Tow Theater is due to open in 2012.

TIPS

» There is a vast underground parking area, if you dare drive in New York.

» Special events take place all year, from summer's Mostly Mozart concert series and swing dancing to live jazz under the stars and the annual run of the Big Apple Circus, which pitches its tent in Damrosch Park at the beginning of November.

Left and below *The Alice Tully Hall, a venue for recitals and chamber music, is part of the Juilliard School of Music campus*

REGIONS CENTRAL PARK AND AROUND • SIGHTS

JEWISH MUSEUM

www.thejewishmuseum.org

A faux Loire Valley chateau, this graystone mansion dating from 1908 contains the Jewish Museum's collection of Jewish ceremonial objects and works of art.

Generous philanthropist Felix Warburg died in 1938 and his widow left the house to the museum in 1944. The permanent exhibit, entitled *Culture and Continuity: The Jewish Journey,* is based on Warburg's collection.

In a re-created 1900s' café, oral histories reveal Jewish life in Europe at that time and explore the immigrant experience in the US. Family workshops and other events celebrate Jewish culture.

✛ 200 D4 ✉ 1109 Fifth Avenue at 92nd Street, 10128 ☎ 212/423-3200 ◉ Fri–Tue 11–5.45, Thu 11–8. Closed Wed and major Jewish holidays 🖐 Adult $12, under 12 free; free Sat 🚇 4, 5, 6 🚌 M1, M2, M3, M4 🏛 💻

LINCOLN CENTER

▷ 218–219.

MOUNT VERNON HOTEL MUSEUM AND GARDEN

www.mvhm.org

In this splendid hotel, eight of the rooms were filled with Federal period furnishings by the Colonial Dames of America when they bought the structure in 1924. In the Gentlemen's Tavern Room, you're welcome to sit down and read a newspaper from 1828, and don't miss the museum's delightful 18th-century gardens.

The museum was a house that belonged to Abigail Adams, daughter of US president John Adams and the wife of George Washington's aide, William Stephens Smith. The Smiths had to sell the property in 1798 before all the buildings were complete and so never lived here. In 1826 the building underwent conversion into a hotel. There are regularly scheduled events.

✛ 201 F7 ✉ 421 East 61st Street at York Avenue ☎ 212/838-6878 ◉ Tue–Sun

11–4 🖐 Adult $8, under 12 free 🚇 4, 6, N, R 🚌 M15, M31, M57

MUSEUM OF ARTS AND DESIGN

www.madmuseum.org

In this museum the American Craft Council displays the nation's biggest exhibition of 20th- and 21st-century American and international crafts. From jewelry to baskets, furniture to teapots, everything is selected to represent the finest in form and function. Stimulating special exhibitions are chosen from the wide-ranging collections, augmented by loans from other collections, to illustrate contemporary trends in technique and design. It's all shown to great advantage in the museum's building in Columbus Circle. The building design provides additional space for exhibitions, educational programing and the rapidly expanding permanent collection. The facade features terracotta panels and fritted glass materials to highlight the museum's craft traditions.

✛ 200 C7 ✉ 2 Columbus Circle ☎ 212/299-7777 ◉ Tue–Sun 11–6, Thu 11–9 🖐 Adult $15, under 12 free (pay-what-you-wish Thu 6pm–9pm) 🚇 59th Street/Columbus Circle (A, B, C, D, 1); 57th Street/Seventh Avenue (N, R, Q); 57th Street/Sixth Avenue (F) 🚌 M5, M7, M10, M20, M31, M104 to Columbus Circle at 59th Street

MUSEUM OF BIBLICAL ART

www.mobia.org

This museum aims to foster an understanding and appreciation of art inspired by the Bible. It opened its new building in 2005 with an inaugural exhibition of works by self-taught Southern folk artists. The museum evolved out of the American Bible Society (1816), which had amassed a huge collection of scripture, now on view behind a glass curtain wall in the main gallery. Exhibitions focus on the collection's highlights, such as *For Glory and for Beauty,* which displayed 29 rare scriptures.

✛ 200 C7 ✉ 1865 Broadway at 61st Street, 10023 ☎ 212/408-1500

◉ Tue–Sun 10–6 (Thu until 8) 🖐 Adult $7, under 12 free 🚇 59th Street/Columbus Circle (A, B, C, D, 1) 🚌 M5, M7, M11, M104

MUSEUM OF THE CITY OF NEW YORK

www.mcny.org

A neo-Georgian, colonial-style villa built in 1929 houses this museum devoted to New York's history and life. The collections here hold more than 1.5 million objects relating to the social and economic life of the city—paintings, photographs, costumes, toys, decorative arts and other artifacts. Some are world-class, like the silver collection and the collection on American theater; the photography, marine and costume collections are also outstanding. The museum has sometimes been criticized for taking a dull approach to display, but lively exhibitions such as *Glamor, New York Style* and *El Barrio: Puerto Rican New York* have helped to change that reputation.

✛ 200 D3 ✉ 1220 Fifth Avenue at 103rd Street, 10029 ☎ 212/534-1672 ◉ Tue–Sun 10–5 (longer hours in summer) 🖐 Suggested admission: adult $10, under 12 free, family $20 🚇 6 🚌 M1, M2, M3, M4, M106 💼 Highlights tour Sat noon 🏛

NATIONAL ACADEMY OF DESIGN

www.nationalacademy.org

The National Academy of Design was founded in 1825 by a group of accomplished artists, architects, sculptors and engravers, including Thomas Cole and artist/inventor Samuel Morse. It is both a museum and a school of fine art, and also owns the largest collection of 19th- and 20th-century American art in the country—with more than 5,000 works ranging from portraiture of the Federalist period, landscapes of the Hudson River School, gritty realism of the Ashcan Movement, and paintings from Fauvism to photo-realism.

The building was the home of Archer Milton Huntington and his wife, the sculptor Anna Hyatt Huntington. In 1913, they expanded and remodeled the house and lived here until 1939, when they gave it to the National Academy of Design, who moved in three years later.

Tours covering the collection's highlights and Edith Wharton's New York are available.

✚ 200 D4 ✉ 1083 Fifth Avenue, 10128 ☎ 212/369-4880 🕔 Wed–Sun 11–6 ✋ Adult $12, under 12 free 🚇 4, 5, 6 🚌 M1, M2, M3, M4 ➤ Docent tours Fri 2pm, $5 ♿

NEUE GALERIE

www.neuegalerie.org

This museum, dedicated to early 20th-century German and Austrian art and design, has a marvelous collection of fine paintings, decorative arts and other media, including works by Gustav Klimt, Paul Klee, Egon Schiele, Josef Hoffmann and Adolf Loos.

On Friday nights there are cabarets in Café Sabarsky, which serves Austrian fare, including delicious pastries.

Some of the furniture is by Adolf Loos, and lighting fixtures are by Josef Hoffmann. The 1914 Carrère & Hastings mansion housing the museum was built for Mrs Cornelius Vanderbilt III, and is every bit as remarkable as the collection.

✚ 200 D4 ✉ 1048 Fifth Avenue at 86th Street, 10028 ☎ 212/628-6200 🕔 Thu–Mon 11–6 ✋ Adult $15, no children; free first Fri of month 6–8 🚇 4, 5, 6 🚌 M1, M2, M3, M4 🍴 ♿

NEW-YORK HISTORICAL SOCIETY

www.nyhistory.org

This Upper West Side museum is fascinating. For nearly 200 years, the Society has been collecting, preserving and interpreting books, paintings, sculpture, photographs and newspapers. The Henry Luce III Center on the fourth floor displays lamps by Louis Comfort Tiffany, Hudson River School landscapes, a complete set of watercolors by John James Audubon for *The Birds of America*, George Washington's inaugural chair, and much more. The library is the oldest research library in the country.

✚ 200 C5 ✉ 170 Central Park West at 77th Street, 10024 ☎ 212/873-3400 🕔 Museum: Tue–Sat 10–6 (Fri to 8), Sun 11–5.45. Library: Tue–Sat 10–5. Print Room by appointment only ✋ Adult $10, Fri 6–8 free, under 12 free 🚇 B, C 🚌 M10, M79 ➤ Audiotours ♿

ROOSEVELT ISLAND

You can take the subway to Roosevelt Island, but the East 60th Street Heliport Aerial Tramway is a much more fun way to travel the 300 yards (274m) over the East River. Today there are 8,000 residents on the island, which is 2 miles (3.2km) long and only 800ft (244m) wide; this is a much sought-after area in which to live.

Up to the 19th century it was farmed by the Blackwell family, then

it housed a prison, a mental health facility, the Octagon Building (1842), as well as the Smallpox Hospital (1854) and, at the northern tip, a lighthouse (1872), both designed by James Renwick, Jr.

✚ 201 F6 ✉ In the East River, between Manhattan and Queens ☎ 212/832-4540 ✋ Tram fare $2.25 🚇 F 🚌 Q102

STUDIO MUSEUM IN HARLEM

www.studiomuseum.org

Specializing in 19th- and 20th-century African-American art, and 20th-century African and Caribbean art and artifacts, this small museum has a lot to offer. Exhibitions have included *Challenge of the Modern: African-American Artists 1925–1945*, which examined the modernist concepts adopted by black artists in the US and the Caribbean; and *Harlem Postcards 2007*. The small sculpture garden is charming. The tempting gift shop offers a good selection of books, postcards and other items.

✚ Off map 200 C2 ✉ 144 West 125th Street between Lenox and Seventh Avenue, 10027 ☎ 212/864-4500 🕔 Thu–Fri 12–6, Sat 10–6, Sun 12–6 ✋ Adult $7, child $3, under 12 free; free Sun 12–6 🚇 2, 3 🚌 M2, M7, M10, M100 🖥 ♿

UPPER WEST SIDE

The Upper West Side is a lively residential area with numerous historic districts, sumptuous landmark buildings, affordable hotels and excellent restaurants, and an affluent crowd that includes many actors, actresses, directors and musicians. The popular American Museum of Natural History (▷ 204–207) is here, as are the city's premier performing arts complex, the Lincoln Center (▷ 218–219), and the Cathedral Church of St. John the Divine. While you stroll, note the San Remo Apartment Building at 145–146 Central Park West, and the Trump International Hotel/Tower on Columbus Circle.

✚ 200 B4 ✉ Between 59th and 125th streets, west of Central Park 🚇 1, 2, 3, A, B, C, D 🚌 M7, M10, M11, M104 🍴 🖥 ♿

Below *Part of the huge collection of scripture at the Museum of Biblical Art*

INFORMATION

www.whitney.org
http://artport.whitney.org/

✚ 200 D6 ✉ 945 Madison Avenue at
75th Street, 10021 ☎ 212/570-3600
🕐 Wed–Thu 11–6, Fri 1–9, Sat–Sun
11–6 ✋ Adult $18, under 18 free
($2 per ticket service charge online),
pay-what-you-wish Fri 6pm–9pm 🚇 6
🚌 M1, M2, M3, M4 🎟 Free exhibition
tours start at the lobby information desk.
Select Saturday family programs free
with museum admission for children
aged under 12 ☎ 212/671-5300 for info
(reservations required for some programs)
📖 🍴 Danny Meyer's Untitled
restaurant (☎ 212/570-3670) serves
breakfast and lunch Tue–Thu 8–3, Fri
8am–9pm, and weekend brunch Sat–Sun
10–9 🍴

Above *The Whitney Museum of American
Art, established in 1931, has occupied its
present building since 1966*

INTRODUCTION

More than 18,000 works by 1,700 prominent 20th- and 21st-century
American artists, including Georgia O'Keeffe, Jasper Johns, Edward Hopper,
Mark Rothko and Jackson Pollock are on display here. The collection also
includes provocative works by innovative and often controversial American
independent film-makers, video artists, multimedia artists and photographers.

Gertrude Vanderbilt Whitney (1875–1942), the daughter of Cornelius
Vanderbilt II (1843–99), studied sculpture at the Art Students League of New
York and went on to become one of the country's most generous patrons
of the arts. In 1914, she launched the Whitney Studio Club, at 8 West 8th
Street in the West Village, next to her MacDougal Alley studio, to exhibit
works of young, avant-garde American artists. She was particularly fond
of revolutionary artists such as John Sloan, Everett Shin and George Luks,
realist painters Edward Hopper and Thomas Hart Benton, and early modernist
painters such as Max Weber and Stuart Davis.

In 1929, after years of collecting, Whitney offered her collection to the
Metropolitan Museum of Art. When the Met refused it, she established
the Whitney Museum of American Art in 1931 with 700 objects. Thus the
museum became one of the few museums anywhere in the world to be
founded by an artist. The Whitney moved to its present building in 1966.

Before entering the museum on Madison Avenue, take a few minutes to
look at the striking granite, modernist building by Marcel Breuer and Hamilton
Smith. In a neighborhood of traditional brownstone, limestone and brick
row houses, this Brutalist architecture attracts attention, and when it was
completed in 1966, many people thought it too heavy and dreary. Today, it is
generally esteemed as daring and innovative as it rises in a series of inverted
stairs above a sunken sculpture garden. The Whitney has broken ground on
a new 200,000sq ft (18,580sq m) building downtown in the Meatpacking

District, designed by Renzo Piano, which will open in 2015. As you enter, the ticket desk is to your left, where there are free museum guides with the current exhibition schedule.

Start your visit with rotating selections from the permanent collection, either on the second floor, or on the fifth floor. New exhibitions are also staged (in the past these have featured individual artists and themed shows).

WHAT TO SEE

ROBERT HENRI, *GERTRUDE VANDERBILT WHITNEY*

Henri (1865–1929) captures the founder of the Whitney Museum, Gertrude Vanderbilt Whitney, in this 1916 portrait. Her granddaughter Flora Whitney Miller donated the painting to the museum, and has remarked that the woman of leisure depicted here is surprising to her, as she remembers her grandmother as an energetic woman, always on the go.

WILLIAM J. GLACKENS, *HAMMERSTEIN'S ROOF GARDEN*

Glackens (1870–1938) depicts wealthy New Yorkers at the beginning of the 20th century enjoying watching tightrope walkers, acrobats and jugglers on a hot summer's evening at Hammerstein's on the corner of Seventh Avenue and 42nd Street. This 1901 oil on canvas captures the mood of the roof gardens, where New Yorkers sought entertainment, as well as relief from the heat.

GEORGIA O'KEEFFE

O'Keeffe (1887–1986) is well represented in the Whitney Collection, which features several of her dazzling flower paintings and *Summer Days* (1936), one of her many cow-skull paintings. The collection also includes her gorgeous *Music Pink and Blue II* (1919) and *Black and White* (1930).

TIPS

» On Fridays from 6pm to 9pm, admission is pay-what-you-wish and there are live musical performances.

» For a good cross section of the latest in American art and to see works by unknown but promising artists, visit when the Whitney Biennial is on (even-numbered years).

» The fifth-floor galleries change from time to time, presenting different aspects of the Whitney's vast collection in themes. Some of the works highlighted on these pages may not be on view when you visit.

Below Dempsey and Firpo *(1924) by George Bellows (left);* Laughing Child *(1907) by Robert Henri (center);* Head *(1926) by Gaston Lachaise (right)*

EDWARD HOPPER

The Whitney Museum holds more than 2,500 works by Hopper (1882–1967), the largest collection in the world. This superb collection includes favorites such as *7am* (1948), the earlier *Small Town Station* (1918–20) and *Italian Quarter From Gloucester* (1912), as well as his particularly haunting painting, *Early Spring Morning* (1930). Notice the curtains and blinds in the windows above the storefronts in this picture. By making each window different, some with yellow blinds and some with white curtains, he gives a sense that people live in each of these dwellings, and that something different is going on inside each one. Hold up your hands to block your view of the barber's pole and the fire hydrant, and notice how they give focus and balance to the painting.

THOMAS HART BENTON, *POKER NIGHT*

Benton (1889–1975) created this commissioned painting in 1948 to represent a scene from Tennessee Williams' Pulitzer Prize-winning Broadway play *A Streetcar Named Desire,* which later became a movie.

LOUISE BOURGEOIS, *QUARANTANIA*

This 1941 sculpture, *Quarantania,* was created by artist Bourgeois (1911–2010) when she was feeling homesick for her native France while she studied in the United States. One of her earliest works, the seven stylized wood figures in this sculpture represent the loved ones she left behind in France and still missed deeply.

Opposite Road and House, South Truro *(1930–33)*, Study for Railroad Sunset, *(1929)* and Cape Cod Sunset *(1934)*, all by Edward Hopper
Below Large Trademark with Eight Spotlights *(1962) by Ed Ruscha (left)*; New Hoover Convertibles, Green, Blue; New Hoover Convertibles, Green, Blue; Double-Decker *(1981–87) by Jeff Koons (right)*

JACKSON POLLOCK, *NUMBER 27*

Pollock (1912–56) was one of the innovators, producing abstracts like *Number 27* (1950) by placing the canvas on the floor and drizzling paint on it in a controlled and deliberate manner. Created gradually, with layer upon layer of paint, his expression of movement and emotion are revealed.

JASPER JOHNS, *THREE FLAGS*

This classic Johns (born 1930) painting, *Three Flags* (1958), captures an everyday object in an unusual composition.

REGINALD MARSH

The Whitney Museum's collection of almost 200 Marsh (1898–1954) artworks includes some of his best-known paintings. *Why Not Use the "L"?* (1930) and *Twenty Cent Movie* (1936) capture details of modern life in the city.

ROY LICHTENSTEIN, *LITTLE BIG PAINTING*

In the Pop Gallery, *Little Big Painting* (1965) is a celebration of mass media and popular culture. The red, white and yellow with harsh black lines resemble an image of an abstract painting. With no trace of the artist's hand, no visible brushstroke, and the dot screen in the background, Lichtenstein (1923–97) evokes mechanical printing, the culture of mass reproduction.

ALEXANDER CALDER, *CIRCUS*

The fascination of Calder (1898–1976) with the circus and his training as a mechanical engineer inspired him to create *Circus* (1926–31) and to breathe life into the tiny wire tightrope walkers, acrobats, weight-lifters and dancers in this mixed-media, miniature reproduction of an actual circus. The sculpture is accompanied by a continuous screening of a film of the affable ringmaster, Calder, in his studio with his wife, winding up the gramophone, as they performed for the Paris avant-garde in the 1920s.

WHITNEY BIENNIAL

Held every second year (even-numbered years) in the spring, this exhibition's focus is on presenting and showcasing the latest in American contemporary art. Typically, works by more than 75 modern artists are on display, boldly capturing the artistic present in a multi-faceted portrayal of contemporary art in a multitude of media and styles.

GALLERY GUIDE

Floors 1, 2, 3 and 4: Temporary exhibits encompass a broad variety of styles and disciplines. Often these exhibits feature a single artist, or a particular style. Some of the exhibitions present works from the Whitney Museum permanent collection.

Floor 5: Displaying works from the Whitney Museum's permanent collection, the current exhibition was installed in 2008 and showcases Whitney artworks in five themes:

"Form Building, Form Breaking": The early 1900s gave rise to a group of innovative American artists, including Max Weber and Georgia O'Keeffe, whose paintings portrayed recognizable subjects in a fragmented manner.

"The Figure and Its Realities": The representational style was used by artists including Edward Hopper and Paul Cadmus who often portrayed cultural and social issues.

"City and Machine": The Precisionism artists celebrated the city and urban experience in a precise style, capturing speed, movement and mechanical precision. Works by Charles Sheeler, Louis Lozowick and others are displayed here.

"Mind, Body, Gesture": In the 1940s and 1950s Abstract Expressionists came to prominence, and artists including Jackson Pollock and Willem de Kooning introduced feelings into their work.

Changing temporary exhibit: Selected from the Whitney Collection.

NORTHEAST CORNER OF CENTRAL PARK TO GRANT'S TOMB

This northeast corner of Central Park boasts beautiful gardens, commissioned by parks commissioner Robert Moses in 1936. You will also find a pretty pond, meandering paths, woods and picturesque waterfalls. Just outside the park is the largest church in the United States, the Cathedral Church of St. John the Divine. Nearby is Grant's Tomb, where the great Civil War general Ulysses S. Grant lies in rest.

THE WALK

Distance: 2 miles (3.2km)
Time: 2 hours
Start at: Fifth Avenue and 105th Street
End at: 122nd Street and Riverside Drive

HOW TO GET THERE

Take bus M4 to Madison Avenue and 104th Street; walk one block west to Fifth Avenue.

★ Leave Madison Avenue by turning left onto East 105th Street. Walk one block west to the entrance gate of the Conservatory Garden, across from El Museo del Barrio (▷ 214) on Fifth Avenue.

❶ The Conservatory Garden— actually a complex of gardens—is at its best in July and August. As you enter, go toward the Classical fountain in the area known as the Italian Garden. Walk to your left to tour the maze-like English Garden. To the right of the Italian Garden is the French Garden, with the charming Untermeyer Fountain (also called "Three Dancing Maidens"). Pass this fountain and walk through the gate toward the pond on your right, whose Dutch name, Harlem Meer, means "little sea."

Skirt around the pond, keeping to the right, with the pond on your left.

❷ The Charles A. Dana Discovery Center, halfway around the pond, displays natural history exhibits in a Victorian-style building.

Continue around the pond and keep to the right of the Lasker Pool and ice-skating rink. Take the path up some steps, then down a few steps, then to the right and walk under the Huddlestone Arch. Still keeping right, with a pretty little waterfall on your left, walk about 300 yards (274m), and you'll come to a very small rustic wooden bridge on your left. Cross the bridge, keeping to the right, and you'll come to the Glenspan Arch. There's a small waterfall beyond the arch and a small pool is just beyond that. Ahead of you, a couple of paths lead to Central Park West, which you can see. The path to the right takes you out to 103rd Street and Central Park West.

On Central Park West, leave the park, turn right and follow the busy street, past Strangers Gate on the right, to Frederick Douglass Circle.

Opposite *The Burnett Fountain in the English Garden, Conservatory Garden*
Right *Peace Fountain, St. John the Divine*

Cross Central Park West at 110th Street and continue left around the circle until you come to the traffic lights. Cross 110th Street and immediately turn left. You are now in Harlem. Continue west on 110th Street for two blocks to Amsterdam Avenue, passing Morningside Park. Turn right and walk north to 111th Street and the Cathedral Church of St. John the Divine.

❸ The enormous Cathedral Church of St. John the Divine is well worth exploring. The Peace Fountain in the Children's Sculpture Garden depicts a bronze Michael the Archangel slaying the devil.

Leaving the cathedral, cross to the west side of Amsterdam Avenue and follow 112th Street west one block to Broadway. Tom's Restaurant, familiar to fans of the TV show *Seinfeld,* is on the right. If you find that you are tired and feel that you do not want to continue, you can catch a bus on the west side of Broadway or take the M4 to Midtown East or the M104 to Midtown West.

To continue the walk, go north up Broadway to 122nd Street, passing Columbia University (▷ 203), New York City's oldest institution of higher learning, on your right. Turn left onto 122nd Street and then walk two blocks west, passing the Manhattan School of Music on your left, to Riverside Drive. Riverside Church is on your left.

❹ From its 392ft (119m) tower, Riverside Church offers a magnificent view across the Hudson River.

❺ Nearby is the General Grant National Memorial (▷ 214), where Grant and his wife, Julia, rest side by side in two black sarcophagi. The Gaudí-style mosaic benches and tables surrounding the tombs are a good spot for a picnic.

From here you can walk back to Broadway and get the M4 or M104 bus downtown.

WHEN TO GO
Do this walk when the weather is pleasant and you want to have a quiet stroll away from crowds. Although the park is generally safe by day and is patrolled, this is not a walk to do alone. Pack a picnic to enjoy along the way.

WHERE TO EAT
Tom's Restaurant, 2880 Broadway at 112th Street (212/ 864-6137).

PLACES TO VISIT
CATHEDRAL CHURCH OF ST. JOHN THE DIVINE
✉ 1047 Amsterdam Avenue at 112th Street
☎ 212/316-7540 ◉ Daily 7–6

RIVERSIDE CHURCH
✉ 490 Riverside Drive ☎ 212/870-6700
◉ Daily 7am–10pm, Claremont Avenue entrance

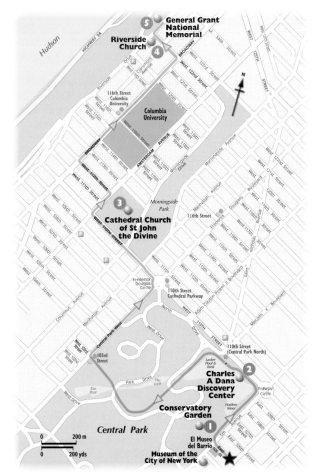

REGIONS CENTRAL PARK AND AROUND • WALK

CENTRAL PARK WEST HISTORIC DISTRICT

This walk begins with a look at the Dakota building, where former Beatle John Lennon was shot in 1980, then stops at his memorial in Central Park. In the 1960s, with private contributions of about $165 million, Upper West Side tenements were razed and the Lincoln Center was built in their stead, a complex of pedestrian open spaces, theaters, concert halls, cinemas and museums. Many actors, actresses and movie directors work and live in the neighborhood—it's fun to see if you can spot any.

THE WALK
Distance: 1.5 miles (2.4km)
Time: 1.5 to 2 hours
Start/End at: 72nd Street subway station

HOW TO GET THERE
Subway B or C; bus M10.

★ Leave the 72nd Street subway at the corner of 72nd Street and Central Park West.

❶ The Dakota (▷ 203) is on the northwest corner of Central Park West and 72nd Street. Look at the front of the building on 72nd Street, where John Lennon was shot. His wife, Yoko Ono, still lives in an apartment in the building.

Walk east across Central Park West and follow the path straight ahead to Strawberry Fields.

❷ Here there is a memorial to Lennon, a black-and-white mosaic called *Imagine*.

Back on Central Park West, turn left, and walk south. Note the residential streets lined with 19th-century brownstones to your right. Turn left into the park at West 67th Street.

❸ Here, Tavern on the Green, the former landmark restaurant of Central Park, has become a visitor center and gift shop (tel 212/874-7874; daily 10–5). You can still buy a snack here from the mobile food vendors who are often found on the outdoor terrace. The Sheep Meadow, straight ahead, is a 15-acre (6ha) expanse created as part of the Olmsted and Vaux design for Central Park; at the time it reminded city-dwellers of the rural landscapes

they had left behind when they emigrated to the United States.

Return to Central Park West and go south for two blocks. Turn right on 65th Street to Columbus Avenue. Cross Broadway and Columbus Avenue. On the west of Broadway is the Lincoln Center.

❹ The Lincoln Center (▷ 218–219) includes the Alice Tully Hall (on the northwest corner of 65th Street) and Avery Fisher Hall (on the southwest corner). Much of the movie *West Side Story* was shot in the tenements that once stood on this spot. Walk south from Avery Fisher about 300 yards (274m) to the Lincoln Center central plaza, with its fountain. On the south side of the plaza is the home of the New York City Ballet, the David H. Koch

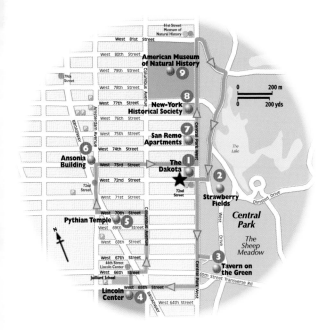

Map showing American Museum of Natural History, West 81st Street through West 64th Street, with numbered walk points including New-York Historical Society, San Remo Apartments, Ansonia Building, The Dakota, Strawberry Fields, Central Park, Pythian Temple, Lincoln Center, Tavern on the Green.

272, are the earliest houses in the neighborhood, dating from 1885. Turn left on Central Park West.

7 Designed in 1930 by architect Emery Roth, the towers of the San Remo Apartments at 145–146 Central Park West grace the skyline. Residents have included Paul Simon and Dustin Hoffman.

Continue north on Central Park West to 77th Street.

8 The New-York Historical Society (▷ 221) is on the corner of 77th and Central Park West. The fascinating collections and unusual variety of gifts in the shop make this worth a stop.

Cross West 77th Street.

9 The enormous American Museum of Natural History (▷ 204–207) is on your left. Go to the main entrance to admire the bronze statue of President Theodore Roosevelt seated upon a horse, then step inside to look at William Mackay's beautiful murals depicting events from Roosevelt's life in the Roosevelt Memorial Hall.

After leaving the museum, walk up Central Park West, and at the 81st Street traffic lights take the entrance to the park straight ahead of you. As soon as you enter, take the path immediately to your right and walk south along this path to West 72nd Street and back again to the 72nd Street subway station.

WHEN TO GO
This walk is very pleasant on Sunday afternoons. Most shops and restaurants are open then.

WHERE TO EAT
CAFÉ LUXEMBOURG
✉ 200 West 70th Street ☎ 212/873-7411

Theater; rising over the plaza on the west is the Metropolitan Opera House with Austrian chandeliers and Marc Chagall murals visible through the glass facade. To the south of the Met is a pleasant open area where open-air concerts are held in summer and the Big Apple Circus holds forth over the year-end holidays. The pond sculpture, Henry Moore's *Reclining Figure*, and the Vivian Beaumont Theater lie to the north of the Met.

Walk up the steps to the Juilliard School to the north, turn right then left down the steps to Broadway. Cross 66th Street, then cross Broadway to your right. Walk east on 66th to Columbus Avenue and turn left. On the right stands the contemporary ABC Building at No. 147 Columbus. Continue along Columbus to West 70th Street and turn left.

5 At 135 West 70th, near the corner of 70th and Broadway is the Pythian Temple, now a condominium; designed by Thomas W. Lamb, and built in 1926, it was dedicated to Pythianism, the cult of

the oracle at Delphi, and Assyrian sages still guard the entrance. Bill Haley and the Comets recorded *Rock Around the Clock* here in 1954. Farther along, at the corner of Amsterdam Avenue, Café Luxembourg is a popular bistro.

Turn right onto Amsterdam Avenue. As you approach West 72nd Street, you'll see one of the few remaining old subway buildings from the early 1900s on your left and a pleasingly harmonious new structure, an expansion of the venerable subway station, across 72nd on the north side of the street. Cross West 72nd Street.

6 The magnificent Beaux Arts Ansonia Building rises at 2109 Broadway between West 73rd and West 74th streets. Caruso, Stravinsky and Toscanini all lived at the Ansonia, and the excellent soundproofing between apartments and floors continues to attract distinguished musicians, singers and conductors.

Turn right on West 73rd Street; 18 row houses, between Nos. 248 and

Opposite *The memorial to John Lennon in Strawberry Fields, Central Park*

SHOPPING
ARGOSY BOOKS
www.argosybooks.com

This store, which has been operating since 1925, is one of the few remaining bookstores in the city for out-of-print and rare books. On its seven floors, it has an extensive stock of books, with strengths in Americana, contemporary first editions, and the history of science and medicine. It also sells prints, autographs and antique maps.

➕ 245 E7 ✉ 116 East 59th Street, between Park and Lexington avenues ☎ 212/753-4455 🕐 Sep–Apr Mon–Sat 10–6; rest of year Mon–Fri 10–6 🚇 59th Street (4, 5, 6) 🚌 M1, M2, M3, M4, M32, M101, M102, M103

BARNEYS
www.barneys.com

Barneys stocks only what's newest and hippest, so you'll find designers whose names everyone knows, as well as those known only to fashion cognoscenti—say, Proenza Schouler, Behnaz Sarafpour and Tess Giberson. The windows always make a statement, and people flock to the sales at the warehouse on 17th Street, between Seventh and Eighth avenues.

➕ 244 D7 ✉ 660 Madison Avenue, between East 60th and 61st streets ☎ 212/826-8900, warehouse 212/450-8400 🕐 Mon–Fri 10–8, Sat 10–7, Sun 11–6 🚇 Fifth Avenue/59th Street (N, Q, R), 59th Street (4, 5, 6) 🚌 M31

BLOOMINGDALE'S
www.bloomingdales.com

Bloomingdale's, opened in 1879, is one of the most venerable names in Manhattan yet keeps up with every trend. It's an icon among its fans, and tourists and locals alike buy logo items emblazoned with the store's name or its sobriquet, "Bloomie's." On weekends locals come along to schmooze.

➕ 245 E7 ✉ Lexington at 59th Street ☎ 212/705-2000 🕐 Mon–Fri 10–8.30, Sat 10–10, Sun 11–7 🚇 59th Street/Lexington (4, 5, 6) 🚌 M1, M101, M102, M103

BORRELLI
www.luigiborrelli.com

The ultimate Italian tailor favored by many a male film star offers exquisite shirts as well as beautiful suits, coats and sweaters, custom-made and off the rack.

➕ 244 D7 ✉ 16 East 60th Street, between Madison and Fifth avenues ☎ 212/644-9610 🕐 Mon–Sat 10–6, Sun 11–5; closed Sun Jul–Aug 🚇 Fifth Avenue/59th Street (N, Q, R) 🚌 M1, M2, M3, M4, M32

CALVIN KLEIN
www.calvinkleininc.com

The beloved Bronx-born designer has expanded beyond refined sportswear into shoes, accessories and home furnishings. He knows how to cut and he knows how to advertise. The boutique is a paragon of minimalism by British architect John Pawson, worth seeing in its own right.

➕ 244 D7 ✉ 654 Madison Avenue at East 60th Street ☎ 212/292-9000 🕐 Mon–Sat 10–6 (Thu until 7), Sun 12–6 🚇 Lexington Avenue/59th Street (N, Q, R, 4, 5, 6) 🚌 M1, M2, M3, M4

CRATE AND BARREL
www.crateandbarrel.com

This chain sells affordable, good-looking designs for your home. The focus is on tableware (from linens to glasses). It also sells attractive outdoor dining stuff.

➕ 244 D7 ✉ 650 Madison Avenue at East 59th Street ☎ 212/308-0011 🕐 Mon–Fri 10–8, Sat 10–7, Sun 12–6 🚇 59th Street/Fifth Avenue (N, Q, R) 🚌 M1, M2, M3, M4, M5

DKNY

www.dkny.com

Donna Karan delivers what New York women want—comfortable clothes that coordinate easily. Black used to be her favorite color, but the current inventory offers plenty of colorful blouses, dresses, miniskirts, combat jackets and accessories. This striking glass-wrapped store opened in 1998. Also at 420 West Broadway and Spring Street.

✚ 244 D7 ✉ 655 Madison Avenue, between East 60th and 61st streets ☎ 212/223-3569 ☻ Mon–Sat 11–8, Sun 11–7 ☻ Fifth Avenue/59th Street (N, Q, R) ☻ M1, M2, M3, M4, M32

DOLCE & GABBANA

www.dolcegabbana.com

Domenico Dolce and Stefano Gabbana have dressed virtually every Hollywood and Broadway star in fashions that exude heat (distressed torn pants and shirts, lots of corset lacing). This spacious and beautiful store is their flagship.

✚ 244 D6 ✉ 825 Madison Avenue, between East 68th and 69th streets ☎ 212/249-4100 ☻ Mon–Sat 10–6 (Thu until 7), Sun 12–5 ☻ 68th Street (6) ☻ M1, M2, M3, M4

DONNA KARAN

www.donnakaran.com

In the elegant and dramatic flagship of this popular American designer, the floating staircase is worthy of Fred Astaire and Ginger Rogers.

✚ 244 D6 ✉ 819 Madison Avenue, between East 68th and 69th streets ☎ 212/861-1001 ☻ Mon–Sat 10–6 (Thu until 7), Sun 12–5 ☻ 68th Street (6) ☻ M1, M2, M3, M4

GIORGIO ARMANI

www.giorgioarmani.com

The ultimate designer for men and women makes suits in understated fabrics with superb detailing.

✚ 244 D7 ✉ 760 Madison Avenue at 65th Street ☎ 212/988-9191 ☻ Mon–Sat 10–6 (Thu until 7) ☻ 68th Street (6) ☻ M1, M2, M3, M4

HUE-MAN BOOKSTORE

www.huemanbookstore.com

This bookstore stocks classic and contemporary African-American fiction and non-fiction, and holds author readings.

✚ Off map 244 C2 ✉ 2319 Frederick Douglass Boulevard, between 124th and 125th streets ☎ 212/665-7400 ☻ Mon–Sat 10–8 ☻ 125th Street (A, B, C, D) ☻ M10

JIMMY CHOO

www.jimmychoo.com

Velvet sofas and satin chairs set the tone at this flagship store selling the exquisite shoes and purses by this legendary Malaysian designer. His line offers a variety of styles from pony boots and evening slides to kitten heels, stilettos and sandals made in all kinds of materials and fabrics, which are decorated with beads, crystals or embroidery, or just beautifully colored.

✚ 244 D7 ✉ 716 Madison Avenue, between 63rd and 64th streets (west side) ☎ 212/759-7078. Also at 645 Fifth Avenue between Fifth and Madison ☎ 212/593-0800 ☻ Mon–Fri 10–6, Sat 10–7, Sun 12–5 ☻ 59th Street (4, 5, 6), 68th Street (6) ☻ M1, M2, M3, M4

KITCHEN ARTS AND LETTERS

www.kitchenartsandletters.com

You can find all of the classic cookery writers here—Julia Child, James Beard and M. F. K. Fisher—plus a host of others organized by category. This store is wonderful for rare and historic culinary volumes, too.

✚ 245 E4 ✉ 1435 Lexington Avenue, between 93rd and 94th streets ☎ 212/876-5550 ☻ Mon 1–6, Tue–Fri 10–6.30, Sat 11–6 (closed Sat Jul–Aug) ☻ 96th Street (6) ☻ M1, M101, M102, M103

MALIA MILLS

www.maliamills.com

Boutique swimwear designed with the variety of female shapes in mind has made this label super popular. There are mix and match pieces to fit everyone, made from beautiful materials in the latest figure-flattering styles. The store has

branched out into ready-to-wear pieces, including dresses, jackets, trousers, shorts, tops, sweaters and lingerie, and there are fun accessories, too.

✚ 244 C6 ✉ 220 Columbus Avenue at 70th Street ☎ 212/874-7200 ☻ Mon–Wed, Fri–Sun 11–6, Thu 12–7 ☻ 72nd Street (1, 2, 3, B, C) ☻ M7, M11, M72

NICOLE MILLER

www.nicolemiller.com

Nicole Miller's innovative, sexy and very wearable fashions attract a number of celebrity clients. She makes cowl-neck halter tops, distressed jersey tunics, bags and shoes, and simple but elegant evening gowns.

✚ 244 D7 ✉ 780 Madison Avenue, between 66th and 67th streets ☎ 212/288-9779 ☻ Mon–Fri 10–7, Sat 10–6, Sun 12–5 ☻ 68th Street (6) ☻ M2, M3, M4

PRADA

www.prada.com

Excellent design, luxury and fine leather are the components that moved the Italian Prada house to fashion prominence. Opulent, high quality men's and women's fashions and a complete line of leather accessories, shoes, luggage and hats are on display here.

✚ 244 D6 ✉ 841 Madison Avenue at East 70th Street ☎ 212/334-8888 ☻ Mon–Sat 10–6 (Thu until 7) ☻ 68th Street/Hunter College (6) ☻ M2, M3, M4

RALPH LAUREN

www.ralphlauren.com

Bronx native Ralph Lauren sells his distinguished cowboy and English country heritage looks in the Rhinelander Mansion. This is one of a handful of such turn-of-the-20th-century houses in Manhattan, renovated to gleaming splendor. There is an amazing hand-carved staircase, some magnificent Baccarat chandeliers and 19th-century oil paintings.

✚ 244 D6 ✉ 867 Madison Avenue, between East 71st and 72nd streets ☎ 212/606-2100 ☻ Mon–Wed 10–7, Thu 10–8, Fri–Sat 10–6, Sun 12–6 ☻ 68th Street (6) ☻ M1, M2, M3, M4

SHERRY-LEHMANN

www.sherry-lehmann.com

Even if you don't buy, this is a shop to browse. In business since 1934, it has a $10-million inventory of wines from every corner of the world, a spacious new flagship store, and a friendly, knowledgeable staff. Besides the premier cru Bordeaux and Burgundies, you'll find ice wines from Canada, Swiss and Lebanese varieties, and selections of sake, port and Madeira. Prices are reasonable, too. Try to stop by for the Wednesday tasting session from 3 to 5.

➕ 244 D7 ✉ 505 Park Avenue at East 59th Street ☎ 212/838-7500 ◉ Mon–Sat 9–7 🚇 Fifth Avenue/59th Street (N, Q, R), 59th Street/Lexington Avenue (4, 5, 6) 🚌 M1, M2, M3, M4, M32

TIME WARNER CENTER

www.shopsatcolumbuscircle.com

This, the first luxury shopping mall in Manhattan, will be familiar to suburbanites. Here under one roof are such big-name stores as Coach, Cole Haan, Davidoff, Godiva, L'Occitane, Hugo Boss, Thomas Pink and Williams-Sonoma.

➕ 244 C7 ✉ 10 Columbus Circle ☎ 212/823-6000 ◉ Mon–Sat 10–9, Sun 11–7 🚇 59th Street/Columbus Circle (A, C, B, D, 1) 🚌 M7, M10

TOD'S

www.tods.com

This Italian designer makes ultra-comfortable shoes, plus boots with classic equestrian styling and detail. They are relatively expensive, but long-lasting.

➕ 244 D7 ✉ 650 Madison Avenue, between East 59th and 60th streets ☎ 212/644-5945 ◉ Mon–Sat 10–6 (Thu until 7), Sun 12–5 🚇 59th Street/Fifth Avenue (N, Q, R) 🚌 M1, M2, M3, M4

ZABAR'S

www.zabars.com

The countermen who wield the knives at this culinary landmark are legendary for their skills and their attitude. Look for the exquisite smoked salmon and other kinds of smoked fish, terrific cheeses, and,

upstairs, top-quality cookware and tableware at great prices.

➕ 244 B5 ✉ 2245 Broadway, between West 80th and 81st streets ☎ 212/787-2000 ◉ Mon–Fri 8–7.30, Sat 8–8, Sun 9–6 🚇 79th Street (1) 🚌 M104

ENTERTAINMENT AND NIGHTLIFE

92ND STREET Y

www.92Y.org

The 92nd Street Y offers some of the city's most varied programs. It hosts music recitals (Guarneri and Tokyo string quartets, Janos Starker), jazz, pop and folk, poetry and literature readings (Thomas Keneally, V. S. Naipaul), and lectures on every conceivable subject by cultural leaders. The 92nd Street Y is a Jewish cultural organization.

➕ 245 E4 ✉ Kauffman Concert Hall, 1395 Lexington Avenue at 92nd Street ☎ 212/415-5500, 212/415-5440 🚇 96th Street (6) 🚌 M96, M98, M101, M102, M103

AARON DAVIS HALL/ HARLEM STAGE

www.harlemstage.org

Harlem's principal center for the performing arts presents established and emerging artists of color in music, dance, theater and multimedia performances.

The Harlem Stage is across the street from the three-theater Aaron Davis Hall.

➕ Off map 244 C2 ✉ City College of New York, West 135th Street and Convent Avenue ☎ 212/281-9240 🚇 137th Street/Broadway (1) 🚌 M4, M5

ALICE TULLY HALL

www.lincolncenter.org

Redesigned in 2009, the 1,100-seat hall is chic and lively with great acoustics for chamber music, vocal recitals, jazz and other outstanding musical events.

The Chamber Music Society (tel 212/875-5788) resides here.

➕ 244 B7 ✉ 1941 Broadway on 65th Street, between Broadway and Amsterdam Avenue ☎ 212/671-4050 or 212/721-6500 ✋ $27.50–$52 🚇 66th Street (1) 🚌 M5, M7, M66, M104

APOLLO THEATER

www.apollotheater.com

Originally a vaudeville theater, the Apollo has been a venue for black entertainers since 1934. Everyone from Duke Ellington and Billie Holiday to Aretha Franklin and Stevie Wonder has performed here. The Wednesday Amateur Night Competition is famous, drawing crowds who register their approval or disapproval with gusto. Today the entertainment ranges from musicians and singers to musicals, starring big names in music.

➕ Off map 244 C2 ✉ 253 West 125th Street, between Frederick Douglass Boulevard and St. Nicholas Avenue ☎ 212/531-5300 🚇 125th Street (A, B, C, D), Lenox (1, 2, 3) 🚌 M104

ASIA SOCIETY

www.asiasociety.org

The downstairs auditorium showcases arts and culture—dance, film, lectures and music—from Asia. Ravi Shankar made his American debut at the Asia Society.

➕ 244 D6 ✉ 725 Park Avenue at East 70th Street ☎ 212/288-6400 🚇 68th Street (6) 🚌 M1, M2, M3, M4, M72

THE AUCTION HOUSE

Sotheby's meets New Orleans bordello at this wood-paneled, split-level lounge. Patrons sip cocktails on velvet sofas beneath gilt-framed portraits.

➕ 245 E4 ✉ 300 East 89th Street, between First and Second avenues ☎ 212/427-4458 ◉ Daily 7.30pm–3am (Fri–Sat until 4am) 🚇 86th Street (4, 5, 6) 🚌 M15, M86

AVERY FISHER HALL

www.lincolncenter.org
www.nyphil.org

Home to the New York Philharmonic, this hall seats 2,700. Many other groups perform here, including the American Symphony Orchestra, under Leon Botstein, and the summer Mostly Mozart Festival. During its season, the Philharmonic opens its morning rehearsals to the public (usually on Thursdays at 9.45 for $15).

244 B7 ✉ 10 Lincoln Center Plaza (Columbus Avenue at 65th Street) ☎ 212/875-5030 or 212/721-6500 🚇 66th Street (1) 🚌 M5, M7, M66, M104

BEACON THEATRE
www.beacontheatre.com
Many different artists perform here, from the likes of Sinead O'Connor and David Gray to modern ballet.
244 B6 ✉ 2124 Broadway at 74th Street ☎ 212/465-6500 🚇 72nd Street (1, 2, 3) 🚌 M72, M104

BEMELMANS BAR
Named for the illustrator of the beloved *Madeline* books, Ludwig Bemelmans, this intimate bar attracts the city's most upscale tipplers with first-class cocktails and perfect piano music from Tony De Sare or the Chris Gillespie Trio most evenings (9.30–1.30).
244 D5 ✉ Carlyle Hotel, 35 East 76th Street, between Park and Madison avenues ☎ 212/744-1600 🕐 Daily noon–1am ✋ Tue–Thu $15–$25 after 9.30pm, Fri–Sat $30 after 9.30pm 🚇 77th Street (6) 🚌 M98, M101, M102, M103

BRUNO WALTER AUDITORIUM
Lectures, seminars, concerts and films are the regular fare at this 212-seat hall. The library is a superb performing arts archive.
244 B7 ✉ The New York Public Library for the Performing Arts, 111 Amsterdam Avenue, between West 64th and 65th streets ☎ 212/870-1630, 212/642-0142 (programs) ✋ Free 🚇 66th Street (1) 🚌 M5, M7, M66, M104

CATHEDRAL CHURCH OF ST. JOHN THE DIVINE
www.stjohndivine.org
Stop by to admire the incomplete edifice, begun in 1892, and you may hear one of the sanctuary's five organs. The repertoire during arts events ranges from choirs singing Bach cantatas or chanting Tibetan monks to music made famous by Duke Ellington and Judy Collins.
244 B2 ✉ 1047 Amsterdam Avenue at 112th Street ☎ 212/316-7540 🚇 Cathedral Parkway/110th Street (1) 🚌 M4, M11

CLASSICAL THEATRE OF HARLEM
www.classicaltheatreofharlem.org
This company, founded in 1988, has been recognized outside Harlem only recently. It has garnered acclaim for recent productions of Genet's *The Blacks* and Euripides' *The Trojan Women*.
Off map 244 C2 ✉ Harlem School of the Arts Theater, 645 St. Nicholas Avenue, near 141st Street ☎ 212/926-4100 or 212/564-9983 🚇 145th Street (A, B, C) 🚌 M3, M10

COTTON CLUB
www.cottonclub-newyork.com
Although its heyday was from 1923 to 1935 (then on 142nd Street), this famous Harlem landmark still has blues, jazz and gospel acts that seem straight out of the 1920s. Monday night is swing night.
Off map 244 B2 ✉ 656 West 125th Street, between Broadway and Riverside Drive ☎ 212/663-7980 🕐 Mon, Thu–Fri 8–midnight, Sat 12–12, Sun 12–8.15 ✋ $15–$40 🚇 125th Street (1) 🚌 M104, Bx15

DANGERFIELD'S
www.dangerfields.com
Rodney Dangerfield is no longer a regular presence, but this classic seedy club, established in 1969, has hosted many legends, from Jay Leno and Jim Carrey to Jackie Mason and Tim Allen.
245 E7 ✉ 1118 First Avenue, between East 61st and 62nd streets ☎ 212/593-1650 🕐 Shows Sun–Thu 8.45, Fri 8.30, 10.30, 12.30, Sat 8, 10.30, 12.30am ✋ $15–$20, plus 2-drink minimum 🚇 59th Street (4, 5, 6) 🚌 M15, M57

DAVID H. KOCH THEATER
www.nycballet.com
www.nycopera.com
This 2,755-seat auditorium is home to the New York City Opera and the New York City Ballet. The New York City Opera is famous for its emphasis on the ensemble rather than soloists, and stimulating productions. The New York City Ballet began in 1933, and is still going strong under artistic director

Peter Martins. The company performs for 23 weeks in the State Theater, then moves to Saratoga.
244 B7 ✉ 20 Lincoln Center Plaza at 63rd Street ☎ 212/870-5570 ✋ City Opera $32–$110 (standing room only $12), NYC Ballet $30–$105 🚇 50th Street (1, 9) 🚌 M5, M7, M11, M66, M104

FEINSTEIN'S AT LOEWS REGENCY
www.feinsteinsattheregency.com
Feinstein's at Loews Regency is a lush, elegant and exclusive club. Michael Feinstein plays on occasion. Dinner is available.
244 D7 ✉ Regency Hotel, 540 Park Avenue at East 61st Street ☎ 212/339-4095 🕐 Shows Tue–Sat, usually at 8, and 10.30 on Sat ✋ $22–$75, plus $40 minimum 🚇 Lexington/63rd Street (F), 59th Street (4, 5, 6), 59th Street (N, Q, R) 🚌 M1, M2, M3, M4, M57

FILM SOCIETY OF LINCOLN CENTER
www.filmlinc.com
This society hosts many different festivals—the New York Jewish Festival, Spanish Cinema Now, and Women in Film, for example.
244 B7 ✉ Walter Reade Theater, 165 West 65th Street ☎ 212/875-5600 ✋ $13 🚇 66th Street (1) 🚌 M5, M7, M66, M104

FLORENCE GOULD HALL
www.fiaf.org (click on "Rentals")
Chamber groups, opera singers, pop and jazz artists, and dance companies entertain in this 400-seat auditorium associated with the Alliance Française.
244 D7 ✉ 55 East 59th Street, between Park and Madison avenues ☎ 212/355-6100 ✋ $30–$35 🚇 Fifth Avenue/59th Street (N, Q, R) 🚌 M1, M2, M3, M4, M5, M57

FRICK COLLECTION
www.frick.org
The classical music concerts and recitals in this exquisite museum are a must.
244 D6 ✉ 1 East 70th Street ☎ 212/288-0700 🚇 68th Street (6) 🚌 M1, M2, M3, M4, M72

GRACE RAINEY ROGERS AUDITORIUM

www.metmuseum.org

Small musical groups and individuals entertain in this mid-size, 700-seat auditorium. And the Met always has chamber music in the Great Hall Balcony on Friday and Saturday evenings.

⊞ 244 D5 ✉ The Metropolitan Museum of Art, Fifth Avenue at 82nd Street ☎ 212/535-7710 or 212/570-3949 ✋ $15–$65 ⏹ 77th Street (6) 🚌 M1, M2, M3, M4, M79

HUDSON BARS

www.hudsonhotel.com

The two bars are central to this hipster hotel. In the Hudson, a long ornate table serves as the bar. Late at night, the backlit floor becomes a dance floor. In the Library, there are leather chairs, ottomans and a fireplace, providing a luxurious backdrop to a relaxing drink.

⊞ 244 C7 ✉ Hudson Hotel, 356 West 58th Street, between Eighth and Ninth avenues ☎ 212/554-6000 ⏹ Hudson Sun–Wed 7–2, Thu–Sat 7–4; Library Sun–Wed noon–1am, Thu–Sat noon–2.30am ⏹ 59th Street/Columbus Circle (A, B, C, D, 1) 🚌 M11, M20, M31, M57

JAZZ AT LINCOLN CENTER

www.jalc.org

Top-drawer jazz artists give stunning performances in the 1,230-seat Rose Theater, the 300- to 600-seat Allen Room (whose 50-foot-high (15m) glass wall overlooks Columbus Circle) and in the more intimate Dizzy's Club Coca-Cola, commemorating the great Dizzy Gillespie.

⊞ 244 B7 ✉ Time Warner Center at Broadway and 60th Street ☎ 212/258-9800 or 212/721-6500 ✋ $30–$150; club has cover and minimum ⏹ 59th Street (1) 🚌 M5, M104

JUILLIARD SCHOOL

www.juilliard.edu

This world-famous performing arts school is especially well known for music. The young artists who train here can be seen in stimulating programs in two auditoriums.

Juilliard also incorporates the School for American Ballet, which is the training ground for the New York City Ballet. Dance aficionados run to secure tickets for the school's annual workshop production in early summer (tel 212/769-7406).

⊞ 244 B7 ✉ 60 Lincoln Plaza ☎ 212/799-5000 ✋ Most are free except for opera programs and dance workshops ⏹ 66th Street (1) 🚌 M5, M7, M66, M104

KOSCIUSZKO FOUNDATION

www.thekf.org

Programs at the Kosciuszko Foundation are varied. Events feature works by Polish composers or artists.

⊞ 244 D7 ✉ 15 East 65th Street ☎ 212/734-2130 ⏹ 68th Street (6) 🚌 M1, M2, M3, M4

LENOX LOUNGE

www.lenoxlounge.com

This long-time Harlem hang-out for musicians has jazz every night except Tuesday.

⊞ Off map 244 D2 ✉ 288 Lenox Avenue, between 124th and 125th streets ☎ 212/427-0253 ⏹ Restaurant Sun–Thu 5–11, Fri–Sat 5–1; bar daily 12–4; shows daily, times vary ✋ Free–$25, plus $16 drinks minimum on Fri and Sat ⏹ 125th Street (2, 3) 🚌 M7, M102

LINCOLN CENTER FOR THE PERFORMING ARTS

www.lincolncenter.org

This huge complex is home to the Metropolitan Opera House, the David H. Koch Theater, Avery Fisher Hall, the Vivian Beaumont and Mitzi E. Newhouse theaters, the New York Public Library of the Performing Arts, the Walter Reade Film Theater and the Juilliard School. In summer there is dancing under the stars on the plaza as well as the Lincoln Center Festival, a free event with hundreds of performing artists. For tours of the first three halls mentioned above call 212/875-5350 to make a reservation.

⊞ 244 B7 ✉ Columbus Avenue, between 62nd and 66th streets ☎ 212/875-5000 or 212/875-5456 ⏹ 66th Street (1) 🚌 M5, M7, M11, M66, M104

LINCOLN PLAZA CINEMA

www.lincolnplazacinema.com

A six-screener showing a select group of critically successful first-run movies and foreign films. For example, Gurinder Chadha's *Bend it Like Beckham* and Almodóvar's *Talk to Her* both played here.

⊞ 244 C7 ✉ 1886 Broadway at 63rd Street ☎ 212/757-2280 ✋ $12 ⏹ 66th Street (1) 🚌 M5, M7, M66, M104

LUKE'S BAR AND GRILL

www.lukesbarandgrill.com

The bar and grill are equal partners at Luke's, which opened in 1990 and appeals to families as well as young professionals. They serve bar food, with great burgers, and there's a stock of good beers, which becomes more evident when the restaurant closes about midnight/1am.

⊞ 245 E5 ✉ 1394 Third Avenue, between 79th and 80th streets ☎ 212/249-7070 ⏹ Restaurant Mon–Thu 11.30am–1am, Sat 10am–2am, Sun 10am–midnight (bar daily until 4am) ⏹ 77th Street (6) 🚌 M79, M98, M101, M102, M103

MAKOR

www.92Y.org

This club, part of a Jewish community center, hosts mainly documentaries and oldies. A new branch of the club (92YTribeca) opened in 2008 at 200 Hudson Street, between Vestry and Desbrosses streets (the telephone number is the same as below).

⊞ 245 E4 ✉ 1395 Lexington Avenue at 92nd Street ☎ 212/601-1000 ⏹ 86th Street (4, 5, 6) 🚌 M1, M2, M86, M96, M101, M102

MANHATTAN SCHOOL OF MUSIC

www.msmnyc.edu

This institution with a world-class reputation has a large concert hall as well as several smaller venues. The programming is diverse—orchestras, chamber ensembles, recitals—and ticket prices are reasonable. Vocal and orchestral master classes take place on a regular basis.

Off map 244 B2 ✉ 120 Claremont Avenue, Broadway at 122nd Street ☎ 212/749-2802 or 917/493-4428 🚇 125th Street (1) 🚌 M4, M104

MERKIN CONCERT HALL

http://kaufman-center.org/
merkin-concert-hall

Part of the Kaufman Center, national and international chamber groups perform here. You might find traditional classical, new music or even a group from Japan.

➕ 244 B6 ✉ 129 West 67th Street ☎ 212/501-3330 ✋ $15–$45 🚇 66th Street (1) 🚌 M5, M7, M104

METROPOLITAN MUSEUM ROOF GARDEN

This venue is classy all the way. What better accompaniment to a drink than a view of the sun setting over Central Park? The balcony bar is chic with its chamber music and jazz groups.

➕ 244 D5 ✉ Metropolitan Museum of Art, 1000 Fifth Avenue at 82nd Street ☎ 212/277-8888 🕐 Roof Garden May–Oct Tue–Thu, Sun 10–4.30, Fri–Sat 10–8; Balcony Bar Fri–Sat 4–8 🚇 86th Street (4, 5, 6), 77th Street (6) 🚌 M1, M2, M3, M4, M86

METROPOLITAN OPERA HOUSE

www.metopera.org

The Metropolitan Opera, which had its first season in 1883–84, moved to this building on the western side of Lincoln Center Plaza in 1966. Although modern, it is glamorous with its Chagall paintings, plush crimson carpeting, chandeliers and gold leaf. The back of each of the theater's 3,800-seats has a screen showing subtitles. Most productions are spectacular, with the best international stars. Season-ticket holders snap up most of the best seats (and the best-priced seats) but individual tickets are usually available. Beginning in May the American Ballet Theatre performs a traditional repertory and modern pieces by such choreographers as James Kudelka and Twyla Tharp.

➕ 244 B7 ✉ 30 Lincoln Center Plaza, between 63rd and 64th streets ☎ 212/362-

6000 ✋ $15–$295, standing room $15–$20 🚇 66th Street (1) 🚌 M5, M7, M11, M66, M104

MILLER THEATRE

www.millertheatre.com

Many cutting-edge classical groups and composers are presented here at Miller Theatre. Among the most notable are John Zorn, Julia Wolfe and John King.

➕ Off map 244 B2 ✉ Columbia University, 2960 Broadway at 116th Street ☎ 212/854-7799 🚇 116th Street (1) 🚌 M104

MITZI E. NEWHOUSE THEATER

www.lct.org

Spalding Gray performed *Swimming to Cambodia* (1996) at this Lincoln Center theater. Its 299 seats are steeply raked.

➕ 244 B7 ✉ 150 West 65th Street ☎ 212/362-7600 🕐 Tue–Sat 8, matinees Wed, Sat 2, Sun 3 🚇 66th Street (1) 🚌 M5, M7, M11, M66, M104

NEW YORK SOCIETY FOR ETHICAL CULTURE

www.nysec.org

All kinds of cultural events are held here. A program of lectures and discussions often complements the performances.

➕ 244 C7 ✉ 2 West 64th Street at Central Park West ☎ 212/874-5210 or 866/468-7619 🚇 66th Street (1) 🚌 M10, M20

SCHOMBURG CENTER FOR RESEARCH IN BLACK CULTURE

www.nypl.org

This African-American cultural archive sponsors an annual Women's Jazz Festival and a performance of Langston Hughes' *Nativity* in December.

➕ Off map 244 D2 ✉ 515 Malcolm X Boulevard at 135th Street ☎ 212/491-2200 🚇 135th Street (B, C) 🚌 M7, M102

SHAKESPEARE IN THE PARK

www.publictheater.org

The Public Theater sponsors this summer Shakespeare festival in Central Park at the Delacorte Theater. Line up for free tickets as early as possible.

➕ 244 C5 ✉ Delacorte Theater, 81st Street (West Side), 79th Street (East Side) ☎ 212/539-8750 🕐 Summer only days vary 🚇 79th Street (1) 🚌 M1, M2, M3, M4, M10, M79

SHOWMAN'S JAZZ CLUB

In the 1940s and 1950s, musicians often dropped into the Showman's Jazz Club after hours to jam or just hang out. Today musicians still frequent the establishment and you might be fortunate enough to find Grady Tate, George Benson or Ed Bradley, for example, whiling away the hours.

➕ Off map 244 C2 ✉ 375 West 125th Street, between St. Nicholas and Morningside avenues ☎ 212/864-8941 🕐 Mon–Thu 8.30pm–12.30am, Fri–Sat 10.30pm–3.30am ✋ $5, 2-drink minimum 🚇 125th Street (A, B, C, D) 🚌 M3

SMOKE

www.smokejazz.com

Intimate and comfortable with excellent acoustics, this club was opened in 1999. Over the years it has headlined great jazz artists including organist Dr. Lonnie Smith and trombonist Slide Hampton, but it is also a good place to see local artists. The food is fresh and seasonal.

➕ 244 B2 ✉ 2751 Broadway, between 105th and 106th streets ☎ 212/864-6662 🕐 Mon–Fri 5–3, Sat–Sun 11.30am–3am ✋ Varies, but there is a cover minimum 🚇 103 Street (1) 🚌 M104

STAND-UP NEW YORK

www.standupny.com

Audiences here can be hard, but comics at this typical comedy club may emerge as the stars of tomorrow.

➕ 244 B5 ✉ 236 West 78th Street at Broadway ☎ 212/595-0850 ✋ Cover varies, 2-drink minimum 🚇 79th Street (1) 🚌 M79, M104

VIVIAN BEAUMONT THEATER

www.lct.org

This is categorized as a Broadway theater despite its address. Its deep-thrust stage allows for innovative directing.

✚ 244 B7 ✉ 150 West 65th Street
☎ 212/362-7600 ⊙ Tue 7, Wed–Sat 8, matinees Wed, Sat 2, Sun 3 ⊜ 66th Street (1) 🚌 M5, M7, M11, M66, M104

SPORTS AND ACTIVITIES
ASPHALT GREEN
www.asphaltgreen.org
This 5.5-acre (2.25ha) complex has Manhattan's only Olympic-size pool. It also has indoor and outdoor running tracks, fields for team sports, a large rooftop terrace with views of the East River, and a multilevel fitness center.
✚ 245 F4 ✉ 555 East 90th Street, between York and East End avenues ☎ 212/369-8890 ⊙ Mon–Fri 5.30am–9.45pm, Sat–Sun 8–7.45 ✋ Day pass $35 ⊜ 96th Street (6) 🚌 M15, M31, M86

BLADES
www.blades.com
This is the most convenient of these stores to Central Park, where you can rent in-line skates. There's also a branch at Chelsea Piers.
✚ 244 C6 ✉ 156 West 72nd Street at Columbus Street ☎ 212/787-3911 ⊙ Mon–Sat 10–8, Sun 10–7 ✋ Rentals $21.65 for 24hr ⊜ 72nd Street (1, 2, 3) 🚌 M7, M11, M72

CENTRAL PARK BICYCLE TOURS
▷ 270.

CENTRAL PARK RESERVOIR
This 1.6-mile (2.6km) gravel path circling the Jacqueline Kennedy Onassis Reservoir is the favorite jogging track for Upper West Siders and Upper East Siders.
✚ 244 D4 ✋ Free ⊜ 86th Street (4, 5, 6), 86th Street (B, C) 🚌 M1, M2, M3, M4, M10, M86

CHARLES A. DANA DISCOVERY CENTER
www.centralparknyc.org
www.centralpark.com
Exhibits at the Discovery Center relate to the natural life in the park, and the center sponsors related activities such as birdwatching. For ranger-led activities call 1-866-NYCHAWK.

✚ 244 D2 ✉ Central Park, 110th Street, between Fifth and Lenox avenues ☎ 212/860-1370 ⊙ Apr–Oct Tue–Sun 10–5; Nov–Mar Wed–Sun 10–5 ✋ Free ⊜ Central Park North (2, 3) 🚌 M1, M2, M3, M4

DEPARTMENT OF PARKS AND RECREATION
www.centralparknyc.org
www.nycgovparks.org
The best tennis courts in this part of the city are: Central Park and 93rd Street (tel 212/280-0205), 30 hard courts; Riverside Drive and 96th Street (tel 212/496-2006), eight clay courts; Riverside Drive and 119th Street (tel 212/496-2006), eight hard courts.
✚ 244 D7 ✉ 830 Fifth Avenue at 64th Street ☎ 212/360-8111 or 212/408-0243 for court reservations ⊙ Tennis courts: early Apr–late Nov daily 6.30am–dusk ✋ Tennis $7 pass for one hour of play obtainable at office above or at Central Park courts ⊜ Fifth Avenue/59th Street (N, Q, R) 🚌 M1, M2, M3, M4

EMPIRE SKATE CLUB
www.empireskate.org
The Empire Skate Club sponsors group skates, a variety of skating events and tours. Year-round skates include the Sunday morning roll from Columbus Circle at 11am and the Tuesday night skate from Blades at 120 West 72nd Street, starting at 8pm.
✚ 244 C7 ☎ 212/774-1774 ✋ Club membership $25 (you don't have to be a member to join group skates)

LARRY & JEFF'S
www.bicyclesnyc.com
This store rents road and mountain bikes and is conveniently close to Central Park.
✚ 245 E5 ✉ 1400 3rd Avenue, between 79th and 80th streets ☎ 212/794-2929 ⊙ Daily 10–7 (until 8 during daylight savings) ✋ $30 day (3hrs 30mins or more) ⊜ 86th Street (4, 5, 6) 🚌 M15, M86

LOEB BOATHOUSE
www.thecentralparkboathouse.com
Weather permitting, you can rent bicycles to ride through the park

and rowboats for use on the lake March through October.
✚ 244 D6 ✉ Central Park, near East 72nd Street and Park Drive North ☎ 212/517-2233 ⊙ Daily 10am–dusk ✋ Bicycles $9–$20 per hr, rowboats $12 per hr ⊜ 68th Street (6), 72nd Street (B, C) 🚌 M1, M2, M3, M4, M10

NEW YORK CITY AUDUBON SOCIETY
www.nycaudubon.org
The New York City Audubon Society allows visitors to the city to join its birdwatching walks in Central Park for a small fee. Call the society for further details.
☎ 212/691-7483

NEW YORK MARATHON
www.nyrr.org
Thirty thousand athletes compete in this marathon, watched by 2.5 million spectators. The finish line is in Central Park.
✚ 244 D4 ✉ New York Road Runners Club, 9 East 89th Street at Fifth Avenue ☎ 212/860-4455 ⊙ First Sun in Nov

WOLLMAN RINK
www.wollmanskatingrink.com
You can skate against the backdrop of the Manhattan skyline at this romantic outdoor rink—or, in summer, roller skate or blade.
✚ 244 D7 ✉ Central Park at 62nd Street ☎ 212/439-6900 ⊙ Mon–Tue 10–2.30, Wed–Thu 10–10, Fri–Sat 10am–11pm, Sun 10–9 ✋ Adult $10.50–$15, skate rental $6.25 ⊜ 59th Street/Fifth Avenue (N, Q, R) 🚌 M5, M66, M72

HEALTH AND BEAUTY
PAUL LABRECQUE SALON AND SPA
www.paullabrecque.com
London-trained Labrecque has coiffed the rich and famous for decades. The ultimate facial at this attractive salon provides five levels of hydration. It also offers sensual body treatments and therapeutic massage treatments (Thai, Reiki, rolfing, phyto-essence and acupuncture).
✚ 245 E7 ✉ 171 East 65th Street, between Lexington and Third avenues

☎ 212/988-7816 🕐 Mon–Fri 8am–9pm, Sat 9–8, Sun 10–8 👋 Facial $135–$210, massage $80–$185 🚇 68th Street (6) 🚌 M98, M101, M102, M103

LA PRAIRIE SPA
www.ritzcarlton.com
A wide range of treatments include detoxification, shiatsu massage and exfoliation. There are also men's and women's steam rooms.
➕ 244 D7 ✉ Ritz-Carlton, 50 Central Park South at Sixth Avenue ☎ 212/521-6135

SPORTS CLUB/LA
www.thesportsclubla.com
The spectacular 61st Street location of this urban country club occupies 150,000 square feet (13,935sq m) and offers 50 fitness classes, five squash courts, two basketball courts, a climbing wall, weights, and a cardio deck with more than 200 machines. There's even rooftop tennis and golf.
➕ 245 E7 ✉ 330 East 61st Street, between First and Second avenues ☎ 212/355-5100 🕐 Mon–Thu 5am–11pm, Fri 5am–10pm, Sat–Sun 7am–9pm. Also at 45 Rockefeller Plaza ☎ 212/218-8600 🕐 Mon–Thu 5am–11pm, Fri 5am–10pm, Sat 8–8, Sun 9–7 👋 Day pass $35 with member only 🚇 59th Street (4, 5, 6) 🚌 M15

FOR CHILDREN
AMERICAN MUSEUM OF NATURAL HISTORY
▷ 204–207.

CENTRAL PARK
▷ 208–213.

CENTRAL PARK ZOO
www.centralparkzoo.com
A perfectly sized zoo for kids, this Manhattan classic is populated by many of the regular youngsters' favorites—sea lions, polar bears, monkeys, pandas, penguins and tropical birds. The Tisch Children's Zoo has fish, birds and llamas, pigs and a host of other small domestic animals.
➕ 244 D7 ✉ Fifth Avenue and 64th Street ☎ 212/439-6500 🕐 Apr–Oct daily 10–5.30; Nov–Mar 10–4.30 👋 Adult

$12, child (3–12) $7, under 3 free 🚇 Fifth Avenue (N, R), 68th Street (6) 🚌 M1, M2, M3, M4

CHILDREN'S MUSEUM OF MANHATTAN
www.cmom.org
The Children's Museum of Manhattan was designed to be a first museum experience for kids from 10 months to 10 years old. It has plenty of sensory exhibits, plus a regular schedule of sing-alongs and other wonderful programs.
➕ 244 B5 ✉ 212 West 83rd Street, between Broadway and Amsterdam Avenue ☎ 212/721-1223 🕐 Sun–Fri 10–5, Sat 10–7 👋 Adults and children $11 🚇 86th Street (1), 81st Street (B, C) 🚌 M7, M11, M79, M104

GUIDED TOUR OF LINCOLN CENTER
www.lincolncenter.org
These one-hour tours take you through the theaters that make up the Lincoln Center. The tour guides tell fascinating stories and you may see a rehearsal in progress.
➕ 244 B7 ☎ 212/875-5350 🕐 Daily 10–4. Reservations recommended 👋 Adult $15, child (under 12) $8 🚇 66th Street (1) 🚌 M5, M7, M11, M104

GUGGENHEIM MUSEUM
▷ 216–217.

LITTLE ORCHESTRA SOCIETY
www.littleorchestra.org
This company organizes two family concert series: Happy Concerts (children aged 6 to 12) and the Lolli-Pops (tots aged 3 to 5). Performances are held at the Kaye Playhouse at Hunter College.
➕ 244 B7 ✉ Avery Fisher Hall, Lincoln Center, Broadway and West 65th Street ☎ 212/971-9500 👋 $40–$99 🚇 66th Street (1, 9) 🚌 M5, M7, M11, M104

LOEWS IMAX THEATER
For some kids, the 3-D IMAX experience is too intense; those who tolerate it are usually enthralled. The screen is eight stories high. Programming changes roughly every two months.

➕ 244 B6 ✉ 1998 Broadway and 68th Street ☎ 212/336-5020 🚇 66th Street (1, 9) 🚌 M5, M7, M66, M104

PAPER BAG PLAYERS
www.paperbagplayers.org
The members of this beloved troupe make their costumes and sets out of cardboard and paper bags and perform offbeat plays and revues at five venues in the city.
➕ 244 B3 ✉ Office at 185 East Broadway ☎ 212/353-2332 🕐 Phone for details, as they tour regularly 👋 $10–$30 🚇 68th Street (6) 🚌 M1, M2, M3, M4, M98, M101, M102, M103

YOUNG PEOPLE'S CONCERTS
www.nyphil.org
www.lincolncenter.org
Sponsored by the New York Philharmonic, these concerts introduce kids to great artists and great music. Children can attend demonstrations and workshops given by members of the orchestra. There's also a program for teens.
➕ 244 B7 ✉ Lincoln Center ☎ 212/875-5656 or 212/721-6500 🕐 Four Saturdays during the year 👋 $12–$34 🚇 66th Street (1) 🚌 M5, M7, M11, M104

Below *New York's public parks are ideal places for sports activities or relaxation*

PRICES AND SYMBOLS

The prices given are the average for a two-course lunch (L) and a three-course dinner (D) for one person, without drinks. The wine price is for the least expensive bottle.

For a key to the symbols, ▷ 2.

AMY RUTH'S

www.amyruthsharlem.com

It's named for the owner's grandmother, who taught her Southern-style cooking. Most items on the menu are named for someone, such as the Reverend Al Sharpton (chicken and waffles). At dinner, look for lusty Southern fried chicken, oxtail stew and fried or baked catfish. No alcohol is served.

✚ Off map 244 D2 ✉ 113 West 116th Street, between Malcolm X Boulevard and Adam Clayton Powell Jr. Boulevard ☎ 212/280-8779 ◷ Mon 11.30–11, Tue–Thu 8.30am–11pm, Fri 8.30am–5.30am, Sat 7.30am–5.30am, Sun 7.30am–11pm ✋ L $18, D $24 ◎ 116th Street (2, 3, B, C) ⊟ M2, M3, M7, M102, M116

ASIATE

www.mandarinoriental.com

Stunning floor-to-ceiling views of Central Park form the backdrop for fine dining in this tranquil haven. The seasonal menu features Asian and international contemporary cuisine supported by an excellent wine cellar. Specialties include butter poached lobster with white polenta, *hon shimeji* mushrooms and kaffir emulsion, and *étuvée* of bay scallops, langoustine, littleneck clams and hearts of palm in coconut herb broth.

✚ 244 C7 ✉ 80 Columbus Circle in the Mandarin Oriental Hotel ☎ 212/805-8881 ◷ Mon–Fri 7–10.30, 12–2, 6–10, Sat 7–10.30, 11.30–2, 6–10, Sun 7–10.30, 11.30–2, 6–9 ✋ L $34, D 3-course prix fixe $85, tasting menu $125, Wine $30 ◎ 59th Street (A, B, C, D, 1, 9) ⊟ M5, M7, M10, M104

AUREOLE

www.charliepalmer.com

Aureole's chef/owner Charlie Palmer is one of the most highly regarded talents on the American culinary scene. This elegant Upper East Side town house with a grand staircase and towers of wine, liquor and flowers, is made for special occasions. Palmer uses ultra-fresh ingredients in such signature dishes as slow-poached Maine lobster with heirloom tomatoes, which is served with lemon-verbena-infused consommé, and seared Hudson Valley foie gras. The wine list features 600 selections, 25 by the glass.

✚ 244 D7 ✉ 34 East 61st Street, between Madison and Park avenues ☎ 212/319-1660 ◷ Mon–Fri 11.45–2.15, 5–10, Sat 5–10 ✋ L $46, D $89, Wine $45 ◎ 59th Street (4, 5, 6), 59th Street/Fifth Avenue (N, Q, R) ⊟ M1, M2, M3, M4

BARNEY GREENGRASS

www.barneygreengrass.com

An Upper West Side tradition since 1929, Barney Greengrass is frantic on weekends, when locals come to feast on huge platters of smoked fish—whitefish, sable, sturgeon and lox—or sandwiches made with similar contents, plus fresh caviar, chopped herring salad, cheese blintzes, borscht and other such specialties. During the week, it's less frenzied. Credit cards are taken only on bills of $25 or more.

✚ 244 B4 ✉ 541 Amsterdam Avenue between West 86th and 87th streets ☎ 212/724-4707 ◷ Tue–Fri 8.30am–4pm, Sat–Sun 8.30am–5pm ✋ L $18, D $25 ◎ 86th Street (1) ⊟ M7, M86, M104

Opposite Rosa Mexicano on Columbus Avenue serves delicious, authentic Mexican food

CAFÉ BOULUD
www.danielnyc.com
Many diners consider this casually smart 1930s-style Parisian neighborhood restaurant their favorite Daniel Boulud restaurant. Three Daniel muses inspire the menu—classics, seasons and ethnic cuisines. You will find a pot-au-feu and a good bouillabaisse; and entrées inspired by Tuscany, Morocco, Vietnam, Spain and the Caribbean. The 450 wine selections are categorized by varietal.
⊕ 244 D6 ✉ 20 East 76th Street, between Fifth and Madison avenues ☎ 212/772-2600 🕐 Mon–Thu 7–10, 12–2.30, 5.45–10.30, Fri 7–10, 12–2.30, 5.45–11, Sat 7–10, 12–2.30, 5.30–11, Sun 8–11, 12–3, 5.45–10.30 ✋ L $54, D $80, Wine $35 🚇 77th Street (6) 🚌 M1, M2, M3, M4, M79

CALLE OCHO
www.calleochonyc.com
Calle Ocho has brought an extensive menu of very good Latin cuisine to the Upper West Side. The atmosphere is trendy and cozy, with a brightly lit high-ceilinged dining room and an intimate lounge serving sherry, brandy, port, cognac, single malts and blends. The Nuevo Latino fusion cuisine provides tantalizing flavor combinations reminiscent of Miami's Little Havana. Start with one of the refreshing ceviches (say, lobster with lemon, lime and jalapeño) or appetizers like *arepa* with spicy braised short ribs. Fish and meat dishes are tasty, both the coffee-glazed tuna or the basil *chimichurri* chicken with roasted almond sauce. The dinner breads and muffins are delicious. The weekend Latin brunch with five kinds of all-you-can-drink Sangria is very popular, with excellent entrées.
⊕ 244 C5 ✉ Excelsior Hotel, 45 West 81st Street, between Columbus Avenue and Central Park West ☎ 212/873-5025 🕐 Mon–Thu 6–11, Fri 6–12, Sat 5–12, Sun

11.30–3, 5–10 ✋ D $45, Wine $28 🚇 81st Street (B, C) 🚌 M7, M11, M10, M79

CESCA
www.cescanyc.com
At this popular Italian trattoria turning out fine cuisine, settle into a booth and order the veal meatballs in broth or the roasted oysters under a spicy tomato zabaglione and crisp pancetta. Settle into a plush booth surrounded by softly lit ivory walls and cast-iron lamps. The food is tasty and eminently affordable, and an extensive Italian wine list complements the Italian cuisine.
⊕ 244 B6 ✉ 164 West 75th Street at Amsterdam Avenue ☎ 212/787-6300 🕐 Mon–Thu 5–11, Fri–Sat 5–11.30, Sun 12–3, 5–10 ✋ D $55, Wine $25 🚇 72nd Street (1, 2, 3) 🚌 M7, M11, M104

COMPASS
www.compassrestaurant.com
Chef Milton Enriquez worked with various 3-star chefs before he arrived at Compass in 2002, and worked his way up through the kitchen. He has maintained its traditions of serving fine contemporary American cuisine with influences (just like New York itself) from all over the world. Dishes like corn risotto and rack of Berkshire pork with Italian prune show how the kitchen brings these tastes together superbly.
⊕ 244 B6 ✉ 208 West 70th Street at Amsterdam Avenue ☎ 212/875-8600 🕐 Mon–Thu 5–11, Fri–Sat 5–12, Sun 11.30–2.30 (except Jul–Aug), 5–10 ✋ D $55 prix fixe 3-course menu $35 Wine $24 🚇 72nd Street (1, 2, 3) 🚌 M5, M7, M72, M104

DANIEL
www.danielnyc.com
Lyons-born chef Daniel Boulud opened this restaurant in 1993. It has all the romance of an Italian Renaissance palazzo, and dining here is a joyous experience. Signature dishes include the creamy oyster velouté with lemongrass and caviar, roast squab stuffed with foie gras and black truffle, and chocolate fondant with nougatine. Warm

madeleines, homemade chocolates and petits fours conclude the meal. The predominantly French wine list offers more than 1,600 selections. Jacket and tie are required.
⊕ 244 D7 ✉ 60 East 65th Street at Park Avenue ☎ 212/288-0033 🕐 Mon–Sat 5.30–11 ✋ D prix fixe 3-course $108, tasting menus $195–$220, Wine $35 🚇 63rd Street/Lexington (F), 68th Street (6) 🚌 M1, M2, M3, M4, M66

JEAN-GEORGES
www.jean-georges.com
Jean-Georges Vongerichten is the toast of the town. He has developed a signature cuisine that is intensely flavored and highly textured, based on vegetable and fruit essences, oils, vinaigrettes and broths. Stellar examples are the peekytoe crab and English pea fondue with rhubarb gelée and shiso purée, and the veal tenderloin with fricassee of mushrooms, fava beans, and Meyer lemon with liquid Parmesan. It's usually hard to snag a table here, so consider the less formal Nougatine at the same address. There's a 700-plus wine list and terrace dining in summer.
⊕ 244 C7 ✉ Trump International Hotel Tower, 1 Central Park West, between 60th and 61st streets ☎ 212/299-3900 🕐 Mon–Thu 12–2.30, 5.30–11, Fri–Sat 12–2.30, 5.15–11 ✋ L $32, 3-course $24 (in Nougatine), 2-course $28; D $60, prix fixe 4-course menu $98, prix fixe 7-course menu $148, Wine $22 🚇 59th Street/Columbus Circle (A, C, B, D, 1) 🚌 M7, M10, M20

LOEB BOATHOUSE
www.thecentralparkboathouse.com
With the demise of Tavern on the Green, the Loeb Boathouse restaurant became the place to dine in Central Park. It sits at the northeast tip of the lake, affording relaxing views of wild fowl and rowboats on the water from the outdoor deck. After starters such as wild bass ceviche or lobster ravioli, entrées range from herb-roasted Cornish game hen to marinated steak Paillard. Rack of lamb and filet mignon feature on the seasonal dinner menu. The restaurant is

particularly popular, so advance reservations are advised.

✚ 244 D6 ✉ East 72nd Street and Park Drive North ☎ 212/517-2233 🕐 Mon–Fri 10–4, Sat–Sun 9.30–4; dinner Apr–Nov only, Mon–Fri 5.30–9.30, Sat–Sun 6–9.30 ✋ L $40, D $70, Wine $38 🚇 72nd Street (B, C), 68th Street (6) 🚌 M1, M2, M3, M4, M72, M79

LONDEL'S
www.londelsrestaurant.com

The South has given the United States its most distinctive cuisine, and this restaurant serves some of the best, from the Southern fried chicken and barbecue back ribs to the blackened catfish. Order collard greens or candied yams on the side, and bread pudding with rum sauce. You'll have had a feast. Live music on Friday and Saturday.

✚ Off map 244 C2 ✉ 2620 Frederick Douglass Boulevard, between 139th and 140th streets ☎ 212/234-6114 🕐 Tue–Sat 11.30am–midnight, Sun brunch 11–5 ✋ L $18, D $30, Wine $25 🚇 145th Street (A, B, C, D) 🚌 M10

MASA
www.masanyc.com

Currently the Holy Grail of dining in Manhattan. Here, sushi chef Masa (from Tokyo via Los Angeles) holds forth behind his hinoki counter creating whatever he has selected as the freshest and best from around the world. It seats only 26 (10 at the sushi bar) and sushi lovers swear it is nirvana.

✚ 244 C7 ✉ Time Warner Center, 10 Columbus Circle, 4th Floor ☎ 212/823-9800 🕐 Tue–Fri 12–1, 6–9, Mon, Sat 6–9 ✋ $400 prix fixe ($200 penalty for cancellations within 48 hours of reservation), Wine $60 🚇 59th Street/Columbus Circle (A, B, C, D, 1, 9) 🚌 M5, M7, M10, M20, M104

MAYA
www.modernmexican.com

Sophisticated Mexican cuisine is the draw here. The *chile relleno* stuffed with seafood and Gouda cheese is a palate-pleasing combination and the guacamole, served in the stone pestle in which it's made,

is among the best in the city. The pork tenderloin marinated with onion-orange salsa is ultra tender and richly flavored—a winner. Credit cards are not accepted.

✚ 245 E7 ✉ 1191 First Avenue, between East 64th and 65th streets ☎ 212/585-1818 🕐 Sun–Thu 5–10, Fri–Sat 5–11 ✋ D $52, Wine $32 🚇 Lexington Avenue/63rd Street (F), 68th Street (6) 🚌 M15

OUEST
www.ouestny.com

This lively, entertaining restaurant helped raise the Upper West Side's culinary reputation with Tom Valenti's fresh seasonal menu. Settle into one of the cherry-red booths and order the luscious short ribs, one of the braised or roasted meats such as the roast free-range chicken with garlic jus, or a fish dish such as seared tuna with white bean purée, black olive-lemon compote and red pepper coulis. The nightly specials attract crowds, especially on Monday, when the kitchen turns out the chef's signature braised lamb shanks. Desserts are Italian-inspired.

✚ 244 B5 ✉ 2315 Broadway, between West 83rd and 84th streets ☎ 212/580-8700 🕐 Mon–Tue 5–9.30, Wed–Thu 5–10, Fri–Sat 5–11, Sun 5–9 ✋ D $55, also prix fixe 3-course menu $38, Wine $32 🚇 86th Street (1, 9) 🚌 M86, M104

PER SE
www.perseny.com

The room has urban chic and fine views, but diners come to taste the superlative cuisine of Thomas Keller, whom many consider America's finest chef. He arrived from the Napa Valley and his famous French Laundry. The menu changes daily, but diners can expect perfectly prepared dishes right down to the finest details. His "oysters and pearls" (oysters, tapioca and osetra caviar) and his "macaroni and cheese"(lobster mascarpone in a lobster broth topped with a wheel of crisp Parmesan) are legendary. The wine list has 500 selections. It's hard to snag one of the 16 tables.

✚ 244 C7 ✉ Time Warner Center, 10 Columbus Circle, 4th Floor ☎ 212/823-9335

🕐 Fri–Sun 11.30–1.30, daily 5.30–10 ✋ Prix fixe tasting menus $295, Wine $55 🚇 59th Street/Columbus Circle (A, B, C, D, 1) 🚌 M5, M7, M10, M20, M104

PERSEPOLIS
www.persepolisnyc.com

Thai chef San Sethachutkul had to master the art of Persian cooking when he took over the kitchens at Persepolis, but there is a similarity in the way the cuisines blend and contrast flavors. The Vermont lamb shank served with almond, raisin and herb couscous is just one example of this Middle Eastern cuisine at its finest, followed by typical desserts like roasted pineapple or baklava.

✚ 245 E6 ✉ 1407 Second Avenue, between 73rd and 74th streets ☎ 212/535-1100 🕐 Daily 12–11.30 ✋ L $25 3-course prix fixe menu, D $40, Wine $26 🚇 Lexington Avenue (6) 🚌 M15

PICHOLINE
www.picholinenyc.com

The Mediterranean cuisine at Picholine is superb. Among the entrées, the licorice-lacquered squab is exquisite, perfectly complemented by foie gras, glazed turnips and spiced rhubarb marmalade. The wild mushroom and duck risotto is a perennial favorite. It's easy to fill up with delicious entrées and main courses—but be sure to save room for one more course. Picholine also has one of the city's most fabulous cheese trays.

✚ 244 C7 ✉ 35 West 64th Street between Central Park West and Broadway ☎ 212/724-8585 🕐 Mon–Thu 5–10, Fri–Sat 5–11, Sun 5–9 ✋ D $85, tasting menu $165, Wine $45 🚇 66th Street (1) 🚌 M10, M20, M66

PIO PIO
www.piopionyc.com

This is the Peruvian version of the Boston Chicken chain. Order a quarter, half or whole chicken, marinated in secret spices. Then add some ceviche tostones, red beans or yuca frita and a beer, and you've got yourself a tasty

meal. Only Amex credit cards are accepted here.

✚ 245 E4 ✉ 1746 First Avenue, between East 90th and 91st streets ☎ 212/426-5800 🕐 Daily 11–11 ♿ L $15, D $35, Wine $25 🚇 86th Street (4, 5, 6) 🚌 M15

ROSA MEXICANO
www.rosamexicano.com

A waterfall studded with sculptures of Acapulco-style divers, among other decorative notes, sets a flashy scene at this authentic Mexican eaterie. The guacamole, which is made at the table, is fragrant with cilantro (coriander) and oregano, and the menu offers unusual regional dishes such salmon *al guajillo,* beef short ribs marinated in lime and beer and *budin Azteca,* a flavorsome tortilla pie.

✚ 244 C7 ✉ 61 Columbus Avenue at West 62nd Street, NE corner ☎ 212/977-

7700 🕐 Sun–Mon 11.30–10.30, Tue–Sat 11.30–11.30 ♿ L $28, D $45, Wine $24 🚇 59th Street/Columbus Circle (A, B, C, D, 1) 🚌 M5, M7, M11, M104

SARABETH'S
www.sarabethseast.com

Sarabeth Levine is most famous for her luscious baking and breakfasts, but that does not mean that she can't turn out equally wonderful lunch and dinner fare. Try her short ribs in Zinfandel or her hazelnut-crusted sea bass, and you'll be a fan. At breakfast, don't miss the cinnamon French toast or the pumpkin waffles—and plan on a light lunch afterwards.

✚ 244 D4 ✉ 1295 Madison Avenue, between East 92nd and 93rd streets ☎ 212/410-7335 🕐 Mon–Sat 8am–11pm, Sun 8am–9.30pm ♿ L $25, D $45, Wine $32 🚇 96th Street (6) 🚌 M1, M2, M3, M4

TOLANI
www.tolaninyc.com

Dine on dishes from around the world at this casual spot, which specializes in global comfort food. Dishes, meant to be shared, might include peri peri prawns, goat curry or North African duck baked in pastry, or more substantial entrées like steak cooked Brazilian style. The restaurant's name means "too good" in South African slang. You can choose between the candlelit downstairs restaurant, the casual bar and lounge, or sidewalk tables.

✚ 244 B5 ✉ 410 Amsterdam Avenue, between 79th and 80th streets ☎ 212/873-6252 🕐 Daily 11–4, 5–2 ♿ L $25, D $38, Wine $30 🚇 79th Street (1) 🚌 M7, M11, M79, M104

Above *The water wall at Rosa Mexicano spans both levels of the restaurant*

PRICES AND SYMBOLS

Prices are the lowest and highest for a double room for one night. Breakfast is included unless noted otherwise. All the hotels listed accept credit cards unless otherwise stated. Note that rates vary widely throughout the year.

For a key to the symbols, ▷ 2.

AFFINIA GARDENS

www.affinia.com

The suites at this well-located hotel have fully equipped kitchens, tranquility kits and guest laundry. There's also a fitness center.

✚ 245 E7 ✉ 215 East 64th Street, between Second and Third avenues, 10021 ☎ 212/355-1230 ✋ Doubles and suites from $399 ⓘ 129 🔽 🚇 68th Street (6) 🚌 M15, M72, M98, M101, M102, M103

CARLYLE

www.thecarlyle.com

This is a striking art deco building. The rooms boast large bathrooms and every conceivable amenity. Bemelmans Bar has charming murals and in the café pianist Bobby Short plays.

✚ 244 D5 ✉ 35 East 76th Street, between Madison and Park avenues, 10021 ☎ 212/744-1600 ✋ $396–$845,

suites from $792 ⓘ 188 rooms and suites 🌊 🔽 🚇 77th Street (4, 5) 🚌 M1, M2, M3, M4

EXCELSIOR

www.excelsiorhotelny.com

One of the few hotels on the Upper West Side, near the Natural History Museum, the Excelsior offers spotless modern rooms equipped with cable TV, dual-line phone with data port, and bathrobes.

✚ 244 C5 ✉ 45 West 81st Street, between Columbus Avenue and Central Park West, 10024 ☎ 212/362-9200 ✋ $204–$399, suites from $359 ⓘ 199 rooms and suites 🔽 🚇 81st Street (B, C) 🚌 M7, M11, M10, M79

GRACIE INN

www.gracieinnhotel.com

Slightly off the beaten track, this inn attracts long-term guests. Each room has a kitchenette and phone with data port. The penthouses have waterbeds, whirlpool tubs and sundecks. Breakfast is in your room.

✚ 245 F5 ✉ 502 East 81st Street, between York and East End avenues, 10028 ☎ 212/628-1700 ✋ Studio $189–$225, 1-bedroom suite from $239 ⓘ 20 rooms, 6 suites 🚇 77th Street (6) 🚌 M15, M31, M79

JUMEIRAH ESSEX HOUSE

www.jumeirah.com

This landmark art deco hotel was thoroughly renovated in 2007 by the Dubai Hotel Group Jumeirah. The sparkling lobby retains its classic art deco look with black-and-white marble floor, columns and classic décor. Cream-colored sofas in a burgundy-draped alcove provide a relaxing environment. Guest rooms are decorated in neutral tones, with plush carpeting, modern furnishings and art deco highlights, HD LCD flat-panel TV, touch-screen controls and mood lighting.

✚ 244 C7 ✉ 160 Central Park South, between Sixth and Seventh avenues, 10019 ☎ 212/247-0300 ✋ From $297, suites from $564 ⓘ 509 🚇 57th Street (N, Q, R) 🚌 M5, M7, M104

LUCERNE

www.thelucernehotel.com

This hotel, in a 1903 landmark building, is a bargain. Rooms are spacious and have marble bathrooms. The suites have sitting areas as well as a kitchenette with refrigerator and microwave.

✚ 244 B5 ✉ 201 West 79th Street, between Broadway and Amsterdam Avenue, 10024 ☎ 212/875-1000 ✋ From $228

(i) 196 rooms and suites 📺 🚇 79th Street (1) 🚌 M7, M11, M79

MANDARIN ORIENTAL

www.mandarinoriental.com

This hotel soars majestically above Columbus Circle commanding views of Central Park, the Hudson River and the Manhattan skyline from floors 35 through 54 of the new Time Warner Center. Rooms are sumptuously furnished. Bathrooms have deep tubs and glass wall showers plus flat-panel TVs. Asiate (▷ 238) is Asian-inspired fine dining. MObar (on the 35th floor) has been attracting a lot of buzz. Facilities include a two-story spa, and a fitness center with 75ft (23m) lap pool. The hotel has access to all the facilities in the Time Warner Center.

➕ 244 C7 ✉ 80 Columbus Circle at West 60th Street, 10023 ☎ 212/805-8800 ✋ From $850, suites from $1,645 (i) 202 rooms, 46 suites 📺 🚇 59th Street (A, B, C, D, 1, 9) 🚌 M5, M7, M10, M104

NEWTON

www.thehotelnewton.com

This reliable hotel caters to the workers in the entertainment industry who appreciate the value of the rooms here. They are equipped with cable TV and phone, and some have microwaves and refrigerators. There is WiFi access throughout.

➕ 244 B4 ✉ 2528 Broadway, between 94th and 95th streets, 10025 ☎ 212/678-6500 ✋ $159–$259 (i) 93 rooms, 12 suites 🚇 96th Street (1, 2, 3) 🚌 M104

ON THE AVE

www.ontheave-nyc.com

A few blocks from the Natural History Museum and Central Park, this small hotel was built in 1922. The rooms, furnished in sleek modern style, feature vibrant paintings by Alfonso Muñoz. There are three floors of penthouse suites.

➕ 244 B5 ✉ 2178 Broadway at 77th Street, 10024 ☎ 212/362-1100 ✋ Doubles from $299, suites from $409 (i) 250 rooms, 16 suites 🚇 79th Street (1) 🚌 M79, M104

PIERRE

www.tajhotels.com

Overlooking Central Park, this 41-story hotel, built in 1930, is the quintessence of luxury. A complete renovation was finished in 2009. The hotel is renowned for its premier service and fabulous guest rooms, many with city or park views. The oversized bathrooms have large soaking tubs and multiple jet sprays. Le Caprice serves eclectic international cuisine.

➕ 244 D7 ✉ Fifth Avenue at 61st Street, 10021 ☎ 212/838-8000 ✋ From $491, suites from $734 (i) 140 rooms, 49 suites 🚇 59th Street/Fifth Avenue (N, Q, R) 🚌 M1, M2, M3, M4

PLAZA ATHÉNÉE

www.plaza-athenee.com

The hotel is on a quiet, tree-lined street one block from Central Park. All rooms are furnished with antique-style European furniture with Belgian linens and writing desks. All rooms also include CD players and high-speed internet, while some suites have dining rooms with atriums and balconies.

➕ 244 D7 ✉ 37 East 64th Street at Madison Avenue, 10065 ☎ 212/734-9100 ✋ Rooms from $495, suites from $1,190 (i) 142 rooms and suites 🚇 Lexington Avenue (F) 🚌 MI, M2, M3, M4

RITZ-CARLTON

www.ritzcarlton.com

This 33-story hotel has magnificent views. The lobby sets an opulent tone with its limestone walls, inlaid onyx floor and Samuel Halpert paintings. The rooms are luxuriously decorated with flat-screen TVs, DVDs, and park-view rooms have telescopes for birdwatching. Bathrooms have deep tubs with neck pillows, Frederic Fekkai toiletries and Frette candles. Pratesi linens and Bang & Olufsen stereos grace the suites. The Ritz-Carlton is famous for its service. BLT Market offers fresh seasonal dishes and The Star Lounge specializes in elegant afternoon tea and classic cocktails. La Prairie spa (▷ 237) is full service.

➕ 244 D7 ✉ 50 Central Park South, 10019 ☎ 212/308-9100 ✋ $695–$895, suites from $995 (i) 272 rooms, 47 suites 📺 🚇 59th Street/Fifth Avenue (N, Q, R), 57th Street (F) 🚌 M5, M7

SHERRY-NETHERLAND

www.sherrynetherland.com

This hotel is a building cooperative—the owners individually decorate their units. The number of guest rooms fluctuates between 100 and 150. The building dates from 1927 and much of its luxury detailing was taken from a Vanderbilt mansion. It has European style and a Harry Cipriani restaurant.

➕ 244 D7 ✉ 781 Fifth Avenue, between 59th and 60th streets, 10022 ☎ 212/355-2800 ✋ $499–$729, suites from $869 (i) 150 📺 🚇 59th Street/Fifth Avenue (N, Q, R) 🚌 M1, M2, M3, M4

TRUMP INTERNATIONAL HOTEL AND TOWER

www.trumpintl.com

The location is superb, with views of Central Park and easy access to the Lincoln Center and Midtown. The rooms, located between the 3rd and 17th floors, are stylish, and each has plasma TV, VCR, CD and DVD; suites have whirlpool tubs and even telescopes. The restaurant Jean-Georges (▷ 239) is a draw.

➕ 244 C7 ✉ 1 Central Park West at Columbus Circle, 10023 ☎ 212/299-1000 ✋ Doubles from $495, suites from $750 (i) 176 rooms and suites 📺 🚇 59th Street/Columbus Circle (A, B, C, D, 1, 9) 🚌 M10, M20

WALES

www.hotelwalesnyc.com

The Hotel Wales is a study in old-fashioned luxury on the quiet Upper East Side near Museum Mile and Central Park. The rooms have plush chairs and luxurious beds. Sarabeth's (▷ 241) and Joanna's Italian Restaurant are bonuses.

➕ 244 D4 ✉ 1295 Madison Avenue, between 92nd and 93rd streets, 10128 ☎ 212/876-6000 ✋ Doubles from $315, suites from $365 (i) 46 rooms, 42 suites 📺 🚇 96th Street (6) 🚌 M1, M2, M3, M4, M96

Londel's
Amy Ruth's
West 111th Street
110th Street Cathedral Parkway
WEST 111th Street
WEST 110TH STREET
110TH STREET
Frederick Douglass Circle
110th Street (Central Park Nth)
Charles A Dana Discovery Center
West 109th Street
East 109th Street
Fraway Circle
West 108th Street
East 108th Street
West 107th Street
East 107th Street
Harlem Meer
West 106th Street
East 106th Street
Conservatory Garden
West 105th Street
El Museo del Barrio
East 105th Street
West 104th Street
Museum of the City of New York
East 104th Street
103rd Street
West 103rd Street
103rd Street
West 102nd Street
The Pool
East 103rd Street
West 101st Street
East 101st Street
Gustave L Levy Place
West 100th Street
Central Park
West 99th Street
East 98th Street
West 98th Street
97th Street Transverse Road
96th Street
West 97th Street
96th Street
East 97th Street
West 96th Street
East 96th Street
Newton
West 95th Street
East 95th Street
West 94th Street
Sarabeth's
East 93rd Street
West 93rd Street
Jewish Museum
Central Park Reservoir
East 92nd Street
Wales
UPPER WEST SIDE
West 92nd Street
Cooper-Hewitt National Design Museum
East 91st Street
West 91st Street
East 90th Street
National Academy of Design
West 90th Street
West 89th Street
Guggenheim Museum
East 88th Street
Barney Greengrass
West 88th Street
West 87th Street
East 87th Street
86th Street
West 86th Street
86th Street Transverse Road
East 86th Street
Neue Galerie
West 85th Street
86th Street
Ouest
West 84th Street
CENTRAL PARK
East 84th Street
West 83rd Street
East 83rd Street
Excelsior & Calle Ocho
West 82nd Street
81st Street Museum of Nat Hist
Metropolitan Museum of Art
East 82nd Street
West 81st Street
East 81st Street
Tolani
West 80th Street
Turtle Pond
East 80th Street
Lucerne
West 79th Street
American Museum of Natural History
79th Street Transverse Road
East 79th Street
West 78th Street
East 78th Street
On the Ave
West 77th Street
East 77th Street
Carlyle
New-York Historical Society
West 76th Street
East 76th Street
Café Boulud
Cesca
West 75th Street
San Remo Apartments
Loeb Boathouse
East 75th Street
Ansonia Building
West 74th Street
Whitney Museum of American Art
East 74th Street
West 73rd Street
Conservatory Water
East 73rd Street
The Dakota
The Lake
West 72nd Street
72nd Street
East 72nd Street
West 71st Street
Strawberry Fields
Frick Collection
East 71st Street
West 70th Street
East 70th Street
Compass
West 69th Street
Olmsted Drive
East 69th Street
West 68th Street
The Sheep Meadow
East 68th Street
West 67th Street
East 67th Street
66th Street Lincoln Center
Tavern on the Green
FIFTH AVENUE
West 66th Street
East 66th Street
Juilliard School
65th Street Transverse
East 65th Street
Dani
Picholine
West 64th Street
Plaza Athénée
Lincoln Center
Rosa Mexicano
West 63rd Street
Wollman Rink
Lowell
East 63rd Street
Museum of Biblical Art
West 62nd Street
The Pond
East 62nd Street
Pierre
West 61st Street
Aureo
Trump International Hotel and Tower, Jean-Georges
Sherry-Netherland
Ritz Carlton
59th Street Columbus Circle
West 59th Street
COLUMBUS CIRCLE
Central Park South
West 58th Street
Mandarin Oriental
Jumeirah Essex House
Asiate, Masa, Per Se
WEST 57TH STREET

Riverside Park
Hudson
HIGHWAY 9A
BROADWAY
Amsterdam Avenue
Columbus Avenue
Central Park West
West End Avenue
Freedom Place
Riverside Drive
Manhattan Avenue
5th Avenue
Madison Avenue
Park Avenue
The Loch
Lasker Pool & Rink
The Pool
West Drive
East Drive
Center Drive
Wollman Rink

A   B   C   D

EAST HARLEM

East 111th Street
East 110th Street
East 110th Street
East 109th Street
East 108th Street
East 107th Street
East 106th Street
East 105th Street
East 104th Street
East 103rd Street
East 103rd Street
East 103rd Street
East 102nd Street
East 101st Street
East 101st Street
101st Street
East 100th Street
100th Street
East 99th Street
98th Street
East 97th Street
EAST 96TH STREET
East 95th Street
East 94th Street
East 93rd Street
East 92nd Street
East 91st Street
East 91st Street
East 90th Street
East 89th Street
East 88th Street
East 87th Street
East 86th Street
East 85th Street
East 84th Street
East 83rd Street
East 82nd Street
East 81st Street
East 80th Street
East 79th Street
East 78th Street
East 77th Street
East 76th Street
East 75th Street
East 74th Street
East 73rd Street
East 72nd Street
East 71st Street
East 70th Street
East 69th Street
East 68th Street
East 67th Street
East 66th Street
East 65th Street
East 64th Street
East 63rd Street
Lexington Avenue 63rd Street
East 62nd Street
East 61st Street
East 61st St
59th Street
Lexington Avenue
East 60th Street
HIGHWAY 25
East 57th Street

3rd Avenue
2nd Avenue
1st Avenue
York Avenue
Lexington Avenue

FRANKLIN DELANO ROOSEVELT DRIVE (FDR)

Pio Pio
Gracie Mansion
Gracie Inn
Carl Schurz Park
John Jay Park
Persepolis
Asia Society and Museum
68th Street Hunter College
Affinia Gardens
Maya
Mount Vernon Hotel Museum and Garden

Mill Rock Park

East River

Wards Island Park
Ralph Demarco Park

Astoria Park
Astoria Park South

Astoria
Astoria Boulevard
Halletts Cove Playground
Welling Court
Socrates Sculpture Park
Rainey Park
Ravenswood Playground
Queensbridge Park

QUEENS

23rd Road
23rd Drive
23rd Terrace
23rd Road
24th Drive
25th Road
26th Avenue
26th Avenue
Newtown
27th Road
28th Avenue
29th Avenue
30th Road
30th Drive
31st Avenue
31st Road
31st Drive
33rd Avenue
33rd Avenue
33rd Road
33rd Road
33rd Road
34th Avenue
34th Avenue
35th Avenue
35th Avenue
36th Avenue
36th Avenue
37th Avenue
38th Avenue
39th Avenue
40th Avenue
41st Avenue
41st Road

Roosevelt Island
Roosevelt Island Bridge
River Road
Main Street
West Road
East Road
Roosevelt Island Main Street

QUEENSBORO BRIDGE
HIGHWAY 25
Queens Plaza South
21st Street Queensbridge
Main Street

Shore Boulevard
Vernon Boulevard
21st Street
Crescent Street

250 m
250 yds

245

E F G H

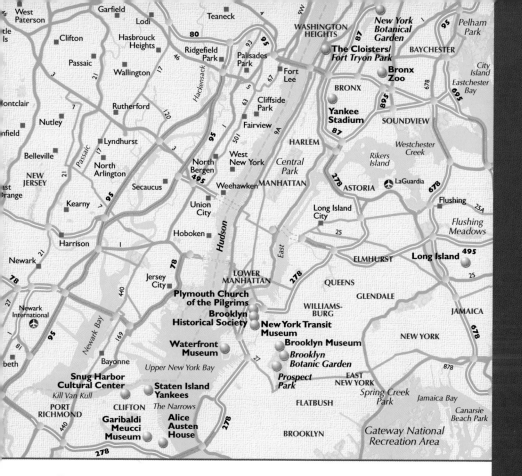

West Paterson · Garfield · Teaneck · WASHINGTON HEIGHTS · New York Botanical Garden · Pelham Park · Lodi · 80 · 95 · 95
tle Is · Clifton · Hasbrouck Heights · Ridgefield Park · Palisades Park · 87 · The Cloisters/Fort Tryon Park · BAYCHESTER · City Island
Passaic · 46 · Fort Lee · Bronx Zoo · 678 · Eastchester Bay
Wallington · 17 · Cliffside Park · BRONX · Bronx Zoo · 678
Montclair · 7 · Rutherford · 120 · Fairview · Yankee Stadium · SOUNDVIEW · 695
Nutley · North Arlington · Fairview · Yankee Stadium · SOUNDVIEW
nfield · Lyndhurst · North Bergen · West New York · Central Park · HARLEM · Rikers Island · Westchester Creek
Belleville · NEW JERSEY · Secaucus · Weehawken · MANHATTAN · 278 · LaGuardia · 678
ast Orange · Kearny · 95 · Union City · Long Island City · Flushing · 25A
Hoboken · Hudson · East · 25 · Flushing Meadows
Harrison · 21 · Jersey City · 78 · ELMHURST · Long Island · 495
Newark · 78 · 440 · LOWER MANHATTAN · 278 · QUEENS · 25
Newark International · Plymouth Church of the Pilgrims · GLENDALE · JAMAICA
Brooklyn Historical Society · WILLIAMS-BURG · NEW YORK · 678
New York Transit Museum · Brooklyn Museum · 878
Bayonne · Waterfront Museum · Brooklyn Botanic Garden · EAST NEW YORK
beth · 81 · Snug Harbor Cultural Center · Prospect Park · Spring Creek Park · Jamaica Bay
Kill Van Kull · Staten Island Yankees · FLATBUSH · Canarsie Beach Park
PORT RICHMOND · CLIFTON · The Narrows · Alice Austen House · BROOKLYN · Gateway National Recreation Area
Garibaldi Meucci Museum · 278

EXCURSIONS

Beyond Manhattan there are four more boroughs that form the largest part, about 73 percent, of New York City in both land mass and population. Many New Yorkers live here in residential neighborhoods, far from the hustle and bustle of congested Manhattan, which is often referred to as "the city." There are many fine attractions here, including museums, the city's largest zoo, gardens and huge sports arenas.

The Bronx, north of Manhattan, is best known as home to the New York Yankees and the city's largest park, Pelham Bay Park, with the Bronx Zoo and New York Botanical Garden. Here, too, is the public garden at Wave Hill, fine seafood and Italian dining, and the Bronx Museum of the Arts.

To the east of the city, Queens boasts the most ethnically diverse population in the world. If you crave ethnic food, there are many small neighborhood restaurants that feature Indian, Peruvian, Greek, Korean and many other regional foods. Here, too, are amazing modern and contemporary art collections at Queens Museum of Art, P.S.1 Contemporary Art Center, Socrates Sculpture Park and the Noguchi Museum.

South of Queens and southeast of the city, Brooklyn is the place to go for atmospheric neighborhoods like DUMBO (Down Under the Manhattan Bridge Overpass) and Williamsburg for the arts, or the specialty shops and boutiques in the young-professional neighborhoods of Brooklyn Heights, Prospect Heights and Cobble Hill.

Take the Staten Island Ferry to Staten Island for sweeping vistas that include the Statue of Liberty and the harbor. On the island, explore the harbor area and dine in a local café before heading to Snug Harbor for the Cultural Center, Botanical Garden and the Staten Island Children's Museum.

Just beyond the city lies Long Island, fringed with miles of beaches along the Atlantic Coast, historic towns, museums and state parks. To the north of the city, the scenic Hudson River Valley, especially beautiful in the fall, offers splendid historic mansions, museums and West Point Military Academy.

EXCURSIONS NEW YORK

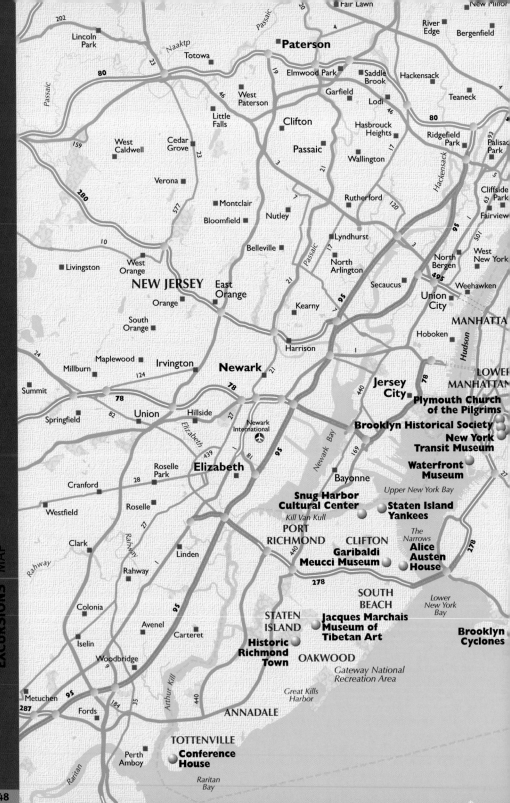

202

Lincoln
Park

Naaktp

Totowa

Passaic

Paterson

20

Fair Lawn

New Milfor

River
Edge

Bergenfield

80

23

West
Paterson

19

Elmwood Park

Saddle
Brook

Hackensack

Teaneck

46

Little
Falls

Garfield

Lodi

Clifton

46

80

93

159

West
Caldwell

Cedar
Grove

23

Passaic

21

Hasbrouck
Heights

17

Ridgefield
Park

Palisa
Park

5

Verona

577

Wallington

Cliffside
Park

63

Fairview

280

Montclair

7

Rutherford

120

95

501

Bloomfield

Nutley

North
Bergen

West
New York

Livingston

10

West
Orange

Belleville

Lyndhurst

17

North
Arlington

Secaucus

495

Weehawken

NEW JERSEY

East
Orange

Passaic

21

Union
City

MANHATTA

Orange

Kearny

7

Hoboken

South
Orange

Harrison

1

Hudson

24

Maplewood

Irvington

Newark

21

**LOWE
MANHATTAN**

Millburn

124

78

**Jersey
City**

78

Summit

78

Union

Hillside

27

**Plymouth Church
of the Pilgrims**

Springfield

82

Elizabeth

Newark
International

81

95

440

Brooklyn Historical Society

**New York
Transit Museum**

Cranford

28

Roselle
Park

Elizabeth

439

1

169

**Waterfront
Museum**

Westfield

Roselle

Upper New York Bay

Clark

27

Rahway

Linden

Bayonne

**Snug Harbor
Cultural Center**

Kill Van Kull

**Staten Island
Yankees**

Colonia

Rahway

Rahway

1

**PORT
RICHMOND**

440

CLIFTON

*The
Narrows*

**Alice
Austen
House**

Iselin

Avenel

Carteret

**Garibaldi
Meucci Museum**

278

Woodbridge

9

278

**SOUTH
BEACH**

278

*Lower
New York
Bay*

Metuchen

95

**STATEN
ISLAND**

**Jacques Marchais
Museum of
Tibetan Art**

**Brooklyn
Cyclones**

287

Fords

184

35

440

**Historic
Richmond
Town**

OAKWOOD

*Gateway National
Recreation Area*

Arthur Kill

Perth
Amboy

ANNADALE

*Great Kills
Harbor*

TOTTENVILLE

**Conference
House**

*Raritan
Bay*

Raritan

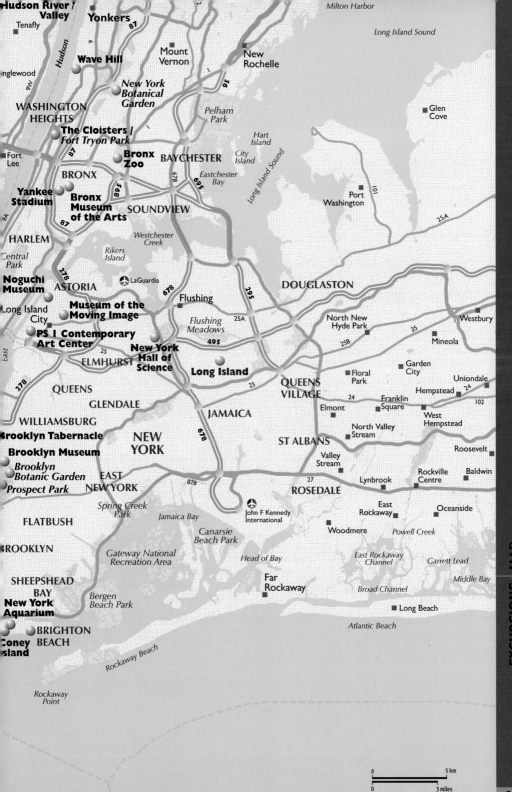

INFORMATION

www.visitbrooklyn.org

🛈 Brooklyn Tourism and Visitors Center, Historic Brooklyn Borough Hall, 209 Joralemon Street, First Floor ☎ 718/802-3846 🕒 Mon–Fri 10–6

WHAT TO SEE
BRIGHTON BEACH

The influx of Russian immigrants to this area on Brooklyn's Atlantic-pounded shore has earned it the nickname Little Odessa by the Sea. You'll appreciate why as you stroll along the ocean's-edge boardwalk and Brighton Beach Avenue. The dozens of supermarkets and delicatessens are stocked with caviar, knishes, vodka, sausages and foods you just don't see back home unless home is Russia. The nightlife recalls Las Vegas, with its scantily clad dancers crowned with elaborate plumage.

✉ Southern tip of Brooklyn 🚇 B, Q 🚌 B1, B68 🍴 🖥 🏛

BROOKLYN BOTANIC GARDEN

www.bbg.org

These 52 acres (21ha), planted with more than 13,000 varieties from around the world, are a place for a quiet stroll when you've had enough of Manhattan. There are water-lily ponds, stately old trees and flowering shrubs, a local plantlife section and a conifer collection. The Cranford Rose Garden shelters more than 1,000 varieties of rose. The stunning Cherry Esplanade draws large crowds in May for the blooming season and the Japanese hill-and-pond garden is one of the best of its type in the country. The Palm House, designed by McKim, Mead & White in 1914, and the greenhouses added in 1987, offer additional spaces. You can see everything in the Botanic Garden in two or three hours.

✉ 900 Washington Avenue, Brooklyn, 11225 ☎ 718/623-7200 🕒 Mar–early Nov Tue–Fri 8–6, Sat–Sun 10–6; Nov to mid-Mar Tue–Fri 8–4.30, Sat–Sun 10–4.30 💲 Adult $10, under 12 free. Free to all Tue and Sat 10–noon 🚇 B, Q to Prospect Park, 2, 3 to Eastern Parkway 🚌 B16, B41, B43, B69 🚶 Guided tours weekends 1pm 🖥 🏛

Above At the southern tip of Brooklyn, broad and sandy Brighton Beach draws New Yorkers on summer weekends

BROOKLYN CYCLONES

www.brooklyncyclones.com

This minor-league club has the fans cheering, because going to the game here is the way baseball used to be. Sitting in the bleachers at this waterfront stadium is just the ticket, especially for old Dodgers fans.

✉ Keyspan Park, 1904 Surf Avenue between 17th and 19th streets, Coney Island ☎ 718/449-8497 🖐 $8–$15 (single tickets available mid-Apr) 🚇 Stillwell Avenue/Coney Island (D, F, N, Q) 🚌 B36, B38, B74 (Stillwell/Surf Avenue)

BROOKLYN HISTORICAL SOCIETY

www.brooklynhistory.org

The Brooklyn Historical Society is a museum, library and educational center dedicated to preserving and exploring Brooklyn's heritage. It occupies a landmark Queen Anne-style building (1881) designed by George B. Post, who embellished the interior with Minton tile floors, elaborately carved black ash, and stained glass by Charles Booth. Post applied bridge engineering techniques to create an open and dramatic two-story space in the center of the building. The museum has a collection of 9,000-plus objects relating to local history. They are used in shows such as *Brooklyn Works,* which traced the history of working people from early farming days through the industrial era (when Brooklyn was the fourth-largest city in the US) to today. The shows are accessible and include fascinating oral history. Prints and Dodger memorabilia are strong elements, too. The society also offers walking tours of Brooklyn neighborhoods and a boat tour of the working waterfront (prices vary). The library (open by appointment) has a premier collection too, including a first edition of Walt Whitman's *Leaves of Grass.*

✉ 128 Pierrepont Street at Clinton Street, Brooklyn, 11201 ☎ 718/222-4111 🕐 Wed–Fri, Sun noon–5, Sat 10–5 🖐 Adult $6, members and under 12 free 🚇 2, 3, 4, 5 🚌 B51 weekdays only �</> Guided tours available

BROOKLYN MUSEUM

www.brooklynmuseum.org

The second-largest art museum in New York City, and one of the largest in the country, attracts half a million visitors every year. The Brooklyn Museum is housed in a grand Beaux Arts building designed by McKim, Mead & White in 1897, with an addition by Polshek Partners completed in spring 2004.

The museum prides itself on its fine collection of Egyptian, Classical and Ancient Middle Eastern Art. It holds the third-largest collection of Ancient Egyptian artifacts dating from predynastic times to the Roman conquest. The Morris A. and Meyer Schapiro Wing contains objects from 1350BC, in the reign of Akhenaten and his wife Nefertiti, through to the time of Cleopatra. Jewelry, reliefs of major deities, decorated sarcophagi, coffins and a 2,600-year-old mummy are on display.

The Arts of Africa, the Pacific and the Americas galleries have astonishing collections. An ivory gong from the Edo people of Benin, works from Polynesia and Indonesia, and important textiles from the Andes are just some of the fascinating items. The Arts of Asia collection has objects from China, India, Iran, Korea, Japan, Tibet, Thailand and Turkey.

The collection of decorative arts, costumes and textiles features a 17th-century Dutch farmhouse and a 20th-century art deco library and fashions of 19th-century America and Europe.

Paintings, sculptures, drawings and photographs include works by Gilbert Stuart, Thomas Cole, George Caleb Bingham, Winslow Homer, Auguste Rodin, Edgar Degas, Camille Pissarro, Edward Steichen and Paul Strand.

First Saturdays of the month are enormously popular. A free program of art and entertainment, with food and drinks supplied, attracts thousands. For example, the entertainment may start with spoken-word artists and members

WHERE TO EAT
BLACK SHEEP PUB

The Irish owners pour a good pint of Guinness at this neighborhood bar that doesn't look too promising from the outside but is a lively place when you get through the doors. The bar food—burgers, sandwiches, salads, and fish and chips—is great value. There's a pub quiz Wednesday nights, movies on Tuesday, sports on TV most other times, and a good price on beers.

✉ 428 Bergen Street at 5th Avenue, Brooklyn ☎ 718/638-1109 🕐 Mon–Wed 4–4, Thu–Fri 2pm–4am, Sat–Sun noon–4am 🚇 Bergen Street (2, 3), Atlantic Avenue/Pacific Street (D, M, N, R)

THE GUTTER

www.thegutterbrooklyn.com

Gutter is a new bar with an old 1950s kind of a feel, and eight bowling lanes. Vintage bowling memorabilia decorates the bar, which looks out over the bowling lanes. There are 12 craft beers on draft, but you can also get pitchers.

✉ 200 North 14th Street at Wythe Avenue, Brooklyn ☎ 718/387-3585 🕐 Mon–Thu 5–4, Fri 2pm–4am, Sat–Sun noon–4am 🖐 $7 a game for bowling 🚇 Nassau Avenue (G), Bedford Avenue (L)

THE LEVEE

www.theleveenyc.com

New Yorkers who know their beer rate this place, which has a few dozen bottled ales as well as six draft brews and a full bar. The Texan owner has made sure there's a friendly Southern feel, and there's a jukebox, pinball and pool table, and a basic bar menu is served until 4am. No frills but a great place to kick back.

✉ 212 Berry Street at Metropolitan Avenue, Brooklyn ☎ 718/218-8787 🕐 Daily noon–4am 🚇 Bedford Avenue (L)

SUPERFINE

Chef Laura Taylor came from Santa Fe, and her innovative seasonal cuisine is Mediterranean inspired. The affordable menu changes daily to take advantage of fresh, organic meat and produce from local markets, and usually offers a main course salad, pasta, steak, chicken and seafood entrées. The restaurant is housed in a casual neighborhood setting with a view of the bridge through the glass doors. Credit cards are not accepted.

✉ 126 Front Street at Pearl Street, DUMBO, Brooklyn ☎ 718/243-9005 🕐 Tue–Fri 11.30–3, 6–11, Sat 3–11, Sun 11–3, 6–10 ✋ L $18, D $32 🚇 York Street (F)

of the Brooklyn Philharmonic in Shakespeare Live alongside a program of Hands-on-Art that allows you to create your own Egyptian-inspired necklaces.

✉ 200 Eastern Parkway, Brooklyn, 11238 ☎ 718/638-5000 🕐 Wed–Sun 11–6 (Thu until 10), first Sat of the month (except Sep) 11–11 ✋ Adult $10, under 12 free; first Sat each month free 5–11 🚇 2, 3 🚌 B41, B45, B69 📷 Audiotour of permanent collection $3 🍴 Museum Café Wed–Fri 10–4, Sat, Sun and holidays 11–5 🏛 Museum shop Wed–Fri 10.30–5.30, Sat–Sun 11–6, until 11pm on first Sat

BROOKLYN TABERNACLE

www.brooklyntabernacle.org

Housed in the renovated old Lowes Metropolitan Theater building, this non-denominational gospel church in the heart of downtown Brooklyn has a congregation of nearly 10,000 from all walks of life. The tabernacle is one of the most renowned inner-city churches in the country. Pastor Jim Cymbala is a powerful orator, and his services are attended by members of all ethnic and national origins as well as visitors from all over the world who come to listen to the 275-voice gospel choir. His wife, Carol, is the choral director of the four-time Grammy award winning Brooklyn Tabernacle Choir, which frequently sings for the 9am and 12pm services.

✉ 17 Smith Street between Fulton and Livingston streets, downtown Brooklyn, 11201 ☎ 718/290-2000 🕐 Services: Sun 9am, noon, 3pm, Tue 7pm 🚇 Jay Street/Borough Hall (A, C, F), Hoyt Street (2, 3), Borough Hall (4, 5), Lawrence Street (M, R)

CONEY ISLAND

www.coneyisland.com

Known as the Playground of the World, Coney Island is a New York treasure, though it's seen tough times. It lost its Thunderbolt roller coaster and Kensington Hotel in 2000; Steeplechase Park was closed in 1964; Astroland Park closed in 2008. In spite of this, the New York Aquarium (opened in 1957) is going strong, the world-famous Cyclone and Wonder Wheel are open and the broad sand beaches remain. The Mermaid Parade, a summer solstice staple, is a "must-see." Nathan Handwerker opened his hot-dog emporium here in 1916, and his famous hot dogs are now sold all over New York. Keyspan Park is the $39-million home of the Brooklyn Cyclones baseball team. It is located behind Parachute Jump on the Boardwalk.

✉ Southern tip of Brooklyn, 11224 🚇 D, F, N, Q 🚌 B36, B74 🍴 📷 🏛

NEW YORK AQUARIUM

www.nyaquarium.com

There are daily dolphin and sea lion shows in summer at this small park, which also houses penguins, walruses, Beluga whales, sharks and seals—300 species in all. Most exhibits are outside. In the Discovery Center kids can pick up starfish, crabs and other small sea creatures.

✉ Surf Avenue and West 8th Street, Coney Island, Brooklyn ☎ 718-265-3474 🕐 Memorial Day–Labor Day, Mon–Fri 10–6, Sat–Sun 10–7; Apr–Memorial Day and Labor Day–Oct 31 Mon–Fri 10–5, Sat–Sun 10–5.30; Nov–Mar daily 10–4.30 ✋ Adult $18.95, child (3–12) $10.95, under 3 free 🚇 Stillwell Avenue (D), 8th Street (F, Q) 🚌 B36, B68

NEW YORK TRANSIT MUSEUM

www.mta.info/mta/museum

The New York Transit Museum occupies a decommissioned subway station in downtown Brooklyn. The permanent and temporary exhibitions explore the history of buses and trolleys in New York City. Highlights are the vintage subway and trolley cars.

✉ Boerum Place and Schermerhorn Street, Brooklyn, 11201 ☎ 718/694-1600 🕐 Tue–Fri 10–4, Sat–Sun noon–5 ✋ Adult $6, child (under 17) $4 🚇 2, 3, 4, 5 🏛 Gallery annex and store at Grand Central Terminal (▷ 157) ☎ 212/878-0106

PLYMOUTH CHURCH OF THE PILGRIMS

www.plymouthchurch.org

The Plymouth Church of the Pilgrims, built in 1849, was the first Congregational Church in Brooklyn and a focal point of the anti-slavery movement at the time. Abraham Lincoln worshiped here twice in 1860, and many eminent writers have spoken here. Elegant and beautiful stained-glass windows by Tiffany adorn this otherwise modest church, and in the courtyard next to it is a superb bronze statue of Henry Ward Beecher (1813–87) with slaves, sculpted by Gutzon Borglum (famous for his work on Mount Rushmore). Beecher, the most famous preacher in America, preached from this pulpit for 40 years, often speaking out against slavery.

✉ 75 Hicks Street, Brooklyn, 11201 ☎ 718/624-4743 ⏰ Guided tour only (1hr 30 min) Mon–Fri 10–4, Sun 11–2, advance reservation required ✋ Phone for prices 🚇 2, 3, A, C

PROSPECT PARK

www.prospectpark.org

Designed by Frederick Law Olmsted and Calvert Vaux, the designers of Central Park (▷ 208–213), this 526-acre (213ha) park is a pleasant place to spend a day. At the main entrance at Grand Army Plaza are a triumphal arch and a monument to President John F. Kennedy.

In Leffert's Homestead is a museum for children. A zoo, skating rink, boathouse and pond, playgrounds, and a lovely 1912 carousel (open same hours as museum; $2) are very popular with children, too. The northeast corner has a rose garden, Japanese gardens, a sculpture garden and the Brooklyn Museum (▷ 251–252). Events throughout the year draw crowds.

The Audubon Center provides maps and guides for self-guiding tours, as well as free guided nature walks and other programs.

✉ Flatbush Avenue at Grand Army Plaza. Information: Prospect Park Alliance, 95 Prospect Park West, Brooklyn, 11215 ☎ Information: 718/965-8999; Lefferts Homestead Historic House Museum: 718/789-2822; Audubon Center: 718/287-3400 ⏰ Daily 5am–1am. Museum: Jul–Aug Thu–Sun and holidays 12–6; Jun 12–5; Apr–May 12–4. Audubon Center: Jul–Labor Day Thu–Sun 12–5; Apr–Jun Thu–Sun 12–4; Feb–Mar, Sat–Sun 12–4 ✋ Adult $3 Sat–Sun, child free 🚇 2, 3, F, Q 🚌 B16, B41, B68, B69 🍴 ♿ 🏛

WATERFRONT MUSEUM

www.waterfrontmuseum.org

An unusual museum in the last surviving railroad barge, the Waterfront stages a summer music series on Saturday nights in July featuring blues to swing and country artists, and a program of Circus Sundays in June. The barge was designated by the UN in 1998 as the Regional Craft of the International Year of the Oceans. Day visitors learn about New York Harbor, barge history and how this barge was rescued.

✉ 290 Conover Street at Pier 44, Brooklyn, 11231 ☎ 718/624-4719 ⏰ Thu 4–8, Sat 1–5 ✋ Free 🚇 F, G 🚌 B61

Above *The Audubon Center in leafy Prospect Park is the place to go for maps and self-guiding tours*

Below *Ancient Egyptian artifacts on display in Brooklyn Museum*

BROOKLYN HEIGHTS
TO MANHATTAN WALK

If Brooklyn were not part of New York City, it would be America's sixth-largest city. Historic Brooklyn Heights, with its many landmark churches, fine brownstones and leafy streets, remains a distinguished residential area. The walk across Brooklyn Bridge provides stunning views of Lower Manhattan.

THE WALK

Distance: 2.5 miles (4km)
Time: 2 to 2.5 hours (allow time to enjoy the view of Manhattan from Brooklyn Bridge)
Start at: High Street/Brooklyn Bridge subway station
End at: Brooklyn Bridge/City Hall subway station

HOW TO GET THERE

Subway A or C from Manhattan to High Street or Brooklyn Bridge subway stations.

★ Leave the High Street/Brooklyn Bridge subway station. As you come out of the station, you see Cadman Plaza Park, with its tall trees, paths and benches. On the right side of the park is Cadman Plaza West. Walk south on this street the length of the park.

❶ Stop for a moment at the large stone monument on your left, dedicated to the Brooklyn men and women who fought during World War II. With its trees and benches, this park is a pleasant place to sit.

Continue on Cadman Plaza West, crossing Tillary Street. Pass the Korean War Veterans Plaza on your left and continue to the Federal Building and the Romanesque Revival US Post Office and Courthouse. Cross Johnson Street.

❷ The enormous building on the left is the Supreme Court of New York. Pause to admire the statue of Christopher Columbus in front of the building and the bronze bust of Senator Robert F. Kennedy, the assassinated brother of President John F. Kennedy.

❸ Straight ahead is an elaborate fountain and behind it is the Greek Revival Brooklyn Borough Hall, built in 1848.

Just past Borough Hall is Joralemon Street. Walk west on Joralemon a block and a half to Sidney Place, on your left. Look down this little street to the big red church, St. Charles Borromeo Roman Catholic Church, built in 1849. Three blocks farther

west on Joralemon, turn right on Hicks Street. Walk one block north.

❹ Grace Church, at 254 Hicks Street, is one of many New York City churches designed by Richard Upjohn; it dates from 1849. Visit the charming entrance court off Hicks Street and cool off in the shade of the enormous elm tree.

Continue a block north on Hicks to Remsen Street, and turn right. Go one block east and cross Henry Street.

❺ On your left is Richard Upjohn's Cathedral of Our Lady of Lebanon, the first round-arched, Early Romanesque Revival ecclesiastical building in the United States. Notice the medallions on the entrance doors. Originally the dining room doors on the French luxury liner *Normandie*, they were bought at an auction in 1945.

Continue another block east on Remsen, and turn left on Clinton

EXCURSIONS | WALK

Street. Walking north, as you cross Montague Street, look at St. Ann and the Holy Trinity Episcopal Church, a major work of James Renwick, Jr., on your left; it is one of the most important Victorian Gothic churches in the United States. At the end of Clinton Street, turn left on Cadman Plaza West, left again on Clark Street and then right on Henry Street. Walk two blocks to Orange Street and turn left.

❻ The Plymouth Church of the Pilgrims, built in 1849 on Orange Street between Henry and Hicks streets, was the center of anti-slavery sentiment during antebellum days. Abolitionist minister Henry Ward Beecher preached against slavery here. Abraham Lincoln worshiped here twice, and the building was a key part of the Underground Railroad, which helped get escaped slaves to freedom. Beautiful stained-glass windows adorn this otherwise modest church, and in the courtyard next to it stands a bronze statue of Henry Ward Beecher by Gutzon Borglum, who sculpted the four

famous presidents' heads at Mount Rushmore, South Dakota.

Return to Henry Street and turn left. There are many cafés, restaurants and delis along here. At the traffic lights, turn right on Middagh Street and, at Cadman Plaza West, take the path ahead across the park. On your left is a plaque with information about the peregrine falcons that often roost here. At the

fork in the path, keep left and you'll come to Washington Street. Turn left, and just before you come to the traffic lights at Prospect Street, go up the steps on your left.

❼ You now leave Brooklyn Heights across Brooklyn Bridge (▷ 68–69), on the wide wooden pedestrian walkway. In 1883 Brooklyn Bridge became the world's longest suspension bridge, spanning the East River and connecting Brooklyn to Manhattan. This spectacular bridge, with its web of steel cables, remains as much a marvel today as it did when it was first built.

When you reach the other side of the bridge you'll see the Brooklyn Bridge City Hall subway, from where you can access lines 4, 5, 6, J, M, Z.

WHEN TO GO
Any day of the week, morning or afternoon, but the walk across the bridge is especially romantic as the sun slowly sets behind Liberty Island and Lower Manhattan's city lights begin to twinkle.

WHERE TO EAT
Henry and Montague streets have a wide selection of cafés and restaurants.

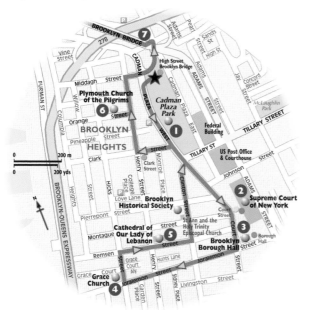

INFORMATION

www.ilovethebronx.com

ℹ The Bronx Tourism Council, The Bronx County Building, 851 Grand Concourse, Suite 123, Bronx ☎ 718/590-3518

WHAT TO SEE

BRONX MUSEUM OF THE ARTS

www.bronxmuseum.org

Founded in 1971, the museum maintains a permanent collection of 20th- and 21st-century works by artists of African, Asian and Latin American descent. The permanent collection of more than 800 works also includes artists for whom the Bronx has been a key component of their artistic development or practice. Exhibitions focus on contemporary and historical cultural issues related to the Bronx, and past exhibitions have featured African-American artist Romare Bearden and photography by Harlem-based Jamel Shabazz.

✉ 1040 Grand Concourse at 165th Street, Bronx ☎ 718/681-6000 🕐 Thu, Sat–Sun 11–6, Fri 11–8 🎟 Adult $5, child $3 🚇 167th Street/Grand Concourse (D, B)

BRONX ZOO

www.bronxzoo.com

The largest metropolitan wildlife park in the country, Bronx Zoo has more than 4,500 animals representing 55 species housed on 265 acres (107ha). This wonderful and hugely popular zoo has no fewer than three names—Bronx Zoo, New York Zoological Park and International Wildlife Conservation Park. The animals, including endangered and threatened species, are well cared for and their surroundings are as near as possible to native habitats.

One of the most impressive areas is the Wild Asia Complex, where you can see Indonesian tigers and Asian elephants, but only from the Wild Asia Monorail. JungleWorld's indoor re-creation of an Asian forest will envelop you,

Above *Bronx Zoo is a fantastic destination for a family day out*

and it's home to leopards, lizards, tree kangaroos and white-cheeked gibbons, among other exotic wildlife from jungles around the world. In the Himalayan Highlands there are rare snow leopards as well as red pandas.

The Congo Gorilla Forest is a 6.5-acre (2.6ha) re-creation of an African rainforest; among the treetop lookouts, wooded pathways and lush greenery are 400 animals, including western lowland gorillas, who can be entertaining. You'll also see okapi and red river hogs.

In the Butterfly Garden (Apr–end Oct) the size of some of the butterflies might surprise you, not to mention the enormous variety and beauty of these complicated insects.

The World of Darkness, as you might imagine, is devoted to the lives of nocturnal creatures, such as fruit-eating bats.

The Children's Zoo (Apr–end Oct) has wonderful activities—kids learn to see like an owl and hear like a fox—and a petting zoo.

The Wild Asia Monorail (late Apr–end Oct) is a 25-minute narrated ride above the roaming Siberian tigers, Indian rhinoceroses, Asian elephants, and other animals of the Indian subcontinent. It's a good way to see a lot without wearing yourself out. Other rides include the Skyfari aerial tram, camel rides and the Zoo Shuttle (Apr–early Nov).

In summer it can get crowded, and if it is a very warm day the animals retreat from open sunny positions and it can be hard to see some of them. If you are planning to visit for a day, you would be advised to eat early or late or bring a picnic and drinks. Lines for the food stands can be long and slow on a busy, hot afternoon.

✉ Bronx River Parkway and Fordham Road, Bronx, 10460 ☎ 718/367-1010 🕒 Apr–Oct Mon–Fri 10–5, Sat–Sun 10–5.30; rest of year daily 10–4.30 💲 Adult $16, child (3–12) $12, under 2 free; Wed suggested donation. Congo Gorilla Forest $5, Children's Zoo $4, Bug Carousel, Zoo Shuttle, Butterfly Zone $3 each. Camel rides $6 and monorail $4. Pay-One-Price ticket that includes admission and all rides except camel rides: adult $29.95, child $19.95 🚇 2 or 5 to Pelham Parkway or East Tremont Avenue 🚌 Liberty Lines Bx11 from Madison Avenue ☎ 718/445-3100 for details 🎫 Tours by Friends of the Zoo ☎ 718/ 220-5141 🍴 🛍 🏛

NEW YORK BOTANICAL GARDEN
www.nybg.org
One of the greatest botanical gardens in the world encompasses 250 acres (100ha) of beautiful landscape, gorgeous gardens and extensive collections of more than 1 million plants. There are 50 indoor and outdoor display gardens, a waterfall, wetlands and 50 acres (20ha) of virgin native forest as well as special programs exhibitions and a range of activities.

The Victorian-style Enid A. Haupt Conservatory glasshouse displays plants from around the world in 11 distinct habitats, including misty rainforests, exotic aquatics and spectacular deserts. In spring and fall the lovely, fragrant Peggy Rockefeller Rose Garden displays antique roses, hybrid teas, floribundas and shrub roses, while every summer the Daylily Garden showcases blooms in rainbow colors. The 12-acre (5ha) Everett Children's Adventure Garden offers the boulder maze for climbing, aquatic plant touch tank and an indoor laboratory with hands-on activities.

✉ Kazimiroff (Southern) Boulevard at 200th Street, Bronx ☎ 718/817-8700 🕒 Tue–Sun 10–6 💲 Prices vary with exhibitions. Grounds only adults $6, child (2–12) $1 🚇 Bedford Park Boulevard (B, D, 4) then walk, or take Bx26 bus 🚌 Bx19, Bx26 🚉 Botanical Garden Station (Metro North)

WAVE HILL
www.wavehill.org
The setting of this park in the Riverdale section of the Bronx is spectacular. This former private estate offers sweeping views of the Hudson River and the New Jersey cliffs as well as 28 delightful acres (11ha) of beautiful intimate

WHERE TO EAT
DOMINICK'S RESTAURANT
Family-style Italian meals are served in a fun, old-style noisy and casual restaurant with no menus. Just tell the waiter what you want for dinner, and listen for today's options. No reservations are accepted and there is almost always a line here. Many tables are communal, and payment is cash only.

✉ 2335 Arthur Avenue near 184th Street, Bronx ☎ 718/733-2807 🕒 Wed–Sun, 12–12 💲 D $45 🚇 182nd Street (B, D)

MARIO'S
www.mariosrestarthurave.com
Five generations of the Migliucci family have prepared food from scratch to order in this family casual eatery known for its authentic recipes. The Neapolitan pies are legendary; pizzas are crusty and bubbling hot, with fresh tomatoes, olive oil, basil and mozzarella cheese. The menu also includes excellent lamb, veal and pasta entrées.

✉ 2342 Arthur Avenue near 184th Street, Bronx ☎ 718/584-1188 🕒 Tue–Thu, Sun 12–9.30, Fri–Sat 12–10.30 💲 L $18, D $35 🚇 182nd Street (B, D)

SPORTS AND ACTIVITIES
BRONX EQUESTRIAN CENTER
www.bronxequestriancenter.com
Located near the lovely Pelham Bay Park, there's an opportunity at this equestrian center to go trail-riding through the woods or enjoy pony and hay wagon rides. ✉ 9 Shore Road, Bronx ☎ 718/885-0551 🕐 Daily 9–7 ✋ Lessons $40 per half-hour, trail rides from $35 per hour, $5 for three pony rides 🚇 Phone for directions

VAN CORTLANDT GOLF COURSE
www.golfnyc.com
The oldest public golf course in the US has been renovated under new management, with seven new greens. Eighteen holes, with clubhouse. ✉ Van Cortlandt Park South and Bailey Avenue, Bronx ☎ 718/543-4595 🕐 Dawn–dusk ✋ $18–$44 plus $8 for non-NY residents 🚇 242nd Street (1)

Below *The new Yankee Stadium, opened in 2009, was built to resemble the original 1923 structure*

gardens, a cultural center that stages art exhibitions, greenhouses full of plants from around the world, a herb garden and gracious wooded paths. On weekends, there's often an imaginative Family Art Project scheduled. ✉ 675 West 249th Street at Independence Avenue, Bronx ☎ 718/549-3200 🕐 Tue–Sun 9–5.30 (Oct 15–Apr 14 until 4.30) ✋ Adult $8, child $2, under 6 free (free Tue and mornings on Sat) 🚇 231st Street (1, 9), then Bx7 or Bx10 🚌 Bx7, Bx10 🚂 Riverdale (Metro North ☎ 212/532-4900)

YANKEE STADIUM
http://newyork.yankees.mlb.com
Yankee Stadium, America's first triple-decker stadium, was the home of the New York Yankees from April 18, 1923, until April 3, 2009, when the new Yankee Stadium, located next door, opened with a victory over the Cubs (7–4). The most famous player of them all, Babe Ruth, hit a three-run homer on that inaugural day in 1923 in front of 74,200 fans and the Yankees were victorious (4–1). After that, the stadium quickly became known as The House That Ruth Built. The stadium was first powered by electric lighting in 1946 and the first electronic message board was installed in 1959. After CBS became its new owner in 1967, the Yankees spent two seasons at Shea Stadium while their own stadium was renovated. Upon their return to Yankee Stadium, the Yankees went on to host the World Series.

The new stadium is designed to resemble the original Yankee Stadium and incorporates many features in honor of the Yankees' history. Groundbreaking ceremonies occurred on August 16, 2006, the 58th anniversary of Babe Ruth's death. The exterior closely resembles the original 1923 stadium, and the modern ballpark interior features a playing field very close in size to the former Yankee Stadium. The new stadium boasts the latest technology and the inside walls are decorated with hundreds of photographs that portray the history of the Yankees.

There are several main entrances, so make a mental note of where you enter to avoid confusion when you leave. Make sure that you have no reason to leave once you are inside, because you cannot re-enter the stadium using the same ticket. Arrive an hour and a half before the game Mondays to Fridays, two hours ahead on weekends to watch the batting practice. It can take some time to get through the entrance, so allow plenty of time to see the beginning of the game.

To get a behind-the-scenes tour it is best to buy advance tickets, but you can take a chance and go to the Advance Ticket window or any of the Clubhouse stores on the day of the tour. The tour covers Yankees' history and you can get a good look at the field, the dugout area, the press box, the Clubhouse and Monument Park.

Alcohol is sold up until the seventh inning of each game, but drunkenness is not tolerated; you can ask to sit in an alcohol-free section when you buy your tickets. Other rules ban bottles, cans, coolers or containers, large bags and briefcases, noisemakers, laser pens, beachballs, firearms and knives; and there's no smoking.

✉ 161st Street and River Avenue, Bronx, 10451 ☎ 718/293-6000 🕓 Baseball season Apr–Oct ✋ Tickets for games $15–$325 ☎ Ticketmaster 212/307-1212 or visit http://newyork.yankees. mlb.com 🚇 4, B, D 🚌 Bx6, Bx13, Bx55 ☞ 45-min behind-the-scenes tour: visit the website to purchase advanced tickets, or buy tickets from Ticketmaster or any Clubhouse store. Tours daily 12–1.40, except when the Yankees play at home. Adult $20 🍴 🛒 Upscale NYY Steak is open till 11pm daily; snacks and drinks throughout the stadium 🏬 Three gift shops and an art gallery. The largest selection of Yankee merchandise is at the Home Plate Store in the Great Hall. Yankee Clubhouse stores have five Manhattan locations; get the location details and opening hours from the website

VAN CORTLANDT PARK

The Caribbean communities brought cricket to New York City, and this is the best place to find a cricket game in progress.

✉ Van Cortlandt Park, Park South and Bailey Avenue 🕓 Dawn–dusk in summer ✋ Free 🚇 242nd Street (1)

YONKERS RACEWAY

www.yonkersraceway.com

One of the premier harness racing tracks in the nation is in the city, just north of the Bronx. The track celebrated its centennial in 1999. The most illustrious race run here is the Night of Champions, with a $1.2 million purse.

✉ 810 Yonkers Avenue, Yonkers ☎ 914/968-4200 🕓 Mon–Tue, Thu–Sat, 7.10pm post time ✋ $2.25–$4.25 🚇 Woodlawn (4) and Beeline 20 bus

Above *Yonkers Raceway is one of the United States' premier harness racing tracks*

INFORMATION

www.metmuseum.org

✉ 99 Margaret Corbin Drive, Fort Tryon Park, 10040 ☎ 212/923-3700 🕐 Mar–Oct Tue–Sun 9.30–5.15; rest of year Tue–Sun 9.30–4.45 ✋ Adult $25, under 12 free. Ticket includes same-day admission to the Metropolitan Museum of Art 🚇 A 🚌 M4 🍴 The Trie Café on the lower level in the Trie Cloister; May–Oct Tue–Sun 10–4.15 🎧 Free guided tours Tue–Fri and Sun 3pm; audioguide adult $7, under 12 $5 ♿

TIPS

» Take the subway ride if you are in a hurry. Get off at 190th Street and take the elevator to street level. Enter Fort Tryon Park and walk up the Promenade to the Cloisters.

» In summer there is a direct bus from the Metropolitan Museum of Art—more expensive than public transportation but quicker.

Above *Designed in the style of a fortified monastery, the Cloisters commands stunning views over the Hudson River*

INTRODUCTION

Perched high above the Hudson River, the Cloisters is in delightful Fort Tryon Park in Washington Heights, at the northern tip of Manhattan, with spectacular views across the river to the steep rock-faced cliffs known as the Palisades. The Cloisters opened in 1938 as a branch of the Metropolitan Museum of Art and is devoted to the art and architecture of medieval Europe. The building includes large sections transported from five 12th- to 15th-century cloisters in southern France and Spain.

WHAT TO SEE

THE COLLECTION

The collection is based on medieval sculptures and segments of architecture acquired by American sculptor George Grey Barnard during trips to Europe, and includes 5,000 sculptures, tapestries, illuminated manuscripts, paintings, stained glass and other priceless objects. He brought them to New York and exhibited them in a brick building on Fort Washington Avenue. In 1925, John D. Rockefeller donated a large sum of money to the Met to purchase the Barnard collection. Then in 1930, Rockefeller gave his Fort Tryon estate to the Met, stipulating that the Cloisters be built to house a medieval collection.

HIGHLIGHTS OF THE COLLECTION

On the main floor is the Fuentidueña Chapel, whose 1160 apse comes from the Church of San Martín in Castile, Spain. The capital on the right side depicts Daniel in the Lions' Den, while the one on the left shows the Adoration of the Magi. The Virgin and Child fresco in the semidome came from a small Catalan church in the Pyrenees. The Romanesque doorway in the nave of the chapel was carved in about 1175 in Tuscany. Also on this floor is the Saint-Guilhem Cloister, whose imposing covered walkway is from a Benedictine abbey near Montpellier, France. The columns have intricately carved capitals and date from the 12th to 13th centuries. In the center of the main floor is the Cuxa Cloister, from a Benedictine monastery near Prades, France. The cloister was abandoned during the French Revolution and was later sold off in parts. Barnard managed to collect about half the original capitals, 25 bases and 12 columns. In the Nine Heroes Tapestries Room are some of the oldest surviving tapestries from a set dating from 1385.

FORT TRYON PARK WALK

Go to Fort Tryon Park for fresh air, a walk in the woods, spectacular views of the Hudson River from Manhattan's highest natural point, gardens and a medieval-style monastery.

THE WALK

Distance: 1.5 miles (2.4km)
Time: 1.5 to 2 hours
Start/End at: Margaret Corbin Circle at 190th Street subway station

HOW TO GET THERE

Subway A to 190th Street or bus M4 to 190th Street.

① One of the earliest battles of the American Revolutionary War was fought here on November 16, 1776. General George Washington's troops lost to the British, who named the fort for colonial governor, Sir William Tryon. Frederick Law Olmsted, Jr. designed the 62-acre (25ha) gardens to recall medieval Europe, using stone walls, arches and terraces. Margaret Corbin Circle is named for a woman who fought in the Fort Tryon battle. On the west side of the circle stands the gatehouse for the Billings estate. Cornelius K. G. Billings spent more than $2 million building Tryon Hill mansion between 1901 and 1905.

Make your way through the huge stone gateway ahead and onto the Promenade. Turn immediately to your left onto this walkway.

② The 3-acre (1.2ha) Heather Garden enjoys a breathtaking view across the Hudson River to New Jersey's Palisades and the George Washington Bridge. With its many heathers, brooms, perennials and shrubs, this garden is one of the largest heather gardens on the east coast. By May, 5,000 bulbs are in full bloom, with more than 30 varieties of daffodils and tulips; 1,000 lilies are in flower from June to September.

From the Heather Garden, return to the Promenade and follow it to Linden Terrace.

③ In 1909, Billings erected a stela in Linden Terrace as a memorial to the Continental Army's defense of the site. There are benches, parapets and splendid river views. At the northeast corner, a flight of steps leads to a flagpole on the highest natural point in Manhattan.

Return down the steps to the Promenade, which veers to the left and down some stone steps. At the bottom of the steps continue along the path to your right.

④ You can see the Cloisters straight ahead to the north. Stroll northward with the river on your left and, if you wish to have a quick look inside the museum, cross the road at the crosswalk (pedestrian crossing) on your right and go straight ahead.

Continue north on the path you left to visit the Cloisters and stroll through the woods and lawns. If you stay on the path closest to Margaret Corbin Drive you'll come to the New Leaf Café (tel 212/568-5323; Tue–Sun), an enterprise of actress Bette Midler's New York Restoration Project.

⑤ The café's stunning location, good food and affordable prices, make it a pleasant rest stop. Proceeds support work in the park.

The path from the café leads back to the park's main entrance.

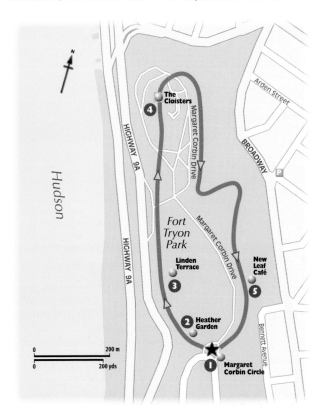

EXCURSIONS | WALK

INFORMATION
HISTORIC HUDSON VALLEY
www.hudsonvalley.org
☎ 914/631-8200

HOW TO GET THERE
🚊 Most of the valley north of New York City is easily visited by train. From Grand Central Terminal, take the Metro-North Hudson Line to the closest station; local taxis meet trains at most stations, or you can book one through Rivertowns Taxi (tel 914/478-2222)

🚗 Follow the West Side Highway to the Henry Hudson Parkway and then the Saw Mill River Parkway (all one road, really, but with three different names). It's best to get specific directions from the Saw Mill by phoning each sight

🚢 The New York Waterway offers day-long excursions (late Oct–Nov only) up the Hudson River, leaving from Pier 78 on Manhattan's west side (tel 1800/533-3779, www.nywaterway.com)

INTRODUCTION
The Hudson River flows 315 miles (507km) from the Adirondack Mountains to New York and out into the Atlantic. The splendor of the valley can be seen in 19th-century paintings by the Hudson River School artists—the area is lovely, especially in the fall, when the colorful foliage brightens the shoreline.

WHAT TO SEE
HUDSON RIVER MUSEUM
The Hudson River Museum (511 Warburton Avenue, Yonkers, tel 914/963-4550; Wed–Sun noon–5) is built around a historic house and a modern addition. Collections encompass art and history, and there's a planetarium. At the Museum Café, you can have a light lunch with splendid views of the Hudson River and the Palisades in New Jersey. Take Metro-North to Yonkers, then grab a cab (about $6).

SUNNYSIDE TO LYNDHURST
Sunnyside, a National Historic Landmark, was the home of Washington Irving, who wrote *The Legend of Sleepy Hollow* and was America's first internationally known author. The cottage (tel 914/631-8200; Apr–Oct Wed–Mon 10–5; Nov–Dec Sat–Sun 10–4) was built in the 18th century and enlarged by Irving in 1835. Guided tours of the house and grounds are available up to one hour before closing time. There is a visitor center, shop and seasonal café. From Grand Central Terminal, catch a train to Tarrytown, where taxis wait.

Lyndhurst, a spectacular Gothic Revival-style mansion (tel 914/631-4481; mid-Apr to Oct Tue–Sun 10–5; rest of year Sat–Sun 10–4), was the home of railroad tycoon Jay Gould. The surrounding lawns have amazing Hudson River views. To get to Sunnyside, you can call a cab, or walk on the footpath.

PHILLIPSBURG MANOR AND KYKUIT
Phillipsburg Manor, on Route 9 in Sleepy Hollow, is a restored colonial farm once owned by the Phillips family (tel 914/631-3992; Apr–Oct Wed–Mon 10–5; Nov–Dec Sat–Sun 10–4). Guided tours are available and buildings are staffed by interpreters in costume who explain early Hudson River Valley life.

Kykuit is a National Trust Historic Site that was home to four generations of the wealthy Rockefeller family. The sumptuous mansion is filled with priceless antiques and works of art, and sculptures fill the landscaped

Above *Wisteria adorns the east facade of Kykuit, the Rockefeller family home*

gardens. Guided tours (early May to early Nov Wed–Mon 10–3) begin at Phillipsburg Manor; tickets go on sale at 9am and are issued on a first-come, first-served basis (children under 10 are not admitted).

VAN CORTLANDT MANOR
This 18th-century Hudson Valley mansion belonged to the Van Cortlandt family for more than 260 years. Pierre Van Cortlandt was the first lieutenant-governor of New York State. The house has original furnishings, and the kitchen is a highlight with its original hearth and beehive oven (tel 914/271-8981; Memorial Day–Labor Day Thu–Sun 10–5, Nov–Dec Sat–Sun 10–4).

WEST POINT, FRANKLIN D. ROOSEVELT NATIONAL HISTORIC SITE TO VANDERBILT MANSION
Farther upstate, there are several other landmarks on the eastern banks of the Hudson, most notably West Point Military Academy. Nearby is Cold Spring, a charming riverfront town known for its antiques shops and garrison, home to another 19th-century mansion **Boscobel** (tel 845/265-3638). Beacon is a riverfront town that is being revived with the help of DIA Arts. Farther north are two sites associated with the Roosevelts. The best way to visit is by car.

The United States Military Academy at **West Point** (tel 845/938-2638) has turned out great generals, presidents and astronauts. The museum has guns, uniforms, medals and flags from conflicts, and the grounds are beautiful.

Franklin D. Roosevelt National Historic Site (tel 845/229-5320; daily 9–5) was the president's birthplace. The house, library and museum have a collection of family memorabilia. Franklin and his formidable wife, Eleanor, are buried in the rose garden; a marble monument marks their graves.

From this point a shuttle bus will take you to the **Eleanor Roosevelt National Historic Site** (daily 9–5) in the grounds of the Roosevelt estate.

Vanderbilt Mansion (tel 845/229-7770; daily 9–5, visit by guided tour only), 2 miles (3.2km) north of the Roosevelt Historic Site, is the lavish Beaux Arts mansion of the grandson of railroad magnate Cornelius Vanderbilt. Inside you will see Renaissance to rococo furniture and works of art. The gardens are exquisite, and there are several walking trails that skirt the river.

WHERE TO EAT
In Tarrytown there are three good places to find something to eat: Equus Restaurant, The Castle (914/631-3646); Horsefeathers, 94 North Broadway (914/631-6606); and Striped Bass, 236 Main Street (914/366-4455).

NATIONAL PARK SERVICE
☎ 845/229-9115

NATIONAL TRUST FOR HISTORIC PRESERVATION
☎ 914/631-4481

Below *Portrait of John D. Rockefeller (1917) by John Singer Sargent, flanked by Meissen birds of prey in the dining room of Kykuit*

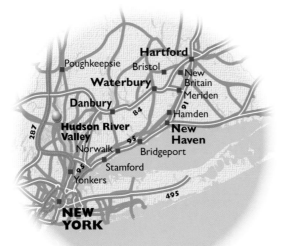

INFORMATION

www.discoverlongisland.com

i Long Island Convention & Visitors Bureau and Sports Commission

☎ 877/386-6654

HOW TO GET THERE

🚆 Go to Pennsylvania Station on Seventh Avenue between 31st and 33rd streets. From here catch a Long Island Railroad train to the town nearest the place of interest

🚌 From New York, travel from Manhattan east on the Long Island Expressway (I-495). Buses and trains are often a better way to get to Long Island, but you usually need a car to get around the various sights, so it's best to take your own wheels

Above Steps leading to the South Terrace of the Charles II-style Westbury House in Old Westbury Gardens

INTRODUCTION

Long Island is 125 miles (201km) long and between 12 and 23 miles (19 and 37km) wide. It lies east of New York City and is washed by the Atlantic Ocean on the south and Long Island Sound on the north. The rocky northern shoreline, scalloped with beaches, coves and bluffs, and sometimes called the Gold Coast, has attracted the affluent since the late 19th century. The Hamptons, at the east of the island, on the Atlantic shore, has become the playground of wealthy families, who have built fine summer houses and mansions. The delightful Atlantic-pounded beaches along the southern shore offer an escape from city heat in summer. The western part of the island, which consists of the Manhattan boroughs of Brooklyn and Queens, is densely populated, but the farther east you go, the more rural it becomes. Here are historic homes, fishing ports, whaling towns, museums and parks.

WHAT TO SEE

OLD WESTBURY GARDENS AND SAGAMORE HILL HISTORIC SITE

Old Westbury Gardens (tel 516/333-0048) was the home of financier John S. Phipps (1874–1958), his wife Margarita and their four children. The Charles II-style manor house is furnished with English antiques and decorative arts. The surrounding 160 acres (65ha), with 88 breathtaking acres (36ha) of formal gardens, walkways, architectural follies and woodlands, are dotted with ponds and lakes. The gardens are between the Long Island Expressway and Jericho Turnpike (Route 25). By car, take Exit 39 (Glen Cove Road) off the I-495. Follow the service road east for 1 mile (1.6km), turn right on Old Westbury Road and continue for half a mile.

Sagamore Hill National Historic Site is northeast of Old Westbury, the home of President Theodore Roosevelt from 1885 until his death in 1919. The house is furnished as it was when he lived here (tel 516/922-4788; Memorial Day–Labor Day daily 10–4; rest of year Wed–Sun). Tours last half an hour and are on a first-come, first-served basis. They are limited in size, so arrive early if possible (by noon in summer they are often sold out). To get there by car, take Exit 41N (Oyster Bay) off I-495 onto Route 106 North. Travel for 4 miles (6km) to Route 25A, where you will turn right and travel 2.5 miles (4km) to the third traffic light. At the bottom of a long hill, turn left onto Cove Road and continue for 1.5 miles (2.4km). Turn right onto Cove Neck Road for 1.5 miles (2.4km).

WALT WHITMAN BIRTHPLACE TO OLD BETHPAGE VILLAGE

Walt Whitman (1819–92) was one of America's finest poets and essayists. At his birthplace (tel 631/427-5240; Jun 15–Labor Day Mon–Fri 11–4, Sat–Sun 11–5; rest of year Wed–Fri 1–4, Sat–Sun 11–4), south of Sagamore Hill, you will see Whitman memorabilia, including photographs and excerpts from his writings and letters. To get there from I-495, take Exit 49N onto Route 110 North. Turn left onto Walt Whitman Road in Huntington Station. As the site is very popular with school groups, you may want to phone ahead.

Old Bethpage Village (tel 516/572-8400; Apr–Oct Wed–Sat 10–4, Sun 11–5; Nov–Dec Wed–Sun 10–4) is an area of shops, farms, a one-room school-house, a church, gardens and homes filled with antiques, staffed by costumed interpreters explaining about life on Long Island in the 19th century. Special events are lively and fun.

Above *A pergola lies at the end of a pretty avenue in the Walled Garden of Old Westbury Gardens*

INFORMATION

www.discoverqueens.info

ℹ Queens Visitor's Center, Queens
Center Mall, 90-15 Queens Boulevard,
Elmhurst, 11373 ☎ 718/592-2082

US OPEN TENNIS CHAMPIONSHIP

www.usopen.org

www.usta.com

This two-week tournament is
one of four in the sport's Grand
Slam. Tickets to any session
admit you to matches played
in Arthur Ashe stadium, and to
other courts. You can see more
tennis if you buy daytime tickets,
since many of the outer courts
are not used at night. Tickets go
on sale at the end of April; most
are sold via subscription or priced
in the stratosphere—but for day
sessions most of the action is on
outer courts.

✉ USTA National Tennis Center,
Flushing Meadows–Corona Park, Queens
☎ 718/760-6200 or 516/354-2590
🕓 Late Aug–end Sep 🚇 Willets Point/
Citi Field Stadium (7) 🚆 LIRR to Citi Field
Stadium

WHAT TO SEE

MUSEUM OF THE MOVING IMAGE

www.movingimage.us

Dedicated to the art, history, technique and technology of motion pictures,
video and television, this fascinating museum doubled in size in 2009.
The main exhibit, *Behind the Screen,* illustrates the processes involved in
producing and exhibiting moving images, using more than 1,000 artifacts,
interactive experiences and demonstrations. There are also exhibits featuring
movie stars' wardrobes, memorabilia and special effects. Interactive exhibits
offer the opportunity to dub your voice, or add sound effects, into a movie.

✉ 35th Avenue at 36th Street, Astoria, Queens ☎ 718/777-6888 🕓 Tue–Thu 10.30–5, Fri
10.30–8, Sat–Sun 10.30–7 ✋ Adult $10, child (3–18) $5 🚇 36th Avenue at 31st Street (N)

NEW YORK HALL OF SCIENCE

www.nysci.org

This museum was one of the first hands-on science museums in the US.
The entire basement is filled with interactive exhibits. Permanent exhibits
demonstrate biology, chemistry and physics, and special shows explore such
topics as Optical Illusions. There's also a large outdoor science playground.

✉ 47-01 111th Street at 48th Avenue, Flushing Meadows–Corona Park, Queens ☎ 718/699-
0005 🕓 Jul–Aug and hol weekends Mon–Fri 9.30–5, Sat–Sun 10–6; Apr–Jun Mon–Thu 9.30–2,
Fri 9.30–5, Sat–Sun 10–6; Sep–Mar Tue–Thu 9.30–2, Fri 9.30–5, Sat–Sun 10–6 ✋ Adult $11,
child (2–17) $8 (free Sep–Jun Fri 2–5, Sun 10–11) 🚇 111th Street (7) 🚌 Q23, Q48

NOGUCHI MUSEUM

www.noguchi.org

Sculpture in clay, metal, stone and wood by noted 20th-century artist Isamu
Noguchi are displayed in 13 galleries along with his *Akari Light Sculptures,*
and a garden displays some of his major granite and basalt works. Housed

in a renovated photo engraving plant, the museum offers public programs to provide an in-depth look at Noguchi's work.

✉ 9-01 33rd Road at Vernon Boulevard, Long Island City, Queens ☎ 718/204-7088 🕐 Wed–Fri 10–5, Sat–Sun 11–6 ✋ Adult $10, child (under 12) free 🚇 Broadway (N)

P.S.1 CONTEMPORARY ART CENTER
www.ps1.org
Dedicated to cutting-edge contemporary art, the museum offers 50 original exhibitions each year, including the prestigious International and National Projects series. The museum's exhibitions showcase emerging artists from throughout the world. P.S.1 Contemporary Art Center has been affiliated with the Museum of Modern Art (▷ 162–163) since the millennium, working together to promote the enjoyment and appreciation of contemporary art. *Warm Up,* the museum's summer music series, is one of New York's favorite summer venues. Performances are held in or near the winning entry of the museum's annual Young Architects Program.

✉ 22–25 Jackson Avenue at the intersection of 46th Avenue, Long Island City, Queens ☎ 718/784-2084 🕐 Thu–Mon 12–6 ✋ $10 donation 🚇 45th Road/Courthouse Square (7)

BELMONT PARK
www.nyra.com
This beautiful 430-acre (174ha) racecourse is the largest in North America. In June, it hosts the Belmont Stakes, the third leg of the Triple Crown.

✉ 2150 Hempstead Turnpike and Plainfield Avenue, Belmont, Queens ☎ 516/488-6000 🕐 May–Jul, Sep–Oct Wed–Sun, 1pm post time ✋ $3–$5 🚆 Long Island Railroad's Pony Express from Penn Station

MORE TO SEE
NEW YORK METS
www.mets.com
When the Brooklyn Dodgers left New York in 1957, the Mets in effect replaced them. Even though they haven't won a championship since 1986 and often finish at or near the bottom of their league, they continue to draw fans to their games. You can usually obtain tickets unless they're playing local rivals the Yankees or the Boston Red Sox. The Citi Field stadium, right underneath the landing approach path to LaGuardia airport, is noisy.

✉ Citi Field, Flushing Meadows–Corona Park, Queens ☎ 718/507-8499 ✋ $8–$60 🚇 Willets Point/Citi Field Stadium (7) 🚢 On Sat–Sun only: New York Waterway (tel 800/533-3779) operates from the South Street Seaport, East 34th Street or East 90th Street for $18 round trip. Reservations recommended

WHERE TO EAT
CHRISTOS STEAK HOUSE
www.christossteakhouse.com
Prime aged steaks, fresh seafood and savory Greek dishes come together in this casual restaurant with indoor and outdoor seating. The steaks are prepared to perfection in classic American steakhouse style, while the salads, sides, appetizers and desserts are influenced by traditional Greek cuisine.

✉ 4108 23rd Avenue, Queens ☎ 718/777-8400 🕐 Mon–Sat 4–12, Sun 3–12 ✋ D $60 🚇 Astoria Boulevard West (B, Q, E)

LA FLOR BAKERY & CAFÉ
Small and charming, this Mexican-fusion café serves good food and exceptional bakery to long lines of hungry folks. Dinner specialties such as grilled snapper with julienne vegetables are offered alongside traditional Mexican favorites like mole enchiladas. Save room for dessert, and pay in cash.

✉ 53-02 Roosevelt Avenue at 53rd Street, Woodside, Queens ☎ 718/426-8023 🕐 Daily 9am–10pm ✋ L $15, D $30 🚇 52nd Street (7)

Opposite *The New York Mets playing the Colorado Rockies at Citi Field*
Below *The P.S.1 Contemporary Art Center*

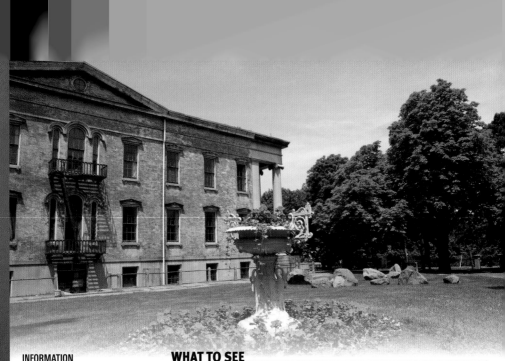

INFORMATION

www.visitstatenisland.com

🔋 SINY Inc., 1110 South Avenue, Suite 57, Staten Island, 10314

☎ 347/273-1257

WHAT TO SEE

ALICE AUSTEN HOUSE

www.aliceausten.org

This unique museum is the Victorian house and garden of Alice Austen (1866–1952), one of America's early female documentary photographers. A visit here is fascinating for the quality of Austen's photographs, but also for the idea it gives of what middle-class life was like at the turn of the 20th century. The house was declared a city landmark in 1971.

The photographs give you a glimpse into the world of a well-traveled young woman, who taught herself to operate the camera, develop heavy glass plates and make prints. Alice took her equipment with her everywhere, despite it weighing as much as 50 pounds (23kg), and photographed the world around her, including New York street scenes, using visual satire to create the effect.

Exhibitions and events take place throughout most of the year and often feature works by other local artists. Take the Staten Island Ferry from Manhattan, then catch the S51 bus to Hylan Boulevard.

✉ 2 Hylan Boulevard, Staten Island, 10305 ☎ 718/816-4506 🕐 Mar–Dec Thu–Sun 12–5 ✋ Adult $2, child free 🚢 Staten Island Ferry 🚌 S51 to Hylan Boulevard ♿

CONFERENCE HOUSE

www.conferencehouse.org

Originally called the Billop Manor House, Conference House was built around 1680. On September 11, 1776, Benjamin Franklin, John Adams and Edward Rutledge (a South Carolina governor and signatory to the Declaration of Independence) came here for a meeting with Admiral Lord Howe, the Commander of Her Majesty's Atlantic Squadron. Howe hoped to persuade the colonists to give up their fight for independence, but the visitors made it clear that they were not interested in his offer.

The two-and-a-half-story house has furnished period rooms and offers a look at life in colonial America. Special events take place throughout the year.

✉ 7455 Hylan Boulevard, Staten Island, 10307 ☎ 718/984-0415 🕐 Apr to mid-Dec Fri–Sun 1–4, guided tours only ✋ Adult $3, child $2 🚢 Staten Island Ferry 🚌 S78 to Craig Avenue

Above *Snug Harbor Cultural Center*

GARIBALDI MEUCCI MUSEUM

www.garibaldimeuccimuseum.org

The Italian national hero, and one of the founders of unified Italy, Giuseppe Garibaldi (1807–82) spent two years in this 1840s' house after fleeing the conquering republicans in Italy. It was the home of one Antonio Meucci (1808–89), who in fact was the inventor of the telephone. He invented a prototype several years before Alexander Graham Bell got into the picture, but, as he failed to patent his idea, he never got the credit.

After Garibaldi's death, in 1884 a committee decided to commemorate his stay in Staten Island and a plaque was placed on the house. After Meucci's death, the house was given to the Italian community to preserve as a memorial to Garibaldi.

Today the house is owned and operated by The Order of Sons of Italy in America and displays artifacts about the lives of these two men.

✉ 420 Tompkins Avenue, 10305 ☎ 718/442-1608 🕐 Wed–Sun 1–5 ✋ Adult $5 ⛴ Staten Island Ferry 🚌 S52, S78

HISTORIC RICHMOND TOWN

www.historicrichmondtown.org

About 15 historic buildings are spread out over 100 acres (40ha) at this museum complex. It stretches across three centuries of daily life and culture on Staten Island, from its earliest days as a rural crossroad to its incorporation into Greater New York. The quaint atmosphere and helpful staff make the whole experience a pleasurable day out. Special events take place throughout the year, including summer fairs, concerts and costumed re-enactments.

✉ 441 Clarke Avenue, Staten Island, 10306 ☎ 718/351-1611 🕐 Wed–Sun 1–5 ✋ Adult $5, child (5–17) $3.50, under 5 free ⛴ Staten Island Ferry 🚌 S74 🎫 Guided tours Wed–Fri 2.30, Sat–Sun 2 and 3.30 🍴

JACQUES MARCHAIS MUSEUM OF TIBETAN ART

www.tibetanmuseum.org

This lovely museum is one of New York's best-kept secrets. The Dalai Lama, when he visited in 1991, attested to the likeness of the stone cottage on Lighthouse Hill to a Tibetan mountain temple, with its peaceful terraced sculpture gardens and an attractive fish pond. The museum exhibits Tibetan, Nepalese and Mongolian art from the 17th to the 19th centuries. The Nepalese metalwork, encrusted with jewels, and the metal figures of deities and lamas, are exquisite. Informative explanations help you understand the significance of the jewelry, dance masks, ritual objects, incense burners, paintings and many other items from the world's Buddhist cultures. Special exhibitions and activities enhance a visit.

✉ 338 Lighthouse Avenue, Staten Island, 10306 ☎ 718/987-3500 🕐 Wed–Sun 1–5 ✋ Adult $6, child under 6 free ⛴ Staten Island Ferry 🚌 S74 to Lighthouse Avenue 🏛

SNUG HARBOR CULTURAL CENTER

www.snug-harbor.org

Snug Harbor, a National Historic Landmark District, spreads out over 83 acres (34ha). Its 26 buildings, a fine collection of Greek Revival, Beaux Arts, Italianate and Victorian architecture, housed "decrepit and worn-out" old sailors during the 1880s. By the 1960s, the buildings had fallen into disrepair. After a vast restoration project, however, they are now a focal point of Staten Island cultural life, with art exhibitions in the Newhouse Galleries (Wed–Sun) and other activities. Be sure to see the Main Hall (Wed–Sun), the oldest building, and its lavish ceiling mural, skylight dome and gilded weathervane.

✉ 1000 Richmond Terrace, Staten Island, 10301 ☎ 718/448-2500 🕐 Grounds daily dawn–dusk. Gallery Museum: Wed–Sun 12–5 ✋ Gallery adult $5, child (under 12) $3. Grounds: free ⛴ Staten Island Ferry 🚌 S40 🎫 🚻 🏛

SPORTS AND ACTIVITIES
STATEN ISLAND YANKEES

www.siyanks.com

This minor-league team plays in a stadium overlooking the harbor. It's fun to take the trip on the Staten Island Ferry.

✉ Richmond County Bank Ballpark at St. George ☎ 718/720-9265 or 718/720-9200 🎫 $15–$35 🚇 South Ferry (1) to Staten Island Ferry ⛴ Staten Island Ferry

New York offers more tours than any city in the world. There are walking tours, bicycle tours, harbor tours, art and theater tours, behind-the-scenes tours, bus tours, limo tours, train tours, multilingual tours and special-interest tours such as ethnic, food and shopping tours. The list of tour operators below is a small sample of what's available.

BICYCLE TOURS
CENTRAL PARK BICYCLE TOURS
www.centralparkbiketours.com
Rent a bicycle and ride around Central Park with a knowledgeable guide for two hours. Tours Monday to Friday at 10am, 1pm and 4pm.
✉ 203 West 58th Street ☎ 212/541-8759 ✋ Adult $49, child (under 18) $40. Rental only: $20 for 2 hours, $30 for 3 hours, $40 all day

BUS TOURS
ON LOCATION TOURS
www.screentours.com
Coaches depart from different locations and reservations are recommended. New York TV Tour is a 3 to 3.5-hour tour to 40 locations; the *Sex and the City* Tour and the *Sopranos* Tour are 4 hours each.
☎ 212/209-3370 ✋ New York TV tour: adult $38, plus $2 ticket fee. *Sex and the City* tour: $42. *Sopranos* tour: $44

A SLICE OF BROOKLYN TOURS
www.asliceofbrooklyn.com
These 4.5-hour bus tours are led by a New York native. There are several tours, but the most popular is the Pizza Tour which includes top Brooklyn attractions like the Brooklyn Bridge, Fulton Navy Yard and Coney Island. You'll visit film locations for *Saturday Night Fever* and *The French Connection*. Best of all, there are two stops for pizza (with no waiting in line): Grimaldi's for a Neapolitan and L&B Spumoni Gardens for a Brooklyn Sicilian.
☎ 212/209-3370 ✋ Adult $75, child (under 12) $65 (includes pizza and soft drinks). Advance tickets required

HELICOPTER TOURS
Helicopters leave from the Downtown Manhattan Heliport at Pier 6 and South Street and from the VIP Heliport at West 30th Street.

LIBERTY HELICOPTER TOURS
www.libertyhelicopters.com
Fly over Manhattan's skyscrapers, New York Harbor and the five boroughs.
☎ 212/967-2099 ✋ $150, 12–15 min; $215, 16–20 min; $995, 18–20 min VIP tour

RIVER TOURS
CIRCLE LINE
www.circleline42.com
Cruises from the Circle Line (Pier 83 at West 42nd Street/12th Avenue or Pier 16, South Street Seaport at Fulton Street and East River) are worth every penny. Take the 3-hour Full Island cruise, the 2-hour Semi-Circle cruise, 2-hour Harbor Lights sunset cruise, 75-minute Liberty cruise, or a combination of packages. Combos are more expensive. Cruises with live music (adults only) operate from May to September. In spring and fall it's at least 10 degrees colder on the water—more when you consider wind chill in a moving boat.
☎ 212/563-3200 ✋ Adult $27–$36, child under 12 $19–$23. Music cruises $35–$50

WALKING TOURS
Here are a few that are highly recommended. Call ahead for up-to-date schedules.

BIG APPLE GREETER
www.bigapplegreeter.org
Big Apple Greeter is a free public service. The greeters—volunteer New Yorkers—are matched with visitors according to languages spoken and areas of interest. Give at least a month's advance notice (longer during peak season).
☎ 212/669-8159 ✋ Voluntary donations

BIG ONION WALKING TOURS
www.bigonion.com
Guides for these 2-hour tours have degrees in American history.
☎ 212/439-1090 ③ Daily, times vary ✋ Adult $18, child $15

GRAND CENTRAL PARTNERSHIP
www.grandcentralpartnership.org
Show up in the sculpture court at 120 Park Avenue, on the southwest corner of East 42nd Street and Park Avenue, for free tours of Grand Central Terminal.
☎ 212/883-2420 ③ Fri 12.30

NEW YORK LIKE A NATIVE TOURS
www.nylikeanative.com
These fast-paced walking tours are designed for energetic folks who are willing to hop aboard public transportation along the walk. Learn more about Brooklyn than an average tourist tour provides.
☎ 718/393-7537 ✋ $15–$20

THEMED WALKING TOURS
MUNICIPAL ARTS SOCIETY
www.mas.org/tours
Architects, historians and writers guide tours of sites including Grand Central Terminal and Ground Zero.
☎ 212/439-1049 ✋ Adult $10–$15

NEW YORK GALLERY TOURS
www.nygallerytours.com
Tour 10 modern art galleries in 2 hours in Chelsea and SoHo.
☎ 212/946-1548 ✋ Adult $20

PATRIOT TOURS
www.patriottoursnyc.com
Historical walking tours of Lower Manhattan specialize in the Civil War and Revolutionary War eras.
☎ 917/716-4908 ✋ Adult $19–$23

PRACTICALITIES

Practicalities gives you all the important practical information you will need during your visit from money matters to emergency phone numbers.

WEATHER

New York City is in the northeast United States. Four of the five boroughs that comprise New York City are islands. Manhattan, the most populous, is bordered on the east by the East River and on the west by the Hudson River. The narrow Harlem River separates it from the Bronx to the north, and Long Island Sound separates it from Long Island to the south. The city has a waterfront of 580 miles (930km). The surrounding landscape is flat, although the highest point, at Todt Hill on Staten Island, is the highest point on the Atlantic coast south of Maine at 409ft (125m).

During the Ice Age, most of New York State was covered by glaciers, with southern Long Island and Staten Island being the exceptions. The movement of the glaciers produced nine physiographic regions. The four seasons are very distinct in this region, and New Yorkers endure, without too many complaints, the cold, damp winters and hot, humid summers.

NEW YORK
TEMPERATURE

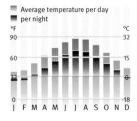

Average temperature per day
per night

RAINFALL

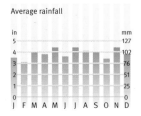

Average rainfall

WEATHER REPORTS

» Radio and television news end with a weather report and a short-range forecast (▷ 283).

» Visit www.weather.com, the Weather Channel's 10-day forecast.

» Visit www.cnn.com/weather for CNN's eight-day forecast and satellite pictures.

DAYLIGHT HOURS

Be aware of the number of daylight hours you have when planning your days out. There are some areas, away from central tourist areas, that are best avoided after dark.

TEMPERATURE

Below are average daily maximum and minimum temperatures for New York City. Precipitation in December, January, February and March can fall as snow.

WINTER

The city's average annual snowfall is 29.2 inches (74cm), most of it falling in January and February. However, even after heavy snowfall, plows quickly remove the snow and disruptions are minimal. The strong winds, more pronounced as you approach the East or Hudson rivers, make it feel colder than it really is.

SUMMER

In July and August, the hottest months, humidity can be as high as 90 percent, and the sun can be fierce. Avoid these months if you suffer from the heat. If you do decide to visit then, make sure to wear sunscreen during the day both in the city and at the beaches.

THE BEST TIME TO VISIT

The most pleasant time to visit, and therefore peak season, is May to early June and September to mid-November. From May to early June, the days are comfortable and the evenings cool; showers are always a possibility. From September to late October, days are still warm but evenings start getting cooler. The leaves change to gold and red in mid- to late October, pretty but less spectacular than New England. By November, days are much cooler and there is more rain and wind.

TIME ZONES

New York is on Eastern Standard Time, five hours behind GMT. Daylight Saving Time, four hours behind GMT, is from early March to November 1.

TIME ZONES

CITY	TIME DIFFERENCE	TIME AT NOON IN NEW YORK
Amsterdam	+6	6pm
Berlin	+6	6pm
Brussels	+6	6pm
Chicago	-1	11am
Dublin	+5	5pm
Johannesburg	+7	7pm
London	+5	5pm
Madrid	+6	6pm
Montreal	0	noon
Paris	+6	6pm
Perth, Australia	+13	1am
Rome	+6	6pm
San Francisco	-3	9am
Sydney, Australia	+15	3am
Tokyo	+14	2am

AVERAGE SUNRISE/SUNSET TIMES

	SUNRISE	SUNSET
Jan	7.15	4.45
Feb	6.50	5.30
Mar	6.10	6.00
Apr	5.15	6.30
May	4.30	7.00
Jun	4.30	7.30
Jul	4.35	7.30
Aug	5.00	7.00
Sep	5.30	6.00
Oct	5.30	5.20
Nov	6.35	4.45
Dec	7.15	4.30

DOCUMENTATION FOR NON-US VISITORS

SECURITY

Since 9/11, security in the US has been stepped up. Restrictions are tight on what baggage you can check in and what you can carry on board, both for domestic and international flights (see www.tsa.gov for the latest information). At airports allow plenty of time to clear security checks and check the current situation before you travel.

Expect your belongings to be searched at airports, at museums and at the entryways of many office buildings. Prohibited items may be confiscated. If you are carrying bottled water, you may be asked to take a sip of it, or, more likely, dispose of it. Cooperation will facilitate easy access. For up-to-date information on security in and around the city, contact multilingual visitor information counsellors (tel 212/484-1222) or New York City non-emergency government agencies (dial 311 or tel 212/639-9675).

VISA AND PASSPORT REQUIREMENTS

Canadian citizens, like all other nationalities, must have a machine-readable passport to enter the United States. Non-resident foreign visitors must show their machine-readable passport, their visa if required, and their round-trip ticket when entering the United States. Upon entry, all visitors should expect to be fingerprinted and photographed.

For up-to-date information on visa requirements and how to obtain one, it is vital that you contact the American embassy in your home country months before your journey. Passport and visa requirements can change at short notice so always check before you travel.

CUSTOMS ALLOWANCES

Visitors arriving in New York from outside the country are required to fill in a Customs Declaration before landing in the United States, and they must declare everything except personal effects, which include either 200 cigarettes or 50 cigars or 2.2lbs (1kg) of smoking tobacco, providing you are 21 or older. You may also bring in 1 liter (33.8fl oz) of alcohol. Visitors are not allowed to bring in any fruits, vegetables, plants, meat or meat products, firearms or ammunition.

If you have any questions, contact your nearest United States consulate or embassy before departing, or visit www.cbp.gov and click on "Travel." If you are bringing more than $10,000 into the country, you must declare it on the customs form given to passengers during your inbound flight. You may bring into the country only $100 worth of gifts duty free, however.

WHAT YOU CAN TAKE HOME

If you buy expensive items, you can often avoid paying New York City's 8.875 percent sales tax by having the items shipped back to your home. Ask when making the purchase, but before paying.

Because rules vary for each country, contact the customs service in your home country.

TRAVEL INSURANCE

The US does not have reciprocal healthcare arrangements with other countries. Ensure you purchase full travel insurance in your country before departing. Check that it covers cancellations, lost luggage and medical expenses up to at least $1 million, including dental care. Medical costs in the US are high, so make sure you have good medical coverage.

The cost of insurance depends on your age, health, type and length of your trip. One-year coverage is very economical if you are planning more than one trip per year. Family coverage can also be very good value if you are traveling with a spouse and children.

US EMBASSIES AND CONSULATES ABROAD		
COUNTRY	**ADDRESS**	**WEBSITE**
Australia	Moonah Place, Yarralumla ACT 2600, tel 61 2 6214 5600	http://canberra.usembassy.gov
Canada	490 Sussex Drive, Ottawa, ON K1N 1G8, tel 1 800 283-4356 or 613 238-5335	http://ottawa.usembassy.gov
France	2 avenue Gabriel, 75382 Paris, tel 33 1 43 12 22 22	http://france.usembassy.gov
Germany	Clayallee 170, 14191 Berlin, Federal Republic of Germany, tel 030 83050	http://germany.usembassy.gov
Ireland	42 Elgin Road, Ballsbridge, Dublin 4, tel 353 1 668 8777	http://dublin.usembassy.gov
Italy	via Vittorio Veneto 121, 00187 Roma, tel 39 06 46741	http://italy.usembassy.gov
New Zealand	29 Fitzherbert Terrace, Thorndon, Wellington, tel 644 462 6000	http://newzealand.usembassy.gov
Spain	Calle Serrano 75, 28006 Madrid, tel 91 587 2200	http://madrid.usembassy.gov
South Africa	PO Box 9536, Pretoria 0001, 877 Pretorius St, Pretoria, tel 27 12 431 4000	http://southafrica.usembassy.gov
UK	24 Grosvenor Square, London, W1A 1AE, tel 020 7499 9000	http://london.usembassy.gov

PRACTICALITIES | ESSENTIAL INFORMATION

MONEY

TAXES

In New York City an 8.875 percent sales tax is added on purchase of goods, except clothing and footwear. The hotel tax is 14.75 percent, plus $3.50 per room per night. The parking garage tax is 18.5 percent.

TIPPING

You must tip people in the service sector because their livelihood depends on tips. If you tip less than expected, you are sending a message that the service was poor.

» **In restaurants,** tip wait staff and bartenders at least 15 percent of the bill. Tip 20 percent in expensive restaurants, and round up for good service. The head waiter in top places expects 5 percent and the cloakroom attendant expects $1.

» **In taxis,** tip the driver 15 to 20 percent, more if the journey is short.

» **In hotels,** tip the bellboy $1 or $2 for each suitcase he carries. The chambermaid expects $2 for a few nights' stay. The hall porter expects $1 or $2 for getting you a taxi.

» **At the airport or train station,** tip the porter $1 or $2 per bag.

FOR NON-US VISITORS

Changing money

Change money before you leave home so that you can pay taxis, trains or buses on arrival. The commission at airport bureaux de change is higher than in most banks. Dollar bills of more than $20 may not be accepted by taxi drivers. There are bureaux de change throughout Manhattan, but you get better service in banks and at the visitor center in Times Square

(▷ 168–170). There are ATMs all over the city. Expect to pay up to $3 per transaction if you are using a bank other than your own.

» **American Express Travel Services** has many offices in the city, including one on the mezzanine level at Macy's in Herald Square (tel 212/695-8075).

» **Travelex** has offices (tel 212/935-9935 or www.travelex.com).

» **Chase Manhattan Bank** (tel 800/935-9935 or www.chase.com) has more than 400 branches with bureaux de change.

How to get money

Most people use credit cards to pay for hotels, restaurant meals and shopping. However, some restaurants accept only cash. If you rent a car, a credit card is essential. MasterCard, Visa and American Express are the cards most often accepted (but occasionally Amex is not accepted). Diner's Club and Carte Blanche are accepted by most restaurants and many hotels. Discover, enRoute, Eurocard and JCB are also often accepted.

Traveler's checks in US dollars remain a safe way to carry money. Keep a separate copy of serial numbers and record those you cash, so that any lost or stolen checks can be replaced quickly. Checks from American Express (tel 800/528-4800 or www.americanexpress.com) are most widely accepted. Most restaurants and large stores will accept traveler's checks as payment but will ask you to produce your passport. Most banks will cash them, but charge between 1 percent and 4 percent on the value

for doing so. American Automobile Association members can avoid fees by purchasing checks from an AAA office.

Stolen cards or traveler's checks

If your credit card is stolen, report the theft to the bank so that charges can be blocked. Also notify the police. It's a good idea to photocopy every card, or at least write down the numbers you need to report a loss, and keep this separately.

Exchange rates

For the latest market conversion rates, visit www.oanda.com or www.x-rates.com.

MONEY-SAVING TIPS

» **CityPass** (tel 888/350-5008, www.citypass.com) is a book of discounted tickets to six attractions and will save you hours of waiting in line at attractions, as well as on two-hour Circle Line harbor cruises (▷ 270). The CityPass costs $79 ($59 for ages 6–17) and can be purchased at any attraction. It is good for nine days.

» **New York Pass** (36 West 44th Street, Suite 1407, New York 10036, tel 877/714-1999, www.newyorkpass.com) is an all-inclusive passport to New York City that gets you discounted admission to more than 50 attractions. Passes cost $80 ($55 children 2–12) for one day, $125/105 for two, $155/135 for three or $200/160 for seven days.

» **"Pay-what-you-wish"** lets you decide how much you will pay for museum entry. Some museums are free one day a week.

MONEY VOCABULARY	
$	dollar
¢	cent
a penny	1 cent
a nickel	5 cents
a dime	10 cents
a quarter	25 cents
a half dollar	50 cents
5 bucks	5 dollars

LOST OR STOLEN CREDIT CARDS	
American Express	
800/992-3404	www.americanexpress.com
Diners Club	
1800 234-6377	www.dinersclub.com
MasterCard	
800/627-8372	www.mastercard.com
Visa	
800/847-2911	www.visa.com

SOME EVERYDAY ITEMS AND HOW MUCH THEY COST	
Takeout sandwich	$8
Bottle of water	$2
Cup of tea or coffee	$2
Pint of beer	$6
Glass of wine	$10
Daily newspaper	50¢–$1.50
20 cigarettes	$7.75
An ice cream	$3.50
A gallon of fuel (petrol)	$3–$4.50

narcotics, such as some cough medicines, diuretics, heart drugs, tranquilizers, sleeping pills, anti-depressants, stimulants, etc., make sure they are properly labeled and that you have a prescription or written statement from your doctor confirming that you are taking these under a doctor's direction and that you require them while traveling.

If you suffer from any sort of heart problems, epilepsy or diabetes, it is a good idea to wear a Medic Alert Identification Tag so that the doctor can easily get access to your medical records through the 24-hour hotline in case of an emergency. You can obtain this tag by phoning 888/633-4298 or visit www.medicalert.org.

HEALTH

New York City has some of the best hospitals and doctors in the country, so if you should be in need of care, you have come to the right place. But make sure you have full insurance (▷ 273).

INOCULATIONS

If you are arriving in the United States from Canada or from a European Union member country, you will probably not need inoculations. However, check with your travel agent or with a US consulate or embassy (▷ 273). All visitors to the United States are advised to be fully immunized against tetanus and diptheria.

WHAT TO TAKE

If you will be in New York during the summer, make sure to have sunscreen, which you can easily purchase from any pharmacy upon arrival. You should bring any medication you require with you and, if it is prescription medicine, pack it in your in-flight baggage. Take copies of your prescription to be on the safe side. If your

medication gets lost or stolen, the copy of the prescription will make it easier to get a replacement.

If you require medication containing habit-forming drugs or

HEALTHY FLYING

» Visitors from Europe, Australia or New Zealand may be concerned about the effect of a long-haul flight on their health. The most widely publicized concern is deep vein thrombosis (DVT). Misleadingly labeled "economy class syndrome," DVT is when a blood clot forms in the body's deep veins, particularly in the legs. The clot can move around the bloodstream and can be fatal.

» You are most at risk if you are elderly, pregnant, using the contraceptive pill, smoke or are overweight. If you think you are at increased risk of DVT, see your doctor before departing. Flying increases the likelihood of DVT because passengers are often seated in a cramped position for long periods of time and may become dehydrated.

» Other health hazards for flyers are airborne diseases and bugs spread by the air-conditioning system on board. These hazards are largely unavoidable but if you have a serious medical condition, seek advice from a doctor before flying.

To minimize risk:

Drink water (not alcohol)

Don't stay immobile for hours at a time

Stretch and exercise your legs periodically

Do wear elastic flight socks, which support veins and reduce the chances of a clot forming

Exercises

1. Ankle rotations	2. Calf stretches	3. Knee lifts
Lift feet off the floor. Draw a circle with the toes, moving one foot clockwise and the other counterclockwise	Start with heel on the floor and point foot upwards as high as you can. Then lift heels high keeping balls of feet on the floor	Lift leg with knee bent while contracting your thigh muscle. Then straighten leg pressing foot flat to the floor

DRINKING WATER

The tap water in New York is safe to drink, as is water from public water fountains. However, bottled water is sold throughout the city in stores, restaurants and vending machines.

BUYING MEDICATIONS

The 24-hour pharmacies listed below are all located in places convenient for visitors. Duane Reade and Rite Aid have locations all over Manhattan and most are open 24 hours.

Travelers from abroad may require a prescription in the United States to purchase certain medications, such as birth control pills, inhalers and codeine, that they can buy over the counter in their own country. Pharmacies are generally open from 9am to 5pm and can be recognized by signs in the window—either a mortar and pestle or a caduceus (a staff with two entwined snakes and two wings at the top, which symbolize a physician).

FINDING A DOCTOR

If you need to find a doctor in New York, contact any one of the health services listed below. They are reputable healthcare providers accustomed to treating visitors.

DOCS at New York Healthcare (55 East 34th Street between Park and Madison avenues, tel 212/252-6001) is a walk-in medical center for non-emergency cases. New York University Downtown Hospital (tel 212/312-5000) offers referrals. N.Y. Hotel Urgent Medical Services (952 Fifth Avenue between 76th and 77th streets, tel 212/737-1212, www.travelmd.com) was set up by a New York City doctor to treat visitors. Whether you need a prescription, a medical examination or a dentist, a specialist will come to your hotel room. He or she will produce appropriate identification. The hotel visit fee is $350 to $400, with higher rates at night and on weekends. You can also go to the office for a fee of $175–$200—either drop in or phone for an appointment. Emergency rooms (ER rooms) in some hospitals have walk-in clinics where you can go for non-emergencies (and pay a slightly lower rate than in the emergency area), but you will probably have to wait for a long time. Or you can always ask the hotel staff to suggest a doctor.

IF YOU HAVE TO GO TO THE HOSPITAL

Before you go, phone your travel insurance company's emergency number to find out which hospitals accept your insurance. You will need to show your insurance card at the hospital before any treatment will be given.

INSURANCE FOR NON-US VISITORS

Although you are not required to have health insurance in order to visit the United States, it would be extremely unwise not to. The US does not have reciprocal health agreements with other countries and the cost of healthcare is very high, whether you need a doctor's visit or dental care or have a medical emergency. An emergency room visit usually carries a minimum charge of $500, and that's before you begin receiving treatment. Make sure that you have a good insurance policy that covers all healthcare, including dental care (▷ 273).

PHARMACIES OPEN 24 HOURS

NAME	ADDRESS	TELEPHONE
CVS	400 West 59th Street at Columbus Avenue	212/245-0617
Duane Reade	224 West 57th Street/Broadway	212/547-9708
Duane Reade	1279 Third Avenue/200 East 74th Street	212/744-2668
Rite Aid	408 Grand Street/Clinton	212/529-7115

OPTICIANS

Lenscrafters has several Midtown locations. Go to 542 Fifth Avenue at 45th Street, tel 212/302-4882 www.lenscrafters.com

Cohen's Optical has numerous locations in Manhattan, including 2565 Broadway, tel 212/666-2615 and 2 West 14th Street, tel 212/989-3937 www.cohensfashionoptical.com

ALTERNATIVE MEDICINE

Alternative medical treatments are widely available in New York City.

American Academy of Medical Acupuncture
www.medicalacupuncture.org

Chiropractic Federation of New York
64 East 34th Street, tel 212/532-0185

North American Society of Homeopaths
www.homeopathy.org

Chinatown offers a wide selection of herbal and alternative treatments, including acupuncture. You will find, among others:

Integrative Healing Arts
50 Greene Street, Second Floor, New York 10013, tel 917/294-3805

Kamwo Herbs
211 Grand Street, New York 10013, tel 212/966-6370

Zon Foo Acupuncture and Medical
36 East Broadway, 2nd Floor, New York 10002, tel 212/925-2501

BASICS
CLOTHING

Casual clothing is acceptable in restaurants, museums and attractions throughout New York City. In summer, men must wear a shirt in most restaurants, although only a handful of places require men to wear a jacket and tie. Of course, there is no shortage of stores where you can buy any clothing that you may have forgotten to bring with you. In public places, you will be expected to wear shoes (no bare feet), and men are expected to remove their hats in churches.

Comfortable walking shoes are a must. In winter, you will need a hat or earmuffs, scarf, gloves or mittens, boots, a sweater and a warm coat or jacket. If you want to go ice skating or sledding in Central Park, you can either bring your own gear or rent skates once you're there.

In spring, bring a sweater and a spring coat or jacket. In summer, prepare for hot, humid weather, and be sure to bring a sun hat or cap and sunglasses. In the fall, pack a sweater and a light jacket or coat as well as lighter clothes in case of warm weather. Rainwear and an umbrella, however, are a must all year round.

SHOPPING

Don't overpack. Shopping in New York is fun, and you can readily find anything you may need—umbrella vendors seem to materialize on almost every significant street corner when it rains (you can pick up an umbrella from $5), and you can readily acquire sunglasses on the street on fine days.

Clothes, accessories, electronic equipment and many other items come in wider selections than in most of the rest of the United States and are cheaper than in many European countries.

For every shopper, bargain-hunting can be rewarding. Be aware, however, that the "Going out of business" sales advertised on posters at electronic equipment stores in the Theater District are bogus—these "sales" are a come-on to attract naïve customers. Before buying, get the model number of the product you want and check other retailers' prices online or you will almost certainly pay too much; if you're spending a significant sum of money, it's better to patronize a reputable specialist retailer. In vintage and second-hand shops it is always worthwhile to ask for a better price—sometimes you will get it.

Keep in mind that many stores close on public holidays; SoHo is fairly closed on Mondays and the Lower East Side is shuttered on Saturdays and very slow on Friday afternoons.

MEASUREMENTS

If you are more used to metric measurements than imperial, the conversion table below will be very useful.

VOLTAGE AND ADAPTERS

The power supply in the US is 110/120 volts AC (60 cycles). American plugs have two-prong flat pins, so you will need an adapter if you have plugs with two round pins, or three pins.

It is best to buy an adapter before departing or in the airport shop as they can be difficult to find in the US, although some department stores and pharmacies stock them. You will also need a voltage transformer for European appliances.

COMFORT AND ETIQUETTE
Public restrooms

Restrooms are normally labeled "Women" and "Men" or use a male/female symbol. You may notice that they are labeled in Spanish as well as English in airports, some restaurants and clubs.

Public restrooms are found in visitor centers (▷ 282) and in Grand Central Terminal (▷ 156–157),

CONVERSION CHART		
FROM	**TO**	**MULTIPLY BY**
Inches	Centimeters	2.54
Centimeters	Inches	0.3937
Feet	Meters	0.3048
Meters	Feet	3.2810
Yards	Meters	0.9144
Meters	Yards	1.0940
Miles	Kilometers	1.6090
Kilometers	Miles	0.6214
Acres	Hectares	0.4047
Hectares	Acres	2.4710
Gallons	Liters	4.5460
Liters	Gallons	0.2200
Ounces	Grams	28.35
Grams	Ounces	0.0353
Pounds	Grams	453.6
Grams	Pounds	0.0022
Pounds	Kilograms	0.4536
Kilograms	Pounds	2.205
Tons	Tonnes	1.0160
Tonnes	Tons	0.9842

but New Yorkers stop in hotels, large bookstores, department stores or cafés—theoretically restrooms in eating places are for patrons only, but in some restaurants it's an option. Restrooms in public buildings are wheelchair-accessible and may offer facilities for baby-changing. Restrooms in most parts of the city are clean and well supplied with soap, hand-dryers and paper. A few in Chinatown are substandard.

Traveling with children

New York is family-friendly for the most part, with special discounts for children, special prices for meals and plenty of attractions to keep them happy. Many hotels let kids stay for free and most museums do not charge for young children.

Look for special things to do in the "Weekend" section of the Friday *New York Times, New York* magazine's "Cue" section and in *Time Out New York*. Special performances can sell out or fill up early, so expect to plan ahead.

For babysitting services there's the Baby Sitters' Guild (tel 212/682-0227 or www.babysittersguild.com).

Laundry services

Most hotels either offer laundry services or will recommend one. Before you make your reservation, check what the hotel offers.

Smoking

When smoking in New York was banned in all public places, including restaurants, clubs, bars and anywhere an employee may be exposed to a patron's smoke, it was very controversial. Today it is widely accepted throughout the city.

People who want to smoke must go outside. There is no smoking on buses, subways or trains, and since 2011 no smoking in parks, on beaches, or in Times Square.

Dealing with beggars

It is your choice whether to give money to beggars. If you would prefer not to, simply keep moving

PLACES OF WORSHIP	
Baptist	Abyssinian Baptist Church (132 Odell Clark Place at West 138th Street between Adam Clayton Powell Blvd. and Lenox Ave., tel 212/862-7474).
Buddhist	New York Buddhist Church (331–332 Riverside Drive between 105th and 106th streets, tel 212/678-0305; www.newyorkbuddhistchurch.org).
Greek Orthodox	Holy Trinity Greek Orthodox Cathedral (319 East 74th Street, tel 212/288-3215; www.thecathedral.goarch.org).
Interfaith	Cathedral of St. John the Divine (1047 Amsterdam Avenue at 112th Street, tel 212/316-7490; www.stjohndivine.org).
Jewish	Temple Emanu-El (1 East 65th Street at Fifth Avenue, tel 212/744-1400; www.emanuelnyc.org) is reform.
Muslim	Mosque of Islamic Brotherhood (130 West 113th Street, tel 212/662-4100; www.mosqueofislamicbrotherhoodinc.org).
Roman Catholic	St. Patrick's Cathedral (960 Madison Avenue, tel 212/753-2261; www.saintpatrickscathedral.org).

if a beggar approaches you on the street and asks for money. Don't make eye contact and don't engage in conversation.

On the subway, you may come across beggars who deliver a monologue or present you with a written notice about their hard times and about how your donation will help their family. Again, if you prefer not to give, don't make eye contact, and shake your head to indicate "no" if you are approached by them personally.

On subways

If all seats are taken, move to the center of the subway car so you don't block the doors. If a senior citizen, an adult with a young child, a pregnant woman or person with a disability gets on and there are no available seats, offer yours. This is polite and it's the civilized thing to do.

GAY AND LESBIAN NEW YORK

The Stonewall Riot on Christopher Street in Greenwich Village is credited with starting the Gay Liberation movement in New York City in 1969.

Today, gay and lesbian visitors will find New York a welcoming and easy place to stay. The West Village, especially Christopher Street, is full of shops, restaurants and services with a gay orientation, as is Chelsea, on Eighth Avenue from 16th to 23rd streets.

» The International Gay & Lesbian Travel Association (tel 800/448-8550 or 954/630-1637, www.iglta.org) is a specialist travel agency.

» Lesbian, Gay, Bisexual & Transgender Community Center (208 West 13th Street, between Seventh and Eighth avenues, tel 212/620-7310, www.gaycenter.org) is an excellent source of information on what's happening in the city and where to stay.

» Gay and Lesbian Switchboard (www.glnh.org) offers counseling and information on events.

What's happening

For current gay and lesbian nightlife options, pick up a copy of *Metro, Go, HX, New York Blade, Next* and *Village Voice*, all of them free publications. *Time Out New York*, available at all street news-stands and many other retail outlets, has an excellent section on what's on in and around the city for gay and lesbian visitors.

PLACES OF WORSHIP

With its rich cultural mix, this city of immigrants offers a place to worship for every kind of belief. A selection of places of worship is listed above. Listings in newspapers note the topic of the current week's theme. For the most extensive list of churches, temples, synagogues and mosques, look in the Yellow Pages.

FINDING HELP

The crime rate in New York has plummeted over the past 10 years and it is now one of the safest large cities in the United States. However, it is big and crowded, and crimes do occur, so always be aware of your surroundings and people around you. If someone does try to steal your property, let them take it, then report the crime to the police.

PERSONAL SECURITY

» Do not keep all your money, credit cards and traveler's checks in the same place.
» Do not carry large sums of money with you. Use the hotel safe if you have brought valuables or have large amounts of cash.
» Do not walk alone at night in deserted areas, and do not go into parks after dark unless there is a concert and a large crowd is there.
» If someone "falls" in front of you, be aware that this may be a ploy to distract you while an accomplice picks your pocket.
» Wear shoulder bags and cameras over one shoulder and across your front—in bandolier style. Do not let your handbag dangle from the back of your chair in restaurants; put it on your lap rather than risk making it an easy target.

OBEY THE LAWS

» Drinking laws are strictly enforced in New York. It is against the law to drive with an open container of alcohol in the car and also, of course, to drive while intoxicated.
» Smoking in all public places, such as restaurants, museums, on public transportation or in public offices, is illegal in New York. Since 2011 it is also illegal to smoke in parks, on beaches, and in Times Square.

IF YOU ARE ARRESTED

» Remember that New York has been on high security alert at different times since 9/11 and that even when these alerts are not in effect, there is a high police presence in the streets, at public places, in airports and at other metropolitan locations. Never joke about matters of security—it's considered a crime.
» Visitors from abroad need to be aware that the police can arrest you if you break the law, if they have a strong suspicion that you have been involved in a crime, or if your behavior or activities make them suspect that you are involved in criminal activities.
» If you are arrested, you have the right to remain silent, to make a telephone call, and to contact a lawyer.
» Anything you say can be used as evidence against you. Your best option is, as soon as possible, to contact your embassy or consulate (see below and right) and ask for their assistance.

LOST AND FOUND TELEPHONE NUMBERS
MTA for buses or trains 212/712-4500
Taxi and Limousine Commission for taxis 311
Police property clerk (lost for more than 48 hours) 646/610-5906

LEGAL AGE	
To purchase tobacco	18 years
To gamble or play the lottery	18 years
To purchase/consume alcohol	21 years
To rent a car	25 years

CONSULATES FOR VISITORS FROM OVERSEAS	
Australia	212/351-6500
Canada	212/596-1628
Ireland	212/319-2555
New Zealand	212/832-4038
United Kingdom	212/745-0200

Below *New York City police officers*

EMBASSIES FOR VISITORS FROM OVERSEAS

COUNTRY	ADDRESS	TELEPHONE	WEBSITE
Australia	1601 Massachusetts Avenue, NW, Washington, D.C. 20036	202/797-3000	www.usa.embassy.gov.au
Canada	501 Pennsylvania Avenue, NW, Washington, D.C. 20001	202/682-1740	www.canadianembassy.org
Ireland	2234 Massachusetts Avenue, NW, Washington, D.C. 20008	202/462-3939	www.embassyofireland.org
New Zealand	37 Observatory Circle, NW, Washington, D.C. 20008	202/328-4800	www.nzembassy.com/usa
United Kingdom	3100 Massachusetts Avenue, NW, Washington, D.C. 20008	202/588-6500	http://ukinusa.fco.gov.uk

COMMUNICATIONS

TELEPHONE CHARGES

Public pay phones

Local calls cost 25 to 50 cents for the first three minutes. Even if you are making a local call, one that has the 212 or 646 area code, you must still dial 1, then the area code, before the seven-digit number. This includes calls from Manhattan to other boroughs (area codes 718 and 347).

All calls that are not local are so-called long-distance calls, which cost more; for these, you again have to dial 1 followed by the area code and seven-digit number.

Paying by card

Prepaid calling cards, sold at many convenience stores and news-stands in various denominations, are the easiest and probably the cheapest way to phone home. Public pay phones throughout New York City take phonecards. Airport public telephones all accept MasterCard, Visa and American Express credit cards.

TELEPHONES AND NON-US VISITORS

Telephone numbers

Local and long-distance calls: dial 1 + area code + 7-digit number

Word telephone numbers: Some numbers are made easy to remember by using the letters on the dial rather than the numbers, for example, 1-800/ WHITNEY. Find the appropriate letters on the dial to call these numbers.

Toll-free numbers

There is no charge for telephone numbers with area codes 800, 888 and 877. The 911 emergency number is also free.

High-toll numbers

Telephone numbers with area codes 700 and 900 are chat lines, dating services or other specialized services that can charge anywhere between 95¢ and $15 per minute.

Cell phones and laptops

If your cell phone is not equipped to make calls from the US, you may as well leave it at home.

If you plan to use a laptop while traveling, make sure that the battery is fully charged before you leave home. At airport security, you may be asked to take the laptop out of the case. Security officers may ask you if it is yours, if it is new and if anyone else has been using it. Make sure that you have an adapter for your laptop, and a converter for voltage if necessary, if it does not have a US two-prong, flat-pin plug and does not work on 110/120 volts. If you plan to use it a lot, bring an extra battery.

EMAIL

Go to www.mail2web.com and type in your email address and password to retrieve your email from any web browser. You can also open a free email account via www.hotmail.com or www.gmail.com.

You can check your email from most hotel lobbies, at internet cafés or FedEx Office outlets (www.fedex.com/us/office), which are found throughout the city.

Alternatively, use the free terminals at the Times Square Visitor Center at 1560 Broadway (▷ 282).

CYBER-CAFÉS

There are more and more of these around town (see below for two well-known cafés).

POST OFFICES

The main post office is at 441 Eighth Avenue between 31st and 33rd streets (tel 212/330-3296). Throughout the city there are numerous branches, which are listed in the Yellow Pages. Most branches are open Monday to Friday 8, 9 or 10am to 6pm. A few open Saturday 9am to 4pm.

TIP

Hotel-room phones may be convenient but they are costly, because most hotels impose a high surcharge on calls dialed from rooms. To avoid these surcharges, use a public pay phone. Many hotels have internet access in the lobby, so you can email, as long as you have a credit card.

COUNTRY CODES FROM THE UNITED STATES	
Dial 011 followed by the country code, the city code, then the telephone number	
Australia	(011) 61
Belgium	(011) 32
France	(011) 33
Germany	(011) 49
Greece	(011) 30
Ireland	(011) 353
Italy	(011) 39
Netherlands	(011) 31
New Zealand	(011) 64
Spain	(011) 34
Sweden	(011) 46
United Kingdom	(011) 44

USEFUL TELEPHONE NUMBERS AND WEBSITES
Emergency (Police, Fire, Ambulance) 911
Traveler's Aid 718/656-4870 or 518/463-2124; www.travelersaid.org
US Postal Information 800/275-8777; www.usps.com
Directory Assistance 411

POSTAGE RATES
A regular letter costs:
Within the US, minimum of 44 cents
Across the border to Canada or Mexico, minimum of 80 cents
Overseas, minimum of 98 cents

CYBER CONNECTIONS	
FedEx Office	**Cybercafé**
60 West 40th Street	250 West 49th Street at Broadway/Eighth Avenue
Tel 212/921-1060	Tel 212/333-4109
www.fedex.com/us/office	Mon–Fri 8am–11pm, Sat–Sun 11am–11pm
Open 24 hours	

OPENING TIMES AND PUBLIC HOLIDAYS

New York never sleeps. The working week is Monday through Friday, 9am to 5pm, but some banks are open on Saturday mornings and many stores are open longer hours; most stores are open all weekend. Some pharmacies are open 24/7, as are some coffee shops and bureaux de change.

Always phone in advance if timing is critical or if you're making a detour to visit a particular place.

PUBLIC HOLIDAYS

On public holidays many museums, some restaurants and all public office buildings close. New Year's Day, Christmas and Thanksgiving are the biggest, most widely celebrated holidays, when most New York businesses grind to a halt. Airports and train stations are particularly busy in the period leading up to these holidays, when many New Yorkers travel out of town to be with family or friends.

However, it is also a time when the city is festive and celebrations are enjoyed by visitors as well as New Yorkers (for a list of parades ▷ 290–291). Much of the city closes down or slows during the Jewish High Holidays—Rosh Hashanah and Yom Kippur—in September and early October.

Above *View of the Chrysler Building and the "city that never sleeps" from the Empire State Building*

OPENING HOURS

	OPEN	CLOSED	COMMENTS
Stores	Mon–Sat, 10–7 Sun noon–6		Many closed Sun Upper East Side, Sat Lower East Side
Banks	Mon–Fri 9.30–3.30	Sat–Sun	Some close at 3, some open Sat morning
Offices	Mon–Fri 9–5	Sat–Sun	
Museums	Tue–Sun		Some open Mon or close another day
Galleries	Tue–Sat 10–6	Mon	
Doctors	Mon–Fri 9–5	Sat–Sun	▷ 276
Pharmacies	Daily 9–7 or 9–9		Shorter hours and Sun closing in commercial neighborhoods, some 24hrs
Grocery stores	Daily 7am–9pm		As above
Restaurants	Daily (see listings)	Some close one day a week	Many serve until 11pm or midnight, a few between 4pm and 5.30pm

PUBLIC HOLIDAYS

January 1	New Year's Day
3rd Monday in January	Martin Luther King Day
3rd Monday in February	Presidents' Day
Last Monday in May	Memorial Day
July 4	Independence Day
1st Monday in September	Labor Day
2nd Monday in October	Columbus Day
November 11	Veterans' Day
4th Thursday in November	Thanksgiving Day
December 25	Christmas Day

TOURIST INFORMATION

EVENTS AND PARADES

Lively events worth planning a trip around take place throughout the year. If you are in New York during a parade, don't miss it. The two biggest are the St. Patrick's Day Parade and the Macy's Thanksgiving Day Parade, which is televised nationwide. The crowd scene is almost as entertaining as the parade. Check local listings for dates, times and parade routes, and plan to show up early for either of them to get a choice viewing spot.

TOURIST OFFICES

Major visitor centers, listed below, are well worth visiting on your first or second day. Many brochures offer discount vouchers, which will save you a few dollars at attractions or restaurants. In addition, most hotels offer a good selection of maps and free brochures.

Times Square Visitor Center

(1560 Broadway between 46th and 47th streets, tel 212/768-1560, www.timessquarenyc.org, daily 8–8) This is New York's central tourist office and has free brochures, maps, helpful staff, a Broadway Ticket Center and a Metropolitan Transportation Authority that sells MetroCards ($\triangleright$ 45), as well as providing ATMs, currency-exchange machines and free internet. It's worth visiting even if you think you don't need to. Some of the free walking tours start from here.

PARADES	
January	
Three Kings' Day	
Martin Luther King Day Parade	
March	
St. Patrick's Day	
March or April	
Greek Independence Day Parade	
Easter Parade, Fifth Avenue	
June	
Puerto Rican Day Parade	
Lesbian and Gay Pride Parade	
September	
West Indian Parade and Carnival	
October	
Columbus Day Parade	
Halloween Parade in Greenwich Village	
November	
Macy's Thanksgiving Day Parade	

NYC & Company Visitor Information Center

(810 Seventh Avenue between 52nd and 53rd streets, tel 212/484-1222, www.nycgo.com, Mon–Fri 8.30 to 6, Sat–Sun 9–5) Smaller than the Times Square complex, this information center has free brochures and leaflets.

The interactive terminal with touch-screen access to visitor information is extremely useful. Buy advance tickets to major attractions here and your CityPass ($\triangleright$ 274), and pick up a copy of the *Official Visitor Guide*. It contains discount vouchers for hotels, stores, restaurants, cruises and museums.

The center provides an ATM (cashpoint), plus telephones that

EVENTS	
January or early February	
Chinese New Year in Chinatown	
April–October	
Baseball season	
May	
Ninth Avenue International Food Festival	
June	
Metropolitan Opera park concerts,	
Museum Mile Festival	
June–September	
Shakespeare in the Park	
July	
Independence Day fireworks over the East River	
August–September	
Lincoln Center Out-of-Doors Festival,	
Harlem Week	
September	
Feast of San Gennaro, in Little Italy	
September–October	
New York Film Festival	
Early November	
New York City Marathon	
December	
Tree lighting at Rockefeller Center,	
New Year's Eve celebrations	

are directly connected to American Express offices.

Lower East Side Visitors Center

(70 Orchard Street between Broome and Grand streets, tel 866/224-0206 or 212/226-9010, www.lowereastsideny.com, Mon–Fri 9.30–5.30, Sat–Sun 9.30–4) Provides pamphlets covering local shopping, dining and entertainment.

Below *The Christmas tree at the Rockefeller Center is ceremoniously lit in December*

USEFUL WEBSITES

ACCOMMODATIONS
» All New York Hotels
www.allnewyorkhotels.net
Search for a hotel (including discount hotels) by name or criteria
» New York Homestay
www.newyorkhomestay.com
Rooms with families for students and those on extended stays
» Manhattan Bed and Breakfast
www.bedandbreakfast.com/manhattan-new-york.html lists inns and bed-and-breakfast options
» Central Reservation Service
www.crshotels.com
A central reservation service for independent hotels in New York City
» YMCA Guest Rooms
www.ymcanyc.org
Main YMCA site with links to YMCAs around Greater New York

BROADWAY AND OFF-BROADWAY TICKETS
» Playbill's Online Theater Club
www.playbillclub.com
A membership club that gives discounts to top shows
» TeleCharge www.telecharge.com
» Broadway.com
www.broadway.com
» TheaterMania
www.theatermania.com
» Ticketmaster
www.ticketmaster.com

MONEY
» Travelex Worldwide Money
www.travelex.com

NEW YORK CITY INFORMATION
» Alliance for Downtown New York
www.downtownny.com
Everything you need to know about Downtown, including links to a free bus service and an interactive map
» The Bronx Tourism Council
www.ilovethebronx.com
» Brooklyn Tourism Council
www.visitbrooklyn.org
» Citysearch
www.newyork.citysearch.com
Attractions, events, hotels, real estate, restaurants and shopping

» Customs information for entering New York City
www.cbp.gov
» New York Convention & Visitors Bureau
www.nycgo.com
» NYC.com
www.nyc.com
» Times Square Business Improvement District
www.timessquarenyc.org
The official site for Times Square and what's going on there

NEWS, REVIEWS AND WHAT'S ON
» *New York*
www.nymag.com
New York magazine website
» New York Today
www.nytoday.com
The *New York Times* site, a guide for New Yorkers and visitors to what's on and what to do
» The *New York Times*
www.nytimes.com
» The *New Yorker*
www.newyorker.com
» *New York Press*
www.nypress.com
A free weekly newspaper
» *Time Out New York*
http://newyork.timeout.com
» *Village Voice*
www.villagevoice.com
A culturally hip publication

RADIO
New York City is the top radio outlet in the United States. The radio bandwidths are cacophonous, and if you live in an area without a similar level or choice, just turning on the radio and flipping the dial is an experience. A few top stations are:
» WNYC-FM 93.9 (820-AM)
www.wnyc.org
» 1010 WINS-AM Radio
www.1010wins.com
» WBGO-FM 88.3 Radio
www.wbgo.org
» WQXR-FM 105.9 www.wqxr.org
Classical music station
» WFAN-AM 660 www.wfan.com
Sports and news talk
» WOR-AM 710 www.wor710.com
Venerable NYC talk radio

TRANSPORTATION
» Airports
www.newyorkairports.com
» Trains
www.amtrak.com
» Airtrain Newark
www.airtrainnewark.com
An on-airport service and shuttle from Newark Liberty International Airport Train Station to Newark Liberty Airport
» American Automobile Association
www.aaa.com
» Subways and buses
www.mta.info

GENERAL
» The Baby Sitters' Guild
www.babysittersguild.com
For child care at any time
» Weather
www.weather.com
www.cnn.com/weather
A comprehensive weather service

Below *Cyber Café on West 49th Street, just off Broadway and Times Square*

MEDIA

At the newspaper stands on many streets throughout the city, you can buy newspapers in English, Spanish and, at some, a few other languages, as well as a wide variety of magazines.

NEWSPAPERS

» *The New York Times* is the city's most widely read daily (www.nytimes.com), published seven days a week. The Sunday edition includes a magazine and special sections for sports, travel, real estate, etc.

» The *Daily News* is a tabloid published seven days a week and offers a large quantity of Sunday supplements.

» The *New York Post* is another tabloid published daily.

» The *Wall Street Journal* is the much-respected New York-based national financial newspaper.

» The *New York Observer* is the pink-hued weekly full of media and political gossip.

MAGAZINES

» *The New Yorker* (www.newyorker.com) is a national literary and news magazine with New York listings and reviews as well as articles; published every Monday.

» *New York Magazine* (www.nymag.com), published every Monday, is a good source of information on restaurants, theaters, movies, books, art, television and bargains around town.

» *The Village Voice* (www.villagevoice.com) is published weekly every Tuesday, with extensive listings of music, clubs, arts and entertainment.

Above The New Yorker *magazine has listings and reviews*

» *Time Out* (http://newyork.timeout.com) is a very good comprehensive weekly magazine with plenty of listings on just about everything going on around town.

To buy newspapers from other countries, go to *Universal News & Magazines* (234 West 42nd Street between Seventh and Eighth avenues, tel 212/221-1809; www.universalnewsusa.com) and nine other locations around Manhattan.

MAJOR TV STATIONS

On cable, NY1 is all about New York, and more than 50 stations on cable, available in most hotels, supply movies, weather updates and home shopping. If you're traveling with kids, ask whether the Disney Channel is available.

NATIONAL TV STATIONS
2 (CBS)
4 (NBC)
5 (Fox)
7 (ABC)
9 and 11 (independent)
13 (PBS)

MAJOR RADIO STATIONS	
www.nyradioguide.com	
AM:	
Sports	660 (WFAN)
News and Talk	820 (WNYC feeds from NPR and the BBC World Service)
Multiethnic	930 (WPAT)
News	1130 (WBBR)
News around the clock	880 and 1010 (WINS)
FM:	
Classic and talk	93.9 (WNYC-FM)
Classical	105.9 (WQXR)
Top 40	100.3 (also known as Z-100)

BOOKS, MAPS, MOVIES AND TELEVISION

BOOKS

Non-fiction

The Historical Atlas of New York City: Eric Homberger, Henry Holt and Company, New York, 1998
A fascinating book on the history of New York, always a pleasure to read. Excellent graphics, maps and photographs.

New York City (A Short History): George J. Lankevich, New York University Press, New York, 2002
A fascinating look at New York's political and social history from the first settlers to the election of Mayor Michael Bloomberg.

New York: Songs of the City: Nancy Groce, Watson-Guptill Publications, New York, 1999
A delightful musical journey through New York's boroughs, with anecdotes and facts about the music industry, lyrics of old tunes about New York, and reproduced music sheet covers and posters.

Fiction

Novelists and short-story writers have long been attracted to New York, and many American classics have been set here. For short stories pick up O. Henry's **The Voice of the City** (1908) or Damon Runyon's **Guys and Dolls** (1932). Novels such as F. Scott Fitzgerald's **The Beautiful and the Damned** (1922), John Dos Passos's **Manhattan Transfer** (1925), J. D. Salinger's **The Catcher in the Rye** (1951) and Truman Capote's **Breakfast at Tiffany's** (1958) are

all popular. More recent novels include Tom Wolfe's **Bonfire of the Vanities** (1987) and **The New York Trilogy** (1988) by Paul Auster.

MAPS AND OTHER PUBLICATIONS

Fodor's 25 Best
Focuses on the top 25 must-see sights. It breaks the city into five areas and recommends the best sights, shops, entertainment venues, nightlife and restaurants.

Fodor's New York City
Information on where to go, what to see and how to get there, written by New York City-based shopping experts, restaurant critics and other specialists. It includes detailed descriptions of hundreds of restaurant and hotel choices, information on sights, and listings of stores and sports opportunities. Useful web links and smart travel tips help in planning.

AIA Guide to New York City: Norval White & Elliot Willensky, Oxford University Press, 2010
The American Institute of Architects' guide to parks and buildings in all five boroughs is truly a treasure store of acknowledged architectural knowledge and informed opinion. Arranged in geographical order, it's fun to have at hand as you amble around town, but it's hefty.

Guide to New York City Landmarks: New York Landmarks Preservation Commission 2008
This guide to the city's landmarks and historic districts is ideal for walking tours.

MOVIES

New York has been the setting of many classic movies by some great directors.

42nd Street (1933), Hal Wallis
King Kong (1933), Merian C. Cooper
Guys and Dolls (1955), Samuel Goldwyn
Breakfast at Tiffany's (1961), Blake Edwards
West Side Story (1961), Robert Wise
Mean Streets (1973), Martin Scorsese
Taxi Driver (1976), Martin Scorsese
New York, New York (1977), Martin Scorsese
Saturday Night Fever (1977), John Badham
Manhattan (1979), Woody Allen
Broadway Danny Rose (1984), Woody Allen
The Cotton Club (1984), Francis Ford Coppola
Radio Days (1987), Woody Allen
When Harry Met Sally (1989), Rob Reiner
A Bronx Tale (1993), Robert De Niro
Gangs of New York (2002), Martin Scorsese
The Devil Wears Prada (2006), David Franke
Sex and the City: The Movie (2008), Michael Patrick King
Julie & Julia (2009), Nora Ephron
Brooklyn's Finest (2010), Antoine Fuqua

TELEVISION

High drama, farce and comedy are played out on the streets of New York daily, and on people's screens throughout the world when they tune into these popular shows set around New York City. Many of can also be seen on video or DVD.
Friends (now in rerun)
Law & Order (now in rerun)
NYPD Blue (now in rerun)
Seinfeld (now in rerun)
Sex and the City (now in rerun)
Will & Grace (now in rerun)
30 Rock

SHOPPING

They say that you can buy anything you want in New York City, and it's true. New York's shopping ranges from large opulent department stores to tiny one-room boutiques. Many visitors come to New York just to shop, especially pre-Christmas, uptown at the flagship designer stores that line Madison and Fifth avenues, or downtown at the cutting-edge designers in SoHo and NoLita. More moderately priced wares can be found at stores around Herald Square and 34th Street, or in the branches of national chains. There aren't any malls of note. Many stores open seven days a week (with late-night hours usually on Thursday). European visitors should note that American sizes differ from British and European sizes. Note too that the sales tax (added at the cash register) is 8.875 percent. There is no tax on clothing or footware. Credit cards are accepted virtually everywhere.

SALES

The largest sales take place in January and July, and also around public holidays—Presidents' Day, Memorial Day and Labor Day, for example.

To keep abreast of current and forthcoming sales check the relevant sections of *New York* magazine and *Time Out* or go online to www.dailycandy.com or http://nymag.com/shopping/articles/sb/. Some of the best deals are found at sample sales, usually held in the spring and fall. Designers and manufacturers hold such sales to make space for their new design samples. Shopping fiends find out about them by subscribing to S & B Report (tel 843/579-0222) or going online at www.lazarshopping.com. Online subscription is $75 a year. For visitors the best way to locate these sales is to go to a favorite designer or store and ask if they hold them. Or try walking around the Garment District, where people often give out flyers announcing them. Bring cash and note you may not be able to try items on. There are no refunds available either.

MARKETS

Unlike European cities, New York has few outstanding markets, although one or two are worth visiting. At the African Market at 2278 Eighth Avenue, textiles, jewelry, bowls made from gourds, wooden stools and other artifacts from Africa are for sale. The Annex Antique Fair and Flea Market in the parking lots at Sixth Avenue and 26th Street (tel 212/243-5343) is very popular. Get there early for the best pickings (it opens at 5am). The Sunday Columbus Avenue market (between 76th and 77th streets) is also fun. In summer, expect small neighborhood street fairs at which people sell all kinds of bric-à-brac, clothing, CDs, food and books. Green markets have become very popular. The most storied is at Union Square (▷ 126), but there are smaller ones around town in Abingdon Square in the West Village or Tompkins Square in the East Village, for example.

Savvy New Yorkers also shop the thrift stores and consignment shops. Some of the best are: Housing Works, 143 West 17th Street (tel 212/366-0820) and 306 Columbus Avenue (tel 212/579-7566), Encore, 1132 Madison Avenue (tel 212/879-2850) at 84th Street, and the Salvation Army, 112 Fourth Avenue (tel 212/673-2741).

Below *Fifth Avenue is one of New York's most prestigious shopping streets*

ENTERTAINMENT AND NIGHTLIFE

The city's performance scene reflects the diversity of the metropolis. Theater patrons will find an array of options. There are 39 or so Broadway theaters, plus 450 non-profit theaters operating in the city. New Yorkers take their nightlife very seriously. You can always find a "scene" somewhere in the city that never sleeps, with the party shifting from bar to dance club and back, and then to the Meatpacking District at dawn.

BARS

There are bars to suit every taste. Great saloons with antique bars often have a lot of history attached. The King Cole Bar claims to have invented the Bloody Mary, while P. J. Clarke's has long been associated with Damon Runyon types. In swank hotel bars such as the St. Regis's King Cole or the Carlyle's Bemelmans you can lounge in luxury. Rooftop bars are spectacular trysting places. Specialty bars serve up every liquor (beer, wine, champagne, vodka and sake). You'll find an extensive gay scene catering to different crowds, concentrated mainly in Chelsea and Greenwich Village. Many lounges now have DJs spinning music, but some don't allow dancing because they lack a cabaret license.

CINEMA

The city is a veritable cinema paradiso. Numerous art houses operate, frequently showcasing individual directors or focusing on particular themes or eras. First-run movies are shown all over town in grand movieplexes.

CLASSICAL MUSIC, DANCE AND OPERA

Musical riches abound, led by the Metropolitan and City Operas and Carnegie Hall and the New York Philharmonic. All kinds of smaller groups and orchestras, plus independent opera companies, play at diverse venues—museums, music schools and churches. The New York City Ballet and American Ballet Theatre are leaders of the traditional dance scene, while Merce Cunningham, Mark Morris, Alvin Ailey, Paul Taylor and Martha Graham are the leading modern dance companies.

CLUBS

Some New York City clubs have a great deal of attitude. At the hottest dance clubs, there's a competition to get in, and people dress à la mode to ensure that they get past the velvet rope and the bouncer at the door. And there's always a VIP room and an A-list for guests (although you can often get on the list by calling in advance or going to www.sheckys.com). So tough has it become to gain entry to the most fashionable clubs, that even a $1,000 bribe will not work. Hence PartyBuddys (tel 866/856-2748, www.partybuddys.com), which promises to shepherd visitors on a nightlife tour for a fee, starting at $275 per person. Still, there are plenty more casual clubs available, especially the gay spots (see *Next,* *HX, Metro Source* and *Go* for listings), which are often a lot more fun.

COMEDY, POETRY AND THE SPOKEN WORD

The spoken word can be heard throughout the city, as the intellectuals and literary lights meet, greet and sign at bookstores, lecture at the 92nd Street Y, or deliver their poetry at poetry fests and St. Mark's Church-in-the-Bowery. And don't forget stand-up comedy, a unique American cultural contribution, celebrated in New York City clubs, which gave birth to such brilliant comedians as Jerry Seinfeld, Jay Leno, Woody Allen, Rosie O'Donnell and Joan Rivers.

CONTEMPORARY LIVE MUSIC

Cabaret is flourishing in alluring rooms at the Carlyle and the Algonquin hotels. Musically, uptown tends to be more traditional; downtown leans to the avant-garde. Indie rock clubs abound on the Lower East Side and in the East Village. Cool jazz and other exotica can be heard at the Knitting Factory and Tonic. Jazz continues to thrive as it has always in New York. The leading venue is still the Village Vanguard, now under the watchful eye of Lorraine Gordon, but it has

THEATER

The Great White Way stretch of Broadway attracts the most visitors with its brightly lit marquees and gilded theaters named after such luminaries as Ethel Barrymore, David Belasco and Eugene O'Neill. The Public Theater and BAM are the shining lights of off-Broadway. The first, founded by Joe Papp, also delivers free summer Shakespeare in the Park, while BAM is famous for its New Wave Festival. Off-Broadway has nurtured many playwrights too, such as Wally

been joined by the $140-million Jazz at Lincoln Center in the Time Warner building on Columbus Circle. World music is featured all over town at Town Hall, Zankel Hall at Carnegie and Symphony Space.

Shawn, Lanford Wilson and Tony Kushner, and several Broadway hits have emerged from here, notably *Rent, Avenue Q, A Chorus Line* and *The Heidi Chronicles*. Off-off-Broadway stages quirky experimental showcases in tiny theaters with fewer than 100 seats, but it has nurtured such players as Eric Bogosian and Laurie Anderson.

PRACTICALITIES

Most box offices open from Monday to Saturday, 10am to 8pm, and Sunday from 11am to 6.30pm. Tickets can be purchased here without paying a fee. Standing Room Only tickets, when available, go on sale on the day of the performance.

Tickets can also be purchased through Telecharge (tel 212/ 239-

6200) and Ticketmaster (tel 212/ 307-7171).

Best performance listings are found in *Time Out New York* magazine, the *Village Voice* and the Friday edition of the *New York Times*. A good website for listings is http://newyork.timeout.com.

Nightlife hot spots are Harlem, Chelsea, the East and West villages, and the Lower East Side. There's also plenty of action in Williamsburg, which now draws its own crowd from Manhattan. Drinking age is 21 (always carry a picture ID). British visitors should note that whiskey is rye, not Scotch.

Above *The Ed Sullivan Theater on Broadway has been home of* Late Show with David Letterman *since 1993; tickets are available for show recordings*

SPORTS AND ACTIVITIES

New York City is a major sports destination, whether you fancy watching a game of baseball, football, basketball, ice hockey or tennis. If you want to take part in something yourself, try jogging in Central Park or working out at one of the many gyms.

PROFESSIONAL SPORTS

Local and regional rivalries drive the professional sports scene. In baseball it's the Yankees (Bronx) versus the Mets (Queens). In addition, whenever the Yankees play the Red Sox, it's a grudge game because Boston has never forgiven New York for stealing Babe Ruth.

The biggest sports are football (Giants and Jets) and basketball (Knicks and New Jersey Nets). Ice hockey has fanatical fans too, supporting the Rangers, Islanders and New Jersey Devils. Despite the American women's global success in soccer, women's professional sports struggle for audience support, although such teams as basketball's Liberty have loyal fans.

Sports seasons are: baseball April–end October; basketball November–end April; soccer March–end October; football and ice hockey September–end April.

TICKETS

Most seats are sold in advance by subscription to corporations and individuals. Tickets are available without fee at the box office; there's an extra fee for phone and online orders. Agencies like TicketMaster (tel 212/307-7171 or www. ticketmaster.com) usually charge a fee of from $4 to $8 per ticket.

Tickets to any of these sports are tough to get and/or expensive, but you can always take a seat in one of the many raucous sports bars around town and see the action there, or at the large ESPN Zone in Times Square.

EXERCISE AND ACTIVITIES

New Yorkers go to the gym, walk, run, cycle, skate, inline skate and play tennis, softball and street basketball. Equestrians ride in Central Park. On the waterfront they enjoy kayaking and sailing from downtown piers. The more sedentary count bowling and pool as sports.

HEALTH AND BEAUTY

Almost every neighborhood in New York has a selection of health clubs with fitness equipment, classes and assorted frills— sometimes a pool. Massages, nutrition consultations and personal trainers may be available by appointment. Most offer day passes for visitors for a price (anywhere from $15 to $50). It's best to go at off-peak hours—between 12 and 2 and from 5 till 8 the clubs may be so crowded you have to sign up to use the machines.

WHAT'S ON OFFER

The city has always had yoga studios and fancy hair salons, but it has seen an enormous growth of day spas and other pampering facilities. Some are world-class, like La Prairie in the Ritz; others cater to New Age constituencies, while still others hustle passers-by for a quick back massage. The Brazilian nail salons are considered extra-special.

FOR CHILDREN

With its towering buildings, vibrant streets, sights and sounds, New York is for kids. Even a ride on the subway can be exciting.

FAMILY-FRIENDLY

A few family-friendly institutions are listed under the individual regions in this book. Also check the Sports and Activities sections and the Shopping sections (especially Niketown and the Disney Store).

In addition, many seasonal events appeal to kids—performances of the Big Apple Circus and the *Nutcracker* at Christmas as well as the Radio City Christmas Spectacular; the Ringling Brothers' circus in spring; and the parades and fairs that take place throughout the year.

SPECIAL EVENTS

As you research your visit, it's worth calling concert halls and museums in advance to find out what special events will be on while you're in town; reserve ahead for those that interest you.

FESTIVALS AND EVENTS

Note that the Convention & Visitors Bureau often has further information about these events. Call 212/484-1222 or check www.nycgo.com. Other useful websites are www.nyc.com and www.nyctourist.com.

JANUARY
NEW YORK WINTER ANTIQUES SHOW
www.winterantiquesshow.com
The city's most prestigious antiques fair in the Park Avenue Armory.
☎ 212/987-0446

FEBRUARY
CHINESE NEW YEAR
www.chinatown-online.com
Firecrackers blast and dragon and lion dancers sashay through the streets of Chinatown.
☎ 212/484-1222 ⊕ Depends on the lunar calendar

WESTMINSTER KENNEL DOG SHOW
www.westminsterkennelclub.org
About 2,500 canines strut their stuff at Madison Square Garden.
☎ 212/213-3165 ⊕ Dates vary

MARCH
ST. PATRICK'S DAY PARADE
http://nyc-st-patrick-day-parade.org
Bagpipers and bands, politicians and New York's finest march down Fifth Avenue from 86th to 44th streets celebrating the patron saint of Ireland.
☎ 212/484-1222 ⊕ March 17

MARCH–APRIL
EASTER PARADE
People with a bent for fashion design stroll along Fifth Avenue between 49th and 57th streets showing off their often wacky and wonderful hats.
⊕ Depending on when Easter falls

NEW YORK INTERNATIONAL AUTO SHOW
www.autoshowny.com
www.javitscenter.com
Heaven for car enthusiasts.
✉ Jacob Javits Convention Center
☎ 800/282-3336 ⊕ Late March/early April

APRIL
MACY'S FLOWER SHOW
More than 30,000 varieties of flower are arrayed in the store in celebration of spring.
☎ 212/494-4495 ⊕ Last two weeks of April

CHERRY BLOSSOM FESTIVAL
www.bbg.org
Traditional Japanese activities and performances take place against a backdrop of pink cherry blossoms in the Brooklyn Botanic Garden.
☎ 718/623-7200 ⊕ Late April, depending on when trees flower

MAY
NINTH AVENUE INTERNATIONAL FOOD FESTIVAL
www.ninthavenuefoodfestival.com
Between 37th and 57th streets, Ninth Avenue is lined with stands selling food of all kinds.
☎ 212/484-1222 ⊕ Second or third weekend of May

Above *Street decorations in Little Italy*

FLEET WEEK
www.fleetweeknewyork.com
The tall ships, active military ships and aircraft carriers sail in a majestic parade into New York Harbor and up the Hudson River. The festival includes military demonstrations, tugs of war and cooking fests, and culminates in a Memorial Day celebration. Posses of sailors roam New York City streets in their crisp white uniforms.
☎ 212/245-0072 ◉ Third week of May

WASHINGTON SQUARE
www.nycgv.com
The streets around Washington Square are lined with artists, photographers and craftspeople selling their work.
☎ 212/982-6255 ◉ Outdoor Art Exhibit Memorial Day weekend

JUNE
BELMONT STAKES
www.nyra.com
The last leg of the horse-racing Triple Crown is run at Belmont on Long Island.
☎ 516/488-6000 ◉ First weekend in June

PUERTO RICAN DAY PARADE
www.nationalpuertoricandayparade.org
The city is awash with Puerto Rican flags.
☎ 718/401-0404 ◉ Second weekend in June

LESBIAN AND GAY PRIDE PARADE
www.nycpride.org
The flamboyant parade from 52nd Street to Greenwich Village, via Fifth Avenue, is the culmination of a week of gay-oriented celebrations.
☎ 212/807-7433 ◉ Last Sunday in June

JULY
INDEPENDENCE DAY HARBOR FESTIVAL AND FIREWORKS
New York City celebrates the nation's birth with a festival in Lower Manhattan and some spectacular fireworks launched from barges on the East River.
☎ 212/484-1222 ◉ July 4

AUGUST
HARLEM WEEK
http://harlemweek.com
A host of Harlem events—film, jazz and food festivals among them—start mid-July and the "week" runs into September.
☎ 212/862-8477 or 212/484-1222 ◉ Most of August

LINCOLN CENTER OUT-OF-DOORS FESTIVAL
www.lincolncenter.org
Over 100 free performances on the plazas at Lincoln Center, including music, dance, theatricals and more.
☎ 212/546-2656

SEPTEMBER
WEST INDIAN PARADE AND CARNIVAL
www.carnaval.com
Thousands flock to Brooklyn to see the dancers and bands sashaying along to reggae, soca and calypso. Caribbean food adds to the festivities.
☎ 212/484-1222 ◉ Labor Day

FEAST OF SAN GENNARO
www.sangennaro.org
The patron saint of Naples is paraded down Mulberry Street at this fiesta, with all kinds of Italian food and street entertainment.
☎ 212/768-9320 ◉ Eleven days in mid-September

NEW YORK FILM FESTIVAL
www.filmlinc.com
The Film Society of Lincoln Center organizes this major film festival. The hub is the Walter Reade Film Theater.
☎ 212/875-5600 ◉ 17 days in late September or early October

OCTOBER
BLESSING OF THE ANIMALS
www.stjohndivine.org
At churches throughout the city, animals are blessed on St. Francis's Day. The biggest event takes place at the Cathedral of St. John the Divine. People bring their pets.
☎ 212/316-7490 ◉ First Sunday

HALLOWEEN PARADE
www.halloween-nyc.com
What started as an impromptu procession of drag queens in Greenwich Village has become a huge event with big-name sponsors. The costumes are amazing, but line up early to get a glimpse.
☎ 212/484-1222

NOVEMBER
NEW YORK CITY MARATHON
www.nyrrc.org
Thousands of runners thunder across the Queensborough Bridge into Manhattan and race for the finish in Central Park.
☎ 212/860-4455 ◉ First weekend in November

MACY'S THANKSGIVING DAY PARADE
Families line the route from 77th Street and Central Park West to Herald Square to see the immense helium balloons.
☎ 212/484-1222 ◉ Last Thursday

DECEMBER
LIGHTING OF THE CHRISTMAS TREE
www.rockefellercenter.com
It's a media event, usually starring popular singers. Stake out your place early—or avoid the area altogether because crowds make it impossible to get through.
✉ Rockefeller Center ☎ 212/332-6868 ◉ Usually the first week in December

RADIO CITY SPECTACULAR
www.radiocity.com
Busloads of revelers come to see the Rockettes kick up a storm in a stylish chorus line for this seasonal show, which always includes a Parade of the Wooden Soldiers.
☎ 212/247-4777 ◉ Through December 30

NEW YEAR'S EVE CELEBRATION
Times Square fills with thousands of partygoers who show up to watch the ball drop announcing the official start of the next year.
◉ December 31

You can dine around the world in New York City, and you can spend a pittance, a fortune, or somewhere in between. The choice is yours. Some New Yorkers dine out every night; others save the top-class choices for special occasions. Dining trends change from season to season. Whether dining at a deluxe restaurant or a casual eatery, healthier, locally grown food is growing in popularity.

RESERVATIONS, DRESS CODES AND OTHER NOTES

In general, it's wise to make a reservation for dinner, especially on weekends. Top-class restaurants require reservations and will ask you to provide a telephone number for confirmation. If you want a table at Jean-Georges, Le Bernardin, Gordon Ramsay or similar, call well in advance. Sometimes, at these "famous" restaurants, it can be tough to get through even to the reservation desk. Just keep trying. If you're on your own and want to eat on the run, you may be able to eat at the bar in one of these fancy restaurants. Note that some restaurants do not take reservations for parties under six people. In Midtown, luncheon reservations are also essential.

The United States is a more casual culture than most and strict dress codes have disappeared. Nonetheless a few places still do require a jacket and tie at dinner so remember to ask when making a reservation. In general, casual smart is the way to go.

Smoking is not allowed in public spaces, period. The majority of restaurants have full bars; some sell beer and wine only, and a few have no liquor but will allow you to bring your own. At premier BYO (bring your own) restaurants, there will be a substantial corkage fee if you bring your own wine.

Vegetarians will find a welcome. Many top-class dining rooms offer vegetarian menus, and fast-food joints are offering healthier options on their menus these days.

Breakfast may be served all day at coffee shops and diners. Otherwise, regular breakfast hours are from 7 to 11am. Lunch usually runs from 11.30am to 2 or 2.30pm and dinner from 5pm to 10 or 11pm, depending on the day of the week. Most top-class restaurants close for lunch on weekends. Many restaurants offer brunch on Sunday or both Saturday and Sunday.

TAXES, TIPPING AND OTHER FINANCIAL CONSIDERATIONS

A sales tax of 8.875 percent will be added to your dining bill. Americans tip more generously than most other nationalities. The minimum (with good service) is 15 percent; many people double the tax for an almost 18 percent tip. Many restaurants offer prix-fixe menus, which often provide good value. In January and late June, a special promotion offers a three-course menu at reduced rates for lunch and dinner at numerous restaurants; this promotion is often extended so it's worth checking if it's available.

DESSERT AND COFFEE

Greenwich Village has been famous for its coffeehouses since the 1950s. Of the few that remain,

Caffe Reggio (119 MacDougal Street, tel 212/475-9557) is a real Italian coffeehouse. Le Gamin (132 West Houston at Sullivan Street, tel 212/475-1543) is a similar French version. Bean Coffee and Tea (446 Sixth Avenue, tel 212/777-0402) is a small, cozy coffee shop serving great coffee, mocha, latte and chai along with cupcakes, muffins, cookies, tarts and fancy pastries. Chef Thomas Keller's Bouchon Bakery and Café (Columbus Circle in the Time Warner Center, tel 212/823-9366) is a celebrated patisserie managed by the head pastry chef from upscale restaurant Per Se. The pastry case displays delectable offerings from Viennoisserie and tarts to handmade chocolates. Crowds make their way to the Magnolia Bakery (401 Bleecker Street, tel 212/462-2572) to taste the cupcakes iced with thick ultrasweet buttercream. In the East Village, Veniero's (342 East 11th Street, tel 212/674-7070) has been making and selling delicious Italian pastries for aeons.

TRADITIONAL AMERICAN FOOD

The United States of America is a nation of immigrants. Traditional American food has evolved out of the traditions of the immigrant populations—German, Jewish, Italian, Scandinavian, Latino, Asian—plus Native American and African-American. Each group has contributed its ingredients and techniques to the food scene. Germans brought sauerkraut, sausages and pumpernickel; Hungarians goulash and stuffed cabbage; Cubans black bean soup and Cuban sandwiches; Irish corned beef and cabbage; Japanese sushi and teriyaki; the Jewish community chopped liver pastrami and knishes; Greeks kebabs; Lebanese baba ganoush and falafel; Mexicans salsa, tacos and refried beans; Moroccans couscous; Russians blinis and caviar; Spanish tapas, chorizo and paella; Swedes gravlax; and Welsh leek and potato pie. Many of these dishes (or American modifications) have become common fare on all-American menus at standard American restaurants and even at neighborhood diners. The United States also boasts some distinctive regional cuisines, most notably Southern, Cajun, Southwestern and Tex-Mex.

DRINKS

The New York bar scene is extremely varied. Bars range from cheap dives charging a few dollars for a drink to luxury lounges charging anywhere from $10 for a cocktail. Despite the campaign against drinking and driving, most bars offer happy hours when they charge half price for drinks or offer two for the price of one. Note that American bartenders expect to be tipped (at least 10 percent). As far as drinks go, international beers and microbrews are readily available; cocktails are in vogue and every day brings a new concoction to light. Food is always available. It ranges from burgers and wings to more sophisticated fare. Most bars open from mid-morning to anywhere from 1am to 4am. Note that the drinking age is 21; expect to be "carded" (to show a photo ID), so carry an identification with photo. Buy wine and liquor at a liquor store; supermarkets sell beer only.

SOME NEW YORK DINING INSTITUTIONS

New York does have some unique dining institutions. The most famous is the deli. Among delis, the most traditional is the Jewish deli, which sells a variety of smoked fish and meats, plus items such as bagels, pastrami and corned beef sandwiches, chopped liver, pickles and knishes. The word deli is also used for small neighborhood grocery stores, often operated by Korean merchants. They sell coffee, bagels, sandwiches, salads and other grocery items.

The coffeeshop/diner is another traditional dining haven. It will have counters and stools as well as table service. Here people secure endless cups of coffee, and breakfast, lunch or dinner selections taken from a vast menu. The city has plenty of fast-food outlets, too (McDonald's, etc.). Look for street vendors also. They sell everything from hot salty pretzels to soups, hot dogs and ethnic snacks. The pizza parlor is also endemic to New York. The most visible coffee vendor is Starbucks, which seems to be on every street corner, but there are plenty of independent cafés, especially in the West and East villages.

LATE NIGHT/24-HOUR

Despite New York's reputation as a 24/7 town, it's not that easy to find food in the small hours. Among tried-and-true late-night oases, the hip but strangely unpretentious Blue Ribbon (97 Sullivan Street, tel 212/274-0404) draws clubbers and workers, including many chefs for sesame-glazed catfish, tofu ravioli, paella, and oysters on the half shell. It's open from 4pm to 4am daily.

The Coffee Shop (29 Union Square West, tel 212/243-7969), looks like what you'd expect, but nothing like you'd find in Peoria with its Brazilian ownership and fare.

At the former Empire Diner, now reopened as the Highliner (210 Tenth Avenue at 22nd Street, tel 212/206-6206), you'll pay for the stylish chrome-and-black art deco setting as well as for the classic egg dishes, sandwiches and meat loaf. It's open daily from 8am to 5am.

At the intersection of SoHo and NoLita, Delicatessen (54 Prince Street at Lafayette Street, tel 212/226-0211) offers international comfort food with Italian, French and American twists. The slick restaurant features a steel and glass wall that opens in warm weather.

Singles can almost always eat at the bar in Manhattan. If the place is full, or if you want to eat on the run, just ask.

Bagel An unsweetened eggless bread cooked in water then baked. It's shaped with a hole in the middle

Boston baked beans Navy beans flavored with molasses and salt pork

Chicken-fried steak Batter-dipped steak

Chowder Thick soup traditionally made with clams or corn

Cobbler Fruit pie topped with a biscuit-style crust

Egg cream A thick drink of chocolate syrup, milk and seltzer

Eggplant Aubergine

Eggs over easy Fried eggs turned over so they are cooked through

Eggs sunnyside up Fried eggs that have not been turned over

French toast Bread coated with beaten eggs and sautéed. Served with maple syrup

Grits Corn kernels with the bran and germ removed

Hero An extra-large long roll

Key lime pie Made with a special lime variety from Florida

London broil A particular cut of flank steak

Lox Cured salmon

Meat loaf Ground beef, turkey and pork combined with breadcrumbs and egg and baked

New York cheesecake Jewish-style dense and creamy cake, which may be plain or topped with fruit

On the rocks With ice

Pot roast Braised beef

Pretzel A long bread, twisted into a knot, sprinkled with coarse salt and sold warm from carts

Salisbury steak A beef patty

Scotch Scottish whisky

Stack of pancakes Three or four thick batter cakes served with maple syrup

Straight up No ice

Sub Short for submarine; another name for an extra-large long roll

Waldorf salad Apples, celery and walnuts in mayonnaise; first created at the Waldorf Astoria

Whiskey American rye

Above *Piles of pretzels on a stand*

RESTAURANTS BY CUISINE

American contemporary
Almond
Annisa
Aureole
The Bailey
Blue Hill
Blue Ribbon Bakery
Compass
Craft and Craftbar
Eleven Madison Park
Gotham Bar & Grill
Gramercy Tavern
The Harrison
Loeb Boathouse
Ouest
Per Se
Prune
The Red Cat
Sarabeth's
Union Square Café
Veritas
WD-50

American traditional
'21' Club
Bridge Café
Manatus

Asian
Asiate
Spice Market

Barbecue
Blue Smoke
Virgil's Real Barbecue

Burgers
Corner Bistro

Caribbean
Negril Village

Chinese
Dim Sum Go Go
Shun Lee Palace

Continental
Four Seasons

Deli
Barney Greengrass
Katz's Deli

Eclectic
The Spotted Pig

French
Artisanal
Balthazar
Bouley
Brasserie
Café Boulud
Daniel
DB Bistro Moderne

Gordon Ramsay at the London
Jean-Georges
Odeon
Paradou
Pastis

Greek
Molyvos
Periyali
Uncle Nick's

Indian
Banjara
Dawat
Devi
Hampton Chutney
Tamarind

International
Tolani

Italian
Babbo
Bar Pitti
Bread
Cesca
Felidia
Gnocco
I Coppi
Lupa
Naples 45
Peasant
Travertine

Japanese
Bond Street
Masa
Nobu
Sugiyama
Sushi Yasuda
Tomoe Sushi

Korean
Bann
Cho Dang Gol

Latin American
Calle Ocho
Pio Pio

Malaysian
Nyonya

Mediterranean
North Square
Picholine

Mexican
Crema Restaurant
Dos Caminos
Hell's Kitchen
La Palapa
Maya
Mesa Grill
Pampano

Rosa Mexicano
Sueños

Middle Eastern
Persepolis

Noodle shops
Big Wong King

Pizza
John's Pizzeria
Kesté Pizzeria
Otto Enoteca Pizzeria

Russian
Uncle Vanya Café

Scandinavian
Aquavit

Seafood
Aquagrill
Blue Fin
Esca
Grand Central Oyster Bar
Le Bernardin
Mermaid Inn
Pearl Oyster Bar

Soul
Amy Ruth's
Londel's

Spanish
Casa Mono
Pipa

Steak
Mark Joseph Steakhouse
Strip House

Thai
Holy Basil
Pam Real Thai

Vegetarian
Angelica Kitchen

Vietnamese
Le Colonial
Nam

HOTELS WITH EXCEPTIONAL DINING ROOMS

Algonquin
Carlyle
Four Seasons
Le Parker Meridien
Mandarin Oriental
Mercer Hotel
New York Palace
Plaza Athénée
Ritz-Carlton (Central Park South)
St. Regis
Sherry-Netherland
Trump International Hotel
W New York – Times Square

Traditionally the priciest hotels in New York have been relatively traditional, formal places. However, the last two decades have seen a number of ultra-chic hotels open around the city, offering guests luxurious amenities in modern, stylish settings. The restaurants, lounges and bars in these places also attract trendy New Yorkers, as well as visitors to the city. There are plenty of hotel rooms, but it is hard to find a comfortable room under $150. If money is no object, reserve a room at the Carlyle or the Four Seasons.

For less expensive options, check out the inexpensive chains—Red Roof, Super 8 and others. The city also has some bed-and-breakfasts, which charge less than the average hotel and provide good-value extras. Hostels are the least expensive lodging options (see below).

It used to be that all the best hotels were in Midtown but that has changed dramatically. Now, there are first-class luxury hotels downtown in SoHo, Greenwich Village and the Financial District. There are bargains away from Midtown. New York City hotels range in size from 2,000-room monstrosities to establishments with 250 rooms or fewer. If you stay at a large convention hotel, expect to find crowded lobbies, more lines and slower service.

Most hotels have similar amenities. The average hotel room comes with air conditioning, private bathroom, cable TV, telephone, coffeemaker, hairdryer, iron and ironing board. The level of luxury and the quality and range of the service are the real distinctions between hotels. Top-class hotel rooms boast luxe fabrics and linens, high-tech electronics and telephony, and high staff-to-guest ratios, which guarantees prompt, courteous service. Space is at a premium in Manhattan, so expect rooms to be on the small side. Double-glazed windows, which are usually standard, help reduce noise. Most hotels have complimentary coffee/tea service, and newspapers in the lobby or delivered to your room.

HOTEL ROOM RATES

Today there is no such thing as a standard rack rate. Prices fluctuate with customer demand. To get the best rate on a hotel room, always call the hotel directly and ask for the best available rate and what special discounts are available. Alternatively, go online to such discount services as www.hotels.com, www.quikbook.com or www.hoteldiscount.com to secure the best rates. Winter (Jan–end Feb) and summer (Jul–end Aug) are the least expensive seasons. Depending on the hotel, weekend rates may be higher or lower than midweek. Parking charges of $40 and up will add substantially to any bill. Note, too, that 14.75 percent room tax will be added to your bill, as well as additional occupancy taxes of $3.50 which are charged for each night's stay.

HOSTELS IN NEW YORK
BIG APPLE HOSTEL
www.bigapplehostel.com

✚ 296 D18 ✉ 119 West 45th Street, between Sixth and Seventh avenues, 10036
☎ 212/302-2603

CHELSEA CENTER HOSTEL
www.chelseacenterhostel.com
🕂 296 D19 ✉ 313 West 29th Street,
between Eighth and Ninth avenues, 10031
☎ 212/643-0214

CHELSEA INTERNATIONAL HOSTEL
www.chelseahostel.com
🕂 296 D20 ✉ 251 West·20th Street,
between Seventh and Eighth avenues, 10011
☎ 212/647-0010

HOSTELLING INTERNATIONAL
www.hinewyork.org
🕂 294 C12 ✉ 891 Amsterdam Avenue
at 104th Street, 10025-4403
☎ 212/932-2300

WHITEHOUSE
www.whitehousehotelofny.com
🕂 297 F22 ✉ 340 Bowery between 2nd
and Great Jones streets, 10012
☎ 212/477-5623

YMCA OF GREATER NEW YORK
www.ymcanyc.org
🕂 294 D16 ✉ 5 West 63rd Street,
between Central Park West and Broadway,
10023 ☎ 212/875-4100

HOTELS BY AREA
LOWER EAST SIDE
Off-SoHo Suites

GREENWICH VILLAGE/
MEAT MARKET/CHELSEA
Abingdon Guest House
Chelsea
Chelsea Lodge

Hotel Gansevoort
The Inn on 23rd
Larchmont
Maritime Hotel
Washington Square

SOHO/TRIBECA
Cosmopolitan Hotel-Tribeca
Hotel Azure
Mercer
SoHo Grand
Tribeca Grand

UNION SQUARE/FLATIRON
DISTRICT/GRAMERCY PARK
Gershwin
Giraffe
Inn at Irving Place

MADISON SQUARE PARK/
MURRAY HILL
70 Park Avenue
Avalon
Grand Union
Hotel Chandler
Marcel
Morgans
Thirty Thirty
Wolcott

MIDTOWN WEST/
THEATER DISTRICT
Algonquin
Americana Inn
Belvedere
Blakely
Casablanca
Dream Hotel
Hudson

Le Parker Meridien
Mansfield
The Michelangelo
Moderne
The Muse
Royalton
Shoreham
Travel Inn
Warwick

LINCOLN CENTER/
UPPER WEST SIDE
Excelsior
Hotel Roger Williams
Jumeirah Essex House
Lucerne
Mandarin Oriental
Newton
On the Ave
Ritz-Carlton
Trump International Hotel and Tower

MIDTOWN EAST
Beekman Tower
Benjamin
Edison
Elysée
Four Seasons
Kimberly
Library
Metro
New York Palace
Peninsula
The Pod Hotel
Renaissance New York Hotel 57
St. Regis
Sherry-Netherland
W New York – Times Square
Waldorf-Astoria Hotel and Towers

UPPER EAST SIDE
Affinia Gardens
Carlyle
Gracie Inn
Pierre
Plaza Athénée
Wales

Opposite and left *The New York Palace*
hotel on Madison Avenue in Midtown

New York is divided into the five boroughs of Manhattan, Brooklyn, the Bronx, Queens and Staten Island, each with their own distinct character.

MANHATTAN

Attractions, many of them world famous, line the streets of Manhattan, the area stretching from Battery Park at its tip to Harlem in the north, beyond Central Park.

FINANCIAL DISTRICT

The oldest part of the city and the nexus of the securities industry anchored by the New York Stock Exchange and Wall Street. It's still primarily a business district, although residents have moved in over the last decade.

BATTERY PARK CITY

A 92-acre (35ha) complex, built on landfill from the creation of the World Trade Center in 1974. It includes housing, commercial and retail space, plus a marina and the Museum of Jewish Heritage.

TRIBECA

It means *Tri*angle *Be*low *Ca*nal and is defined by Canal and Barclay streets and Broadway and the Hudson River. In 1980, the Odeon restaurant opened and pioneer residents followed, settling into the warehouses and manufacturing buildings. It now has the highest real-estate values in the city and plenty of celebrity cachet. Home to TriBeCa Film Center, it's still a mixed-use neighborhood of gritty warehouse lofts, loft-style restaurants and low-end retail.

CIVIC CENTER

The focal point of city government, incorporating the courts, police and immigration. City Hall is at the center of the area. It's dwarfed by the Municipal Building, designed by McKim, Mead & White.

CHINATOWN

In the 1840s, Chinatown was just eight blocks. Today it includes about 30 blocks, from Kenmare and Delancey streets to East Broadway and Worth Street, and from Broadway to Allen Street. Shop for fish, meat, vegetables and herbal remedies or dine in the many affordable restaurants.

LITTLE ITALY

Little of the once vibrant community survives. Most of the Italians have moved to the suburbs and Chinese residents have replaced them. It consists largely of Mulberry Street, which is lined with tourist-oriented restaurants, plus genuine delis.

NOLITA

It stands for *No*rth of *Li*ttle *Ita*ly. The narrow streets around St. Patrick's

Old Cathedral, once the heart of the Italian community, are now lined with hip designer boutiques.

SOHO
In 1973 the 20 blocks between Houston, Canal, West Broadway and Broadway were designated a Historic District, protecting the best stock of cast-iron buildings in the city. Artists had already begun reclaiming the manufacturing and warehouse spaces and pioneering a loft lifestyle. Today the artists and most galleries have moved on; the area is now an ultra-expensive, chic shopping area crowded with non-residents on weekends.

BOWERY
A long street connecting Chinatown to the East Village, it was once the city's Skid Row, lined with flophouses and numerous stores selling kitchen supplies and lighting fixtures. Today it is being gentrified.

LOWER EAST SIDE
The traditional gateway for every wave of immigrants, from the Jewish and the Italians to the Puerto Ricans, this was the last Manhattan neighborhood to be updated. Today, young professionals and artists occupy the tenements and congregate at the clubs and bars along Orchard, Clinton and other streets. Remnants of the Puerto Rican community survive, and so does the bargain bazaar on Sunday along Orchard Street. The boundaries stretch from 14th Street to Fulton and Franklin and from the East River to Broadway, incorporating Chinatown, Little Italy and the East Village neighborhoods.

GREENWICH VILLAGE/ WEST VILLAGE
This area stretches from 14th to Houston streets and from the Hudson River to Bowery and Fourth Avenue. Originally a poor neighborhood housing the workers

and stevedores who worked the waterfront, it became a bohemia around 1900, attracting a mixture of artists, writers and anarchists. Today, it's a mixed neighborhood. The gay population has mostly moved to Chelsea, and now "successful" singles and families occupy the town houses and apartments. Small boutiques line the west end of Bleecker Street. The southern section around Bleecker Street and Sixth Avenue still has an Italian flavor.

MEATPACKING DISTRICT
Sandwiched between the West Village and Chelsea around 14th Street, this gritty neighborhood is being redeveloped. Restaurants, bars, clubs and stores are opening, and hotels, too.

NOHO
Between SoHo and Greenwich Village (from Houston to Eighth streets and Mercer to Bowery/Third Avenue), this youth-oriented neighborhood has plenty of fashionable shopping, bars and restaurants. The acronym stands for *North of Houston*.

EAST VILLAGE
This was originally an extension of the Lower East Side, settled by Jewish and Ukrainian/Polish communities. In the 1960s–70s it became the center of the counter-culture. East Village has been rapidly redeveloped and is now filled with restaurants, bars and a young street scene.

ALPHABET CITY
It refers to avenues A, B, C and D between Houston and 14th streets. In the 1970s, First Avenue marked the DMZ and the streets east of First were considered dangerous drug supermarkets. Gentrification began in 1983 when Operation Pressure Point started cleaning up the drug trade, and buildings on Tompkins Square became co-ops. Today young professionals occupy the tenement apartments; there's

a thriving dining and bar scene, including a substantial number of gay bars and clubs. The original Hispanic population has been dispersed.

GRAMERCY PARK
This genteel and dignified neighborhood radiating from the eponymous gated garden square remains primarily residential. It stretches from 18th to 23rd streets and from Park Avenue South to Third Avenue.

UNION SQUARE/ FLATIRON DISTRICT
This hot neighborhood, leading south from the Flatiron Building on 22nd Street and around Madison Square, has bars, restaurants and clubs. The Green Market at Union Square is a must on Saturday. The former Ladies' Mile along Sixth Avenue between 15th and 24th streets is now occupied by large national chain stores. The boundaries are 14th and 23rd streets, and Park and Sixth avenues.

CHELSEA
Today Chelsea is the center of the gay community and the new focus for contemporary art anchored by numerous warehouse/garage galleries around and along 24th Street. It has a lively club and restaurant scene. The boundaries stretch from 14th to 30th streets and from Sixth Avenue to the Hudson River.

MURRAY HILL
A quiet residential neighborhood between 34th and 40th streets and Madison and Third avenues. It is becoming increasingly commercial on the fringes. The Morgan Library and the Episcopalian church, where the Roosevelts worshiped, set the tone.

MIDTOWN
The commercial heart of the city, between 34th and 59th streets on the West Side and from 40th to 59th streets on the East Side.

It includes major attractions, shops, restaurants, theaters, TV studios, Nasdaq and corporate offices.

TIMES SQUARE/ THEATER DISTRICT
The old peep shows, hookers and junkies have been displaced, and the area around 42nd Street and Broadway is now occupied by major corporations and national chain stores—Condé Nast, Reuters, ESPN Zone, Toys "R" Us and many others, who share the area with new hotels, clubs and theaters.

CLINTON/HELL'S KITCHEN
Real-estate developers have rediscovered this neighborhood from 42nd to 59th streets between Eighth Avenue and the Hudson River. Formerly known as Hell's Kitchen, it was the site of slaughterhouses and freight yards.

UPPER EAST SIDE
It stretches from 59th to 96th streets from Fifth Avenue to the East River. The section from 59th to 78th streets between Fifth and Park avenues is often referred to as the Gold Coast, where those who can afford it live. Farther east it was not always elegant, but it became more so in 1956 when the Third Avenue "El" was demolished and Madison Avenue became an ultra-chic shopping street. Today it is filled with private clubs, consulates, art galleries, restaurants and fine residences. Museum Mile extends along Fifth Avenue from 81st Street north past the Metropolitan Museum of Art.

YORKVILLE
High-rise apartments line the streets of what was formerly the German section between Lexington and Third avenues on 86th Street.

CARNEGIE HILL
Between 86th and 96th streets and Fifth and Third avenues, this is primarily a low-key wealthy residential district, anchored by the Carnegie mansion (now the Cooper-Hewitt National Design Museum). The area is home to such prestigious private schools as Dalton, Spence and Horace Mann, plus the Guggenheim and the Jewish Museum.

EAST HARLEM/SPANISH HARLEM
From 96th to 142nd streets, between Park Avenue and the East River, this area is still home to El Barrio, the community established by the Puerto Ricans, who first arrived at the end of World War I and increased in numbers after World War II. Today it's a mixed neighborhood of Italians, African-Americans and Hispanics.

LINCOLN SQUARE
The square is the area around the Lincoln Center. Wealthy individuals, many of them successful performers, occupy the towers, and the area buzzes with bars, restaurants and stores. The ABC and CNN studios are a major presence.

UPPER WEST SIDE
Broadway cuts right through this section that extends from 59th to 125th streets between the Hudson River and Central Park West. The blocks around 72nd Street were the center of an old German/East-European, primarily Jewish, liberal intellectual community. In the 1970s and 1980s, Columbus and Amsterdam avenues were gentrified and the old single-room occupancy hotels returned to handsome residences. Today, it's often referred to as a Manhattan suburb, because of its family orientation, although it has become more fashionable recently, as new chic restaurants have opened. Central Park West is lined with expensive cooperatives overlooking Central Park. Notable attractions include the American Museum of Natural History.

MORNINGSIDE HEIGHTS
Columbia University dominates this neighborhood, along with Barnard, Teachers College, the Cathedral of St. John the Divine and the Union Theological and Jewish Theological seminaries.

HARLEM
Stretching from 110th Street to the Harlem River and from Fifth to St. Nicholas avenues, Harlem is the city's most famous black community. Originally a suburb for the wealthy, it was settled in the late 19th century by Jewish immigrants from Germany. When the subway arrived in the early 20th century, most of the black community moved in from midtown Manhattan and also from the southern states; it drew black artists, writers and musicians. In the 1920s the Harlem Renaissance brought whites and blacks together to the clubs, theaters and jazz joints. Later it became a blighted community, destroyed by the riots of the 1960s. Today it has been rediscovered by the middle classes and increasingly by whites in search of reasonably priced houses. The restaurants and churches attract visitors.

WASHINGTON HEIGHTS/ INWOOD
This is the last stop in Manhattan. It has been home to many different immigrant groups. Today, it's largely a Dominican community, although young professionals are moving in. It's also home to the Cloisters and Fort Tryon Park.

BROOKLYN
With the highest population of the five boroughs (2.5 million), Brooklyn is a healthy rival to Manhattan. It's full of world-class museums, spacious parks, landmark buildings and lively neighborhoods.

GREENPOINT
This is an old Polish neighborhood where young professionals have moved in because of its proximity to Manhattan.

WILLIAMSBURG
Primarily a Jewish and African-American neighborhood, recently

Williamsburg has been discovered by the young and hip. Its ambience is now reminiscent of 1950s' Greenwich Village.

DUMBO

One developer alone has created this neighborhood (Down Under the Manhattan Bridge Overpass) by renting to artists and musicians. Today it is becoming a "hot" neighborhood à la SoHo with expensive lofts.

BROOKLYN HEIGHTS

This is a former premier residential neighborhood. The Promenade offers magnificent views of the Manhattan skyline.

COBBLE HILL

Cobble Hill is an affluent residential neighborhood where the streets are lined with elegant brownstones. Atlantic Avenue supports a major Middle Eastern community.

PROSPECT PARK

The Brooklyn Botanic Gardens are in Prospect Park and the Brooklyn Museum of Art is adjacent to the gardens.

CARROLL GARDENS

Fine brownstones made this primarily Italian neighborhood an attractive residential area for those who could not afford to buy property in Manhattan.

FORT GREENE

After it was designated a historic district in 1978, professionals started buying the handsome brownstones. It's home to the Brooklyn Academy of Music.

PARK SLOPE

Brooklyn's "alternative" village on the western edge of Prospect Park. The main commercial streets are Seventh and Fifth avenues.

CROWN HEIGHTS

The city's largest West Indian community, plus a thriving Hasidic Jewish community.

BRIGHTON BEACH/ CONEY ISLAND

Often called Little Odessa due to its Russian Jewish community, Brighton Beach has a boardwalk, clubs, restaurants and stores servicing the Russian community. Next door, Coney Island was the city's great blue-collar playground from the late 1890s to the early 1930s. In the 1960s it became drug infested and dangerous. Today it is being revived. It's home to the New York Aquarium.

QUEENS

An international melting pot, Queens has the most diverse population of the five boroughs, and is also the largest. Named for Queen Catherine of Braganza, Charles II's wife, it is a good place to go to sample ethnic life and cuisine.

ASTORIA

The old Greek neighborhood has survived. Astoria was also a film-making area and some of the studios have been revived, including one that houses the American Museum of the Moving Image.

LONG ISLAND CITY

This is Queens' most industrialized area. The gritty waterfront area is being revamped.

FOREST HILLS

This wealthy, largely Jewish enclave, only a short commute from Manhattan, has handsome apartment houses, and good restaurants and social services.

JACKSON HEIGHTS

There is a major South American and Indian enclave on 82nd Street.

CORONA, CITI FIELD AND FLUSHING MEADOWS PARK

The Citi Field stadium is the home of the Mets. The park has the National Tennis Center, the New York Hall of Science and the Queens Museum of Art. Corona is mainly a Dominican, Colombian and Mexican community.

FLUSHING MEADOWS

This is an area populated by Chinese, Koreans, Vietnamese, Malaysians and Japanese.

THE BRONX

The Bronx was once an expensive retreat for the wealthy. Development in the 1920s brought more well-heeled residents, then it got a reputation as a crime-laden area, and now has been turned into a much more tourist-friendly borough, with plenty of attractions and some beautiful parks.

FORDHAM

The Bronx Zoo and the New York Botanical Garden are in this neighborhood. Arthur Avenue is a colorful Italian area.

RIVERDALE

The most desirable residential neighborhood in the borough and the location of Wave Hill, an 1843 estate once home to Mark Twain and Teddy Roosevelt and now a public garden and cultural center.

VAN CORTLANDT PARK AND WOODLAWN CEMETERY

Many famous people are buried at Woodlawn, including F. W. Woolworth, Irving Berlin and Duke Ellington. Van Cortlandt Park is a delightful space with forests and hills to explore.

CITY ISLAND

New Yorkers come to this historic fishing community for fresh fish.

STATEN ISLAND

Staten Island is more than twice the size of Manhattan. Its residents are largely blue collar, still living a fairly autonomous, rural life away from busy Manhattan. Attractions include the Alice Austen House, Snug Harbor Cultural Center and Historic Richmond Town.

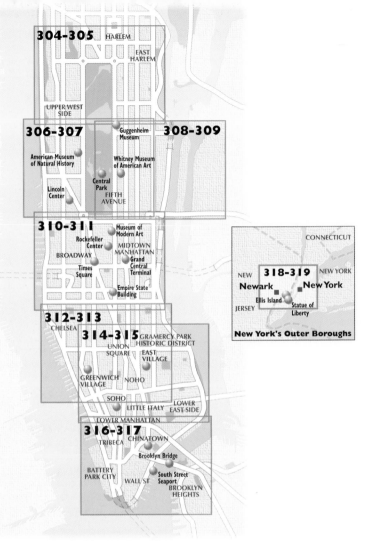

304-305 HARLEM

EAST HARLEM

UPPER WEST SIDE

306-307

Guggenheim Museum

308-309

American Museum of Natural History

Whitney Museum of American Art

Lincoln Center

Central Park

FIFTH AVENUE

310-311

Museum of Modern Art

Rockefeller Center

MIDTOWN MANHATTAN

BROADWAY

Grand Central Terminal

Times Square

Empire State Building

312-313

CHELSEA

314-315 GRAMERCY PARK HISTORIC DISTRICT

UNION SQUARE

EAST VILLAGE

GREENWICH VILLAGE

NOHO

SOHO

LITTLE ITALY

LOWER EAST SIDE

LOWER MANHATTAN

316-317

TRIBECA

CHINATOWN

Brooklyn Bridge

BATTERY PARK CITY

WALL ST

South Street Seaport

BROOKLYN HEIGHTS

CONNECTICUT

NEW

318-319

NEW YORK

Newark

New York

Ellis Island

JERSEY

Statue of Liberty

New York's Outer Boroughs

304-317

| 0 | 250 m |
| 0 | 250 yds |

318-319

| 0 | 8 km |
| 0 | 5 miles |

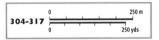 Motorway

Main road

Secondary road

Other road

- - - Road in tunnel

===== Footpath

Railway station

Park or garden

Building of interest

 Recommended sight

✝ Church

🅿 Car parking

Subway station:

1, 2, 3

4, 5, 6

7

A, C, E

B, D, F

L

M, J, Z

N, R, Q

S (42 St Shuttle)

MAPS | NEW YORK

302

MAPS

Map references for the sights refer to the individual locator maps within the regional chapters. For example, the Empire State Building has the reference ✚ 147 D10, indicating the locator map page number (147) and the grid square in which the Empire State Building sits (D10). These same grid references can also be used to locate the sights in this section. For example, the Empire State Building appears again in grid square D10 within the atlas, on page 311.

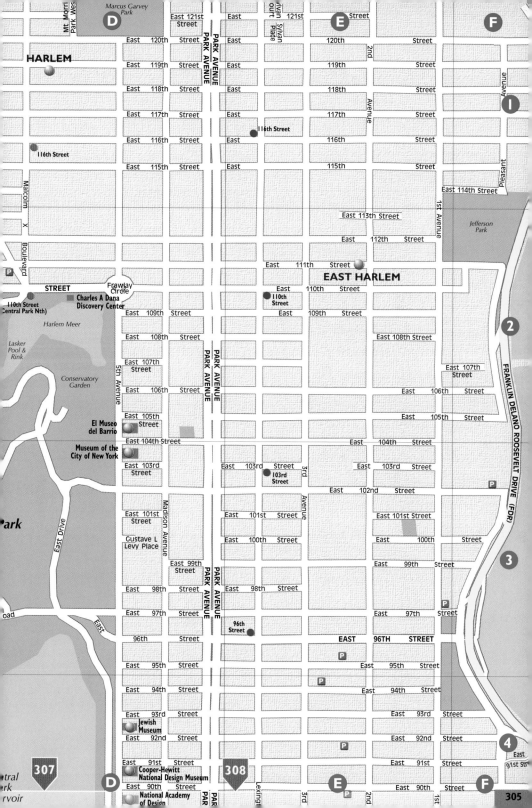

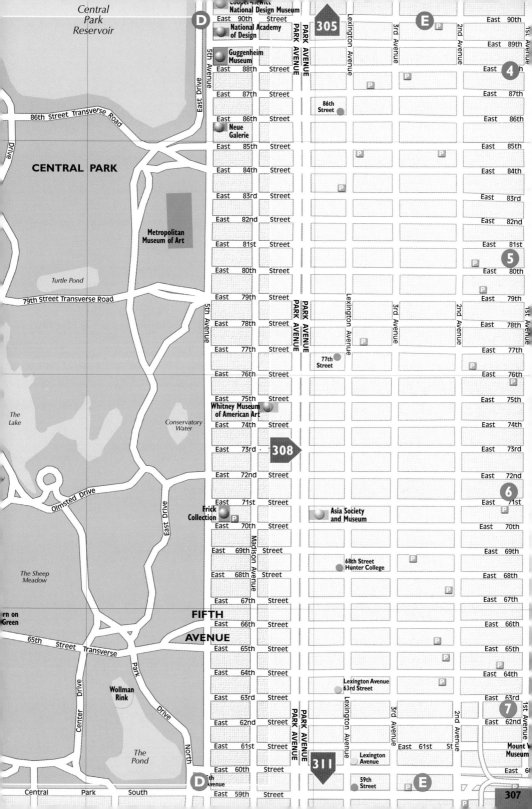

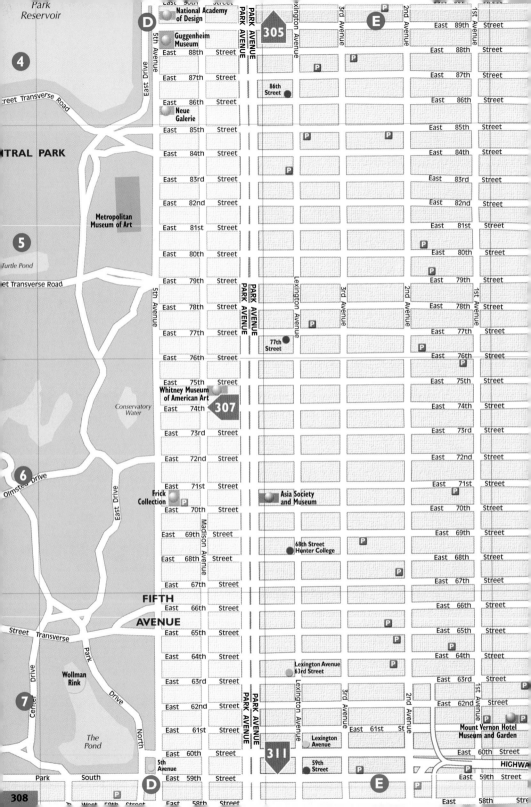

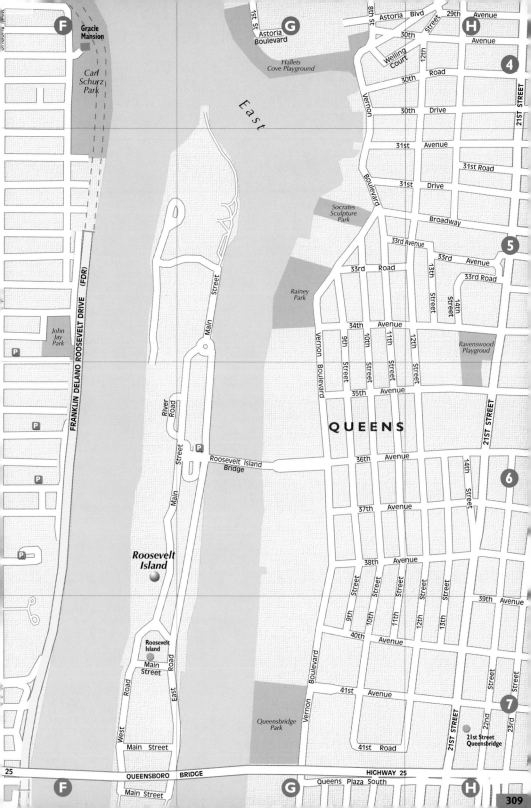

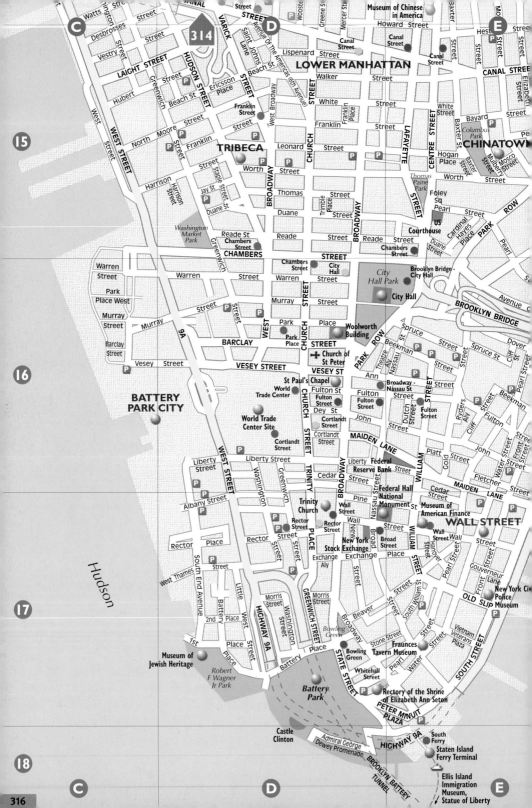

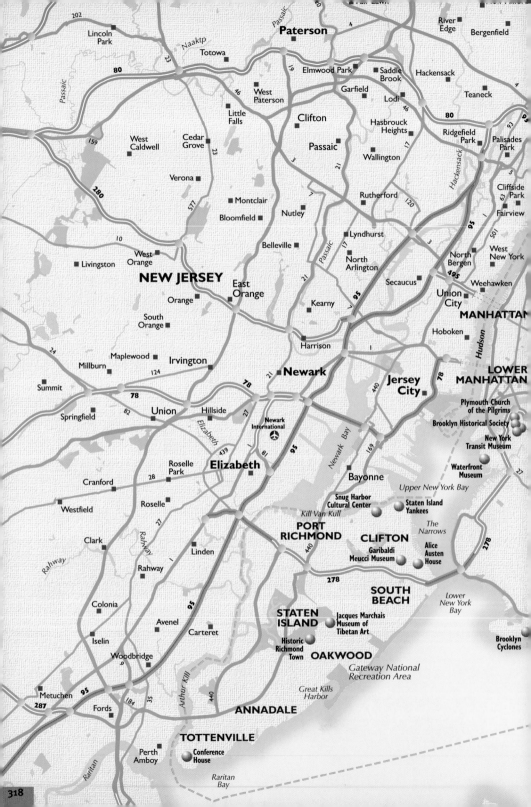

Lincoln
Park

202

Naaktp

Totowa

80

23

West
Caldwell

159

Cedar
Grove

23

Verona

Montclair

577

Bloomfield

Little
Falls

46

West
Paterson

Paterson

Passaic

19

Elmwood Park

Saddle
Brook

Garfield

Clifton

Passaic

Lodi

Hasbrouck
Heights

Wallington

Rutherford

Hackensack

Teaneck

80

Ridgefield
Park

17

120

Palisades
Park

Cliffside
Park

Fairview

93

95

4

501

North
Bergen

West
New
York

Nutley

Belleville

Lyndhurst

Passaic

17

North
Arlington

Secaucus

3

495

Weehawken

Union
City

Hoboken

MANHATTAN

West
Orange

Livingston

NEW JERSEY

East
Orange

Orange

South
Orange

10

Kearny

21

Harrison

95

1

LOWER
MANHATTAN

Hudson

78

Maplewood

Irvington

Newark

Jersey
City

24

Millburn

124

Summit

78

Springfield

82

Union

Hillside

27

Newark
International

81

440

Jersey
City

78

Plymouth Church
of the Pilgrims

Brooklyn Historical Society

New York
Transit Museum

Cranford

28

Roselle
Park

Elizabeth

439

95

Bayonne

169

Waterfront
Museum

27

Westfield

Roselle

Elizabeth

1

Upper New York Bay

Clark

27

Linden

440

Snug Harbor
Cultural Center

Kill Van Kull

Staten Island
Yankees

The
Narrows

278

Rahway

Rahway

PORT
RICHMOND

CLIFTON

Garibaldi
Meucci Museum

Alice
Austen
House

Colonia

95

Avenel

Carteret

278

SOUTH
BEACH

Lower
New York
Bay

Iselin

Woodbridge

9

STATEN
ISLAND

Jacques Marchais
Museum of
Tibetan Art

Brooklyn
Cyclones

Metuchen

95

287

Fords

184

35

440

Arthur Kill

Historic
Richmond
Town

OAKWOOD

Gateway National
Recreation Area

Great Kills
Harbor

ANNADALE

TOTTENVILLE

Perth
Amboy

Conference
House

Raritan

Raritan
Bay

318

PICTURES

The Automobile Association would like to thank the following photographers, companies and picture libraries for their assistance in the preparation of this book.

Abbreviations for the picture credits are as follows – (t) top; (b) bottom; (c) centre; (l) left; (r) right; (AA) AA World Travel Library.

2 AA/J Tims;
3t AA/J Tims;
3c AA/J Tims;
3b AA/J Tims;
4 AA/J Tims;
5 AA/J Tims;
6 AA/J Tims;
7 AA/J Tims;
8 AA/J Tims;
9 AA/D Corrance;
10 AA/J Tims;
11 AA/J Tims;
12 AA/J Tims;
13bl AA/J Tims;
13tr AA/J Tims;
14 AA/J Tims;
15tl AA/J Tims;
15br AA/J Tims;
16 AA/J Tims;
17bl AA/J Tims;
17br AA/J Tims;
18 AA/J Tims;
19t AA/J Tims;
19b AA/J Tims;
20 Julie Lemberger/Corbis;
21tl Photo courtesy of Steinway & Sons;
21tr AA/J Tims;
22 AA/J Tims;
23bl AA/J Tims;
23tr AA/J Tims;
24 AA/J Tims;
25bl AA/J Tims;
25br AA/J Tims;
26 AA/J Tims;
27 AA/J Tims;
28 AA;
29bl Mary Evans Picture Library;
29br Mary Evans Picture Library;
30 AA/C Sawyer;
31 AA;
32 Mary Evans Picture Library;
33tl AA/J Tims;
33br AA/J Tims;
34 Mary Evans Picture Library;
35bl AA;
35br AA/J Tims;
36 AA/J Tims;
37bl AA/J Tims;
37tr AA/J Tims;

38 AA/J Tims;
39tl Stephane de Sakutin/AFP/Getty Images;
39br Bettmann/Corbis;
40 AA/J Tims;
41 AA/J Tims;
42 Digitalvision;
44 AA/J Tims;
48 AA/J Tims;
49t AA/J Tims;
49b AA/J Tims;
50 AA/J Tims;
51 AA/J Tims;
53 AA/J Tims;
55bl AA/J Tims;
55cr AA/Clive Sawyer;
56 AA/J Tims;
57 AA/J Tims;
58 AA/J Tims;
59 AA/J Tims;
60 AA/E Rooney;
64 AA/J Tims;
65 AA/J Tims;
66 AA/J Tims;
67 AA/J Tims;
68 AA/J Tims;
69bl AA/J Tims;
69br AA/J Tims;
70 AA/J Tims;
71 AA/J Tims;
72 AA/J Tims;
75 AA/C Sawyer;
76 AA/J Tims;
77 AA/J Tims;
78 AA/J Tims;
79 AA/J Tims;
80 AA/J Tims;
81bl AA/J Tims;
81br AA/S McBride;
82 AA/J Tims;
83 AA/J Tims;
84 AA/C Sawyer;
85 AA/J Tims;
86 AA/J Tims;
87 Terese Loeb Kreuzer/Alamy;
88 AA/J Tims;
89 AA/C Sawyer;
90 AA/J Tims;
92 AA/J Tims;
94 AA/J Tims;

95 AA/C Sawyer;
97 Jon Kamantigue;
98 Resurrection Vintage;
100 AA/J Tims;
101 AA/J Tims;
102 ImageState;
105 AA/J Tims;
108 AA/J Tims;
112 AA/J Tims;
113 AA/J Tims;
114 AA/J Tims;
115bl AA/J Tims;
115br AA/J Tims;
116 AA/J Tims;
117 AA/J Tims;
119 AA/J Tims;
120t AA/J Tims;
120b AA/J Tims;
121 AA/J Tims;
122 AA/J Tims;
124 AA/J Tims;
134 AA/S Collier;
139 AA/J Tims;
140 AA/J Tims;
144 AA/C Sawyer;
148 AA/J Tims;
149 AA/J Tims;
150 AA/J Tims;
151t AA/J Tims;
151b AA/J Tims;
152 AA/C Sawyer;
153 AA/J Tims;
155 AA/J Tims;
156 AA/J Tims;
157 AA/J Tims;
158 Pierpont Morgan Library/Art Resource/Scala, Florence;
159 AA/J Tims;
160 AA/J Tims;
161 Stephen Finn/Alamy;
162 MOMA, New York/Scala, Florence;
163 AA/J Tims;
164 AA/J Tims;
165 AA/J Tims;
166bl AA/J Tims;
166br AA/J Tims;
167 AA/J Tims;
168 AA/J Tims;
169 AA/J Tims;

170 AA/J Tims;
171 AA/C Sawyer;
172 AA/J Tims;
174 AA/C Sawyer;
175 AA/J Tims;
176 AA/J Tims;
186 Ingram;
190 AA/J Tims;
193 The New York Palace;
194 AA/C Sawyer;
198 AA/J Tims;
202 AA/C Sawyer;
203 AA/J Tims;
204 AA/J Tims;
205 AA/J Tims;
206 AA/J Tims;
208 AA/J Tims;
209 AA/J Tims;
210t AA/J Tims;
210b AA/J Tims;
211 AA/J Tims;
212 AA/J Tims;
213t AA/J Tims;
213b AA/J Tims;
214 AA/C Sawyer;
215 Michael Bodycomb;
216 AA/J Tims;
217 AA/C Sawyer;
218 AA/J Tims;
219bl AA/J Tims;
219br AA/J Tims;
221 AA/J Tims;
222 AA/J Tims;
223 Whitney Museum of American Art;
224 Whitney Museum of American Art;
225 Whitney Museum of American Art;
226 AA/J Tims;
227 AA/J Tims;
228 AA/J Tims;
230 AA/J Tims;
237 AA/J Tims;
238 AA/J Tims;
241 AA/J Tims;
242 AA/J Tims;
246 AA/J Tims;
250 AA/J Tims;
253t AA/J Tims;
253b AA/J Tims;
254 AA/J Tims;
255 AA/J Tims;

256 AA/J Tims;
258 New York Yankees;
259 Photorush/Photolibrary;
260 AA;
262 Mick Hales/Historic Husdon Valley;
263 Historic Husdon Valley;
264 Vince Kish, Courtesy of Old Westbury Gardens;
265 Vince Kish, Courtesy of Old Westbury Gardens;
266 G Fiume/Getty Images;
267 Rick Shupper/Photolibrary;
268 AA/J Tims;
271 AA/J Tims;
275 AA/J Tims;
277 AA/J Tims;
279 AA/J Tims;
281 AA/J Tims;
282 AA/C Sawyer;
283 AA/J Tims;
284 AA/J Tims;
285 AA/J Tims;
286 AA/J Tims;
287 AA/J Tims;
288 AA/J Tims;
290 AA/J Tims;
292 AA/J Tims;
294 AA/C Sawyer;
296 The New York Palace;
297 The New York Palace;
298 AA/J Tims;
303 AA/J Tims.

Every effort has been made to trace the copyright holders, and we apologise in advance for any accidental errors. We would be happy to apply any corrections in the following edition of this publication.

CREDITS

Series editor
Sheila Hawkins

Project editor
Lodestone Publishing Ltd

Design
Low Sky Design Ltd

Cover design
Chie Ushio

Picture research
Elisabeth Stacey

Image retouching and repro
Jacqueline Street

Mapping
Maps produced by the Mapping Services Department of AA Publishing

Text updated by Donna Dailey

Indexer
Marie Lorimer

Production
Lorraine Taylor

See It New York City
ISBN 978-0-87637-136-7
Fifth Edition

Published in the United States by Fodor's Travel and simultaneously in Canada by Random House of Canada Limited, Toronto.
Published in the United Kingdom by AA Publishing.
Fodor's is a registered trademark of Random House, Inc., and Fodor's See It is a trademark of Random House, Inc.
Fodor's Travel is a division of Random House, Inc.

Color separation by AA Digital Department
Printed and bound by Leo Paper Products, China
10 9 8 7 6 5 4 3 2 1

Special Sales: This book is available for special discounts for bulk purchases for sales promotions or premiums. Special editions, including personalized covers, excerpts of existing books, and corporate imprints, can be created in large quantities for special needs.
For more information, write to Special Markets/Premium Sales, 1745 Broadway, MD 6-2, New York, NY 10019 or e-mail specialmarkets@randomhouse.com
Important Note: Time inevitably brings changes, so always confirm prices, travel facts, and other perishable information when it matters. Although Fodor's cannot accept responsibility for errors, you can use this guide in the confidence that we have taken every care to ensure its accuracy.

A04723
Maps in this title produced from cartographic data © Tele Atlas N.V. 2003   Tele Atlas
Transport map © Communicarta Ltd, UK
Weather chart statistics supplied by Weatherbase © Copyright 2003 Canty and Associates, LLC

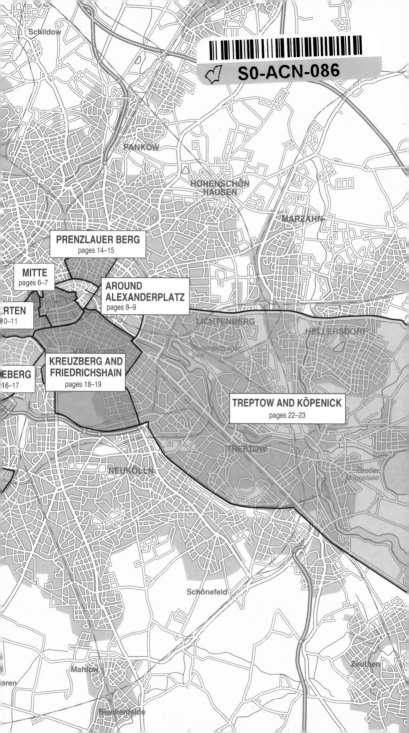

S0-ACN-086

Schildow

PANKOW

HOHENSCHÖN
HAUSEN

MARZAHN

PRENZLAUER BERG
pages 14–15

MITTE
pages 6–7

**AROUND
ALEXANDERPLATZ**
pages 8–9

LICHTENBERG

HELLERSDORF

RTEN
0–11

Rummelsburger
See

**KREUZBERG AND
FRIEDRICHSHAIN**
pages 18–19

EBERG
16–17

TREPTOW AND KÖPENICK
pages 22–23

Spree

NEUKÖLLN

Großer
Müggelsee

Dahme

TREPTOW

Schönefeld

Mahlow

Zeuthen

eren

Blankenfelde

INSIGHT GUIDES

BERLIN

smart guide

Part of the Langenscheidt Publishing Group

Contents

Areas

A–Z

Below: the iconic East German car: the Trabant.

2

Left: the Berlin Sculpture.

Atlas

Below: in Karl Friedrich
Schinkel's graceful square,
Gendarmenmarkt.

Berlin

More than any other major European city, Berlin still bears the scars of the last 100 years. The new Berlin does not hide its ghosts. Instead, they live among the bold architecture and hotspots of this gritty, trendy city, which exudes the energy of a capital reborn, but remembers being on the frontline of many pivotal and, at times, dark moments in the 20th century.

Berlin Facts and Figures

Population: 3.4 million (of which 86 percent ethnically German; 23.4 percent between ages of 18 and 35)
Area: 891 sq km (344 sq miles)
Buildings destroyed in World War II: 34 percent
Visitors staying overnight per year: 14.6 million
Hotels, hostels and pensions: 576
Theatres: 52
Museums: 125
Cinemas: 288
Number of bezirke (boroughs): 12
Largest lake: Grosser Müggelsee
Tallest building: the Fernsehturm (368m/1,207ft)

Division and Reunification

On 9 November 1989, with the eyes of the world watching, the Berlin Wall fell. The frontier at which East met West, the Wall had ripped through the centre of Berlin since 1961 and been the most visible and poignant emblem of the Cold War. After a century of profound tumult in Germany – wars, privation, dictatorships, division – at which Berlin had often found itself at the epicentre, the city was finally in a position to move forward.

And move forward it has. The history of Berlin since that night has been one of the most complete urban transformations in history. In the years since reunification, the redesigned Reichstag is once again the centre of government, Europe's biggest construction site has turned out a glittering new architectural playground, and many parts of central Berlin that had remained piles of rubble since the final days of World War II have finally been regenerated. Meanwhile, musicians, artists, students and entrepreneurs from around the world have flocked to Berlin to be a part of the city's re-emergence.

Berlin's Neighbourhoods

Visitors to Berlin who knew the city 20 years ago would no doubt be astounded by the shifts in the personalities of the various *bezirke* (boroughs). Located in the eastern part of Germany, less than 100km (62 miles) from the Polish border, Berlin is buffered by the leafy Grunewald forest and the Havel river to the west. The Spree river crosses the centre of the city and is a main inland waterway; the city is criss-crossed with many canals. The centre of Berlin is Mitte, where the major cultural institutions are located. Tiergarten with its leafy park is to Mitte's west and leads to Charlottenburg, which is upscale, if less prominent since the fall of the Wall. South of the centre is Kreuzberg, home to many of the newer landmarks and a neighbourhood legendary for its alternative youth culture and large Turkish population. Schöneberg sits just west and is more gentrified, with a prominent gay scene. Meanwhile, northern district Prenzlauer Berg has transformed from a grey, poor district into a trendy hub of café culture and boutiques.

Below: in line with German tradition, when the sun comes out, locals head to a beer garden.

Berlin Today

Two decades since the fall of the Wall, the subway system is reconnected and the centre of Berlin is again a thriving hub of business and politics, not to mention riches of culture. This has come at a literal price: Berlin has considerable municipal debt due to redeveloping the city, while unemployment runs above the national average. Nevertheless, as Mayor Klaus Wowereit quipped, Berlin is 'poor but sexy'. He might be on to something. Compared to London and Paris, Berlin certainly appears less affluent and more gritty. Yet it maintains an avante-garde flair that has been largely priced out of these other capital cities; the cost of living in Berlin is still comparatively cheap. Mean-while, though it is not the hotbed of Weimar-era decadence depicted in the film *Cabaret*, Berlin is still permissive. The city's nightlife scene is legendary, heavy drinking and smoking do not yet raise eyebrows, and Berliners generally take a liberal view of others' sexual proclivities.

Gradually, Berlin is becoming more established, with increasing tourism and fewer cranes, as the landscape of the city settles down. Nevertheless, there is still a good deal of edgy energy to keep Berlin distinct. With so much recent history that it can almost be touched, an exploding cultural scene and the sense of a city still building its identity, what better time to explore the old and the new in Berlin?

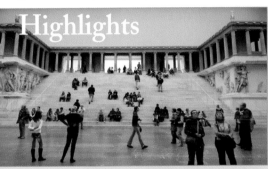

Highlights

▲ **Pergamonmuseum** An immense ancient collection: do not miss the Pergamon Altar.
▶ **Berlin Wall** Bernauer Strasse and the East Side Gallery are the best places to see the remains of this potent Cold War symbol.

▲ **Fernsehturm** An icon of communist East Berlin; ascend to the observation deck to take in the great panoramic city views.

▶ **Reichstag** From Sir Norman Foster's dazzling glass cupola, see the history-packed seat of the German parliament.

▲ **Schloss Charlottenburg** The palace reflects Berlin's Hohenzollern past, while the park is idyllic.
▶ **Jüdisches Museum** Striking architecture houses a broad and unflinching look at Jewish history.

Mitte

Mitte means 'middle', and this central Berlin district is truly both the geographical and historical centre of the city. It includes the two islands where Berlin began, the remnants of the old Hohenzollern Kaisers' residences and many of its contemporary cultural institutions, from the Museumsinsel to the Berliner Ensemble. Mitte is also the home of some of Berlin's most bombastic icons, such as the Brandenburger Tor, as well as some of its most sombre monuments. Sidelined during its days in East Germany, Mitte has sprung back into life since the Wall came down and regained its rightful place at the administrative and cultural heart of the city.

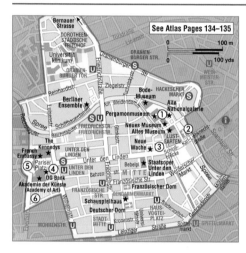

Berlin was actually founded on two islands, but they have been physically merged for years. Still, Fischerinsel, the island where the city's fishermen lived, is a nice break from the hustle of Mitte, with old boats in the historical harbour district, and shaded waterfront walks.

Museumsinsel

Running down the centre of Mitte is **Unter den Linden**, the city's grand promenade. At its start, it is bisected by the **Museumsinsel** ①, the island that is home to much of the city's immense collection of art treasures, divided up between the **Altes Museum**, the **Neues Museum, Alte Nation-algalerie, Pergamonmuseum** and the **Bode-Museum**. The Altes Museum not only contains masterpieces, it is itself a masterpiece of neoclassicism designed by Karl Friedrich Schinkel, the architect who did so much to shape Berlin's look

in the early 19th century. It is framed by the huge lawn, the **Lustgarten** (Pleasure Garden) of the Kaisers, as well as the imposing hulk of the **Berliner Dom** ②, the Protestant cathedral of the Evangelical Church in Germany, in whose basement much of the Hohen-zollern dynasty is buried.

SEE ALSO ARCHITECTURE, P.28; CHURCHES, SYNAGOGUES AND MOSQUES, P.44; MUSEUMS, P.86, 89

Unter den Linden

Across the **Schlossbrücke**, with its statues glorifying Prussian military virtues, the large pink building is the

former Prussian armoury, which today houses the **Deutsches Historisches Museum** ③ (German Historical Museum), with its surprising addition by I.M. Pei out of view in the rear. On the other side of the street stands the Kommandatur, the Prussian army headquarters.

Next to the Zeughaus is another Schinkel building, the **Neue Wache**, the guardhouse for the palace, which today is a memorial to the victims of German fascism and contains a statue by Käthe Kollwitz, *Mother with Her Dead Son*. Across the street is the **Staatsoper Unter den Linden**, still a major opera house.

Next door is **Bebelplatz**, where in 1933 the Nazis, including many students from the University, burned books by authors they deemed un-German; there is a sunken memorial to the book-burning in its centre. Most of the

Left: the Brandenburger Tor, Berlin's most iconic site.

the **Französischer Dom**, both Protestant churches. Today, the Französischer Dom is a museum dedicated to the Huguenots who settled in Berlin and played an instrumental part in starting the local Industrial Revolution.

Across the Spree is the **Berliner Ensemble**, the theatre built by the East Germans for returning playwright Berthold Brecht. Continuing up Friedrichstrasse, the **Dorotheenstädtische Friedhof** is Berlin's celebrity cemetery, with the graves of Bertolt Brecht, Heinrich Mann, G.W.F. Hegel, Karl Friedrich Schinkel and many others. Next door stands Brecht's house, which contains a **museum** and a fine **restaurant** in its basement.

Bernauer Strasse, the infamous **death strip** of the **Berlin Wall**, contains two of the remaining stretches of the Wall, as well as numerous historical markers provided by the Wall Documentation Centre at Bernauer Strasse and Ackerstrasse.

SEE ALSO ARCHITECTURE, P.30; LITERATURE, P.80; MONUMENTS AND MEMORIALS, P.82; MUSIC, P.96; RESTAURANTS, P.112; THEATRE AND DANCE, P.126

Below: classical sculpture in the Pergamonmuseum.

books were looted from the Staatsbibliothek, the national library next to the University. The huge building overlooking Bebelplatz is the law school of Humboldt, nicknamed the 'Kommode' (Chest of Drawers). The **Reiterdenkmal Friedrichs des Grossen** (statue of Frederick the Great) in the centre of the street marks the end of the monuments of Imperial Berlin.

SEE ALSO MONUMENTS AND MEMORIALS, P.82–5; MUSEUMS, P.87–8; MUSIC, P.97

Brandenburger Tor

Continuing down the street, one of the few remaining relics of Russian post-war power stands, the Russian Embassy. Nearby, the **Hotel Adlon** ④ (a reproduction of the one which burned down in 1945) marks the beginning of Pariser Platz, which is dominated by the most recognisable symbol of Berlin, the **Brandenburger Tor** (Brandenburg Gate) ⑤.

The structures around the Brandenburger Tor are all recent, including the Akademie der Künste (Academy of Art), the French Embassy and the **DG Bank**, a Frank Gehry building. **The Kennedys**, a small museum, is in one of the buildings flanking the Gate, and beyond it is the recent **Denkmal für die ermordeten Juden Europas** (Memorial to the Murdered Jews of Europe) ⑥.

SEE ALSO HOTELS, P.71; MONUMENTS AND MEMORIALS, P.83; MUSEUMS, P.88

Elsewhere in Mitte

A couple of blocks south of Unter den Linden, near Friedrichstrasse, stands the group of buildings which are considered Schinkel's masterpiece, the impressive **Gendarmenmarkt** complex. Centred on the **Konzerthaus Berlin**, a theatre which is now used as a symphony hall, it is flanked by the **Deutscher Dom** and

Around Alexanderplatz

A lexanderplatz was once Berlin's commercial centre, a booming district of shops, trams and pedestrians. The German Democratic Republic (GDR) rebuilt much of this area after it was flattened in World War II, in a reconstruction which does little credit to East German architecture, being mostly the prefab buildings known as *Plattenbau*. Still, the iconic Fernsehturm is just one of the attractions here. With grandiose architecture, cutting-edge galleries and the historical districts of the Nikolaiviertel and Scheunenviertel, Alexanderplatz and the areas around it are distinctive parts of Mitte that are well worth visiting.

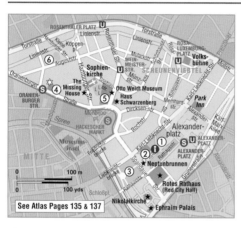

See Atlas Pages 135 & 137

Alexanderplatz

Alexanderplatz is dominated by two of Berlin's tallest buildings. The **Park Inn** hotel was previously one of three in which visitors from outside East Germany could spend the night instead of returning to the West at midnight. The other sky-scraping edifice is the **Fernsehturm** ① (Television Tower), built in the late 1960s to show East German superiority over the West, in particular the **Funkturm** (Radio Tower) in far West Berlin. From the observation deck there is an unparalleled view of the city.

Back on the ground, the **Rotes Rathaus** (Red City

Hall), named for the bricks, not the politics practised therein, is a welcome early 20th-century relief from the Socialist architecture that dominates this area. During the city's division, East Berlin was administered from here, while West Berlin used Rathaus Schöneberg.

In the park in front of it, one of the last remnants of the Prussian castle, the **Neptunbrunnen**, spouts water from all manner of bronze sea creatures. At the north-western corner of Alexanderplatz, the **Marienkirche** ②, one of Berlin's oldest churches, is worth a visit for its Plague-era *Dance of*

Death fresco and, if you're lucky, a recital on the 18th-century Walther organ.
SEE ALSO ARCHITECTURE, P.30–31; CHURCHES, SYNAGOGUES AND MOSQUES, P.44; HOTELS, P.73

The Nikolaiviertel

Just west of Alexanderplatz lies the **Marx-Engels-Forum** ③, a park dominated by the twin statues of the founders of communism and a collection of impressive stainless-steel stelae, in which are engraved photographs of the history of socialism and world revolution. Just beyond it, dominated by the twin steeples of the **Nikolaikirche**, is the Nikolaiviertel neighbourhood, which contains some of Berlin's oldest buildings, many of which were imported for the 750th anniversary of the city's founding in 1987. The church itself is now a museum of early Berlin history. Other historic buildings nearby include the **Ephraim Palais**, once the home of the court jeweller. On nice days, the restaurants and bars along the river here are a great place to relax.
SEE ALSO CHURCHES, SYNAGOGUES AND MOSQUES, P.44; PALACES AND HOUSES, P.105

Left: the Fernsehturm (Television Tower).

The rest of the courtyard, known as **Haus Schwarzenberg,** is one of the prominent collections of artists' studios in the Mitte area. Apart from being a treasure chest of classical art, Mitte is known as a gallery hub and international art venue, due largely to the **Kunst-Werke Institute of Contemporary Art** ⑥ in Auguststrasse, which launched the Berlin Biennial for Contemporary Art in 1997. The art scene is part of what makes Scheunenviertel such a trendy area, packed with bars and restaurants.
SEE ALSO ARCHITECTURE, P.28–9; CHURCHES, SYNAGOGUES AND MOSQUES, P.44; GALLERIES, P.62; MONUMENTS AND MEMORIALS, P.83

Karl-Marx-Allee

East of Alexanderplatz is Karl-Marx-Allee, formerly Stalinallee, a massive architectural project undertaken by the GDR. The overall effect is a study in Russian bombast; the history is given on bilingual placards placed along both sides of the avenue. Starting at Strausberger Platz and extending to Frankfurter Tor, it makes an interesting walk on a day with good weather.
SEE ALSO ARCHITECTURE, P.30

Monbijou Park, on Oranienburger Strasse, is named for a minor palace which stood there until destroyed by bombing. It was built in 1703, and had numerous outbuildings in various fanciful styles. Today, its location on the banks of the Spree hosts the Strandbar, a fake beach which comes to life each summer and is hugely popular with locals and visitors.

The Scheunenviertel

North of Alexanderplatz, several bridges lead to the Scheunenviertel, a neighbourhood mostly built in the 19th century for Eastern European immigrants, many of whom were Jews. The Scheunenviertel has a rich Jewish history, and fittingly, its skyline is dominated by the **Neue Synagogue** ④, built in the 1860s as a sign of Jewish Berlin's prosperity. A park on Grosse Hamburger Strasse is the former site of the Alte Synagogue's **ceme-**tery; only the grave of Moses Mendelssohn remains.

Next to it, the **Grosse Hamburger Strasse Memorial** commemorates the Jews who were gathered in a former building there, before being deported to concentration camps. Similarly sombre is the **The Missing House** art installation by French artist Christian Boltanski, on the other side of the street. Here, the names and occupations of the former residents of a bombed-out house are affixed to the wall next to where their apartments once were.

The **Sophienkirche** is a masterpiece of Northern German Baroque architecture. Sophienstrasse, to the rear of the church, contains a number of restored 18th-century houses, as well as an entrance to the **Hackescher Höfe** ⑤, one of the most impressive collections of linked courtyards, now full of shops and bars.

Below: the Nikolaikirche, in one of Berlin's prettiest areas.

Tiergarten

The Tiergarten district is named after one of Berlin's most agreeable features, the huge 'central park' once used as a hunting preserve (its name means 'animal garden') by the Electors. It contains many monuments and sculptures, as well as the Zoo Berlin. The Tiergarten district is something of a showcase for post-reunification architecture, containing Potsdamer Platz, entirely rebuilt after the city's reunification in 1989. This is now the home of the annual Berlinale, Berlin's film festival, but the area around here yields many year-round cultural pleasures. For many, though, the highlight of this area will be a trip to the Reichstag.

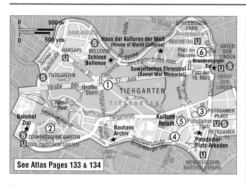

See Atlas Pages 133 & 134

In 1955, an architectural competition was held to build new 'classic modern' residences in a bombed area just off the Tiergarten known as the Hansaviertel. Architects like Aalvar Aalto, Walter Gropius and Oscar Niemeyer were among the winners, and today, architecture students still walk its streets taking notes. A map on Bartningallee near the Hansaplatz S-Bahn station is the most convenient one for matching up architects with buildings.

The Tiergarten

Past the Brandenburger Tor (Brandenburg Gate), Unter den Linden becomes the Strasse des 17 Juni, its name commemorating a workers' uprising in East Berlin in 1953 that was put down by Soviet tanks. The broad boulevard stretches towards the **Siegessäule** ①, the victory column raised after the Franco-Prussian War. Just past the Brandenburger Tor is the **Sowjetisches Ehrenmal** (Soviet War Memorial), on the site of a mass grave of Russian soldiers killed in battle for Berlin.

Venturing north into the park brings you to the **Haus der Kulturen der Welt** (House of World Cultures), known to the locals as the 'pregnant oyster', a gift to West Berlin from the United States. It serves as a venue for exhibitions and concerts.

At the end of John-Foster-Dulles-Allee is **Schloss Bellevue**, an 18th-century hunting lodge which is now the residence and office of Germany's President, a ceremonial figure whose presence is signalled by a flag atop the building.

South and west of the Siegessäule, trails lead past artificial lakes fed by the nearby Landwehrkanal along the periphery of the **Zoo Berlin** ②. The Zoo itself is immense, one of the largest collections of animals in the world, with one of its residents being an international star, the orphaned polar bear Knut. Across from the Zoo's main entrance is Bahnhof Zoo, once West Berlin's

main train station, now replaced by the shiny new **Hauptbahnhof**.

SEE ALSO ARCHITECTURE, P.31; CHILDREN, P.41; MONUMENTS AND MEMORIALS, P.84–5; PARKS AND GARDENS, P.108

Potsdamer Platz

Next to Alexanderplatz, Potsdamer Platz was the most important square in pre-war Berlin and a centre of local culture. Bombed flat, it was caught in the no man's land between the Wall, languishing until unification made it the hottest piece of real estate in Europe. A campaign to bring corporate headquarters and commercial activity there resulted in a flurry of high-

Left: the roof of the Sony Center in Potsdamer Platz.

legislature. Its burning in 1933 was the catalyst for the Nazis seizing complete power, and the staged images of the victorious Russian army raising the hammer and sickle are part of Berlin's iconography. Standing on the western side of the Wall, with the border running just metres from its back door, the Reichstag lay empty for years after being reconstructed. With the country's reunification, it regained its former prominence as the home of the *Bundestag* (government). Sir Norman Foster designed a new dome and made it a focal point for the public, who can look down and watch the parliament at work. It is Berlin's top tourist attraction for Germans and always has long queues on the steps, although they move relatively quickly.

Past the Reichstag, lining the banks of the Spree, is the **Spreebogen** complex of government buildings, notable for their transparent architecture and occasional grandiosity. Some feature outdoor cafés and bars, which are extremely popular during the summertime.
SEE ALSO ARCHITECTURE, P.31

profile architectural projects. A huge cinema complex was built to house the **Berlinale**, and several grand hotels were built to house visitors. Despite all this, there's little to do in Potsdamer Platz itself once you've visited the excellent **Deutsche Kinemathek** and admired Helmut Jahn's **Sony Center** ③ and some of the other buildings; the Potsdamer Platz Arkaden is principally a shopping mall, and the majority of the restaurants are undistinguished.

It is, however, the jumping-off point to see two of Berlin's most important museums, the **Neue Nationalgalerie** ④ and the **Gemäldegalerie** at the **Kulturforum**, as well as being within walking distance of the **Philharmonie** ⑤, home of the renowned Berlin Philharmonic and the **Musikinstrumenten-museum**.

Not far from them, across a narrow section of the park, is the **Bauhaus Archiv**,

which documents the important 1920s architectural and crafts movement with regular exhibitions.
SEE ALSO ARCHITECTURE, P.31; FESTIVALS AND EVENTS, P.54; FILM, P.57; MUSEUMS, P.90–91; MUSIC, P.96

The Regierungsviertel

Few of Berlin's buildings are invested with as much history as the **Reichstag** ⑥, built in 1894 to house Germany's

Below: posing outside the Reichstag.

Charlottenburg

Before reunification, Charlottenburg *was* Berlin for Western visitors. Hotels and shops lined the Kurfürstendamm (or Ku'damm, as the locals call it), and a visit to the KaDeWe department store and its legendary food floor was mandatory. With a visit to Mitte or the palace of Sanssouci in Potsdam requiring going into GDR territory, the best glimpse of the Hohenzollern past was a tour of Schloss Charlottenburg. Today, the East is open and the choice of hotels is wider, but although less trendy, Charlottenburg retains its attractions and remains the best place to get a sense of the most established and sophisticated side of Berlin.

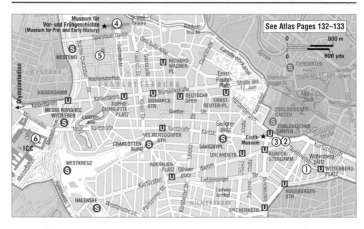

See Atlas Pages 132–133

The Kurfürstendamm

For visitors, the Ku'damm starts in the section of Tauentzienstrasse by Wittenbergplatz U-Bahn station, a beautifully reconstructed Weimar-era facility with vintage advertisements on its walls. **Wittenbergplatz** is home to an understated memorial for victims of the concentration camps. At the end of Wittenbergplatz is the **KaDeWe** ①, Berlin's most famous and legendary department store. The Kaufhof des Westens, as it is officially called, opened in 1907 and has served as a temple of luxury goods ever since. Its luxurious and decadent

food hall, on the sixth floor, is particularly worth a visit.

Other large department stores can be found nearby, and at the point where Tauentzienstrasse becomes the Ku'damm stands one of Berlin's rare skyscrapers, the **Europa-Center** ②, with its Mercedes star revolving on top. Next door, the **Kaiser-Wilhelm-Gedächtniskirche** (Kaiser Wilhelm Memorial Church) ③ was left in its partially bombed state by the Evangelical Church as a war memorial. Services are held in the tubular building adjacent. From here, the Ku'damm becomes the familiar tree-lined boulevard that evokes

pre-war Berlin, although increasing real-estate prices have seen a rise in chain stores and fast-food outlets and a decline in luxury retailers. A surprising discovery is the X-rated **Erotik-Museum** upstairs from the huge Beate Uhse store on Joachimsthaler Strasse near Zoo Station, home to a serious collection of historic erotica.

In the waning days of the Weimar Republic, Christopher Isherwood (or his alter ego in his *Berlin Stories*) would come over here for louche entertainment. At that time, numerous wealthy theatre people and other arty bohemians lived in huge apartments, whose

Left: shopping on the Kurfürstendamm.

with artefacts collected by Heinrich Schliemann and local Bronze Age discoveries. Across from the Schloss is the **Bröhan-Museum** ⑤, one of Europe's best collections of Art Nouveau, Art Deco, and Functionalism.
SEE ALSO MUSEUMS, P.91; PALACES AND HOUSES, P.104; PARKS AND GARDENS, P.108–9

Western Charlottenburg

South and to the west of the Schloss, Berlin's immense **Internationales Congress Centrum (ICC)** houses regular trade shows and conventions. Hard as it may be to believe now, its Eiffel Tower-like **Funkturm** ⑥ caused the envious East Germans to raise the Fernsehturm in Alexanderplatz *(see p.8)*.

A couple of U-Bahn stops away is the **Olympiastadion**, erected by Hitler for the 1936 Olympics and completely modernised for the 2006 World Cup. Some of the monumental Nazi sculpture is still plainly visible. Berlin's Hertha soccer team calls it home, and it also plays host to the likes of the Rolling Stones on tour.
SEE ALSO SPORTS, P.125

To immerse yourself fully in the feeling of a shopping stroll up the Ku'damm in the old days, stop for *Kaffee und Kuchen* (coffee and cake) at the Kranzler-Eck (Kurfürstendamm 21) or soup at Bovril (Kurfürstendamm 184).

buildings can still be seen, even if the apartments have long been subdivided.

Shoppers are advised to visit the Ku'damm side streets to the south, like elegant Fasanenstrasse, for interesting boutiques and galleries with a Berlin flair. This is where **Wilmersdorf** starts, with its upscale residential quarters and Wilhelminian buildings. For a taste of bourgeois lifestyle, try the smart street cafés and sophisticated shops around **Ludwigkirchplatz**.
SEE ALSO CHURCHES, SYNAGOGUES AND MOSQUES, P.45; FOOD AND DRINK, P.59; LITERATURE, P.80; MUSEUMS, P.91; SHOPPING, P.120

Schloss Charlottenburg

Best approached by walking up Schlossstrasse, **Charlottenburg palace** ④ was built by Frederick III as a summer residence for his wife, Sophie Charlotte, in 1699, back when this part of the city was deep in the countryside. New parts were added to the building over the years, and it was used as a secondary palace until the start of the 20th century. Today, it contains a museum with the largest collection of 18th-century French art outside of France and a large Baroque garden, which takes up the majority of the property and is a must-see in summer. Schloss Charlottenburg is one of Germany's most elegant houses, something of a rarity in austere Prussia.

In the palace grounds, there is another museum, the **Museum für Vor- und Frühgeschichte** (Museum for Pre- and Early History),

Below: at the gates of Schloss Charlottenburg.

13

Prenzlauer Berg

Prenzlauer Berg is the New Berlin writ large. Formerly a grey, working-class district, its large number of undamaged buildings attracted the first redevelopers after the fall of the Wall, and a new population demographic followed. Today, Prenzlauer Berg is one of the hippest and most revitalised parts of the city. More upscale than bohemian, its streets are filled with galleries, boutiques, restaurants and bars that serve an upwardly mobile, international populace. There are few traditional sights here, but the café culture and attractive streets make this an enjoyable place in which to wander.

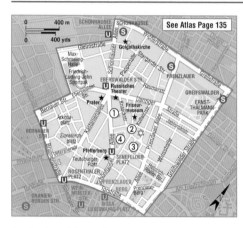

frenzy of construction to house the thousands of new Berliners attracted by the industry which had grown up in the city. With so little industry, and so much housing, the district was spared the bombing of World War II, and although the GDR did little to rebuild or renovate the *mietskasernen*, they survived. The spacious apartments attracted East German intellectuals and artists, particularly around **Kollwitzplatz** ②, the park across from where artist Käthe Kollwitz, memorialised by a statue in the park, once lived. The Café Westphal at Kollwitzstrasse was a meeting place for dissident intellectuals during the years before 1989 (it is now the **Istoria** restaurant). Another famed centre of dissent was the Golgotha Church on

Windmills and Breweries

Berlin is so flat that the gentle rise on which this neighbourhood sits earned it the half-ironic status of a 'mountain'. Until the last half of the 19th century, that rise was sufficient to catch the prevailing winds, and so Prenzlauer Berg was Berlin's milling centre, with dozens of windmills providing flour to the city's bakeries. Then came the breweries, with Joseph Pfeffer opening the first in 1841 at the site on Schönhauser Allee which is now the entertainment complex **Pfefferberg**. In 1853, Jost Schultheiss took over a brewery at Schönhauser Allee and built his

empire there. Today it is the **Kulturbrauerei** ①, a mixed-use complex of bars, restaurants, cinemas, offices and shopping. Others followed, such as the Bötzow on Prenzlauer Allee and Königstadt on Saarbrücker Strasse.
SEE ALSO NIGHTLIFE, P.103

Prenzlauer Berg in the 20th Century

The district's real expansion came towards the end of the century, when workers' housing, the so-called *mietskasernen* (rental-barracks) were thrown up in a

Right: Prenzlauer Berg has a thriving café culture.

14

Left: stall selling GDR-era clothes in Kollwitzplatz.

prisoners during Nazi times, and the **Jüdischer Friedhof** (Jewish Cemetery) ④ on Schönhauser Allee, which dates from 1827 and has been rebuilt in recent years. It contains the remains of composer Giacomo Meyerbeer, painter Max Liebermann and publisher Leopold Ullstein.

Reflecting its popularity, Prenzlauer Berg is Berlin's first district with its own tourism bureau. Located in the Kulturbrauerei cultural centre, the Tourist Information Centre sells tickets and provides English-language cultural and architectural tours of Prenzlauer Berg (TIC Kulturbrauerei Maschinenhaus, Schönhauser Allee 36; tel: 4435 2170; www.tic-berlin.de; Sun–Wed noon–6pm, Thur–Sat noon–8pm; tram: M1, M10, U2: Eberswalder Strasse; map p.135 D4).

SEE ALSO MUSIC, P.99

StarStargarder Strasse, some of whose parishioners had been involved with sheltering Jews during the Nazi regime.

After the Wall came down, the cheap apartments drew a new group of bohemians from around the world, and the so-called LSD district (named for the boundary streets, Lychener Strasse, Stargarder Strasse and Danziger Strasse) became a hot centre of Berlin creativity, although the area south of Danziger Strasse between Schönhauser Allee and Prenzlauer Allee was also notably chic. Today, Prenzlauer Berg attracts a young, multilingual going-out crowd from all over Berlin every night, filling up the countless bars, clubs and restaurants.

Kastanienallee

In a spherical building on Prenzlauer Allee there is a huge Zeiss planetarium, and many of Berlin's large-scale concerts take place in the nearby **Max-Schmeling-Halle**. The area makes for great walking, particularly on **Kastanienallee** (dubbed 'Casting Alley' by the locals), or in the streets around Kollwitzplatz, where there is great people-watching during the Saturday organic market.

Historical attractions in Prenzlauer Berg are few, but there are a couple of notable sights: the **Wasserturm** (Water Tower) ③ near Kollwitzplatz was a secret detention centre for political

Neighbouring sub-district Weissensee has Europe's largest Jewish cemetery, covering 42 hectares (105 acres) and containing over 110,000 graves, including those of hotelier Berthold Kempinski and department store magnate Hermann Tietz. The mausoleum of opera singer Joseph Schwartz has a secret passage leading to a small room, where Jews hid during World War II. Dedicated in 1880, the cemetery survived the Nazi era largely unscathed, but is now in a dilapidated state and largely overgrown by vegetation. With its simple tombstones and imposing marble mausoleums, it tells the stories of humble and famous Jewish Berliners (Jüdischer Friedhof Weissensee; Markus-Reich-Platz 1; tours by appointment; tel: 925 3330).

Schöneberg

Schöneberg is one of Berlin's most architecturally pleasant areas. It is not awash with historical sights, but has been the scene of many of Berlin's famed cultural moments: John F. Kennedy made his famous *'Ich bin ein Berliner'* speech outside Rathaus Schöneberg. Meanwhile, its established gay and party scene drew Christopher Isherwood and Marlene Dietrich in the 1920s, while David Bowie and Iggy Pop made Schöneberg their home in the 1970s. The media rediscover it as a *szenekiez* (scene-neighbourhood) every few years, and there are numerous bars and restaurants that set the tone for the rest of Berlin culture.

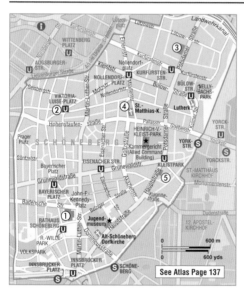

See Atlas Page 137

At Goebenstrasse and Potsdamer Strasse there is a housing project which is built across the street. What gives it its structural integrity is a huge Nazi air-raid bunker, which would have cost more to tear down than the property was worth, so the city simply used it as part of the building's foundation.

Around Rathaus Schöneberg

Each of Berlin's *bezirke* (districts) has an administrative building, or *Rathaus* and it was in **Rathaus Schöneberg** ① that the West Berlin government was housed after the traditional Berlin city hall wound up in East Berlin. It was here, on 26 June 1963, that President John F. Kennedy gave his famed *'Ich bin ein Berliner'* speech, which solidified American support for West Berlin. A model Liberty Bell within the building commemorates this.

Nearby is Bayerischer Platz, which displays another commemoration. This area was the site of a real-estate development of luxury apartments which were marketed to wealthy Jews by Jewish developers, people who were among the first victims of the Nazis' anti-Semitic laws. In 1993 two artists, Renata Stih and Frieder Schnock, erected signs with excerpts from the

laws ('Jews are allowed to buy foodstuffs only from 4.00 to 5.00 in the afternoon. 4 July 1940') around the Bayerisches Viertel neighbourhood. Maps of their location are in the park and elsewhere in the area. Keep walking north from Bayerischer Platz and you'll find **Viktoria-Luise-Platz** ②, one of Berlin's most charming pocket parks, surrounded by outdoor cafés which are great for lingering in on warm afternoons.

The Motzkiez

When the British writer Christopher Isherwood came to Berlin in the 1930s to write the stories which eventually became the play *I Am A Camera* and the musical *Cabaret*, it was largely because it was possible to live as an openly gay man. He is remembered with a plaque on his house at Nollendorfs-

Left: the weekend flea market by Rathaus Schöneberg.

where else in the city, but the customers are a perfect example of the neighbourhood's bourgeois residents. Continuing out of the square, past the church, is the start of Goltzstrasse, the hot centre of Schöneberg's 'scene', which continues as the street crosses Grunewaldstrasse and becomes Akazienstrasse. The bars, restaurants, cafés and shops change with bewildering speed, but if you can find a local versed in this week's line-up of happening hangouts, you'll be presented with glimpses of the lifestyles of the cool and the stylish.
SEE ALSO FOOD AND DRINK, P.59

Hauptstrasse

Hauptstrasse is, as its name makes clear, Schöneberg's 'main street' and has a couple of points of interest, starting at Kleistpark, where there is a building in which the Allied command was housed. **Neues Ufer** ⑤, an unprepossessing gay bar formerly known as Das Anderes Ufer, entered Berlin lore when David Bowie rented an apartment behind it at number 155 in the mid-1970s and used the bar as his main hangout.

Many of the houses on this part of Hauptstrasse were built by nouveau riche farmers who sold their property in the late 19th century to developers desperate to throw up apartments; those which were spared bombing are still impressive. At the end of Hauptstrasse stands the **Alt-Schöneberg Dorfkirche**, an 18th-century reconstruction of an older village church from when the *bezirk* was an independent town.
SEE ALSO GAY AND LESBIAN, P.66

trasse 17 (although whether it is on the right house remains a subject of debate), which is right in the Motzkiez, as the area around **Motzstrasse** has been dubbed. It has been a gay hub since the 1920s; a plaque commemorating the homosexuals killed by the Third Reich is affixed to Nollendorfplatz U-Bahn station. Motzstrasse is also the epicentre of the annual **Christopher Street Day** and **Gay Pride Day** celebrations in the spring. Local bars, shops, small hotels and cinemas all cater to gay men (and women, to a lesser extent), as does the helpful drop-in centre **Mann-O-Meter**.

Not in the Motzkiez itself, but still in Schöneberg, is the renowned **Wintergarten Varieté** ③, where acrobats, magicians and other performers provide entertainment with an edge in the decadent style of Weimar-era Berlin.
SEE ALSO CABARET, 39; FESTIVALS AND EVENTS, P.55; GAY AND LESBIAN, P.64–5; LITERATURE, P.80

The Szenekiez

The quintessential Schöneberg experience can be had on a Wednesday or Saturday in summertime by walking around the outdoor market in **Winterfeldplatz** ④. Not only are the goods on display, mainly food, of a quality you won't find anywhere

Below: the plaque at Nollendorfplatz U-Bahn.

TOTGESCHLAGEN
TOTGESCHWIEGEN
DEN
HOMOSEXUELLEN OPFERN
DES
NATIONALSOZIALISMUS

Kreuzberg and Friedrichshain

When the Wall went up, Kreuzberg found itself isolated. Many buildings were abandoned, and the cheap rents attracted Turkish guestworkers, while the empty houses enticed squatters; before long, it was one of Berlin's most vibrant areas. Today, Kreuzberg is known for being a buzzing centre of art, culture and nightlife, not to mention the thriving Turkish-German culture. Neighbouring Friedrichshain retains its gritty charm and is home to the last big stretch of the Wall, now the East Side Gallery.

See Atlas Pages 138–139

In years past, May Day was riot day in East Kreuzberg, with supermarkets ritually trashed and regular confrontations with the police. This has abated considerably in recent years, but the walls of Kreuzberg are still filled with graffiti and political posters year-round, and are a good barometer of the hot issues of the day.

Landwehrkanal, the twice-weekly **Turkischer Markt** (Tuesday and Friday) on Maybachufer sells fresh vegetables, as well as household goods and more kinds of olives than seem possible. The banks of the canal on the other side of Kottbusser Damm are a favourite place to lounge in the sun, and **Böcklerpark** and **Görlitzer Park** come alive at weekends, with locals grilling outdoors. SEE ALSO FOOD AND DRINK, P.59; RESTAURANTS, P.119

East Kreuzberg

East Kreuzberg refers to the part that was closest to the Wall, with **Oranienstrasse** its main street. Also referred to by locals as 'Kreuzberg 36', in contrast to the slightly more bourgeois 'Kreuzberg 60' in the West, it is packed from one end to the other with Turkish shops, cafés and alternative bookshops, and remains a definitive slice of radical, edgy Berlin life.

The **SO 36** bar was an early hot centre of alternative art and had already made its mark when it became an important venue for Berlin punk rock. Just off Oranien-strasse, on Adalbertstrasse, is **Hasir**, a Turkish restaurant where in 1971, the *döner kebap* was invented, as a variation on Turkish cuisine to suit German tastes. An old hospital on Mariannenplatz was a squat for artists in the 1970s and has become the **Künstlerhaus Bethanien**, where artists from around the world receive grants to work.

The former warehouses along the river on Köpenicker Strasse now play host to clubs and luxury condominiums, as well as providing space for Berlin's IT industry. Further south, down **Kottbusser Damm** where it intersects the

North Kreuzberg

At the border with Mitte are some of Berlin's most famous sights, such as **Checkpoint Charlie** ①, although the hut there is a reproduction and the 'soldier' is an actor. A **museum** across the street has a strident political agenda, but some fascinating

Left: the Turkischer Markt on Maybachufer.

SEE ALSO BARS AND CAFÉS, P.37; GAY AND LESBIAN, P.65; PARKS AND GARDENS, P.109

Friedrichshain

Connected by the neo-Gothic red-brick **Oberbaumbrücke** ⑥ bridge that spans the Spree river at Warschauer Strasse station, both Kreuzberg and Friedrichshain have come from largely run-down-edgy to trendy-edgy since the Wall came down, and both boast offbeat shopping and a lot of nightlife options.

In recent years, the latter has become a favourite with Berlin's younger crowd; some even consider it the most happening district. The streets around **Simon-Dach-Strasse** brim with bars and restaurants, most of them packed all night. Parts of Friedrichshain are still quite rough around the edges, rents are cheap and the punk spirit is alive.

However, developers have now arrived, and even parts of the **East Side Gallery** ⑦, the artist-painted longest stretch of Wall still intact, have had to make way for a new entertainment complex.

SEE ALSO GALLERIES, P.63

exhibits on escape attempts. Turning east on Kochstrasse from Checkpoint Charlie will bring you to a small museum district containing the bold **Jüdisches Museum** ② and the **Berlinische Galerie**, while turning west takes you to the **Martin-Gropius-Bau**, which usually has a couple of fine exhibitions and the **Topography of Terror** ③, located in the excavated remains of the Gestapo headquarters.

SEE ALSO MONUMENTS AND MEMORIALS, P.82; MUSEUMS, P.93–4

West Kreuzberg

Southern and Western Kreuzberg is more bourgeois than its neighbour, with houses in a better state of repair. **Bergmannstrasse** is also lined with alternative businesses and Turkish shops, from its market hall (one of the few remaining indoor markets from the 19th century) to Mehringdamm.

On Hasenheide's southern perimeter is **Flughafen Tempelhof**, the Nazi-built airport. Tempelhof had the world's eyes on it during the Berlin Airlift, when planes loaded with crucial supplies landed, unloaded and took off again in minutes, breaking the Russian blockade of Berlin. It has ceased to serve as a commercial airport and at the moment its future is uncertain.

On Mehringdamm, you'll find the **Schwules Museum** (Gay Museum) ④. Crossing Mehringdamm leads to **Viktoriapark** ⑤, which contains the 'cross hill' which gives the entire district its name. The monument with the cross marking the Napoleonic Wars on top of the hill is by Schinkel and dates from 1821. On summer nights, the nearby beer garden is packed. The hill, one of Berlin's few natural ones, is high enough to be a perfect place to orient yourself with the city.

Below: the Oberbaumbrücke, Berlin's prettiest bridge.

Western Districts

Zehlendorf and Spandau form the western edge of Berlin. Rich in forests, lakes and waterways, as well as historical landmarks, they are always good for an outing. Spandau, on the western edge of Berlin, has large forests and more than 100km (62 miles) of shoreline, comprised by the Havel river and several lakes. While Spandau is traditionally also an industrial area, Zehlendorf has always been the residence of the rich and famous, with its villas set in leafy surrounds. Dahlem, meanwhile, is best-known for its collection of excellent museums, and those looking for a break from urbanity will find relief in Grosser Wannsee and beautiful Pfaueninsel (Peacock Island).

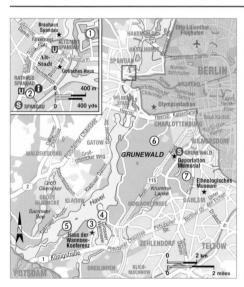

Outside Germany, Spandau was long associated with the **War Criminals Prison** south of the old town, where several prominent Nazis sentenced at the Nuremberg Trials were imprisoned after World War II. Inmates included Albert Speer and Rudolf Hess, Hitler's deputy, who, after the release of the others, was the only prisoner here for two decades until he committed suicide in 1987. The prison was torn down soon after his death.

Spandau

Founded as a Slavic settlement at the confluence of the Spree and Havel rivers, Spandau was a town in its own right until 1920 and is still distinctive from Berlin proper. The Spandauers are proud of this, as well as of their preserved buildings, which reflect 500 years of history. Spandau has a distinct medieval small-town atmosphere: it is best experienced at its Christmas Market, which stands out as one of Berlin's most picturesque.

The **Zitadelle Spandau** (Citadel) ① is one of the best-preserved Renaissance fortresses in Germany, with some parts dating back to the 12th century. The Zitadelle has a history museum, a great medieval-style restaurant, and provides a perfect backdrop for open-air concerts. Less known, it also serves as winter quarters for 10,000 bats.

The **Gotisches Haus** (Gothic House) ② dates back to the 15th century and is the

oldest residence in all of Berlin. Today it houses the Spandau Information Office and is the starting point for town walks. Don't miss the crooked medieval half-timbered houses near Marien-kirche (St Mary's church) at the quiet north end of the old-town island. Pay a visit to the fortress-like **Brauhaus Spandau** brewery nearby and have a home brew in the charming beer garden. SEE ALSO FESTIVALS AND EVENTS, P.55

Zehlendorf

Zehlendorf is the city's most genteel district, a leafy suburb in Berlin's southwest. This is where the well-to-do reside, while the less affluent flock to

Left: the Zitadelle Spandau is in an idyllic setting.

The Grunewald

The Grunewald is an enormous forest stretching between the districts of Charlottenburg, Wilmersdorf, Zehlendorf and the Havel river, shared by city-worn humans, their dogs and several wild boar that habitually appear on nearby roads, raiding the rubbish bins for leftover lunches.

The Grunewald has a few sights. **Teufelsberg** ('Devil's Mountain') ⑥ was constructed from rubble after World War II. The abandoned US radar station at its summit (crowned by a white ball-shaped dome) was one of the premier listening posts of the Cold War. Other history is felt at the Grunewald S-Bahn station, where platform 17 is the **Deportation Memorial** to the 55,000 Berlin Jews sent from this station on trains bound for concentration camps.

the district's woods and beaches at the weekend. The glamour of past times can be felt in the **Max-Liebermann-Villa** ③ (now a museum) at Grosser Wannsee, where the famous painter lived until his death in 1935. Just around the corner is the **Haus der Wannsee-Konferenz**, the notorious villa where the 'Final Solution' was devised by Nazi bureaucrats in January 1942. It houses a museum telling the story of how the hatred towards Jews was fuelled and how the terror that led to the Holocaust was organised.
SEE ALSO PARKS AND GARDENS, P.110

Around Wannsee

Europe's largest inland beach, **Strandbad Wannsee** ④, boasts almost a mile of sandy beaches and can be found on the shores of **Grosser Wannsee**. For the past century, Berliners have come here for a day out, a boat ride, a

steamer cruise to Potsdam or coffee and cake at the café overlooking the lake.

Located south of Grosser Wannsee in the southern Havel river is **Pfaueninsel** ⑤, where 60 peacocks strut the grounds. Accessible only by ferry, it is listed as a Unesco World Heritage Site and is probably Berlin's most beautiful natural sanctuary.
SEE ALSO PARKS AND GARDENS, P.110; SPORTS, P.125

Below: Glienicker Brücke.

Dahlem

Dahlem is a residential part of Zehlendorf, distinguished by its number of exquisite museums, such as the **Brücke Museum** ⑦, dedicated to the German Expressionist painters group of the same name whose works were defamed as 'degenerate art' by the Nazis, as well as the **Ethnologisches Museum** (Ethnological Museum), with 500,000 artefacts from all over the world, and the **Museum für Asiatische Kunst** (Museum of Asian Art).
SEE ALSO MUSEUMS, P.94–5

> The inconspicuous **Glienicker Brücke** (left) spanning the Havel river connecting Berlin and Potsdam became known as the Cold War trading post for spies and other undesirables.

Treptow
and Köpenick

Treptow and Köpenick form a large district stretching from the city centre to the southeastern suburbs of Berlin. For visitors, Treptow's main point of interest is the large park named for the area, where the bombastic Soviet war memorial stands. Köpenick, meanwhile, gained fame through 'The Captain of Köpenick' and his antics. Today both districts, with their lakes, waterways and forests, offer plenty of recreational options, while Friedrichshagen is a picturesque place in which to spend time.

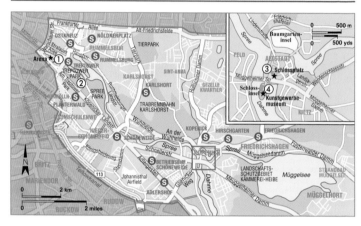

Treptow

Treptow is a mostly industrial district in the former East Berlin that is, however, rich in waterways and parks. The giant modern sculpture of the **'Molecule Man'** ① in the Spree river connects the glistening **'Treptowers'** skyscrapers of post-Wall Treptow with **Treptower Park**, a monument to its past. The **Sowjetisches Ehrenmal** (Soviet War Memorial) ② found here recalls World War II and the Stalinist period to follow. **Treptower Park** is also home to the 1896 Archenhold observatory, housing what was then the world's longest refractor telescope.

The area of Treptow was once best-known for the Johannisthal Airfield, Germany's first airport, where competing Fokkers and Junkers built in the local workshops were tested and the first commercial flights took off in the 1920s. Parts of the aviation laboratories, wind tunnels and hangars have been preserved and are historical landmarks today.

Some former industrial sites were reinvented as cultural venues or party locations, the largest of them being the **Arena** (a former bus depot) on the banks of the Spree that comes with a floating swimming pool in an old barge.

Treptow is a convenient starting point for boat tours of the southeast lakes of Berlin and to Köpenick and Grünau.
SEE ALSO MONUMENTS AND MEMORIALS, P.85; MUSIC, P.98; PARKS AND GARDENS, P.110–11

Köpenick

For many people, Köpenick is associated with 'The Captain of Köpenick'. Founded as a Slavic settlement back in the 9th century, Köpenick is one of Berlin's oldest parts. The former fishermen's village raised on an island (**Schlossinsel**, the location of Schloss Köpenick) has preserved its small-town charm with narrow lanes,

Left: in Treptower Park, the Sowjetisches Ehrenmal.

Kunstgewerbemuseum (Museum of Decorative Arts). SEE ALSO PALACES AND HOUSES, P.104–5

Friedrichshagen

A very lovely part of Köpenick is the Friedrichshagen quarter. From the S-Bahn station of the same name, walk down picturesque 18th-century **Bölschestrasse** with its small ornate buildings, charming shops and good restaurants to **Müggelsee**, Berlin's largest lake. In one of the many beer gardens by the water, you can sit under old chestnut trees and enjoy the view of sailing boats passing by. Even more attractive is **Neu-Venedig** ('New Venice'), a lagoon neighbourhood where the Müggelspree river branches into numerous canals, lined by cottages and fish restaurants.

Overlooking the Grösser Müggelsee are the Müggel-berge hills, a large forested area popular with hikers and mountain bikers. The somewhat derelict 1960s Müggel-turm tower offers scenic views. Swimmers flock to **Strandbad Müggelsee** beach, a lido similar to its counterpart on Grösser Wannsee in the West.

The story of *Der Hauptmann von Köpenick* (The Captain of Köpenick) is legendary. In 1906, ex-convict Wilhelm Voigt exposed the Prussian blind belief in military authority when he marched into the Köpenick town hall disguised as a captain and confiscated the town finances.

restored old buildings and the red-brick *Rathaus* (town hall). As three-quarters of Köpenick are covered by lakes and forests, this is a popular place to visit for fresh air and the outdoors.

The colourful history of Köpenick is reflected in the **Altstadt**, the car-free old town around Schlossplatz, uniquely located at the confluence of the Spree and Dahme rivers. Here, where little old ladies with hats idle away the day in the cafés near the old parish church, clocks seem to tick more slowly.

At the neo-Gothic town hall, **Rathaus Köpenick** ③, a bronze statue commemorates the Captain *(see box, left)*. Hearty German cuisine is served in the Ratskeller restaurant here, which is also a popular venue for jazz concerts.

Divided from the old town by wooden bridge and located right on the water is **Schloss Köpenick** ④, the restored palace, housing the

Below: Schloss Köpenick.

Potsdam

Potsdam is Berlin's neighbour, a small city with a historical importance that outweighs its size. Its main attraction is the Sanssouci Palace, built for Frederick the Great. The entire park is a Unesco World Heritage site and contains numerous buildings, large and small, which can take an entire day to explore. Potsdam also has a charming city centre studded with 18th-century buildings, including entire neighbourhoods built to look Dutch and Russian. The nearby Babelsberg film studios provide the central impetus for the Film-museum Potsdam, housed in 17th-century military stables.

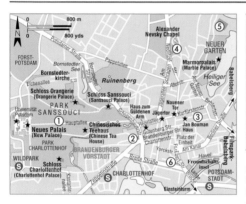

Potsdam Tourist Information can be found at Brandenburger Strasse 3, Potsdam, and at the BerlinInfostore in Berlin HauptBahnhof station; tel: 0331 275 580; www.potsdamtourismus.de. For general information in English: www.potsdam.de and for details on Sanssouci park and palaces: www.spsg.de.

Sanssouci

Sanssouci ① was begun in 1747 on the orders of Frederick the Great, who found the royal palace in Berlin not to his liking. With construction continuing into the 19th century, this ensemble of palaces, gardens and pleasure spots is considered by many to be the equal of Versailles. The park itself can be enjoyed for free, although small vending machines by the entrances ask for a voluntary admission charge to help maintain the grounds. With the majority of attractions here being open only from May to October, most visitors get to see the gardens in their full formal splendour, with fountains splashing in the sunlight.

The **New Palace** is open year-round and is central to Frederick the Great's history, since it was his main residence. **Sanssouci Palace**, the older of Frederick's two palaces here, is adjoined by the **Picture Gallery**, stuffed with 18th-century art, and the **New Chambers** is a former orangery turned into a guest palace for noble visitors.

Elsewhere in the grounds, perhaps the most charming building is the **Chinese Tea House**, built 1754–7 from a sketch by Frederick and used for tea parties on fine porcelain which is displayed there today. Frederick is buried, along with his dogs, who also merit tombstones, next to Sanssouci Palace. Post-

Frederician Sanssouci includes the **Charlottenhof Palace**, the **Orangery Palace** and the **Church of Peace**, all built in the early to mid-19th century by Friedrich Wilhelm IV.

Historic City Centre

Just outside Sanssouci, by the exits by the Picture Gallery or Church of Peace, one can see Potsdam's own **Brandenburger Tor** (Brandenburg Gate) ②, dating from 1770. This provides an entrance to the historic city centre, which continues down Brandenburger Strasse and its surrounding side streets, most of which are pedestrianised. At Hermann-Elfleim-Strasse 3 is the **Haus zum Güldenen Arm**, built and brilliantly decorated by the brewer and wood-sculptor August Melchior Erhart. Across

Left: Sanssouci.

that the 1945 Potsdam Conference, which decided the fate of post-war Germany, was held. The round table where the Allies sat is still on view, and the surrounding grounds also contain the **Marble Palace**, created as a summer residence on the Heiliger See, and dating from 1791.

Outside of Potsdam proper, but easily reached by public transport, the suburb of Babelsberg has not only its own park with a palace designed by Schinkel, but also the **Filmpark Babelsberg**, on the site of the UFA Studios, where much classic German cinema was made. Today, it is an amusement park not unlike Universal Studios in California, with rides and stunt shows mostly geared towards the German television-viewing audience. People with a serious interest in what was accomplished in Babelsberg by directors such as Fritz Lang and G.W. Murnau would be better off in central Potsdam at the **Filmmuseum Potsdam** ⑥, which has well-curated exhibitions on German film history, as well as a cinema programme in the evenings.

Friedrich-Ebert-Strasse, the building materials abruptly change from plaster to brick. The **Holländisches Viertel** (Dutch quarter) ③ was erected in the 1730s to house Dutch builders who were invited by the Kaiser to build in Potsdam. The 134 houses have been reconstructed from the disrepair they had fallen into and now house galleries and restaurants as well as private residences and offices. The **Jan Bouman Haus** at Mittelstrasse 8 has reconstructed a typical residence of an 18th-century Dutch builder and provides a good history of the area in its museum.

Heading up Friedrich-Ebert-Strasse, one comes to **Alexandrowka** ④, a cluster of wooden Russian peasant houses built by Friedrich Wilhelm III in 1826 to house Russian musicians who had been taken by the Kaiser as spoils of war in the Napoleonic Wars. The Alexander

Nevsky Chapel above the settlement contains a number of important icons, and the area is another Unesco World Heritage Site.

Cecilienhof and Babelsberg

The last palace built by the Hohenzollerns, the **Cecilienhof** ⑤, was finished in 1917 and became a luxury hotel after World War I. It was here

Below: the distinctive shape of the Einsteinturm.

One of the most distinctive buildings in Potsdam is the Expressionist **Einsteinturm** (Einstein Tower), built in 1921 as an astrophysics observatory for the astronomer Erwin Finlay-Freundlich to conduct experiments in support of the Theory of Relativity. Albert Einstein's verdict on the avant-garde building? 'Organic.' Despite a large-scale conservation project in 1999, the tower is fragile, so take a guided tour while you can (tours run Oct–May).

A–Z

In the following section Berlin's attractions and services are organized by theme, under alphabetical headings. Items that link to another theme are cross-referenced. All sights that fall within the atlas section at the end of the book are given a page number and grid reference.

Architecture

Like no other European capital, Berlin's buildings bear witness to the chaotic history of the 20th century, from the beginning of urban planning for a working-class population, the creative, experimental years of the Bauhaus and the birth of modernism, the hubris and destruction during the Nazi period, the city divided in the Cold War to its rebirth as Germany's capital after the fall of the Berlin Wall. These listings demonstrate Berlin's tumultuous modern history through its architecture, as well as some key buildings from the Prussian era that have survived; for more of these, *see Palaces and Houses, p.104–5*.

The Prussian Legacy

St Hedwigs Cathedral (1773)

Bebelplatz; S1, S2, S25, S5, S7, S75, S9, U6: Friedrichstrasse, U2: Französische Strasse; map p.136 C1

Built by Johann Baumann, this Baroque Catholic cathedral was meant to demonstrate the predominately Protestant state's support for religious freedom.

Neue Schönhauser 8 (1785)

U8: Weinmeister Strasse; map p.135 C3

This apartment house is believed to have been built by Georg Christian Unger and is a typical Berlin residence from during the city's expansion in the late Baroque period. There are several houses on this street, such as numbers 12–14, with well-preserved facades and back courtyards that are exemplary of their time. This building demonstrates early classicism in Berlin.

Neue Synagoge (1866)

Oranienburger Strasse 28–30; S1, S2, S25, S26: Oranienburger Strasse; map p.134 C3

Berlin's Jewish citizens erected what was once the city's largest synagogue with an oriental appearance, reflecting the tastes of the time. It was built by Eduard Knoblauch and Friedrich August Stüler. Ironically, it was largely undamaged during the Nazis' Kristallnacht pogrom but nearly destroyed by Allied bombing and later demolished under the GDR. It was restored after unification.

> Karl Friedrich Schinkel gave Mitte much of the appearance that we recognise today, being responsible for the **Altes Museum** *(see Museums, p.86)*, the first museum in Germany and only the third in Europe, after the Prado in Madrid and the British Museum in London. Other Schinkel masterpieces include the **Neue Wache** *(see Memorials and Monuments, p.85)*, the **Konzerthaus** *(see Music, p.96–7)* and the **Schinkel-Pavillion** in the grounds of Schloss Charlottenburg *(see Palaces and Houses, p.104)*.

SEE ALSO CHURCHES, SYNAGOGUES AND MOSQUES, P.44

City Life, Pre-World War I

Proskauer Strasse Apartments (1898)

Proskauer Strasse 14/15/17; U5: Frankfurter Tor

In the years before World War I, it was the German Mietshaus, a combination apartment building and rented space for shops, that shaped the face of the city. Proskauer Strasse, designed by Alfred Messel, was cutting-edge. It opened up the traditional inner courtyard to bring in light and create room for children. The building won a prize at the Paris World's Fair in 1900.

Hackescher Höfe (1907)

Rosenthalerstr 40–41; S3, S5, S7, S9: Hackescher Markt; map p.134 C3

Built by Kurt Berndt and August Endell, this was the largest combined residential and commercial complex in Europe. Its inner courtyards were a labyrinth of working class apartments, shops and small factories. The neighbouring station Hackescher Markt and the surrounding

Left: GDR-era architecture on Karl-Marx-Allee.

biel, who also designed Flughafen Tempelhof. After the war, East Germany used it for its Central Planning Commission. A GDR-era mural can be seen on the Leipzigerstrasse side of the building. In 2000, it became the finance ministry.

Olympiastadion (1936)
Olympischer Platz 3; U2, S75, S9: Olympiastadion
The stadium was designed by Werner March with some adjustments by Albert Speer. After the war, Germans feared that National Socialist architecture would breed fascism and so they destroyed many buildings such as Hitler's new chancellery. But if any building was meant to demonstrate Hitler's vision for Germany as an empire in the classic sense, it is the Olympiastadion, modelled on Rome's Colosseum. To get a true feel for this venue, try to get tickets to a Hertha BSC football match and absorb the atmosphere of where the 1936 Olympics were held. The tribune where Hitler and his cohorts watched Jesse Owens triumph over German athletes is still intact.
SEE ALSO SPORTS, P.125

Flughafen Tempelhof (1941)
Platz der Luftbrücke 1–6; U6: Platz der Luftbrücke; map p.138 B3

neighbourhood still give an impression of turn-of-the-century Berlin.

Modernism

Hufeisen-Siedlung (Horseshoe Housing Project) (1927)
Fritz-Reuter-Allee, Buschkru-gallee, Parchimer Allee; U7: Parchimer Allee
This was a joint project of architects Bruno Taut and Martin Wagner and is a classic Bauhaus. It is one of the first big German housing estates, with more than 1,000 apartments. Simplification and mass production was meant to make the homes affordable for the working class. Nevertheless, workers still couldn´t afford to live there. Clerks and civil servants moved in.

Berolina-Haus (1932)
Alexanderplatz 1; U2, U5, U8, S5, S75, S9: Alexanderplatz; map p.137 E2
The Berolina-Haus and the neighbouring Alexanderhaus are all that remain of the planned Weimar-era redesign of busy Alexanderplatz. Designed by Peter Behrens, the two buildings were meant

to serve as gates to this central traffic hub and commercial district. On the top floor of Berolina-Haus was the very hip Swing-era Café Braun, accessible via ultra-modern escalators and paternosters.

National Socialism

Bundesfinanzministerium (Ministry of Finance) (1936)
Wilhelmstrasse 97, Leipziger-strasse 6–7; U2, S1, S2, S25: Potsdamer Platz; map p.134 B2
It was from here that Hermann Göring's *Reichsluftfahrtminis-terium* (aerospace ministry) directed the air war against Britain. It was designed by Hitler's architect Ernst Sage-

Below: the redeveloped Hackesche Höfe.

In its day, Tempelhof Airport was the largest building in the world. While the building was doubtless meant to demonstrate Nazi power and Germany's technological prowess, Sagebiel's efficient design also became a model for airports around the world. Nazi symbols were removed from public after the war, but you can still see the German eagle adorning Tempelhof buildings.

Hochbunker (1943)
Albrechtstrasse 24–25; S3, S5, S7, S9, S75, U6, Tram M1 and 12: Friedrichstrasse; U6, Tram M1, M6 and M12: Oranienburger Tor, S1, S2: Oranienburger Strasse

Planning for war, Hitler built a massive civilian bomb-shelter system – enough to contain 7 percent of the population. To speed up the process after the war began, he built huge above-ground bunkers. This one was too costly to tear down and it served as a venue for an underground raver club after the Berlin Wall fell; today, it is sometimes used for art exhibits.

East Berlin

Karl-Marx-Allee (1951–4)
Block C: Karl-Marx-Allee 71–91B, Karl-Marx-Allee 72-90; U5: Strausberger Platz Station, Weberwiese; map p.135 E2

The Frankfurter Tor welcomed visitors from the East to central Berlin and was designed by Hermann Henselmann for Stalinallee,

One of a series of three *Unités d'Habitation* that Le Corbusier designed as a solution to the housing shortages across Europe following World War II, the Corbusierhaus in Charlottenburg is possibly the ultimate example of Berlin's modern-architecture housing blocks. You can even choose to stay in one of the furnished flats available (www.domizil-berlin.com).

later renamed Karl-Marx-Allee, which was intended to be Germany's first Socialist boulevard in the style of Moscow. As you drive down the boulevard, you are flanked left and right for 260m (284yds) by what were luxurious housing blocks reserved for state functionaries in the days of East Berlin. Architect Richard Paulinck combined elements of classicism with Socialist aesthetics. This is where East German leaders held their annual military parades. Its value as architecture is disputed, but it is reminiscent of a Berlin that is rapidly disappearing. Take the subway to Frankfurter Tor, then walk back along Karl-Marx-Allee and visit old East Berlin landmarks like Café Moskau, a popular Soviet restaurant back in the day that now sports a dance club, or the egg-shaped Filmtheater Kosmos, East Germany's cinema for film premières.

Berlin Wall (1961)
Bernauer Strasse; www.die-

berliner-mauer.de; U8: Bernauer Strasse, Schwarzkopfstrasse, U6: Schwarzkopfstrasse, Niederkirchnerstrasse, Kochstrasse, or U2, S1, S2, S25: Potsdamer Platz; map p.134 B4

The other major East German construction project, the Berlin Wall was erected in a single night and became the world's symbol of the Cold War. There are few stretches of the original Wall left standing; the best places to see it are here at the former 'Death Strip' on Bernauer Strasse or at the **East Side Gallery** across from the Ostbahnhof.
SEE ALSO GALLERIES, P.63

Fernsehturm (1969)
Alexanderplatz; U2, S5, S7, S75, S9: Alexanderplatz; map p.135 C3

When construction was completed, East German leaders praised the futuristic TV tower as the 'work of the working class'. However, locals say the arch-Socialist GDR head of state, Erich Honecker, hated the fact that the sun setting in the west

Below: the Olympiastadion, modelled on the Colosseum in Rome.

reflected in a cross on the East's tower. Nevertheless, the Fernsehturm has become a Berlin icon, and the rotating restaurant on top with its stunning view of the city is a popular tourist stop.
SEE ALSO CHILDREN, P.43

West Berlin

Haus der Kulturen der Welt (1957)

John-Foster-Dulles-Allee 10; S3, S5, S7, S9, S75: Hauptbahnhof; map p.134 A3

Post-war building in West Berlin was largely functional and unsensational. That's why the former Kongress-halle stands out as a West Berlin icon and the optimism of the early 1960s. Built by Hugh Stubbins, it was a gift from the US.

Neue Nationalgalerie (1968)

Potsdamer Strasse 50; tel: 266 2951; www.neue-national galerie.de; U2, S1, S2, S25: Potsdamer Platz; map p.134 A1

The first building to open as part of West Berlin's new

Left: the Corbusierhaus.

culture forum at Potsdamer Platz, the steel-and-glass construction is the only building that Mies van der Rohe would build in post-war Germany. The former head of the Bauhaus in Dessau, van der Rohe had fled from the Nazis in 1938.

The New Berlin

Jüdisches Museum (1998)

Lindenstrasse 9–14; tel: 2599 3300; www.juedisches-museum-berlin.de; U6, U1: Hallesches Tor; map p.134 C1

The Jewish Museum was designed by the architect Daniel Libeskind and is one of the most interesting buildings constructed in unified Germany. The building is based on the shape of an exploded Star of David. Libeskind created empty spaces between the folds that can neither be entered nor crossed, as if to express the unspeakable, the annihilation of Jews under Hitler.
SEE ALSO MUSEUMS, P.93–4

Reichstag (1999)

Platz der Republik 1; S3, S5, S7, S9, S75: Hauptbahnhof. map p.134 A3

Representative for all of the new buildings in Berlin's new government quarter, Sir Norman Foster placed special emphasis on transparency in redesigning the parliament's plenary hall in this building that was the parliament of Weimar's fragile democracy and later Hitler's stage. The glass cupola on the roof of the Reichstag allows citizens visiting to observe their elected officials at work.

Potsdamer Platz 1 (2000)

S1, S2, S25, U2: Potsdamer Platz; map p.134 B2

The 20-storey flat iron-shaped red-brick office building recalls Potsdamer Platz's

pre-war role as Europe's busiest intersection, architects Hans Kollhoff and Helga Timmermann creating a building that combines contemporary design with elements of a classic New York-style skyscraper.

Sony Center (2000)

Potsdamer Strasse 2; daily 24 hours; S1, S2, S25, U2: Potsdamer Platz; map p.134 A2

A massive tent-like roof seems to whirl above the main square of this entertainment and office complex designed by German-American architect Helmut Jahn. One of the most impressive new complexes in post-Wall Berlin, the Sony Center is a popular attraction for Berliners and tourists alike, and is conveniently only a short walk from all the other new sites on Potsdamer Platz.

Bundeskanzleramt (2001)

Willy-Brandt-Strasse 1; S3, S5, S7, S9, S75: Hauptbahnhof; map p.134 A3

Berliners nickname everything, and have dubbed the new chancellery the 'washing machine' for its squat shape and glass front. Architects Axel Schultes and Charlotte Frank designed the building to symbolise the unification of Germany's two halves.

Below: the slick exterior of the Sony Center.

Bars and Cafés

A lot of time is spent in bars and cafés in Berlin. In fact, the distinction between the two can be hard to make, as the same place will often host people enjoying the ritual *Kaffee und Kuchen* (coffee and cake) in the middle of the afternoon and then another crowd sipping beer, wine and cocktails at night. Of course, there are also *Konditorei*, which are bakeries with dining facilities, not to mention bars that are just bars. Of the thousands in the city, those listed below provide a taster of Berlin drinking and café culture. *Prost! See also Gay and Lesbian, p.65–7; Nightlife, p.102–3; and Restaurants, p.112–19.*

Mitte

Opernpalais
Unter den Linden 7; tel: 202 683; www.opernpalais.de; daily 8am–midnight; U2, S5, S7, S9: Hackescher Markt; map p.137 C1
In a 1733 building which was once the residence of the Hohenzollern princesses, a well-dressed clientele sips coffee and tea and enjoy a bewildering selection of pastries; there are over 40 types of cake alone on offer each day. In winter, it serves as a great break from one of Berlin's best Christmas markets, held right outside.

Strandbar
Monbijoupark; www.alteseuropa.com; daily 10am–late; S3, S5, S7, S9: Hackeschèr Markt; map p.137 C2
It's a simple enough concept: dump a bunch of sand on the shore of the Spree river opposite the Bode-Museum, set up a couple of shacks with beer taps and refrigerators, and people will come. In fact, so many of them come that this popular evening spot is often full. The nearby Hexenkessel Hoftheater (either on its fixed stage or on the ship Marie in

Berlin is not as noted for its *Kaffee und Kuchen* culture as some other German cities, but that doesn't stop the locals from stopping each afternoon around 3pm for refreshment. You can often get breakfast until late in the afternoon, particularly in establishments favoured by Berlin's huge student population, and a bite to eat late at night is also easy come by at these places.

the river, depending on production) draws crowds to its performances of Shakespeare in German. The enticing sight of people stretched out in the sun makes you want to join the fun.

Weinbar Rutz
Chaussestrasse 8; tel: 2462 8760; www.rutz-weinbar.de; Mon–Sat 5pm–midnight; U6: Zinnowitzer Strasse; map p.134 B4
Top-drawer wines from around the world are on offer at this upscale bar. It is pricey, but one of the best places to taste excellent vintages in Berlin. Light snacks are also available, and there is a restaurant upstairs.

Around Alexanderplatz

Altes Europa
Gipsstrasse 11; tel: 2809 3840; www.alteseuropa.com; daily noon–late; U8: Weinmeisterstrasse; map p.134 C3
Idiosyncratic bar on the site of the Gipsdiele, a notorious dive of the inter-war years made famous by Joseph Roth, decorated with kitschy oil paintings and the odd obscene fresco. The food is all but inedible, but there's excellent beer and, surprisingly for a Berlin bar, the featured wine is usually both superb and a bargain.

Café Silberstein
Oranienburger Strasse 27; tel: 281 2095; www.silberstein-cafe.de; daily 10am–2am; S1, S2: Oranienburger Strasse, U6: Oranienburger Tor; map p.134 C3
Although it was one of the first places in Berlin to offer sushi, Silberstein is still best-known as a bar. Its odd furniture mirrors the strange abstract decorations from the 1920s which were discovered on the walls during a spate of renovation.

Right: Weinbar Rutz.

Left: lunchtime at Café Einstein.

Tiergarten

Café Einstein
Kurfürstenstrasse 58; tel: 261 5096; daily 10am–2am; U1, U15: Kurfürstenstrasse; map p.133 E1

A Berlin institution in the mansion of a once-famous silent-screen actress. A Viennese coffee house with style, and staffed by haughty waiters. The apple cake sets a high standard, though, and the brew is good enough to have given birth to a city-wide franchise of coffee houses.

Caffé e Gelato
Alte Potsdamer Strasse 7, Potsdamer Platz Arkaden (top floor); tel: 2529 7832; www.gelato-berlin.de; Mon–Sat 10am–10pm; S1, S2, U2: Potsdamer Platz; map p.134 A1

This ice-cream parlour is a hit among locals and visitors alike. Always packed and with long queues for takeaway cones but worth the short wait. As close as you can get to real Italian ice-cream in Berlin and with so many flavours to chose from, you are bound to make a return trip.

A classy place for a drink on Oranienburger Strasse.

Gorki Park
Weinbergsweg 25; tel: 448 7286; www.gorki-park.de; daily 10am–2am; U8: Rosenthaler Platz; map p.135 C4

This offshoot of Prenzlauer Berg's Pasternak Restaurant is a popular meeting place for locals, as well as a fine place to have an authentic Russian lunch. Free wi-fi, good coffee, Russian beer and vodka,

and a popular Sunday brunch from 10am onwards.

Hackbarths
Auguststrasse 69a; tel: 282 7706; daily 9am–3am; U8: Weinmeisterstrasse; map p.134 C3

Hackbarths was a bakery once upon a time, and it still opens to serve breakfast. A crucial part of the early post-Wall scene in the Mitte area, it is still the favourite wateringhole of local artists and curators. Light meals available.

Above: when in Germany... do as the Germans do.

Schleusenkrug
Müller-Breslau Strasse; tel: 313 9909; www.schleusenkrug.de; daily 10am–midnight; S3, S5, S7, S9, U7, U2: Tiergarten or Zoologicher Garten; map p.133 D2
Located by a lock in the Landwehrkanal and within earshot of the Zoo, this popular spot in the Tiergarten has been a favourite since it opened in 1954, although since 1996, new management has made it as noted for its organic sausages as its central location and pleasant grounds. A perfect retreat after a visit to the Zoo.

Charlottenburg
Café Hardenberg
Hardenbergstrasse 10; tel: 312 2644; www.cafe-hardenberg.de; daily 9am–1am; U2: Ernst-Reuter-Platz; map p.133 C2
The Café Hardenberg pretty much defines the West

Want a beer? Be prepared to wait: German tradition says seven minutes is what it takes to draw a decent beer, waiting for the head to subside and then shooting a bit more in. Does it make a difference? Probably not, but tradition is tradition.

Berlin student café: located near both the Technical University and the Art College, it hums day and night with students and others out and about in the neighbourhood enjoying a light meal, breakfast, or one of those huge cups of *milchkaffee*.

Café im Literaturhaus
Fasanenstrasse 23; tel: 882 5414; daily 10am–midnight; U15: Uhlandstrasse; map p.137 D4
Housed in a beautiful 1889 Belle Époque villa off the Ku'damm and frequented by accomplished and aspiring writers, this small café-cum-restaurant in the building's winter garden makes for a great break from city-trotting, even if it is just for a cup of coffee. The Mediterranean-inspired food does not quite come up to the setting.

Café Kranzler
Kurfürstendamm 18; tel: 887 183 925; www.cafekranzler.de; daily 8.30am–8pm; S5, S7, S9: Zoologischer Garten, U2: Kurfürstendamm; map p.133 D1
The refined ladies who gathered for *Kaffee und Kuchen* here in days gone by would hardly recognise the Kranzler today. Not that there aren't still refined ladies and *Kaffee und Kuchen* here, but this Ku'damm landmark, a survivor of an institution which opened on Unter den Linden in 1835, moved to the Ku'damm a century later and was destroyed in World War II, to be rebuilt after the conflict. It has now been integrated into a huge office and

shopping complex, its vintage architecture intact. A defining old-school Berlin place every bit as much as the KaDeWe and the Ku'damm itself.

Schwarzes Café
Kantstrasse 148; tel: 313 8038; daily 24 hours; U2, S5, S7, S9: Savignyplatz; map p.133 C1
If ever there were a typical Berlin café, this raucous institution would be it. Rough around the edges and full of attitude, it has always been there, is always open and everyone else goes there, which gives it a certain distinct charm.

Universum
Kurfürstendamm 153; tel: 8906 4995; www.universum lounge.com; daily 6pm–late; U7: Adenauerplatz; map.136 B4
With a space-age theme, this is one of Berlin's most distinctive concept bars. Situated in the same building as the Schaubühne theatre, Universum has a clock set to Houston time and a fun ambience thanks to all the moon mission emphemera.

Vienna Bar
Kantstrasse 152; tel: 3101 5090; www.vienna-bar.de; daily 11am–4am; U2, S5, S7, S9: Zoologischer Garten; map p.133 D1

A bit friendlier than next-door neighbour Paris Bar, although owned by the same folks, the Vienna Bar's high-end international clientele is a cross section of the movers and shakers around Berlin's media and business worlds. It has yet to develop a distinctive style, but it is in the right location, so expect it to find a niche.

Zwiebelfisch

Savignyplatz 7; tel: 312 7363; www.zwiebelfisch-berlin.de; daily 24 hours; S5, S7, S9: Savignyplatz; map p.133 C1

An older, well-educated crowd gathers here to peruse the many magazines and newspapers on offer and discuss the news and views contained therein. If your German and your knowledge of current events are up to it, you can join in. If you're lucky enough to be able to go with a regular, you'll be royally entertained.

Prenzlauer Berg

Café Schwarz Sauer

Kastanienallee 13; tel: 448 5633; www.schwarzsauer.com; daily 8pm–late; U2: Eberswalder Strasse

The central location on

Above: perfectly in-season fruit pastries.

'Casting Allee', so called because of the beautiful people posing at the kerbside tables during the summer. Schwarz Sauer is probably the best-known, best-loved bar on the street and is a favourite meeting place for young and budget-conscious residents of the neighbourhood, many of whom are British and American expats.

Prater-Garten

Kastanienallee 7–9; tel: 448 5688; www.pratergarten.de; daily noon–1am, garden open Apr–Sept; U2: Eberswalder Strasse

Claiming to be Berlin's oldest beer garden, the Prater has been around since 1837, when someone named Porath opened a beer bar on the site. In 1852, the Kalbo family took it over and soon established a small theatre to entertain the drinkers with songs and revues. In 1946, the property was taken over by the Volksbühne theatre, which became the focus of activity on the property, but in 1996, a major remodelling of the property put the beer garden back in business, where it remains an extremely popular gathering place today.

Left: drinking at a bar in Hackescher Höfe.

A good café will never offer fruit pastries out of season. This means berries in the spring, peaches and plums later in the year, and apples, pears and dried fruit in the autumn.

Enjoy a Prater Pilsner, a charcoal-grilled Wurst, and an ambience that looks not too unlike the photo on the 1912 postcard pictured on the Prater's website.

Weinstein

Lychener Strasse 33; tel: 442 1842; Mon–Sat 5pm–2am, Sun 6pm–2am; U2: Eberswalder Strasse

Somewhere between a restaurant, a café and a wine bar, Weinstein has grown out of a wine wholesale business into one of the neighbourhood's top tips. The food is good, and the selection of wines from obscure corners of Europe, particularly Eastern Europe, is incredible.

Wohnzimmer

Lette Strasse 6; tel: 445 5458; www.wohnzimmer-bar.de; daily 10am–late; U2: Schönhauser Allee

In this bohemian-chic dive bar, the residents of Prenzlauer Berg come and hang out on vintage furniture. *Wohnzimmer* translates as 'living room', and with breakfast, cakes and drinks available, this laid-back pub is ideal for relaxing in like it was your own trendy lounge.

Yes

Knaackstrasse 14; www.yes berlin.de; Mon–Sat 8pm–late; U2: Senefelderplatz; map p.135 D4

Very eccentric bar owned and presided over by a very eccentric Spaniard with excellent taste in background music, beer and spirits. Yes also sits right by the Wasserturm, making it a good stop during an evening out in Prenzlauer Berg. If the owner

Left: the longest bar in Berlin, at Bar am Lützowplatz.

the ceiling. In recent years, they've started serving ice-cream in the summertime in the tiny front garden during the day. English is spoken at the bar, although note that one of the owners is named Chaos for a reason.

Kreuzberg and Friedrichshain

Barcomi's
Bergmannstrasse 21; tel: 694 81 38; www.barcomis.de; Mon–Sat 9am–midnight, Sun 10am–midnight; U7: Gneisenaustrasse; map p.138 B3

Cynthia Barcomi, an American, got tired of Berlin's bad coffee and became the first person in town to introduce home-roasted beans in her house blend. There are also cookies and brownies; unsurprisingly, this is the American cake-lover's home from home.

Café Milagro
Bergmannstrasse 12; tel: 692 2303; www.milagro.de; daily 9am–1am; U7: Gneisenaustrasse; map p.138 B3

A fixture of the Bergmannstrasse scene since 1990, the Milagro is open round the clock, and offers food until midnight. Its two floors are often packed with locals of every description, eating, drinking and trying to read in the dim light on a winter's afternoon.

CSA
Karl-Marx-Allee 96; tel: 2904 4741; www.csa-bar.de; daily May–Oct: 8pm–late, Nov–Apr: 7pm–late; U5: Weberwiese; map p.135 E2

This upmarket drinking den is somewhat different from most of the drinking options in scruffy, anarchic Friedrichshain. CSA has been sleekly designed from the former offices of the

---

> As of January 2008, smoking has been theoretically prohibited in Berlin's bars and restaurants, although a separate smoking area is legal. Many bars have resisted this, but the chances are you'll be able to drink in a smoke-free environment.

offers you some of his whisky, though, just say no.

Schöneberg

Bar am Lützowplatz
Lützowplatz 7; tel 262 6807; www.baramluetzowplatz.de; daily 4pm–4am; U3, U7: Nollendorfplatz; map p.133 E1

Berlin's longest cocktail bar, stretching throughout the length of the block, is a favourite of visitors. Seeing Mao Zedong's visage at the head of it may set off some cognitive dissonance though, even without the help of one of their superb selection of single malts, champagnes (one of the largest collections in the world) or distinctive cocktails.

Café Berio
Maassenstrasse 7; tel: 216 1946; www.cafe-berio.de; Sun–Thur 8am–midnight, Fri–Sat 8am–1am; U2, U3, U4: Nollendorfplatz; map p.137 E4

A mainstay of Berlin's gay and lesbian community for over 50 years, the Berio is also a favourite place to stop after shopping at the Winterfeldtplatz market for its excellent coffee and pastries. Friendly service, and lovely tables outside during summer months.

Pinguin-Club
Wartburgstrasse 54; tel: 781 3005; www.pinguin-club.de; daily 6pm–4am; U7: Eisenacher Strasse; map p.137 E3

Since 1986, this merry pub has been serving a mix of Germans and expats, most of whom have remained regulars as they've aged. Elvis, Billy Wilder and Horst Buchholz on the set of One, Two, Three, as well as various forgotten German pop stars stare down from the walls, there's a kiddy-car made into a table and a disco ball on

One daunting fact about Berlin is that its bars can, legally, be open round the clock. This, however, doesn't mean 24 hours: an hour a day has to be set aside for cleaning, although customers can remain in the house while service is suspended. Bars tend just to close when they close, usually late at night after the customers stop coming.

Czech Republic's airline of the same name, and has put an elegant spin on the Soviet-era architecture, to make this bar something quite special.

Floating Lounge

Mühlenstrasse 73–7; tel: 6676 3806; www.eastern-comfort.de; Tue–Sat 2pm–late, Sun 11am–late; S3, S5, S7, S9: Warschauer Strasse; map p.135 E1

Part of the Eastern Comfort Hostel Boat, this chilled out lounge is ideal for having a drink in while watching the sun set over the Oberbaumbrücke.

Golgatha Tanzbar und Biergarten

Dudenstrasse 40 (in Viktoriapark); tel: 785 2453; www.golgatha-berlin.de; 21 Mar–Sept daily noon–late; U7: Yorckstrasse, U6: Platz der Luftbrücke, S1, S2: Yorckstrasse; map p.138 B3

Leave it to irreverent Berliners to name a beer garden on a hill with a cross on top of it after the garden where Jesus spent his last night,

Above: enjoying a sunny day at an outdoor table.

even if they do (intentionally) misspell it. Live bands, occasional firework displays and lots of beer make this a lively and occasionally rowdy place in the summertime. Best to go with a local if you don't speak *Berlinisch*, but it's a genuine slice of Berlin life. Enter on Katzbachstrasse where Monumentenstrasse ends, then take the first right inside the park. You should hear it before you see it.

Solar

Stresemannstrasse 76; tel: 163 765 2700; www.solarberlin.com; daily 6pm–late; S1, S25: Anhalter Bahnhof; map p.134 B1

Step into the glass lift on the side of a nondescript high-rise building near the Anhalter Bahnhof and

whoosh up to a glamorous cocktail lounge with killer views out over the city.

Western Districts

Loretta am Wannsee

Kronprinzessinnweg 260, Zehlendorf; tel: 803 5156; www.loretta.de; daily 10am–at least 11pm; S1, S7: Wannsee

Berlin's Wannsee is a large lake with the biggest inland beach in Europe, so it's not surprising that there is a tree-shaded, 1,000-seat beer garden serving a variety of food and Berlin, Bavarian and Czech beers on draught just 150m (164yds) from the S-Bahn station. A perfect way to finish a day's boating, a visit to the Pfaueninsel, or any of the other activities in the region.

Below: the view of the Oberbaumbrücke from Floating Lounge.

Overseas visitors who've never experienced Continental ice-cream concoctions can be in for a shock: piles of ice-cream and fruit are often doused with liquor and then topped with whipped-cream, with a few cookies stuck in for good measure. A quality *Eiscafe* will have an illustrated menu.

Cabaret

Since the days of Christopher Isherwood's experiences in Berlin's sexual underground during the Weimar Republic years, the city has been widely considered to be a capital of cabaret shows, an impression compounded by the famous musical and film *Cabaret*, inspired by Isherwood's stories. Today, there remain a few venues in Berlin to experience top-class performances, including on some of the legendary old stages, such as the Wintergarten Varieté, while general theatres often provide a platform for well-known *travestie* artists. For further listings of theatres, see *Theatre and Dance, p.126–7.*

Entertainment Forms

Be aware of the distinctions between cabaret, *travestie* and *varieté*, or you could be in for something of a surprise. *Travestie* is effectively revue in drag, while *varieté* is more of a mixed, circus-like show with a sprinkling of all different types of entertainment.

Cabaret

Bar Jeder Vernuft
Schaperstrasse 24, Wilmersdorf; tel: 883 1582; www.bar-jeder-vernunft.de; shows Tue–Thur 8.30pm, Fri–Sat 8pm, other shows vary; admission charge; U3, U9: Spichernstrasse; map p.137 D4
In a multi-mirrored circus-style tent, see popular performers in slick, entertaining shows, some in English. This is a fun place to indulge in classic Berlin entertainment.

Kleine Nachtrevue
Kurfürstenstrasse 116, Schöneberg; tel: 784 5539; www.kleine-nachtrevue.de; show Tue–Sat 11pm; admission charge; U1, U2, U3: Wittenberg-platz; map p.133 E1
Burlesque, nude ballets and torch songs by a male Mar-

lene Dietrich impersonator make up the late-night programme at this playful cabaret, ideal for experiencing the decadent fantasy.

La vie en Rose
Tempelhof Airport; tel: 6951 3000; www.lavieenrose-berlin.de; show Tue–Fri 8pm, Sat 9pm, Sun 8pm; admission charge; U6, S41, S42: Platz der Luftbrücke; map p.138 B3
This is a small cabaret with a revue show that includes *travestie* and erotic dancers. There is also a restaurant with singing waiters and magicians who entertain the guests as they wait to be seated.

Scheinbar Varieté
Monumentenstrasse 9; tel: 784 5539; www.scheinbar.de; show 8.30pm, check programme for performance dates; admission charge; S2, S25, U7: Yorck-strasse; map p.138 A3
This theatre is about as big as your living room, seating up to 60 guests for its popular 'open stage' evenings when anyone can perform and the stage hosts professional and amateur clowns, jugglers or pantomime artists. Make reservations, by phone only.

Travestie

Cabaret Chez Nous
Marburger Strasse 14, Charlottenburg; tel: 213 1810; www.cabaret-chez-nous.de; show daily 8.30pm, Fri–Sat second show 11pm; admission charge; U2: Wittenbergplatz, Kurfürstendam; map p.133 D1
Considered Berlin's best *travestie* club, Chez Nous is also a travelling show. They describe themselves as a 'pompous demonstration of music, dance and conversation' with charm, extravagant costumes and fascinating rhythm.

First Ladies
Tel: 4465 3172; www.thefirst ladies.de
The First Ladies is a Berlin-based travelling *travestie* group. They have performed together on stages around the world for the past 20 years and also take part in a special *travestie* event called *Familie Wunderlich*, that performs two to four times a year. Check the Ladies' website and local listings for up-to-date details.

Ikenna Cabaret Berlin
Marlene-Dietrich-Platz 1; tel: 6272 0093; www.ikenna.de; show Wed–Sun 8pm; admission

Left: Wintergarten Varieté in its heyday.

Friedrichstadtpalast

Friedrichstrasse 107; tel: 2326 2326; www.friedrichstadt palast.de; show Tue–Thur 8pm, Sat–Sun 4pm; admission charge; S3, S5, S7, S9, S75, U6, Tram M1, 12: Friedrichstrasse; map p.134 B3

One of the biggest attractions in Berlin for more than a century, Friedrichstadtpalast has survived two world wars, two dictatorships, and continues to draw crowds from all over to its musical and dance shows.

Wintergarten Varieté

Potsdamer Strasse 96; tel: 2500 8888; www.wintergarten.de; show Mon–Tue, Thur–Fri 8pm, Wed 4pm and 8pm, Sat 5pm and 9pm, Sun 3pm and 6pm; admission charge; U1: Kurfürstenstrasse, or S1, S2: Potsdamer Platz; map p.134 A1

Wintergarten has been described as Europe's most beautiful varieté theatre, and its extravagant shows are reminiscent of 1920s Berlin.

charge; U2, S1, S2: Potsdamer Platz; map p.134 A1

The *travestie* artist Ikenna performs regularly in New York, Los Angeles, Paris, Cannes and Salzburg, and is known for her soulful singing. In Berlin, Ikenna hosts a number of visiting *travestie* artists. There are two shows each night.

Theater im Keller

Weserstrasse 211; tel: 4799 7444; www.theater-im-keller.de; admission charge; U7, U8: Herrmanplatz; map p.139 D3

Below: a glamorous cabaret performer.

This is a cosy basement theatre with just 43 seats and a changing programme. Check local listings for current events.

Varieté

Belle et Fou Theatre

Marlene-Dietrich-Platz 1; tel: 2559 9550; www.belle-et-fou.de; show Wed–Sat 8pm; admission charge; S1, S2, U2: Potsdamer Platz; map p.134 A1

This is a new *varieté* group that aims to hark back to Berlin's permissive past with a playful erotic performance. Popular with tourists, it has received mixed reviews in the local press.

Chamäleon Theater

Rosenthaler Strasse 40–41; tel: 4000 5930; www.chamaeleon berlin.com; show Tue–Fri 8pm, Sat 7pm and 10pm, Sun 5pm; admission charge; S3, S5, S7, S9, S75, U8: Hackescher Markt; map p.135 C3

A major attraction at Hackescher Höfe, Chamäleon's influence on the development of German *varieté* extends well beyond Berlin. A beautiful theatre in one of the city's original theatre venues.

German-speakers will delight in the many venues for sharp-witted *Kabarett*, that particularly German brand of political satire. The best venues include **Wühlmäuse** (Berliner Kabarett-Theater, Pommernallee 2–4; tel: 3067 3011; www.wuehl maeuse.de), where the programme includes top *Kabarett* artists such as Kurt Krömer and Georg Schramm; **Distel** (Friedrichstrasse 101; tel: 204 4704; www.distel-berlin.de), once a thorn in the side of the political class in GDR-era East Germany; and **Kneifzange** (Friedrichstrasse 176–179; tel: 4799 7480; www.kneifzange-berlin.de), which has been going for 50 years, raising irreverence to an art form.

Children

Berlin's prime attractions might not seem immediately suitable for travelling with children, but the city is surprisingly child-friendly. Walking the wide streets of Berlin can be a tiring experience for little feet, but there are exciting alternatives: a front-seat ride past all the sights on a city double-decker bus, a visit to the world's largest dinosaur skeleton, petting a koi in the Zoo Aquarium, licking ice-cream 200m (656ft) above the city on the TV tower or exploring Berlin in miniature at the city's Legoland. Meanwhile, playgrounds and parks can be found in virtually every neighbourhood.

Activities

Domäne Dahlem (Dahlem Domain)

Königin-Luise-Strasse 49, Zehlendorf; tel: 666 3000; www.domaene-dahlem.de; farm grounds daily 24 hours, museum Wed–Mon daily 10am–6pm; farm grounds: free, museum: admission charge; U3: Dahlem-Dorf

Germany's only working farm with underground access. In the 15-hectare (37-acre) open-air museum of farming, kids can tour the fields on a tractor, pet the hogs, learn old crafts and learn about nutrition and organic farming in the old manor. A shop sells organically grown products, and for the parents there is an on-site beer garden (May–Oct 11am–8pm).

Jacks Kids World

Joachimstaler Strasse 19, Charlottenburg; tel: 8862 4464; www.jacks-kids-world.de; Mon–Fri noon–7.30pm, Sat–Sun 10am–8pm; admission charge, half-price after 6pm; S5, S7, S75, S9: Zoologischer Garten, U1, U9: Kurfürstendamm; map p.133 D1

Mini-Go Karts, trampolines, jungle gyms, climbing maze, tunnel slides, cinema showing Disney cartoons and a nap room for infants and toddler area. Kids over 4 can be dropped off while parents go shopping and sightseeing.

Kinderbad Monbijou

Oranienburger Strasse 78, Mitte; tel: 282 86 52; www.berliner baederbetriebe.de (German only); Mon–Fri 11am–7pm, Sat–Sun 10am–7pm; admission charge; S1, S2, S25, S26: Oranienburger Strasse; map p.134 C3

On a hot summer day, there is hardly a better alternative than cooling off in centrally located Monbijou children's pool. Officially, only children are allowed to bathe here, but you can accompany your toddler in the shallow pool. Camp out on the lawn under old trees. Good to combine with a visit to Hackesche Höfe.

Legoland Discovery Centre

Potsdamer Strasse 4, Tiergarten; tel: 301 0400; www.legolanddiscoverycentre.com; daily 10am–7pm, last admission 5pm; admission charge; S1, S2,

> A good deal for very active families is the 'Welcome Card Berlin and Potsdam' (sold in tourist offices), which is a two- or three-day public transport and discount pass valid for one adult and up to three children.

S25, U2: Potsdamer Platz; map p.134 A2

A small indoor amusement park in the Sony Center on Potsdamer Platz, complete with rides, 4D cinema, a build-and-test area for creative lovers of the little bricks, a miniature Berlin, a cafeteria and a gift shop. Best for kids aged 3–7, but beware, no child discounts mean it is expensive.

Loxx MiniaturWeltenBerlin

Grunerstrasse 20, Mitte; tel: 4472 3022; www.loxx-berlin.com; daily 10am–7pm; admission charge; U2, U5, U8, S5, S7, S75, S9: Alexanderplatz; map p.135 D3

One of Berlin's newest attractions. A huge computer-controlled model railway world on 2,500 air-conditioned sq m (3,000 sq yds). Trains and highlights of

Left: considering a splash in the Lustgarten.

and Zoo; U2, U9, S, S5, S7, S75, S9: Zoologischer Garten; map p.133 D1

A hands-on experience of biodiversity, this aquarium has a record number of species in fish tanks and terrarium, including breathtaking displays of sharks, stingrays, piranhas and coral reef fish, as well as the opportunity to pet the kois.

Zoo Berlin
Hardenbergplatz 8, Tiergarten; tel: 25 40 10; www.zoo-berlin.de; 15 Mar–14 Oct: daily 9am–6.30pm, 15 Oct–14 Mar: daily 9am–5pm; admission charge; combined tickets for Zoo and Aquarium; U2, U9, S5, S7, S75, S9: Zoologischer Garten; map p.133 D1

The Zoo Berlin, home to famous hand-raised polar bear Knut, is a centrally located classic with a compact yet pleasant display of the largest variety of animals shown anywhere in Germany. There are public feedings, a petting zoo and huge playgrounds. Parents will also be interested to note the Zoo's blend of historic architecture, like the Elephant Gate, as well as the modern animal houses like the fascinating, glass-domed Hippopotamus House.

Berlin are presented on a 1:87 scale, including an airport serviced by model planes: big fun for kids and dads.

Sea Life Berlin
Spandauer Strasse 3, Mitte; tel: 992 800; daily 10am–7pm; admission charge; S5, S7, S75, S9: Hackescher Markt; U2, U5, U8: Alexanderplatz; map p.135 C3

Displays of local and European water life. The attached Aquadom is really something: a slow elevator ride through a huge round fish tank full or coral fish. Overall though, the cost means the Aquarium is better value for families.

Stadtbad Schöneberg
Hauptstrasse 39, Schöneberg; tel: 780 9930; www.berliner baederbetriebe.de (German only); admission charge; Sept–May: Mon 2–10pm, Tue–Fri 7am–10pm; Sat–Sun 9am–10pm; U7: Eisenacher Strasse; bus M48: Hauptstrasse, Albertstrasse; map p.137 E3

Indoor swimming pool and a small water park.
SEE ALSO SPORTS, P.125

Zoo-Aquarium
Budapester Strasse 32, Tiergarten; tel: 254 010; www.aquarium-berlin.de; daily 9am–6pm; admission charge; combined tickets for Aquarium

Below: the Elephant Gate at Zoo Berlin leads to many creatures, from flamingos to a curious giraffe.

Left: playgrounds can be found in many Berlin parks.

tel: 902 540; www.dtmb.de; Tue–Fri 9am–5.30pm, Sat–Sun 10am–6pm; admission charge; U1, U7: Möckernbrücke; U1, U2: Gleisdreieck; S1, S2, S25: Anhalter Bahnhof; map p.138 B4

The Mecca for young railway, car and engineering aficionados. A few steps from the main building is the SPECTRUM Science Centre (entrance Möckernstrasse 26), offering several floors of playful physics experiments suited to kids aged from 4 upwards.

Museum für Kommunikation

Leipziger Strasse 16, Mitte; tel: 2029 4204; www.museumsstiftung.de/berlin (German only); Tue–Fri 9am–5pm, Sat–Sun 11am–7pm; free; U2: Mohrenstrasse; U2, U6: Stadtmitte, S1, S2, S25: Potsdamer Platz, map p.134 B2

Kids can play football with cute-looking robots in the museum's foyer, while parents may marvel at the architecture of this beautifully renovated 19th-century building, the world's oldest postal museum. In the basement, you can admire the Blue Mauritius and Bell's first telephone.

Museum für Naturkunde (Museum of Natural History)

Invalidenstrasse 43, Mitte; tel: 2093 8591; www.naturkundemuseum-berlin.de; Tue–Fri 9.30am–5pm, Sat–Sun, holidays 10am–6pm; admission charge; U6: Zinnowitzer Strasse; S3, S5,

General Information

ACCOMMODATION

Some hotels have family rooms sleeping up to four; one extra bed or cot in a double is usually not a problem. Renting an apartment with a full kitchen is often good value.

SEE ALSO HOTELS, P.70–77

BABYSITTING

Although you can almost certainly arrange a babysitter for a few hours through your hotel, this is an alternative:

Kinderinsel (Children's Island)

Eichendorffstrasse 17, Mitte; tel: 4171 6928; www.kinderinsel.de; S2: Nordbahnhof; U6: Zinnowitzer Strasse; map p.134 B4

Kinderinsel is a day care centre-cum-hotel. The multilingual professional staff look after children aged 0–14 around the clock, entertain them with ghost parties or take them out on city adventure tours. In emergencies (sick children or parents), they pay house visits.

DISCOUNTS

Almost everywhere, there are discounts for children under 14. Toddlers are mostly admitted for free. Most Berlin museums are free for kids under 16.

EATING OUT

Children are welcome but expected not to disturb other guests in restaurants. Most places have children's menus or serve an extra plate if you want to split a meal. Most restaurants will also have high chairs for young guests.

HOSPITALS

DRK Krankenhaus Westend

Spandauer Damm 130; tel: 3035 4848; S41, S42, S46: Westend and 5 minutes' walk

A hospital with 24-hour children's emergency service and English-speaking staff.

SEE ALSO ESSENTIALS, P.48–9

SUPPLIES

Baby food and supplies such as nappies are sold at every larger supermarket and at pharmacies.

Museums

Deutsches Technikmuseum

Trebbiner Strasse 9, Kreuzberg;

In winter, ice rinks are set up on Alexanderplatz and Potsdamer Platz where the winter playground (Winterwelt) is completed by a huge tobogganning hill (see p.55).

Make the trip up to one of Berlin's best viewpoints as a treat for both parents and little ones. The **Fernsehturm** (Television Tower) has good views of the city from the observation deck or the Telecafé restaurant with its rotating floor, over a meal or an ice-cream sundae *(see also p.30–1)*. Alternatively, you can avoid the queues at the **Reichstagskuppel** (dome of the **Reichstag** building) by entering the building on its right side entrance, which is reserved for families with young children *(see also p.31)*.

S7, S9: Hauptbahnhof; S1, S2: Nordbahnhof; map p.134 B4
The star of Berlin's Natural History Museum's newly arranged dinosaur exhibition is the world's largest Brachiosaurus skeleton, measuring 12m high by 22m long (40ft by 70ft). SEE ALSO MUSEUMS, P.88–9

Sightseeing

BY BOAT

Give those little feet a rest on one of the many sightseeing boats cruising on the Spree river and canals. Several companies operate on similar routes.
SEE ALSO TRANSPORT, P.129

Reederei Riedel
Landing Märkisches Ufer, Mitte; tel: 693 4646; www.reederei-riedel.de (German only); Mar–Oct; U2: Märkisches Museum; S3, S5, S7, S75, S9, U8: Jannowitzbrücke; map p.135 D2
Go on a three-hour *'Brückenfahrt'* (tour of bridges) along the Spree and the Landwehrkanal and discover that Berlin actually has more bridges than Venice.
Reederei Winkler

Landing Bahnhof Friedrichstrasse (outside the railway station), Mitte; tel: 349 9595; www.reedereiwinkler.de/en; Apr–Oct; S5, S7, S75, S9: Friedrichstrasse; map p.136 B2
Easy-to-find landing, one-hour city tours. Longer ones depart from Schloss Charlottenburg landing.

BY BUS

Kids will love seeing the city from the top deck of bus No. 100 or 200, or any official hop-on hop-off bus tour.

BY CYCLE-RICKSHAW

Call or simply hail at Brandenburg Gate, Potsdamer Platz, Kurfürstendamm or Hauptbahnhof for individual guided tours of the city.
Berlin Rikscha Tours
Tel: 0163 307 7297; www.berlin-rikscha-tours.de; spring–autumn: daily 24 hours
Velotaxi
Tel: 443 194 28; www.velotaxi.de; spring–autumn: daily 24 hours

BY HORSE-DRAWN CARRIAGE
Berliner Kremser

Tel: 03 33 936 5701; www.berliner-kremser.de; Mon–Fri noon–9pm, Sat–Sun 10am–9pm
Departure points: near the Adlon Hotel on Unter den Linden avenue, at the Holocaust Memorial and the Lustgarten (Altes Museum). 30- or 60-minute guided tours can be had across the centre of Berlin.

Toy Shops
Ratzekatz

Raumerstrasse 7, Prenzlauer Berg; tel: 681 9564; www.ratzekatz.de; Mon–Fri 10am–7pm; U2: Eberswalder Strasse
Angelina Jolie bought dinosaurs here for her son; the crammed shop stores everything from baby toys to model trains.
T.O.T.S.
The Original Toy Store

Unter den Linden 69, Mitte; tel: 2267 9081; map p.136 A1
Quality toy paradise just a block away from Brandenburg Gate. Traditional Anker stone building sets and puzzles. Wooden toys. English-language children's books.

Right: a tour boat sets sail on the Spree.

43

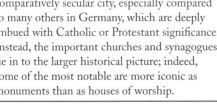

Churches, Synagogues and Mosques

There's no Notre-Dame or Hagia Sophia here: for a European capital city, Berlin is a comparatively secular city, especially compared to many others in Germany, which are deeply imbued with Catholic or Protestant significance. Instead, the important churches and synagogues tie in to the larger historical picture; indeed, some of the most notable are more iconic as monuments than as houses of worship.

Mitte

Berliner Dom (Berlin Cathedral)

Lustgarten; tel: 2026 9136; www.berliner-dom.de; Oct–Mar: Mon–Fri 9am–7pm; Sun, holidays noon–7pm, Apr–Sept: until 8pm; admission charge; S3, S5, S7, S9, S75: Hackescher Markt; map p.137 D1

The central administrative building of the Evangelical Church was built in 1905 to replace a classic Schinkel structure. It's typical Wilhelmine bombast and the sanctuary's acoustics are not

At the end of the 19th century, the Kaiser's wife, the Kaiserin, decreed that each of the city's *bezirke* (districts) should have its own Evangelical church, which resulted in the skyline being dotted with steeples. None are particularly architecturally distinguished. Another decree was that non-Evangelical churches were permitted, but not allowed to have their front doors on the street, so neighbourhood Catholic and other Protestant churches are often hidden from view.

ideal for the many concerts held there, but the sheer detail of its interior is impressive. Admission also includes access to the dome, which has a fine view of Mitte, and the crypt, which contains 90 sarcophagi of various Hohenzollerns.

Around Alexanderplatz

Marienkirche

Karl-Liebknecht-Strasse 8; tel: 242 4467; www.marienkirche-berlin.de; Mon–Thur 10am–4pm, Sat–Sun noon–4pm, Sunday services 10am, organ recital and meditation May–Oct: Sat 4.30pm; free; S3, S5, S7, S9, S75, U2, U5, U8: Alexanderplatz; map p.137 E2

Begun around 1270 and gradually added to and rebuilt until Carl Gotthard Langhans, the architect of the Brandenburg Gate, finished it in 1790, this is one of Berlin's oldest structures. The *Dance of Death* fresco in the entrance hall is from 1485, during the time of the Plague. The Walther organ is one of Germany's finest. The church gained further prominence in 1989 as a centre for anti-government

dissidence in East Germany, one of the few in Berlin.

Neue Synagogue

Oranienburger Strasse 28–30; tel: 8802 8316; www.cjudaicum. de; Apr–Sept: Sun–Mon 10am–8pm, Tue–Thur 10am–6pm, Fri 10am–5pm; Nov–Feb: Sun–Mon 10am–6pm, Tue–Thur 10am–6pm, Fri 10am–2pm; admission charge; guided tour in English Thur 4pm; S1, S2, S25, S26: Oranienburger Strasse; map p.134 C3

Built in 1866 as a symbol of pride in Berlin's Jewish community, the New Synagogue, its Moorish dome filigreed with gold, towers over the Scheunenviertel. Although attacked on Kristallnacht in 1939, the thugs were turned away by a brave policeman, Wilhelm Krützfeld, who is honoured with a plaque on the synagogue front. The real damage came from an Allied bombing raid in 1945, which destroyed the sanctuary. Today, the structure is a museum for the Centrum Judaicum, a foundation which maintains a permanent collection celebrating the building's history and various temporary exhibitions dealing

Left: the Neue Synagogue.

Kaiser Wilhelm I, and bombed in 1943, this church has become famous for its ruin. Instead of rebuilding it, the Evangelical Church shored up the remains and left it as a stark reminder of war amidst its gleaming modern surroundings. Services take place in the glass-encased tower next door.

Kreuzberg and Friedrichshain

Mosques

Although Berlin's mostly Turkish Muslim community has over 200,000 members, mosques tend to be hidden from view, with worship being conducted in converted factory buildings and unlabelled storefronts. As recently as April 2007, the laying of a cornerstone for a mosque in Kreuzberg attracted angry demonstrators. One of the few visible mosques is the **Ahmadiyya Mosque** in Wilmersdorf (Brienner Strasse 7–8; tel: 873 5703); a very impressive one is the **Sehitlik Mosque** in Neukölln (Columbiadamm 128; tel: 692 1118, tours on request), its minarets towering over the Hasenheide park. None of Berlin's mosques are open for inspection by the general public without prior notice.

Note that there is an armed police presence in front of all synagogues and other Jewish buildings in Berlin. This is a normal security procedure and not a cause for alarm.

---

with various aspects of Berlin's Jewish history.

Nikolaikirche
Nikolaikirchplatz; tel: 2400 2162; www.stadtmuseum.de; Tue, Thur–Sun 10am–6pm, Wed noon–8pm; free, donations welcome; S3, S5, S7, S9, S75, U2, U5, U8: Alexanderplatz; map p.137 E1
Originally constructed in 1220 and added to through the 19th century, the Nikolaikirche forms the centre of the Nikolaiviertel historical district and today is a museum of early Berlin history throughout the 17th century, as well as a concert venue. Bombed heavily during World War II, it was reconstructed in 1987.

Charlottenburg
Kaiser-Wilhelm-Gedächtniskirche
Breitscheidplatz; tel: 0171 313 9328; www.gedaechtniskirche-berlin.de; daily 9am–7pm, Sunday services 10am, 6pm; free; S3, S5, S7, S9, U1, U2, U9: Zoologischer Garten; map p.133 D1
Built in 1891–5 to honour

Below: the impressively detailed altar and ceiling of the Berliner Dom.

Environment

Berlin is a surprisingly 'green' city; surprising because of the scale of development the city is always undergoing and the cash-flow problems that the local government is suffering. However, there are measures in place to reduce once chronic problems of air pollution, while recycling is an inbuilt feature of the German lifestyle. Visitors will notice the provision made for recycling as well as the changes wrought by the recent smoking ban. Meanwhile, with 18 percent of the Greater Berlin area covered by greenery, many local species are thriving, and the urban population is never too far from a park, forest or even a beach.

Construction

Berlin is constantly renewing itself. Hard as it may be to believe, there is still damage from bombing raids during World War II, and unexploded bombs even turn up from time to time. In addition, much of the renovation done by the East German government was rather lacking, whether covering up a beautiful old facade with concrete or working with low-quality materials, and this, too, is having to be repaired. The days when the sky over Potsdamer Platz looked like a crane convention may be gone, but the building of new buildings continues at a lesser pace, especially in the East, where bombed buildings tended to be torn down and the lot left vacant.

Air Quality

A piece of good news for those who never felt at home in Berlin's smoke-infested bars and cafés: smoking is now banned in indoor public areas, apart from specially identified rooms. However, many Berliners still smoke, so some bars have avoided

Due to high-tech water purification and less industry in Berlin, the water quality of the Spree river has improved considerably over the past 20 years, but swimming is still neither allowed nor advisable here. However, 17 species of fish have recently been counted in the Spree, and the quality of the Berlin tap water is excellent.

the ban by re-inventing themselves as 'smoking clubs'.

With the replacement of coal stoves in old apartment buildings by more modern heating systems, the Berlin air *(Berliner Luft)* has lost the pungent smell that used to be so characteristic of winter in the city. Another measure aimed at improving the proverbial *Berliner Luft* has been the recent introduction of *Umweltplaketten*, green, yellow or red tags for cars, depending on their contribution to pollution. Without such a sticker, cars are not allowed into the Green Zone or *Umweltzone*, the inner-city area within the S-Bahn ring. If

you are planning to drive to Berlin, you can have a badge mailed to your house in advance by online registration at www.umweltplakette.de.

Flora and Fauna

Berlin is committed to protecting and preserving its 2,500 public parks, green spaces and old trees in the city, realising how much they contribute to Berliners' quality of life. The efforts pay: Berlin is considered a very habitable place by two- and four-legged creatures: Mandarin ducks, herons, wild boar and foxes can all be spotted in city parks, with a bit of luck. Recent surveys have shown that the number of species found per hectare of urban land in Berlin is actually higher than in rural areas of Germany. This is partly due to the slightly higher average temperatures in the city, providing comfortable conditions for some Mediterranean species.

Among animals feeling particularly at home in Berlin are bats: 10,000 of them spend the winters in the Spandau Citadel, making it

Left: cranes are an everyday presence in Berlin.

the Wall. The city pumped €4.5 million into laying it out.
SEE ALSO PARKS AND GARDENS, P.108–11; SPORTS, P.124; TRANSPORT, P.129

Eco-initiatives

Berliners, like all good Germans, are renowned for separating their rubbish neatly into colour-coded bins or containers (plastic goes in yellow, paper in blue). What they are less conscientious about is cleaning up after their dogs, assuming that they are not paying their dog tax for nothing, so keep an eye on where you step.

Although the sky over Berlin is not often a sunny one, solar power is hot here. SolarEnergy, one of the world's most important renewable energy trade shows, is held under the Funkturm tower every two years, partly to meet the rising demand for the latest heating technologies. You can even charter a solar-powered boat for a tour on the Berlin canals (www.solarpolis.de). However, so far solar power only accounts for 1 percent of the city's energy consumption, but with the increasing popularity of this energy form in sunnier southern Germany, this may increase in the future.

one of Europe's most important hibernation areas for the winged mammals. Surviving old bunkers and abandoned buildings in the city are just as popular with them. The more natural setting of the Berlin forests includes a number of nature sanctuaries that are refuges for protected species.

An area well-suited to study how quickly nature reclaims abandoned developed sites is the Schöneberger Südgelände, barely 20 minutes away from Potsdamer Platz by S-Bahn. A unique landscape emerged here on 18 hectares (45 acres) of a former marshalling yard. Trees have grown between railway tracks ever since the yard was given up after the building of the Wall, resulting in a 'primary forest'. Public protests prevented a development of the area in the 1970s, so it was left untouched for decades. Numerous species of birds, butterflies, grasshoppers and wild flowers are flourishing

here now on dry meadows and in robinia forests.

Berlin also has 17,000 hectares (42,500 acres) of forest, several dozen lakes with beaches and 180km (112 miles) of navigable waterways, resulting in plenty of recreational options. A great way of exploring the city and its surroundings is by bicycle – Berlin has 620km (385 miles) of bike paths, and rental bikes are available from many places. For a bit of history with your nature, try the Berliner Mauer-Radweg path, a 160km (100-mile) bicycle trail along the former death strip, passing by the few surviving relicts of

Right: a recycling bin at an S-Bahn station.

Essentials

Berlin is an easy city to get around, and there is certainly no lack of things to do. Locals tend to be reserved but polite with strangers, and younger Berliners in particular may be happy to practise their English on you. The police in Berlin are generally friendly and helpful to tourists, but note that their command of English may be limited. Still, don't hesitate to approach them if you feel lost. The following listings detail practical information to help you get to grips with, among other things, locating an address, getting out cash and finding information on what events are happening during your stay.

Addresses

House numbers in Berlin do not necessarily progress in one direction. The name of the street and the numbers on that block are marked on street signs at most corners.

Climate

Summers are fairly warm in Berlin, with highs around 25°C (77°F) from June to August, but rainy days are not uncommon. Spring and autumn are pleasant seasons to visit, with moderate temperatures. Winters tend to be wet and cold, with few sunny days.
www.berlin-life.com/weather.php

Electricity

You will need an adaptor or transformer for most British and US plugs. German sockets have two round holes and supplies are 220 volts.

Embassies and Consulates

Australia
Wallstrasse 76–79, Mitte;
tel: 880 0880
Canada
Leipziger Platz 17, Mitte;
tel: 203 120

Republic of Ireland
Friedrichstrasse 200, Mitte;
tel: 220 720
UK
Wilhelmstrasse 70, Mitte;
tel: 2045 7579
US
Consulate: Clayallee 170, Zehlendorf; tel: 832 92
Embassy: Neustädtische Kirchstrasse 4–5, Mitte; tel: 238 6290

Emergencies

Polizei (Police): 110
Feuerwehr/Rettungsstelle (Fire Department/ Ambulance): 112
These numbers can be called toll-free from public phone boxes and mobile phones.

Health

DOCTORS AND HOSPITALS
Call a doc
Tel: 01804-22 55 23 62
Arranges appointments with English-speaking doctors.
Charité
Schumann Strasse 20–21; tel: 420 50; U6, S1 S2, S7, S9, S75: Friedrichstrasse; map p.134 B3
St Hedwig Krankenhaus
Grosse Hamburger Strasse 5; tel: 231 10; S5, S7, S9, S75: Hackescher Markt; map p.134 C3

MEDICAL TREATMENT
EU Nationals
Visitors from EU member states are entitled to reduced-cost (usually 70 percent) emergency treatment from doctors and dentists with a European Health Insurance card (EHIC). UK citizens can obtain it from post offices or online at www.dh.gov.uk.
North Americans
International Association for Medical Assistance to Travellers (IAMAT); 40 Regal Road, Guelph, Ontario N1K 1B5, Canada; tel: 519 836 0102
This is a non-profit group that offers members fixed rates for medical treatment. Members

Below: if in need of a pharmacy, look out for one of these.

Left: a good map is always useful for navigating city streets.

(phone cards) are sold at T-Punkt telecom shops.

Tourist Information

EX-BERLINER
The monthly *Ex-Berliner* English-language city maga-zine is good for listings of all kinds of events. Available from all better news-stands and tourist offices (limited contents on www.exberliner.de).

TOURIST OFFICES
The city tourist offices are called 'Berlin Infostore', and branches can be found at: Hauptbahnhof; ground floor; daily 8am–10pm.
Brandenburg Gate, Pariser Platz; daily 10am–6pm
Berlin Pavilion at the Reichstag, Scheidemannstrasse; daily 10am–6pm
Neues Kranzler Eck mall, Kurfürs-tendamm 21; daily 10am–6pm
Apart from making reserva-tions, providing maps and information, these places sell the **Berlin WelcomeCard** (travelcard and 50 percent dis-count on admission charges) and the new **WelcomeCard Culture** that includes free entry into 70 museums.

Visas

Visitors from the EU, the US, Canada and Australia don't need a visa for visiting Ger-many, just a valid national identity card (EU citizens) or a passport. Visitors from other countries need a valid passport and should check regulations with their local German Consulate.

receive a medical record com-pleted by their doctor and a directory of English-speaking IAMAT doctors in Germany, who are on call 24 hours a day. Membership is free.

PHARMACIES
Over-the-counter drugs are sold at *apotheke* (pharmacies) which can be found every-where, marked by a red 'A'.

Internet

Many hotels, hostels and cafés, especially in the tourist areas, provide wireless inter-net, and there are numerous internet cafés all over town:
easyEverything
Kurfürstendamm 224; daily 6.30am–2am; U1, U15: Kurfürstendamm; map p.133 D1
The biggest internet café is very centrally located. Other branches, with shorter open-ing hours, at the **Sony Center** and **Friedrichstrasse** station.

Money

Germany's currency is the euro. For up-to-date exchange rates, consult: www.xe.com.
Credit cards are not as universally accepted here as

elsewhere in the world. Always carry some cash; small items are never paid for by card. ATMs are located all over the city but not as frequently as you might want. Many are situated in banks; after hours, open the doors with your card. Most have an English menu but require numeric PINs.
Wechselstuben (Bureaux de Change) offer slightly better exchange rates than banks. You find them at railway stations and airports.

Post

Post offices are rare these days, but they are about the only places selling stamps.
Postamt Friedrichstrasse
Georgenstrasse 12, Mitte; daily 8am–10pm; S1, S7, S9, S75, U6: Friedrichstrasse; map p.136 B2
The longest-opening branch.

Telephones

Berlin has many telephone shops where you can make long-distance calls at low fares. Compare prices, though, since most have a focus region in the world.
Most phone boxes are card-operated. *Telefonkarte*

Fashion

Berlin fashion has always been edgy. From the erotic masculinity of Marlene Dietrich to today's street-savvy style, it has long been known for its elegant toughness. In Marlene's day, Berlin was a fashion centre, a role it lost after World War II and did not recover until after the Berlin Wall fell and designers rediscovered the German capital. While those looking for the big international names will find them, Berlin's speciality is innovative, individual designers housed in quirky boutiques, as well as cutting-edge streetwear. For department stores that stock clothing, *see Shopping, p.120.*

The Berlin Fashion Map

International brands can be found in posh boutiques on **Kurfürstendamm** or **Friedrichstrasse**, while Berlin's new, young fashion is mainly situated in the Eastern part of the city, in small shops on **Kastanienallee** in Prenzlauer Berg, or in the winding side streets around **Hackescher Markt** in Mitte.

Berlin Designers and Boutiques

Adddress

Rosa-Luxemburg-Strasse 28, Mitte; tel: 2887 3365; www.adddress.de; Mon–Sat noon–7pm; U2: Rosa-Luxemburg-Platz; map p.135 C3

Andrea Vrajitoru launched her shop in 2003, determined to add a touch of elegance to

West Berlin's famous Kurfürstendamm is still a major fashion venue, where many high-street and international brands are found. Explore the side streets that lead off Ku'damm to find smaller boutiques with local designers.

daily life. Her womenswear mixes high-quality design with utilitarian sophistication, resulting in a raft of trendy designs fit for any occasion.

Anuschka Hoevener

Kastanienallee 47, Prenzlauer Berg; tel: 4431 9299; www.anuschkahoevener.de; Tue–Fri 2–6pm; U8: Rosenthaler Platz; map p.135 C4

One of Berlin's avante-garde designers, Hoevener celebrates natural materials like silk and wool, incorporating sculptural forms into her minimalist designs for women. She is also gaining a devoted following in the US and Japan.

Butterflysoulfire

Lehderstrasse 74, Prenzlauer Berg; tel: 4210 5335; www.butterflysoulfire.com; Mon–Fri 10am–6pm; Sat by appointment; S8, S41, S42: Greifswalder Strasse

As its name suggests, this young label for men and women seeks a metamorphosis of styles that combine street cool with evening elegance. Proud of its Berlin roots, it calls its label A1, 'a tribute to the hood'.

Above: the hallmark knitwear at Claudia Skoda Level.

C'est tout Berlin

Mulackstrasse 26, Mitte; tel: 2759 5530; www.cesttout.de; Mon–Sat noon–8pm; U8: Rosenthaler Platz; map p.135 C3

As its designer, Katja Fuhrmann defined MTV Germany's look. Now she's turned to the appearance of women everywhere with urban, elegant and feminine designs.

Claudia Skoda Level

Alte Schönhauser Strasse 35, Mitte; tel: 280 7211; www.claudiaskoda.com; Mon–Fri noon–8pm, Sat noon–7pm; U8: Weinmeisterstrasse; map p.135 C3

An icon of the Berlin avantgarde and the city's most

Left: shopping at the clubwear and streetwear shop, Planet.

captures the spirit of change in the new Berlin.

Heimspiel
Niederbarnimstrasse 18, Friedrichshain; tel: 2068 7870; www.heimspiel-berlin.de; Mon–Fri 1–8pm; U5: Samariter-strasse

At this multi-label store, small is beautiful. It is a retail outlet for no less than 30 young Berlin designers, offering everything from clothes and accessories to art and crafts.

Molotow
Gneisenaustrasse 112, Kreuzberg; tel: 693 0818; www.molotowberlin.de; Mon–Fri 2–8pm, Sat noon–4pm; U7: Mehringdamm; map p.138 B4

This boutique is a showcase for both established and emerging local designers and sells fresh, elegant items that are both innovative and wearable.

Stoffrausch
Gabelsbergerstrasse 8, Friedrichshain; tel: 2966 5151; www.stoffrausch.com; Mon–Fri noon–8pm, Sat noon–4pm; U5: Samaritrstrasse

Designers Steffi di Freddi and Dominik Muun say their clothes are for 'crazy city-

established local designer, Claudia Skoda transformed knitwear into a modern design statement and became known internationally. She hung out with Bowie and Iggy Pop in West Berlin and spent the '80s in New York before returning home to take part in the revival of Berlin. Men's and women's lines available.

Creation Pia Fisher
Eisenacher Strasse 69, Schöneberg; tel: 7895 0915; www.creationpiafischer.de; Mon–Tue, Thur–Fri noon–6pm, Sat 10am–2pm; U7: Eisenacher Strasse; map p.137 E3

Pia Fischer is definitely not a disciple of the No Logo school; her unique creations are akin to an extravagant patchwork of 'utensils of haute couture': labels, buttons, zippers and ribbons.

Ebner Hosen Berlin
Schlesische Strasse 36, Prenzlauer Berg; tel: 5369 6486; www.florindaschnitzler.de; Tue–Sat 1.30–7.30pm; U1: Schlesisches Tor; map p.135 E1

In addition to its collections of hip trousers, shirts, capes and skirts, Ebner offers a

'racing and tuning' service to breathe new life into your favourite old clothes.

Firma
Neue Schönhauser Strasse 6, Mitte; tel: 2804 5666; www.firma.net; Mon–Fri noon–8pm, Sat noon–7pm; U8: Weinmeisterstrasse; S3, S5, S7, S9: Hackescher Markt; map p.135 C3

One of the most internationally celebrated of the new designers, the men's fashion by design duo Carl Tellessen and Daniela Biesenbach

Below: women's and men's fashions at Molotow.

Above: popular street fashion at IrieDaily.

dwellers and other lunatics', and indeed, their street hip jackets, trousers and sweatshirts are ideal for the urban individualist.

Thatcher's Shop
Hackesche Höfe IV, Rosenthaler Strasse 40–41, Mitte; tel: 2758 2210; www.thatchers.de; Mon–Fri 11am–8pm, Sat 11am–6pm; S3, S5, S7, S9: Hackescher Markt; map p.134 C3

Inspired by photography, music, architecture and digital arts, Ralf Hensellek and Thomas Mrozek have been among the most popular Berlin designers since they first opened Thatcher's in 1995 (also at: Kastanienallee 21; tel: 2462 7751; Tue–Fri noon–8pm, Sat noon–6pm; U2: Eberswalder Strasse).

Other Designer Boutiques and Department Stores

Peek & Cloppenburg
Tauentzienstrasse 19, Charlottenburg; tel: 212 900; www.peekundcloppenburg.de; Mon–Sat 10am–8pm; U2: Wittenbergplatz; map p.133 D1

This is the flagship store of the Düsseldorf fashion house. It offers a wide variety of brands, from casual wear and business attire to young fashion and designer brands, often at a discount.

Quartier 206
Friedrichstrasse 71, Mitte; tel: 2094 6800; www.department store-quartier206.com; Mon–Fri 11am–8pm, Sat 10am–6pm; U2: Stadtmitte, Französische Strasse; map p.134 B2

This is where the stars shop when they come to Berlin. A sophisticated temple to shopping, Quartier 206 restores Friedrichstrasse's cosmopolitan flair. The heart of the Quartier is Anne Maria Jagdfeld's, with her stunning collection of top designers, beauty products and flowers.

Specialist Clothing

Devils Child
Kreuzbergstrasse 31, Kreuzberg; tel: 7889 5002; www.devils-child.com; Mon–Fri noon–6pm, Sat noon–2pm; S2, S25, U7: Yorckstrasse; map p.138 B3

This local t-shirt maker has a wide variety of Berlin prints, but customers can also choose their own designs.

> ### Size Conversions
> **Women:** 36 (UK 8, US 6); 38 (UK 10, US 8); 40 (UK 12, US 10); 42 (UK 14, US 12); 44 (UK 16, US 14); 46 (UK 18, US 16).
> **Men:** 87 (UK/US 34); 91 (UK/US 36); 97 (UK/US 38); 102 (UK/US 40); 107 (UK/US 42); 112 (UK/US 44)

Rocking Chair
Gabriel-Max-Strasse 13, Friedrichshain; tel: 2936 4291; www.rockingchair-berlin.de, Mon–Fri noon–7pm, Sat 10am–4pm; U5: Samariterstrasse

Look closely and you might spot Elvis at this fashion shop that features '50s clothes, rockabilly attire, punk outfits and a large selection of retro-style bowling jerseys and Hawaiian shirts.

Sexy Mama
Lychener Strasse 52, Prenzlauer Berg; tel: 5471 4338; www.sexy-mama.de; Mon–Fri noon–7pm, except Tue, Wed 10am, Sat 11am–5pm; U2: Schönhauser Allee or Eberswalder Strasse

Catering to an influx of young families in Berlin's hippest neighbourhood, this boutique offers locally designed clothing for fashion-conscious mothers-to-be.

Trüffelschwein
Rosa-Luxemburg-Strasse 22, Mitte; tel: 7022 1225; www.trueffelschweinberlin.com; Mon–Sat noon–8pm; U2: Rosa-Luxemburg-Platz; map p.135 C3

Named for the pig used to sniff out delicious truffles in the woods, this men's fashion store is arranged like an attic to go rummaging in for timeless clothing that defies any passing trend. No suits or tuxedos here, but everything else a man might need.

Streetwear

East Berlin
Kastanienallee 13, Prenzlauer Berg; tel: 4404 6090; www.east berlin.net; Mon–Fri noon–8pm, Sat 11am–7pm; U2: Ebers-walder Strasse
Trendy young fashion that screams out its love of Berlin on t-shirts and sweatshirts bearing local icons such as the TV Tower on Alexander-platz or the Bundesadler, the eagle that is Germany's national symbol.

IrieDaily
Depot 2, Oranienstrasse 9, Kreuzberg; tel: 611 4655; www.iriedaily.com; Mon–Fri 11am–8pm, Sat 11am–6pm; U1: Görlitzer Bahnhof; map p.135 D1
Beloved, iconic Kreuzberg brand selling skater-influenced urbanwear. Very Berlin and increasingly suc-cessful, but still true to its edgy, street-style roots. Pick up a classic hoodie.

Planet
Schlüterstrasse 35, Charlotten-burg; tel: 885 2717; www.planet wear.de; Mon–Fri 11am–8pm, Sat 11am–6pm; U1: Uhland-strasse; map p.132 C1
Looking for some proper rave kit to hit Berlin's legendary club scene in? Planet is brim-ming with dancefloor-ready clothes and shoes, in addition to more standard streetwear styles. Pumping music helps get clients in the mood.

Accessories

Bless
Mulackstrasse 38, Mitte; tel: 2759 6566; www.bless-service. de; Mon, Wed–Fri 2–7pm, Sat noon–6pm; S3, S5, S7, S9: Hackescher Markt; map p.135 C3
Designers Ines Kaag and Parisian Desirée Heiss met as students in 1993 and began collaborating on creating accessories that range from exclusive designs to daily wear and yet always retain their unmistakable signature.

Footwear

Budapester Schuhe
Kurfürstendamm 43, Charlotten-burg; tel: 8862 4206; Mon–Fri 10am–7pm, Sat 10am–6pm; U1: Uhlandstrasse; map p.133 C1
For the latest in designer shoes, this is a one-stop shop, packed with designs from the most coveted brands, as well as some spe-cialists in handmade footwear.

Riccardo Cartillone
Savignyplatz 5, Charlottenburg; tel: 312 9701; www.riccardo cartillone.com; Mon–Sat 10am–8pm; S5, S7, S9, S75: Savignyplatz; map p.133 C1
Cartillone emigrated to

Above: Berlin is a great place for finding funky shoes.

Germany and discovered a demand for well-designed Italian shoes. At nine stores in Berlin he sells top brands as well as his own creations for men and women, often marked down (also at: Dircksen-strasse 48; tel: 2804 0711; Mon–Sat 11am–8pm; S3, S5, S7, S9: Hackescher Markt; map p.137 E2).

Solebox
Nürnberger Strasse 16, Charlot-tenburg; tel: 9120 6690; www.solebox.de; Mon–Sat noon–8pm; U2: Wittenbergplatz; map p.133 D1
Solebox sells streetwear and sneakers ranging from well-known labels to their own designs and rare, hard-to-find brands (also at: Alte Schönhauser Strasse 50; Mon–Fri 1–8pm, Sat 1–6pm; U8: Weinmeisterstrasse, U2: Rosa-Luxemburg-Platz; map p.135 C3).

Below: utter elegance at Riccardo Cartillone.

Festivals and Events

The city of Berlin is chronically broke, but certainly not in spirit. It seems that there is always something to celebrate here, with many events culminating in ceremonial fireworks. The biggest one of these, on New Year's Eve at the Brandenburger Tor (Brandenburg Gate), attracts a million visitors every year. In the months preceding this big party, Berlin plays host to a number of special events and large-scale festivals. Of these, the most famed is the prestigious Berlinale International Film Festival.

January

Grüne Woche (Green Week)
Late January; exhibition ground Messe Berlin, Wilmersdorf; tel: 3069 6969; www.gruene woche.de; admission charge; S41, S42, S46: Messe Nord, ICC; map p.132 A1
The annual Green Week farming and food fair is a spectacular gourmet extravaganza. Visitors come to sample exotic goods, while proud farmers present their organic produce.

Lange Nacht der Museen
Late January; museums throughout the city; www.lange-

Below: crowds gather outside a cinema during the Berlinale.

nacht-der-museen.de; admission charge
A hundred museums keep their doors open until 2am, presenting not just their collections but an ambitious programme of video installations, concerts, shows and recitals. All venues are connected by free shuttle busses leaving in front of the Berliner Rathaus near Alexanderplatz.

February

Berlinale International Film Festival
Early/mid-February; cinemas around Potsdamer Platz; www.berlinale.de; admission charge; map p.134 B2
Playing in the same league as Venice and Cannes, the Berlinale is one of Europe's most important film festivals and the largest cultural event of the year. All of Berlin seems to go film-mad for two weeks. With 200,000 tickets sold, the Berlinale is the place where film professionals and the audience meet; dedicated cineastes take two weeks off so they can watch five films a day.
SEE ALSO FILM, P.57

March

Spandauer Frühlingsfest (Spandau Spring Festival)
Early/mid-March; Festplatz am Brauhaus, Oranienburger Tor; www.spandauer-fruehlings fest.de; free; daily 2–10pm; U7: Altstadt Spandau
Admission is free to this fun-fair in idyllic Spandau. Enjoy the rides and the hearty German food and beer.

May

Karneval der Kulturen
Blücherplatz; www.karneval-berlin.de; Whitsun weekend; free; map p.138 B4
The Carnival of Cultures is an immensely popular four-day street festival that reflects Berlin's diversity. All around Kreuzberg, dancers and musicians take to the streets in Mardi Gras style and draw huge crowds of onlookers. Bands, acrobats, wizards, percussionists perform on every corner around Blücherplatz.

June

ISTAF Golden League Athletics
Olympiastadion, Olympischer Platz 3; tel: 3068 8100;

Welhnachts Zauber
GENDARMENMARKT

Left: the famous Christmas market at Gendarmenmarkt is a winter treat not to be missed.

For two weeks in October, dozens of public and private buildings, major landmarks on Unter den Linden and around the Ku'damm are illuminated. 'Lightseeing' tours are provided by various operators.

November/December

Christmas markets

Berlin hosts more than 50 Christmas markets in all parts of the city, each with distinct atmospheres. Most open in late November and close at Christmas or in early January. The most notable ones are:

Gendarmenmarkt The square of the same name provides a beautiful setting for one of the most exquisite Christmas markets in Germany.

Nostalgischer Weihnachtsmarkt on Unter den Linden offers a wealth of traditional German crafts and seasonal food and drink.

Spandauer Weihnachtsmarkt in the pedestrian old town of Spandau has a small-town feel.

Winterwelten on Potsdamer Platz. Apart from hosting an Alpine-style Christmas market, the area is transformed into a giant winter playground complete with an ice rink and sledging hill.

New Year's Eve Party at the Brandenburg Gate

31 Dec, from 6pm around Brandenburg Gate and on Strasse des 17. Juni, up to Siegessäule, Tiergarten

Every year, a million Berliners and visitors see in the New Year in a festive mood, watching the spectacular midnight fireworks and listening to live music at the Brandenburger Tor, once marking the separation of East and West.

Public Holidays

1 Jan: Neujahr (New Year); Karfreitag (Good Friday); Ostermontag (Easter Monday); 1 May: Tag der Arbeit (Labour Day); Himmelfahrt (Ascension Day); Pfingsten (Whit Monday); 3 Oct: Tag der Deutschen Einheit (Day of German Unity); 25–6 Dec: Weihnachten (Christmas)

---

www.olympiastadion-berlin.de; admission charge; U2, S75, S9: Olympiastadion

A day of highly competitive athletics action hosted at the Olympiastadion. The ISTAF meeting, part of the Golden League series, attracts the top athletes in the world.

Christopher Street Day (CSD)

Late June; city centre; www.csd-berlin.de; free

Christopher Street Day sees thousands of scantily clad gay and lesbian folk proudly take to the streets on decorated floats, demonstrating for equal rights and having fun, cheered by the onlookers, many of them in town for a 'Pride Week' of events preceding the CSD.

August

Berliner Gauklerfest

Two weeks in August; around the Opernpalais restaurant, Unter den Linden 5; tel: 206 2673; www.gauklerfest.de; admission charge; bus: 100, 200: Staatsoper, U2: Hausvogteiplatz; map p.137 C1

In one of Berlin's most charming annual street festivals, the city's best restaurants and bars run a gourmet trail, while visitors can shop for crafts and antiques in an intimate market atmosphere, entertained by jugglers, tightrope walkers and puppeteers.

September

Berlin Marathon

Start at Brandenburg Gate; tel: 3012 8810; www.real-berlin-marathon.com; registration fee for participants

Watch and cheer 40,000 runners, skaters and wheelchair athletes attracted by this fast course past all the major Berlin sights.

October

Festival of Lights

Mid-October; tel: 3267 9887; www.city-stiftung-berlin.eu

Film

Berlin has been Germany's cinema central since the medium began. The UFA Studios in nearby Babelsberg produced some of the most famous and, during the Nazi era, notorious films Germany has made, including Fritz Lang's *Metropolis* and Josef von Sternberg's *The Blue Angel*. The Berlinale, Berlin's international film festival, is one of the top cinematic showcases, and films like *Goodbye, Lenin!, Downfall* and the Oscar-winning *The Lives of Others* are bringing Berlin cinema to a new audience. However, for many, the myth of Berlin is embodied cinematically in the 1972 film of *Cabaret*.

The Beginnings of Berlin Cinema

Berlin is the birthplace of cinema. In 1895, a film was projected onto a screen in the Wintergarten, a month before the Lumière brothers showed their first film in Paris. With the rise of film occuring during the artistic years of the Weimar Republic, it's not a coincidence that Berlin was the setting of much early German cinema. One of the first abstract documentaries was Walter Ruttmann's *Berlin: Symphony of a Great City* (1927), which 'orchestrated' images of Berlin in motion.

A young Billy Wilder began his film career here with *People on Sunday* (1929). At Babelsberg Studios near Potsdam, Fritz Lang's seminal classics *Metropolis* (1927) and *M* (1931) were filmed, as was the film that made Marlene Dietrich famous, *The Blue Angel* (1930).

Post-War Cinema

The coming of the Nazis saw the near-wholesale defection of German film's talent, most of whom were Jewish or anti-Nazi. The most notorious film of this period is Leni Riefenstahl's *Olympia* (1938), a still controversial piece of Nazi propaganda.

After the war, Berlin slowly re-emerged as a film setting, in Roberto Rossellini's *Germany Year Zero* (1948), a story of post-war corruption, and in Billy Wilder's lighter tale, *A Foreign Affair* (1948). George Seaton's *The Big Lift* (1950) is a comedy about the Berlin Airlift and was filmed in and around the actual scene of events, Flughafen Tempelhof.

Filmed on location in West Berlin and in other parts of Germany, Bob Fosse's 1972 adaptation of the musical *Cabaret*, itself adapted from Christopher Isherwood's *Berlin Stories (see also Literature, p.80)* and subsequent play, *I am a Camera*, is enduringly popular and critically acclaimed. The on-screen portrayal of Weimar Republic-era Berlin is key to how many visitors imagine the city. For a taste of the nightlife portrayed so evocatively here, *see Cabaret, p.38–9.*

Berliners' favourite film about their city is probably Billy Wilder's comedy *One, Two, Three* (1961). In a development Wilder couldn't have anticipated, the Wall went up during shooting and was deftly incorporated into the film.

The city has served as a backdrop for numerous Cold War spy thrillers, most notably Martin Ritt's *The Spy Who Came in from the Cold* (1965), as well as in lighter films such as the Bond caper *Octopussy* (1983). Wim Wenders's cult clasic, *Wings of Desire* (1987), uses the divided city as a character equal to the human actors and is an invaluable look at Berlin in the last years of the Wall.

Contemporary Film

Post-Wall, Berlin has turned into a choice location, and it is common to come upon a film crew set up on a backstreet somewhere, filming in an apartment or restaurant. Berlin as a location was used to great effect in Tom Tykwer's *Run, Lola, Run!* (1998). The traumas of 20th-century history have been revisited

Left: Liza Minelli evokes Weimar-era Berlin in *Cabaret*.

new, historic and documentary fare in its original language. Once there at the Filmhaus, you may want to check out the exhibits of the Deutsche Kinemathek and the fabulous museum shop.
SEE ALSO MUSEUMS, P.90

Cinemaxx Potsdamer Platz
Potsdamer Strasse 5; tel: 01805 2463 6299; www.cinemaxx.de; U2, S2, S25: Potsdamer Platz; map p.134 B2
The biggest multiplex in town, showing English-language films on at least two of its 19 screens.

CineStar Berlin
Sony Center, Potsdamer Strasse 4; tel: 2606 6400; www.cinestar.de; U2, S2, S25: Potsdamer Platz; map p.134 B2
Comfortable multiplex screening all the US blockbusters and a few art-house films in their original format.

Hackesche Höfe Filmtheater
Rosenthaler Strasse 40–41; tel: 283 46 03; www.hackesche-hoefe.org; S5, S7, S75, S9: Hackescher Markt; map p.135 C3
Once you've mastered five flights of stairs, you can sit back and watch original-language movies.

Below: still from Fritz Lang's *Metropolis*, at the Deutsche Kinemathek *(see p.90)*.

recently, in Oliver Hirschbiegel's *Downfall* (2004), while the East Germans' story has joined the narrative and made a great impact, with the comedy *Goodbye Lenin!* (2003) and the Oscar-winning tragedy, *The Lives of Others* (2006).

Festivals

The **Berlinale** is a prestigious international film festival held each year, with major films from around the world vying for the high prize of the Golden Bear. There are so many screenings that it is often possible for the general public to see a film. If you are hoping to attend any part of the Berlinale, it is wise to make all your plans at least six months in advance. The event runs a very comprehensive website with all the information you'll need about what's playing and where to get tickets at: www.berlinale.de.
SEE ALSO FESTIVALS AND EVENTS, P.54

The Berlinale is far from the only show in town, however. There's a **Fantasy Film Festival** in July and August, a

Human Rights Film Festival in the autumn, **Verzaubert**, a gay film festival, in April and plenty of smaller festivals at independent cinema houses throughout the year.

Cinemas

The majority of Berlin's big cinemas play dubbed versions of Hollywood films, although the Potsdamer Platz houses frequently show them in the original version with subtitles. The best way to find out what's on is to pick up a listings magazine like *tip* or *Zitty* and look for films labelled *OF* (*Originalfassung*, original version), *OmU* (*Original mit Untertiteln*, original with subtitles) or, for non-German or English-language films, *O m engl U*, indicating English subtitles. Note that cinemas tend to use the German titles for films, even when they are going to be screening in English.

Arsenal
Potsdamer Strasse 2; tel: 2695 5100; www.fdk-berlin.de; U2, S2, S25: Potsdamer Platz; map p.134 A1
The Arsenal is devoted to art-house cinema, screening

Food and Drink

E ven within Germany, Berlin has never really been considered a food destination; even famous German specialities like bread and beer are not considered particularly special. However, quality is on the up generally, with increasingly good Italian, Japanese and German regional cuisines on offer; meanwhile, there is a certain rough charm to traditional Berlinese food, although it is becoming harder to hunt it down. Nevertheless, you can indulge in Berliners' favourite street foods, such as *currywurst* and *döner kebap*, all over the city. For food and drink vocabulary, *see Language, p.79,* and *Restaurants, p.119.*

Local Dishes

Berlin's signature dish is considered to be *eisbein*, a pig's trotter. Served with boiled potatoes and mashed peas or sauerkraut, it's hardly exalted fare and today only turns up on the most traditional menus.

Another famous concoction is *königsberger klopse*, pork meatballs served with a white, caper-studded gravy. There are also various roast pork dishes, like *schweinehaxe* (*eisbein*, but roasted) and *krustenbraten* (roast pork with a crunchy crust).

Beef is hardly eaten, although *tafelspitz*, sliced

roast beef pounded very thin and sautéed with an egg-wash crust, is an Austrian dish common in restaurants. Chicken and saltwater fish outside of various preparations of herring and smoked salmon is not common, but a few freshwater fish like *zander* (pike-perch) and *viktoriabarsch* (a type of perch) can be found on some menus.

Street Food

Street food is more likely to provide a satisfactory taste of Berlin cuisine. A *thüringer bratwurst*, a pale sausage seasoned with powdered caraway, is a recommended lunch, as is *currywurst*, which sounds much worse than it

tastes: a sausage, cut into coins, has mild curry powder and paprika sprinkled heavily over it and is then doused in warm curry ketchup. Served with *pommes* (french fries) and ketchup or mayonnaise, it is not healthy food by any means, but at **Bier's** outside Friedrichstrasse Station or **Konnopke's** in Prenzlauer Berg, it can be seen how this is often considered the definitive Berlin cuisine.

Oddly enough, this status is also conferred on the *döner kebap*, which has become a ubiquitous European snack. The sandwich-style version was invented in Berlin in 1971, consisting of meat shaved off a column, packed into a toasted quarter of Turkish *peda* bread, dressed with tomato, cabbage, onion and cucumber and topped off with one of several sauces.

Beer

Local beer took a huge leap in quality when the Wall opened up, as East Berlin beer was still made like it always had been, unlike the factory-processed Western variations.

Frühstück (breakfast) is a big deal in Berlin, with weekend brunches being particularly popular. Almost all cafés that open in the morning will serve some sort of *frühstück*, and it will often be served most of the day to accommodate party animals sleeping off the previous night's excesses. A typical *frühstück* will involve a variation on scrambled eggs, bread, cheeses and cold cuts, served with juice and coffee.

Below: *frühstück.*

Left: eating local favourite,
currywurst.

the likes of Paul Bocuse.

Kollwitzplatz Market
Kollwitzplatz, Prenzlauer Berg;
Thur noon–7pm, Sat 9am–4pm;
U2: Senefelder Platz; map
p.135 D4
Saturday at Kollwitzplatz is
packed with local families, but
you will find some of Berlin's
finest produce, pasta and
bread for sale if you can make
your way to the stands. Thursday is calmer and smaller.

Rogacki
Wilmersdorfer Strasse 145–146,
Charlottenburg; tel: 343 8250;
www.rogacki.de; Mon–Wed
9am–6pm, Thur 9am–7pm, Fri
8am–7pm, Sat 8am–4pm; U2:
Bismarckstrasse; map p.132 B2
Since 1928, the Rogacki family has been selling fish and
meat to a select clientele.
There is also some cheese
and other deli items, but the
emphasis is on fish you cannot get anywhere else, every
kind of sausage imaginable,
and game in season. A major
draw is the dining area, where
many locals come for lunch.

Turkischer Markt
Maybachufer, Kreuzberg; Tue, Sat
noon–6.30pm; U1, U8: Kottbusser
Tor; map p.139 D4
Shop for fruit and vegetables
of widely varying quality, nuts
and sweetmeats, oils and
seasonings and Turkish
breads in the company of
local Turkish housewives.

Wochenmarkt Winterfeldplatz
Winterfeldplatz, Schöneberg;
Wed 8am–2pm, Sat 8am–4pm;
U1, U2, U4: Nollendorfplatz;
map p.137 E4
Well-dressed locals come out
for high-quality organic vegetables and baked goods,
olives, Spreewald pickles and
potted herbs. It is all fun to
look at, but prioritise the food,
some of the best in town.

Although the Eastern firms
have long since been gobbled
up by the Western ones, the
quality remains the same,
thanks to a large consumer
base. Try *Berliner Pilsner* or
Berliner Bürgerbräu. *Berliner
Weisse* is a sour, lactic beer
that is never drunk straight,
but mixed with raspberry or
woodruff syrup and drunk with
a straw in the summer.

Buying Food
Some of the best food on offer
can be found on the lower
levels of department stores
like **Kaufhof**, **Hertie** and
Karstadt, instead of Berlin's
supermarkets, which gener-
ally lag behind. Individual fruit and
vegetable shops will also generally have higher-quality produce. 'Bio' stores such as
Demeter, **LPG** and **eo** can
also be a good choice.

Galeries Lafayette
Friedrichstrasse 76–78, Mitte;
tel: 209 480; www.galeries-
lafayette.de; Mon–Sat
10am–8pm; U6: Französische
Strasse; map p.134 B2
The basement food depart-
ment is a bit of France in the
middle of Berlin. Here, you can

Above: fresh chillies on display
at the Turkischer Markt.

get genuine Poilâne bread,
registered chickens from
Bresse, a serious selection of
cheese, and an unparalleled
French wine selection.

KaDeWe
Tauentzienstrasse 21–24,
Charlottenburg; tel: 21 210;
www.kadewe-berlin.de;
Mon–Thur 10am–8pm, Fri 10am–
9pm, Sat 9.30am–8pm; U1, U2:
Wittenbergplatz; map p.133 D1
Ordering for much of the
legendary department store's
food halls has been taken over
by a supermarket chain, and it
shows. However, many independent boutiques remain,
as do mini-restaurants run by

59

Galleries

esides all the treasures of the past in
Berlin's museums, the city is fairly bursting
with commercial galleries showing off the
works of some of today's finest talents. Many
artists have been drawn to live here because of
the low rents for studio space and the creative
energy of the city, as well as the buzzing scene
this has created. For an idea of what is on
display during your visit, free programme
folders are available in most reputable galleries
and list the current shows, as well as provide a
map showing the locations of all the galleries
listed. For art museums, see *Museums, p.86–95*.

Art Galleries

MITTE
Arndt & Partner
Zimmerstrasse 90–91; tel: 283
3738; www.arndt-partner.com;
Tue–Sat 11am–6pm; U2: Stadtmitte; map p.134 B1
Long-established gallery representing a wide range of
emerging talents and the
occasional underground star
(Joe Coleman), Arndt & Partner has positioned itself as a
champion of the international
avant-garde.

Contemporary Fine Arts
Am Kupfergraben 1; tel: 2887
8726; www.cfa-berlin.com;
Tue–Sat 11am–6pm; S3, S5,
S7, S9: Friedrichstrasse;
map p.136 C2
Contemporary Fine Arts lives
up to its name, with a roster
that pretty much defines Ger-
many's favourite contem-
porary artists, among them
Georg Baselitz, Peter Doig,
Jörg Immendorf, Raymond
Pettibon, Jonathan Meese,

A good resource for information on the current exhibitions
showing around town is:
www.indexberlin.de.

Above: at Galerie Eigen + Art.

Chris Ofili and Daniel Richter.
Its glittering new headquarters opposite Museuminsel
just confirms its position as
one of Berlin's most
important galleries.

Klosterfelde
Zimmerstrasse 90–91; tel: 283
5305; www.klosterfelde.de;
Tue–Sat 2pm–6pm; U2: Stadtmitte; map p.134 B1
Another pioneer in Mitte's
gallery boom, Klosterfelde
long outgrew its tiny backyard space and moved into
more spacious digs in the
Zimmerstrasse group of former warehouses. Working
with a number of conceptual
artists and others far outside

the mainstream, it has
helped build the reputations
of the likes of Matt Mullican,
Dan Peterman, Rivane
Neuenschwander and
Kirsten Pieroth.

Mehdi Chouakri
Edisonhöfe, Invalidenstrasse
117; www.mehdi-chouakri.de;
tel: 2839 1153; Tue–Sat
11am–6pm; S1, S2, S25: Nordbahnhof; U6: Zinnowitzer
Strasse; map p.134 B4
Iranian-born Chouakri cruises
the outer limits of the avant-
garde to present some of the
most challenging art on the
scene, often with a wry sense
of humour. Shows here can
be quite outrageous.

60

Left: a photography exhibit at Kicken Berlin.

Thumm rode the wave of the 'New British Artists', introducing several of them to Berlin before they became famous back home. She continues to seek out fresh young talent while holding on to many of her old clients, including Julian Opie and Fiona Banner.

Galerie Berinson
Auguststrasse 22; tel: 2838 7990; www.berinson.de; Tue–Sat 11am–6pm; S1, S2, S25: Oranienburger Strasse; map p.134 C3
Hendrik Berinson is one of the best-known dealers of historical photography, including many important German photographers of the 1920s and 1930s. Among the artists he shows are Georg Grosz, Stanley Kubrick, Friedrich Seidenstücker, Lee Miller and Marianne Brandt.

Galerie Eigen + Art
Auguststrasse 26; tel: 280 6605; www.eigen-art.com; Tue–Sat 11am–6pm; S1, S2, S25: Oranienburger Strasse; map p.134 C3
Eigen + Art made its splash by arriving early on Auguststrasse and aggressively promoting artists from the

AROUND ALEXANDERPLATZ
Alexander Ochs Galleries
Sophienstrasse 21; tel: 2839 1387; www.alexanderochs-galleries.com; Tue–Fri 10am–6pm, Sat 11am–6pm; U8: Weinmeisterstrasse; map p.134 C3
Nobody has been more instrumental in promoting the art of the new Chinese avant-garde in Berlin and building bridges to allow artists from the Far East to come and work in Berlin than Alexander Ochs. As a result, he's had his pick of the finest young talent China has to offer, whose work is often shown first in the West – or in the world – at this gallery in an impressive red-brick courtyard.

DNA
Auguststrasse 20; tel: 2859 9652; www.dna-galerie.de; Tue–Fri 2–6pm, Sat 11am–6pm; S1, S2, S25: Oranienburger Strasse; map p.134 C3
Die Neue Actionsgalerie came about after Johann Nowak was turfed out of his popular bar-cum-gallery at Hackescher Markt and found

that the international, Berlin-based artists he had been showing in its basement were beginning to attract attention. This cavernous, two-level space has some of the most audacious, hair-raising artists on the scene, which makes it a must on the Augustrasse gallery-crawl.

Galerie Barbara Thumm
Dircksenstrasse 41; tel: 2839 0347; www.bthumm.de; Tue–Fri 11am–6pm, Sat 1–6pm; S3, S5, S7, S9: Alexanderplatz; map p.137 E2

Below: Adam Szymczyk and Elena Filipovic, curators of the 5th Berlin Biennial for Contemporary Art.

61

former East Germany, including Neo Rauch, who went on to become its first big star. A small but very select roster now includes Carsten Nicolai, Matthias Weischer and Christine Hill. The gallery wisely maintains a presence in Leipzig, where many new stars are rising.

Kicken Berlin

Linienstrasse 155; tel: 2887 7982; www.kicken-gallery.com; Tue–Sat 2–6pm; S1, S2, S25: Oranienburger Strasse; map p.134 C4

Kicken represents a virtual who's who of photography, from pioneers like Eugène Atget, through Arnold Newman and contemporaries like Robert Mapplethorpe. They've almost always got a fantastic show up, and serious collectors can make an appointment to view prints in their private gallery down the street.

Kuckei + Kuckei

Linienstrasse 158; tel: 883 4354; www.kuckei-kuckei.de; Tue–Fri 11am–5pm, Sat 11am–5pm; S1, S2, S25: Oranienburger Strasse; map p.134 C4

You'll either respond immediately to the Kuckei + Kuckei aesthetic or you won't; some find the works of the artists it represents cold and flat, while others find them filled with ideas. They prefer artists with a conceptual element to their work and have launched important careers.

Kunsthaus Tacheles

Oranienburger Strasse 54–56; tel: 2826 185; www.tacheles.de; U6: Orainenburger Tor; map p.134 B3

After the Wall came down, the bombed-out former department store on Oranienburger Strasse attracted young artists looking for studios. With minimum investment, the squatters from all over the world turned the ruin into a centre of creativity. While a few studios are still there and the courtyard is a playground for scrap-metal art, the building is now covered with random graffiti and beleaguered by tourists attracted by its morbid charm. There is a pleasant bar and a comfy cinema on the top floor but not for long – eviction orders have been issued by the owner.

Kunst-Werke (KW Institute for Contemporary Art)

Auguststrasse 69; tel: 243 4590; www.kw-berlin.de; Tue–Sun noon–7pm, Thur 9pm; admission charge; S5, S7, S9: Hackescher Markt; S1: Oranienburger

Strasse; map p.134 C3

Kunst-Werke is located in a former margarine factory in the Scheunenviertel area in Mitte. In 1997 Kunst-Werke initiated the Berlin Biennale for Contemporary Art and partnered with New York's art-space P.S.1, with which it remains identified.

Wohnmaschine

Tucholskystrasse 35; tel: 3087 2015; www.wohnmaschine.de; Tue–Sat 11am–6pm; S1, S2, S25: Oranienburger Strasse; map p.134 C3

The only major gallery in Mitte before the Wall opened, Wohnmaschine moved out of its rickety quarters in 1998 and into this medium-sized space, where sometimes the art is so playful you'll see little kids pulling their parents over to look. Few of the

Left: innovative displays at the Kunst-Werke Institute for Contemporary Art.

artists who show here are household names yet, but this is one gallery that's always worth a visit.

KREUZBERG AND FRIEDRICHSHAIN

Galerie Volker Diehl
Lindenstrasse 35; tel: 2248 7920; www.dv-art.com; Tue–Sat 11am–6pm; U6: Kochstrasse; map p.134 C1

Diehl often shows representational work by his roster of international artists, but none of it could be accused of being merely decorative. There's often an edge, psychological or physical, to the paintings, prints and occasional photographs on display here.

Street Art and Murals

It was a policy of the East Berlin government to paint murals 'beautifying' the blank sides of buildings, preferably with murals glorifying socialist virtues. Since 1989, most of these have vanished,

Left: inside the Kunsthaus Tacheles.

although the mosaic one on the **Haus des Lehrers** (House of Teachers) on the east side of Alexanderplatz remains as a good example. One thing that Berlin excels at is street art, often extremely ephemeral. Well-known guerrilla artists like Banksy and Swoon have cut swathes through the city, primarily in Mitte, Prenzlauer Berg and Kreuzberg, but lots of locals get into the action and a close look at walls will turn up some very clever pieces.

East Side Gallery
Mühlenstrasse; www.eastside gallery.com; daily 24 hours; S3, S5, S9, S75: Ostbahnhof; map p.135 E1

Probably Berlin's best-known murals are the ones painted on the 1.3km (0.8-mile) remaining stretch of the Berlin Wall on Mühlenstrasse, known as the East Side Gallery. The largest open-air gallery in the world, its 106 wall sections were painted by groups of artists

Thanks to a subsidy to bring culture to the Eastern half of the city, a major gallery mile has sprung up on Auguststrasse and the surrounding streets, and Mitte remains the hot centre of Berlin's art market. Note that the location and existence of galleries is as volatile as the art market itself, with galleries opening and closing all the time.

from all over the world after reunification as a memorial to freedom of expression. There are also some newer murals representing contemporary graffiti artists. Unfortunately, the heavy automotive traffic on Mühlenstrasse and the degradations of vandals have conspired to destroy large parts of the gallery, including the famous image of Honecker and Brezhnev locked in a passionate kiss. Nevertheless, a non-profit organisation has been working on restoring the original images bit by bit, to preserve these unique images.

Below: a new mural at the East Side Gallery in progress.

63

Gay and Lesbian

Berlin has almost always been one of Europe's most gay and lesbian-friendly cities, and it is particularly so today. Pretty much anything goes here, so whichever side of the scene you are looking for, there is something happening to suit it. In Berlin, information is plentiful and easy to come by, the bars and clubs are inclusive and the scene goes on 24 hours a day. Meanwhile, the locals are welcoming and tolerant; indeed, in 2002, the city elected Klaus Wowereit as its first openly gay mayor and did not blink an eye when he declared, 'I'm gay and that's a good thing.'

History

In 1897, Dr Magnus Hirschfeld formed a committee in Berlin to look into the question of whether homosexuality was a disease or a naturally occurring condition. He lobbied tirelessly for the decriminalisation of homosexuality. His Institute for Sexual Research, founded in 1919, offered a huge library and doctors for medical consultations, but the Nazis burned the library and its papers in 1933. Hirschfeld went into exile in Nice, where he died in 1935. A monument to him now stands behind the Haus der Kulturen der Welt in the Tiergarten, near where the Institute was located.

By the 1920s, the area around Motzstrasse was already a center of gay activity, thanks in part to the Eldorado club, where Christopher Isherwood was a regular *(see Literature, p.80)*. When the Nazis came to power, homosexuals were forced to wear a pink triangle on their clothing and many were sent to concentration camps; the number estimated to have perished at the hands of the Nazis ranges from 5,000 to 15,000. A monument to them is affixed to the Nollendorfplatz U-Bahn station near Motzstrasse today.

After the war, the West Germans held homosexuality in legal limbo, but the East Germans decriminalised it in the early 1950s, which meant that when the Wall opened, there was a ready-made scene for all to explore in East Berlin. Today, the gay scene is still very much where it used to be: in the **Motzkiez** in the West and in **Prenzlauer Berg** in the East. One distinction between the East and West Berlin scenes is that the tradition in the East was for there to be mixed venues for gays and lesbians, while the two scenes were separate in the West. This has relaxed on both sides of town since the Wall opened up, but if you would rather not mix, choose your venue accordingly.

Resources

SCHÖNEBERG
Mann-O-Meter
Bülowstrasse 106; tel: 216 8008; www.mann-o-meter.de; Mon–Fri 5–10pm, Sat–Sun 4–10pm; U1, U2, U4, U12, U15: Nollendorf-platz; map p.137 E4

Below: exhibits at the Schwules Museum.

Left: out and proud at the Christopher Street Day parade.

Mixed Bars and Clubs

MITTE
Ackerkeller
Bergstrasse 67; tel: 3646 1356; http://ackerkeller.de; daily 7pm–late; S1, S2, S25: Nord-bahnhof
Young club run by a non-profit organisation for gay and lesbian youth, frequented by students and alternative types.

AROUND ALEXANDERPLATZ
Sharon Stonewall
Linienstrasse 136; tel: 2408 5502; www.sharon stonewall.com; U6: Oranien-burger Tor; map p.134 B3
Stylish mixed bar with affordable and well-mixed cocktails just behind the madness of Oranienburger Strasse.

PRENZLAUER BERG
Schall und Rauch
Gleimstrasse 23; tel: 448 0770; www.schall-und-rauch.de; daily 10am–3am; U2, S45, S46: Schönhauser Allee
The name may mean 'shallow words' in German, but there's no mistaking the friendly atmosphere here. The food's good, the company's good, and a small guesthouse on the premises is well furnished.
Sonntagsclub
Greifenhagener Strasse 28; tel: 449 7590; www.sonntags-club.de; U2, S45, S46: Schönhauser Allee
Traditional pre-1989 East

Each of the more central city districts has its own gay neighbourhood or street. In Schöneberg, it is the **Motzstrasse** quarter, in Kreuzberg, it is **Oranienstrasse** and **Mehringdamm** and in Prenzlauer Berg, it is **Gleimstrasse** and **Greifenhagener Strasse**.

Berlin's central gay resource centre has multilingual staff in touch with every facet of gay life in the city. Its website has a downloadable gay guide to the city, as well as a searchable database of bars, clubs, medical resources and anti-violence programmes. Men only.

KREUZBERG AND FRIEDRICHSHAIN
Schwules Museum (Gay Museum)
Mehringdamm 61; tel: 6959 9050; www.schwulesmuseum.de; Wed–Mon 2–6pm, Sat until 7pm; admission charge; U6, U7: Mehringdamm; map p.138 B4
For years, this was the world's only museum devoted to gay life and culture, and its research division contributed greatly to the understanding of homosexuality. The library is probably the most thorough in Europe, containing archives of noted sexologists and thousands of books and periodicals. All information is available in English.

Publications and Websites
Siegessäule
Berlin's most established magazine for gay men, available free everywhere in the city gay men might conceivably go (including some inconspicuous bakeries). Great listings and a website at www.siegessaeule.de. German only.
L-Mag
Bimonthly free magazine for lesbians, Siegessäule's sister, is the best print resource around. Website at www.l-mag.de has podcasts, listings and more. German only.
Out in Berlin
Klaus Wowereit's grinning visage greets visitors to this bilingual website at www.out-in-berlin.com, and a full array of queer listings and information is just a click away.

Gay pride annual mega-events include the **Christopher Street Day parade** (late June) and the **Schwul-Lesbisches Stadtfest** (street fair) around Nollendorf-platz in Schöneberg (mid-June). *(See Festivals and Events, p.55.)*

65

Left: dolls and a friendly
atmosphere greet you at the
Barbie Bar.

damm; map p.138 B4
Gay and lesbian culture centre
in the same complex as the
Schwules Museum offers
weekend events, including an
all-lesbian event on the fourth
Friday of the month and the
Safer-Sex-Party at Christmas
and New Year.

SO 36
Oranienstrasse 190; tel: 6140
1306; www.so36.de; 11am–late;
U2, U8: Kottbusser Tor; map
p.135 D1
Long-time venue for alternative
lifestyles of all sorts. Current
events include Gayhane on the
fourth Saturday of the month,
featuring Turkish and oriental
dance music, and MfS, an all-
female hip-hop party on the
first Friday of the month.

Gay Bars and Clubs
PRENZLAUER BERG
Zum Schmutzigen Hobby
Rykestrasse 45;
www.ninaqueer.com; daily
6pm–late; U2, S45, S46: Schönhauser Allee; map p.135 D4
Zum Schmutzigen Hobby is
the hobby of celebrity drag
queen Nina Queer, who presides every Wednesday over
the Glamourquizz at 9pm. A
bit touristy, but then, some of
the tourists are celebrities.

Berlin gay and lesbian hang-
out that is still a meeting
place of choice for politically
minded queers due to its mix
of club nights, discussion
events and film screenings.
Closed early 2008 due to a
fire; check webpage for
reopening and events in
other nearby locations.

SCHÖNEBERG
Hafen
Motzstrasse 16; tel: 211 4118;
www.hafen-berlin.de; 8pm–late;
U2, U3: Nollendorfplatz; map
p.137 E4
A bar that advertises itself
as being for 'Sally Bowles
and her friends' is certainly
trading on neighbourhood
tradition, and the crowd here
celebrates everything from
Playboy bunnies to the
Queen of Holland's birthday:
any excuse for a party.
Neues Ufer
(formerly Anderes Ufer)
Hauptstrasse 157; tel: 7895

7900; 11am–2am; S1, S2, S25:
Schöneberg; map p.138 A3
Under new management since
2003, when the legendary
gay/lesbian pair who formerly
owned the bar retired, this
friendly, relaxed spot was cat-
apulted to fame when David
Bowie, who lived next door,
started hanging out there in
the 1970s because nobody
paid him any mind. Nothing
has changed but the name.

KREUZBERG AND
FRIEDRICHSHAIN
Barbie Deinhoff's
Schlesische Strasse 16;
www.barbiedeinhoff.de; daily
6pm–late; U1: Schlesisches Tor;
map p.139 E4
Trashy, slightly naughty bar
catering to a youngish crowd
of playful, sex-positive gay
and lesbian folk.
SchwuZ
Mehringdamm 61; tel: 693
7025; www.schwuz.de; Fri–Sat
11pm–late; U6, U7: Mehring-

The opportunities for indulging
in the sex scene are plentiful in
Berlin generally, but most of the
options are men-only. Listings
of the latest happenings can be
found in the main gay
publications and websites (see
p.65). Saunas are also popular
cruising grounds, as are the
local parks. Anti-gay violence is
less common than in other
European cities, but does occasionally happen, so do keep
alert and, of course, protected.

SCHÖNEBERG

**Brasil Sauna
(formerly Apollo)**
Kurfürstenstrasse 101; tel: 213
2424; www.gaysaunaclub
brasil.de; Tue–Thur 10pm–6am;
Fri 1pm–Mon 7am; map
p.133 D1
Tropical theme in the bar;
always crowded. Attention:
pros at work. Admission
includes robe, towels, slippers. Foam parties; private
rooms for rent.

Heile Welt
Motzstrasse 5; tel: 2191 7507;
U1, U3, U2, U4: Nollendorfplatz;
map p.137 E4
Long-standing, relaxed bar
in the Motzkiez makes a
good introductory stop in
the evening on a first night
in Berlin.

Prinzknecht
Fuggerstrasse 33; tel: 2362
7444; www.prinzknecht.de;
daily 3pm–3am; U4: Viktoria-
Luise-Platz; map p.137 E4
Refreshing to find a bar in
this part of town which isn't
fixated on the cult of youth.
Large beer garden and rooms
catering to all tastes.

Tom's Bar
Motzstrasse 19; tel: 213 4570;
www.tomsbar.de; Mon–Sat
10pm–late, Sun 10pm–6am;
U1, U2, U3, U4: Nollendorfplatz;
map p.137 E4
Named in honour of the
artist Tom of Finland, this
Motzstrasse institution is not
for the timid, although the
front bar is friendly. Upstairs
is the new Tom's Hotel,
featuring pleasant rooms
equipped with flat-screen
TVs and free WLAN.

KREUZBERG AND
FRIEDRICHSHAIN

Barbie Bar
Mehringdamm 77; tel: 6956
8610; www.barbiebar.de; daily
2pm–late; U7: Mehringdamm;
map p.138 B3
Unsurprisingly, Barbie dolls

decorate this camp but
relaxed and welcoming bar.
Special events held regularly;
check the website for details.

Berghain
Am Wriezener Bahnhof;
www.berghain.de; Sat
midnight–late; S5, S7, S9:
Ostbahnhof; map p.135 E2
Stylish, post-industrial nightclub in a former power station, attracting buff young
men with its top-shelf dance
music and sound system. It
even has its own label, Ost-
Ton, to release some of it. A
super-trendy hotspot for
after-hours clubbing.

Lesbian Bars and Clubs

PRENZLAUER BERG

Freizeitheim
Schönhauser Allee 157;
www.freizeitheim-berlin.de;
Tue–Thur 8pm–2am, Fri–Sat
8pm–4am; U2: Senelder Platz;
map p.135 D4
Place to meet hip, culture-
worker types from 20 to 40,
with a small dancefloor that
plays a mixture of electro-
clash and disco classics.
Also has table football,
booths, for one-on-one
action and affordable drinks.

SCHÖNEBERG

Pour elle
Kalckreuthstrasse 10; tel: 218

7533; daily 10pm–late; U1, U2,
U3, U4: Nollendorfplatz; map
p.137 E4
Still going strong after 30
years, this traditional hangout
in the Motzkiez gay nexus of
West Berlin is where the
femmes are femmes and
butches are butches.

KREUZBERG AND
FRIEDRICHSHAIN

Schokocafé
Mariannenstrasse 6; tel: 615
2999; www.schoko-cafe.de;
Wed–Mon 5pm–late; U1: Görlitzer Bahnhof; map p.135 D1
One of the last surviving
first-wave all-female lesbian
'movement' hangouts, catering to an older, established
crowd. The all-women Turkish bath Hamam is in the
same building.

Below: drag queens at Sage Club *(see Nightlife, p.102).*

67

History

1244
Berlin, situated on the Spree on an adjacent island to the town of Cölln, is mentioned in contemporary records for the first time.

1307
Berlin and Cölln become a joint city under the Ascanian dynasty.

1319
The death of the last Ascanian precipitates the collapse of law and order in the province.

1411
Burgrave Frederick of Nuremberg, a member of the Hohenzollern family, brings peace by becoming governor and subsequently Elector of the Marches.

1448
A citizens' rebellion is crushed by Frederick II.

1535
The first Protestant elector, Joachim I Nestor, accedes to the throne, heralding the arrival of the Reformation in Berlin.

1618–48
Berlin is severely affected by the Thirty Years' War, losing half its population of 12,000. In 1640, Friedrich Wilhelm, the Great Elector, accedes to the throne.

1672
Jews and French Huguenot refugees are welcomed to Berlin. The city benefits from their industry and culture. A mass influx of persecuted European Protestants is sparked.

1701
After the Hollenzollern's acquisition of Polish land up to the Russian frontier, the Great Elector's successor, Elector Friedrich II, declares himself King of Prussia.

1740

The ascension to the throne of Friedrich II (Friedrich the Great) is the start of military expansion and administrative reform.

1791
The Brandenburger Tor, a monument to Prussian glory, is completed.

1806
During the Napoleonic Wars, Napoleon marches through the Brandenburger Tor, marking the start of two years of French occupation.

1813
Russia, Austria and Prussia defeat Napoleon at the Battle of Leipzig.

1840
Friedrich Wilhelm IV takes the throne and brings cultural greats to Berlin, but the poverty of the lower classes continues.

1848
Following revolutions in Paris and Vienna, Berliners take to the streets in the 'March Revolution', which results in the loss of 200 lives.

1862
Otto von Bismarck becomes Minister-President of Prussia and, later, the North-German Alliance.

1871
The German states' victory in the Franco-Prussian War is marked by the proclamation of the Second German Empire, with Berlin as its imperial capital.

1914–18

World War I, expected to be a six-month fight with a victorious outcome, results in rationing and famine in Berlin, as Germany experiences a blockade.

1918
Kaiser Wilhelm abdicates in November after the navy mutinies. Philip Scheidemann declares Germany a republic and Karl Liebknecht declares it socialist.

1919
The socialist Spartacus uprising is stopped as its leaders Karl Liebknecht and Rosa Luxemburg are murdered by government troops. The government of the Weimar Republic is formed, but has to aquiesce to demanding peace terms at the Treaty of Versailles.

1920
The Kapp Putsch sees 6,000 soldiers occupy the government district. Only a general strike by workers

forces the coup to end after four days. Greater Berlin takes today's geographical form after territorial reform unites the city with several surrounding towns.

1923
Hyperinflation hits its peak, with a US dollar buying 4.2 billion Reichsmarks. Mass poverty prevails and it is only when the Rentenmark is introduced that the economy becomes more stable. In November, Adolf Hitler's attempted putsch collapses in Munich, before his plan to march on Berlin is realised.

1923–9
Berlin becomes the focal point for the European arts and bohemian scene.

1929
The Wall Street Crash precipitates the worldwide Depression. By the end of the year, 2.9 million Germans are unemployed.

1933
Poverty and desperation leads to a surge in support for both the Communist Party and the Nazis. Hitler becomes Chancellor. Shortly after, the Reichstag is burnt down. A left-wing anarchist is blamed and Hitler tightens his grip over the country.

1936
Nazi tyranny is suspended for two weeks as Berlin hosts the 11th Olympic Games.

1938
During Kristallnacht (9 November) the SA target Jewish shops, homes and businesses.

1939
Outbreak of World War II.

1945
The Battle of Berlin. Hitler takes his own life in his bunker as Soviet troops close in. Germany surrenders. The de-Nazification of Berlin begins as the city is divided into four sectors.

1948–49
Conflicts between the occupying Allied forces result in the Soviets cutting off all transport into West Berlin for nearly a year. France, Britain and the US airlift supplies into the stranded city during the Berlin Blockade.

1949
The Federal Republic of Germany, with Bonn as its capital, and the German Democratic Republic (GDR) are formed.

1953
On 17 June, Soviet tanks hit the streets to crush the Workers' Uprising.

1961

With one in every nine GDR citizens having fled to West Germany and tension between Russia and the US at a high, transport links between the East and West are cut and the Berlin Wall is erected overnight.

1963
US President John F. Kennedy gives his 'Berliner' speech at Rathaus Schöneberg. Berlin is at the epicentre of the Cold War throughout the 1960s.

1972
The Berlin Agreement allows travel between West Berlin and the GDR.

1989
Hungary opens its border with Austria, leading to a mass exodus of East Germans to the West and bringing the local economy to the point of collapse. On 9 November, the Wall is declared open.

1990
On 3 October, Germany is officially reunified.

1999
The capital of Germany is moved to Berlin.

2001
Klaus Wowereit is elected mayor. A programme of cuts is announced in the face of Berlin's huge debts.

2006
Berlin hosts the FIFA World Cup final.

2008
Smoking is banned in most indoor public places.

2011
Berlin's new international airport is scheduled to open.

Hotels

B erlin hotels are quite reasonably priced compared with other capitals in Europe, and if you avoid landing during peak periods, such as the Berlinale, some real bargains can be found. Hotels include the high-end and opulent, as well as the arty and boutique, but some of Berlin's guesthouses and hostels are a worthwhile alternative. For families or long-term stays in Berlin, a catered apartment, available in almost every district, may be the best option. Whether you have come to surround yourself with art and culture, to party all night or for a romantic weekend, there's a hotel in Berlin to suit your needs.

Mitte

Apartments am Brandenburger Tor

Wilhelmstrasse 93; tel: 200 7570; www.apartments-mitte.de; €€€€; S1, S2, S25, bus TXL, bus 100: Unter den Linden; bus 200: Behrenstrasse; map p.134 B2

Self-catered modern apartments of different sizes in an unbeatable location just a stone's throw away from Unter den Linden and Brandenburger Tor, adjacent to the Holocaust Memorial. There are many restaurants and a supermarket within walking distance. Furniture is a little basic but comfortable. Best for families and groups: there is a washing machine and separate bedrooms. Great value for money.

Hotel price ranges including tax, given as a guide only, for a standard double room in peak season, with bathroom but without breakfast unless otherwise stated:

€	under €50
€€	€50–€80
€€€	€80–€150
€€€€	over €150

Arte Luise Kunsthotel

Luisenstrasse 19; tel: 284 480; www.luise-berlin.com; €€–€€€; S3, S5, S7, S9: Friedrichstrasse; map p.136 A2

Every room in this hotel has been created by a noted artist, including some big names, but this can mean the decor is not necessarily for the timid. Fortunately, you can look through the selection available in the hotel's 50 rooms on the website before you book, choosing from themes that range from the whimsical to the downright bizarre. Close to the main train station, it is in an ideal location and is a one-of-a-kind experience.

Artotel Berlin-Mitte (Ermelerhaus)

Wallstrasse 70–73; tel: 240 620; www.artotel.de; €€€–€€€€ U2: Märkisches Museum; map p.135 D2

An 16th-century Rococo mansion on the banks of the Spree has been converted into a luxurious contemporary hotel with a fine collection of Georg Baselitz paintings. Located on Fischerinsel, a charming, quiet village-like area that is nonetheless quite accessible by public transport from the rest of the city, it offers a number of rooms with wheelchair access. A favourite of art-loving visitors and those in search of something a bit different.

Hilton am Gendarmenmarkt

Mohrenstrasse 30; tel: 302 0230; www.hilton.de; €€€€; U2, U6: Stadtmitte; map p.134 B2

Superb location on Gendarmenmarkt square (grand neoclassical architecture and one of Berlin's best Christmas markets), with a metro station right outside the hotel. Numerous sights and museums and Friedrichstrasse high-end shopping within walking distance. Excellent restaurants, but not much nightlife in the area. Friendly service, high-speed internet, spa, pool, 24-hour gym and an in-house Trader Vic's. Reserve a room overlooking the Gendarmenmarkt.

Honigmond and Honigmond Garden Hotel

Tieckstrasse 12 and Invalidenstrasse 122; tel: 284 4550;

Left: the grand lobby of the Hotel Adlon.

ered. In 1945, having survived the war, it was destroyed by an accidental fire, and although bits of it remained, it was finally demolished in 1984. After reunification, the building was rebuilt from original plans, and the new Kempinski Adlon opened its doors in 1997. Its many rooms and suites are some of the most luxurious in Berlin and have prices to match, but no other Berlin hotel offers a view of the iconic Brandenburger Tor and such quick access to Berlin's cultural centres.

Hotel de Rome

Behrenstrasse 37; tel: 460 6090; www.hotelderome.com; €€€€; U2: Hausvogteiplatz; bus TXL, bus 100, 200: Staatsoper; map p.134 C2

A Sir Rocco Forte hotel with a very central and yet quiet location just off Unter den Linden, mere steps away from the opera and Museum-insel. One of the few luxury hotels in Berlin housed in a historical building (it was once the head office of Dresdner Bank), it was recently converted into an elegant 5-star designer hotel, where most rooms are large with high ceilings and

---

It is not essential to book your room with breakfast. If you get a good rate, go for it. Otherwise, there are plenty of affordable alternatives in neighbourhood bakeries and coffee houses. Curiously, lower-priced hotels tend to include breakfast in the price of the room. Expect to spend anywhere from 5 to 20 euros for breakfast if it's not included.

---

www.honigmond.de; €€–€€€; U6: Zinnowitzer Strasse, S1, S2: Nordbahnhof; map p.134 B4

Small, lovingly renovated romantic hotels (the name translates as 'honeymoon') in a central yet somewhat hidden old neighbourhood. Elegant rooms with stucco, parquet floors and colonial-style furniture. A good choice for summer, when breakfast is served in the lush back garden with a pond, fountains and pet rabbits. If you prefer croaking frogs over street noise, ask for a garden room. Within walking distance of happening Scheunenviertel with its boutiques and nightlife and the

Dorotheenstädtischer Friedhof cemetery.

Hotel Adlon

Unter den Linden 77; tel: 22 610; www.hotel-adlon.de; €€€€; U1, U2, U25: Unter den Linden; map p.136 A1

Probably Berlin's most famous address since it went up in 1907, the Adlon has paid host to scores of luminaries, from the crowned heads of Europe to Thomas Edison, Albert Einstein and Charlie Chaplin. Readers of Isherwood's *Berlin Stories* will recognise the name, and it was here that Marlene Dietrich was discov-

---

Below: a luxurious marble bathroom and a 'lady's bedroom' at the opulent Hotel Adlon.

> Expect air conditioning only in hotels from 4 stars upwards. If these are out of your reach and you are planning to travel in the summer, opt for accommodation in an old (pre-war) building rather than a new one, as they tend to be cooler. However, do note that these may not have a lift.

dramatic modern decor. The former bank vault was converted into a 20m (66ft) swimming pool.

Maritim Pro Arte

Friedrichstrasse 151; tel: 20 335; www.maritim.de; €€€; S3, S5, S7, S9, U6: Friedrichstrasse; map p.136 B1

The entire Maritim hotel chain seems just a little bit old-fashioned, but that's not necessarily a bad thing, as this fine hotel right by Friedrichstrasse station attests. The 'Pro Arte' part of its name comes from a changing collection of first-rate contemporary German art in the lobby and some of the rooms, which are comfortable without being overdone. With easy walking access to the Brandenburger Tor, Unter den Linden and shopping on Friedrichstrasse, it's an affordable place right in the middle of things.

Meliá

Friedrichstrasse 103; tel: 2060 7900; www.meliaberlin.com; €€€; S3, S5, S7, S9, U6: Friedrichstrasse; map p.134 B3

This luxurious but affordable hotel on the banks of the Spree is a new arrival and being part of a Spanish hotel group, is something of a favourite with Spanish travellers. Bright, comfortable rooms offer a nice relief on one of Berlin's gloomy days and there is a good and authentic tapas bar.

The Regent

Charlottenstrasse 49; tel: 20 338; www.theregentberlin.com; €€€€; U2: Hausvogteiplatz; S5, S7, S75, S9: Friedrichstrasse; map p.134 B2

One of the world's best places to stay according to Condé Nast, The Regent Berlin is probably the hotel most popular with visiting American celebrities like Brad Pitt and Tom Cruise. If you are into old-world elegance and opulent decor, this is the place for you. The de luxe rooms and suites overlook Gendarmenmarkt, and Fischers Fritz is the in-house gourmet restaurant, boasting two Michelin stars for its renowned fish and seafood dishes.

The Westin Grand

Friedrichstrasse 158; tel: 20 270; www.starwoodhotels.com/westin; €€€€; S5, S7, S75, S9: Friedrichstrasse; TXL bus, bus 100, bus 200: Unter den Linden; map p.136 B1

In a choice location on the corner of Friedrichstrasse and Unter den Linden, this 5-star non-smoking hotel boasts a grand sweeping lobby and old-world charm despite being newly renovated. The beautiful suites come with free butler service. Marble pool area, gym, spa and a beauty salon make it an ideal setting for weddings or honeymoon trips. Ask for the quiet rooms overlooking the courtyard garden.

Around Alexanderplatz

Alexander Plaza

Rosenstrasse 1; tel: 243 1020; http://alexanderplaza.com; €€–€€€; S3, S5, S7, S9: Hackescher Markt; map p.137 D2

An excellent choice for the Mitte area, this quiet hotel is located within walking distance of the Scheunenviertel and Alexanderplatz and just steps from the S-Bahn and a

major tram depot. The Thursday and Saturday markets at Hackescher Markt are minutes away, as are numerous dining possibilities.

The Circus

Weinbergsweg 1a; tel: 2839 1433; www.circus-berlin.de; €; U8: Rosenthaler Platz; map p.135 C4

Looking for a quiet, romantic getaway? This isn't it. It is, however, one of Berlin's best-loved hostels, located within minutes of Kastanienallee in Prenzlauer Berg or the historical Scheunenviertel. It can get loud and raucous, but the staff are great at orienting first-timers, and have tips and tricks the overwhelmingly youthful clientele finds useful. There is bicycle rental available, a travel service, wi-fi and tickets for various events around town.

Citystay Hostel Berlin Mitte

Rosenstrasse 16; tel: 2362 4031; www.citystay.de; €; TXL

Left: distinctive decor at the Arte Luise Kunsthotel.

doorstep. It is also very easy to reach by direct TXL bus from Tegel airport.

Hotel Hackescher Markt
Grosse Präsidentenstrasse 8; tel: 280 030; www.loock-hotels.com; €€–€€€; S5, S7, S9: Hackescher Markt, S1, S2: Oranienburger Strasse, map p.134 C3

A hotel in the middle of trendy Scheunenviertel with its galleries, up-and-coming designer stores, bars and restaurants, where you can sleep peacefully in a feel-good room overlooking an ivy-overgrown courtyard and have breakfast in the sun. This small and charming boutique hotel has it all; just remember to ask for a garden room. If you want to arrive in style, the hotel provides limousine pick-up at very little extra cost compared to an ordinary taxi.

Park Inn
Alexanderplatz 7; tel: 23 890; www.parkinn-berlin.com; €€–€€€; S3, S5, S7, S9, U2, U5: Alexanderplatz; map p.137 E2

Formerly the Stadt Berlin, one of only a couple of hard-currency hotels in East Berlin where Westerners were permitted to stay, the Park Inn is a favourite with discount-

travel sites because, with 1,012 rooms and suites, there is almost always a vacancy. Rooms can be tiny indeed, although with 39 floors, the views can be as breathtaking as Berlin gets. The 'classic' rooms on the top 10 floors tend to be bigger and more expensive, but there is no denying the central location here is a plus. Book a room on the Fernsehturm side.

Radisson-SAS Hotel
Dom Aquareé, Karl-Liebknecht-Strasse 3; tel: 238 280; www.berlin.radissonsas.com; €€€€; S5, S7, S75, S9: Hackescher Markt; map p.137 D1

When was the last time you stayed in a hotel with a 25m-(82ft-) high cylindrical aquarium stocked with 2,500 tropical fish in its lobby? That's the astonishing sight which greets you at this newly reconstructed luxury hotel across the Spree river from the Berliner Dom. Depending on your room, you'll have either the cathedral or the fish as a view. Rooms are not big, but they are comfortable and the location is excellent.

Tiergarten

Grand Hyatt
Marlene-Dietrich-Platz 2 (Potsdamer Platz); tel: 2553 1234; www.berlin.grand.hyatt.com; €€€€; S1, S2, S25, U2: Pots-

bus, bus 100, bus 200: Spandauer Strasse, Marienkirche; S5, S7, S9: Hackescher Markt; map p.137 D2

Housed in a converted 19th-century department store, this new hostel recommends itself for its superb yet quiet location, design and service. It has all the mod cons you can ask for, but they come in a charming historical package. The hostel has shared but lockable facilities and is sparklingly clean and secure. Alexanderplatz, Unter den Linden, Scheunenviertel and Museuminsel are all on your

Hotel price ranges including tax, given as a guide only, for a standard double room in peak season, with bathroom but without breakfast unless otherwise stated:
€   under €50
€€   €50–€80
€€€   €80–€150
€€€€   over €150

Below: a friendly welcome at the Hotel Brandenburger Hof.

indoor pool landscape, complete with cocktails served on a sun terrace.

Ritz-Carlton

Potsdamer Platz 3; tel: 337 777; www.ritzcarlton.com; €€€€; S1, S2, S25, U2, bus 200: Potsdamer Platz; map p.134 B2

Nice high-rise tucked away from the honky-tonkier bits of Potsdamer Platz, although with easy access to all the Berlinale's cinemas. Famous for its luxurious feather beds, it also features heated floors in its marble bathrooms. Ask for a room overlooking the Tiergarten or Potsdamer Platz's collection of modern architecture. An added plus is a very authentic French brasserie, Desbrosses & Desbrosses.

Charlottenburg

Hecker's Hotel

Grolmanstrasse 35; tel: 88 900; www.heckers-hotel.com; €€–€€€; S1, S2, S25: Savignyplatz; map p.133 C1

Stylish 4-star boutique hotel in a quiet street off the Kurfürstendamm, a perfect

damer Platz; map p.134 B2

The hot centre of the annual Berlinale film festival, the Grand Hyatt seems a bit austere at first glance, but the lobby furnishings of black marble and polished wood are echoed in the room decor, which is both minimal and warm. Smart touches, like Bang & Olufsen flat-screen televisions and Aveda cosmetics in the luxurious bathrooms, are first-rate, not to mention the fresh flowers which greet you each day, and you're well sealed away from the tacky atmosphere of Potsdamer Platz.

Intercontinental

Hotel Berlin

Budapester Strasse 2; tel: 26 020; www.berlin. intercontinental.com; €€€€; S3, S5, S7, S9, U2: Zoologischer Garten; bus 200 to Budapester Strasse; map p.133 E1

The Interconti, as abbreviation-prone Berliners call it, has been a part of central West Berlin's skyline for 50 years, and its rooms are both up to date and yet redolent of the era in which it was built. Close to the Kurfürstendamm, it may not be as close to the action as it once was, but is still nice to return to in the evening.

Pullman

Budapester Strasse 25; tel: 26 960; www.schweizerhof.com; €€€€; U2, S5, S7, S9, bus X9: Zoologischer Garten; bus 200: Budapester Strasse; map p.133 E1

Huge, modern 4-star hotel with a clear commitment to design in a convenient location near the Zoo, the Tiergarten and the Ku'damm. It is worth asking for a quiet room and a rate with breakfast included. In the hotel's 'Le Spa' pampering zone, you will find a gym, three saunas and Berlin's largest

Hotel price ranges including tax, given as a guide only, for a standard double room in peak season, with bathroom but without breakfast unless otherwise stated:

€	under €50
€€	€50–€80
€€€	€80–€150
€€€€	over €150

shopping location. Savignyplatz with its bars and restaurants is a block away. Spacious rooms with king-sized beds and theme suites in colonial, Tuscan or Bauhaus style. Roof terrace, lavish buffet breakfast and lunch. The air of privacy and luxury makes it a preferred haunt for many a shy showbiz star.

Hotel Art Nouveau
Leibnitzstrasse 59; tel: 327 7440; www.hotelartnouveau.de; €€€; U7: Adenauerplatz; S5, S7, S9, S75: Savignyplatz; map p.132 C1
Charming boutique-style pension, decorated with a mix of discreet modernity and well-chosen antiques. Rooms feel like havens after a long day of sightseeing,

and not only is breakfast included, but there is an 'honour' refrigerator packed with goodies for those midnight cravings.

Hotel Bleibtreu
Bleibtreustrasse 31; tel: 884 740; www.bleibtreu.com; €€€; U1: Uhlandstrasse; S5, S7, S9, S75: Savignyplatz; map p.133 C1
A good choice for the eco-conscious traveller, as a recent renovation of this hotel made extensive use of environmentally friendly materials. In keeping with the theme, options such as reflexology sit alongside traditional pampering services. Rooms are snug in size but smart, with an aesthetic somewhere between the earthy and the urban.

Hotel Brandenburger Hof
Eislebener Strasse 14; tel: 214 050; www.brandenburger-hof.com; €€€€; U3: Augsburger Strasse; map p.133 D1
Discreet, warm elegance at a grand, but not at all stuffy hotel. The rooms' decor is in the Bauhaus style, and the winter garden is a lovely place to while away some time.

Breakfast is included, and the Michelin-starred restaurant **Die Quadriga** is excellent.
SEE ALSO RESTAURANTS, P.116

Hotel Pension Dittberner
Wielandstrasse 26; tel: 884 6950; www.hotel-ditterberner.de; €€€; U7: Adenauerplatz; S5, S7, S9, S75: Savignyplatz; map p.133 C1
If you are looking to live out a fantasy of Alte Berlin life, this traditional pension is an ideal place in which to do it. Well-chosen paintings and prints adorn the walls, and the decor is solidly luxurious, with tactile fabrics and immaculately elegant furnishings. Yet for all the glamour, the proprietor is charming, making all guests feel at home. Amidst the vintage style, guests also have access to free wifi and DSL.

Propeller Island City Lodge
Albrecht-Achilles-Strasse 58; tel: 891 9016; www.propeller-island.com; €€–€€€; U7: Adenauerplatz; bus 109, X10, M19, M29: Adenauerplatz; map p.136 B4
Eccentric self-described 'habitable work of art in the heart of Berlin'. Every piece of furnishing is an artist-created, one-of-a-kind object; no two rooms resemble each other. Get inspired amid surreal colours, slanted floors, 'sound sculptures' and suspended beds. Alternatively, you can sleep in a coffin, a cage or a prison cell. Not all rooms have full bathrooms. There are no traditional reception services or a restaurant – not a problem since the lodge is just a block away from the Ku'damm.

Q! Hotel
Knesebeckstrasse 67; tel: 810 0660; www.loock-hotels.com; €€€; U1: Uhlandstrasse; S5, S7,

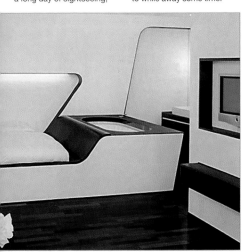

Left: note the bathtub by the bed at the futuristic Q! Hotel.

75

Left: elegant style at the Hotel-Pension Dittberner *(see p.75).*

lined street three blocks away from a metro station and lively Kollwitzplatz square with its organic farmers' market on Saturdays.

City Guesthouse Pension Berlin
Gleimstrasse 24; tel: 448 0792; www.pension-guesthouse-berlin.de; €–€€; U2: Schönhauser Allee
Friendly, B&B-style boarding house in a renovated 19th-century building. The pleasant, comfortable and well-equipped guest rooms and apartments with hardwood floors are very affordable, and the accommodating staff go out of their way to make your stay a memorable one. Only 10 minutes from Alexanderplatz by underground, and surrounded by bars, restaurants and shops.

Hotel Pension Kastanienhof
Kastanienallee 65; tel: 443 050; €€; www.kastanienhof.biz; U8: Rosenthaler Platz, then Tram 1: Schwedter Strasse; map p.135 C4
The 150-year-old Kastanienhof is a find: in a quiet location between Mitte and Prenzlauer Berg, it offers simply furnished rooms with incredibly helpful service. It has a rustic charm which is atypical for Berlin, and which the large number of repeat guests find restful. The huge, free breakfast buffet is another plus, and the short walk to the sights and sounds of the neighbourhood makes it a great place for travellers on a budget.

Kreuzberg and Friedrichshain

Die Fabrik
Schlesische Strasse 18; tel: 611 7116; www.diefabrik.com;

S9, S75: Savignyplatz; map p.133 C1
A truly sexy hotel, decked out in futuristic style and popular with design-conscious magazines and their trendy readers. Despite its hipness, it is surprisingly comfortable, with a playfulness that belies its aesthetics, such as the bath that can be rolled into from the bed. There is also a fantastic spa on-site and a super-chic bar and restaurant.

Swissotel Berlin
Augsburger Strasse 44; tel: 220 100; www.swissotel.com; €€€–€€€€; S3, S5, S7, S9, U2: Zoologischer Garten; map p.133 D1
With its soaring atrium lobby

and ultra-modern decoration, the Swissotel is located on the corner of the Ku'damm. Rooms are comfortable, and the ones which don't look out onto the atrium have splendid views across the rooftops of Berlin. Each room is fitted with a Lavazza espresso machine.

Prenzlauer Berg

Ackselhaus/Bluehome
Belforter Strasse 21; tel: 4433 7633; www.ackselhaus.de; €€€; U2: Senefelder Platz; map p.135 D4
The Ackselhaus boarding house is a unique retreat in young and trendy Prenzlauer Berg. The terracotta-coloured 19th-century converted residential building offers a Mediterranean ambience, complete with a charming courtyard garden. It is easy to feel at home in tastefully decorated rooms with a personal touch. The Bluehome twin building next door focuses on a water theme, and the Balinese-style studios are a dream. It's located in a tree-

Hotel price ranges including tax, given as a guide only, for a standard double room in peak season, with bathroom but without breakfast unless otherwise stated:
€ under €50
€€ €50–€80
€€€ €80–€150
€€€€ over €150

€–€€; U1: Schlesisches Tor; map p.139 E4

Great value in the heart of the vibrant Kreuzberg district with loads of live music, bars, cafés and nightlife at your fingertips. There are shared bathrooms and no lift, televisions or telephones in the rooms, or credit cards accepted, but this hostel is ideal for backpackers, families, groups or individuals on a budget. Housed in a converted red-brick factory building, the quiet rooms are basic but cosy, with wooden floors and rugs.

Generator

Storkower Strasse 160; tel: 417 2200; www.generatorhostels. com; €–€€; S41, S42, S8, S85: Landsberger Allee

If you are over 25, you may not like this place, but for party-loving teenagers from all over the world, the Generator is the place to be, and it can put up 900 of them at a time. Its futuristic design gives it an edge over most other hostels. The rooms are small and Spartan, but safe and clean. Breakfast is plentiful and included. It is a bit of a hike to the more interesting parts of town, but the Generator is well connected. If the nightly in-house parties are not your thing, just join one of the pub crawls offered. Don't bother to be back early: a fair share of the Generator guests are kids on school trips and tend not to sleep anyway.

Home-from-Home Hotel & Hostel Friedrichshain

Warschauer Strasse 57; tel: 9700 2030; http://friedrichshain.home-from-home.de; €–€€; S5, S9: Warschauer Strasse

In German, twin beds are zwei Einzelbetten. A double bed is a Doppelbett.

Interested in staying at a budget place in a neighbourhood with an average age of 21? With kinky shops, bars, nightlife, breakfast until 4pm? Then this is for you: choose from single, twin-bed, triple rooms or dorms with or without private bathroom and TV.

Hotel Sarotti-Höfe

Mehringdamm 57; tel: 6003 1680; www.hotel-sarotti hoefe.de; €–€€; U6: Mehringdamm; map p.138 B4

Very reasonable accommodation in a beautifully converted 19th-century red-brick building in trendy Kreuzberg, populated by a young crowd. The Kreuzberg ethnic restaurants, offbeat shops and nightlife are at hand, while the more traditional sights are just a few metro stops away. Cosy rooms in warm colours and wireless LAN for free throughout the hotel are plus points, as are helpful staff, a €5 buffet breakfast and 10 percent discount if you pay in cash.

Riemers Hofgarten

Yorckstrasse 83; tel: 7809 8800; www.hotel-riehmers-hofgarten.de; €€; U6, U7: Mehringdamm; map p.138 B4

A favourite with insiders and gay travellers for many years,

Pension 11. Himmel

Perhaps you never dreamed of staying in an original communist-era prefab. But you've got to give credit to the young people who set up and run this place on the 11th floor (hence the name '11th Heaven') of a high-rise in Marzahn, East Berlin's largest housing development. Their efforts resulted in eclectically decorated rooms with balconies and full bathrooms, offered for incredibly little money. Marzahn is more than a place to sleep: go and see the old windmill and the impressive Gardens of the World, and enjoy your young hosts' company (Pension 11. Himmel, Wittenberger Strasse 85, Marzahn; tel: 937 720 52; www.pension-11himmel.de; S7: Ahrensfelde).

Riemers Hofgarten is a bit out of the way for the main tourist attractions, but located in a charming corner of Kreuzberg not terribly far from Schöneberg. Its affordability and friendly service have won it a devoted clientele, and the elegant 19th-century courtyard after which it is named is a fine piece of bombast. Good restaurant, too.

Below: *zwei Einzelbetten* at the Hotel Bleibtreu *(see p.75).*

Language

Since most Berliners speak some English, it is generally easy enough to get by. Younger people in particular will enjoy practising their English on you. Learning a few phrases in German is a good idea, however, especially as the German language can be a little tricky. Germans have a habit of joining words together (chances are that you run into '*Schienenersatzverkehr*', literally 'rail replacement traffic', when trains are replaced with buses) or even splitting them (to go out is '*ausgehen*' but '*Ich gehe heute abend aus*' is what you say when you're going out tonight). Happily, at least everything is pronounced the way it is spelt.

The Alphabet
a=ah, ä=ay, b=beh, c=tseh,
d=deh, e=eh, f=eff, g=geh,
h=hah, i=eeh, j=yot, k=kah,
l=ell, m=emm, n=enn, o=oh,
ö=oeh, p=peh, q=koo, r=err,
s=ess, t=teh, u=ooh, ü=uyuh,
v=fow, w=veh, x=iks,
y=ypsilon, z=tsett

ä is like the 'e' in 'get'
ö is like the 'er' in 'Bert'
ü as in 'true'
ie as in 'thief'
ei as in 'wine'
ß like 's' in 'sit'

General Words and Phrases

yes *ja*
no *nein*
maybe *vielleicht*
please *bitte*
thank you *danke*
you're welcome
gern geschehen
hi/hello *Hallo*
Good morning *Guten Morgen*
Good evening *Gute Abend*
Goodbye *Auf Wiedersehen*
see you tomorrow *bis morgen*
I'm looking for... *Ich suche…*
Where is...? *Wo ist…?*
What is...? *Was ist…?*
When is...? *Wann ist…?*

What is your name?
Wie heisst du? (informal)
Wie heissen Sie? (formal)
My name is... *Ich heisse...*
What is your name?
Wie heisst du? (informal)
Wie heissen Sie? (formal)
How are you?
Wie geht es Ihnen?
I'm fine, and you?
Mir geht es gut, und Ihnen?
I'm... *Ich bin...*
I don't understand
Ich verstehe nicht
I understand *Ich verstehe*
I don't know *Ich weiss nicht*
Can you repeat?
Können Sie das wiederholen?
I'm sorry *Es tut mir leid*
In Ordnung *Okay/Agreed*
Excuse me *Verzeihung*
Where are the toilets?
Wo sind die Toiletten?
Ladies/gentlemen
Damen/Herren
free *kostenlos*
here *hier*
there *dort*
right *rechts*
left *links*
straight on *geradeaus*
upstairs *oben*
downstairs *unten*
near *nah*
far *weit*

opposite *gegenueber*
beside *neben*
today *heute*
tomorrow *morgen*
now *jetzt*
later *später*
open/closed
geöffnet/geschlossen
Help! *Hilfe!*
street *die Strasse*
palace *das Schloss*
church *die Kirche*
art *die Kunst*

On Arrival

How do I get to...?
Wie komme ich zu…?
I want to get off at...
Ich möchte aussteigen...
How far is it? *Wie weit ist es?*
departure/arrival
Abfahrt/Ankunft
train station *der Bahnhof*
bus stop *die Bushaltestelle*
train *der Zug*
car *das Auto*

It should be noted that in Germany, words that feature a double 's' after a long vowel, such as '*Schloss*', may be spelled with the German letter 'ß' and appear as '*Schloß*'. For pronunciation, *see box, left.*

Left: a street sign using the traditional German letters.

How much is it?
Was kostet das?
a different size
eine andere Grösse
Do you take credit cards?
Nehmen Sie Kreditkarten?

Health

doctor *der Arzt*
dentist *der Zahnarzt*
hospital *das Krankenhaus*
pharmacy *die Apotheke*
prescription *Rezept*
I'm sick *Ich bin krank*
It's an emergency
Es ist ein Notfall
police *Polizei*
Was ist deine Handy-Nummer?
What is your mobile (phone) number?

Numbers

one *eins*
two *zwei*
three *drei*
four *vier*
five *fünf*
six *sechs*
seven *sieben*
eight *acht*
nine *neun*
ten *zehn*
eleven *elf*
twelve *zwölf*
thirteen *dreizehn*
fourteen *vierzehn*
fifteen *fünfzehn*
sixteen *sechzehn*
seventeen *siebzehn*
eighteen *achtzehn*
nineteen *neunzehn*
twenty *zwanzig*
thirty *dreissig*
fifty *fuenfzig*
one hundred *einhundert*
one thousand *eintausend*

ticket *der Fahrschein*
return ticket
die Rückfahrkarte
platform *der Bahnsteig*
city map *der Stadtplan*
I'd like to change
Ich möchte Geld
money *wechseln*
I'd like a single-
Ich möchte ein Einzel-
double room
zimmer/Doppelzimmer
with bathroom *mit Bad*
Please show me
Bitte zeigen Sie mir
another room
ein anderes Zimmer
Is breakfast included?
Mit Frühstück?
to book *reservieren*
lift *Fahrstuhl*
key *Schlüssel*

Eating Out

I would like to...
Ich möchte einen Tisch
...reserve a table for four
für vier Personen bestellen
What do you recommend?
Was empfehlen Sie?
breakfast *Frühstück*
lunch *Mittagessen/Lunch*
dinner *Abendessen*
the menu *die Karte*
Do you have vegetarian

dishes? *Haben Sie vegetarische gerichte?*
The bill, please
Die Rechnung, bitte
We'd like separate cheques
Wir möchten getrenn-bezahlen
together *zusammen*
change *Wechselgeld*
SEE ALSO RESTAURANTS, P.119

Shopping

shop *der Laden, das Geschäft*
department store *Kaufhaus*
I'm just browsing
Ich schaue mich nur um
I'd like to buy...
Ich möchte kaufen...
Do you have... *HabenSie...*

Below: it is useful to be able to read a few basic German words.

There are five different words for 'the', depending on the gender of the word: *der, die, das, ein* and *eine*. No one minds if you get these wrong, though.

79

Literature

B erlin was a late arrival in the world of literary metropolises. Having only become the German capital in 1871, it had a way to go to catch up with sister capitals Paris and London, long-time national literary hubs. However, in 1929, Expressionist author Alfred Döblin put the city on the literary map with his novel *Berlin Alexanderplatz*, and it has been there ever since. Today, there is a buzzing creative scene, and the annual International Literature Festival Berlin brings together young and acclaimed authors from all over the world, who introduce new works to the public; see www.literaturfestival.com.

Der Berl
Alexander

Berlin Writers

Bertolt Brecht

Bertolt Brecht (1898–1956) moved to Berlin from provincial Augsburg in the 1920s and matured into a groundbreaking poet and playwright. He fled Nazi Germany in 1933 and returned to post-war East Berlin, where he staged internationally acclaimed productions at the Berliner Ensemble theatre that still shows Brecht plays like *The Threepenny Opera* (1928), *Galileo* (1938) or *The Caucasian Chalk Circle* (1948).

Like many other poets and writers, Bertolt Brecht was buried at the **Dorotheenstädtischer Friedhof** (Chausseestrasse 126; daily in summer 8am–8pm; S1; S2, S25: Nordbahnhof; U6: Zinnowitzer Strasse; map p.134 B4). Famous people interred here include philosophers Hegel and Fichte and authors Heinrich Mann and Anna Seghers. At the entrance to the cemetery is the **Brecht-Weigel-Gedenkstätte**, Bertolt Brecht's house, now a museum and Brecht archive.

Alfred Döblin

Alfred Döblin's (1878–1957) *Berlin Alexanderplatz* (1929) is a powerful depiction of hero Franz Biberkopf's struggle for survival in a tough, frantic Berlin in the years after hyperinflation. The best-selling novel became and still is a source of inspiration for scores of authors, theatre directors and film-makers.

Günter Grass

German-Polish Günter Grass (1927–) set his most famous novel, the magical realist classic *The Tin Drum* (1958) against the backdrop of the Nazi and post-war years. Out-

Below: Bertolt Brecht's grave.

Bertolt Brecht

spoken, political and prolific, he continues to be a high-profile figure and was awarded the Nobel Peace Prize in 1999.

Christopher Isherwood

Anglo-American Christopher Isherwood's (1904–86) *Berlin Stories*, including *Mr Norris Changes Trains* (1935) and *Goodbye to Berlin* (1939), are among the best-known Berlin literature, due in large part to their adaptation as the play *I am a Camera* and later, as the popular musical and film *Cabaret (see Film, p.56)*. In the 1920s, tolerance of homosexuality in Weimarera Berlin was what attracted Isherwood. His semiautobiographical account reflects the years of decadence before the Nazi regime.

Berlin Reading List

FICTION

Thomas Brussig
Heroes Like Us, The Harvill Press (1998)

Christopher Isherwood
The Berlin Stories, New Directions Publishing Corporation (1963)

Erich Kästner Fabian
The Story of a Moralist,

Left: books about the city for sale in Berlin Story.

and media shop is a popular late-night refuge of book and music lovers. It has a fairly good selection of new English-language paperbacks and hard-cover best-sellers.

Marga Schoeller Bücherstube
Knesebeckstrasse 33, Charlottenburg; tel: 881 1112; Mon–Wed 9.30am–7pm, Thur–Fri 9.30am–8pm, Sat 9.30am–4pm; S5, S7, S75, S9: Savignyplatz; map p.133 C1
A Berlin establishment since 1929, Marga Schoeller's was a hub of West Berlin's literary scene during the times of the Wall. It is less of a focal point now but remains a cosy, welcoming place with a superb selection of English titles.

Saint George's English Bookshop
Wörther Strasse 27, Prenzlauer Berg; tel: 8179 8333; www.saintgeorgesbookshop.com; Mon–Fri 11am–8pm, Sat 11am–7pm; U2: Senefelder Platz, Eberswalder Strasse; map p.135 D4
The quaint shop just off Prenzlauer Allee offers an array of well cared for, mostly second-hand fiction and non-fiction books. Chances are you drop on a comfy leather sofa with a book in hand and forget the world around you for hours.

Cyrus Brooks (1993)
Ian McEwan
The Innocent, Vintage (1990)
Peter Schneider
The Wall Jumper, University of Chicago Press (1983)

NON-FICTION
David Clay Large
Berlin, Basic Books (2001)
Anthony Read, David Fisher
Berlin Rising: Biography of a City, W.W. Norton (1994)
Frederick Taylor
The Berlin Wall: 13 August 1961–9 November 1989, Bloomsbury (2007)

Bookshops

Another Country
Riemannstrasse 7, Kreuzberg; tel: 6940 1160; www.anothercountry.de; Mon–Fri 11am–8pm, Sat 11am–4pm; U7: Gneisenaustrasse; map p.138 C3
A book lover's home away from home: part bookshop, part library. Another Country has 20,000 volumes on its shelves and also runs film, TV and cooking nights.
Berlin Story
Unter den Linden 40, Mitte; tel: 2045 3842; www.berlinstory.de; daily 10am–7pm; S1, S2, S25,

bus 100, 200: Brandenburger Tor; map p.136 B1
This multilingual bookshop has the best range of Berlin-related books in English, as well as paraphernalia of all kinds. Ask the staff for up-to-date insider tips on the city, as they tend to be well informed. The website is also a good place to browse if you want to do some homework before coming to Berlin.
Books in Berlin
Goethestrasse 69, Charlottenburg; tel: 313 1233; www.booksinberlin.de; Mon–Fri noon–8pm, Sat 10am–4pm; S5, S7, S75, S9: Savignyplatz; map p.132 C2
This shop is an excellent source for English and American literature, both new and second-hand. Check the website for occasional lectures and readings.
Dussmann das Kulturkaufhaus
Friedrichstrasse 90, Mitte; tel: 2025 1111; www.kulturkaufhaus.de (German only); Mon–Sat 10am–midnight; S5, S7, S75, S9, U6: Friedrichstrasse, bus 100, 200: Unter den Linden; map p.136 B1
Berlin's largest general book

Below: a local heavyweight.

81

Monuments and Memorials

Berlin lives with the memory of its past like no other city, and its atonement for the deeds committed in World War II can be seen everywhere, from large-scale projects to the small golden paving stones, *Stolpersteine* (stumbling blocks), hammered by artist Gunter Demnig into the pavements in front of houses where people were taken to concentration camps. You'll also see many other monuments of historical interest in Berlin, marking the conflicts that have shaped the city over the last two centuries.

Cold War Memorials

Checkpoint Charlie
Friedrichstrasse/corner Zimmerstrasse, Mitte/Kreuzberg; U6: Kochstrasse; map p.134 B1
Not much is left of this former border crossing point between East and West Berlin, but some of its history is told in the nearby **Checkpoint Charlie Museum**. As the naming of checkpoints was based on the American spelling code and this one was the third to open, it was given the name Charlie. It was reserved for diplomats, tourists from abroad and military personnel from the Western powers. Today, a 'You are now leaving the American sector' border sign, some sandbags and a copy of a soldier's post commemorate the place where American and Soviet tanks stood face to face during the Cold War. Part-time actors in Soviet and American uniforms pose for photographs.
SEE ALSO MUSEUMS, P.93

Gedenkstätte Berliner Mauer (Berlin Wall Documentation Centre)
Bernauer Strasse 111, Wedding;

Above: reminders of the Cold War at Checkpoint Charlie (left) and at Gedenkstätte Berliner Mauer (right).

tel: 464 1030; www.berliner-mauer-dokumentation szentrum.de; Tue–Sun Apr–Oct: 10am–6pm, Nov–Mar: 10am–5pm; S1, S2, S25: Nordbahnhof; map p.134 B4
There are a number of memorials along the route of the Berlin Wall, many of them clustered on Bernauer Strasse, the 'death strip' on which so many potential escapees were shot, but this small museum and information clearing-house is the place to start if you want to see them. The observation tower gives a good view of where a long stretch of the

Wall stood, and the official city memorial, with its controversial inscription, is right across the street.

Jewish Monuments

Bebelplatz
Mitte; U6: Französische Strasse, bus 100, bus 200: Staatsoper; map p.136 C1
On 10 May 1933, Nazi students from Berlin University (now Humboldt University) across Unter den Linden from this huge square looted the National Library (just west of the University) and piled the books here to burn. Israeli artist Micha Ullman

Left: the Holocaust Memorial.

being taken to concentration camps. On the right is a group of 13 figures by artist Will Lammert. On the left is a plaque in memory of the 55,000 Jews from Berlin who were deported. (The stones piled atop it are a traditional Jewish gesture of remembrance.) The area behind the monument is the site of the Alter Judischer Friedhof (Old Jewish graveyard), which was desecrated by the Nazis.

Kristallnacht 50th Anniversary Memorial
Koppenplatz, around Alexanderplatz; U8: Weinmeisterstrasse, Rosenthaler Platz; map p.134 C4
Commissioned by the East German government to commemorate the 50th anniversary of the Gestapo rampage against Jewish businesses and synagogues in 1939, this moving sculpture by Karl Biedermann, a table and chairs, one of which has been knocked over, is surrounded by a memorial text by poet Nelly Sachs.

Triumphal Monuments

Brandenburger Tor
Pariser Platz, Mitte; www.brandenburger-tor.de; bus 100, 200: Brandenburger Tor; S1, S2, S25: Unter den Linden; map p.136 A1
The Brandenburg Gate, a focal point and iconic symbol

rose brilliantly to the challenge of memorialising this event with his sunken room of empty white bookcases which can be glimpsed through a window set in the plaza. A plaque nearby quotes Heinrich Heine: 'Where one burns books, it is only a prelude; in the end one also burns people.'

Denkmal für die ermordeten Juden Europas (Memorial to the Murdered Jews of Europe)
Wilhelmstrasse 72–73, Mitte; tel: 2639 4311; guided tours and reservations: 2639 4336; Field of Stelae daily 24 hours, Information Centre Apr–Sept: 10am–8pm, Oct–Mar: 10am–7pm; free; S1, S2, S26: Unter den Linden; U2: Mohrenstrasse; map p.134 B2
Also known as the Holocaust Memorial, this controversial project was first planned in 1988–9 and went through much discussion before Peter Eisenman's design was chosen and realised in 2003. Opened in December 2004, it consists of a 1.9-hectare (4.7-acre) site covered with a grid of 2,700 concrete stelae,

which are blank. Each visitor seems to form his or her own idea of what it means. The Information Centre underground has the names of all known Jewish victims of the Holocaust.

Grosse Hamburger Strasse Memorial
Grosse Hamburger Strasse 24, Around Alexanderplatz; S3, S5, S7, S9: Hackescher Markt; map p.134 C3
This two-part memorial stands on the site of the first Jewish community's old-age home, which was used as a collection point for Jews

Below: the Grosse Hamburger Strasse Memorial.

One of the most photographed views in Berlin is that of the Kaiser-Wilhelm-Gedächtnis-kirche *(see p.85)* framed by the 'Berlin Sculpture', which was erected to mark the city's 750th anniversary in 1987. Symbolising the east and west interlocking, but not touching, it is a fitting monument to the division of the pre-reunification years *(see picture, p.2–3)*.

83

Left: the statue of Frederick the Great rears up in front of the Fernsehturm.

completed in 1851, based on the design by Christian Daniel Rauch, after decades of discussing how best to honour the much-revered monarch. The 13m (44ft) bronze statue of Frederick, known by Berliners as 'Der Alte Fritz' ('The Old Fritz'), on his favourite horse, Conde, is wonderfully ornate, with a pedestal depicting the most outstanding generals of Frederick's army and other leading Germans of the time. Under Frederick the Great, the Forum Fredericianum, the complex of neighbouring buildings including Humboldt University, the former royal library and the opera house, was laid out.

Siegessäule

Grosser Stern/Strasse des 17. Juni, Tiergarten; Apr–Oct: daily 9.30am–6.30pm, Nov–Mar: 9.30am–5.30pm; S5, S7, S9: Tiergarten; bus 100: Grosser Stern; map p.133 E2

of Berlin and German history, is a neoclassical structure built by Carl Gotthard Langhans in 1788–91 as a triumphal arch and city gate on the road to Brandenburg. It was commissioned by King Friedrich Wilhelm as a symbol of peace, and its design was based on the Propylaea, the gateway to the Acropolis in Athens. After the 1806 Prussian defeat, Napoleon took the Quadriga, the statue of a horse-drawn chariot crowning the gate, to Paris where it remained until his defeat in the Battle of Waterloo in 1814. During the Third Reich, the Nazis used the Gate as a backdrop for their torchlight parades. The building of the Wall in 1961 left the Gate in no-man's land between the inner and outer border fortifications. It remained inaccessible to the public until its reopening in December 1989. Ever since, it has served as a symbol of

German unity, and provides the location for one of the world's most famous New Year's Eve parties.

Reiterdenkmal Friedrichs des Grossen

Unter den Linden, Mitte; U6: Französische Strasse; S5, S7, S9: Friedrichstrasse; map p.136 C1
This large equestrian statue of Frederick the Great (1786) positioned on the traffic island in the middle of Unter den Linden boulevard was

Shiny 'Goldelse' ('Golden Else'), as the Berliners disrespectfully refer to the 35-tonne gold-covered Goddess of Victory crowning the Victory Column, can be spotted from almost everywhere in the Tiergarten, as it overlooks

Below: the icon of Berlin: the Brandenburger Tor.

a large roundabout in the middle of the park. In Wim Wenders's film *Wings of Desire,* it was the place where angels congregate. The triumphal column, standing 69m (226ft) high, was built in 1864–73 at the request of Kaiser Wilhelm to commemorate the Prussian victories over France, Austria and Denmark. The sandstone blocks the column is made of are decorated with cannon pipes captured from the enemy in the above-mentioned wars. Originally located opposite the Reichstag, the Victory Column was in the way of Hitler's plans for Germania, the grand new 'Capital of the World' that he envisaged, and was moved to its present location in 1939. It can be reached through four tunnels built to plans by Albert Speer in 1941. After a 285-step hike on a spiral staircase, the view from the top is breathtaking.

War Memorials

Kaiser-Wilhelm-Gedächtniskirche
Breitscheidplatz, Charlottenburg; tel: 0171 313 9328; www.gedaechtniskirche-berlin.de; daily 9am–7pm, Sunday services 10am, 6pm; free; S3, S5, S7, S9, S75, U1, U2, U9: Zoologischer Garten; map p.133 D1
The husk of a neo-Romanesque church that sustained bombing damage in an Allied air raid in 1943 has been preserved as a reminder of the horror of war.
SEE ALSO CHURCHES, SYNAGOGUES AND MOSQUES, P.45

Neue Wache
Eastern end of Unter den Linden, Mitte; bus 100, 200: Deutsche Staatsoper; map p.137 C1
The New Guard House was constructed in neoclassical style in 1816–18 to plans by

Karl Friedrich Schinkel as a memorial to those killed in the Napoleonic Wars. With its portico of Doric columns, the building resembles a Greek temple. From 1818 to 1918, it housed the royal guard. Badly damaged in World War II and rebuilt in the 1950s with an eternal flame burning inside, it served as the GDR's 'Memorial to the Victims of Fascism and Militarism' and saw a grotesque weekly changing of the goose-stepping guard of honour. Re-dedicated once again after the fall of the Wall, it is now officially the 'Central Memorial of the Federal Republic of Germany to the Victims of War and Tyranny'. The centre of the chamber, with its austere and solemn atmosphere, is now occupied by the enlarged *pietà* sculpture by Käthe Kollwitz, *Mother with Her Dead Son.*

Sowjetisches Ehrenmal (Russian War Memorial)
Strasse des 17. Juni, Tiergarten; S1, S2, S26: Unter den Linden; map p.134 A2
Located near the Reichstag, this imposing memorial is constructed out of stone taken from Hitler's Reichs Chancellery and commemorates the Soviet soldiers who died in the battle to take Berlin in 1945. Built almost immediately after the war, it was one of Berlin's biggest headaches for years: the property was owned by the Soviets, yet stood in the British sector, necessitating a British military enclosure guarded by Berlin police to protect the two Russian soldiers whose job it was to be on guard there. Two artillery pieces and two tanks (supposedly the first two into the city, although that is doubtful) flank a monumental statue of a soldier on a column.

Above: the Siegessäule.

Sowjetisches Ehrenmal (Russian War Memorial)
Treptower Park, Treptow; S6, S8, S9, S10: Treptower Park
Erected over a mass grave for soldiers killed in the battle for Berlin, this is the largest Soviet war memorial in Germany. Its central figure is a Russian soldier holding a young girl, a smashed swastika under his feet. Arranged on the periphery of the field which stretches in front of him are 16 coffin-like structures which have scenes of the liberation of Germany by the Russians and cautionary texts in German and Russian in bas-relief. Unparalleled as a powerful piece of Soviet propaganda in Berlin, it is nonetheless a popular picnic spot for people strolling in Treptow Park.
SEE ALSO PARKS AND GARDENS, P.110–11

Many of the monuments that reveal much about Berlin's history are in fact the city's architecture, such as the surviving neoclassicist constructions of the Nazi era and the bombastic GDR projects around Alexanderplatz.
See Architecture, p.28–31.

85

Museums

Berlin has an extraordinary and vast collection of museums and galleries. It is true that the Dog Museum and the Hairdressing Museum are gone, as is the Gründerzeit Museum of the famed East German transvestite Charlotte von Mahlsdorf, but it is still easy enough to spend a couple of weeks in Berlin doing nothing but soaking up the art and history which has been curated over the years and is displayed here in often striking and audacious ways. Note that most museums close on Mondays but stay open late on Thursday nights. For information on commercial art, *see Galleries, p.60–63*.

Mitte

Alte Nationalgalerie

Bodestrasse 1–3, Museums-insel; tel: 2090 5801; www.museen-berlin.de; Tue–Wed 10am–6pm, Thur–Sun 10am–8pm; admission charge; S3, S5, S7, S9: Hackescher Markt; bus 100, 200: Lustgarten; map p.137 D2

The Alte Nationalgalerie

Berlin's central collection of museums stretches across what is known as **Museums-insel** (Museum Island), the skinny island in the Spree river on which the city was founded. Berlin's collection of art was divided during the Allied occupation and is still being sewn back together, a process which is not due to be completed until 2009, but a visit to at least a couple of the ones which are open now is pretty much mandatory for art lovers. A three-day ticket good for a great many Berlin museums is available from the box offices of all participating institutions. Children and youths under 16 have free access to most museums.

assembles the Berlin National Museums' massive collection of 19th-century art under one roof. The third floor displays entirely German painters, including masterpieces by Caspar David Friedrich, as well as architectural render-ings by Karl Friedrich Schinkel. On the second floor, a large number of French Impressionists, including Manet, Monet and Renoir, are joined by their German contemporaries, including Feuerbach, Böcklin and Liebermann. The first floor has a display of Adolf Menzel's paintings and an extensive collection of 19th-century German sculpture.

Altes Museum

Am Lustgarten, Museumsinsel; tel: 2090 5577; www.museen-berlin.de; Mon–Wed 10am–6pm, Thur–Sun 10am–8pm; admission charge; S3, S5, S7, S9: Hackescher Markt; bus 100, 200: Lustgarten; map p.137 D1

The Altes Museum is itself an art treasure, being one of Karl Friedrich Schinkel's master-pieces of neoclassicism. Inside, the central attraction is the bust of Nefertiti, still

radiant after 1,750 years, but there are other Egyptian and classical works on display here as well. In 2009, the Egyptian Museum collection will be transferred to the Neues Museum.

Bode-Museum

Monbijoubrücke, Museumsinsel; tel: 2090 5601; www.museen-in-berlin.de; Mon–Wed 10am–6pm, Thur–Sun 10am–8pm; admission charge; S3, S5, S7, S9: Friedrichstrasse; S1, S2, S25: Oranienburger Strasse; map p.137 C2

Housing the Sculpture Museum, the Byzantine Museum and the Numismatic Collection of the city's art treasures, the Bode-Museum was designed in the 19th century to maximise light and display space. Its church-like interior makes it an ideal venue for its medieval and Renaissance sculpture collec-tion, which includes wooden carving masterpieces by Erasmus Grasser and Tilman Riemenschneider. There are also French, Dutch, Spanish and Italian works from this period and sculptures from the Baroque and Romantic

Left: sculpture at the Pergamonmuseum.

Museumsinsel; tel: 2030 4444; www.dhm.de; daily 10am–6pm; admission charge; S3, S5, S7, S9: Hackescher Markt; map p.137 C1

The German Historical Museum used to be a joke with Western visitors to East Berlin because the East German regime's idea of German history was at such wide variance with the rest of the world's. Today, after a thorough rebuilding of the former Prussian armoury's interior and the addition of a striking annexe in the rear, designed by I.M. Pei, it is one of Berlin's must-see museums. The exhibit starts upstairs with the coming of the Romans and their impact on the Germanic tribes, then quickly moves to the establishment of Christianity and the rise of the German city-states and on through the centuries to World War I. A map or other guide is essential for seeing this in order if you're not already well familiar with the sequence of events. Downstairs, one is plunged into the chaos of the Great War's aftermath, the inflation, rise of Hitler and the Nazis, World War II, the Cold War and the reunification of Germany.

periods. The Byzantine collection has many early Christian works, including carved ivory devotional items and an impressive mosaic chapel. Other highlights here are the Basilica, a great hall in which altarpieces from European churches are displayed with paintings appropriate to the period, and the Numismatic Collection, one of the best collections of coins in the world.

Deutsche Guggenheim
Unter den Linden 13–15; tel: 202 0930; www.deutsche-guggenheim-berlin.de/e/; Fri–Wed 10am–8pm, Thur 10am–10pm; admission charge, free on Monday; S1, S2: Unter den Linden; S3, S5, S7, S9, S75: Friedrichstrasse; map p.136 C1

Located on the ground floor of the Deutsche Bank building on Unter den Linden, this tiny space mounts three to four shows a year by important contemporary artists who have often been commissioned to produce works specifically for the show by either the Guggenheim or Deutsche Bank.

Deutsches Historisches Museum (German Historical Museum)
Unter den Linden 2,

Below: the Alte Nationalgalerie wears its treasures on both the inside (left) and the outside (right).

This is all presented without flinching, admirably straight-forward and sometimes grue-some. The I.M. Pei annexe is used for temporary, more specialised shows amplifying individual aspects of the permanent collection.

Hamburger Bahnhof: Museum für Gegenwart (Museum of Contemporary Art)

Invalidenstrasse 50–51; tel: 3978 3411; www.hamburger bahnhof.de; Tue–Fri 10am–6pm, Sat 11am–8pm, Sun 11am–6pm; admission charge, free Thur 2–6pm; U6: Zinnowitzer Strasse; S3, S5, S7, S9: Haupt-bahnhof; S1, S2: Nordbahnhof; map p.134 A4

Located in a building which once housed one of Europe's first train stations (and which later found itself at the Berlin Wall), this space has been provided by the Berlin City Museums as a place for noted private collectors to house their art, as well as for large-scale touring exhibitions curated elsewhere and by the museum staff. The core is built from Erich Marx's collection of late 20th-century works, including many Warhols, Rauschenbergs, Kiefers and Beuys. In 2004, the museum was granted a seven-year loan of the Friedrich Christian

Above: propaganda displays at the Deutsches Historiches Museum.

Flick Collection, which is housed in the Rieckhallen, a former warehouse. This collection is particularly strong in such contemporary European artists as Candida Höfer, Pipilotti Rist, Luc Tuymans and Franz West.

The Kennedys

Pariser Platz 4a; tel: 2065 3570; www.thekennedys.de; daily 10am–6pm; admission charge; S1, S2, S25, bus 100, 200: Unter den Linden; map p.136 A1

This small museum houses the renowned Camera Work collection of photos, docu-ments and memorabilia of the Kennedy family and com-memorates JFK's 1963 visit to the divided city, when he made his famous statement, 'Ich bin ein Berliner'.

Medizinhistorisches Museum an der Charité (Medical History Museum)

Charitéplatz 1; tel: 4505 36156; www.bmm.charite.de; Tue–Sun 10am–6pm, Wed 10am–7pm; admission charge, minimum age for admission 16; U6: Zinno-witzer Strasse; S3, S5, S7, S9: Hauptbahnhof; map p.134 B3

Charité Hospital was the site of the development of Robert Koch's germ theory of dis-ease in the 19th century, and the historical buildings on its campus date back further than that. At this museum one can see over 750 preserved wet and dry specimens,

collected over the years for display to medical students of pathology, as well as displays showing the evolu-tion of surgery and medicine over the past four centuries. The entire museum is an outgrowth of the work of Dr Rudolf Virchow, a pioneer in public health and the dis-coverer of cellular function.

Museum für Naturkunde (Museum of Natural History)

Invalidenstrasse 43; tel: 2093 8591; www.naturkundemuseum-berlin.de; Tue–Fri 9.30am–5pm, Sat–Sun 10am–6pm; admission charge; U6: Zinnowitzer Strasse; S3, S5, S7, S9: Hauptbahnhof; S1, S2: Nordbahnhof; map p.134 B4

If you go to the Museum of Natural History in your kids, it is entirely possible you may get no further than the first hall, with its incredi-ble dinosaur display (includ-ing a brachiosaurus which is the largest mounted dinosaur skeleton in the world), much of which was dug up in the early 20th century at Tenda-guru, Tanganyika, by scien-tists from this museum. Video displays have interac-tive features showing how these remarkable animals lived and moved, and the flat-screen displays bring the skeletons to life. Get past this, though, to find a hall of

Below: a Nazi uniform at the Deutsches Historiches Museum.

Berlin's Best Museums...
...For Art
Alte Nationalgalerie *(see p.86)*
Hamburger Bahnhof *(see p.88)*
Neue Nationalgalerie *(see p.91)*
...For History
Deutsches Historisches
Museum *(see p.87)*
Pergamonmuseum *(see p.89)*
Jüdisches Museum *(see p.93)*
...For Science
Medizinhistorisches Museum
an der Charité *(see p.88)*
Museum für Naturkunde
(see p.88)

hoofed mammals, a thorough set of dioramas showing the fauna of Berlin and Brandenburg, minerals galore and Alfred Kieler's famed insect models, including a mosquito at 60 times life-size and a flea at 100 times. Much of the museum is still being renovated and bilingual signage is sporadic, but in most cases the displays are so well done that it is not a problem.

SEE ALSO CHILDREN, P.42

Neues Museum
Bodestrasse, Museumsinsel;
reopening 2009; www.museen-berlin.de; map p.137 D2
Upon its reopening, scheduled for autumn 2009, the Neues Museum will house the Egyptian Museum's collection and parts of the Museum for Pre- and Early History's collection, which is currently in Charlottenburg.

Pergamonmuseum
Am Kupfergraben 5, Museumsinsel; tel: 2090 5201;
www.museen-in-berlin.de;
Mon–Wed 10am–6pm,
Thur–Sun 10am–8pm; admission charge; S3, S5, S7, S9:
Friedrichstrasse, Hackescher Markt; map p.137 C2
With over a million visitors annually, this is one of Germany's most popular museums, and with good rea-

son: what other museum can boast not only an entire Greek temple complex, but also the approach to the city of Babylon and its fabled Ishtar Gate? The Pergamon temple complex was excavated by Carl Umann in 1864–5 with the cooperation of the Turkish government and moved, stone by stone, to this museum, built especially to house it. The frieze showing a battle between the Greek gods and the Giants is one of Hellenic art's masterpieces. Other pieces of classical sculpture can be seen in the wings off the central temple room. The ancient Near Eastern collection is just as impressive, not only because of the Babylonian walls, but the Desert Palace of Mshatta from Jordan. In addition, the Museum of Islamic Art is upstairs and forms a small but inclusive survey of the subject, including the impressive Aleppo Room from the Syrian city's Christian quarter. A major reconstruction of this museum commenced in 2008, and while parts of it will be closed, the museum will remain open.

Around Alexanderplatz
DDR Museum
Karl-Liebknecht-Strasse 1;
tel: 8471 23731; www.ddr-museum.de; Mon–Sun 10am–8pm, Sat 10am–10pm; admission charge; S3, S5, S7, S9: Hackescher Markt; bus 100, 200: Lustgarten; map p.137 D1
This small, private museum, below the Radisson SAS DomAquaree Hotel, on the banks of the Spree across from the Berliner Dom, is not nearly the scholarly institution its neighbours are, but it certainly is a lot of fun. With a stated goal of showing everyday life in the former Deutsche Demokratische Republik (East Germany) and with a particular emphasis on East Berlin, it emphasises a hands-on approach, with a Trabant car you can climb into and 'start', a screening room featuring propaganda films and Erich Honecker's private projector, a hidden corner with a Stasi listening-area, and a reconstructed apartment from a Plattenbau apartment building. It does not shrink from the unpleasant aspects of life in the old regime, nor does it edit

Below: Brice Marden poses in front of his painting *The Propitious Garden of Plane Image* in 2007, at the Hamburger Bahnhof.

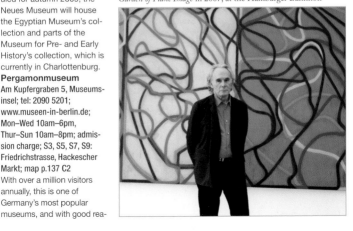

S25: Potsdamer Platz; bus 200: Philharmonie; map p.134 A2
The Prussian royal family's 13th- to 18th-century holdings are displayed at this recently built 7,000-sq m (8,370-sq yd) museum, which uses ingeniously filtered natural light and special artificial light to show each of the thousand paintings on the main floor to its best advantage. The art is arranged chronologically in galleries around a central atrium, with the octagonal Rembrandt room, displaying 16 of the master's works, at its apex. Particularly strong in Dutch and Flemish masters, as well as German artists, the collection at the Gemäldegalerie is the result of the painstaking reunion of works from East and West Berlin, as well as ones taken as war booty by the Soviet Union. Downstairs are an additional 400 paintings in a study collection, as well as computers connected to a digital gallery.

Kupferstichkabinett (Museum of Prints and Drawings)
Matthäikirchplatz 8; tel: 266 2002; www.museen-in-

Below: design at the Bauhaus Archiv.

out the enjoyable moments. Recommended for teenagers.
Märkisches Museum
Am Köllnischen Park 5; tel: 3086 6215; www.stadtmuseum.de; Tue, Thur–Sun 10am–6pm, Wed noon–8pm; admission charge, free Mon; U2: Märkisches Museum; S3, S5, S7, S9: Jannowitzbrücke; map p.135 D2
This rather stodgy display has been the closest thing Berlin had to a city historical museum, although the rebuilding currently under way will likely result in something better when it reopens, scheduled for October 2008. The fragments of Berlin Wall on the outside, however, are worth seeing.

Tiergarten

Bauhaus Archiv Museum of Design
Klingelhöfer Strasse 14; tel: 254 0020; www.bauhaus.de; Wed–Mon 10am–5pm; admission charge; U2, U3, U4: Nollendorfplatz; map p.133 E1
The Bauhaus Archive presents the history and impact of the important Bauhaus (1910–33) school of architecture, design and art in the 20th century. Although the Bauhaus move-

ment started in Weimar and moved to Dessau, it ended up in Berlin, and this small museum hosts regular exhibitions of its work along with interactive terminals which tell its story in German and English. An audioguide is included in the admission.

Deutsche Kinemathek (Museum of Film and Television)
Potsdamer Strasse 2; tel: 300 9030; www.filmmuseum-berlin.de; Tue–Sun 10am–6pm, Thur 10am–8pm; admission charge; U2, S1, S2, S25, bus 200: Potsdamer Platz; map p.134 A2
The permanent exhibition on German film history includes gems such as a model of the robot in *Metropolis*, and has compelling stories to tell about early stars like Marlene Dietrich and the making of classics like Fritz Lang's *Caligari*. One room is dedicated to Leni Riefenstahl.

Gemäldegalerie (Picture Gallery)
Matthäikirchplatz 4–6; tel: 266 29 51; www.museen-in-berlin.de; Tue–Wed, Fri–Sun 10am–6pm, Thur 10am–10pm; admission charge; U2, S1, S2,

One of the most high-profile names in fashion, Berlin-born photographer Helmut Newton died in 2004, shortly after reaching an agreement with the Prussian Heritage Foundation to donate many of his photographs to a joint foundation venture. The resulting **Museum für Fotografie** (Jebensstrasse 2; tel: 266 2188; www.smb.spk-berlin.de; Tue–Sun 10am–6pm; admission charge; U2: Zoologischer Garten; map p.133 D1) is the largest dedicated photography gallery in the city.

berlin.de; Tue–Wed, Fri–Sun 10am–6pm, Thur 10am–10pm; admission charge; U2, S1, S2, S25: Potsdamer Platz; bus 200: Philharmonie; map p.134 A2

With half a million prints and 110,000 drawings, watercolours and pastels ranging from Botticelli to Warhol, this is one of the world's most important collections of works on paper. Illuminated manuscripts, early Italian, Dutch and German masters and 19th-century works are among its strongest points, and a contemporary collection emphasises artists working in Berlin. Owing to the fragile nature of the works, however, only a small part of them are on display at any given time. Scholars can gain access to the entire collection, but visitors are assured of a small but comprehensive central collection and a rotating series of temporary exhibitions.

Musikinstrumentenmuseum (Museum of Musical Instruments)

Tiergartenstrasse 1; tel: 254 810; Tue–Wed, Fri–Sun 10am–6pm, Thur 10am–10pm; admission charge; U2, S1, S2, S25: Potsdamer Platz; bus 200: Philharmonie; map p.134 A2

Tucked away in the complex housing the Philharmonie, the Musical Instrument Museum is a must-see for music fans, spanning the centuries between Stradivarius (not only violins, but also guitars) and synthesisers. CDs at most displays will show you how an instrument sounds, and occasionally there are live musicians playing them. On Sundays, the huge Wurlitzer theatrical organ is fired up, to the delight of all.

Neue Nationalgalerie

Potsdamer Strasse 50; tel: 266 2951; www.neue-national galerie.de; Tue–Wed, Fri–Sun 10am–6pm, Thur 10am–10pm; admission charge; U2, S1, S2, S25: Potsdamer Platz; map p.134 A1

When the Cuban Revolution chased Bacardi Rum out of Havana, Mies van der Rohe wasn't able to build the glass-encased corporate headquarters he had designed for them, but West Berlin needed a modern art museum and the design proved easily adaptable to that purpose. The cornerstone of the Kulturforum near Potsdamer Platz, the Neue Nationalgalerie is best known to Berliners as the venue for blockbuster shows, not only the selection from New York's Museum of Modern Art which broke records a couple of years ago, but also such unexpected hits as 'Art in the DDR'. Mies's design lets in plenty of natural light, so works are shown to great advantage. When travelling shows aren't busy pulling in the crowds, the museum's own impressive collection of art hangs on the walls, including works by Klee, Munch, Picasso and Kirchner.

Charlottenburg

Bröhan Museum

Schlossstrasse 1a; tel: 3069 2600; www.broehan-museum.de; Tue–Sun 10am–6pm; admission charge; U2: Sophie-Charlotte-Platz; U7: Richard-Wagner-Platz; S8, S45, S46: Westend; map p.132 B3

Located directly across the street from Schloss Charlottenburg, this museum specialises in Art Nouveau, Art Deco and Functionalism, three related movements in fine and applied arts covering the period 1889–1939. Paintings, furniture and objects are arranged in rooms of the same style on the ground floor, a painting gallery is one floor up, and the third floor is reserved for special exhibitions.

Erotik-Museum

Joachimsthaler Strasse 4; tel: 886 0666; www.erotik museum.de (German only);

Below: the exterior of the Neue Nationalgalerie, with Henry Moore's bronze *Archer* in front.

91

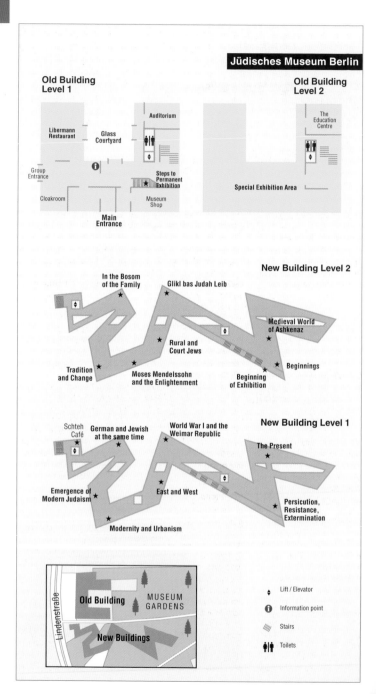

Jüdisches Museum Berlin

Old Building Level 1

Libermann Restaurant
Glass Courtyard
Auditorium
Group Entrance
Steps to Permanent Exhibition
Cloakroom
Museum Shop
Main Entrance

Old Building Level 2

The Education Centre
Special Exhibition Area

New Building Level 2

In the Bosom of the Family
Glikl bas Judah Leib
Medieval World of Ashkenaz
Rural and Court Jews
Tradition and Change
Moses Mendelssohn and the Enlightenment
Beginning of Exhibition
Beginnings

New Building Level 1

Schteh Café
German and Jewish at the same time
World War I and the Weimar Republic
The Present
Emergence of Modern Judaism
East and West
Persicution, Resistance, Extermination
Modernity and Urbanism

Lindenstraße
Old Building
MUSEUM GARDENS
New Buildings

↕ Lift / Elevator
ⓘ Information point
/// Stairs
🚻 Toilets

Above: the Jewish Museum's striking design makes as much of an impact as the exhibits.

daily 9am–midnight; admission charge; S5, S7, S9, U2, U9: Zoologischer Garten; map p.133 D1
Formerly the private collection of a Munich scholar of erotica, the contents of the Erotik-Museum were bought by sex-shop entrepreneur Beate Uhse, who installed it in her flagship store. Artefacts include obsidian dildos from ancient China and depictions of the act in every nook imaginable. The section on the late Beate Uhse, a former Luftwaffe pilot and the mother of the sex industry in postwar Germany, is actually quite interesting. The attached museum shop is a good place for offbeat souvenirs.

Käthe-Kollwitz-Museum and Graphic Collection
Fasanenstrasse 24; tel: 882 5210; www.kaethe-kollwitz.de; Wed–Mon 11am–6pm; admission charge; U9, U15: Uhlandstrasse or Kurfürstendamm; map p.133 D1
This private museum shows a permanent collection of 200 mainly graphic works and some poignant sculptures by the Expressionist artist and pacifist who spent 50 years of her life in Berlin. An enlarged version of Käthe Kollwitz's famous *Mother with Her Dead Son (pietà)* sculpture can be found in the **Neue Wache** building (New Guard House) on Unter den Linden avenue, now the National Memorial to the Victims of War and Tyranny.
SEE ALSO MONUMENTS AND MEMORIALS, P.85

The Story of Berlin
Kurfürstendamm 207–8; tel: 8872 0100; www.story-of-berlin.de; daily 10am–8pm, admission charge; free after 6pm; U1, bus M19, M29, 109: Uhlandstrasse, map p.133 C1
The multimedia exhibition in this modern counterpart to the Märkisches Museum takes visitors through 800 years of Berlin history. The visit to the exhibition includes a guided tour through an original nuclear shelter underneath the Ku'damm-Karree shopping centre, with pretty realistic (and for children, possibly frightening) sound effects.

Kreuzberg and Friedrichshain

Berlinische Galerie
Alte Jakobstrasse 124–8; tel: 7890 2600; www.berlinische galerie.de; Wed–Mon 10am–6pm; admission charge; U1, U6: Hallesches Tor; map p.134 C1
The city museum of modern art, photography and architecture is renowned for staging excellently curated exhibits such as a recent one on German Expressionism. It also has a fine permanent collection, spanning the period from World War I to the 1970s.

Checkpoint Charlie Museum
Friedrichstrasse 43–5; tel: 253 7250; www.mauermuseum.de; daily 9am–10pm; admission charge; U6: Kochstrasse; map p.134 B1
A fascinating exhibition of attempts to get through the Berlin Wall to West Berlin, including elaborate devices used to hide escapees, marred only by some heavy-handed right-wing polemics.

Jüdisches Museum (Jewish Museum)
Lindenstrasse 9–14; tel: 2599 3300; www.juedisches-museum-berlin.de; Tue–Sun 10am–8pm, Mon 10am–10pm, closed Rosh ha-Shanah, Yom Kippur, Christmas Eve; admission charge; U1, U6: Hallesches Tor; U6: Kochstrasse; map p.134 C1
Controversial in about every

Below: erotic art on display at the Erotik-Museum.

93

Right: Topography of Terror.

way possible, from its much-discussed Daniel Libeskind architecture to the content of its exhibits, Berlin's Jewish Museum makes a provocative supplement to visiting the Deutsches Historisches Museum and is every bit as much of a must-see. Concentrating as it does on Jewish life in Germany, it tells the story from the earliest Jewish settlements in German cities and towns to renewed Jewish life in the country today through a huge collection of art, artefacts, documents, films and innovative interactive terminals. Jewish contributions to German culture are made plain, and Germany's anti-Semitism is addressed without blinking, as is the Holocaust which resulted from it. Plan an entire day to thread through Libeskind's difficult layout and rest assured that you'll have a lot to talk about after your visit.

Martin-Gropius-Bau
Niederkirchnerstrasse 7, Kreuzberg; tel: 254 860; www.gropiusbau.de; Wed–Mon 10am–8pm; admission charge; S1, S2, U2, bus 200: Potsdamer Platz; map p.134 B1
This huge exhibition hall in an imposing 19th-century red-and-gold neo-Renaissance building plays host to numerous, often excellent, touring collections of archaeological, historical and art exhibitions.

Topography of Terror
Niederkirchnerstrasse 8; tel: 2548 6703; www.topographie.de; Oct–Apr: daily 10am–6pm, May–Sept: 10am–9pm; free; U2: Mohrenstrasse; map p.134 B1
The remains of the Prinz Albrecht Palais, from which the Gestapo operated, were unearthed during routine

excavation here and today house a largely open-air exhibit. A further exhibition on the workings of the Gestapo is housed in a permanent building over the ruins.

Western Districts

Brücke Museum
Bussardsteig 9, Dahlem; tel: 831 2029; www.bruecke-museum.de; Wed–Mon 11am–5pm; admission charge; U3: Oskar-Helene-Heim, then bus 115 to Pücklerstrasse
This private museum is not part of the Dahlem museum complex and is located some way away. It is dedicated to the works of the first group of important German Expressionist artists, who banded together in Dresden under the collective title of 'Die Brücke', the bridge. With over 400 works by Ernst Ludwig Kirchner, Fritz Bleyl, Karl Schmidt-Rottluff, Erich Heckel, Max Pechstein, Emil Nolde and Otto Mueller, it is an essential stop for people interested in 20th-century German art.

Ethnologisches Museum (Ethnological Museum)
Lansstrasse 8, Dahlem; tel: 830 1438; www.museen-in-berlin.de; Tue–Fri 10am–6pm, Sat–Sun 11am–6pm; admission charge; U3: Dahlem-Dorf
The ethnological collections in Dahlem, covering the Americas, the South Seas, Africa, East Asia and musical ethnology, are an unparalleled resource for those interested in non-European peoples and their cultures. They are displayed with a very contemporary regard for the meanings of the objects, the curators having long ago decided not to show objects which have sacred meaning to the peoples who created them. The American Indian collection, for instance, was largely formed by German explorers in the 19th century, who were taking the scientific study of America's natives seriously at a time when Americans were not; as a result, many items on display are unique. Ritual religious items, however, are only available to recognised

scholars, and the stereotyping of Indians by American culture is addressed in a straightforward manner.

The American archaeological rooms show artefacts of the many Central and South American native cultures as they existed up to the time of the arrival of the Spanish, and the South Seas collection not only includes typical buildings and carved and woven items, but entire boats in the huge boat room, which make palpable the immense distances early Polynesian peoples traversed as their culture spread. The East Asian area concentrates on folk art of both China and Japan, while the 'Art from Africa' exhibit, which has won awards, emphasises the link between the sacred and secular in everyday items, thus illuminating the belief-systems of the cultures which created them. In addition to all of this, the Ethnological Museum has a unique treasure in its musical ethnology display: not only are a wide variety of instruments on display, but sound recordings are, too, as an extension of the Berlin Phonogram Archive, which has existed since 1900 to document European and non-European musics, and which was the first project of its type. In its collection are examples of musics which are no longer performed, and it is listed in Unesco's registry Memory of the World.

Museum für Asiatische Kunst (Museum of Asian Art)

Lansstrasse 8, Dahlem; tel: 266 3666; www.museen-in-berlin.de; Tue–Fri 10am–6pm, Sat–Sun 11am–6pm; admission charge; U3: Dahlem-Dorf

> Other museums are everywhere and are often in private hands. There's a Sugar Museum, a U-Bahn Museum and a Hemp Museum, among dozens of others.

This museum is distinct from the East Asian collection at the Ethnological Museum, and collects items from India and East Asia with an eye towards their artistic more than their utilitarian value. Displaying work from Afghanistan to Indonesia, the Collection of South, Southeast and Central Asian Art highlights not only India and Tibet, but the varied cultures of Southeast Asia and the Chinese province of Xinjiang. The Collection of East Asian Art has Chinese, Japanese and Korean artworks. Eventually, this museum will be re-housed in the rebuilt Hohenzollern Schloss on Museum Island.

Museum of European Cultures

Arnimallee 25, Dahlem; tel: 8390 1287; www.museen-in-berlin.de; Tue–Fri 10am–6pm, Sat–Sun 11am–6pm; admission charge; U3: Dahlem-Dorf

The central collection here was created by merging the European part of the Ethnological Museum with the for-

mer Museum of Folklore, and shows the commonality and differences of everyday life on the European continent via traditions and celebrations and the items created for them from the 18th century to the present day.

Treptow and Köpenick

Stasi Museum

Ruschestrasse 103, Haus 1, Lichtenberg; tel: 553 6854; www.stasimuseum.de; Mon–Fri 11am–6pm, Sat–Sun 2–6pm; admission charge; U5: Magdalenenstrasse; S8, S45, S46: Frankfurter Allee

From this grim building the Ministry for State Security, better-known as the Stasi, East Germany's secret police, was directed. Pervading every level of life in East Germany, the Stasi depended on a web of informers and enforcers, collecting vast amounts of information about its citizens. Here, you can visit Erich Mielke's office, from which he directed operations, see spy technology used to gather information and learn about the links with other countries' espionage services. You will also find information about the resistance to the Stasi, which was an important factor in bringing down the East German regime.

Right: remembering the Wall at the Checkpoint Charlie Museum.

Music

From Eastern European street musicians to smoky jazz clubs, *klezmer* combos, Finnish rock bands and world-class orchestras, Berlin is a crossroads of musical wealth. With two halves of the city sewn back together, Berlin boasts twice the classical music repertoire of most cultural metropolises, alongside a deeply eclectic range of other musical forms. Meanwhile, Berlin's fluid contemporary music scene features influences from all over the world; home-grown talent today covers all genres from techno to electronica to rock to reggae. For listings of more nightclubs that feature live acts, *see Nightlife, p.102–3.*

Classical and Opera

THE SCENE

With several major orchestras, including the Grammy-winning, world-renowned Berlin Philharmoniker, not to mention a number of grand opera houses, visitors to Berlin are spoiled for choice when it comes to classical music. For the chance truly to indulge, visit during September's **MusikFest Berlin** (www.berlinerfestspiele.de), which features several guest ensembles in addition to the local orchestras; the Berlin Philharmoniker tops the bill.

MAJOR VENUES AND ORCHESTRAS

Berliner Philharmonie und Kammermusiksaal
Herbert-von-Karajan-Strasse 1, Tiergarten; ticket hotline tel: 2548 8999; www.berliner-philharmoniker.de; S1, S2, U2: Potsdamer Platz; map p.134 A2
The Berliner Philharmoniker, under the direction of Sir Simon Rattle, is considered by many to be the best symphony philharmonic orchestra in the world, and classical music lovers may want to

plan their trip around their ability to purchase hard-to-get tickets. Even if attending a performance is impossible, the building itself is unique. Completed by Hans Scharoun in 1963, its walls seem to flow like the music that fills them.

Deutsche Oper Berlin
Bismarckstrasse 35, Charlottenburg; tel: 341 0249; www.deutscheoperberlin.de; advance sales 11am–6pm; U2: Deutsche Oper; map p.132 C2
Originally built in 1912, this opera building was destroyed in World War II and not rebuilt until 1961, during the former West Germany's 'economic miracle'. Deutsche Oper is best-known for its innovative interpretations of classic works and for hosting internationally renowned performers.

Komische Oper
Behrenstrasse 55–57, Mitte; tel: 4799 7400; www.komische-oper-berlin.de; advance sales: Unter den Linden 41, Mon–Sat 11am–5.30pm; U6: Französische Strasse, or S1, S2: Unter den Linden; map p.136 B1
This venue is for fans of lighter classical music. The in-

Tickets to classical concerts can be bought at the box office of the relevant concert house, or through *Theaterkassen* (ticket agencies). Note that many will charge a hefty commission on top of the price of the ticket. Alternatively, **Hekticket** is a good bet for last-minute tickets at discounted rates for the same day (Hardenbergstrasse 29D, Charlottenburg; tel: 230 9930; www.hekticket.de; map p.133 D1).

house comic opera performs operettas and is well known for extraordinary productions. The orchestra's repertoire also includes symphonies and opera for children.

Konzerthaus Berlin
Gendarmenmarkt, Mitte; ticket hotline tel: 2030 92101; www.konzerthaus.de; advance sales: Mon–Sat noon–7pm, Sun and holidays noon–4pm; U6: Hausvogteiplatz; map p.134 B2
Weber's opera *Der Freischütz*, the first major German Romantic opera, had its debut performance here. The Baroque concert house at the elegant

Left: performing in a Mozart opera at the Komische Oper.

belsdorff, the Staatspoer features a repertoire that focuses on classical opera and ballet. The opera was destroyed in World War II, and rebuilt. Located in East Berlin during the Cold War, it is now one of the main attractions in the historic renovation of the palace area on Unter den Linden.

OTHER ORCHESTRAS
Akademie für Alte Musik in Berlin
Adalbertstrasse 20, Kreuzberg; tel: 6165 8640; www.akamus.de; U8: Moritzplatz; map p.135 D1

The academy was founded in East Germany in 1980 and specialises in old music, especially of the baroque period. Outside Berlin, it has performed at New York's Carnegie Hall.

Deutsches Symphonie Orchester (DSO)
Im RBB-Fernsehzentrum, Masurenallee 16–20, Charlottenburg; tel: 2 0298 7530; www.dso-berlin.de; U2: Theodor-Heuss-Platz; map p.132 A1

Founded in 1946, the Symphonie has performed around the world. The principal conductor and artistic director is Ingo Metzmacher.

Gendarmenmarkt was built by Friedrich Schinkel. After its destruction in the war, it was rebuilt and reopened in 1984. It is home to the Berlin Symphonic Orchestra.

Neuköllner Oper
Karl-Marx-Strasse 131, Neukölln; tel: 6889 0777; www.neukoellneroper.de; advance sales Mon–Sat 9am–8pm, Sun and holidays 2–8pm; U7: Karl-Marx-Strasse; map p.139 E2

The influence of this neighbourhood or *kiez theatre*, as the Berliners say, extends well beyond Neukölln. Its 11 productions each year are almost exclusively premières by young authors in genres that range from opera to musicals and musical theatre.

Orangerie Charlottenburg
Schloss Charlottenburg, in the park area, Spandauer Damm 10, Charlottenburg; www.concertsberlin.com; S41, 46, 47; U7: Richard-Wagner-Platz; map p.132 B3

This Baroque palace was once the summer residence of Prussian kings, and has been a cultural focal point since its earliest beginnings. The concert series in the Grand Orangerie gives visitors a small taste of Baroque Berlin.
SEE ALSO PALACES AND HOUSES, P.104

Staatsoper Unter den Linden
Unter den Linden 7, Mitte; tel: 2035 4555; www.staatsoperberlin.org; advance sales Mon–Sat 10am–6pm; U6, S1, S2, S5, S7: Friedrichstrasse; map p.136 C1

Built in 1741 for Frederick the Great, by the famous architect Georg Wenzeslaus von Kno-

Left: American saxophonist Earl Von Freeman performs at the Berliner JazzFest.

Platz der Luftbrücke; admission charge; map p.138 B3
Together with its smaller sister venue, the Columbia Club, this concert hall has room for 3,500 people and is a popular venue for indie and alternative rock bands as well as other events. Check listings.

Fritz Club im Postbahnhof
Strasse der Pariser Kommune 3–10, Friedrichshain; tel: 698 1280; www.fritzclub.de; S3, S5, S7, S75, S9: Ostbahnhof; admission charge; map p.135 E2
A large warehouse that has been turned into a popular venue for rock and pop concerts by bands ranging from the almost famous to the internationally acclaimed. Near the East Side Gallery, it has a nice beer garden and popular after-show dancefloor with DJs. Check listings.

Knaack
Greifswalder Strasse 152, Prenzlauer Berg; tel: 442 7060; www.knaack-berlin.de; Wed 9pm–late, Fri–Sat from 10pm; admission charge; S8, S10, Tram M2: Prenzlauer Allee
On Wednesday nights, the stage belongs to local Berlin bands dreaming of stardom. Weekends rock, swing and groove on four floors with live bands and DJs from around Europe. Fridays offer free student admission.

Lido
Cuvrystrasse 7, Kreuzberg; tel: 6956 6840; www.lido-berlin.de; Fri–Sat, from 8pm (concert) or 11pm (party); admission charge; U1, U12, U15: Schlesiches Tor
One of Berlin's newest live music bars, this club hosts young not-yet-famous rock, soul and pop bands. A long bar at one end, a stage at the other, a room full of dancers in-between.

Mahler Chamber Orchestra
Hasenheide 54, Kreuzberg; tel: 417 1790; www.mahler-chamber.de; U7: Südstern; map p.139 C3
The Mahler Chamber Orchestra, founded in 1997, has recorded with Anna Netrebko and performs internationally.

Contemporary
THE SCENE
Kreuzberg and Neukölln, with their large migrant communities, have produced a new generation of German rap and soul musicians. Meanwhile, rock clubs like Knaack, Lido or Columbiahalle often present new Britpop and US bands long before they've made it on the world stage, as well as hot German rock bands. Germany's music industry is largely centred in Berlin, and **PopKomm** (www.popkomm.de) in September/October, is Berlin's mega music event, bringing together fans, bands, DJs and the entertainment industry for business and hundreds of house, electro, reggae and rock concerts. On PopKomm club night, €12 buys access to 30 clubs across the city.

VENUES
Arena
Eichebstrasse 4, Treptow; tel: 533 2030; www.arena-berlin.de; U1: Schlesisches Tor; S8, S9, S41, S42: Treptower Park; admission charge
Arena is located in an old bus garage that dates from 1927 and was designed by the architect Franz Ahrens. There are two concert venues, a swimming pool that floats on the Spree river and a sauna with a full-length river-front window. Arena is a popular venue for concerts, festivals and theatre, especially in summer.

Columbiahalle
Columbiadamm 13–21, Kreuzberg; tel: 698 0980; www.columbiahalle.de; U6:

Max-Schmeling-Halle
Am Falkplatz, Prenzlauer Berg; tel: 443 045; www.max-schmeling-halle.de; admission charge; U2: Schönhauser Allee; S8, S41, S42: Schönhauser Allee

Named after the famous boxer, it was built in the former no man's land along a strip of the Berlin Wall. It hosts sporting events and is home to professional basketball team Alba Berlin, as well as being the venue for many concerts.

Tempodrom
Möckernstrasse 10, Kreuzberg; tel: 747 370; www.tempodrom.de; S1, S2: Anhalter Bahnhof; admission charge; map p.138 B4

This venue seats 3,500 for concerts of all sorts, from rock and pop to musicals. Check listings for information about upcoming concerts.

Velodrom
Paul-Heyse-Strasse 26, Friedrichshain; tel: 443 045; www.velodrom.de; S8, S41, S42: Landsberger Allee; admission charge

Like the Schmeling-Halle, Velodrom was built as part of Berlin's bid to host the Olympics. It's a world-class venue for indoor cycling competition and also hosts big-ticket concerts.

Jazz

THE SCENE
The avant-garde and experimental continues to thrive in the local jazz scene. Night owls might catch local jazz greats, such as trumpet player Til Brönner, or rising star-on-sax Mark Wyand, at the legendary midnight jam session at A Trane. Stars like Wynton Marsalis have been known to join in and test the chops of Berlin's young stars.

Right: Berlin's premier jazz club, the A Trane.

Major festivals include **Berlin JazzFest** (www.berlinerfest spiele.de) in the mid-autumn.

VENUES
Acud Café
Veteranenstrasse 21, Mitte; tel: 4435 9499; U8: Rosenthaler Platz; S1, S2: Nordbahnhof; map p.134 C4

This venue is a survivor of the Wild East days that gripped Mitte after the Wall fell. It's not a place to hear big names, but you will catch young jazz and blues musicians from around the world passing through Berlin, searching for their voice. Concert times and quality vary.

A Trane
Pestalozzistrasse 105, Charlottenburg; tel: 313 2550; www.a-trane.de; Sun–Thur 9pm–2am, Fri–Sat 9pm–late; S5, S9, S75: Savignyplatz; admission charge; map p.133 C1

This is Berlin's best and best known jazz club, hosting local and international performers in an intimate atmosphere. Reserve seats online.

Aufsturz
Oranienburger Strasse 67, Mitte; tel: 2804 7407; www.aufsturz.de; daily 10pm–2am; U6: Oranienburger Tor; S1, S2: Oranienburger Strasse; map p.134 B3

On Fridays and Saturdays,

Over the years, Berlin's left-field and creative reputation has intrigued legendary musicians, most notably David Bowie and Iggy Pop, who lived in Schöneberg in the 1970s and recorded some of their most significant albums here. U2 also spent time in Berlin, recording their seminal album, *Achtung Baby*, which makes many references to Zoo Bahnhof.

the Aufsturz features local and international jazz. The styles vary from modern to electronic jazz. During the week, the club also plays rock and folk. The club area measures 150 sq m (180 sq yds) and has room for 120 grooving people.

Badenscher Hof
Badensche Strasse 29, Wilmersdorf; tel: 861 0080; www.badenscher-hof.de; Mon–Fri 4pm–late, Sat 6pm–late; U7: Berliner Strasse, Blissestrasse; map p.137 D3

An old West Berlin icon, this is a restaurant and venue for local jazz and blues acts. The crowd is not as young and trendy as you'll find in Mitte or Prenzlauer Berg; it remains more a popular after-work bar for 50-somethings.

b-flat
Rosenthaler Strasse 13, Mitte; tel: 283 3123; www.b-flat-

The **Karneval der Kulturen** *(see p.54)* is a great place to get a taste of the breadth of Berlin's world music scene, which takes in virtually every crossover of global music imaginable.

berlin.de; daily 9pm–open end; U8: Rosenthaler Platz or Weinmeisterstrasse; admission charge; map p.134 C3
Founded in 1995 by musicians Jannis Zotos and Thanassis Zotos and the actor André Hennecke, b-flat has a great club atmosphere and a long bar, and plays host to a cross-section of European and German bands playing a variety of styles. Be sure to drop in on Wednesday night for Robin's Nest, the jam session hosted by Berlin bass player Robin Draganovich.

Junction Bar
Gneisenaustrasse 18, Kreuzberg; tel: 694 6602; www.junction-bar.de; Sun–Thur concerts 9–11.30pm, DJs 11.30pm–5am, Fri–Sun concerts 10pm–12.30am; U7: Gneisenaustrasse; admission charge; map p.138 C4
A Kreuzberg establishment featuring live jazz, soul, funk and chansons every night of the week.

Kunstfabrik Schlot
Chausseestrasse 18, Mitte; tel: 448 2160; www.kunstfabrik-schlot.de; opening depends on event; U6: Zinnowitzer Strasse; S1, S2, S25: Nordbahnhof; admission charge; map p.134 B4
A somewhat larger and sometimes noisy club, Schlot is still one of the best places to hear live jazz musicians in Berlin. Live music most nights, starting around 9pm. There is a popular jazz brunch on Sunday with a live band.

Quasimodo
Kantstrasse 12a, Charlottenburg; tel: 312 8086;
www.quasimodo.de;

daily 9pm; S3, S5, S7, S9, S75: Savignyplatz; admission charge; map p.133 D1
A cellar bar with stage and dancefloor, Quasimodo is a Berlin institution that hosts live jazz, funk & soul, Latin, blues and rock bands. Check listings and get there a little early for good seats.

Yorckschlösschen
Yorckstrasse 15, Kreuzberg; tel: 215 8070; www.yorck schloesschen.de; Sun–Thur 9am–3am, Fri–Sat 9am–4am; U7: Mehringdamm, S1, S2, S25: Yorckstrasse; admission charge; map p.138 B4
This place is proof that West Berlin never died. Located in the heart of Kreuzberg, from breakfast until late at night this venue swings with local disciples of traditional jazz, blues and funk.

Record Shops

Alberto Records
Gneisenaustrasse 56, Kreuzberg; tel: 693 3517; Mon–Fri 12.30–7.30pm; U7: Südstern; map p.139 C3
Alberto sells used records ranging from 1960s classics to contemporary sounds.

Core Tex
Oranienstrasse 3, Kreuzberg; tel: 6128 0051; www.coretex

Below: instruments are also sold at Musikalienhandlung Hans Riedel.

records.com; Mon–Fri 11am–8pm, Sat 11am–6pm; U1: Görlitzer Bahnhof; map p.135 D1
Offers hardcore and punk import recordings and their own labels: Bad Dog, Mad Mob and Grapes of Wrath.

Da Capo
Kastanienallee 96, Prenzlauer Berg; tel: 448 1771; www.da-capo-vinyl.de; Tue–Fri 11am–7pm, Sat 11am–4pm; U2: Eberswalder Strasse
A vinyl lover's nirvana, especially if you are looking for old East German rock recordings.

DNS Recordstore
Eberswalder Strasse 30, Prenzlauer Berg; tel: 247 9835; www.dns-music.de; Mon, Wed–Thur 11am–8pm, Tue, Fri 11am–11pm, Sat 11am–6pm; U2: Eberswalder Strasse
This shop has an amazing selection of club music: anything from techno, minimal, house and drum 'n' bass to electro, electro-pop and ambient. Recordings are on CD or vinyl. They also sell DJ equipment.

Freizeitglauben
Petersburger Strasse 81, Friedrichshain; tel: 2904 9151;

Left: the hefty classical music selection at Musikalienhandlung Hans Riedel.

soul, downbeat, headz, reggae/dancehall and electronic music.

L&P Classics
Knesebeckstrasse 33–4, Charlottenburg; tel: 8804 3043; www.lpclassics.de; Mon–Sat 10am–8pm; U2: Uhlandstrasse; S9, S75: Savignyplatz; map p.133 C2

This shop stocks a wide range of CDs and DVDs, focusing on classical music.

Musikalienhandlung Hans Riedel
Uhlandstrasse 38, Wilmersdorf; tel: 882 7395; www.musik-riedel.de; Mon–Fri 8am–6.30pm, Sat 9am–2pm; U1: Ulandstrasse; map p.137 C4

Enormous classical music specialist, selling everything from CDs to sheet music to instruments.

Musik unter den Gleisen
Friedrichstrasse 128, Mitte; tel: 285 9144; www.musik-drehscheibe.de; Mon–Fri 11am–7.30pm, Sat 11am–6pm; U6, S1, S2, S5, S7: Friedrichstrasse; map p.134 B2

This store is located under the S-Bahn tracks and has over 20,000 recordings on CD and vinyl, with a focus on alternative rock.

www.freizeitglauben.de; Mon–Fri noon–8pm, Sat 1–6pm; U5: Frankfurter Tor

Freizeitglauben is a recording label and a record shop under one roof, focusing on techno, house and electro. It is also a gathering place for local musicians and lovers of the genres they promote. You can also investigate their select choice of CDs, t-shirts and DJ equipment.

Gelbe Musik
Schaperstrasse 11, Wilmersdorf; tel: 211 3962; Tue–Fri 1–6pm, Sat 11am–2pm; U3: Augsburger Strasse; map p.137 D4

This avant-garde specialist stocks the most out-there, left-field music in Berlin: industrial, electronica and world feature heavily.

Hiphop Vinyl
Grünberger Strasse 54, Friedrichshain; tel: 4201 2516; www.hhv.de; Mon–Fri 2–7.30pm, Sat noon–4pm; U5: Frankfurter Tor

The name says it all. HHV has more than 50,000 recordings in its catalogue of hip hop, *Deutschrap* (German-language rap),

Oye Records
Oderberger Strasse 4, Prenzlauer Berg; tel: 6664 7821; www.oye-records.com; Mon–Fri 1–8pm, Sat noon–6pm; U2: Eberswalder Strasse, Senefelder Platz

Oye has a large selection of techno, house, electro, new rave, funk, soul, disco and new boogie on vinyl and CD, both new releases and used recordings.

Platten Pedro
Tegeler Weg 102, Charlottenburg; tel: 344 1875; www.platten-pedro.de; Mon–Fri 10am–6pm, Sat 10am–1pm; U7: Mierendorffplatz; map p.132 B3

This is the place to come to hunt down rare vinyls. Pedro stocks more than 131,000 vinyl recordings, including hard-to-find Rolling Stones and Beatles singles and other rarities.

Vopo-Records
Danziger Strasse 31, Prenzlauer Berg; tel: 442 8004; www.vopo-records.de; Mon–Fri noon–8pm, Sat noon–4pm; U2: Eberswalder Strasse

They took their name from the nickname for the East German police, *'Volkspolizei'*, and are into hardcore sounds: punk, metal, garage, hip hop and rock 'n' roll available on CDs, vinyl LPs and singles. They also sell concert tickets.

Below: a listening post at Gelbe Musik.

Nightlife

To survive a night out in Berlin, get some sleep first. The best clubs don't get interesting until well after midnight and keep rocking until after sunrise. Each neighbourhood has its own scene, but you will find the best venues in Mitte, Prenzlauer Berg, Kreuzberg and Friedrichshain. Public transport gets you close to the action and there are late buses, but do not worry about missing the last train home; most U and S lines have an all-night service at the weekend. For information on other places to have a drink or see live music, *see Bars and Cafés, p.32–7, Gay and Lesbian, p.64–7 and Music, p.96–100.*

Mitte

Cookies
Friedrichstrasse 158–164; tel: 2749 2940; Tue, Thur 10pm–6am; admission charge; S1, S2, S25, S5, S7, S75, S9, U6: Friedrichstrasse; map p.134 B2
This is Berlin's hippest DJ club, the icon of the Mitte style, laid-back elegance. It can be tough to get in, so show up early. The crowd is young and includes many Berlin celebrities.

Rio
Chausseestrasse 106; tel: 202 50; www.kulturkaufhaus.de; Sat 11.30pm–late; admission

Below: spinning the decks at Watergate.

charge; U6: Zinnowitzer Strasse; map p.134 B4
With a vibe mixing the stylish and the gritty, this club offers an authentic New Berlin experience, with an excellent electro soundtrack that gets everyone dancing.

Around Alexanderplatz

Kaffee Burger
Torstrasse 60; tel: 2804 6495; www.kaffeeburger.de; Mon–Thur 8pm–late, Fri–Sat 9pm or 10pm–late, Sun 7pm–late; admission charge, some events free; U2: Rosa-Luxemburg-Platz; U2, S5, S7, S75, S9: Alexander-platz; map p.135 C4
A Mecca for East Berlin intellectuals under communism, this dance bar is now an icon of Ostalgia (nostalgia for the East). Its 'Russian Disco' nights with author and DJ Vladimir Kaminer are legendary. Check local listings.

Sage Club
Köpenicker Strasse 76; tel: 278 9930; www.sage-club.de; Thur 10pm–6am, Fri–Sat 11pm–6am; admission charge; U8: Heinrich-Heine-Strasse; map p.135 D2
This is the favourite of Berlin's hip hop scene, though rock,

The main S-Bahn and U-Bahn lines run all night Friday, Saturday and the evening before a holiday, except for the U4, S45 and S85. The rest of the week, night buses are available between 12.30am and 4.30am (Sun until 7am) every 30 minutes along the U-Bahn and S-Bahn lines. Night buses are numbered N1 to N3 and N5 to N9. Taxi service is reliable and can be flagged down on the street or called out by dialling 261 026.
See also Transport, p.129.

electro and techno also get a look in through the week. Popular with the hip and fashion-conscious.

Tiergarten

40 Seconds
Potsdamer Strasse 58; tel: 8906 4241; www.40seconds.de; Fri–Sat 11pm–late; admission charge; S1, S2, S25, U2: Potsdamer Platz, Nightbus N2; map p.134 A1
A penthouse DJ club for devoted house fans that got its name from the time it takes the lift to reach the

Left: Berlin is renowned as a hardcore party town.

klatt.com; Wed–Sat 8pm–1am, Fri–Sat 10pm–5am; free; U1, U12, U15: Schlesisches Tor; Night bus N65; map p.135 E1

Its laid-back Zen lounge style makes this combination restaurant, bar and DJ club a favourite for refined clubbers. Dinner is taken on lounge chairs with a spectacular view of the Spree river. Later, tables are pushed aside to make room to dance. Reservations recommended.

Watergate Club

Falckensteinstrasse 49; tel: 6128 0396; www.water-gate.de; Wed–Fri 11pm–late, Sat midnight–late, opening times vary in summer; admission charge; U1, U12, U15: Schlesisches Tor; Night bus N65; map p.135 E1

This riverside house and techno club is where the ravers meet. In summer, dance outside on the waterfront patio.

club. The bird's-eye panorama of downtown Berlin is not to miss.

Prenzlauer Berg

Club 23

Kulturbrauerei; Schönhauser Allee 36; tel: 4431 5100; www.soda-berlin.de; Thur 7pm–late, Sun from 8pm, Fri–Sat 11pm; admission charge; U2: Eberswalder Strasse; map p.135 D4

The best dance club at the Kulturbrauerei, an old brewery transformed into a cultural factory with no fewer than eight clubs. Friday and Saturday offer ladies' admission free, with drinks free until 1am.

Magnet

Greifswalder Strasse 212–213; tel: 4400 8140; www.magnet-club.de; Tue–Sun 8pm–late; admission charge; S8, S10, Tram M4, M10, N54: Greifswalder Strasse; map p.135 D4

This is the heart of Berlin's Indie and Britpop scene. Popular with students, who hop between the club's two rooms, one for live bands and the other a dancefloor with DJ.

White Trash Fast Food

Schönhauser Allee 6–7; tel:

5034 8668; www.whitetrash fastfood.com; daily 6pm–late; admission charge; U2: Senefelder Platz, Rosa-Luxemburg-Platz; map p.135 C4

If Russ Meyer and Jim Morrison were looking for a place to hang, this would be it. A trash roadhouse in a former Chinese restaurant, it has two bars, the best burgers in Berlin, its own tattoo parlour and diverse live music on offer, from Finnish punk to jazz to Japanese new wave.

Kreuzberg and Friedrichshain

Matrix

Warschauer Platz 18, Gewölbe 3; tel: 2936 9990; www.matrix-berlin.de; Mon–Sat 10pm–late; admission charge; S3, S5, S6, S7, U1, U12, U15: Warschauer Strasse

This popular dance club is built into the vaulted roofs of a railway overpass. As the trains roll by overhead, dance the night away on four floors and six cocktail bars. Or dip in the indoor pool.

Spindler & Klatt

Köpenicker Strasse 16–17; tel: 695 6675; www.spindler

There are all-night *döner kebap* stands throughout the city, but word on the street is that the **Grill und Schlemmerbuffet** at Rosenthaler Platz in Mitte makes the best *döner* in Berlin. Other popular late or all-night *döner* and *currywurst (see Food and Drink, p.58)* stands include: **Döneria Fantasia** (Brückenstrasse 2; 24 hours; U8: Heinrich-Heine-Strasse), **Currywurst** (Kantstrasse, under S-Bahn bridge; until 3am or later; S3, S5, S7, S9, S75: Zoologischer Garten), **Bagdad** (Schlesische Strasse 2; 24 hours; U1, U12, U15: Schlesisches Tor), **Döner-Imbiss**, Corner of Boxhagener Strasse-Münzstrasse; until late; U5: Frankfurter Tor or Samariterstrasse), **Max & Moritz** (Bötzowstrasse 51; until 5am; tram M4: Hufelandstrasse)

103

Palaces and Houses

Given the amount of bombing damage Berlin suffered in World War II, it is quite remarkable that any old buildings at all remain in the city. Because of that and the fact that Berlin is, on the whole, a very young city by European standards, there is little to see here in terms of magnificent relics of the past. However, those such as Schloss Charlottenburg and Schloss Köpenick, which remain or have been restored, offer fine examples of how the royal and wealthy lived in bygone days.

Palaces

Schloss Charlottenburg

Spandauer Damm 10–22, Charlottenburg; tel: 320 910; www.spsg.de; (Old Palace) Tue–Sun 9am–5pm, (New Wing) Apr–Oct: Tue–Sun 10am–5pm, Nov–Mar: Tue–Sun 11am–5pm; admission charge; U2: Sophie-Charlotte-Platz; S45, S46: Jungfernheide; map p.132 B3

Easily the most spectacular building in Berlin, this magnificent structure was built by the Elector Frederick III (later known as Kaiser Frederick I of Prussia) as a summer palace for his wife, Sophie-Charlotte, in 1699 so that she could escape the unhealthy air around the Stadtschloss. She did not enjoy many summers there, dying in 1705, but the property was used by many subsequent Hohenzollerns, who added bits and pieces as they went along. The Old Palace consists of over 20 rooms furnished in high 18th-century style, with exhibits of royal porcelain and silver. The New Wing was built by Frederick the Great and contains his state apartments, as well as the winter quarters of

Berlin is historically a working-class city, with fewer grand homes but some interesting worker-housing solutions, such as Le Corbusier's *Unités d'Habitation (see Architecture, p.30)*.

Wilhelm III, his successor. A large number of Frederick the Great's collection of French paintings is on view here, including some masterpieces. As notable as the palace are the formal gardens, which contain an 18th-century teahouse, a Neapolitan-style villa (the New Pavilion), and the mausoleum of Queen Luise.
SEE ALSO PARKS AND GARDENS, P.108–9

Schloss Friedrichsfelde

Am Tierpark 125 (Lichtenberg Tierpark Zoo), Lichtenberg; tel: 666 35035; www.stadt museum.de; tours hourly 11am–4pm in summer, 11am–2pm in winter; Zoo admission charge; U5: Tierpark

This 18th-century palace was home to Princess Anna Charlotta Dorothea, as well as various minor nobility. Period paintings and tapestries are displayed along with metal-

work, including a fine selection of pieces from the Royal Ironworks. Note that admission to the Schloss is only available with a tour, and that you will also have to buy a ticket for the Lichtenberg Zoo (called Tierpark Berlin).
SEE ALSO PARKS AND GARDENS, P.111

Schloss Köpenick

Kunstgewerbemuseum, Schlossinsel; tel: 266 2902; www.smb.spk-berlin.de; Tue–Sun 10am–6pm; admission charge; S3: Köpenick; Tram 60, 61, 62, 68: Schlossplatz Köpenick

Divided from the old town by wooden bridge and located right on the water is Schloss Köpenick, the Köpenick palace (1677–82), a significant example of 17th-century Baroque architecture that has been wonderfully restored. The Hohenzollerns used it as a summer palace and hunting lodge and, occasionally, as a court room. In 1730, King Frederick I put his son Frederick II (later 'the Great') on trial here for desertion. The heir to the throne narrowly escaped the death sentence. Today, the palace houses the

Left: Schloss Charlottenburg.

finest, although Ephraim himself was despised for having devalued Prussia's currency in order to help the Kaiser finance the Seven Years War. The current structure is a thorough re-creation of the house which had been torn down in 1935 so that Mühlenstrasse could be widened. The facade was carefully dismantled and stored and in 1989, placed back on a new structure erected for Berlin's 750th anniversary. Today, temporary art exhibitions are held inside.

Knoblauch-Haus

Poststrasse 23, Mitte; tel: 2400 2162; www.stadtmuseum.de; Tue, Thur–Sat 10am–6pm, Wed noon–8pm; free; U2: Klosterstrasse; map p.135 C2

Johann Christian Knoblauch built this house for his family between 1759 and 1761. For many years the family lived there, sharing the space with the silk-ribbon business which provided them with their fortune. Its original Baroque facade was replaced in 1806 by a more classical one which remains today. Inside is a small museum dedicated to the family, housed in rooms decorated in typical Biedermeier style. A wine restaurant occupies the ground floor.

Museum of Decorative Arts (Kunstgewerbemuseum), showing Baroque and Renaissance furniture and other objects. A nice alternative way to reach the palace is by boat from Treptower Hafen.

Stadtschloss

Karl-Liebknecht-Strasse opposite Lustgarten and Altes Museum, Mitte; map p.137 D1

The castle complex of the Hohenzollern dynasty was heavily damaged during World War II bombing, and its remains destroyed by the East German regime in 1952. One part remains, integrated into the former Council of State building on Werderscher Markt and plainly standing out from its functional architecture. From the topmost balcony, Karl Liebknecht announced the Socialist Republic of Germany in 1918 after the Kaiser had fled. This event made it worth preserving by the GDR. The rest of the land facing onto Karl-Liebknecht-Strasse has been earmarked by the city for a complete restoration of the Stadtschloss from the original plans, which still exist. Upon its completion, the city

will move the Dahlem collections of non-European art into it. In order to reconstruct the Stadtschloss, the Palast der Republik, the central administrative building of the GDR, had to be destroyed, a move which angered many in the Eastern part of the city. Its remains, facing onto the river, can still be seen, although they will eventually be totally obliterated. Funds for the construction of the Stadtschloss are still uncertain, so a date for completion is not yet set.

Houses

Ephraim Palais

Poststrasse 16, Mitte; tel: 2400 2121; www.ephraim-palais.de; Tue, Thur–Sat 10am–6pm, Wed noon–8pm; admission charge; U2: Klosterstrasse; map p.135 C2

Veitel Heine Ephraim was a 'court Jew', a position which allowed him to trade loans and financial advice to the Kaiser in return for protection, and he was made court jeweller to Frederick the Great in 1745. This house, originally built in 1765, was considered Berlin's

Right: Schloss Köpenick.

Pampering

Berlin is rich in options to relax, detox and be pampered; you can lose your sense of time in a floatation tank or enjoy a Balinese temple massage, though for the most local forms of relaxation, opt for one the city's fantastic saunas or a traditional hamam. Berlin boasts some unusual venues for unwinding, particularly with the options for swimming in special floating constructions on the Spree river. Meanwhile, even if a stay at one of the smartest hotels in town is financially out of reach, day passes at their luxurious in-house spas are often available.

Saunas

Liquidrom

Möckernstrasse 10, Kreuzberg; tel: 2580 07820; www.liquidrom-berlin.de (German only); daily 10am–midnight, Fri–Sat until 1am; S1, S2, S25, bus 29, M41: Anhalter Bahnhof; map p.138 B4

A contemporary art spa: minimalist architecture, quality materials and 'liquid sound', an experience for all senses that combines bathing in warm Dead Sea waters with sound and light therapy. While you float in the pool, listen to whale sounds or new age music from the underwater speakers. The use of the sauna and steam bath is included in the admission charge. Back rubs, hot stone or Balinese herbal massages should be reserved in advance.

Sauna auf dem Badeschiff

Eichenstrasse 4, Treptow; tel: 01789 500 163; www.badeschiff.de; opening hours subject to change; robes, towels, slippers for hire; S41, S42, S8, S85, S9: Treptower Park

Left: glamorous natural beauty products at Belladonna.

For a unique Berlin experience, rub shoulders with a hip crowd in the floating sauna on the Spree. Throughout the cold months, the Badeschiff floating swimming pool on the river is converted into a futuristic-looking sauna-ship. Fantastic view of illuminated Oberbaumbrücke bridge. Open daily, but check times.
SEE ALSO SPORTS, P.125

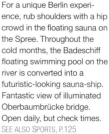

Thermen am Europa-Center

Nürnberger Strasse 7, Charlottenburg; tel: 257 5760; www.thermen-berlin.de; daily 11am–8pm; U1, U2: Wittenbergplatz; S5, S7, S75, S9: Zoologischer Garten; map p.133 D1

The Thermen is a 1970s retro-style Berlin classic. You can indulge in head-to-toe pampering (facials, body-wraps, depilation, thalasso treatments, massages) or detox in what is still Berlin's largest sauna landscape, complete with 32-degree indoor and outdoor rooftop thermal-water swimming pool and terrace overlooking the city. The Thermen is mixed; clothing is optional in the pools but not allowed in the saunas.

Left: the pool at Thermen am Europa-Center.

shop, which specialises in natural products. Also a great place to buy make-up and essential oils.

Float-store am Gendarmenmarkt

Kronenstrasse 55–58, Mitte; tel: 2061 9933; www.float-store.de (German only); Mon–Sat 10am–8pm; U2, U6: Stadtmitte; map p.134 B2

Classy anti-ageing oasis. Float in an egg-shaped saltwater tank, inhale pure oxygen or enjoy a classic anti-cellulite or Ayurvedic massage.

Hamams

Hamam

Mariannenstrasse 6, Kreuzberg; tel: 615 1414; www.hamam-berlin.de (German only); Mon 3–11pm, Tue–Sun noon–11pm; map p.135 D1

A Turkish bath reserved for women only, offering traditional Turkish soap massage, exfoliation, depilation and various treatments. Excellent massage therapists on staff. Bring your own towels and slippers or rent them.

Sultan Hamam

Bülowstrasse 57, Schöneberg; tel: 2175 3375; www.sultan-hamam.de; daily noon–11pm, Mon men only, Tue–Sat women only, Sundays mixed; U2: Bülowstrasse; U7, S1, S2, S25: Yorckstrasse; map p.138 A4

An authentic oriental steam bath, complete with a lounge offering shishas and oriental snacks. There are steam and exfoliation rooms, as well as a bio-sauna with coloured light therapy. Treatments for both men and women include waxing, massages and facials, all at very reasonable prices. Try the Sultan Package. It can be tricky to find the backyard entrance in the dark, so come early.

Hotel Spas

Adlon Day Spa

Unter den Linden 77, Mitte; tel: 3011 17200; www.adlon-day-spa.de; Mon–Fri 8am–10pm, Sat–Sun 8am–8pm; U1, U2, U25, bus 100: Unter den Linden; map p.136 A1

The Adlon Day Spa, open to non-guests, allows you to luxuriate in style. A spacious pool, water shiatsu and treatments of all kinds, from the 'True Romance Package' for two to 'Executive De-stress', will help you regenerate in no time and in a private atmosphere: no mixed saunas here.

Day Spa Berlin

Friedrichstrasse 106, Mitte; tel: 284 900; www.day-spa-berlin.de; daily 10am–11pm; S5, S7, S75, S9, U6: Friedrichstrasse; map p.136 B2

This impressive, nicely decorated new day spa is part of the Artist Riverside Hotel. Open to everyone, it provides everything you might need – dressing gowns, towels, slippers – and offers a wellness trip around the world. You can choose from Hawaiian, Balinese, Egyptian, Tibetan and more treatments and baths,

> Going to the sauna is very much part of the German lifestyle. Be aware that public saunas are usually co-ed and the dress code is birthday suits. Large hotels tend to have separate saunas.

have a hot chocolate massage, float in a saltwater tank or just enjoy the view over the Spree from one of the saunas.

Beauty

Aveda Lifestyle Salon and Spa

Kurfürstendamm 26a, Charlottenburg; tel: 8870 8799; www.aveda.de; Mon–Fri 10am–8pm, Sat 9am–6pm; U1, bus M46, 110, 249: Kurfürstendamm; map p.133 D1

Come for a facial, a body-wrap, a new hairstyle or makeover. By appointment only; services for both women and men. All products for sale.

Belladonna

Bergmannstrasse 101, Kreuzberg; tel: 694 3731; www.bella-donna.de; Mon–Fri 10am–7pm, Sat 10am–6pm; U7: Gneisenaustrasse; map p.138 B3

Beauty heaven at this pretty

107

Parks and Gardens

Berlin has a lot to offer in terms of leafy respites from hectic urban life. Enjoy the scenery in the sprawling Tiergarten and the variety of plant life and solitude in the Botanical Garden, or get off the beaten path and discover a mix of fine horticulture and active recreation in Britzer Garten in Neukölln. Apart from providing viewpoints, garden art and occasional concerts, all the green spaces are great for people-watching: Berliners love their gardens and tend to live life outside in the short summers.

Tiergarten

Tiergarten
Free; U2, U9, S5, S7, S75, S9: Zoologischer Garten; S5, S7, S75, S9: Tiergarten, Bellevue; S1, S2, S25: Unter den Linden, Potsdamer Platz; bus 100: Grosser Stern, Schloss Bellevue; map p.133 E2/134 A2

Berlin's largest park, the Tiergarten ('Animal Garden') was originally laid out as a game reserve for the Hohenzollern kings. The 252-hectare (630-acre) expanse of woods and gardens stretches from the Brandenburg Gate in the East to the Zoological Garden in the West, bordering on Potsdamer Platz and the Reichstag. It is best to explore by bicycle or Velotaxi. Pedal along waterways and ponds,

Cycle rickshaws for leisurely tours of the Tiergarten can be found at the Brandenburg Gate. The red-and-silver Deutsche Bahn rental bikes parked in strategic locations all over the city can be unlocked by mobile phone. You need to register so that your credit card can be debited.

past islands, statues and vintage gas lamps from all over Europe, and take a break in the rose garden or the beer garden at Café am Neuen See, on the western edge of the park, where you can rent a boat and row across the lake. Sights in the park include the Siegessäule and the **Sowjetisches Ehrenmal** (Soviet War Memorial). At least equally impressive, albeit only in May and June, are the multicoloured rhododendron woods. At weekends, Tiergarten turns into a heavy-duty recreation park shared by joggers, walkers, cyclists, t'ai chi

aficionados, sunbathers and Turkish barbecue lovers.
SEE ALSO MONUMENTS AND MEMORIALS, P.84–5

Charlottenburg

Schlossgarten Charlottenburg
Württembergische Strasse 6; daily 6am–10pm; voluntary admission charge; S41, S42, S46: Westend; bus M45: Schloss Charlottenburg; map p.132 B3

Also known as the Schlosspark, this Baroque garden and English-style park has been restored to its 18th- and 19th-century glory. In addition to the Charlotten-

Below: cycling in the Tiergarten.

Left: relaxing in the idyllic surrounds of the Schlossgarten Charlottenburg.

stage uses the idyllic setting as a welcome backdrop for films and performances.

Western Districts

Botanischer Garten

Unter den Eichen 5–10; tel: 8385 0100; www.botanischer-garten-berlin.de; winter daily 9am–4pm, summer 9am–8pm; admission charge; S1, bus M48: Botanischer Garten

The beautifully landscaped 50-hectare (126-acre) botanic garden is home to 22,000 different species of plants, offering a botanical journey around the world in one day. Best to enjoy the serene surroundings during the week, when you have the garden almost to

Below: the varied features of Volkspark Friedrichshain.

There is even a vineyard on one of the slopes of the Kreuzberg. The Kreuz-Neroberger is grown here, one of Europe's northernmost wines.

burg palace and the manicured greenery, points of interest here include a carp pond, a mausoleum for Queen Luise and the Belvedere, a former teahouse and outlook point that now houses a collection of porcelain. There is a landing for boats to Potsdam nearby, at Schlossbrücke.
SEE ALSO PALACES AND HOUSES, P.104

Kreuzberg and Friedrichshain

Viktoriapark

Kreuzbergstrasse/Katzbachstrasse; free; U6: Platz der Luftbrücke; map p.138 B3
With its winding trails, rocky areas and a deep waterfall, Viktoriapark is not your average urban park. Located on the Kreuzberg ('Cross Mountain'), it is a great vantage point offering interesting views from the national mon-

ument crowning the steep hill. It was built by great Karl Friedrich Schinkel to commemorate the Napoleonic Wars. Great people-watching here, and the park reflects Kreuzberg's diversity.

Volkspark Friedrichshain

Am Friedrichshain/Landsberger Allee; free; tram M4: Platz der Vereinten Nationen; bus 200: Am Friedrichshain; map p.135 E3/4
The Friedrichshain Public Park is Berlin's oldest park. One popular attraction for children is the beautiful fountain adorned with fairytale characters, the Märchenbrunnen (Fairytale Fountain). However, this park has something for everyone: large, well-kept playgrounds, the shade of old trees overlooking a pond, a hike up the 78m (256ft) high Grosser Bunkerberg, or 'Mont Klamott' ('Rubble Mountain'), as it was made from debris after World War II, as well as a picnic and a ball game on the heavily used lawn at the northern corner of the park. With its well-lit, versatile pathways, it is also a popular running spot. After dark, an open-air

yourself. It is a wonderful retreat from the city, not too central to be packed out but still easy to reach from Alexanderplatz or Potsdamer Platz. Once a month, the local registry performs marriage ceremonies in the Mediterranean greenhouse.

Liebermann Villa at Lake Wannsee
Colomierstrasse 3; tel: 8058 5900; www.max-liebermann.de; Apr–Oct: Thur–Mon 10am–6pm, Nov–Mar: Wed–Mon 11am–5pm; admission charge; S1, S7: Wannsee, then bus 114: Colomierstrasse

After many years of being used by a diving club, the Lake Wannsee residence of famous Berlin painter Max Liebermann was painstakingly restored, including the grounds, which are complete with the floral opulence and diversity in his garden that inspired many of his paintings. They can now be viewed where they where created and compared with the subjects Liebermann depicted.

Pfaueninsel (Peacock Island)
Pfaueninselchausee 1, Zehlendorf; free; May–Aug 8am–9pm, shorter hours in winter; bus 218: Pfaueninsel, then ferry

King Friedrich Wilhelm II bought this island in the middle of Havel river in 1793 and conceived it as a park. He and his successor Friedrich Wilhelm III turned it into a world of its own, filled with artificial ruins, exotic plants and free-range peacocks. The winding pathways offer changing views of the natural beauties and picturesque buildings, some of them designed by Karl Friedrich Schinkel. A romantic, magical place, it can only be reached by ferry.

Directly across Invalidenstrasse from the Hauptbahnhof is a brick wall, behind which is one of Berlin's newest and least-known parks, **Moabit Prison Historical Park**. The prison which once stood here housed Wilhelm Voigt, the notorious 'Captain of Köpenick' *(see Treptow and Köpenick, p.22–3)*, as well as poet Albrecht Haushofer, who wrote the *Moabit Sonnets* there. Today it is a large, grassy park with some enigmatic monuments.

Treptow and Köpenick

Treptower Park
Between Puschkinallee and Am Treptower Park; free; S4, S6, S8, S9, S85: Treptower Park, Plänterwald

Leafy Treptower Park is located on the banks of the Spree in the East of Berlin, not far from the impressive red-brick Oberbaumbrücke bridge and the huge 'Molecule Man' sculpture in the middle of the river. Archenhold Observatory, the oldest of its kind, is located here, complete with the world's largest refractor telescope. Don't miss the imposing **Sowjetisches Ehrenmal** (Soviet War Memorial) at the entrance from Puschkinallee avenue, dedicated to the 5,000 Soviet soldiers who were killed in the Battle of Berlin and buried here. The grand

Below: catching a boat is the only way of getting to Pfaueninsel (Peacock Island); once there, it is a lovely spot for relaxing.

Left: explore gardens of the world at the tranquil Marzahner Erholungspark.

Park, Britzer Garten's twin in the East, is also worth a trip. Here, the 'Gardens of the World' are the main attraction. Chinese, Japanese, Korean, Balinese and Islamic theme gardens represent the very distinct fine garden art of the respective region, including authentic plants and materials. The Chinese 'Garden of the Reclaimed Moon', complete with a teahouse and waterscape, is particularly noteworthy and the largest of its kind in Europe. Other park features include a Renaissance-style hedged maze, a rhododendron grove, a herbal garden and several playgrounds.

Tierpark Berlin
Am Tierpark 125, Lichtenberg; tel: 515 310; www.tierpark-berlin.de; daily 9am–4pm/5pm/6pm depending on season; admission charge; U5: Tierpark

If you want to experience 10,000 animals in more natural habitats than in the crowded Zoologischer Garten and you enjoy walking around beautiful gardens, try the sprawling Tierpark in the East, Europe's largest landscape zoo. It is renowned for its elephant-breeding programme, the concerts in **Schloss Friedrichsfelde** palace and the fine flower and shrubbery displays.
SEE ALSO PALACES AND HOUSES, P.104

layout includes gravestones carrying Stalin quotes and a huge monument of Soviet soldier crushing a swastika and carrying a German child. With its grand layout, the memorial is well worth visiting. Elsewhere in Treptower Park, locals picnic on the lawn along the river, hang out at the old 'Zenner' beer garden, rent a rowing boat or cross over to 'Insel der Jugend' island.
SEE ALSO MONUMENTS AND MEMORIALS, P.85

Further Out

Britzer Garten
Sangerhauser Weg 1, Neukölln; tel: 700 9060; www.gruen-berlin.de/britz; daily 9am–dusk; admission charge; U6: Alt-Mariendorf, then bus: 179, or taxi from station

This park, landscaped in 1985 as a national garden show venue and maintained for Berliners, who were at that time cut off from the surrounding countryside by the Wall, is now a beautifully grown-in garden well worth the longish trip. On an area of 90 hectares (225 acres) are hills, lawns with free deckchairs, big lakes, playgrounds, modern sculptures, theme gardens and animal enclosures. A great family outing for next to nothing. Dogs and bicycles are not allowed.

Marzahner Erholungspark
Eisenacher Strasse, Marzahn; tel: 700 9060; www.gruen-berlin.de; daily 9am–dusk; admission charge; S7, bus 195: Marzahn

The Marzahn Recreational

Every spring in Britzer Garten, 'Tulipan', a spectacular tulip show, attracts thousands of flower-lovers and photographers, just like the 'Dahlia Fire' exhibit in autumn.

Restaurants

Berlin has never been known as a restaurant town, due to a combination of the austere local cooking and the city's overwhelmingly working-class nature, but in the past decade, there's been a notable change. As more Germans have started taking holidays out of the country and Berlin's status as the country's capital has swung into action, the quality of food available in its restaurants has improved remarkably, with increasing numbers of cheap ethnic eateries and an ever-growing array of Michelin-starred fine dining establishments. For more information about Berlinese food, *see Food and Drink, p.58–9.*

Mitte

GERMAN

Guy Restaurant
Jägerstrasse 59–60; tel: 2094 2600; www.guy-restaurant.de; €€€€; Mon–Fri noon–3pm, 6pm–1am, Sat 6pm–1am; U6: Französische Strasse; map p.134 B2
In the courtyard of a converted mansion which also houses Berlin's Rolls-Royce dealership, half-German, half-French chef Hartmut Guy presents virtuoso cuisine in a remarkably relaxing atmosphere. Of particular note is the seasonal menu, which takes advantage of the best that farmers from the surrounding region have to offer. The business lunch is a particular bargain, given its quality. The sommelier has some wonderful surprises, and the service is top-notch.

Restaurant Vau

Approximate prices per person for a three-course meal with a glass of house wine:

€	under €20
€€	€20–€35
€€€	€35–€50
€€€€	over €50

Jägerstrasse 54–55; tel: 2029 730; www.vau-berlin.de; €€€€; Mon–Sat noon–2.30pm, 7–10.30pm; U6: Französische Strasse; map p.134 B2
Where the renowned Jewish intellectual Rachel Varnhagen had her salon in the late 18th century, chef Kolja Kleeberg now presides over a different kind of forum. The prix-fixe €110 menu is filled with variations on traditional themes given a fascinating twist by Kleeberg's philosophy of no more than three ingredients on a plate. The €14-per-plate lunch menu even has intriguing offerings for vegetarians.

AUSTRIAN

Kellerrestaurant im Brecht-Haus
Chausseestrasse 125; tel: 282 3843; €€; May–Oct noon–12.30am, Nov–Apr 6pm–midnight; U6: Oranienburger Tor; map p.134 B4
Photographs of Bertolt Brecht, the great playwright and poet, show him gaining weight after moving back to Berlin after World War II, but you don't have to be a literary critic to find out why:

> You will sit at your table all night and day waiting for the server to volunteer the bill. Germans signal they are finished eating by placing their napkin on the plate.

many of the dishes on the menu here in the restaurant beneath the house he lived in are from a notebook kept by his wife, Helene Weigel. Her Bohemian roots show in the *fleischlabberln* (ground-meat patties) and the *paradiessuppe* (tomato soup), among other dishes. In the summer, you can dine outdoors in the garden, if you can ignore the fact that Berti and Helene are buried just over the wall. If there's a lecture at the Literaturforum upstairs when you plan to dine, make reservations.

Lutter & Wegner
Charlottenstrasse 56; tel: 2029 5410; €€–€€€; daily 11am–2am, kitchen open until midnight; U2, U6: Stadtmitte; map p.134 B2
Lutter & Wegner were wine merchants who opened a restaurant in 1811, where the Regent Hotel stands today at

Left: preparing for a smart dinner at the Lorenz Adlon.

www.hotel-adlon.de; €€€€; Tue–Sat 7–10.30pm; U1, U2, U25; Unter den Linden; map p.136 A1

A luxury hotel has to have a luxury restaurant, and this spot, named after the hotel's founder, certainly fits the bill. Chef Thomas Neeser's impeccably French cuisine makes use of ingredients from around the world, including Iranian caviar, Madagascan vanilla and Italian beef. The hotel's stature also attracts special events, with star chefs and vintners showing off their skills.

Margaux
Unter den Linden 78 (entrance on Wilhelmstrasse); tel: 2265 2611; www.margaux-berlin.de; €€€€; Mon–Sat 7–10.30pm; S1, S2, bus 100, 200; Unter den Linden; map p.136 A1

Chef Michael Hoffmann calls his style 'classic avant-garde', which describes it perfectly: a combination of roast pork or steamed fish with molecular gastronomy. It works most of the time, especially when he's dealing with seafood, but stumbles do occur. The interior is a bit austere, but the service is friendly and the wine list is extraordinary.

Charlottenstrasse 49. Famed for their *sekt* (sparkling white wine), their gastronomy took second place. Today it is the other way around: with an Austrian-based menu, including what is probably Berlin's best *wiener schnitzel*, Lutter & Wegner's Gendarmenmarkt location is a top restaurant destination. Strictly traditional, strictly high-quality ingredients and a wine list which reminds you of their original business.

FRENCH
Borchardt
Französische Strasse 47; tel: 2038 7110; €€€–€€€€; daily noon–1am; U6: Französische Strasse; map p.134 B2

An old standby with politicians and opera patrons since the 19th century, Borchardt used to be the only 'good' restaurant in this part of town. Competition saw it reinvent itself as a French-style bistro, which has kept the tables full. The food can be inconsistent, and you're better off going with the more traditional offerings than some of the chef's flights of fancy.

Gourmet Restaurant Lorenz Adlon
Hotel Adlon, Unter den Linden 77; tel: 2261 1960;

Below: for those who like literary interest with their dinner, the Kellerrestaurant im Brecht-Haus.

Left: eating out has become more common for Berliners.

southern Italy have become a force to be reckoned with in Berlin's Italian restaurant scene. This is their high-end restaurant; there is also a trattoria on Fuggerstrasse in Schöneberg and a superb pizzeria in Monbijou Park. There is not much messing with tradition here, although when there is, like a shrimp-and-strawberry salad with balsamic dressing, it's still good. Appetisers (the caponata is legendary), pastas (squid-ink pasta with truffles) and main courses (stew of organic lamb) are all excellent and served on handmade plates. There is a superb wine selection, which the sommelier will guide you through. The only downside is that the menus are in Italian only, which forces the server to translate, a problem for large parties.

Around Alexanderplatz

GERMAN
Honigmond
Borsigstrasse 28; tel: 285 7505; www.honigmond-berlin.de; €–€€; Mon–Fri noon–2am, Sat–Sun 9am–2am; S1, S2, S25: Nordbahnhof, Oranienburger Strasse; map p.134 B4

A neighbourhood gem, this place is so successful that it has spawned two hotels. And no wonder: Berlin specialities like *königsberger klopse*, an unbeatable beef stew with fried slices of dumpling and vegetarian *maultaschen* (a Swabian speciality which resembles oversized ravioli) are regulars on the menu here. The real treasures are on the weekly selection, which is seasonal and in German only. Soups are creative, and only the rare forays into Chinese-like food do not live up to the restaurant's otherwise impeccable quality. Even the bread is addictive.

EAST ASIAN
Makoto
Alte Schönhauser Strasse 13; tel: 9789 3857; €; Mon–Sat noon–4pm, 6–11.30pm; U8: Weinmeisterstrasse; map p.135 C3

Where do homesick, impoverished Japanese students and artists go for a taste of home? This welcoming little noodle joint. Specialising in ramen in countless variations, with both soy and miso broth, it also does udon and soba dishes and a few rice-bowls. Japanese beer, sake and a full range of shochu cocktails add to the authenticity.

ITALIAN
Al Contadino
sotto le Stelle
Auguststrasse 34; tel: 281 9023; www.alcontadino.com; €€–€€€; daily 6pm–midnight; U8: Weinmeisterstrasse; map p.134 C3

The Mutagnola family from

SOUTHEAST ASIAN
Monsieur Vuong
Alte Schönhauser Strasse 46; tel: 9929 6924; www.monsieur vuong.de; €–€€; Mon–Sun noon–midnight; U8: Weinmeisterstrasse; map p.135 C3

There really is a Monsieur Vuong, although he's not the handsome devil with the rolled sleeves in the big photo here (that's his father). A decade ago, he and his German partner started providing Berlin with authentic Vietnamese soups and noodle dishes, and, although the current location is five times the size of the one they started with, it is still impossible to

A reminder: as of January 2008, all restaurants in Germany are now non-smoking.

get a seat quickly, but worth it to wait as reservations cannot be made. Nice touches include a slice of grapefruit in the mineral water.

SPANISH
Pata Negra
Instituto Cervantes, Rosenstrasse 18–19; tel: 8471 2812; www.pata-negra-berlin.de; €€; Mon–Fri 8.30pm–midnight, Sat 5pm–midnight; S5, S7, S75, S9: Hackescher Markt; map p.137 D2

Welcome to Spanish high-tech cuisine. If you don't want liquid nitrogen to get near your food and would rather not put on goggles while it is applied, avoid. Not without entertainment value though, and the efforts of Enrique Serván's young staff to explain the secrets of experimental cuisine are laudable. The results, like the Pata Negra soup with grilled watermelon pearls are excellent. 16-course menus available, but better to order à la carte.

Tiergarten
GERMAN
First Floor
Budapester Strasse 45 (at Palace Hotel, Europacenter); tel: 2502 1182; www.palace.de; €€€; Tue–Sat noon–3pm, 6.30–11pm; S5, S7, S75, S9, U2; U9: Zoologischer Garten; bus 100, 200: Breitscheidplatz; map p.133 D1

Reopened in 2007 under master chef Matthias Buchholz, the Michelin-rated First Floor offers haute cuisine in a salon-like classical ambience. Go with the recommended food and wine pairings as they are excellent. The sommelier is in command of an outstanding collection of 12,000 bottles.

Charlottenburg
GERMAN
Florian
Grolmanstrasse 52; tel: 313 9184; www.restaurant-florian.de; €€; daily 6pm–3am; S3, S5, S7, S9: Savignyplatz; map p.133 C1

Owned by two sisters from Swabia, armed with one of Germany's best culinary traditions, this gathering place for stars of stage and screen and the media who report on them is also welcoming to non-celebrities. Hearty portions of rigorously traditional Swabian dishes at fair prices make it one of the neighbourhood's best bargains, and there are a few outdoor tables during the summer for unparallelled people-watching on one of central Berlin's most upscale streets.

Marjellchen
Mommsenstrasse 9; tel: 883 2676; www.marjellchen-berlin.de; €€; daily 5pm–midnight; S3, S5, S7, S9: Savignyplatz; map p.132 C1

No-nonsense Prussian, Silesian and Pomeranian food served in a welcoming atmosphere. Recommended dishes include *schlesisches himmelreich* (smoked meats stewed with dried fruit, served with a yeast dumpling), *mecklenburger kümmelfleisch* (leg of lamb stewed with root vegetables

and caraway seed) and *falscher gänsebraten* (pork chops stuffed with apples, plums and dark bread). They also know their German wines here, so ask for a recommendation.

FRENCH
Paris Bar
Kantstrasse 152; tel: 313 8052; www.parisbar.de; €€; daily noon–2am; S3, S5, S7, S9: Zoologischer Garten; map p.133 D1

The Paris Bar is famous, and if you are, too, you'll enjoy the food and service. If you are not, you may find the service less than friendly. However, this remains one of Berlin's iconic restaurants. The walls are adorned with art traded for meals, and there are pictures of various German celebrities around, as well as, on occasion, the celebrities themselves. If you are with one of them, you will be in luck.

ITALIAN
12 Apostel
Bleibtreustrasse 49; tel: 312 1433; www.12-apostel.de;

Right: Marjellchen.

115

€–€€; daily 24 hours; S3, S5, S7, S9: Savignyplatz; map p.133 C1

It's not often that 24-hour restaurants are this good, or even that pizza in Berlin is this good, although conceptually it is a bit of a shame they've added to the original 12, each named for an Apostle: 'Judas' features spicy salami and chilli pepper. Pasta, salads and a few meat and fish dishes round out the menu. Also at: Georgenstrasse 49, Mitte; tel: 201 0222; www.12-apostel.de; daily 24 hours; S3, S5, S7, S9: Friedrichstrasse; map p.136 C2.

Grünfisch

Fasanenstrasse 42; tel: 3937 1523; www.gruenfisch.de; €€–€€€; Mon–Sat 6pm–midnight; U3: Spichernstrasse; map p.137 D4

Finely prepared Sicilian food is the draw at this elegant, award-winning place, which focuses on modern and traditional seafood preparations seasoned with mint, fennel and oranges. The original location is in Kreuzberg and proved so popular that the owners added this more central one. An exclusive wine list includes Nero d'Avola vintages from little-known but high-quality producers. Reservations essential. Also at: Willibald-Alexis-Strasse 27, Kreuzberg; tel: 616 21252; www.gruenfisch.de; Tue–Sat 6pm–midnight; U6: Platz der Luftbrücke; U7: Gneisenaustrasse; map p.138 B3.

MODERN EUROPEAN

Die Quadriga

Eislebener Strasse 14; tel: 2140 5650; www.brandenburger-hof.com; €€€€; Tue–Fri noon–2pm, Mon–Sat from 7pm; U3: Augsburger Strasse; map p.133 D1

High temple of gourmet cuisine inside the Hotel Brandenburger Hof, where Michelin-starred chef Bobby Bräuer creates exquisite, seasonal dishes with international influences. There is also a cellar of 850 excellent German wines at its disposal to go alongside the food. This very upscale restaurant is intimate, only capable of seating a small number per sitting, so be sure to book in advance.

Prenzlauer Berg

ALSATIAN

Gugelhof

Knaackstrasse 37; tel: 442 2929; www.gugelhof.com; €€–€€€; Mon–Fri 4pm–1am, Sat–Sun 10am–1am; U2: Senefelder Platz; map p.135 D4

Berlin's most famous Alsatian restaurant offers excellent versions of *tarte flambée* (melted cheese over bits of

Below: gourmet dining at Die Quadriga.

meat on a crackery crust), *bäckeoffe* (the Alsatian answer to *pot-au-feu*) and *choucroute garni*, along with ever-changing weekly specials. The wine list has a fine selection of German and Alsatian wines, particularly rieslings, and the after-meal selection of *eaux de vie* is the best in town. Weekends see the entire neighbourhood arriving for breakfast or lunch, and reservations are mandatory.

AMERICAN
The Bird
Am Falkplatz 5; tel: 5105 3283; www.thebirdinberlin.com; €€–€€€; Mon–Sat 6pm–late, Sun noon–late; U2, S45, S46: Schönhauser Allee

Despite its name, The Bird is about red meat, specifically, that hard-to-find commodity in Berlin, beef. Burgers and cut-to-order steaks are just about all that's on the menu (although there are incredibly hot chicken wings available as appetisers), served with hand-cut french fries. It is an authentic piece of American Germany (the owners are from New York) and always packed with homesick Americans and Americanophilic Germans, to the point where a reservation is almost always a must.

CHINESE
Ostwind
Husemannstrasse 13; tel: 441 5951; €–€€; Mon–Sat 6pm–1am, Sun 10am–1am; U2: Eberswalde Strasse

Given that most 'Chinese'

Approximate prices per person for a three-course meal with a glass of house wine:

€	under €20
€€	€20–€35
€€€	€35–€50
€€€€	over €50

---

restaurants in Berlin serve up a caricature of the cuisine, it is a pleasure to come across this basement restaurant which is as dedicated to Chinese culture generally as it is to Chinese cuisine. Eschewing MSG, it strives for authenticity. Service can be slow and some dishes are oddly bland, but a careful perusal of the menu can result in a fine meal.

EAST ASIAN
Omoni
Kopenhagener Strasse 14; tel: 361 9244; €–€€€; daily 5pm–midnight; U2, S45, S46: Schönhauser Allee

This understated Korean-Japanese restaurant not only offers some of the best sushi in town from a huge menu, but some of the only authentic Korean cuisine, epitomised by *bibimbap*, a huge, heated bowl of rice dressed with raw egg, vegetables and Korean pickles, which you then mix up with the spoon provided. Organic produce when available, friendly service and reservations essential.

ITALIAN
Due Forni
Schönhauser Allee 12; tel: 440 17 333; €; open daily noon–midnight; U2: Senefelder Platz; map p.135 D4

This once elegant building housed the Polish Consulate back in communist times and now plays host to a frantic bunch of yelling, gesticulating waiters scurrying from the two ovens that give the place its name, to the customers, who will tuck into one of the bewildering number of pizzas on offer. There is also a blackboard full of pasta dishes and salads, but clearly pizza's the star. Good, inexpensive carafe wine, too.

If, in some of the lower-end establishments, your server seems a bit snarly, don't worry: it's Berliner *Schnauze*, best translated as 'attitude'. The locals find it charming, visitors usually less so.

Trattoria Paparazzi
Husemannstrasse 35; tel: 440 7333; €–€€; daily 6pm–1am; U2: Eberswalder Strasse

Ignore the name and book a table for some remarkable southern Italian food at this long-time neighbourhood favourite, run by a German woman who returned from holiday fired with enthusiasm for what she had been eating and went to culinary school in Italy to learn the tricks. Yes, they do pizza, but look beyond that to the *malfatti* (rolled, stuffed pasta) and *strangolapreti* (hand-cut pasta with cheese, spinach, and ham). Check for daily specials, which are often dishes found nowhere else in town.

RUSSIAN
Restaurant Pasternak
Knaackstrasse 22–24; tel: 441 3399; www.restaurant-pasternak.de; €–€€; daily 10am–1am; U2: Senefelder Platz; map p.135 D4

Comrades! Collectively endeavour to avail yourself of the traditional specialties of the Russian people! Don't let the somewhat silly retro-communist trappings of the menu put you off of some excellent Russian cuisine. Be it tea and blinis or a full meal of herring, borscht and *shashlik*, this place delivers the goods. Of particular note are the Jewish specialities: *latkes*, *kreplach* and more, cooked just as authentically as the rest of the menu. Incredibly popular, so booking is essential.

117

Schöneberg

ALSATIAN

Storch

Wartburgstrasse 54; tel: 784 2059; €€; Mon–Sat 6pm–1am; U7 Eisenacher Strasse; map p.137 E3

Berlin's first Alsatian restaurant is still one of its best, serving up superb *flammekuchen*, *choucroute*, hearty stews and Alsatian and German wines and beers to diners seated at long tables. The friendly waiting staff are a plus in a city not known for them, and the vintage advertisements on the wall, from the owner's extensive collection, add a lot to the warm atmosphere.

INDIAN

India Haus

Feurigstrasse 21; tel: 213 8826; €; Mon–Fri 5pm–midnight, Sat–Sun noon–1am; U4: Innsbrucker Platz; map p.137 E3

Maybe it is due to the fact that it is located just behind the Odeon, Berlin's oldest English-language cinema, but this veteran Indian restaurant is one of the very few recommendable ones in the city. It could be that British visitors who know korma from kofta have allowed the owners to make a profit on traditionally prepared and seasoned dishes. As with most British restaurants, it is all from the northern Indian tradition, so while there are no surprises, there are no let-downs, either. They will make it properly spicy if you ask.

ITALIAN

Café Aroma

Hochkirchstrasse 8; tel: 782 5821; www.cafe-aroma.de; €€; Mon–Fri 6pm–midnight, Sat 2pm–midnight, Sun 11am–midnight; S1, S2, S25, U7: Yorckstrasse; map p.138 A4

Café Aroma has been Berlin's top northern Italian restaurant

Above: an authentically Italian cappuccino at Café Aroma.

for years and has a large and devoted clientele, much of it made up of Italians living in Berlin. The gathering place for the local 'Slow Food' movement, it is also something of an embassy for Italian culture in general, with language classes often being offered. There is always something unusual on the blackboard and classics on the printed menu. The atmosphere is loud and somewhat chaotic, and the service is friendly.

Kreuzberg and Friedrichshain

GERMAN

Altes Zollhaus

Carl-Herz-Ufer 30; tel: 692 3300; www.altes-zollhaus-berlin.de; €€–€€€; Tue–Sat 6pm–midnight; U1: Prinzenstrasse; map p.139 D4

It is hard to believe you are in Berlin while dining at this canalside, half-timbered cottage, which served as a customs depot in the 19th century. Rather, it is until you see the menu, on which the produce of the surrounding

Brandenburg countryside is subjected to chef Günter Beyer's alchemy. Duck is a speciality, but seasonal specials change week by week as fruit and vegetable crops come and go. There's a range of choices from traditional to slightly avant-garde, and the restaurant has its own exclusive winery making wines to complement the cuisine.

Henne

Leuschnerdamm 25; tel: 614 7730; www.henne-berlin.de; €; Tue–Sat 7pm–midnight, Sun 5pm–midnight; U8: Moritzplatz; map p.135 D1

Does it seem absurd to have to make a reservation for a bar that serves a roasted half-chicken for €6.50 and pretty much nothing else? Not after you've tasted the chicken, an organic, milk-marinated one from Bavaria raised by the owner's brother. Add another €3 for a portion of potato or cabbage salad and a couple more for a draught beer, and you have a quintessential Berlin dining experience. You will feel sorry for John F. Kennedy, who wrote them a letter (displayed above the bar) expressing his disappointment that he couldn't come for dinner after his *'Ich bin ein Berliner'* speech.

Jolesch

Muskauerstrasse 1; tel: 612

3581; www.jolesch.de; €–€€; daily 10am–1am; U1: Görlitzer Bahnhof or Schlesisches Tor; map p.135 E1

A wonderful neighbourhood restaurant, Jolesch offers a wide selection of German and Austrian dishes, from the very basic to almost fancy. The locals gather for breakfast, lunch (a particular bargain, with a three-course meal for €7.90) and dinner, or hang out at the bar in the front. Unpretentious, friendly and affordable.

FRENCH
Le Cochon Bourgeois

Fichtestrasse 24; tel: 693 0101; €€–€€€; Tue–Sat 6pm–midnight; U7: Südstern; map p.139 D3

Given Kreuzberg's political leanings, it is hardly surprising that its best French restaurant should be known as the 'bourgeois pig', but the irony stops at the name. In a city with few top-notch, authentic French places, this is a magnet for the city's French population, as chef Benjamin Stoeckel prepares a crisp salad with warm cheese, adds Moroccan accents to the fish and has assembled a wine list of some distinction.

SPANISH
Sol Y Sombra

Oranienplatz 5; tel: 6953 3887; www.solysombra-berlin.de; €; daily 5pm–late; U8: Moritzplatz; map p.135 D1

Your typical neighbourhood tapas bar, frequented mostly by a local Kreuzberg crowd. Pick from a wide selection of Andalusian goodies on display. All the staples of Spanish cuisine, including a delicious gazpacho.

TURKISH
Hasir

Adalbertstrasse 10; tel: 614 2373; www.hasir.de; €–€€; daily 24 hours; U1, U8: Kottbusser Tor; map p.135 D1

There are actually six Hasirs: one next door to this and others in Wilmersdorf, Schöneberg, Spandau and Mitte, the latter featuring a liveried doorman. This is the one where it all started, though, from the invention of the döner kebap to the idea that Germans might want to eat Turkish cuisine. From a light soup to heartier appetisers to the grilled meat specialities which put the place on the map originally, through the traditional closing rice pudding, it's dead-on authentic and tasty. Note that only this location is open day and night; check their website for other locations' addresses and opening hours.

Eating Out Vocabulary
Vorspeise **appetiser**
Hauptgericht **main course**
Beilage **side dish**
Fleisch **meat**
Gemüse **vegetable**
Salat **salad** (also lettuce)
Getränke **drinks**
Schweinefleisch **pork**
Rindfleisch **beef**
Hänchen **chicken**
Kalbsfleisch **veal**
Pute, Truthahn **turkey**
Ente **duck**
Gans **goose**
Wildschwein **wild boar**
Kaninchen **rabbit**
Wurst **sausage**
Schinken **ham**
Lachs **salmon**
Kabeljau **cod**
Hering **herring**
Zander **pike-perch**
Barsch **perch**
Thunfisch **tuna**
Krabben **small shrimps**
Garnelen **prawns**
Kohl **cabbage**
Rotkohl **red cabbage**
Blumenkohl **cauliflower**
Rosenkohl **Brussels sprouts**
Gurke **cucumber** (also pickle)
Kartoffel **potato**
Bohnen **beans**
Erbsen **peas**
Tomate **tomato**
Champignon **mushroom**
Knoblauch **garlic**
Zwiebel **onion**
Wasser **water**
Mineralwasser **mineral water**
mit/ohne Kohlensäure
with/without gas
Milch **milk**
Saft **juice**
e.g. *Orangensaft* **orange juice**
Tee **tea**
Kaffee **coffee**
Bier **beer**
helles/dunkles **light/dark**
Weissbier **wheat beer**
Wein **wine**
Rotwein **red wine**
Weisswein **white wine**
Schnaps **spirits/liquor**
See also Language, p.79.

Below: the dining scene is becoming ever more lively and stylish.

Shopping

While you will have no trouble hunting down the big names in Berlin, there is a considerable amount of idiosyncratic shopping to be done here, in offbeat boutique stores and the myriad markets; when looking for distinctive purchases, you will notice that nostalgia for East Germany (ostalgia) is a big theme. Germany liberalised its once restrictive shop opening hours a while back and Berlin, typically, scrapped just about all restrictions. Shopping for basic needs is possible at just about any time, but generally department stores and most shops open at 10am and close at 8pm or 10pm, with many still closing on Sundays.

Department Stores

F95
Frankfurter Allee 95–97; tel: 4208 3358; www.f95store.com; Mon–Fri noon–8pm, Sat 11am–6pm; S4, S10, U5: Frankfurter Allee
A self-described lifestyle concept store, this shop even transforms the arrangement of its products into art installations. Goods are arranged on wooden pallets; jeans hang from the ceiling as if floating in space. Berlin's young, trendy clientele love it.

Galeries Lafayette
Friedrichstrasse 76–78; tel: 209 480; www.galeries-lafayette.de; Mon–Sat 10am–8pm; U2: Stadtmitte or Französische Strasse; map p.134 B2
A short walk from Unter den Linden, this is the Berlin branch of the famous Parisian department store and the stunning, glass centrepiece of a new shopping district in central Berlin. Be sure to visit the French deli and exquisite collection of wines in the basement.

KaDeWe
Tauentzienstrasse 21–24; tel: 21 210; www.kadewe-berlin.de; Mon–Thur 10am–8pm, Fri 10am–9pm, Sat 9am–8pm; U1, U2: Wittenbergplatz; map p.133 D1
Opened in 1907 by the Jewish merchant Adolf Jandorf, it belongs today to Karstadt Quelle. For a full century, its concept has remained the same: to rival London's Harrods with a massive display of luxury and everyday goods and name brands, as well as eating extravagance at its 30 gourmet bars. The luxury food hall takes up the whole sixth floor. A Berlin institution and a must-see.
SEE ALSO FOOD AND DRINK, P.59

Shopping Malls

Alexa
Grunerstrasse 120; tel: 269

Below: shopping at the Galeries Lafayette.

Left: quirky bargains at the Berliner Antik and Flohmarkt.

German stamps, lighting, chairs, dishes and leather jackets worn by the East German police. They also have trendy bags in contemporary designs.

Flea Markets

Antique Market at Ostbahnhof

Erich-Steinfurth-Strasse; tel: 2900 2010; Sun 9am–5pm; S3, S5, S7, S9, S75: Ostbahnhof; map p.135 E2

This market near East Berlin's former central station has had its ups and downs, but is now experiencing a healthy revival. Come early to find the best antiques before professional shop dealers scoop up the bargains.

Berliner Antik und Flohmarkt

Georgenstrasse; Wed–Mon 11am–6pm; S3, S5, S9, S75, S25, U6: Friedrichstrasse; map p.136 B1

Follow the S-Bahn away from the Friedrichstrasse station down Georgenstrasse and you will find this and other antique shops under the arches of the S-Bahn. Everything from antique jewellery and vintage furniture to Jugendstil lamps.

Berliner Kunst-und Nostalgiemarkt

Am Kupfergraben; Sat–Sun 11am–5pm; U2, S5, S7, S75, S9: Alexanderplatz; map p.137 C2

This is a pretty flea market along the banks of the Spree river on the way to Pergamonmuseum. Visitors can find stalls full of books and clothes, antiques, souvenirs and sundry items. Popular with tourists; bargain hard to pare down inflated prices.

Flea Market at Arkonaplatz

Arkonaplatz; tel: 786 9764;

3400; www.alexacentre.com; Mon–Sat 10am–8pm; S3, S5, S7, S9, S75, U2, U5, U8: Alexanderplatz; map p.135 D3

Alexanderplatz has been a Berlin crossroads and meeting place for over a century. Alexa is the latest addition, a massive shopping mall in neo-Art Deco design with 180 shops offering everything from food and fashion to computers and music.

Stilwerk Berlin

Kantstrasse 17; tel: 315 150; www.stilwerk.de; Mon–Fri 8am–8pm, Sat 10am–6pm; S9, S75, S5, S3: Zoologischer Garten, or U15: Uhlandstrasse, map p.133 D1

This is a distinctive shopping mall concept, with boutiques and sales outlets offering high-quality luxury and lifestyle accessories for the home, from furniture by international designers to lighting, kitchenware and fine textiles.

Second-Hand and Retro Stores

Colours

Bergmannstrasse 102; tel: 694 3348; www.kleidermarkt.de; Mon–Fri 11am–7pm, Sat

Being Continental Europe's largest department store, the KaDeWe is not much fun to explore with kids in tow. You can, however, park them in the nice childcare facility on the third floor, right next to the toys. Exclusive kidswear and a children's hair designer are also available here.

11am–6pm; U7: Mehringdamm; map p.138 B3

At this popular shop in the heart of Kreuzberg you can buy retro clothing priced by the kilogram. It is a quick walk from the Mehringdamm station. Combine a trip here with a visit to the Turkish open-air market on Bergmannstrasse.

Waahnsinn Berlin

Rosenthaler Strasse 17; tel: 282 0029; http://waahnsinn-berlin.blogspot.com; Mon–Sat noon–8pm; U8: Weinmeister Strasse; map p.135 C3

This is the place to go for 'ostalgia'-infleunced retro. They have got everything from 1968 East German egg-shaped chairs to buttons with images from East

www.troedelmarkt-arkona
platz.de; Sun 10am–4pm,
closed in winter; U8: Bernauer
Strasse

Located on one of the most
beautiful neighbourhood
squares in Mitte, this market
caters to those hunting
down artefacts from daily life
in the old East Germany. But
you can also find antique
books and second-hand
clothing, linen and other
odds and ends. After shopping, relax in one of the
cafés on the square.

Flea Market at
Boxhagener Platz

Boxhagener Platz; tel: 0174 946
7557; Sun 10am–6pm; U5:
Frankfurter Tor, Samariter
Strasse

This is a bargain-hunter's
paradise and a favourite of
students or anyone on a low
budget looking for cheap
treasures in the cardboard
boxes and on the tables of
the merchants. After shop-

ping, visit the many local art
galleries and cafés.

Flea Market at
John-F.-Kennedy-Platz

John-F.-Kennedy-Platz; tel: 332
224 6723; Sat–Sun 8am–4pm;
U4: Rathaus Schöneberg; map
p.137 E3

This is a popular local market
on the square in front of the
Rathaus Schöneberg.
Reflecting its neighbourhood
character, this market lacks
the 'scene' feel of markets in
Mitte and Prenzlauer Berg,
but is more intimate and
relaxed for it.

Flea Market at Mauerpark

Bernauer Strasse 63–64; tel:
0176 2925 0021; Sun 8am–
6pm; U8: Bernauer Strasse;
U2: Eberswalderstrasse

Perhaps Berlin's most
bohemian market, it takes its
name from the Berlin Wall.
The park is located on a
stretch of land where the Wall
once stood, and the market
occupies land that was once

Cash is king. With few exceptions, German retailers loathe
credit cards. Many restaurants
and clothing stores will not
take them. The upside is that
you can often request 'Skonto',
a discount of 3 percent or more
if you agree to pay in cash,
especially for big items like furniture. Maestro debit cards are
accepted almost everywhere.

mined and guarded with
lethal force. It's a great place
to look for old vinyl albums,
CDs and East German para-
phernalia. Be sure to take
time to kick back in one of
the beach bars, with real
sand, house music DJs and
cool drinks. Note, though,
that the annual left-wing May
Day riots are often launched
from Mauerpark.

Flea Market at Strasse
des 17. Juni

Strasse des 17. Juni; tel: 2655
0096; Sat 11am–5pm, Sun
10am–5pm, S3, S5, S7, S9, S75:
Tiergarten; map p.133 D2

Russian military paraphernalia,
Art Deco lamps, Biedermeier
furniture, handmade clothing,
CDs, doorknobs and other
hardware, it's all here at one
of Berlin's most popular flea
markets. Popular among
tourists, but it's also a
favourite of locals. One tip:
barter hard to push down
inflated prices.

Rare and Used Book
Market at the
Bodemuseum

Am Kupfergraben/Museums-
insel; tel: 0171 710 1662;
Sat–Sun, Holidays 11am–5pm;
S3, S5, S7, S9, S75: Hackescher
Markt; map p.137 C2

Located on Berlin's picturesque Museuminsel, this
market specialises in rare and
used books. There are also

Left: browsing records at the
Berliner Antik und Flohmarkt.

vendors selling prints and lithographs. A bit pricey, so stay firm when you haggle.

Gift and Specialist Shops

Ach Berlin
Markgrafenstrasse 39; 9212 6880; www.achberlin.de; Mon–Sat 11am–7pm; U2, U6: Stadtmitte; U2: Hausvogteiplatz; map p.134 C2

It took Berlin a long time to adopt the self-confidence of New York's 'I Love NY' campaign. But the city is changing, and Ach Berlin is a sign of that change, a collection of gifts from coffee mugs to shoe brushes with every imaginable Berlin motif: the Berlin bear, the TV Tower, Brandenburg Gate. All that's missing is the slogan, 'I Love Berlin'.

Ampelmann Shops
Potsdamer Platz Arcaden; tel: 2592 5691; www.ampelmann.de; Mon–Sat 9am–9pm, Sun noon–6pm; S1, S2, S25, U2: Potsdamer Platz; map p.134 B1

A fierce battle erupted between East and West Berliners when after unification the Westerners tried to remove the East's 'traffic light man', a

Above: 'ostalgic' gifts at Mondos Art.

Below: book-shopping at the Kunst-und Nostalgiemarkt.

green striding figure for go and a standing red figure for wait. The East won, and the 'Ampelmann' became an icon, adorning T-shirts, bags, sweets, lamps and many other objects. (Also at: Karl-Liebknecht-Strasse 1; tel: 2758 3238; Mon–Sat 10am–8pm, Sun 11am–8pm; S1, S2, S25: Unter den Linden; map p.137 D1; and Rosenthaler Strasse 40–41; Hackesche Höfe, Hof 5; tel: 4404 8801; Mon–Sat 10am–10pm, Sun 11am–8pm; S/Tram Hackescher Markt; map p.135 C3)

Herrlich Männergeschenke
Bergmannstrasse 2; tel: 784 5395; www.herrlich-online.de; Mon–Sat 10am–8pm; U7: Gneisenaustrasse; map p.138 B3

Everything a man needs: kitchen stuff, compasses, camping knives, pens and warm blankets. This gift shop specialises in presents for boyfriends, husbands, fathers and grandfathers. Forget the

tie and socks this year.

Misses & Marbles
Raumerstrasse 36; tel: 4978 6282; www.misses-marbles.de; Mon–Sat 10am–7pm, Sun 11am–6pm; U2: Eberswalder Strasse

A cosy hole-in-the-wall shop that exemplifies a Berlin trend: the combination coffee bar, gift and newspaper shop. Souvenirs on sale are largely from Berlin designers and include blankets, kids' T-shirts and odd accessories, purses made out of used sail cloth and much more.

Mondos Art
Schreiner Strasse 6; tel: 4201 0778; www.mondosarts.de; Mon–Fri 10am–7pm; U5 Samariterstrasse

East German retro, this shop carries it all, from DVDs of old East German Defa film studio movies to board games, East German passports and a beer called Red October.

123

Sports

The 2006 World Cup inspired a new lease of life for Berlin's sporting world, not least the iconic Olympiastadion, which benefited from an extensive renovation. Yet with the Berlin Marathon attracting tens of thousands of runners every year, Berlin was already known for its participatory activites. It has a lot on offer in addition to the traditional sports: water activities on Grosser Wannsee, ice-skating on Unter den Linden and cycling just about everywhere. For the less active, spectator events like watching local football side Hertha BSC or the Six-Day Cycling Race are reasonably priced and accessible.

Participant Activities

CYCLING

Berlin is flat, green and laced with bike paths. In fact, cycling is so much a part of the local culture and city structure that renting a bike for a day is easy. Start by biking around the Reichstag, through the Brandenburger Tor, then follow the Spree, or cut through the Tiergarten. With its many back roads and quiet neighbourhoods, Berlin is a great city to explore by bike. If you can, start on a Sunday morning, when you have the city almost to yourself. Most streets have bike lanes, and drivers tend to be careful. If you feel more comfortable in a group, choose from a variety of organised English-language sightseeing tours by bicycle, such as www.berlinonbike.de.

SEE ALSO TRANSPORT, P.129

INDOOR CLIMBING
Magic Mountain
Böttgerstrasse 20–26, Wedding; tel: 88715 7900; www.magic mountain.de (German only); admission charge; Mon–Fri noon–midnight, Sat–Sun 11am–10pm; U8, S1, S2, S25, S41, S42: Gesundbrunnen
With the nearest mountains hundreds of miles away, this is an alternative. Magic Mountain, a bright new place, has 200-plus appealing climbing routes that challenge everyone from novices to veterans. You can also work out in the gym or relax in the sauna after you are done. Children six and older welcome.

INLINE SKATING
For everyday inline skating, join the Berliners on Kronprinzessinnenweg along the Grunewald forest or start at Brandenburger Tor and go

Below: rental bicycles.

west on wide pavements on Strasse des 17. Juni, past the Siegessäule, cutting through the Tiergarten park.
Skate Night Berlin
www.skate-night-berlin.com
Skaters used to have the run of the city every summer Sunday night (bringing traffic to a standstill), but now skate nights are confined to just a few nights a year. Check for dates and courses.

RUNNING AND WALKING
Banks of the Landwehrkanal
U1: Prinzenstrasse
A flat and beautiful, if urban route, following the Landwehr channel. Get to know upmarket parts of Kreuzberg district, with stately old buildings and shading trees. The path is lit up in the evening if you keep to the streets.
Berlin Marathon
Start at Brandenburger Tor, Mitte; tel: 301 28 810; www.real-berlin-marathon.com; annually in September; registration charge
The flat and fast course takes you past all the major sights,

Left: at the Olympiastadion.

Stadtbad Schöneberg

Hauptstrasse 39, Schöneberg; tel: 780 9930; www.berliner baederbetriebe.de (German only); admission charge; Sept–May: Mon 2–10pm, Tue–Fri 7am–10pm, Sat–Sun 9am–10pm; U7: Eisenacher Strasse, bus M48: Hauptstrasse/ Albertstrasse; map p.137 E3

Beautifully renovated public indoor pool, airy and flooded with light, includes a 25m (82ft) sports pool, diving boards, jacuzzis and a hot saltwater pool, plus a tunnel water slide, toddler pools and a small counter-current outdoor pool. Extra charge for the sauna.

SEE ALSO CHILDREN, P.41

Spectator Sports

CYCLING

Berlin Six Day Race

Velodrom, Paul-Heyse-Str. 29, Prenzlauer Berg; tel: 9710 4204; www.sechstagerennen-berlin.de (German only); admission charge; every January; S41, S42, S8, S85: Landsberger Allee

A Berlin society event bringing together people from all walks of life over a glass of beer or champagne. Some are so eager to see and be seen, they never look at the track.

FOOTBALL

Olympiastadion

Olympischer Platz 3, Charlotten- burg; tel: 3068 8100 (stadium) or 01805 189 200 (Hertha service hotline); www.olympiastadion- berlin.de; U2, S75, S9: Olympiastadion

The Olympiastadion, a city landmark refurbished for the World Cup finals in 2006 and capable of seating almost 75,000, is home to 'Berlin's old lady', Hertha BSC, the capital's premier league football team. Games run from August until May.

---

while enthusiastic crowds and mostly pleasant temper- atures make it one of the world's most popular marathons, always good for a world or personal record. It attracts up to 40,000 runners, skaters and wheelchair ath- letes. Register early if you want to take part.

Tiergarten

S5, S7, S75, S9: Tiergarten, Bellevue or Zoologischer Garten; S1, S2, S25: Unter den Linden; map p.133 E2/134 A2

Berlin's 'Central Park' is flat, safe and pleasant to run or walk in. You can jog on wide avenues or narrow paths along the ponds and water- ways and take in blooming rhododendrons or colourful foliage. The adjoining govern- ment district with the Reich- stag and Kanzleramt is easy to include. Wider paths are partly illuminated at night.

WATER SPORTS AND SWIMMING

Badeschiff (Swimming Ship)

Eichenstrasse 4, Treptow; tel: 01789 500 163; www. badeschiff.de; opening hours

> Ice-rinks are set up in attractive locations during the winter sea- son – one on Unter den Linden avenue, more at Potsdamer Platz and Alexanderplatz. Skates can be rented for little money – go with the flow and enjoy Berlin's skyline.

subject to change; admission charge; robes, towels, slippers for hire; S41, S42, S8, S85, S9: Treptower Park

A floating swimming pool anchored on the Spree river, part of the Arena venue and complete with an artificial beach and beach bar. Mix with a hip young crowd and float in the illuminated pool. The Badeschiff is converted into a sauna landscape with heated pool in the winter.

SEE ALSO PAMPERING, P.106

Strandbad Wannsee

Wannseebadweg 25, Zehlen- dorf; Apr–Sept: Mon–Fri 10am– 7pm, Sat–Sun 8am–8pm; admission charge; S1, S7: Nikolassee

Have a swim in the clear water of Lake Wannsee, go windsurfing or rent a boat at this long, sandy beach.

Theatre and Dance

German theatre has always been political, and you can journey through the city's many theatres and plays to encounter the country's turbulent past. Major playwrights such as Bertolt Brecht, Ferdinand Bruckner, Gerhard Hauptmann and Heiner Müller have lived and worked in Berlin, and the city retains its reputation as a fertile ground for innovative forms of theatre. Similarly, the local classical and contemporary dance scenes are thriving, and modern productions often overlap with theatre, music and other art forms.

Theatre

MAJOR THEATRES

Berliner Ensemble

Bertold-Brecht-Platz 1; tel: 2840 8155; www.berliner-ensemble.de; S3, S5, S7, S9, S75, U6, Tram M1, 12: Friedrichstrasse; map p.136 B2

This is the house that Brecht built. His famous *Threepenny Opera* had its première here, and after the war he was the theatre's director. For years after his death, the BE saw itself as the guardian of Brecht's legacy. More recently, playwright Heiner Müller has found a home here, and today performances cover a broad range of German playwrights.

Deutsches Theatre

Schumannstrasse 13a; tel: 2844 1225; www.deutsches theater.de; S3, S5, S7, S9, S75: Friedrichstrasse; map p.134 B3

This is considered the most conservative of Berlin's main theatres. It focuses on classic German theatre.

Maxim Gorki Theatre

Am Festungsgraben 2; tel: 202 210; U6, S3, S5, S7, S9, S75, S9: Friedrichstrasse; S1, S2: Unter den Linden; map p.137 C1

This is not a Russian theatre, but a venue for contemporary pieces and classics from German and international theatre.

Schaubühne

Kurfürstendamm 153; tel: 890 023; www.schaubuehne.de; U7: Adenauerplatz; S5, S7, S9: Charlottenburg; map p.136 B4

Founded in 1962, The Schaubühne has always been edgy, with a focus on political and social themes. It is also known for providing a venue for new international dramatists and avant-garde dance.

Volksbühne

Linienstrasse 227; tel: 240 655; www.volksbuehne-berlin.de; U2: Rosa-Luxemburg-Platz; S5, S75, S9: Alexanderplatz; map p.135 D3

The visually interesting Volksbühne makes a habit out of its total disregard for political correctness. It is provocative and willing to take risks.

FRINGE THEATRES

English Theatre Berlin

Fidicinstrasse 41; tel: 693 5692; www.etberlin.de; U6: Luftbrücke; map p.138 B3

More than a venue for ex-pats, the ETB has earned a solid reputation in Berlin for its English-language perform-ances, which include Ameri-can and British classics and new writers.

Grips-Theater

Altonaer Strasse 22; tel: 3974 7477; www.grips-theater.de; U9: Hansaplatz; map p.133 D3

Grips, which is German slang for being clever, is theatre for children and young adults. It is best-known for its award-winning play *Linie 1*, which takes place on Berlin's U1 and has been running since 1986.

Hebbel-Theater

Hau 1: Stresemannstrasse 29, Hau 2: Hallesches Ufer 32, Hau 3: Tempelhofer Ufer 10; tel: 259 0040; www.hebbel-am-ufer.de; Hau 1: S1, S2, S25: Anhalter Bahnhof; Hau 2, 3: U1, U6: Hallesches Tor; Hau 1: map p.134 B1; Hau 2,3: map p.138 B4

This ensemble of three theatres in close proximity to each other provides a venue

Left: the ornate lobby of
the Deutsches Theatre.

Staatsballett Berlin

Deutsche Oper, Bismarckstrasse
35; tel: 341 0249; www.deutsche
operberlin.de; advance sales
11am–6pm; U2: Deutsche Oper;
U7: Bismarckstrasse;
map p.132 C2

Berlin's dance tradition goes
back to 1794, when the first
independent ballet company
was founded. In 2004, the
dance companies of the city's
three opera houses merged to
create the Staatsballett. The
programme is a mix of modern dance and classical ballet.

FESTIVALS

Tanz im August – Inter-
nationales Tanzfest Berlin

www.tanzimaugust.de; different
venues; TanzWerkstatt Berlin,
Mitte, Klosterstrasse 68–70; tel:
2474 9756; www.tanzwerkstatt.
bkv.org; U2: Klosterstrasse;
map p.137 E1

Germany's biggest dance
festival, this four-week programme is the highlight of
Berlin's dance community. It
is organised by Hebbel-The-
atre and Tanzwerkstatt
Berlin. Performers include
dancers such as Pina
Bausch or the Jirí Kyliáns
Nederlands Dans Theater, as
well as newcomers.

Heiner Müller (1929–95),
widely considered the most
significant German dramatist of
the 20th century after Brecht,
wrote and staged many
provocative plays in Berlin,
such as *Die Umsiedlerin*, until
the communist authorities cen-
sored him and prevented most
of his works from being performed in East Germany.

for contemporary German
and international theatre,
dance and performance art.

Kleines Theater

Südwestkorso 64; tel: 821 2021;
www.kleines-theater.de; U9:
Friedrich-Wilhelm-Platz; U3:
Rüdesheimer Platz

In this small theatre, with just
99 seats, a small troupe of
actors perform drama by
local authors as well as
musical pieces and comedy.

Dance

COMPANIES

Minako Seki

Venues vary; tel: 618 5211;
www.minakoseki.com

Minako Seki, born in Japan,
has been dancing in Berlin
since 1986. A third generation

butoh dancer, she co-founded
the 'Tatobea: Théâtre Danse
Grotesque', the first German-
Japanese butoh ensemble.
She performs her own pieces
in Berlin and internationally.

MS Schrittmacher

Zossener Strasse 52; tel: 6981
4344; www.msschrittmacher.de;
U6, U7: Mehringdamm; map
p.138 C4

This is a growing independent
dance company. Founded by
choreographer Martin Stiefer-
mann in 1998, Schrittmacher
uses dance to confront issues
such as suicide, the loss of
balance, trust and the failure
of human relationships.

Sasha Waltz & Guests

Sophienstrasse 3; tel: 246 2800;
www.sashawaltz.de; U8: Weinmeisterstrasse; map p.134 C3

This is the most innovative
and popular dance company
in Berlin. Waltz founded the
company together with
Jochen Sanding in 1993 and
from 1999 to 2004 was artistic
manager of the Schaubühne.
Now, as an independent company, Waltz puts on more than
140 performances a year. Get
tickets early; performances
are often sold out.

Below: Jasmin Wagner in
Cassandra/Elektra.

Transport

Getting to Berlin is straightforward, with several scheduled daily international flights and a historic role as a European rail hub. Given that Berlin sprawls over a vast area, getting around the city is surprisingly easy, too. The city's public transport, made up of underground trains, light rail and buses and sewn back together following the fall of the Wall, penetrate every corner of the city and its near suburbs. Tickets can even be used on a couple of boats. Note that the Berlin Public Transit Authority (BVG) website (www.bvg.de) is a useful resource for all public transport information.

Getting To Berlin

BY RAIL

As the halfway point between Paris and Moscow and also Stockholm and Rome, Berlin has been a European rail hub since train travel started; the Hamburger Bahnhof (now an art museum, *see p.88*) is one of the oldest stations in Europe. Today, the gleaming new **Hauptbahnhof** on the banks of the Spree river near the Reichstag is where most passengers disembark from one of Deutsche Bahn's trains. It is easily connected to all of Berlin's public transport, and if you can get to your destination via S-Bahn, your train ticket will cover you for this portion of your journey, too.

BY AIR

Berlin currently has three airports, although the historic **Tempelhof** one only serves private planes and its future is in doubt. Most international flights on regular carriers continue to arrive at **Tegel** in the north, and travellers can connect to either the TXL express bus, serving central Berlin, or buses 109 and 128 to less

The round-trip flight from London to Berlin will set back your carbon balance by 0.45 tonnes. To feel better, you can buy a carbon offset certificate from www.myclimate.org, www.climatecare.org or www.terrapass.com.

central destinations. Budget airlines are served by **Schöne-feld**, in the southeast, which is preparing to become Berlin's main airport. The city centre is about 30 minutes away by Airport Express Regionalbahn, or 50 minutes on the S-Bahn.

Getting Around Berlin

A single ticket is good for two hours' travel in one direction on the **U-Bahn** (Untergrund-bahn) and **S-Bahn** (Schnell-bahn) lines, **trams**, **buses** and **ferries** within **A–B zones**. Single tickets, good for one-way travel for two hours, are €2.10. Day tickets, valid for travel until 3am, are €6.10. Week tickets, valid until midnight a week later, cost €25.50 and also allow travel with another adult and up to three children aged 6–13 after 8pm.

BY U-BAHN AND S-BAHN

The U-Bahn often runs above ground, and the S-Bahn below. The system is fast, and the map is clear; many U-Bahn stations display maps showing the time taken between stations. Note that Berlin tradition has the crowd on the platform charge the doors the second they open, meaning that sometimes passengers have to push their way out.

Some lines run 24 hours a day; if you're going to be out late it pays to check for the last train before leaving the station. Most have extended operating hours at weekends and holidays. Most central U-Bahn and S-Bahn stations are safe, although you may be approached by beggars or drug-dealers at some of the seamier ones, as well as those looking to sell used tickets.

BY BUS AND TRAM

Berlin has an extensive bus network which connects U-Bahn and S-Bahn stations with the city's smaller streets, particularly in outly-ing areas. Maps are available at all BVG kiosks, located in

Left: a U-Bahn train.

doubling as bike lanes, Berlin is easy to traverse by bicycle. Find bike rental addresses at www.fahrradstation.de (German only) or get one of the red-and-silver Deutsche Bahn rental bikes parked in strategic locations all over town (Apr–Nov). You can register by mobile phone and unlock the bike with a code that is texted to you. Currently, the fare is 7 cents a minute, charged to your credit card.

If you prefer some guidance, call **Berlin On Bike** (tel: 4373 9999; www.berlinonbike.de) and book one of their many guided bike tours leaving from Kulturbrauerei in Prenzlauer Berg, to explore major sights or hidden places, or go along the former death strip. Guides speak English.

Guided tours with American-owned **www.fattirebiketours.com** leave from Alexanderplatz (Panoramastrasse 1a, at the foot of the TV Tower) or Zoologischer Garten station. Rental rates get cheaper if you rent for more than one day (tel: 2404 7991).

It is possible to take bicycles on U-Bahn and S-Bahn trains, but you need to buy an extra *Fahradkarte* (discounted ticket).
SEE ALSO SPORTS, P.124

major stations. Bus stops are identified by a green H in a green-and-yellow circle. There is a reduced service at night, with night lines taking different routes and identified by the N suffix.

Eastern Berlin is largely served by a network of modern, Swiss-built trams, whose stops are marked the same way. They usually stop running around midnight.

BY BOAT
Treptower Hafen
Puschkinallee 15; tel: 536 3600; www.sternundkreis.de; Mar–Oct daily; S3, S41, 42 (ring train), S6, S8, S9: Treptower Park
Berlin's port and marina is the place to board boat tours on Berlin waters or all the way up to Poland.
SEE ALSO CHILDREN, P.43

BY TAXI
In crowded areas, you can normally hail a taxi. If you are out of luck, call one of the major taxi companies:
City-Funk: 210 202
Funk-Taxi Berlin: 261 026
TaxiFunk Berlin: 0800 443 322 (freecall)

All single, day and week tickets must be validated at time of purchase by cancelling them in the machine next to the vending machine. Exceptions are tickets bought on trams or buses, which are pre-validated.

Taxi-Ruf Würfelfunk: 0800 222 2255 (freecall)
Taxis are beige in Berlin, have meters and are safe. Taxis in Berlin tend to be cheap, and taxi ranks are everywhere. Hailing a taxi in the street is not a problem, unless you are in a very deserted part of town. In that case, go to a café or bar and ask the bartender to call a taxi. The *Kurzstrecke* is a €3 fare for a ride of less than 2km (1¼ miles) if you hail the taxi in the street and tell the driver you want a *Kurzstrecke*. Taxis can also be arranged to get you from bus stops at night. Ask your driver or staff at the station.

BY BICYCLE
Do as the locals do and get a bike. With its many kilometres of bike paths and bus lanes

Below: a guided bike tour.

Atlas

The following streetplan of Berlin
makes it easy to find the attractions
listed in our A–Z section. A selective
index to streets and sights will help
you find other locations throughout
the city

Map Legend

Autopista		Railway
Dual carriageway		U-Bahn Station
Main road		S-Bahn Station
Minor road		Bus station
Footpath		Airport
Pedestrian area		Tourist information
Notable building		Sight of interest
Park		Cathedral / church
Hotel		Mosque
Urban area		Synagogue
Non urban area		Statue / monument
Cemetery		Hospital

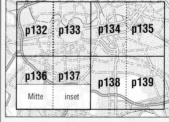

p132	p133	p134	p135
p136	p137	p138	p139
Mitte	inset		

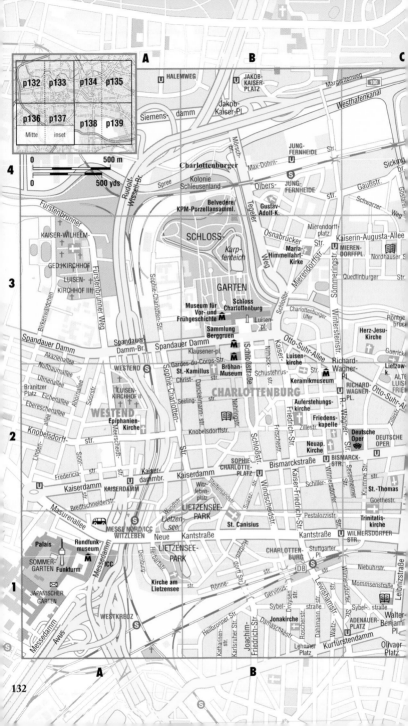

A   B   C

4

0   500 m
0   500 yds

Nord-hafen

Schwartzkopffstr.
Boyenstr.

PARK AM NORDBAHNHOF

Dokumentationszentr. Berliner Mauer

KIRCHHOF VON ST-ELISABETH

FRIEDHOF DER SOPHIENKIRCH-GEMEINDE

Bergstr.

Elisabethk.

Anklamer

Brunnenstraße

Veter

SCHWARTZKOPFF. STR.

INVALIDEN-FRIEDHOF

Schwartzkopffstr.

Chausseestraße

Gartenstr.

NORDBAHNHOF

Zinnowitzer

Pappel-platz

Invalidenstraße

VOLKSPARK WEINBERG

Rosenth

Museum für Naturkunde

ZINNOWITZER STR.

Schwedter

Golgatha-Kirk

H.-ZILLE-PARK

ROSENTHALER PLATZ

Postdad

FRITZ-SCHLOSS-PARK

Lehrter Str.

Minna-Cauer-Str.

GE-SCHICHTS-PARK

Hamburger Bahnhof Mus. für Gegenwartskunst

INVALIDEN-PARK

Zoologisches Museum

Platz vor dem Neuen Tor

DOROTHEEN-STÄDT. & FRANZ. FRIEDHOF

Linienstr.

Kunst-Werke

Augustr.

Neue Synagoge

Linienstr.

Sophie

GE-SCHICHTS-PARK

Europaplatz

HAUPTBAHNHOF

Humboldt-hafen

Invalidenstraße

Robert-Koch-Platz

Universitäts-klinikum

Hannoversche Str.

Torstraße

ORANIENBURGER TOR

Oranienburger

St.-Joh.-K.

Sophien-kirche

Hackesche Höf.

Seydlitzstraße

Jugend-gästeh.

Otto-Dix-Str.

Alt-Moabit

Washington-platz

G.-Heinemann-Brücke

Spree

Kammerspiele Deutsches Th.

Friedrichstadtpalast

Ziegelstr.

ORANIENBURGER STR.

MONBIJOU-PARK

Bode-Museum

Mon

3

SEE PAGES 136-137

Reinhardt

str.

Am Weidendamm

Museums-insel

Pergamon-museum

Alte National-galeri

Wertstr.

Moltke-brücke

SPREEBOGEN-PARK

Karlpl.

Marienstr.

FRIEDRICHSTR.

DB

FRIEDRICHSTR.

Neues Museum

Ber

KANZLER-GARTEN

Bundeskanzler-amt

REICHS-TAG

Str.

Reichstags-gebäude Deutscher Bundestag

Robert-Koch-Mus.

Georgenstr.

Deutsches Historisches Museum

Alles Museum

LUST-GARTEN

Joachim-Karnatz-Allee

Haus der Kulturen der Welt

Paul-Löbe-Haus

Gagern-Str.

Tirpitz-Ufer

Heinrich-v.-Gagern-Str.

Platz der Republik

Dorotheenstr.

MITTE

MOABITER WERDER

John-Foster-Dulles-Allee

Carttton

Scheidemannstr.

Dorotheen-

str.

Großfürstenpl.

Kurfürstenplatz

Sowjetisches Ehrenmal

Platz des 18. März

Pariser Platz

UNTER DEN LINDEN

Unter den Linden

UNTER DEN LINDEN

Weil

2

Straße des 17. Juni

Bremer Weg

Brandenburger Tor (Brandenburger Gate)

Ebert-

str.

Akademie d. Künste

Komische Oper

Französische Str.

Friedrichs-werdersche K. (Schinkelmuseu

Flora

Bellevueallee

Amazone

Löwen-brücke

Behrenstr.

FRANZÖSISCHE STR.

Französischer Dom

HAUS-VOGTEI-PLATZ

Herkules mit der Lyra

TIERGARTEN

Friedrich Wilhelm III.

Musiker-denkmal

Goethe

Lessing

Denkmal für die ermordeten Juden Europas

Jägerstr.

Taubenstr.

Wilhelm

Schjaupiel-haus

STADT-MITTE

Deutscher Dom

Hausvogtei-platz

Königin Luise

Musikinstr.-mus.

Wilhelm I.

Sony Center

Beisheim-Center

Mauerstr.

Kronenstr.

Kronenstr.

Spi

Wagner

Kunstgewerbe-museum

Kulturforum

Matthai-kirchpl.

Deutsche Kinemathek

IMAX

POTSDAMER PLATZ

DB S

Potsdamer Platz

Leipziger Pl.

Voßstr.

Leipziger Straße

Leipziger Straße

Krausenstr.

ma

Österre

Gemälde-galerie

St.-Matthäus-Kirche

Phil-harmonie

POTSDAMER PL.

MÖHRENSTR.

Museum für Kommunikation

Schützen-

Haus am Checkpoint Charlie

Zimmerstr.

Musical-Th.

Potsdamer-Platz-Arkaden

Niederkirchner

Martin-Gropius-Bau

Checkpoint Charlie

Mauermuseum

Axel-Springer-Str.

Neue National-galerie

TILLA-DURIEUX-PARK

Stresemannstr.

Topographie des Terrors

Anhalter

KOCHSTR.

Kochstraße

Rudi-Dutschke-Str.

Markgrafenstr.

Charlottenstr.

Reichpietschufer

Schöneberger Ufer

George-C.-Marshall-Str.

Bernburger Str.

Lukas-Kirche

MENDELSSOHN-BARTHOLDY-PARK

Askanischer Platz

Dreifaltigkeits-kirche

St.-Clemens Kirche

Lindenstr.

Jüdisches Museum Berlin

Rie

1

Genthiner

Lützow-

Winterganten

Potsdamer Straße

Bissing-zalle

MENDELSSOHN-BARTHOLDY-PARK

ANHALTER BAHNHOF

Tempodrom

Hallesche Str.

Willy-Brandt-Pl.

E.-T.-A.-Hoffmann-Promenade

St.-Agnes Kirch

Apostelk.

Klucks

Kronen

Pohlstr.

GLEIS-DREIECK

Möckernstr.

Postbank

Hebbel-theater

Mehring-platz

Friedenssäule

A.d. Apostel-kirche

KURFÜRSTEN-STR.

Kurfürstenstr.

KURFÜRSTEN-STR.

Schöneberger Ufer

Halleschen Ufer

Willy-Brandt-Straße

Stampfer

Franz-Klühs-Str.

Neuenburger Str.

A   B

Map index labels (top-left overview grid):

p132	p133	p134	p135
p136	p137	p138	p139
Mitte	inset		

Grid rows (right margin): 4, 3

Top map labels:

Lehniner Platz · ADENAUER-PLATZ · Xantener Str. · Olivaer Platz
Neue Schaubühne · Dulsburger Str. · dorfer Str.
Kurfürstendamm · Nestorstr. · Ciceerostr. · Paulsborner Str. · Brandenburgische Str. · Düssel-
Westfälische Str. · Joachim- · Zähring
A. Magnus-Kirke
HALENSEE · Sensener Str. · Hochmeister-kirche · Wittelsbac
Rathenau-platz · Seeser Str. · Eisenzahnstraße · Danielk.
Hugenottenk. · KONSTANZER STR. · PREUSS PARK
Halen-see · Koenigsallee · 100 · Neue Kirke · Fehrbellin Platz
Trabener Str. · Caspar- · Theuß-Str. · Cicerostr. · FEHRBELLINER PL.
Kirche d. Nazareners · genlein · Auguste- · Nestorstr. · Russ. Kathedrale · Hohenzollern-
Erdener Str. · Humboldt- · Paulsborner · HOHENZOLLERN-DAMM · Hoffmann- v.-Fallers-leben-Pl. · Dän.
Johanna-platz · Hubertusallee · Lynarstr. · Charlottenbrunner Str. · Hohenzollern-dammbr · Berliner
Bismarckallee · Warmbrunner · Kudowa · Salzbrunner · FRIEDHOF WILMERS-DORF
Grunewaldk. · Hubertus-see · Dietruck · Auguste-Viktoria · Cunostr. · Kalischer Str. · Fennsee
Bismarckallee · Berkaer · Str. · allee · Reinerzstr. · Flinsberger Platz · Hohenzollerndamm · Rudolstädter Str. · Wallenber
Wernerstr. · Richard- · Strauss- · Str. · Hubertus- · Joseph-Joachim-Pl. · Kreuzk. · Brat

500 m / 500 yds · 0 · 0

MITTE
(enlargement from page 134-135)

Grid rows (left margin): 2, 1

Schumannstraße · Friedrichstadtpalast · Dietrich-Bonhoeffer-Haus
Mensa · Reinhardtstraße · Ziegelstraße · Max-Planck Institut Frauenklinik
Kapelle-ufer · Karlplatz · Amelie · Am Zirkus · Friedrichstr. · Universitäts-kliniken
Spree · Kron- · Margarete- · Reinhardtstraße · Albrechtstr. · Berthold-Brecht-Pl. · Am Zirkus · Weidendammer Brücke · Am Kupfergra
Prinzen- · Schiffbauerdamm · Marienstr. · Albrechtshof · Am Weidendamm · Ebert- brücke
prücke · Bundespresse- amt · Steffin- · Berliner Emsemble · Reichstagufer · Geschwister-Scholl-Str.
Schiffbauerdamm · Str. · Luisenstraße · Bundestags-verwaltung · Metropol-Theater · Philosophische Fakultät IV der Universität
Marie-Elisabeth-Lüders-Haus · Bundesamt für Güterverkehr · Reichstagufer · FRIEDRICH-STRASSE
Paul-Löbe-Haus · Institute der Humboldt-Universität Berlin · Spree · FRIEDRICHSTRASSE · Universitätsstr.
Paul-Löbe-Allee · Reichstagufer · Neustädtische · Georgenstr. · Georgenstr. · Theater Kneitzange · Planckstr.
Reichstagsgebäude Deutscher Bundestag · Marschall- · brücke · Kirchstr. · Jolly Hotel Vivaldi · Dorotheenstr.
Herkules · Jacob-Kaiser-Haus (Verwaltungsgebäude) · Institute der Humboldt-Universität Berlin · Bundespresseamt · Charlottenstr. · Universitäts-bibliothek
Friedrich-Ebert-Platz · Wilhelm- · Dorotheenstr. · Dorotheenstr. · Maritim pro Arte · Deutsche Staatsbibliothek · Frie
Simsonweg · Dorotheenstraße · Robert-Koch-Museum · Schadowstr. · Mittelstr. · Linden · Friedrichstr.
Jacob-Kaiser-Haus (Verwaltungsgebäude) · Bundes-vermögensamt · Neustädtische · Haus der Schweiz · Unter den Linden · d
Brandenburger Tor · French Embassy · Fraktionsbüros der SPD · Gouverneurshaus · Alte Bibliothek
Pariser Platz · UNTER DEN LINDEN · Unter den Linden · Glinkastr. · Komische Oper
Straße des 17. Juni · 18. März · Platz des · Adlon · Rossija · The Westin Grand · Rosmarinstr.
United Kingdom · Ebertstraße · Charlottenstr. · Friedrichstr.

Column labels (bottom): A · B

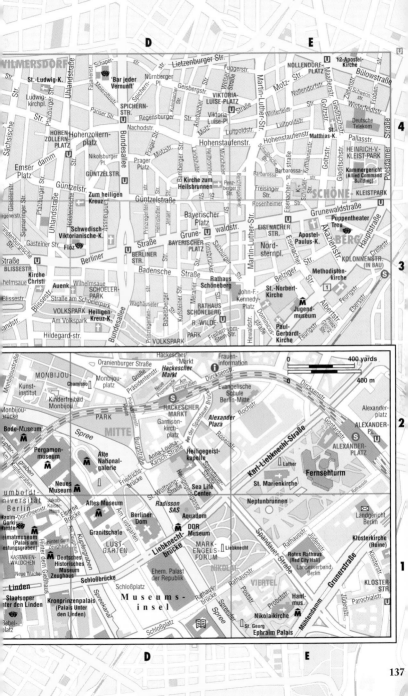

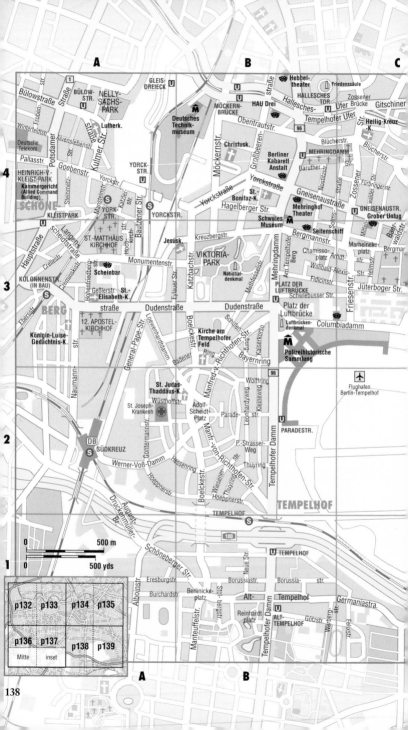

Bülowstraße　Straße

BÜLOW-STR.

NELLY-SACHS-PARK

GLEIS-DREIECK

Hebbel-theater

Friedenssäule

HALLESCHES TOR

Zossener Brücke

Gitschiner

MÖCKERN-BRÜCKE

HAU Drei

Halllesches- Ufer

Tempelhofer Ufer

Heilig-Kreuz-K.

Winterfeldtstr.

Frobenstr.

Potsdamer Straße

Alvenslebenstr.

Kulmer Str.

Lutherk.

Deutsches Technik-museum

Obentrautstr.

Großbeerenstr.

96

Blücherstr.

Blücherstr.

Deutsche Telekom

Pallasstr.

Goebenstr.

YORCK-STR.

Möckernstr.

Christusk.

Berliner Kabarett Anstalt

MEHRINGDAMM

Baruther Str.

Zossener Straße

Nostitzstr.

Fürbringerstr.

HEINRICH-V.-KLEIST-PARK

Steinmetzstr.

Mansteinstr.

Kleiststr.

Yorckstr.

Yorckstraße

St.-Bonifaz-K.

Gneisenaustraße

Solmsstr.

Zossener

GNEISENAUSTR.

Großer Unfug

Kammergericht (Allied Command Building)

YORCK-STR.

Katzler str.

Bautzener Str.

YORCKSTR.

Hagelberger Str.

Mehringhof Theater

Schwules Museum

Bergmannstr.

Marheineke-platz

Bergmar

Baer-waldstr.

SCHÖNE-

KLEISTPARK

Langenscheidtstr.

Hochkirchstr.

Jesusk.

Kreuzbergstr.

Seitenschiff

Am Tempelhofer Berg

Chamisso-platz

Amdt-str.

Hellmit

Friesenstr.

Jüterboger Str.

Hauptstraße

Scheidtstraße

ST.-MATTHÄUS KIRCHHOF

Monumentenstr.

Katzbachstr.

VIKTORIA-PARK

National-denkmal

Willibald-Alexis-

Fidicinstr.

Crellestr.

Scheinbar

St.-Elisabeth-K.

Mehleistraße

PLATZ DER LUFTBRÜCKE

KOLONNENSTR. (IN BAU)

Heinrichbergstr.

Geßlerstr.

Hohenfriedbergstr.

Czemirstraße

straße

Dudenstraße

Eylauer Str.

Dudenstraße

Schulen-burg

Platz der Luftbrücke

BERG

Ebersstr.

12. APOSTEL-KIRCHHOF

Loewenhardtdamm

Boelckestr.

Kirche am Tempelhofer Feld

Kaiserkorso

Columbiadamm

Luftbrücken-denkmal

Königin-Luise-Gedächtnis-K.

General-Pape-Str.

Badener

Ring

Bayernring

Manfred-Richthofen-Str.

Polizeihistorische Sammlung

Naumann str.

St. Judas-Thaddäus-K.

Wüsthoffstr.

Adolf-Scheidt-Platz

Wolffring

Leonhardyweg

Kleinweg

96

Flughafen Berlin-Tempelhof

St. Joseph-Krankenh

Parade-str.

PARADESTR.

Tempelhofer Damm

DB

SÜDKREUZ

Werner-Voß-Damm

Hoeppnerstr.

Gontermannstr.

Hessenring

Boelckestr.

Manfr.-von-Richthofen-Str.

P-Strasser-Weg

Wiesaer-str.

Thuyring

Thuyring

TEMPELHOF

Hoeppnerstr.

August-Druckenmüller-Br.

Schöneberger Str.

TEMPELHOF

100

TEMPELHOF

0　　　　500 m

0　　　　500 yds

Alboinstr.

Eresburgstr.

Borussiastr.

Neue Str.

Borussia-　str.

U TEMPELHOF

Germaniastra.

Burchardstr.

Berlinicke-platz

Sto-bergstr.

Alt-Tempelhof

Manteuffelstr.

Reinhardt-platz

Tempelhofer Damm

ALT-TEMPELHOF

Götzstr.

Warberg str.

Felixstr.

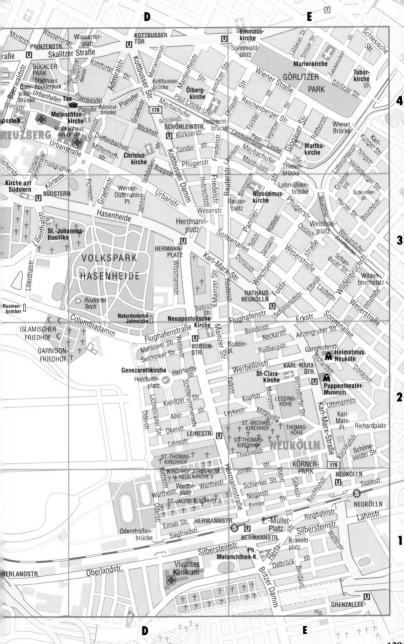

Selective Index for Street Atlas

Note that the ß in 'Straße' (street) appears as 'ss' throughout the book ('Strasse')

PLACES OF INTEREST

STREETS

PARKS

U-BAHN / S-BAHN

141

Index

R

Insight Smart Guide: Berlin
Compiled by: Claudia Himmelreich, Ed Ward, William Boston
Proofread and indexed by: Neil Titman
Edited by: Sarah Sweeney

All photos by: John Santa-Cruz/APA; Except: archivberlin Fotoagentur GmbH/Alamy 34/35; Action Press/Rex Features 54/55; Adenis/Laif 67; Debbie Bragg/Every night images 102; Geoffrey M. R. Hammond/istock photo 39BL; Claudia Himmelreich 111; Katja Hoffmann/Laif 102/103; JazzSign/Lebrecht 98; Naki Kouyioumtzis/ Axiom 114; Monika Rittershaus/ Lebrecht 96/97; Nigel Treblin/Getty images 89; Corrie Wingate/APA 118; World Pictures/Photoshot 112/113; www.visitBerlin.de 54/64/65/119/124/125/130/131
Picture Manager: Steven Lawrence

Maps: James Macdonald and Mapping Ideas Ltd
Art Director: Ian Spick
Series Concept: Maria Lord
Series Editor: Jason Mitchell
First Edition 2008

© 2008 Apa Publications GmbH & Co. Verlag KG Singapore Branch, Singapore.
Printed in Singapore by Insight Print Services (Pte) Ltd

Worldwide distribution enquiries:
Apa Publications GmbH & Co. Verlag KG (Singapore Branch) 38 Joo Koon Road, Singapore 628990; tel: (65) 6865 1600; fax: (65) 6861 6438
Distributed in the UK and Ireland by:
GeoCenter International Ltd
Meridian House, Churchill Way West, Basingstoke, Hampshire RG21 6YR; tel: (44 1256) 817 987; fax: (44 1256) 817 988

Distributed in the United States by:
Langenscheidt Publishers, Inc.
36–36 33rd Street 4th Floor, Long Island City, New York 11106; tel: (1 718) 784 0055; fax: (1 718) 784 0640l
Contacting the Editors
We would appreciate it if readers would alert us to errors or outdated information by writing to: Apa Publications, PO Box 7910, London SE1 1XF, UK; e-mail:insight@apaguide.co.uk